NICHIREN

日蓮

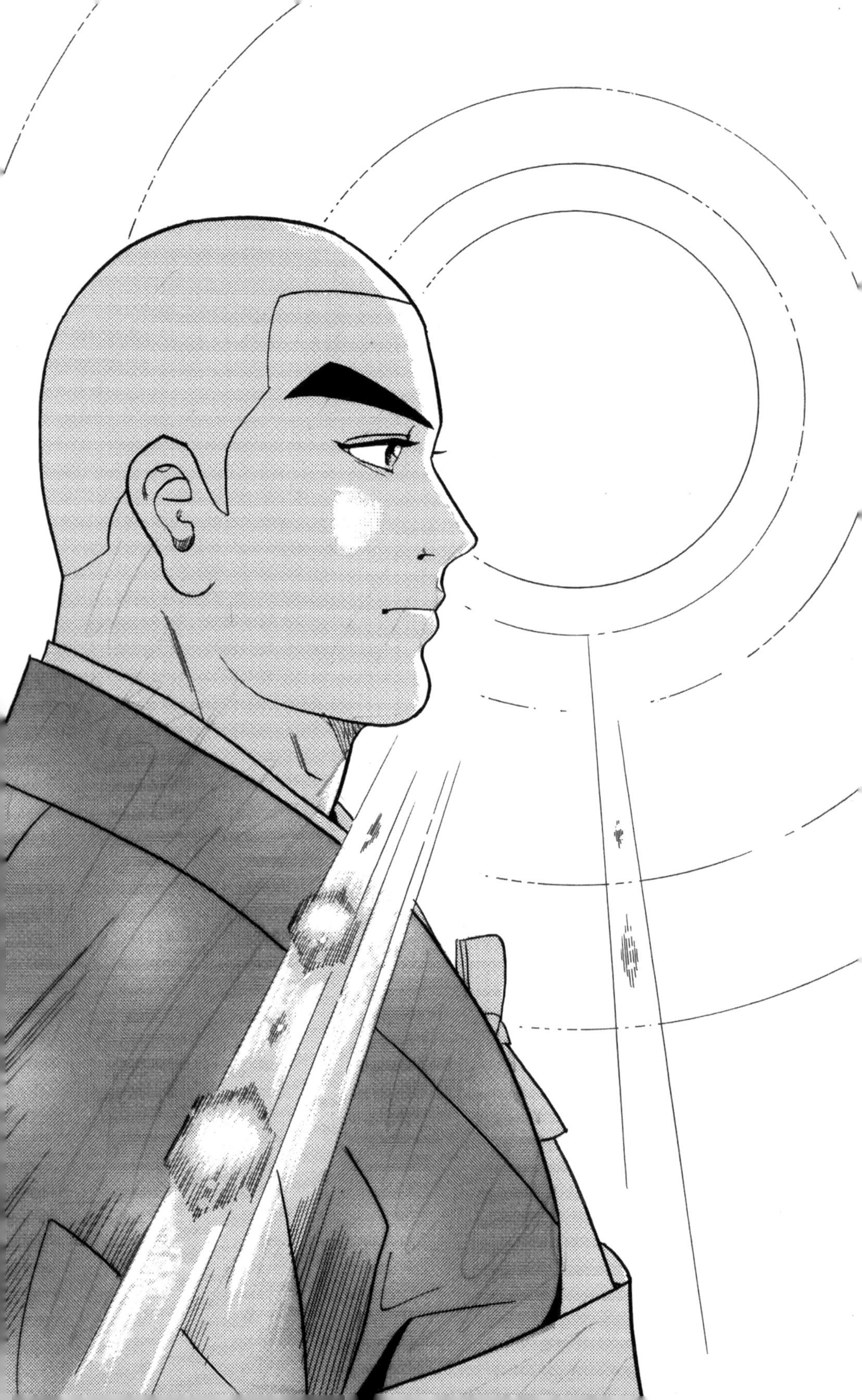

NICHIREN

WRITTEN BY MASAHIKO MURAKAMI
ILLUSTRATIONS BY KEN TANAKA

MIDDLEWAY
PRESS

Published by Middleway Press
A division of the SGI-USA
606 Wilshire Blvd., Santa Monica, CA 90401
© 2015 Soka Gakkai

Printed in Korea.
Lettering by Richard Starkings & Comicraft's Jimmy Betancourt
Design by John Roshell of Comicraft
Richard Starkings and Stuart Moore, Editorial Consultants
Cover color by Steve Buccellato
10 9 8 7 6 5 4 3 2 1
ISBN: 978-0-9779245-7-8

Library of Congress Cataloging-in-Publication Data
Tanaka, Ken.
  Nichiren / written by Masahiko Murakami ; illustrations by Ken Tanaka.
      pages cm
  ISBN 978-0-9779245-7-8 (trade paper : alk. paper)
1. Comic books, strips, etc. 2. Nichiren, 1222-1282--Comic books, strips, etc. I.
Murakami, Masahiko, 1958- II. Title.
  PN6728.N53 2015
  294.3'928092--dc23
  [B]
                                    2015006828

CONTENTS

PREFACE

Nichiren, the main character of this story, was a Buddhist monk who lived in thirteenth-century Japan. Although based on historical events, the story was conceived and written by Masahiko Murakami as a work of fiction, weaving together fictional characters and events with those that existed in real life. In interpreting the script, illustrator Ken Tanaka added his personal touches to breathe life into the characters.

While striving to remain true in substance, the writer and illustrator have taken the liberty of drawing from their imagination and inspiration to create and develop the characters and plot for the story.

We hope readers will enjoy this comic book with the above in mind.

MASAHIKO MURAKAMI   KEN TANAKA
Author   Illustrator

Masahiko Murakami is a well-known Japanese novelist and playwright. Ken Tanaka is an illustrator of several Japanese manga on Buddhist history. Both live in Japan.

INTRODUCTION

A LONG TIME AGO, WHEN SAMURAI RULED JAPAN...

It is a period of great disaster. Society is in turmoil. Yet those in power turn their backs on the misery all around them.

Buddhist priests enjoy great influence among the rulers, who use religion as a way to control the people. Both care more about wealth and power than helping the suffering masses.

But when a young priest named Nichiren challenges the authorities, showing the way to bring peace and happiness to society, they will stop at nothing to silence him....

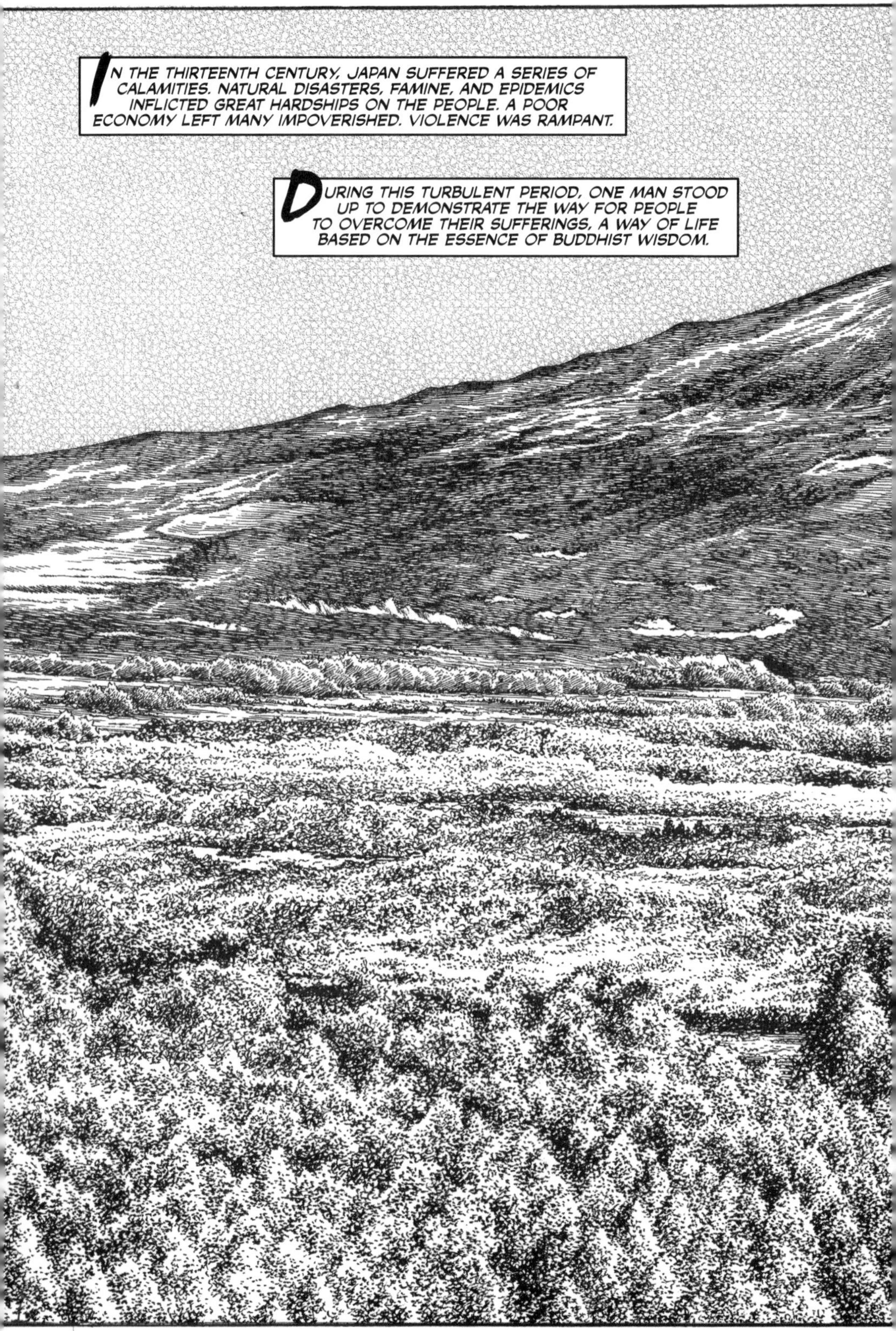
IN THE THIRTEENTH CENTURY, JAPAN SUFFERED A SERIES OF CALAMITIES. NATURAL DISASTERS, FAMINE, AND EPIDEMICS INFLICTED GREAT HARDSHIPS ON THE PEOPLE. A POOR ECONOMY LEFT MANY IMPOVERISHED. VIOLENCE WAS RAMPANT.
DURING THIS TURBULENT PERIOD, ONE MAN STOOD UP TO DEMONSTRATE THE WAY FOR PEOPLE TO OVERCOME THEIR SUFFERINGS, A WAY OF LIFE BASED ON THE ESSENCE OF BUDDHIST WISDOM.

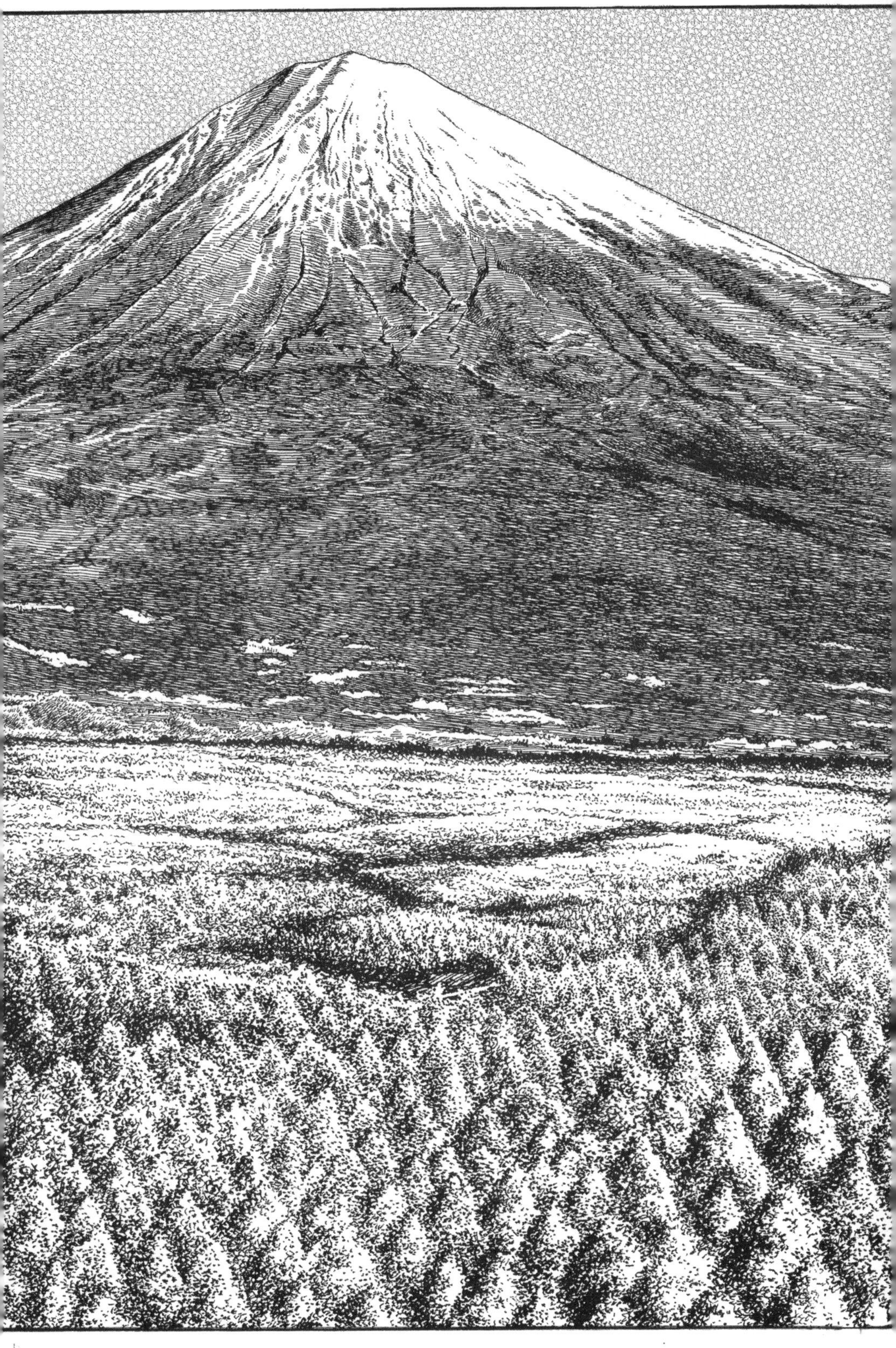

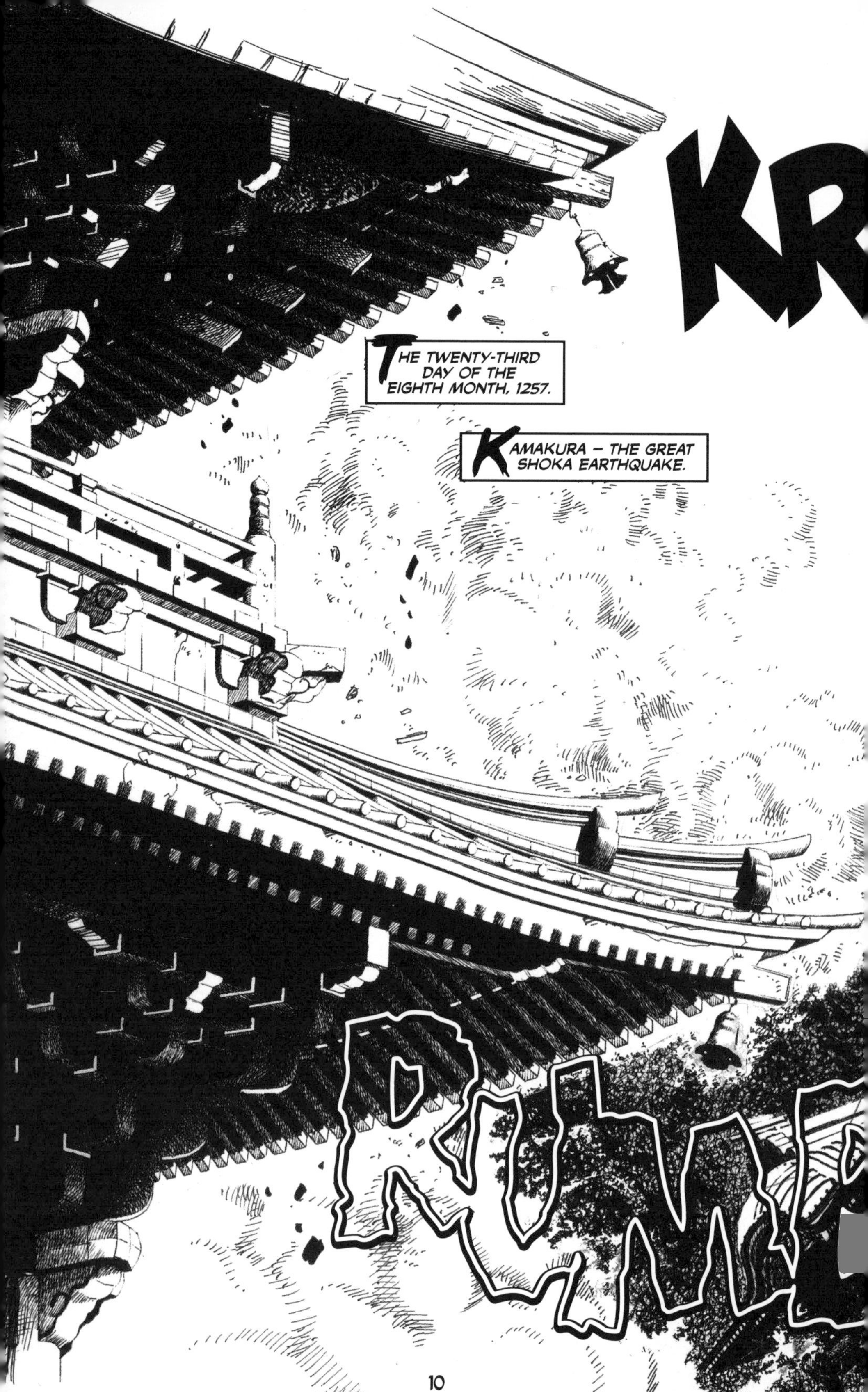

KR
THE TWENTY-THIRD DAY OF THE EIGHTH MONTH, 1257.
KAMAKURA – THE GREAT SHOKA EARTHQUAKE.
RUMB

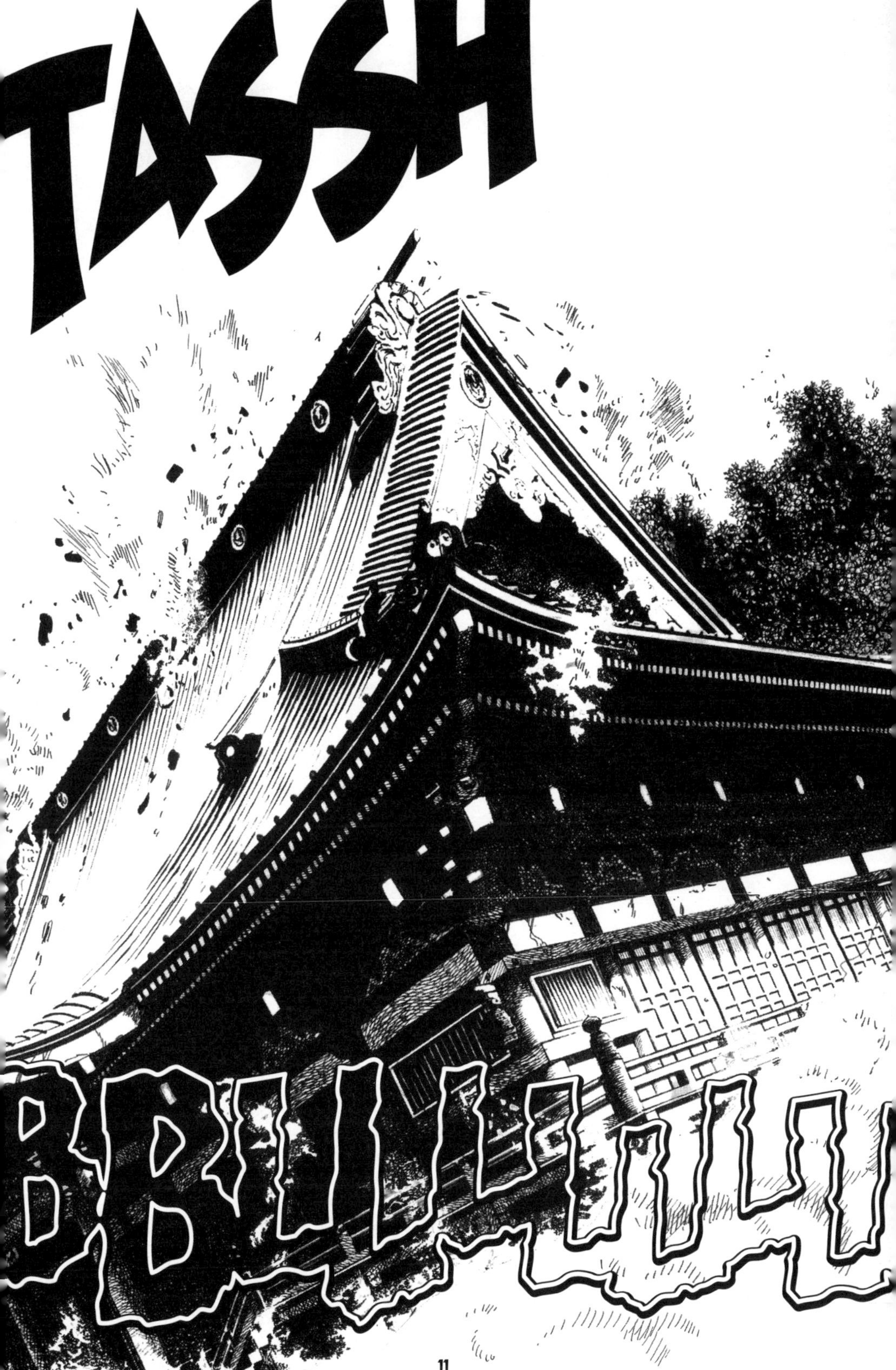
TASSH
BBUUUUU

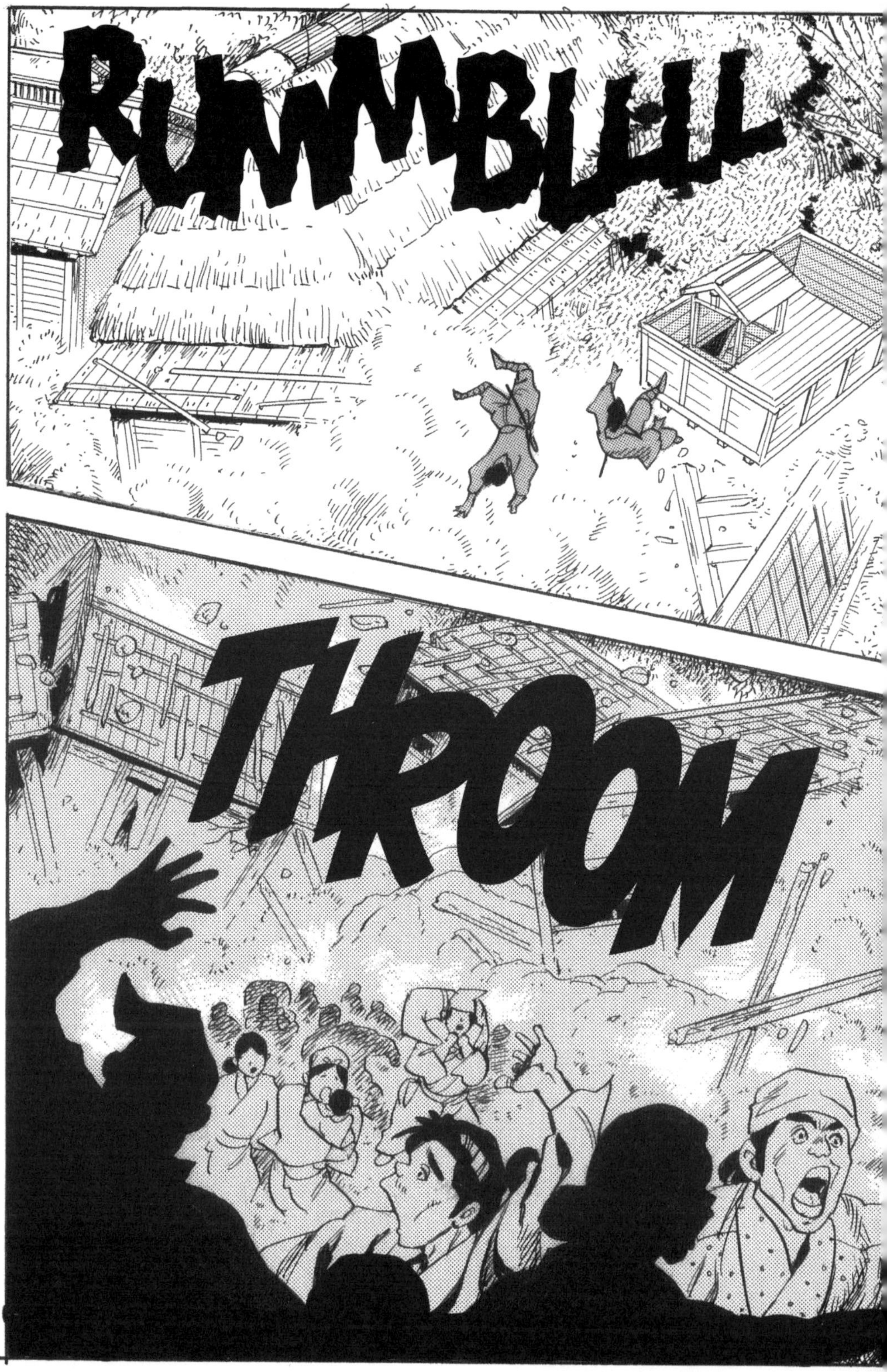
RUMBLLL
THROOM

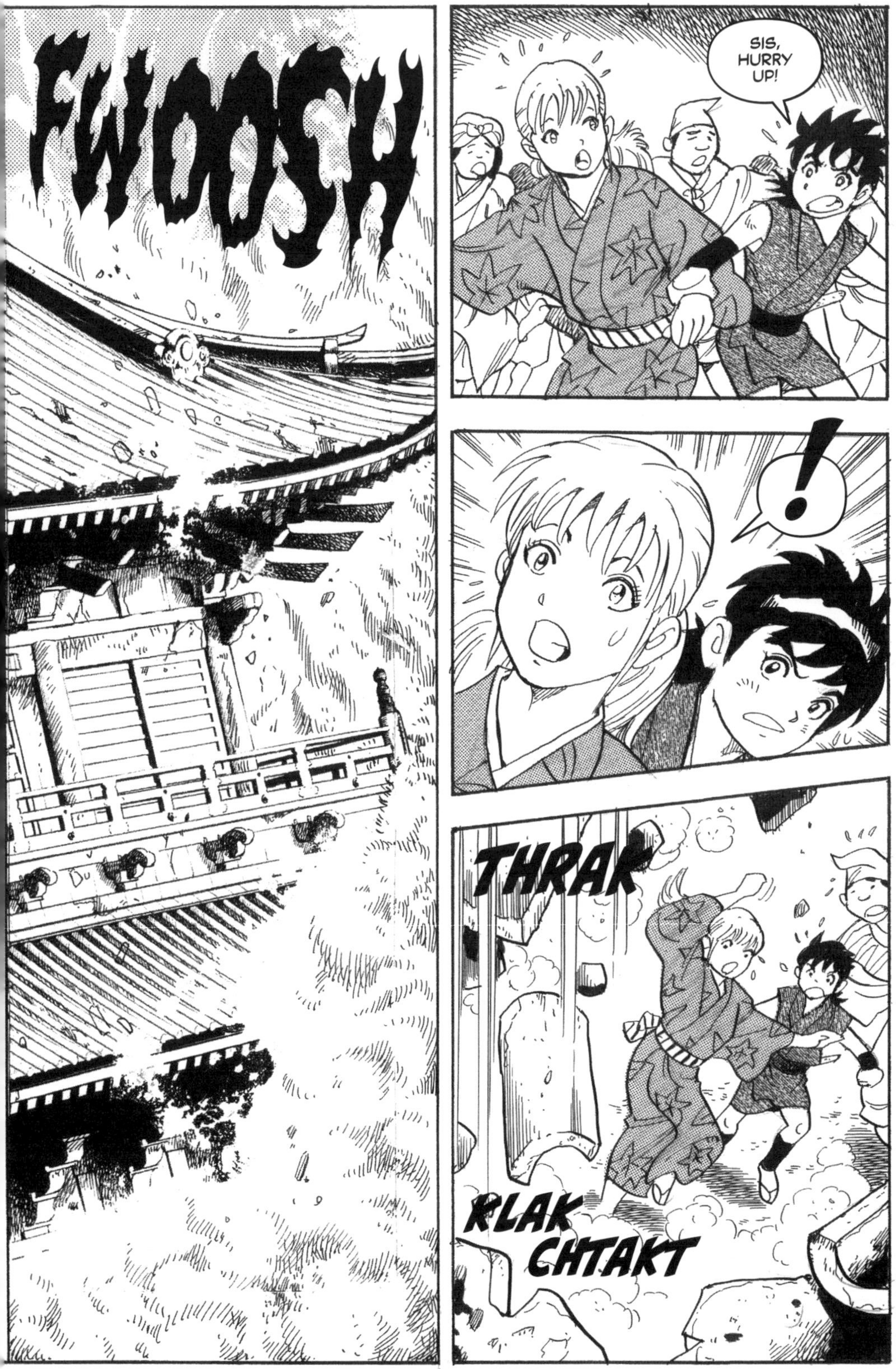
FWOOSH
SIS, HURRY UP!
!
THRAK
KLAK
CHTAKT

Dawn.

HELP!

WATER!

GIVE ME WATER!

WATER!

UGHH...

AAGH!

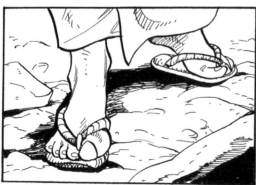

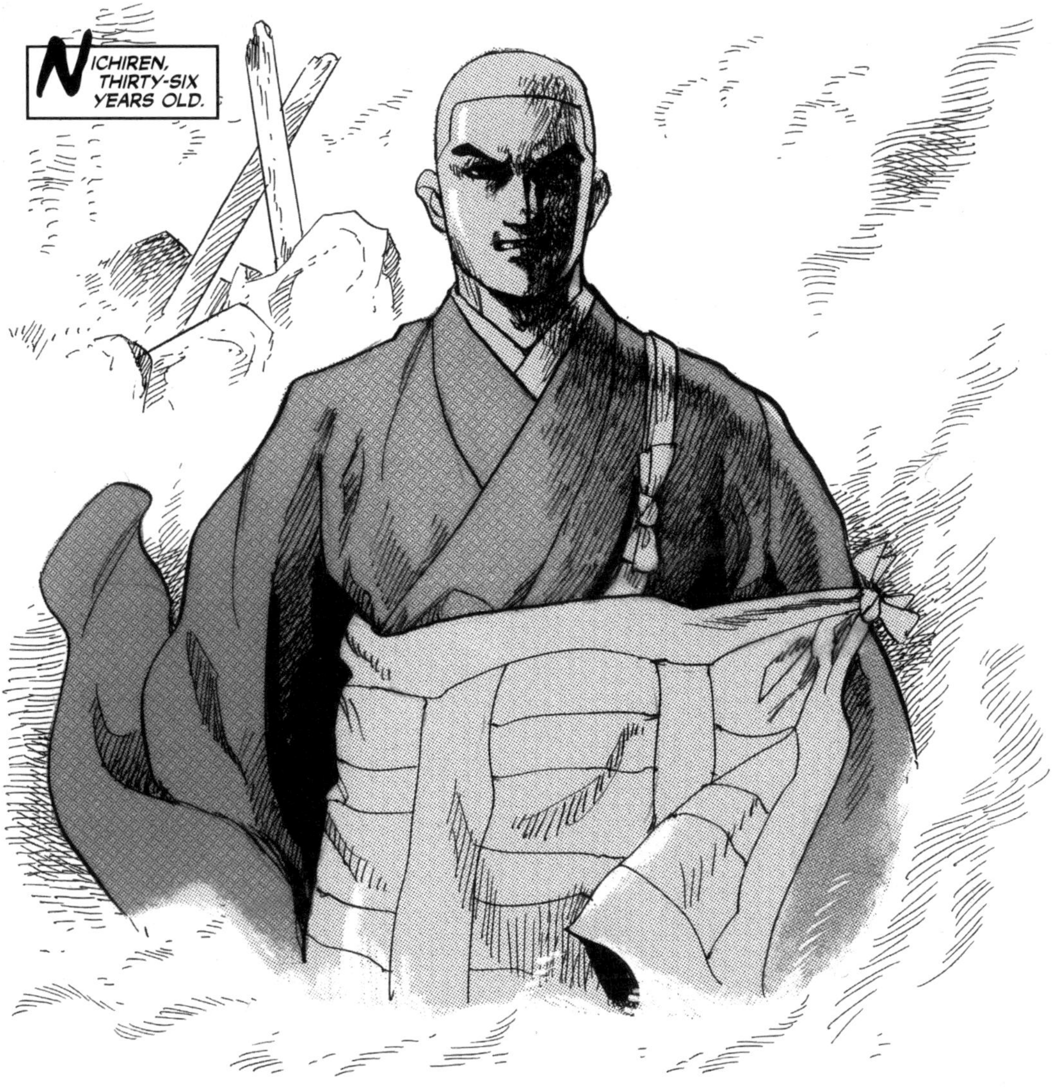
NICHIREN, THIRTY-SIX YEARS OLD.
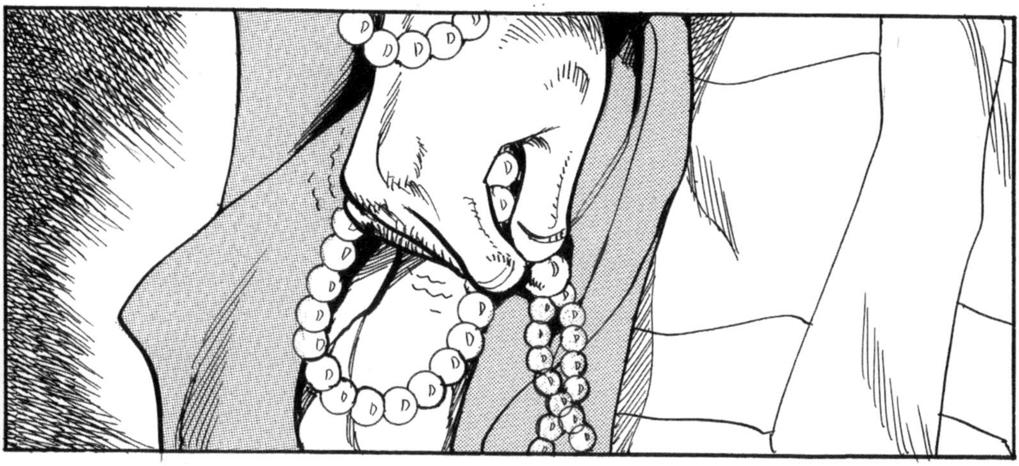

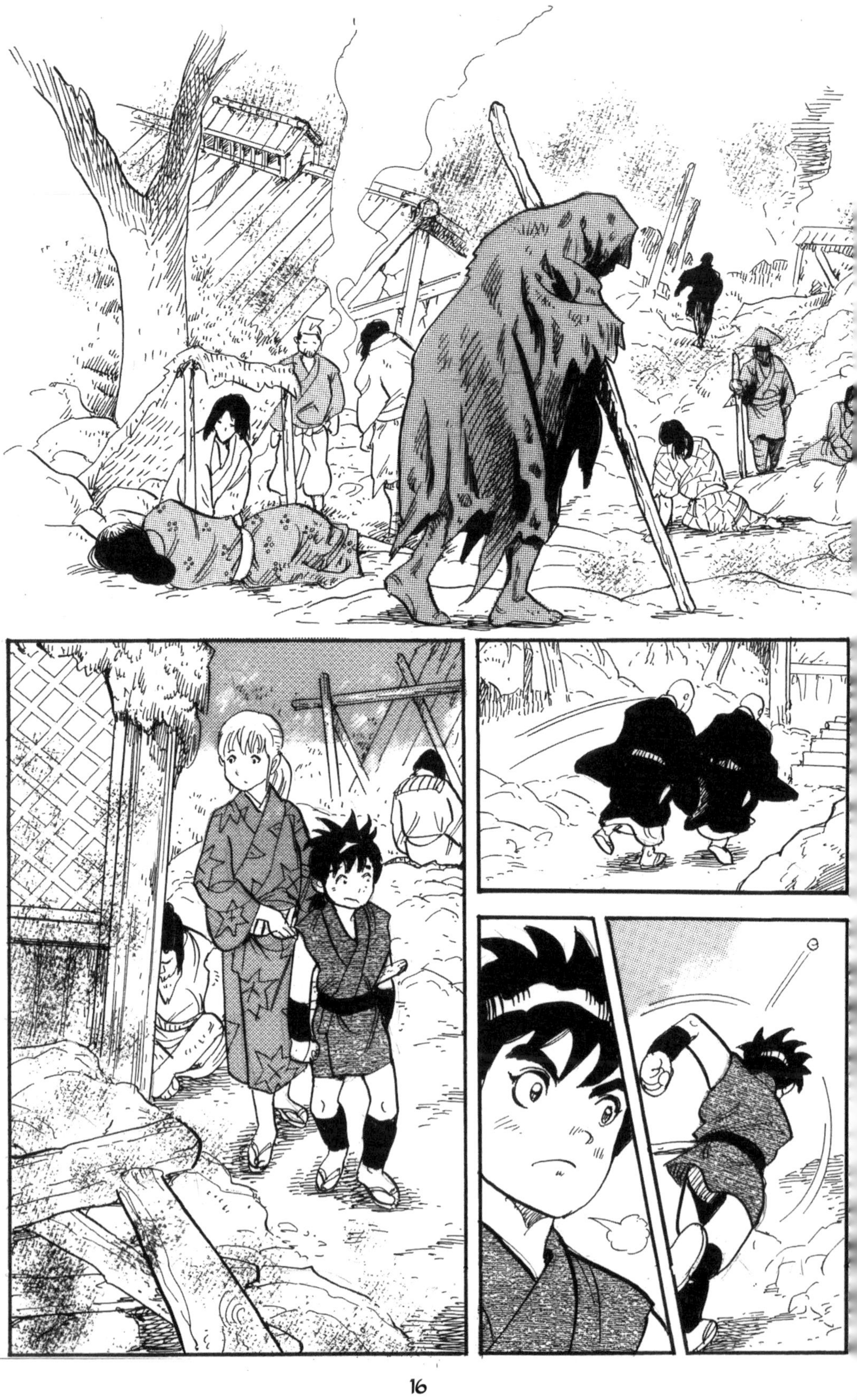

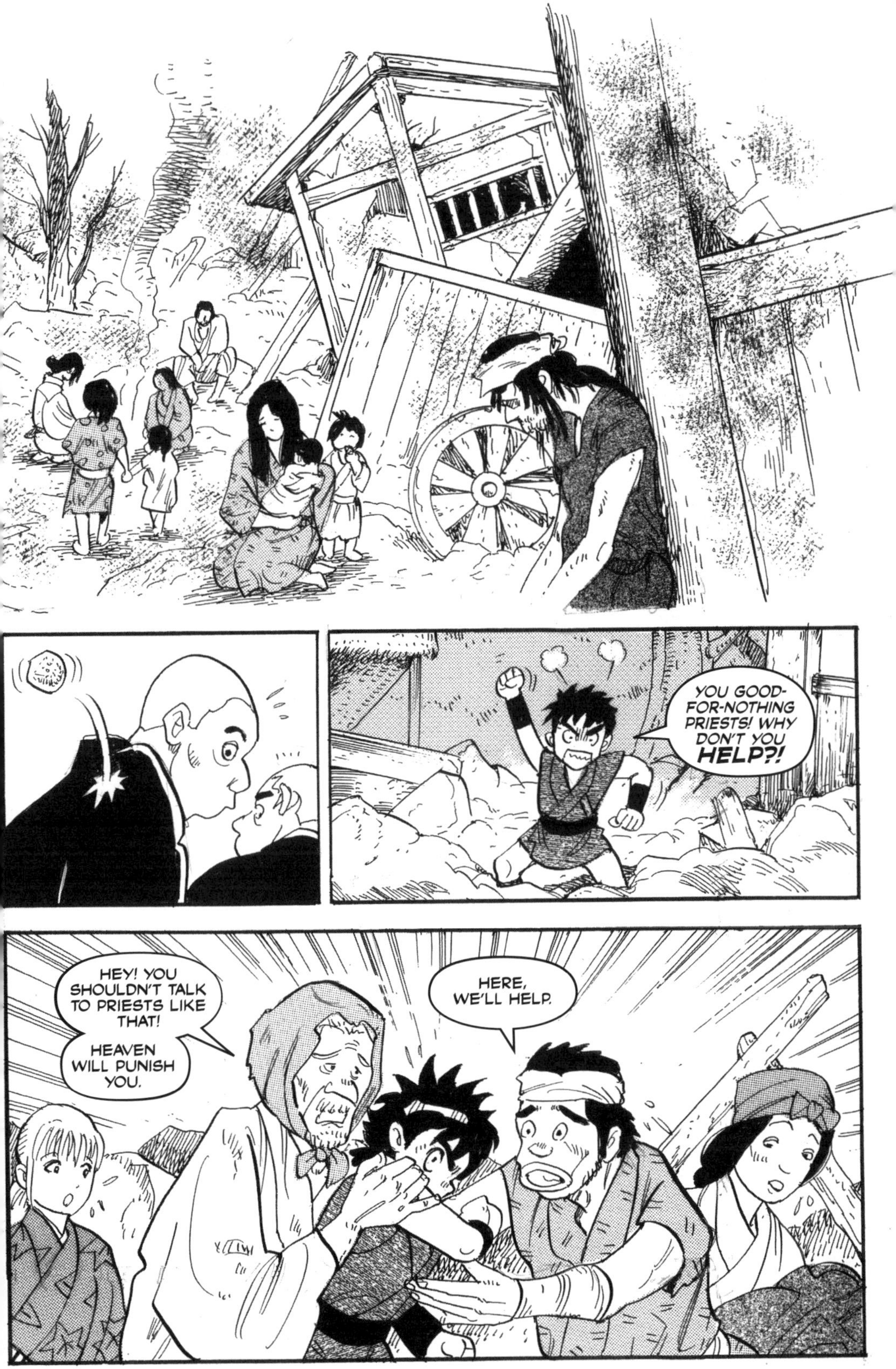
YOU GOOD-FOR-NOTHING PRIESTS! WHY DON'T YOU **HELP?!**
HEY! YOU SHOULDN'T TALK TO PRIESTS LIKE THAT!
HEAVEN WILL PUNISH YOU.
HERE, WE'LL HELP.

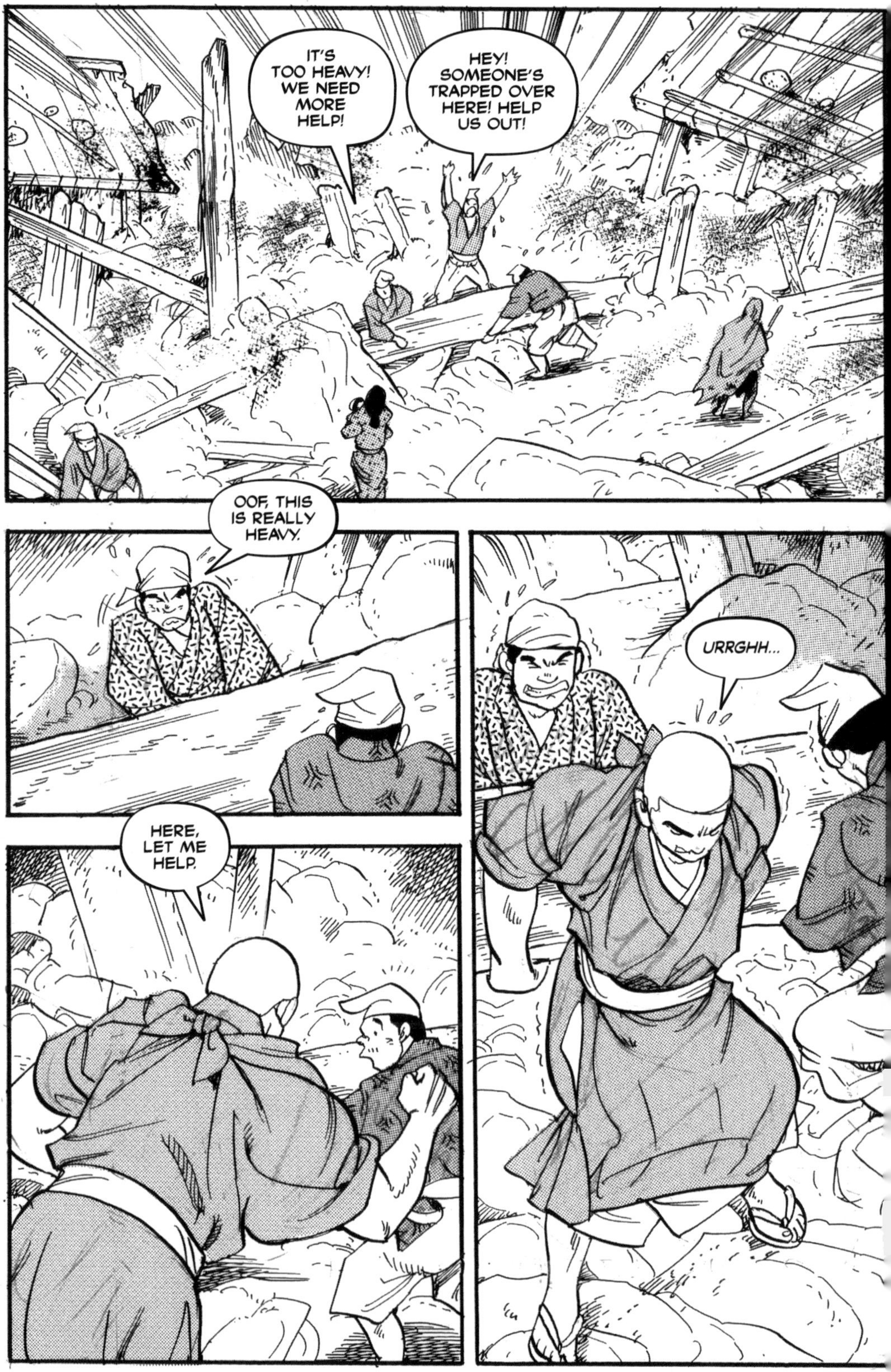
IT'S TOO HEAVY! WE NEED MORE HELP!
HEY! SOMEONE'S TRAPPED OVER HERE! HELP US OUT!
OOF, THIS IS REALLY HEAVY.
URRGHH...
HERE, LET ME HELP.

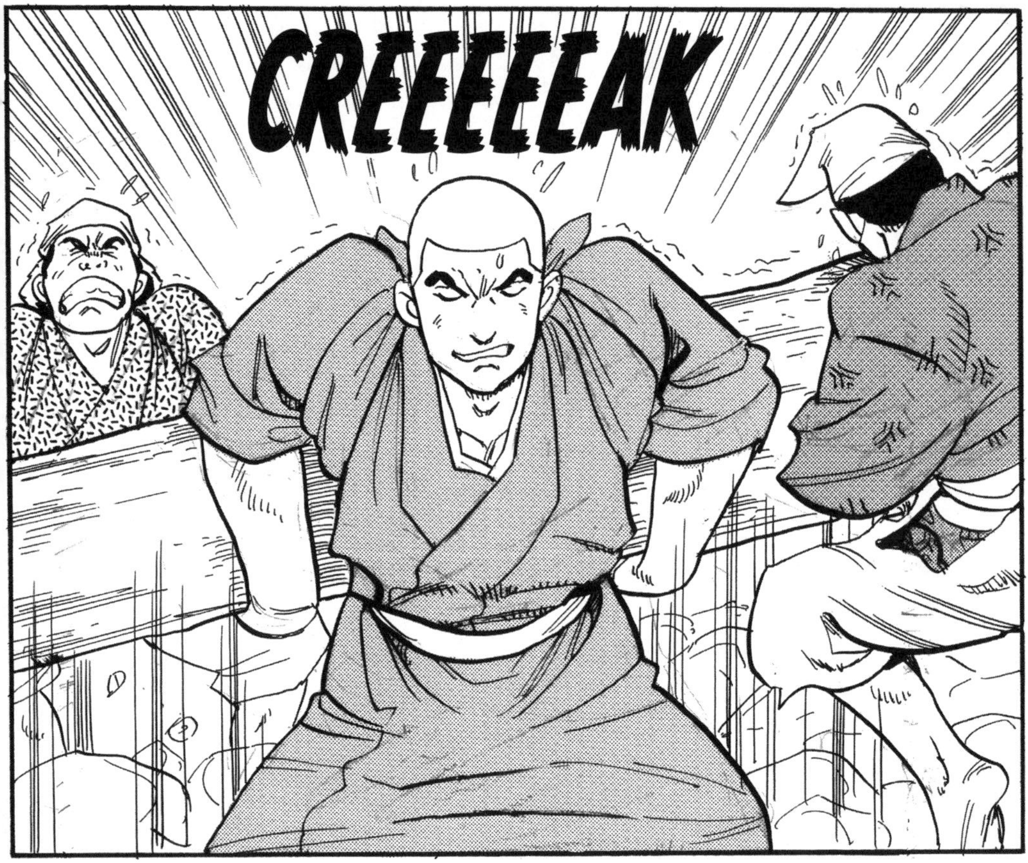
CREEEEEAK

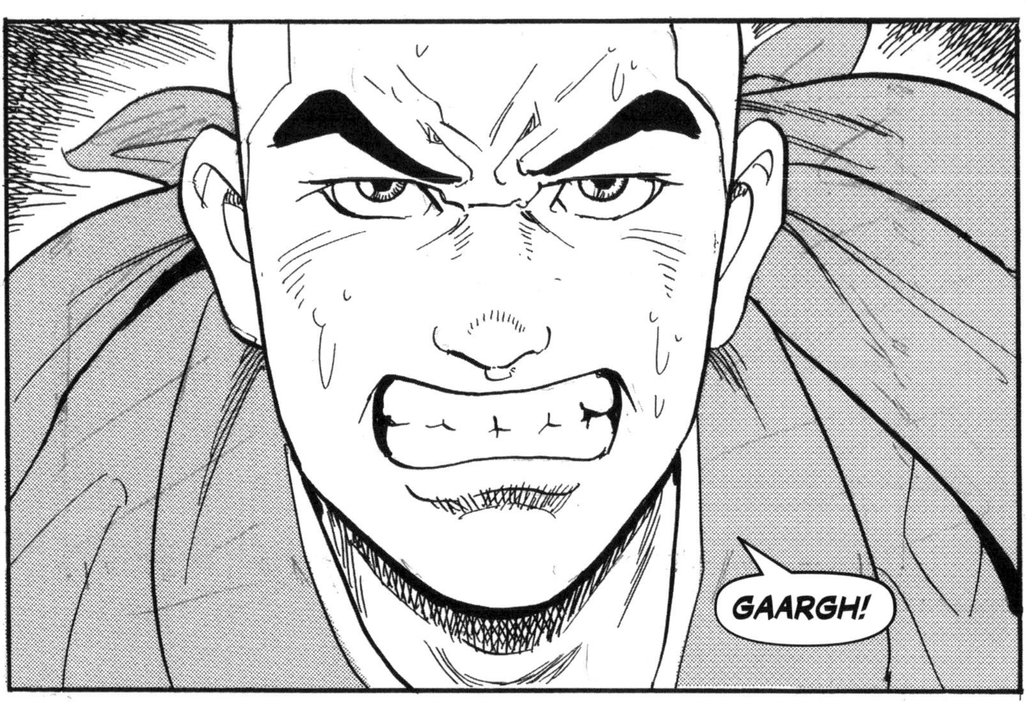
GAARGH!

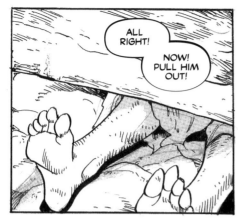

ALL RIGHT!

NOW! PULL HIM OUT!

CAN YOU HELP TOO, PLEASE?

YAY! WE DID IT!

PHEW! I'M GLAD...

YOU'RE A PRIEST?!

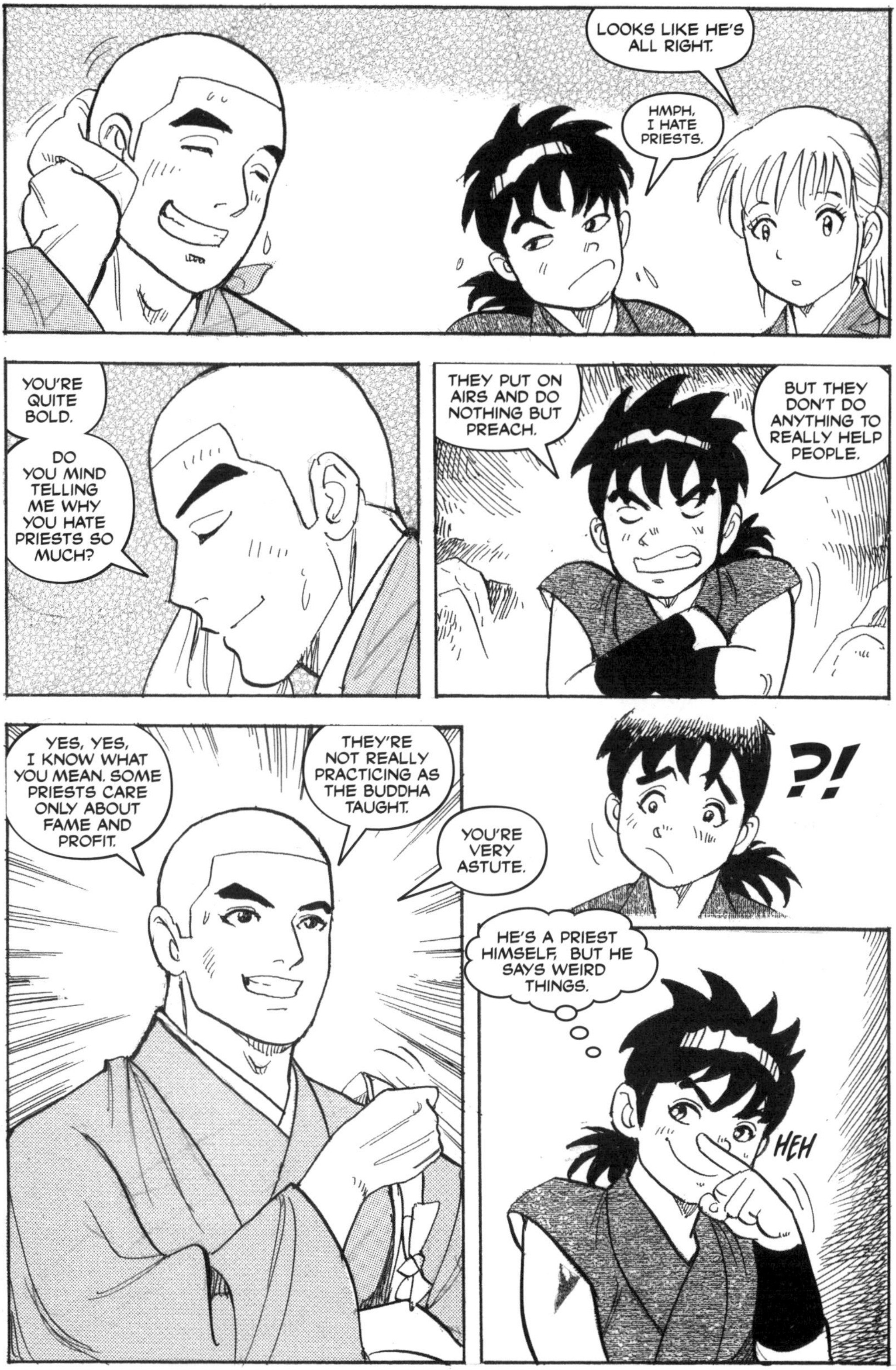

LOOKS LIKE HE'S ALL RIGHT.
HMPH, I HATE PRIESTS.
YOU'RE QUITE BOLD.
DO YOU MIND TELLING ME WHY YOU HATE PRIESTS SO MUCH?
THEY PUT ON AIRS AND DO NOTHING BUT PREACH.
BUT THEY DON'T DO ANYTHING TO REALLY HELP PEOPLE.
YES, YES, I KNOW WHAT YOU MEAN. SOME PRIESTS CARE ONLY ABOUT FAME AND PROFIT.
THEY'RE NOT REALLY PRACTICING AS THE BUDDHA TAUGHT.
YOU'RE VERY ASTUTE.
?!
HE'S A PRIEST HIMSELF, BUT HE SAYS WEIRD THINGS.
HEH

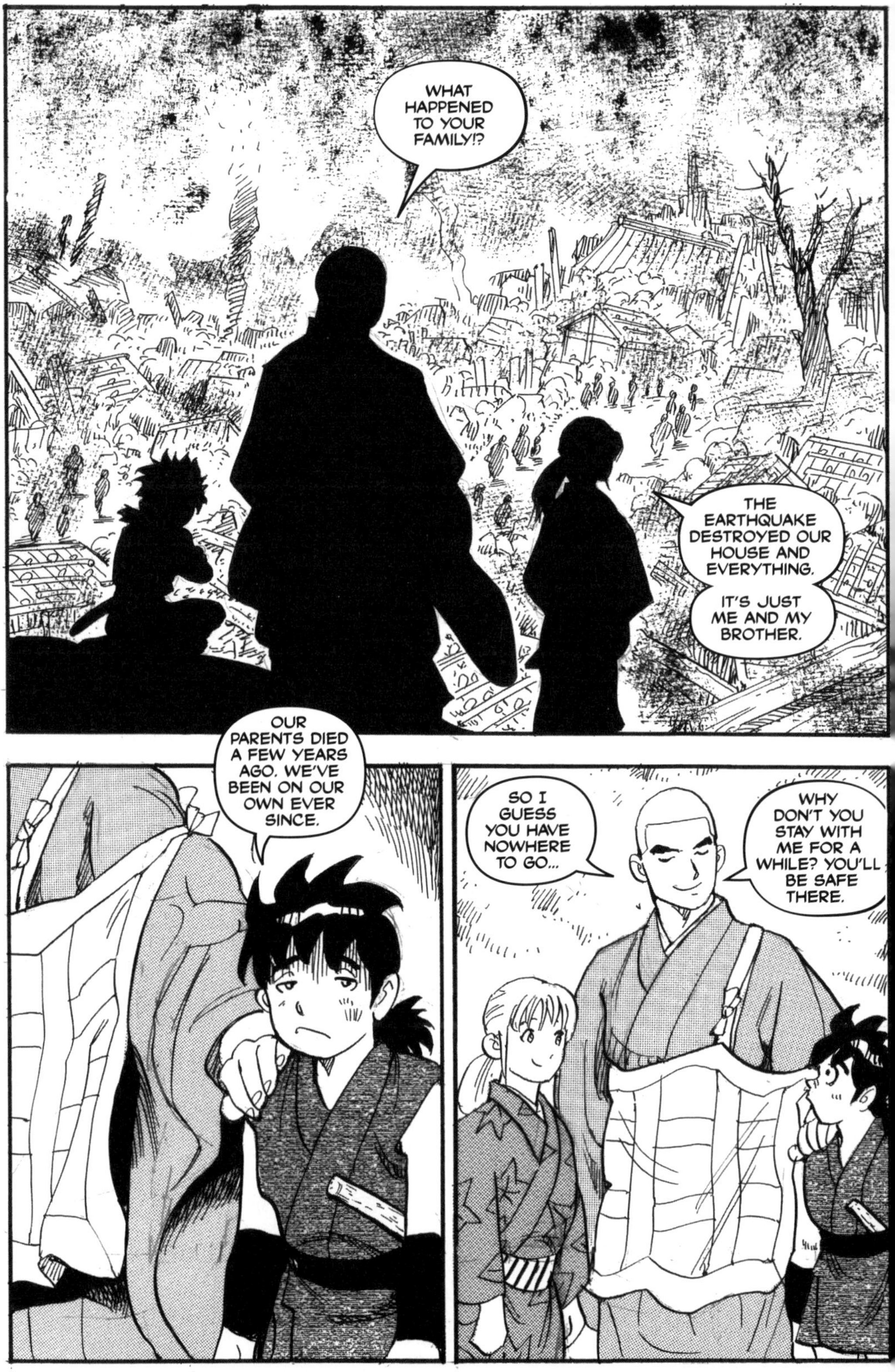
WHAT HAPPENED TO YOUR FAMILY!?
THE EARTHQUAKE DESTROYED OUR HOUSE AND EVERYTHING.
IT'S JUST ME AND MY BROTHER.
OUR PARENTS DIED A FEW YEARS AGO. WE'VE BEEN ON OUR OWN EVER SINCE.
SO I GUESS YOU HAVE NOWHERE TO GO...
WHY DON'T YOU STAY WITH ME FOR A WHILE? YOU'LL BE SAFE THERE.

CHAPTER 1

"ON ESTABLISHING THE CORRECT TEACHING
FOR THE PEACE OF THE LAND"

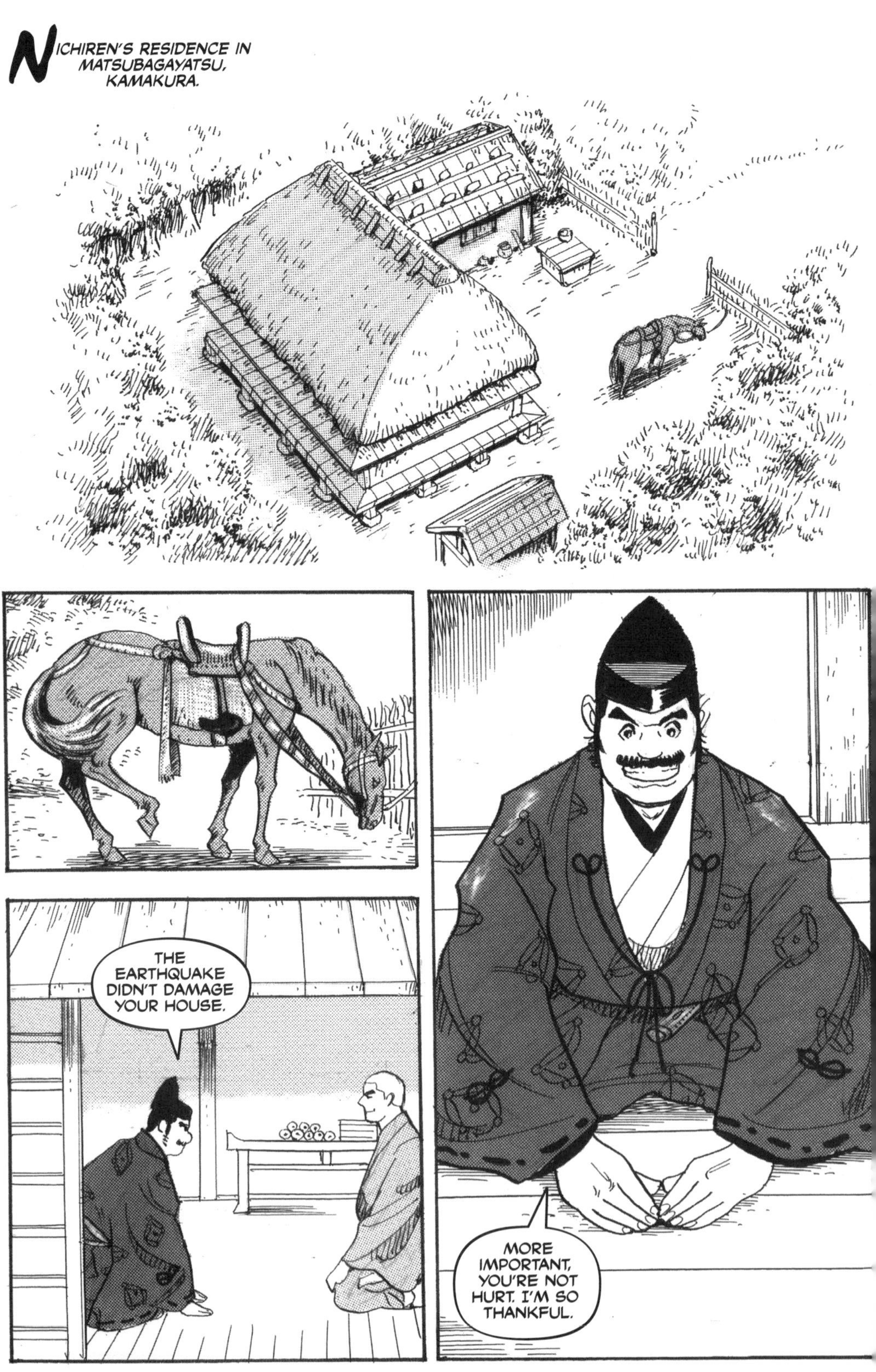
NICHIREN'S RESIDENCE IN MATSUBAGAYATSU, KAMAKURA.
THE EARTHQUAKE DIDN'T DAMAGE YOUR HOUSE.
MORE IMPORTANT, YOU'RE NOT HURT. I'M SO THANKFUL.

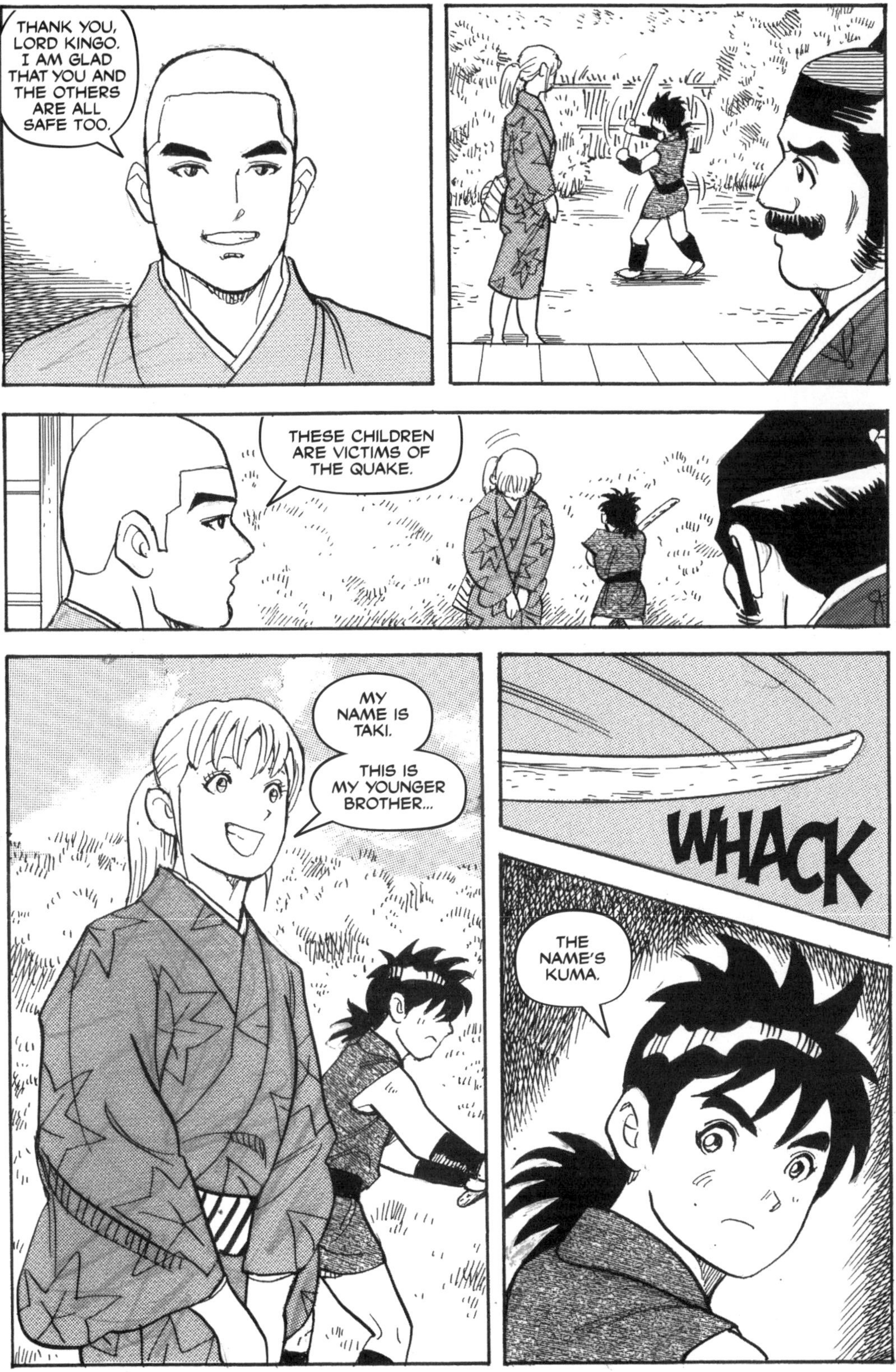

THANK YOU, LORD KINGO. I AM GLAD THAT YOU AND THE OTHERS ARE ALL SAFE TOO.
THESE CHILDREN ARE VICTIMS OF THE QUAKE.
MY NAME IS TAKI.
THIS IS MY YOUNGER BROTHER...
WHACK
THE NAME'S KUMA.

HAH! YOU'RE A *FIERY* ONE!

KUMA SAYS HE HATES PRIESTS.

HA HA HA

YEAH, BUT YOU'RE NOT REALLY *LIKE* A PRIEST.

YOU'RE DIFFERENT.

SO YOU MEAN YOU'RE LOOKING AFTER BOTH OF THEM?

I CAN MANAGE... WITH NISSHO'S AND NICHIRO'S HELP.

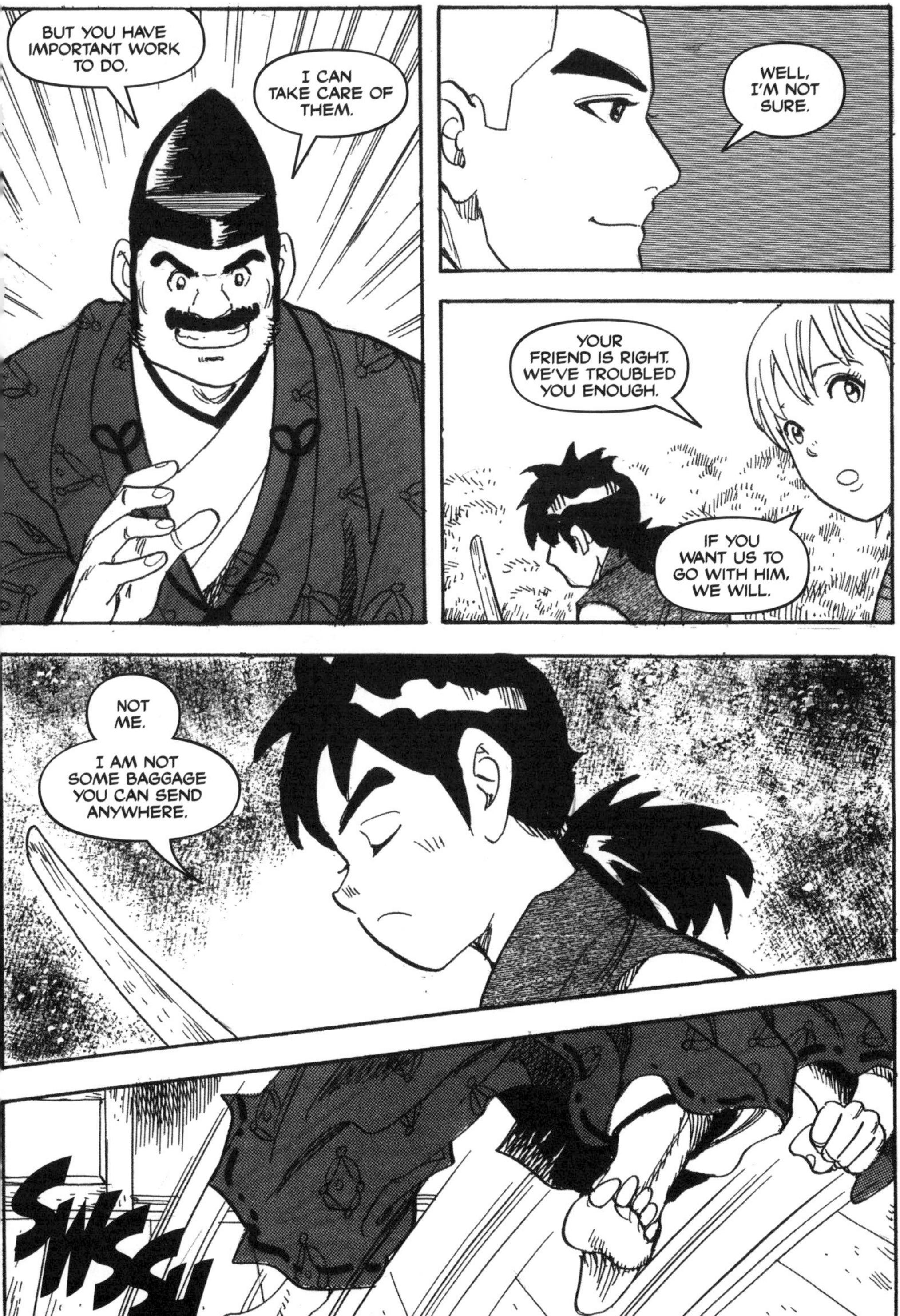
BUT YOU HAVE IMPORTANT WORK TO DO.
I CAN TAKE CARE OF THEM.
WELL, I'M NOT SURE.
YOUR FRIEND IS RIGHT. WE'VE TROUBLED YOU ENOUGH.
IF YOU WANT US TO GO WITH HIM, WE WILL.
NOT ME.
I AM NOT SOME BAGGAGE YOU CAN SEND ANYWHERE.
SWSH

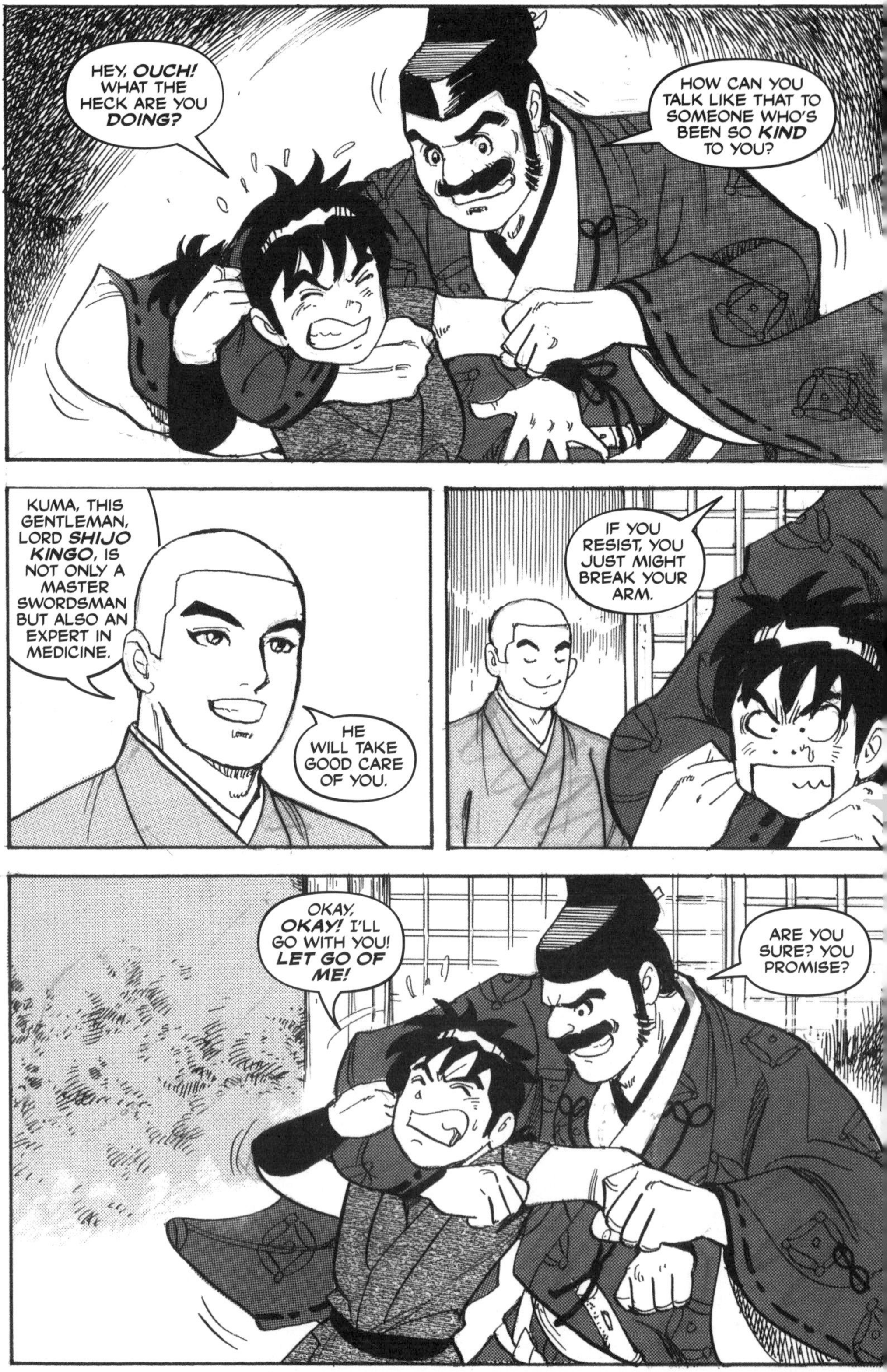
HEY, OUCH! WHAT THE HECK ARE YOU DOING?
HOW CAN YOU TALK LIKE THAT TO SOMEONE WHO'S BEEN SO KIND TO YOU?
KUMA, THIS GENTLEMAN, LORD SHIJO KINGO, IS NOT ONLY A MASTER SWORDSMAN BUT ALSO AN EXPERT IN MEDICINE.
HE WILL TAKE GOOD CARE OF YOU.
IF YOU RESIST, YOU JUST MIGHT BREAK YOUR ARM.
OKAY, OKAY! I'LL GO WITH YOU! LET GO OF ME!
ARE YOU SURE? YOU PROMISE?

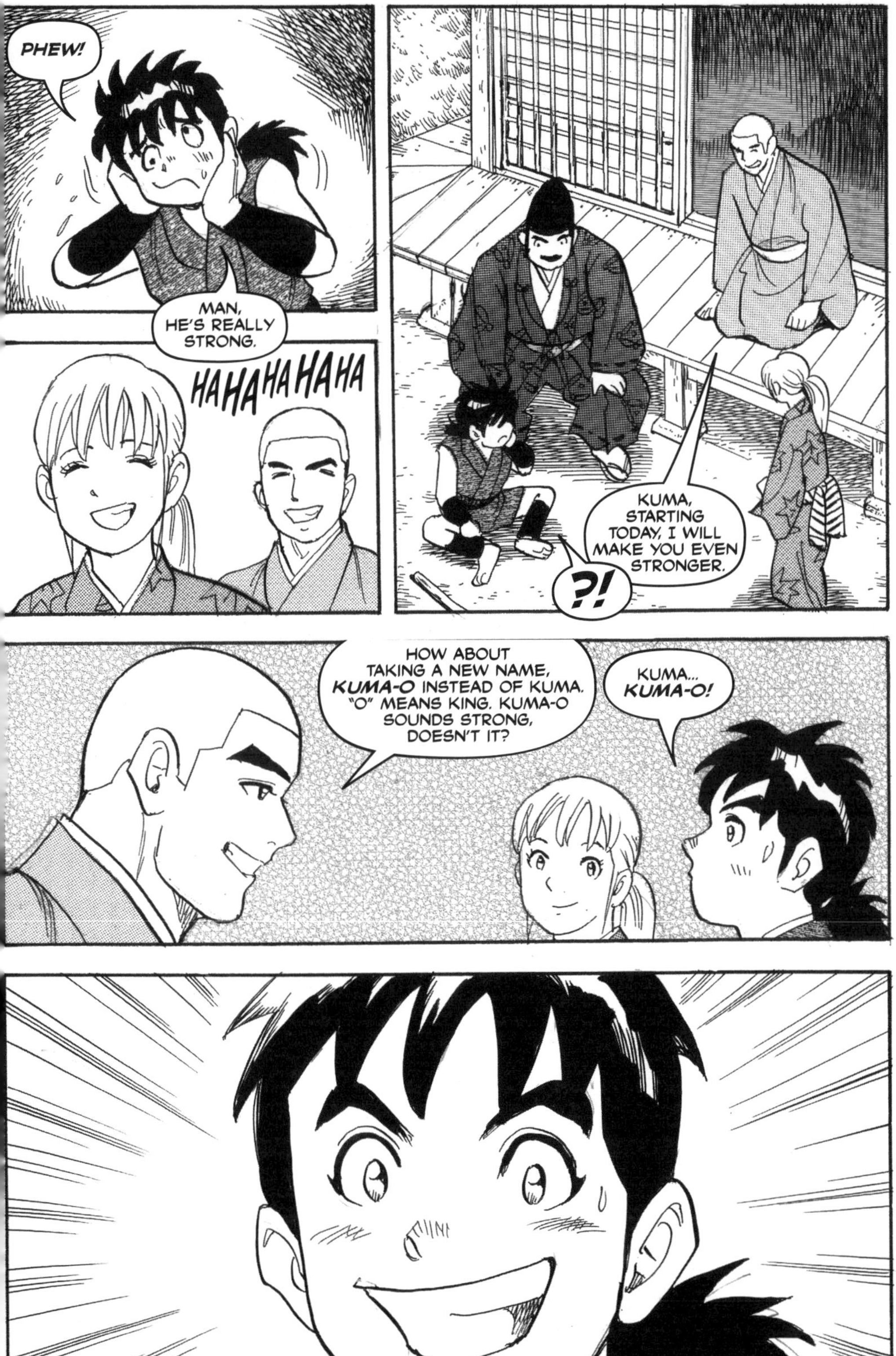
PHEW!
MAN, HE'S REALLY STRONG.
HAHAHAHAHAHA
KUMA, STARTING TODAY, I WILL MAKE YOU EVEN STRONGER.
?!
HOW ABOUT TAKING A NEW NAME, KUMA-O INSTEAD OF KUMA. "O" MEANS KING. KUMA-O SOUNDS STRONG, DOESN'T IT?
KUMA... KUMA-O!

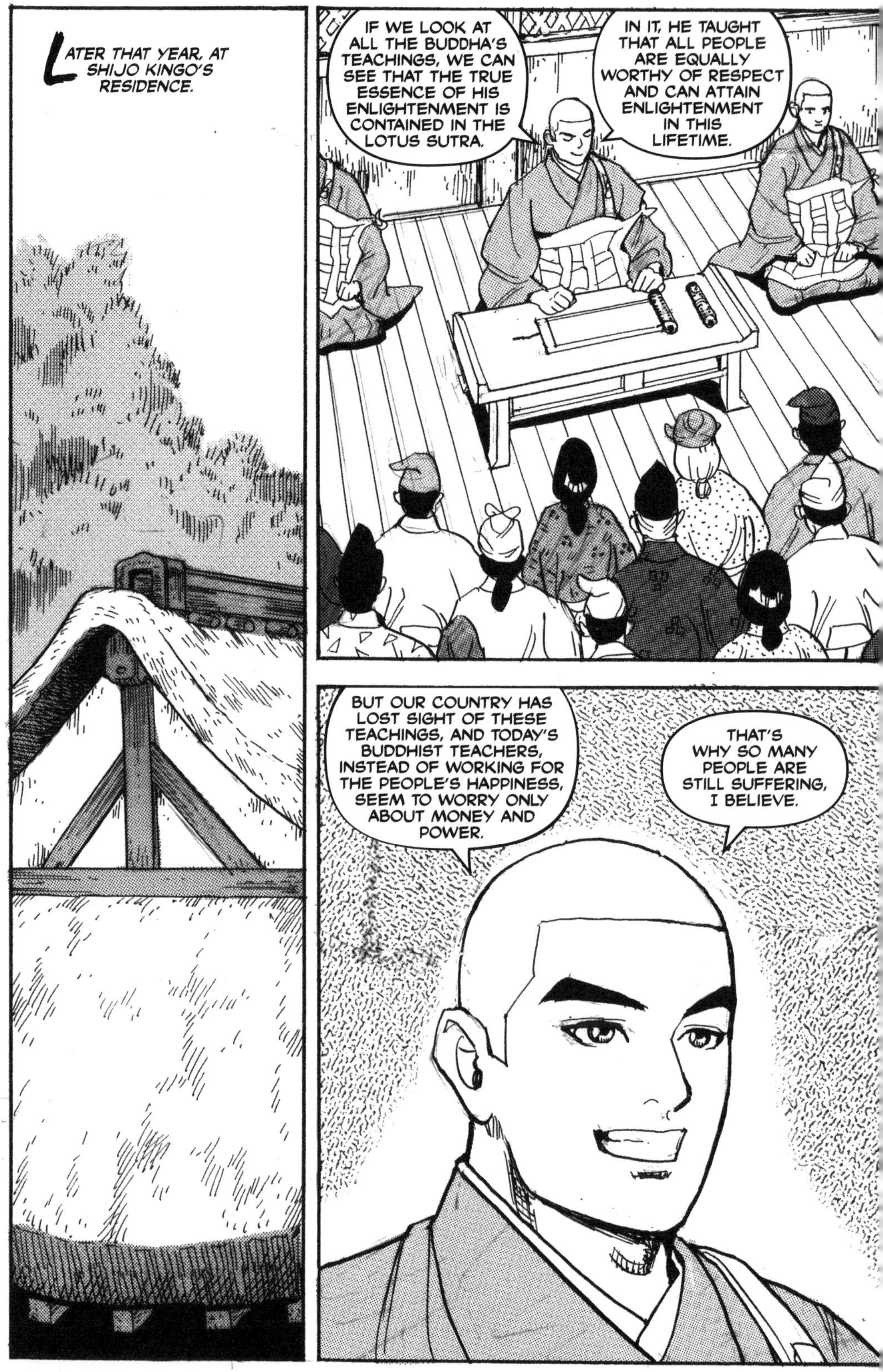
LATER THAT YEAR, AT SHIJO KINGO'S RESIDENCE.
IF WE LOOK AT ALL THE BUDDHA'S TEACHINGS, WE CAN SEE THAT THE TRUE ESSENCE OF HIS ENLIGHTENMENT IS CONTAINED IN THE LOTUS SUTRA.
IN IT, HE TAUGHT THAT ALL PEOPLE ARE EQUALLY WORTHY OF RESPECT AND CAN ATTAIN ENLIGHTENMENT IN THIS LIFETIME.
BUT OUR COUNTRY HAS LOST SIGHT OF THESE TEACHINGS, AND TODAY'S BUDDHIST TEACHERS, INSTEAD OF WORKING FOR THE PEOPLE'S HAPPINESS, SEEM TO WORRY ONLY ABOUT MONEY AND POWER.
THAT'S WHY SO MANY PEOPLE ARE STILL SUFFERING, I BELIEVE.

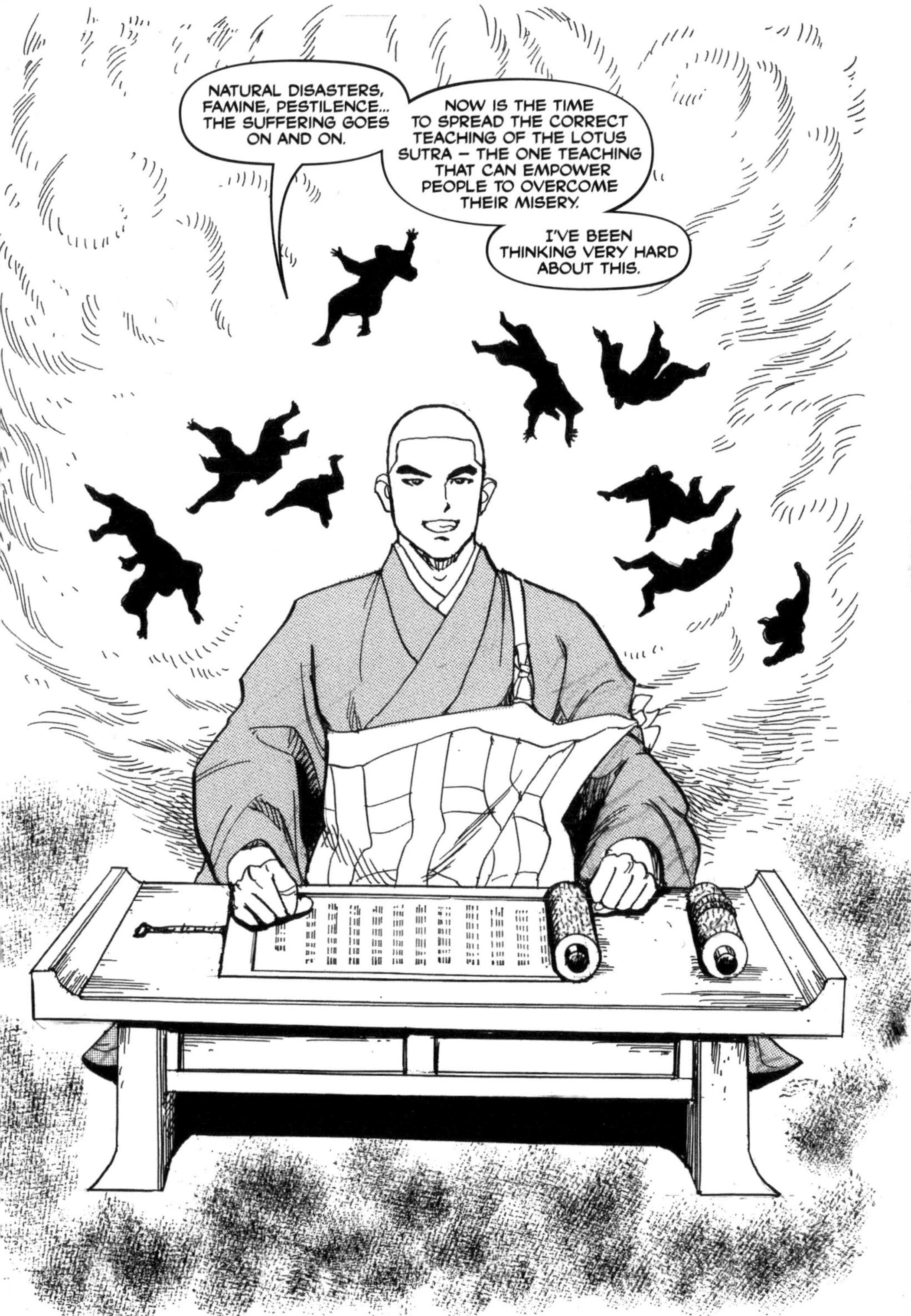
NATURAL DISASTERS, FAMINE, PESTILENCE... THE SUFFERING GOES ON AND ON.
NOW IS THE TIME TO SPREAD THE CORRECT TEACHING OF THE LOTUS SUTRA – THE ONE TEACHING THAT CAN EMPOWER PEOPLE TO OVERCOME THEIR MISERY.
I'VE BEEN THINKING VERY HARD ABOUT THIS.

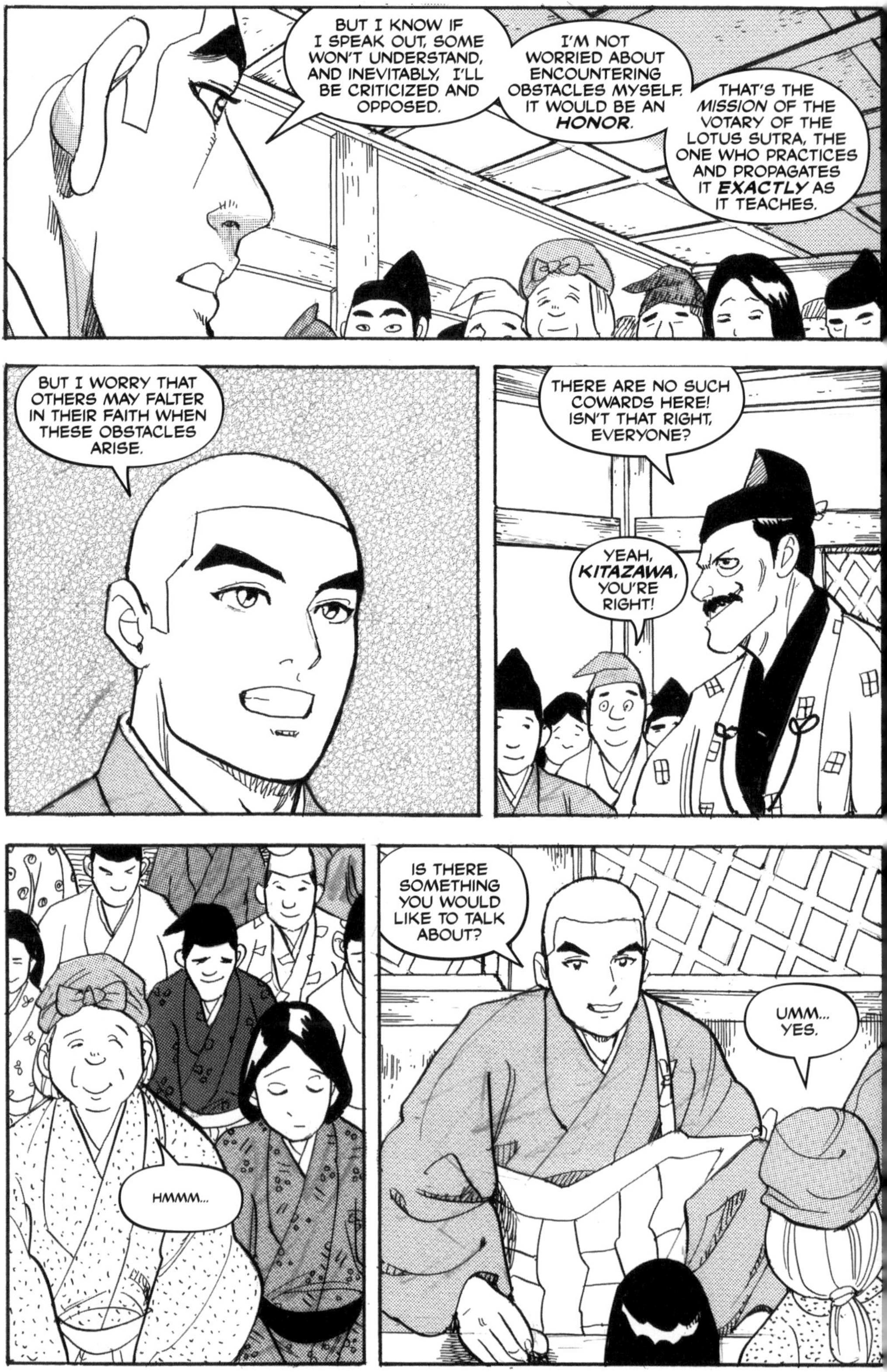
BUT I KNOW IF I SPEAK OUT, SOME WON'T UNDERSTAND, AND INEVITABLY, I'LL BE CRITICIZED AND OPPOSED.
I'M NOT WORRIED ABOUT ENCOUNTERING OBSTACLES MYSELF. IT WOULD BE AN **HONOR**.
THAT'S THE *MISSION* OF THE VOTARY OF THE LOTUS SUTRA, THE ONE WHO PRACTICES AND PROPAGATES IT ***EXACTLY*** AS IT TEACHES.
BUT I WORRY THAT OTHERS MAY FALTER IN THEIR FAITH WHEN THESE OBSTACLES ARISE.
THERE ARE NO SUCH COWARDS HERE! ISN'T THAT RIGHT, EVERYONE?
YEAH, ***KITAZAWA***, YOU'RE RIGHT!
HMMM...
IS THERE SOMETHING YOU WOULD LIKE TO TALK ABOUT?
UMM... YES.

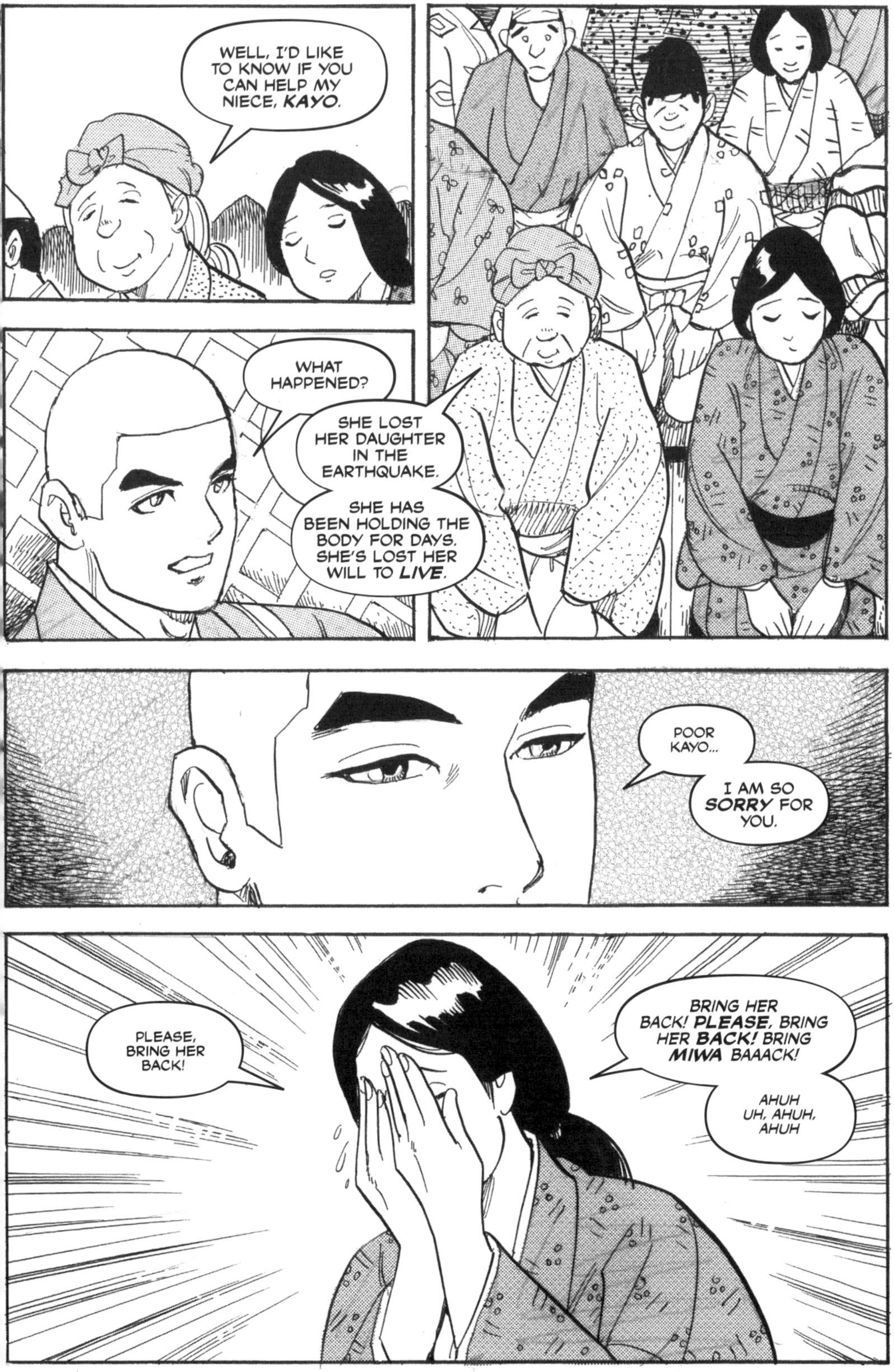
WELL, I'D LIKE TO KNOW IF YOU CAN HELP MY NIECE, KAYO.
WHAT HAPPENED?
SHE LOST HER DAUGHTER IN THE EARTHQUAKE.
SHE HAS BEEN HOLDING THE BODY FOR DAYS. SHE'S LOST HER WILL TO LIVE.
POOR KAYO...
I AM SO SORRY FOR YOU.
PLEASE, BRING HER BACK!
BRING HER BACK! PLEASE, BRING HER BACK! BRING MIWA BAAACK!
AHUH UH, AHUH, AHUH

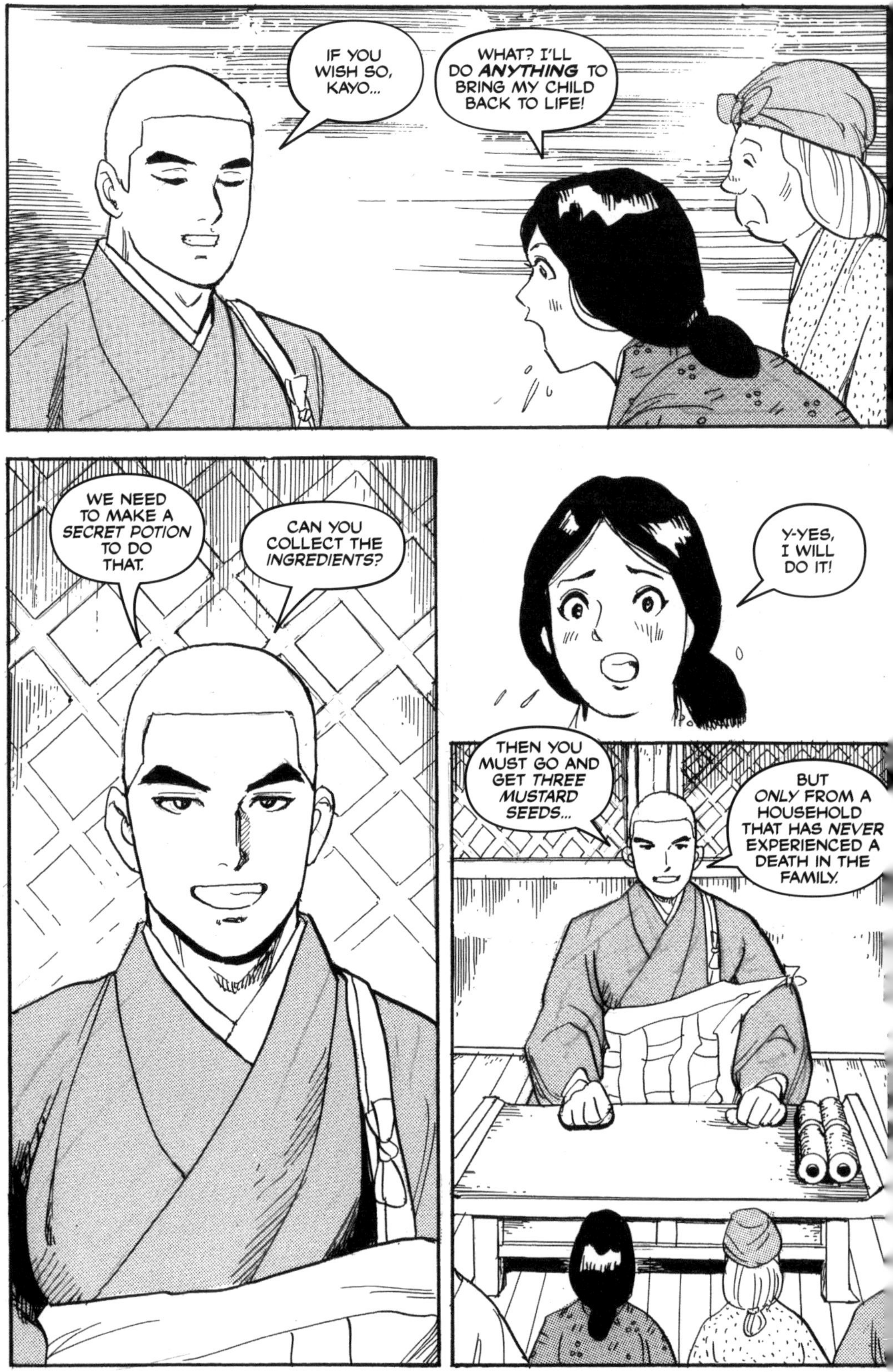
IF YOU WISH SO, KAYO...
WHAT? I'LL DO ***ANYTHING*** TO BRING MY CHILD BACK TO LIFE!
WE NEED TO MAKE A *SECRET POTION* TO DO THAT.
CAN YOU COLLECT THE *INGREDIENTS?*
Y-YES, I WILL DO IT!
THEN YOU MUST GO AND GET *THREE MUSTARD SEEDS...*
BUT *ONLY* FROM A HOUSEHOLD THAT HAS *NEVER* EXPERIENCED A DEATH IN THE FAMILY.

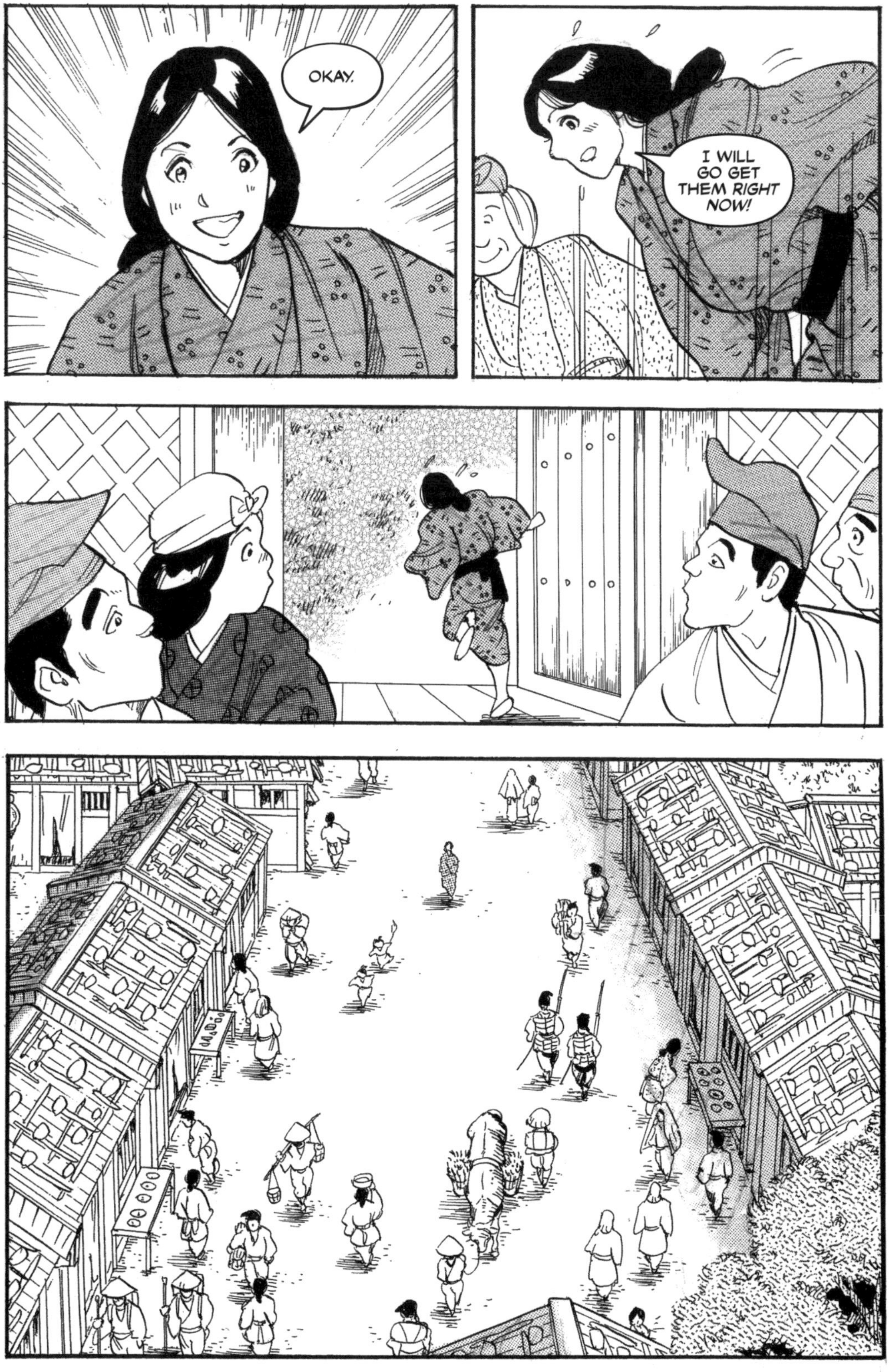
OKAY.
I WILL GO GET THEM *RIGHT* NOW!

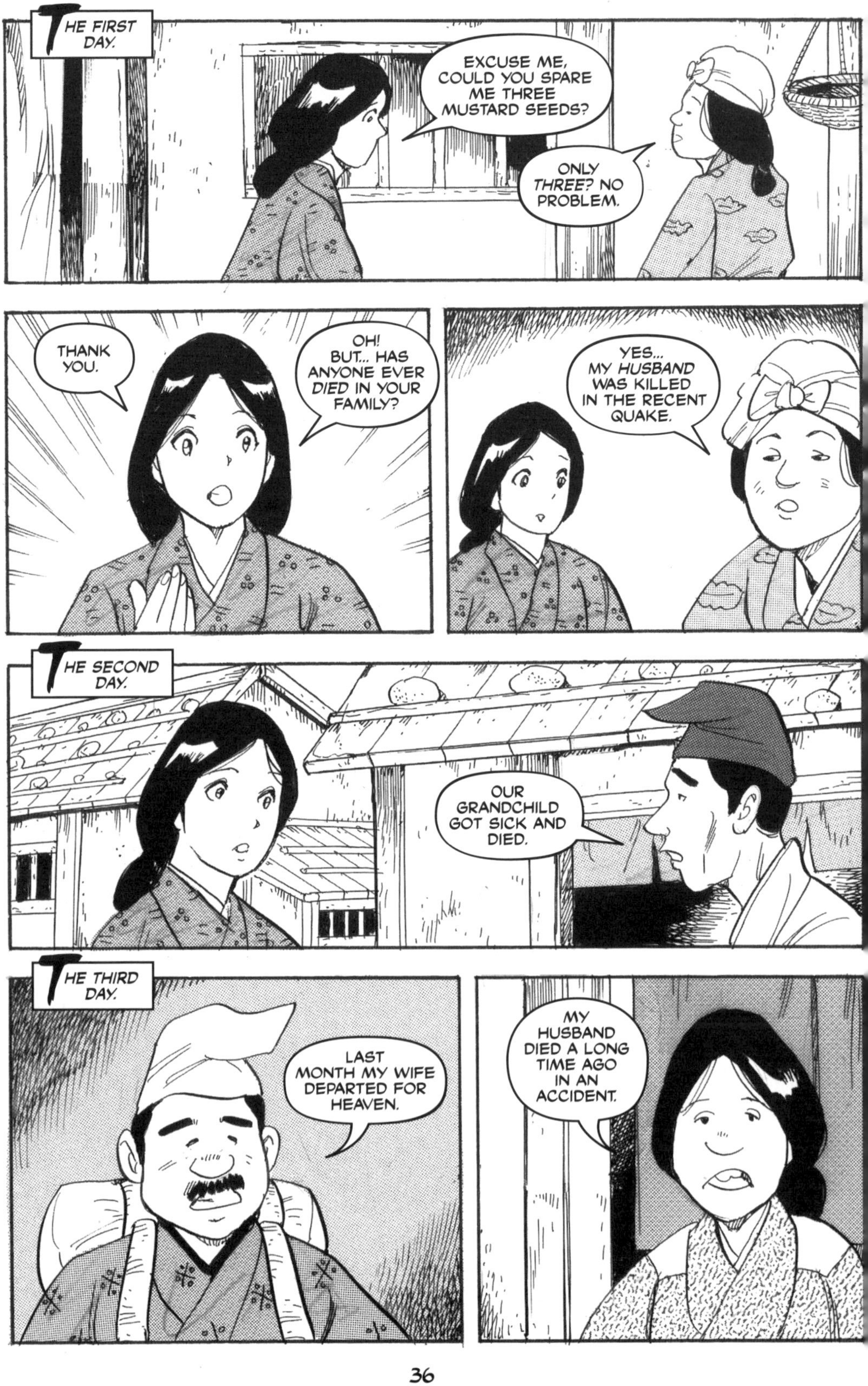
THE FIRST DAY.
EXCUSE ME, COULD YOU SPARE ME THREE MUSTARD SEEDS?
ONLY *THREE*? NO PROBLEM.
THANK YOU.
OH! BUT... HAS ANYONE EVER *DIED* IN YOUR FAMILY?
YES... MY *HUSBAND* WAS KILLED IN THE RECENT QUAKE.
THE SECOND DAY.
OUR GRANDCHILD GOT SICK AND DIED.
THE THIRD DAY.
LAST MONTH MY WIFE DEPARTED FOR HEAVEN.
MY HUSBAND DIED A LONG TIME AGO IN AN ACCIDENT.

...

...

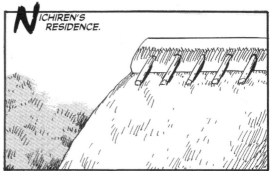

NICHIREN'S RESIDENCE.

I... COULD NOT COLLECT THE INGREDIENTS FOR THE SECRET POTION.

EVERY HOUSEHOLD I VISITED HAS EXPERIENCED DEATH.

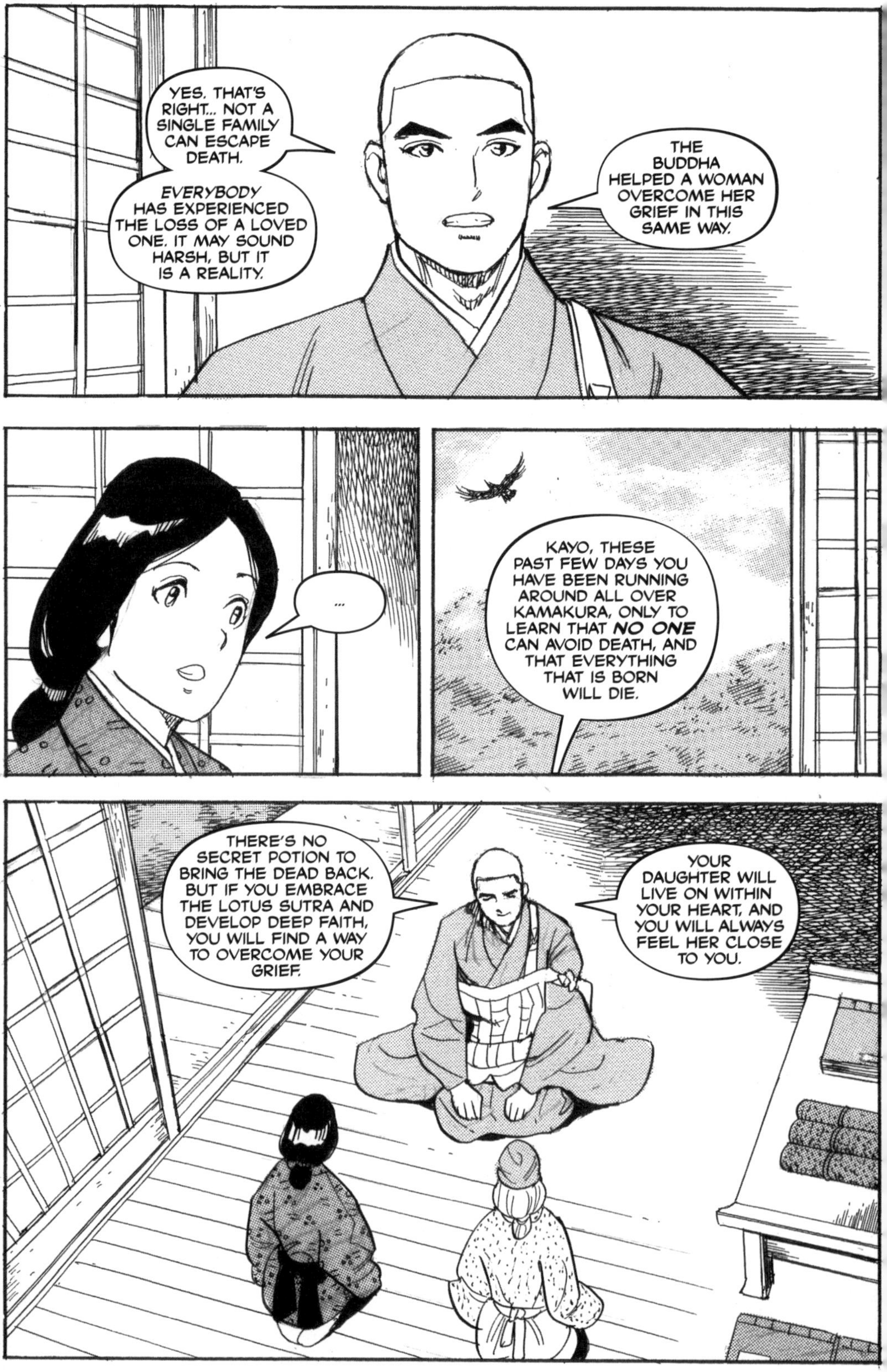
YES, THAT'S RIGHT... NOT A SINGLE FAMILY CAN ESCAPE DEATH.
EVERYBODY HAS EXPERIENCED THE LOSS OF A LOVED ONE. IT MAY SOUND HARSH, BUT IT IS A REALITY.
THE BUDDHA HELPED A WOMAN OVERCOME HER GRIEF IN THIS SAME WAY.
...
KAYO, THESE PAST FEW DAYS YOU HAVE BEEN RUNNING AROUND ALL OVER KAMAKURA, ONLY TO LEARN THAT **NO ONE** CAN AVOID DEATH, AND THAT EVERYTHING THAT IS BORN WILL DIE.
THERE'S NO SECRET POTION TO BRING THE DEAD BACK. BUT IF YOU EMBRACE THE LOTUS SUTRA AND DEVELOP DEEP FAITH, YOU WILL FIND A WAY TO OVERCOME YOUR GRIEF.
YOUR DAUGHTER WILL LIVE ON WITHIN YOUR HEART, AND YOU WILL ALWAYS FEEL HER CLOSE TO YOU.

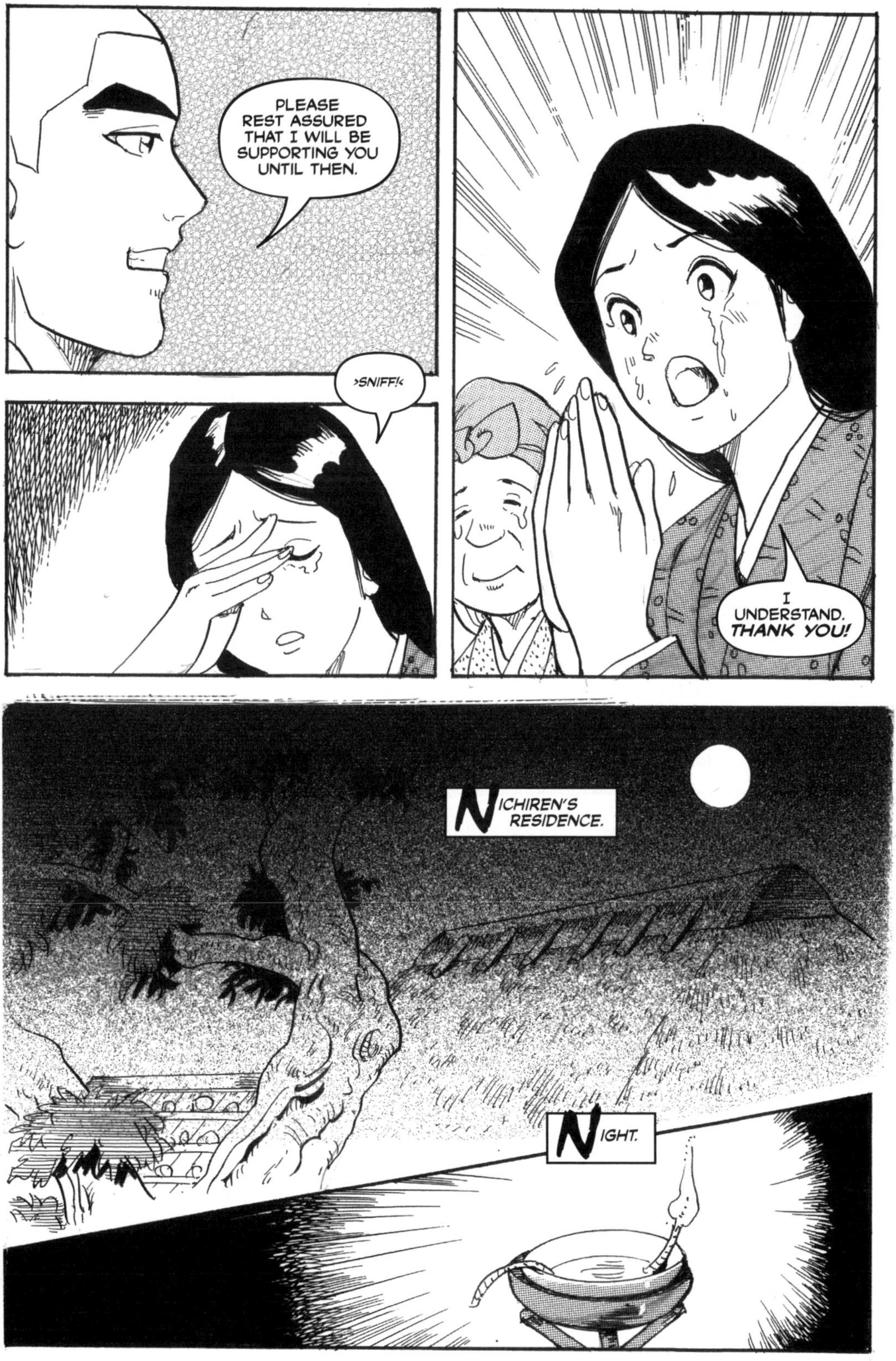
PLEASE REST ASSURED THAT I WILL BE SUPPORTING YOU UNTIL THEN.
›SNIFF!‹
I UNDERSTAND. THANK YOU!
NICHIREN'S RESIDENCE.
NIGHT.

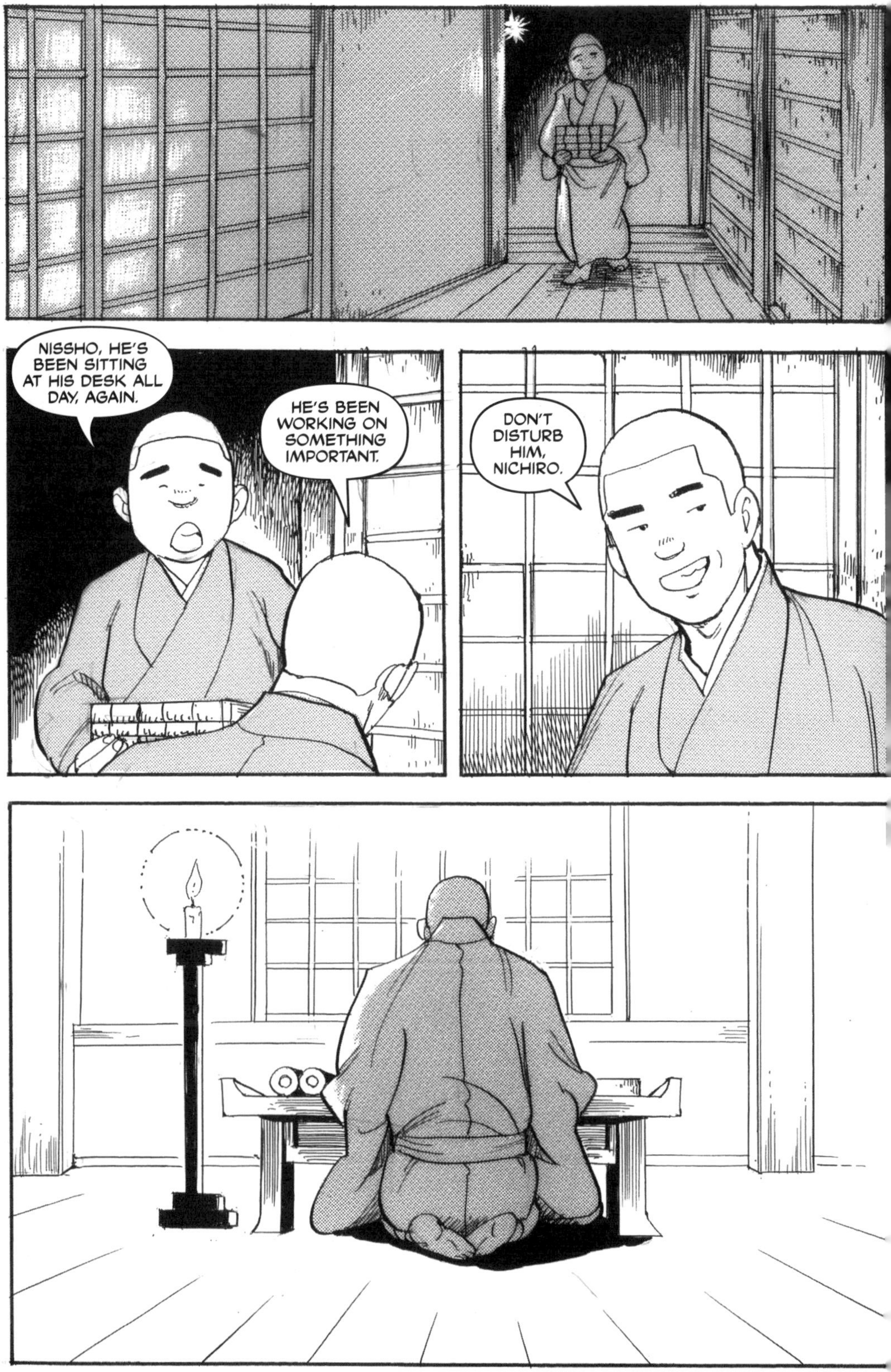
NISSHO, HE'S BEEN SITTING AT HIS DESK ALL DAY, AGAIN.
HE'S BEEN WORKING ON SOMETHING IMPORTANT.
DON'T DISTURB HIM, NICHIRO.

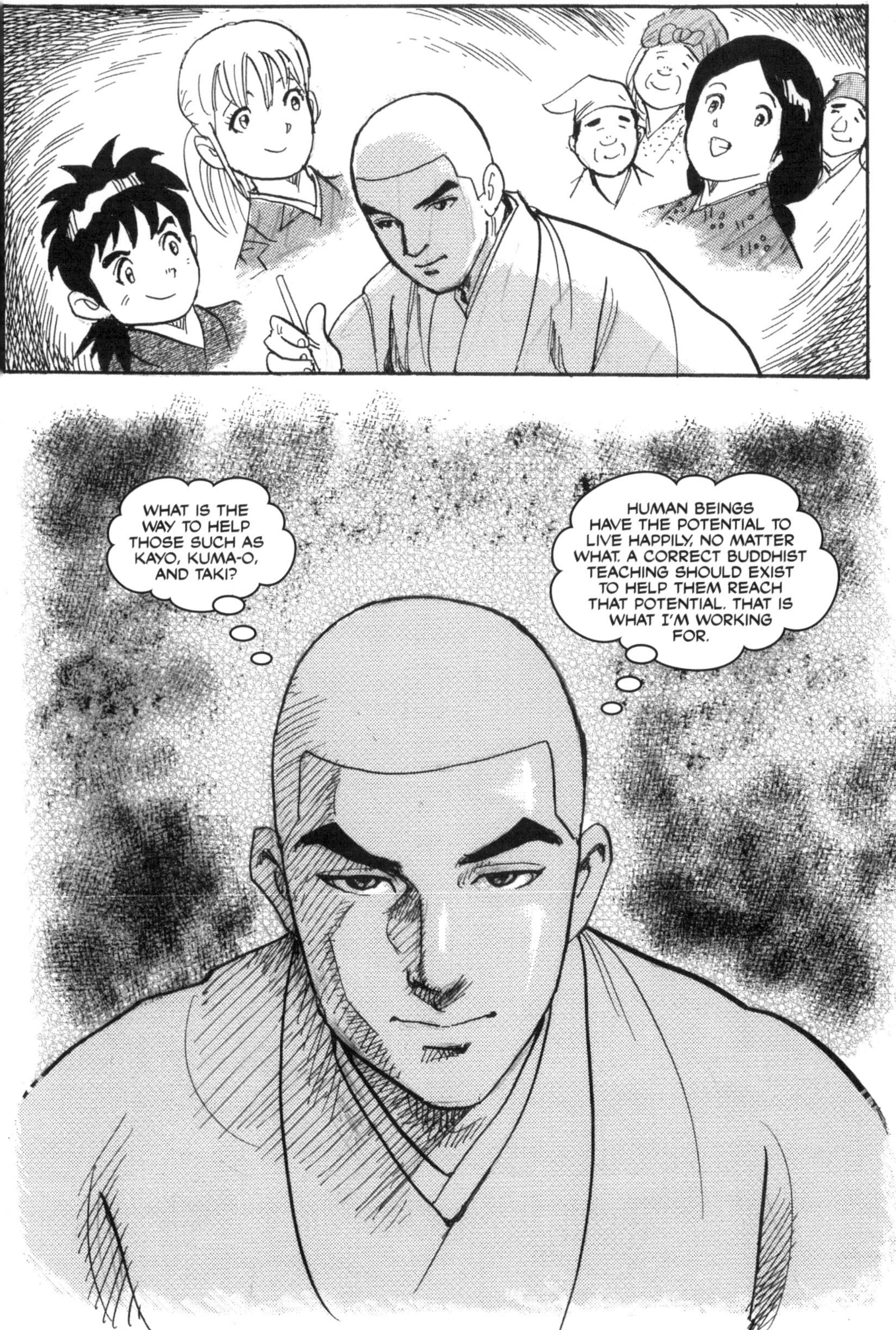
WHAT IS THE WAY TO HELP THOSE SUCH AS KAYO, KUMA-O, AND TAKI?
HUMAN BEINGS HAVE THE POTENTIAL TO LIVE HAPPILY, NO MATTER WHAT. A CORRECT BUDDHIST TEACHING SHOULD EXIST TO HELP THEM REACH THAT POTENTIAL. THAT IS WHAT I'M WORKING FOR.

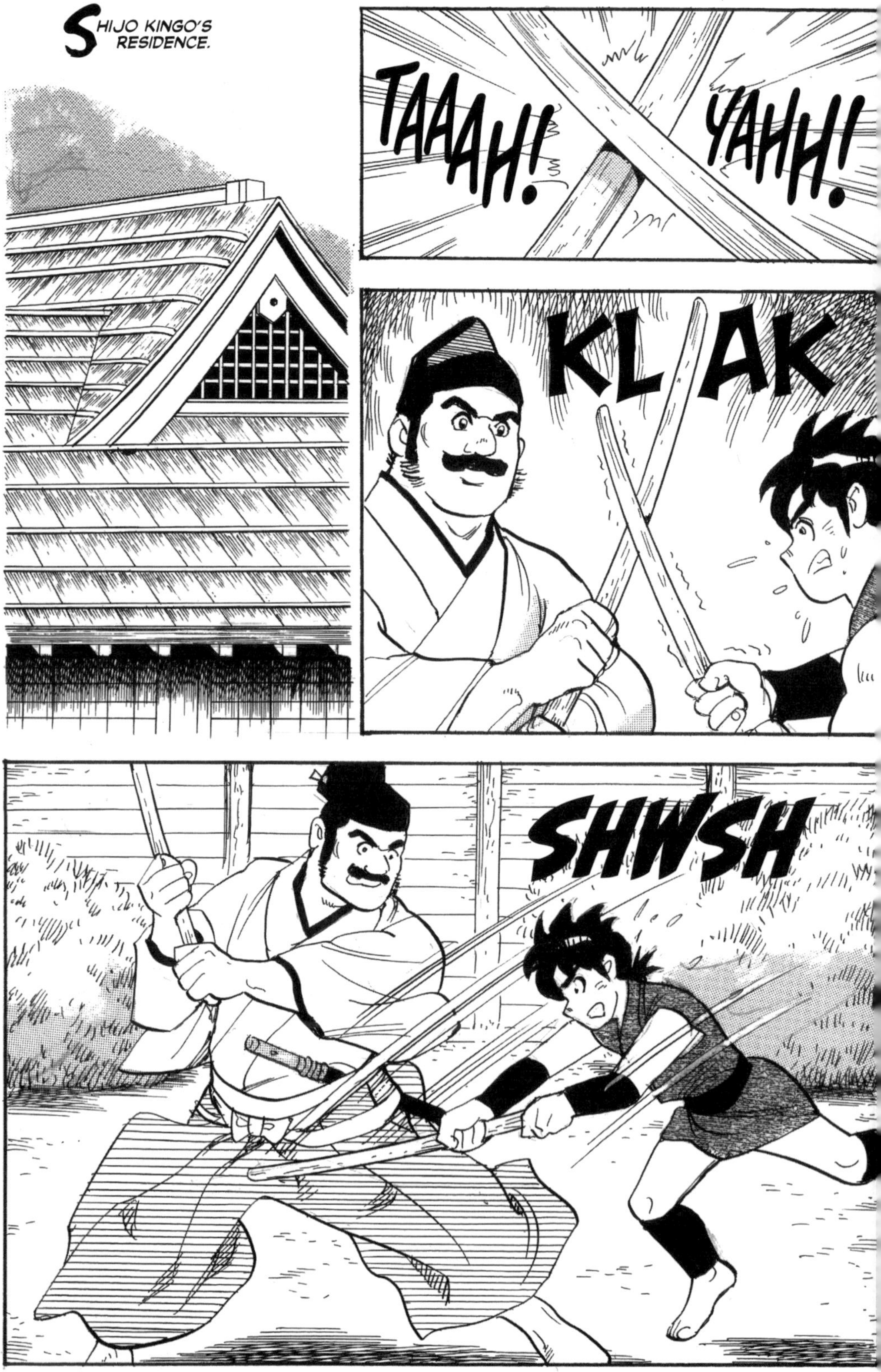
SHIJO KINGO'S RESIDENCE.
TAAAH!
YAHH!
KLAK
SHWSH

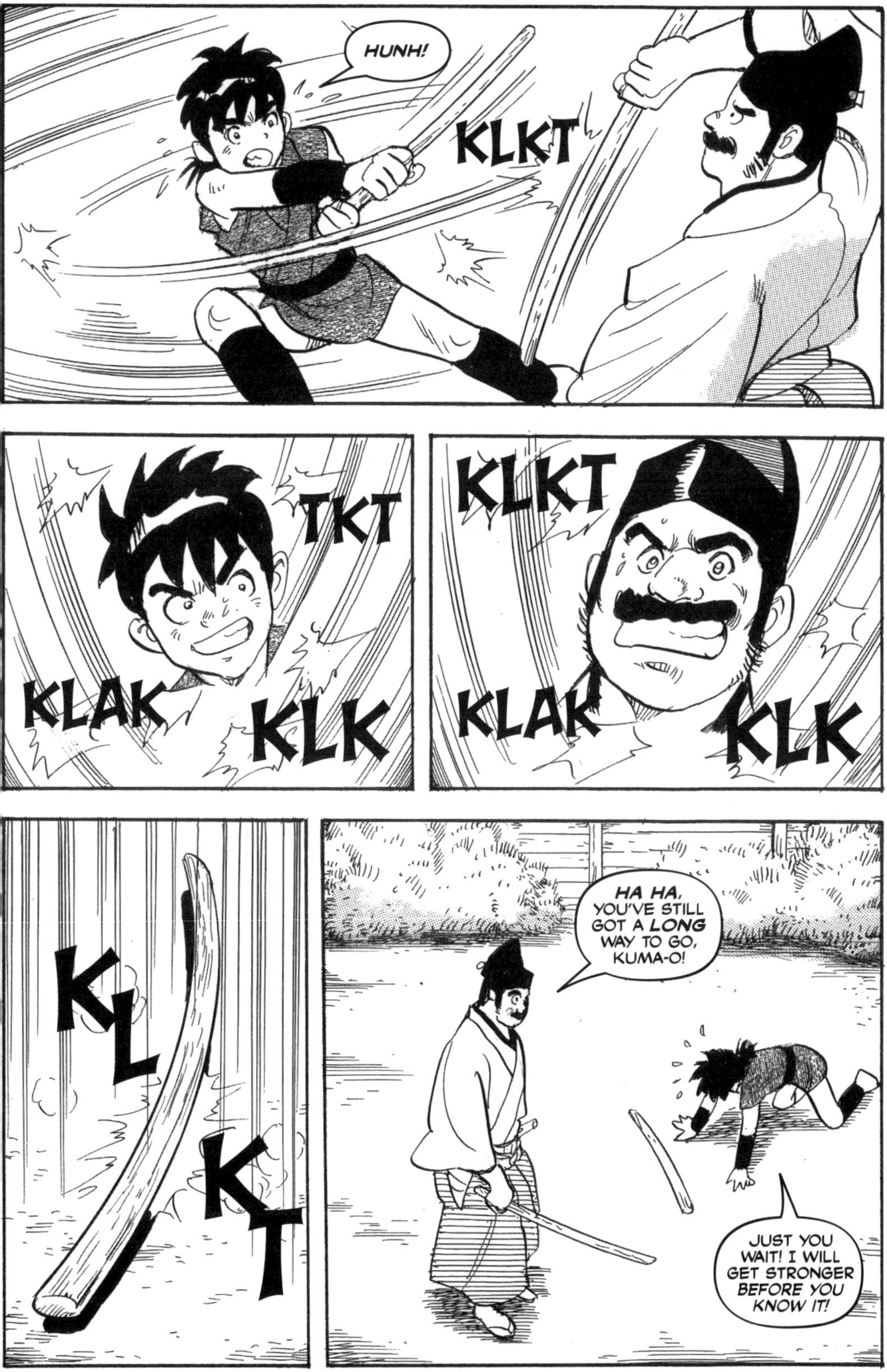
HUNH!
KLKT
TKT
KLAK
KLK
KLKT
KLAK
KLK
KLKT
HA HA, YOU'VE STILL GOT A LONG WAY TO GO, KUMA-O!
JUST YOU WAIT! I WILL GET STRONGER BEFORE YOU KNOW IT!

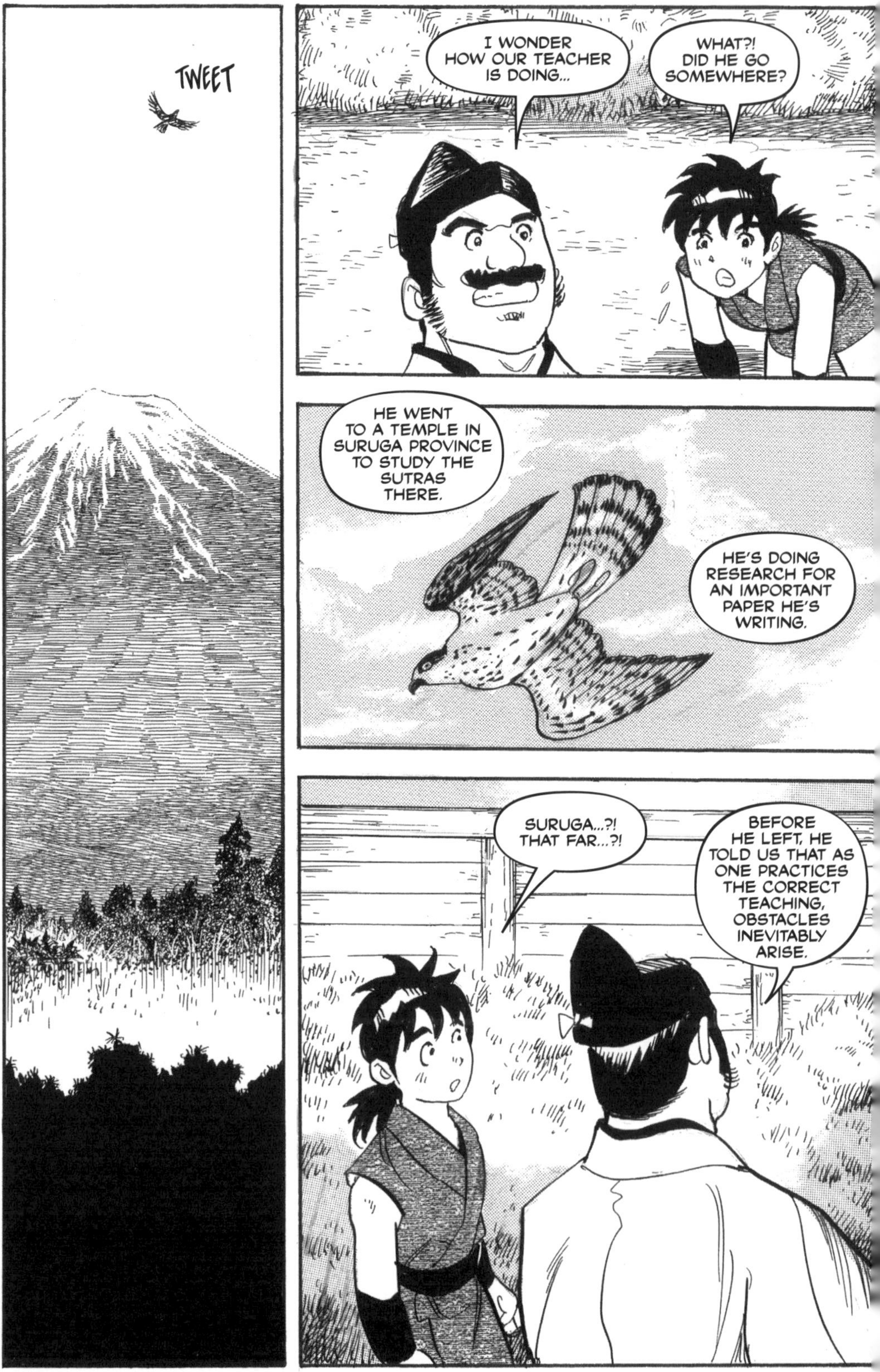
TWEET
I WONDER HOW OUR TEACHER IS DOING...
WHAT?! DID HE GO SOMEWHERE?
HE WENT TO A TEMPLE IN SURUGA PROVINCE TO STUDY THE SUTRAS THERE.
HE'S DOING RESEARCH FOR AN IMPORTANT PAPER HE'S WRITING.
SURUGA...?! THAT FAR...?!
BEFORE HE LEFT, HE TOLD US THAT AS ONE PRACTICES THE CORRECT TEACHING, OBSTACLES INEVITABLY ARISE.

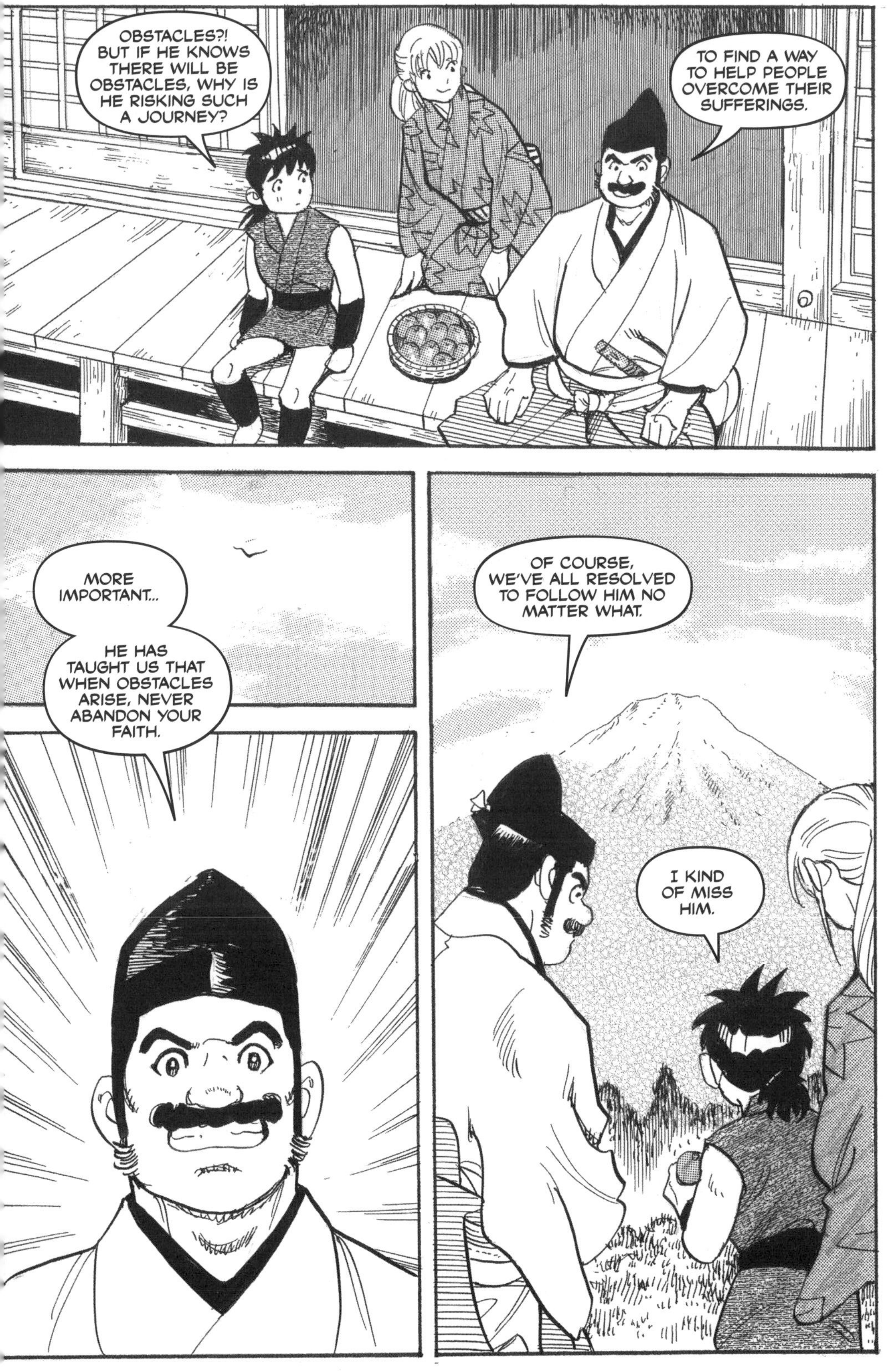
OBSTACLES?! BUT IF HE KNOWS THERE WILL BE OBSTACLES, WHY IS HE RISKING SUCH A JOURNEY?
TO FIND A WAY TO HELP PEOPLE OVERCOME THEIR SUFFERINGS.
MORE IMPORTANT...
HE HAS TAUGHT US THAT WHEN OBSTACLES ARISE, NEVER ABANDON YOUR FAITH.
OF COURSE, WE'VE ALL RESOLVED TO FOLLOW HIM NO MATTER WHAT.
I KIND OF MISS HIM.

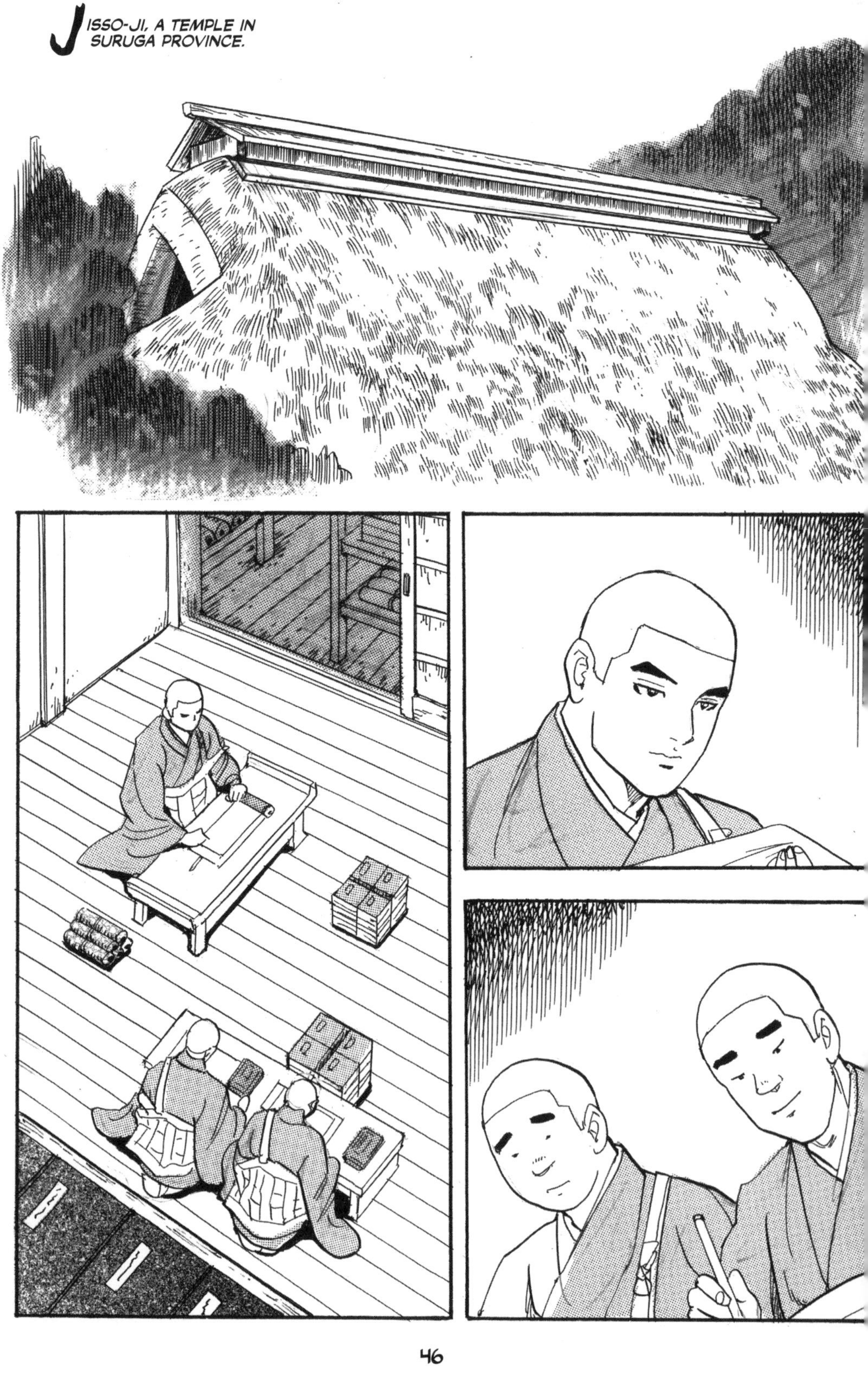
JISSO-JI, A TEMPLE IN SURUGA PROVINCE.

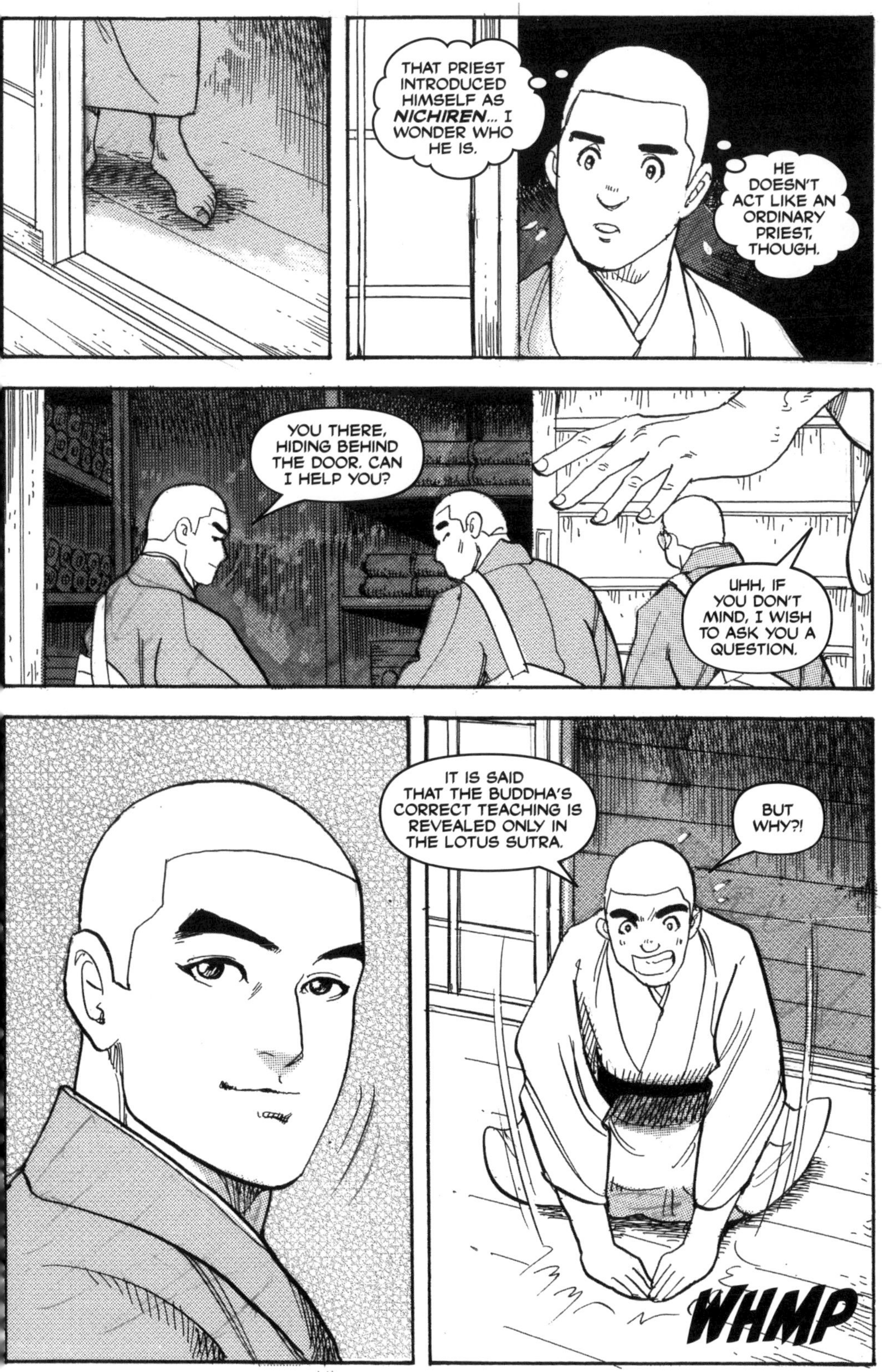
THAT PRIEST INTRODUCED HIMSELF AS NICHIREN... I WONDER WHO HE IS.
HE DOESN'T ACT LIKE AN ORDINARY PRIEST, THOUGH.
YOU THERE, HIDING BEHIND THE DOOR. CAN I HELP YOU?
UHH, IF YOU DON'T MIND, I WISH TO ASK YOU A QUESTION.
IT IS SAID THAT THE BUDDHA'S CORRECT TEACHING IS REVEALED ONLY IN THE LOTUS SUTRA.
BUT WHY?!
WHMP

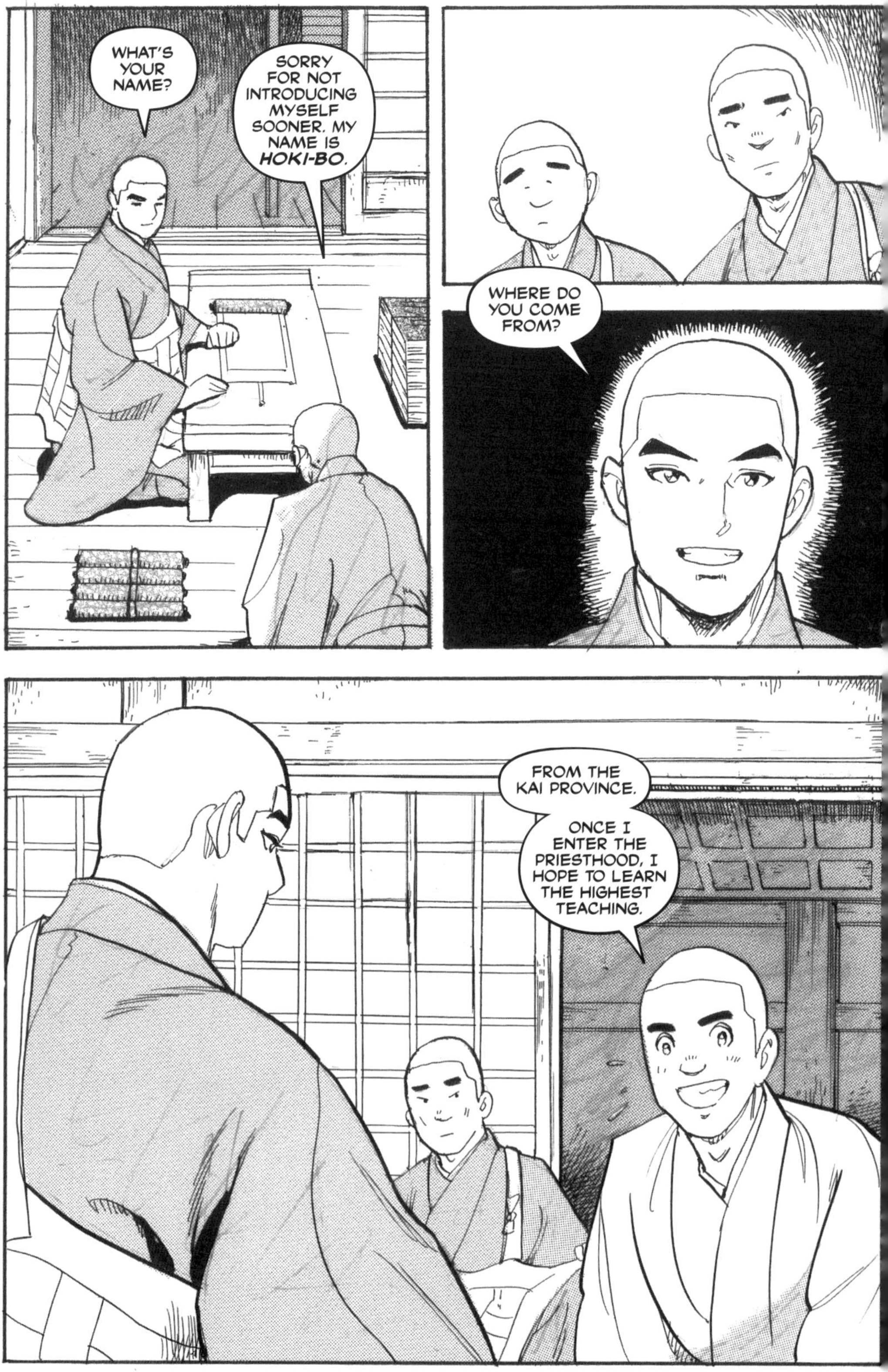
WHAT'S YOUR NAME?
SORRY FOR NOT INTRODUCING MYSELF SOONER. MY NAME IS HOKI-BO.
WHERE DO YOU COME FROM?
FROM THE KAI PROVINCE.
ONCE I ENTER THE PRIESTHOOD, I HOPE TO LEARN THE HIGHEST TEACHING.

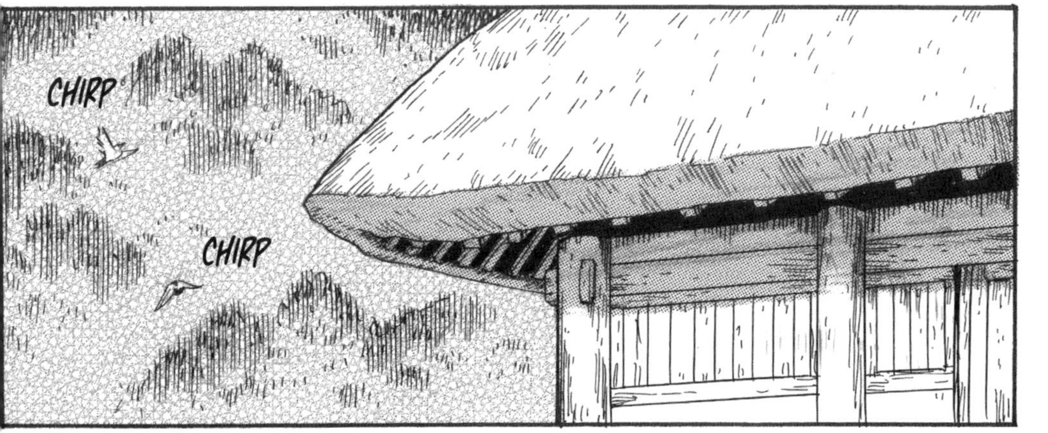
CHIRP
CHIRP

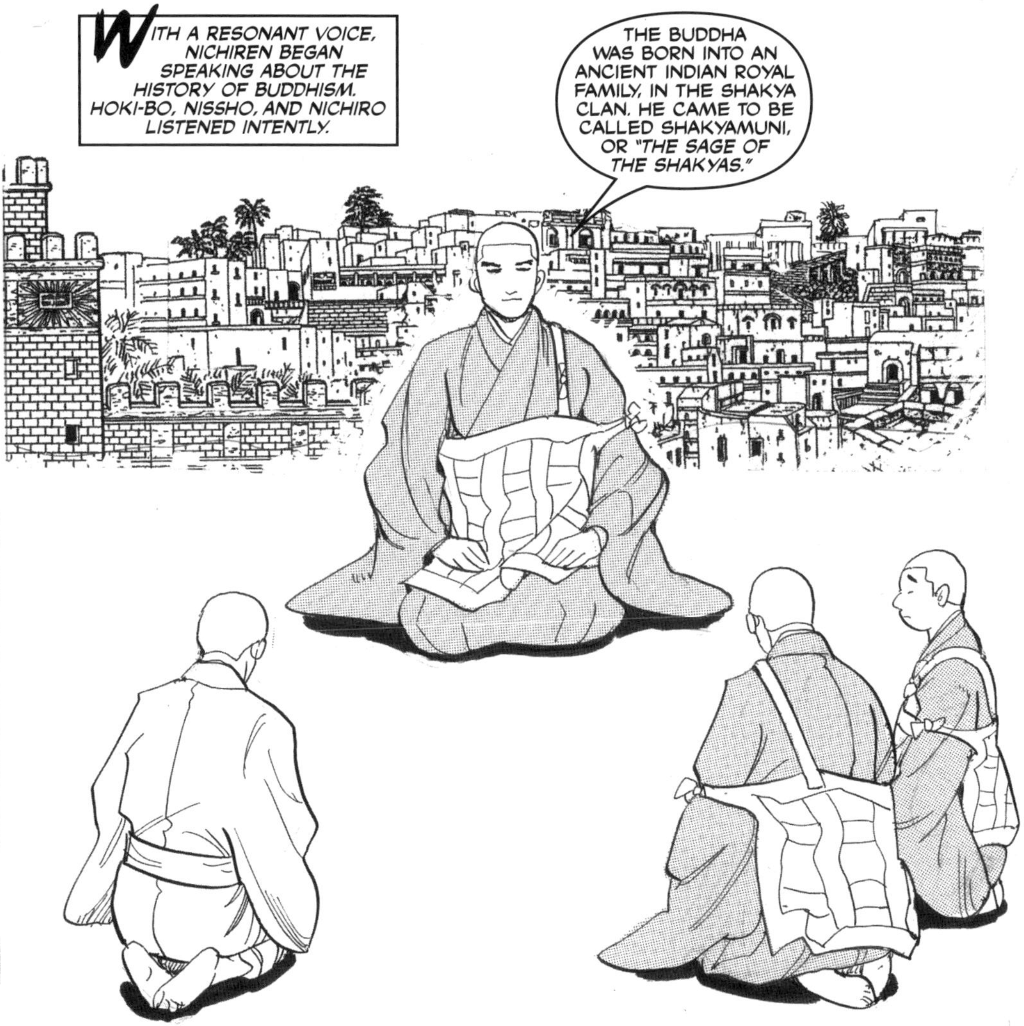
WITH A RESONANT VOICE, NICHIREN BEGAN SPEAKING ABOUT THE HISTORY OF BUDDHISM. HOKI-BO, NISSHO, AND NICHIRO LISTENED INTENTLY.
THE BUDDHA WAS BORN INTO AN ANCIENT INDIAN ROYAL FAMILY, IN THE SHAKYA CLAN. HE CAME TO BE CALLED SHAKYAMUNI, OR "THE SAGE OF THE SHAKYAS."

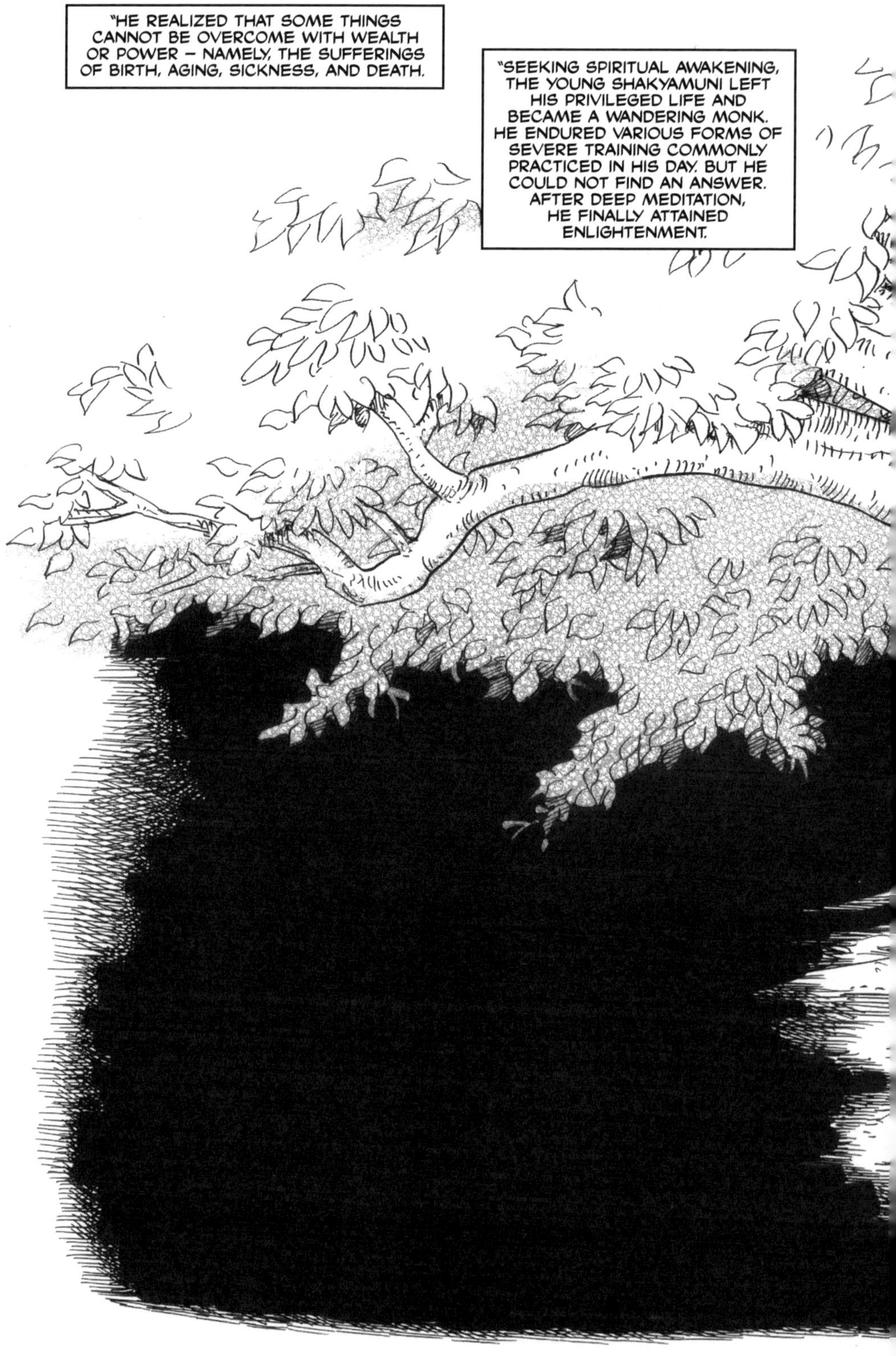
"HE REALIZED THAT SOME THINGS CANNOT BE OVERCOME WITH WEALTH OR POWER – NAMELY, THE SUFFERINGS OF BIRTH, AGING, SICKNESS, AND DEATH.
"SEEKING SPIRITUAL AWAKENING, THE YOUNG SHAKYAMUNI LEFT HIS PRIVILEGED LIFE AND BECAME A WANDERING MONK. HE ENDURED VARIOUS FORMS OF SEVERE TRAINING COMMONLY PRACTICED IN HIS DAY. BUT HE COULD NOT FIND AN ANSWER. AFTER DEEP MEDITATION, HE FINALLY ATTAINED ENLIGHTENMENT.

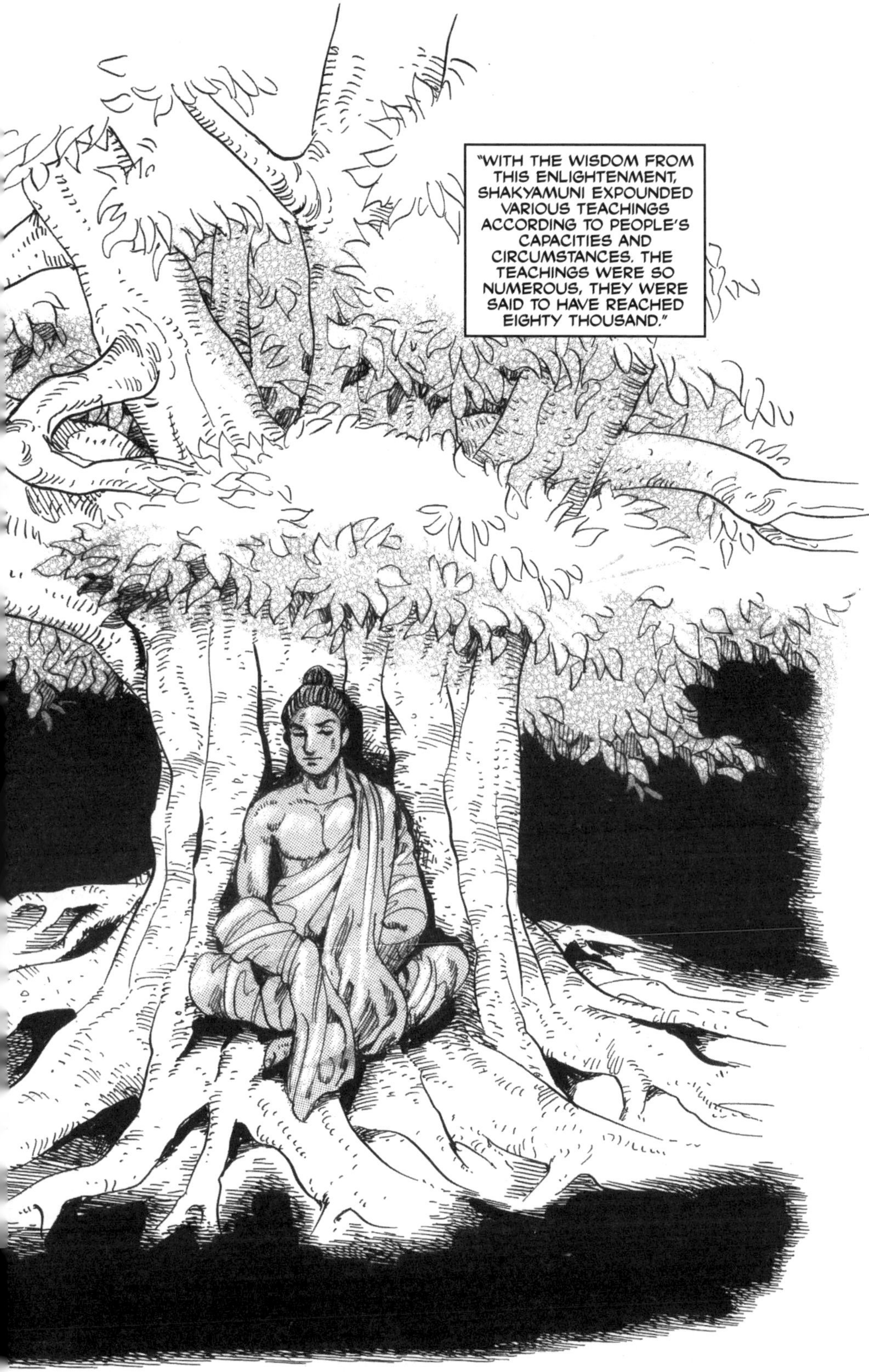
"WITH THE WISDOM FROM THIS ENLIGHTENMENT, SHAKYAMUNI EXPOUNDED VARIOUS TEACHINGS ACCORDING TO PEOPLE'S CAPACITIES AND CIRCUMSTANCES. THE TEACHINGS WERE SO NUMEROUS, THEY WERE SAID TO HAVE REACHED EIGHTY THOUSAND."

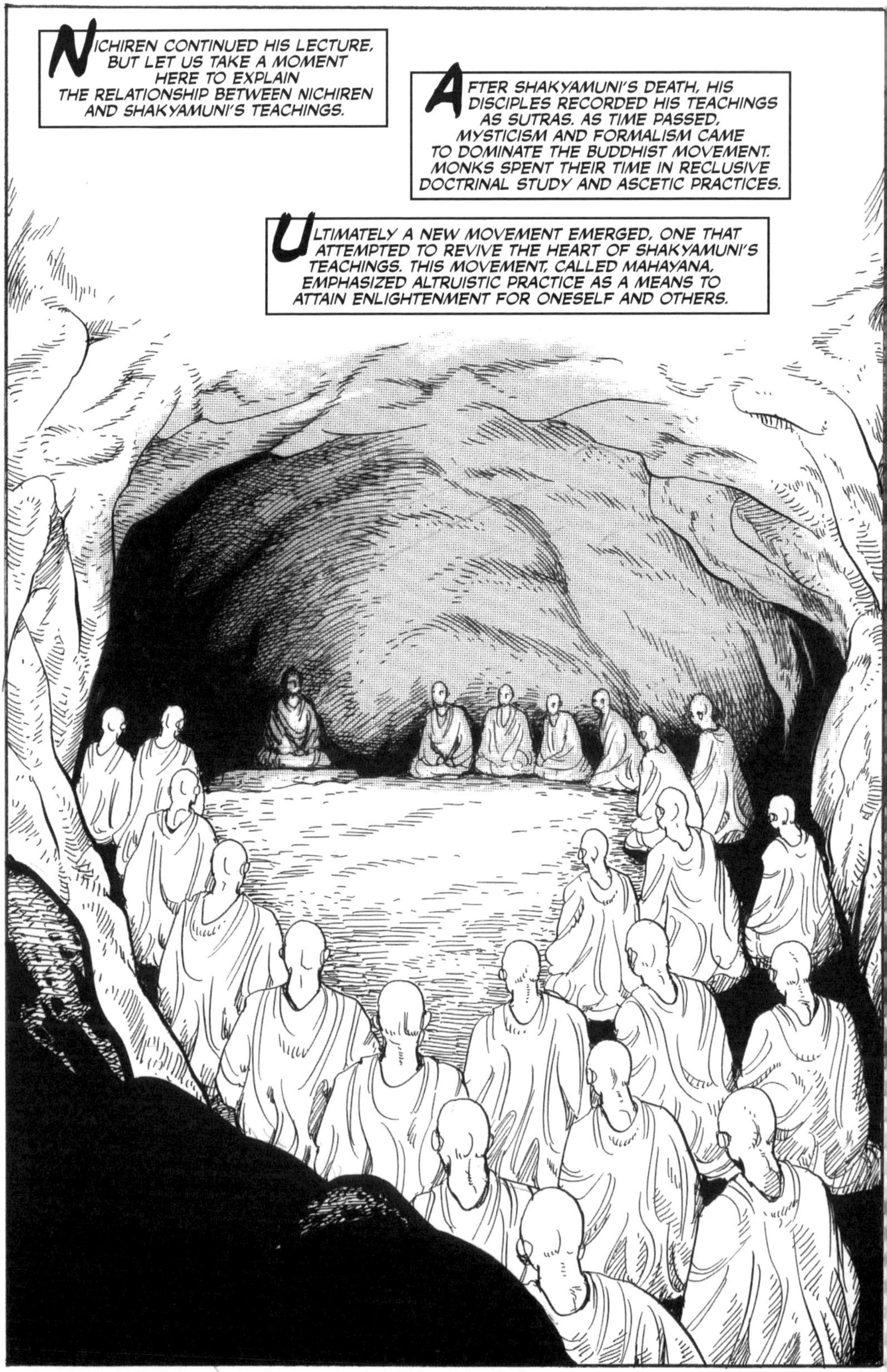
NICHIREN CONTINUED HIS LECTURE, BUT LET US TAKE A MOMENT HERE TO EXPLAIN THE RELATIONSHIP BETWEEN NICHIREN AND SHAKYAMUNI'S TEACHINGS.
AFTER SHAKYAMUNI'S DEATH, HIS DISCIPLES RECORDED HIS TEACHINGS AS SUTRAS. AS TIME PASSED, MYSTICISM AND FORMALISM CAME TO DOMINATE THE BUDDHIST MOVEMENT. MONKS SPENT THEIR TIME IN RECLUSIVE DOCTRINAL STUDY AND ASCETIC PRACTICES.
ULTIMATELY A NEW MOVEMENT EMERGED, ONE THAT ATTEMPTED TO REVIVE THE HEART OF SHAKYAMUNI'S TEACHINGS. THIS MOVEMENT, CALLED MAHAYANA, EMPHASIZED ALTRUISTIC PRACTICE AS A MEANS TO ATTAIN ENLIGHTENMENT FOR ONESELF AND OTHERS.

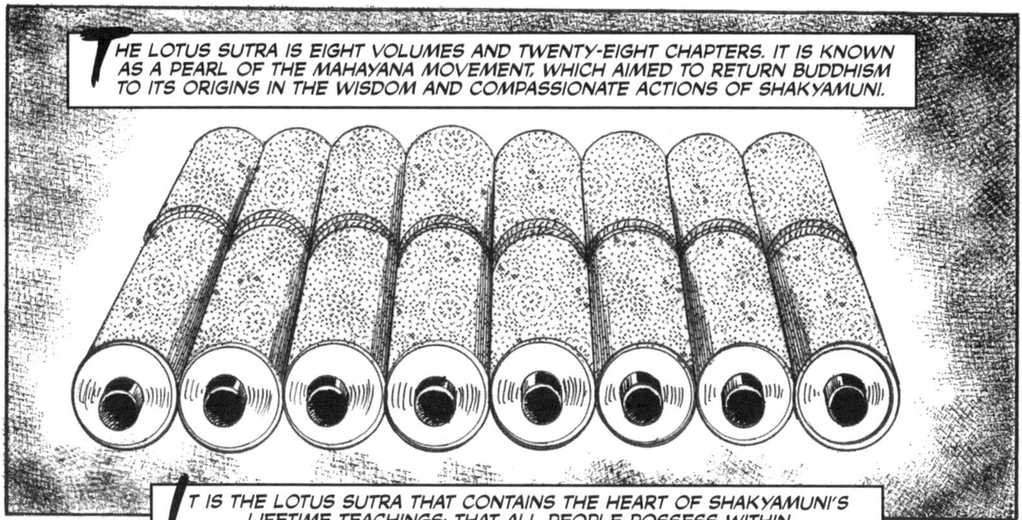
THE LOTUS SUTRA IS EIGHT VOLUMES AND TWENTY-EIGHT CHAPTERS. IT IS KNOWN AS A PEARL OF THE MAHAYANA MOVEMENT, WHICH AIMED TO RETURN BUDDHISM TO ITS ORIGINS IN THE WISDOM AND COMPASSIONATE ACTIONS OF SHAKYAMUNI.
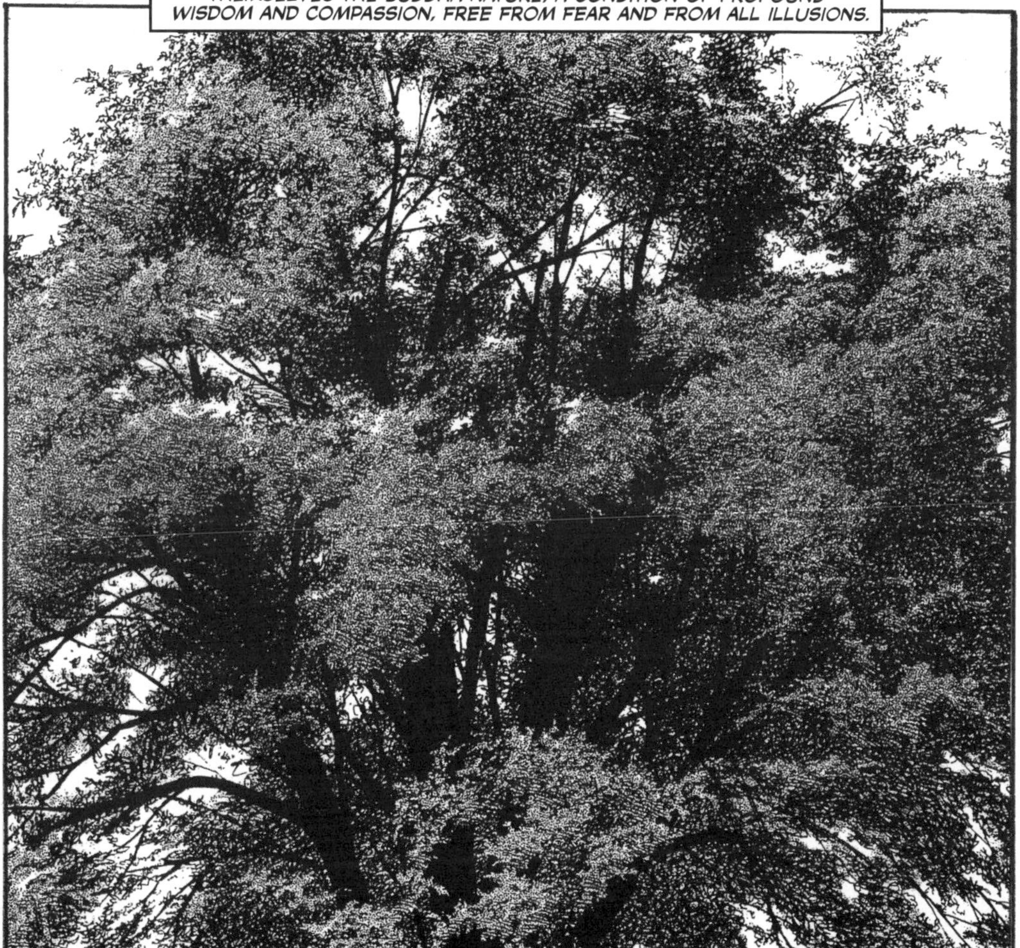
IT IS THE LOTUS SUTRA THAT CONTAINS THE HEART OF SHAKYAMUNI'S LIFETIME TEACHINGS: THAT ALL PEOPLE POSSESS WITHIN THEMSELVES THE BUDDHA NATURE, A CONDITION OF PROFOUND WISDOM AND COMPASSION, FREE FROM FEAR AND FROM ALL ILLUSIONS.

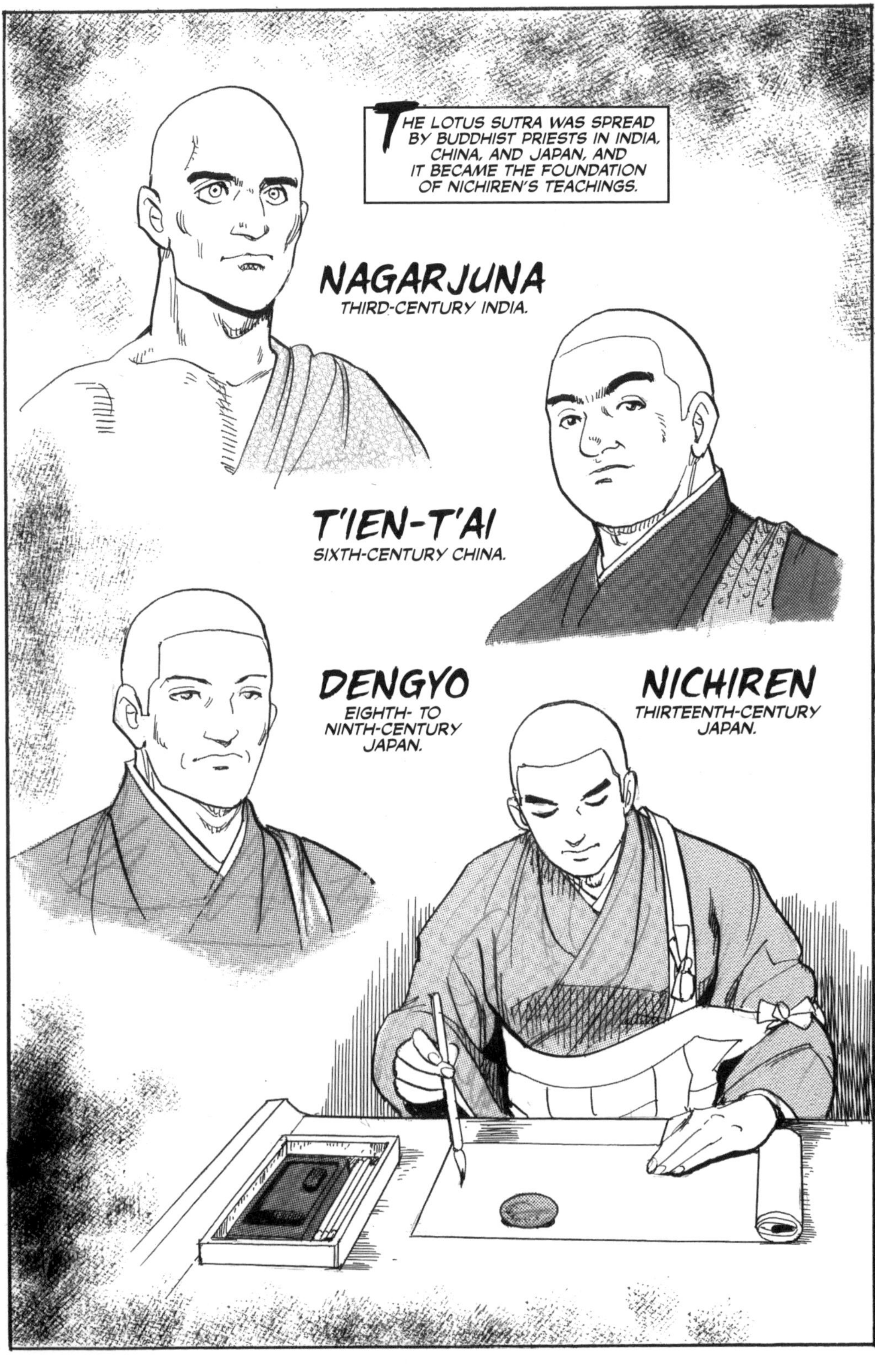
THE LOTUS SUTRA WAS SPREAD BY BUDDHIST PRIESTS IN INDIA, CHINA, AND JAPAN, AND IT BECAME THE FOUNDATION OF NICHIREN'S TEACHINGS.
NAGARJUNA
THIRD-CENTURY INDIA.
T'IEN-T'AI
SIXTH-CENTURY CHINA.
DENGYO
EIGHTH- TO NINTH-CENTURY JAPAN.
NICHIREN
THIRTEENTH-CENTURY JAPAN.

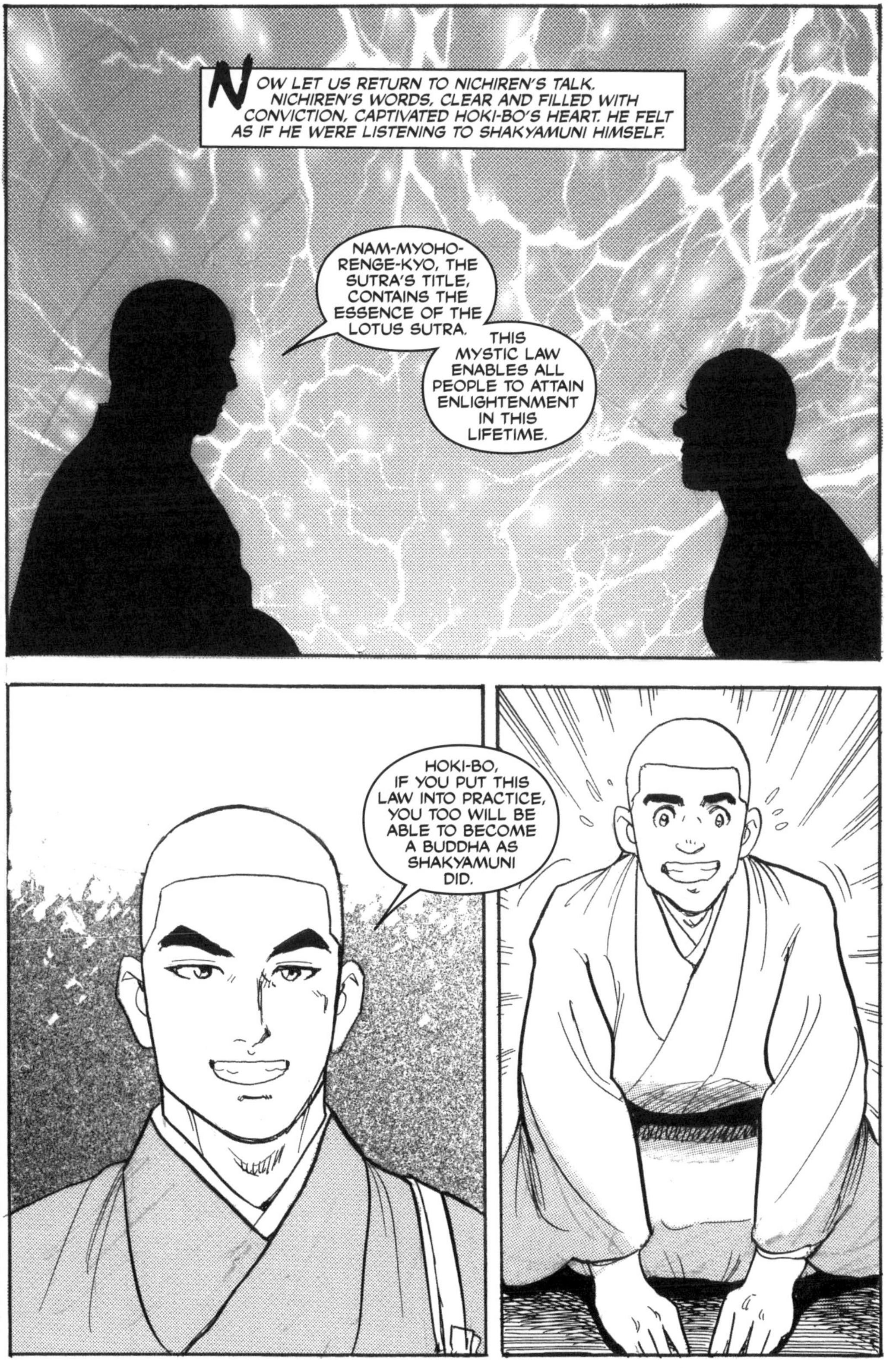
NOW LET US RETURN TO NICHIREN'S TALK. NICHIREN'S WORDS, CLEAR AND FILLED WITH CONVICTION, CAPTIVATED HOKI-BO'S HEART. HE FELT AS IF HE WERE LISTENING TO SHAKYAMUNI HIMSELF.
NAM-MYOHO-RENGE-KYO, THE SUTRA'S TITLE, CONTAINS THE ESSENCE OF THE LOTUS SUTRA.
THIS MYSTIC LAW ENABLES ALL PEOPLE TO ATTAIN ENLIGHTENMENT IN THIS LIFETIME.
HOKI-BO, IF YOU PUT THIS LAW INTO PRACTICE, YOU TOO WILL BE ABLE TO BECOME A BUDDHA AS SHAKYAMUNI DID.

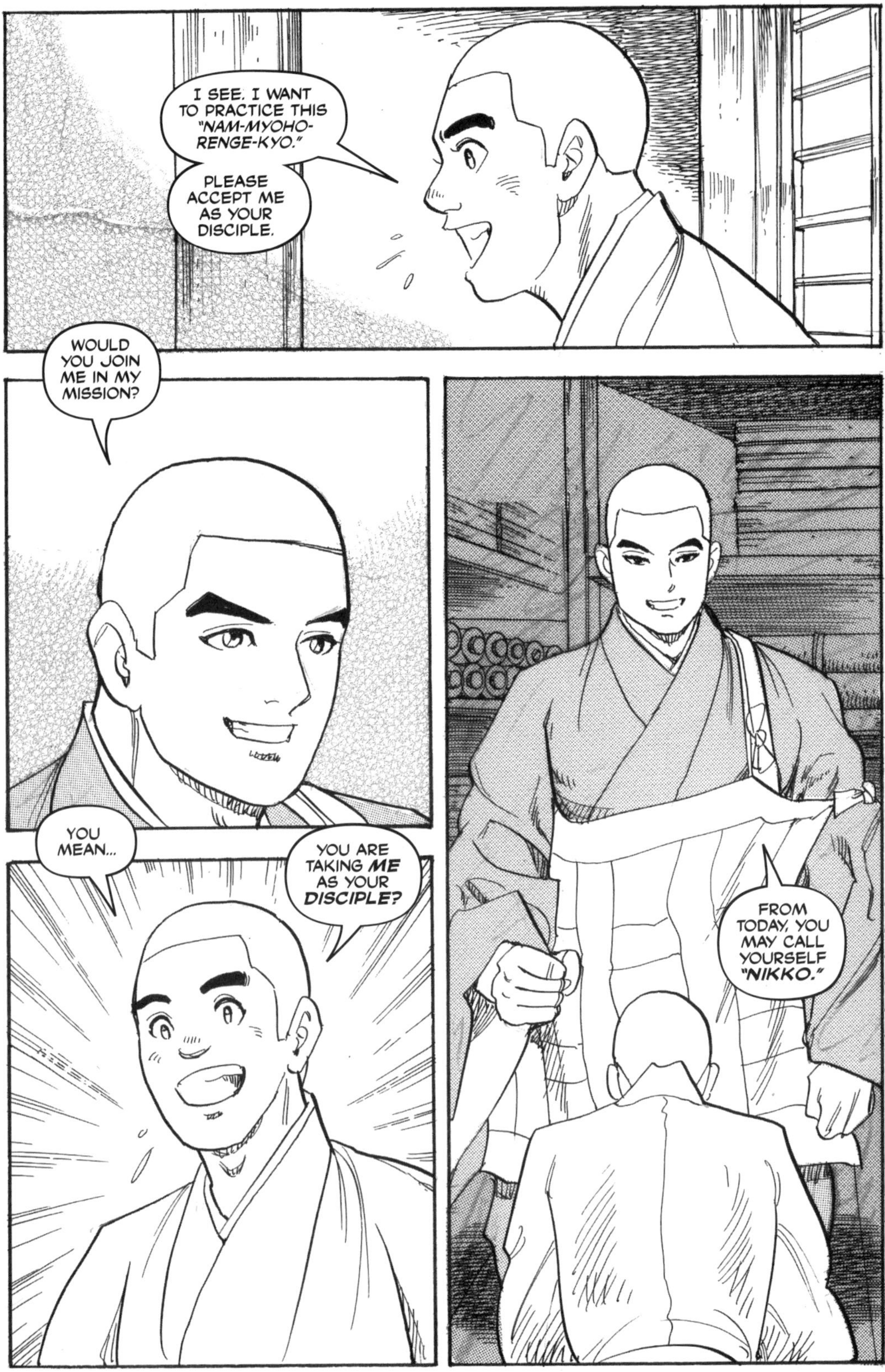
I SEE. I WANT TO PRACTICE THIS *"NAM-MYOHO-RENGE-KYO."*
PLEASE ACCEPT ME AS YOUR DISCIPLE.
WOULD YOU JOIN ME IN MY MISSION?
YOU MEAN...
YOU ARE TAKING ***ME*** AS YOUR ***DISCIPLE?***
FROM TODAY, YOU MAY CALL YOURSELF ***"NIKKO."***

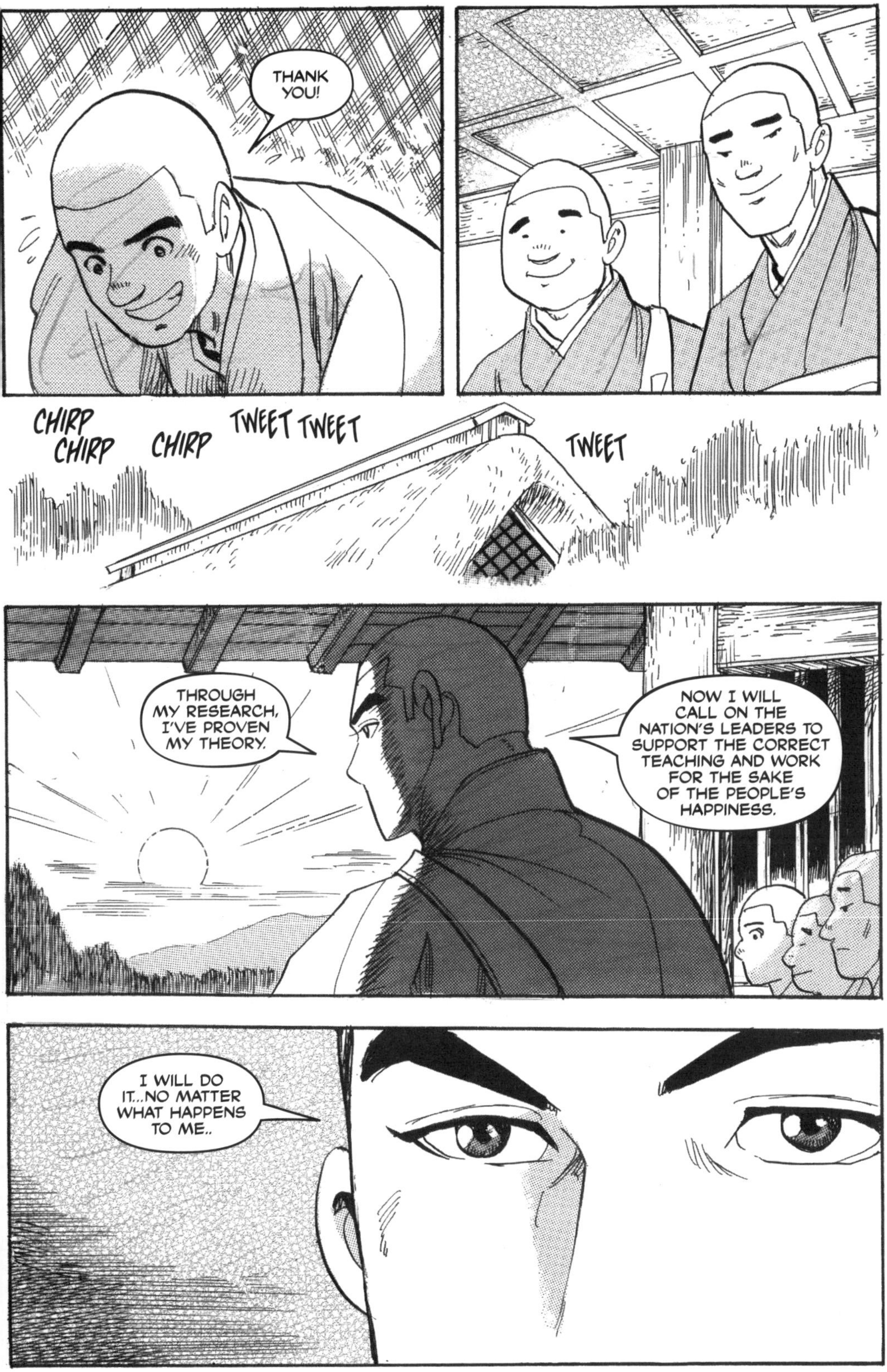
THANK YOU!
CHIRP CHIRP
CHIRP
TWEET TWEET
TWEET
THROUGH MY RESEARCH, I'VE PROVEN MY THEORY.
NOW I WILL CALL ON THE NATION'S LEADERS TO SUPPORT THE CORRECT TEACHING AND WORK FOR THE SAKE OF THE PEOPLE'S HAPPINESS.
I WILL DO IT...NO MATTER WHAT HAPPENS TO ME..

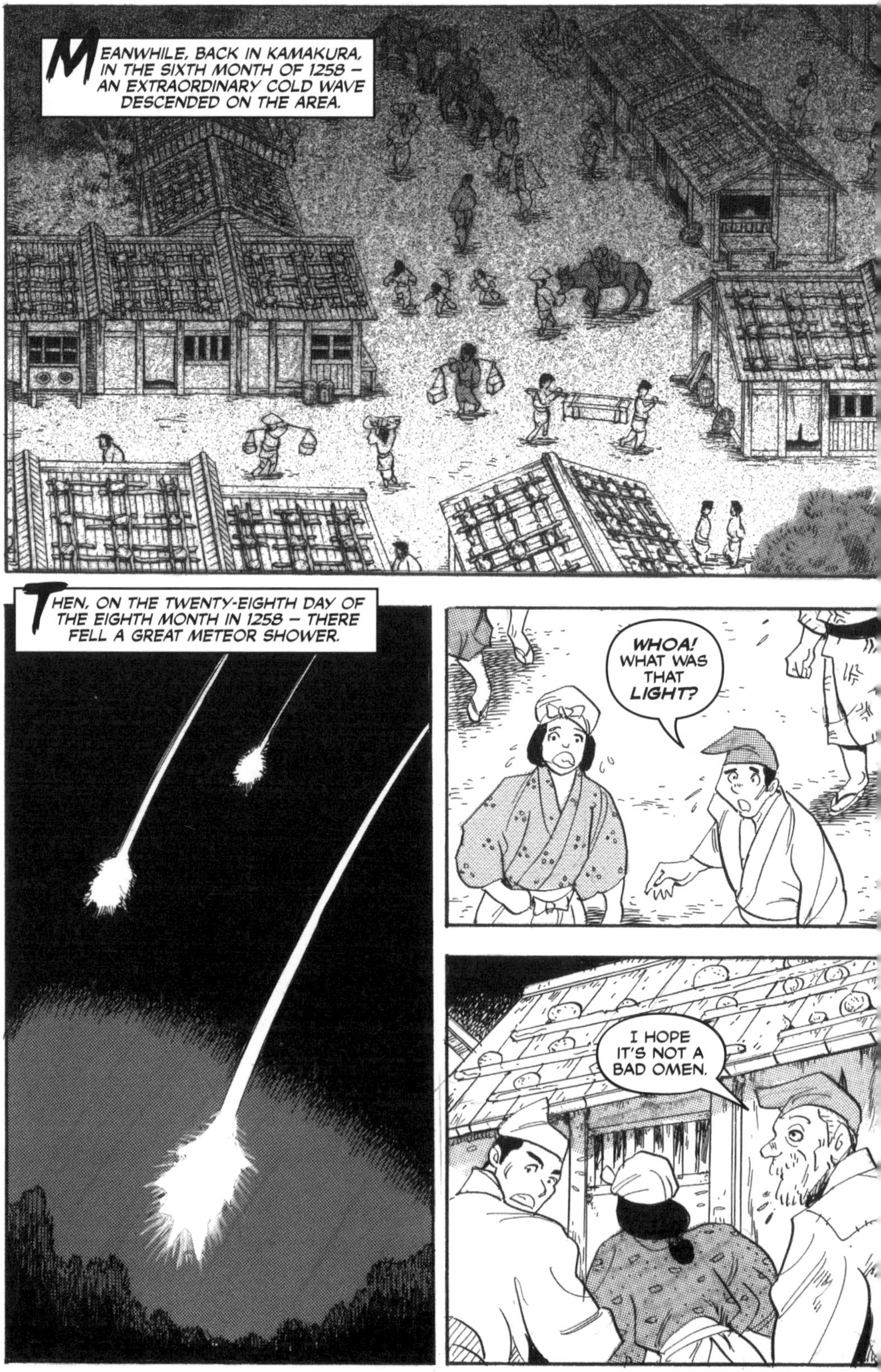
MEANWHILE, BACK IN KAMAKURA, IN THE SIXTH MONTH OF 1258 – AN EXTRAORDINARY COLD WAVE DESCENDED ON THE AREA.
THEN, ON THE TWENTY-EIGHTH DAY OF THE EIGHTH MONTH IN 1258 – THERE FELL A GREAT METEOR SHOWER.
WHOA! WHAT WAS THAT LIGHT?
I HOPE IT'S NOT A BAD OMEN.

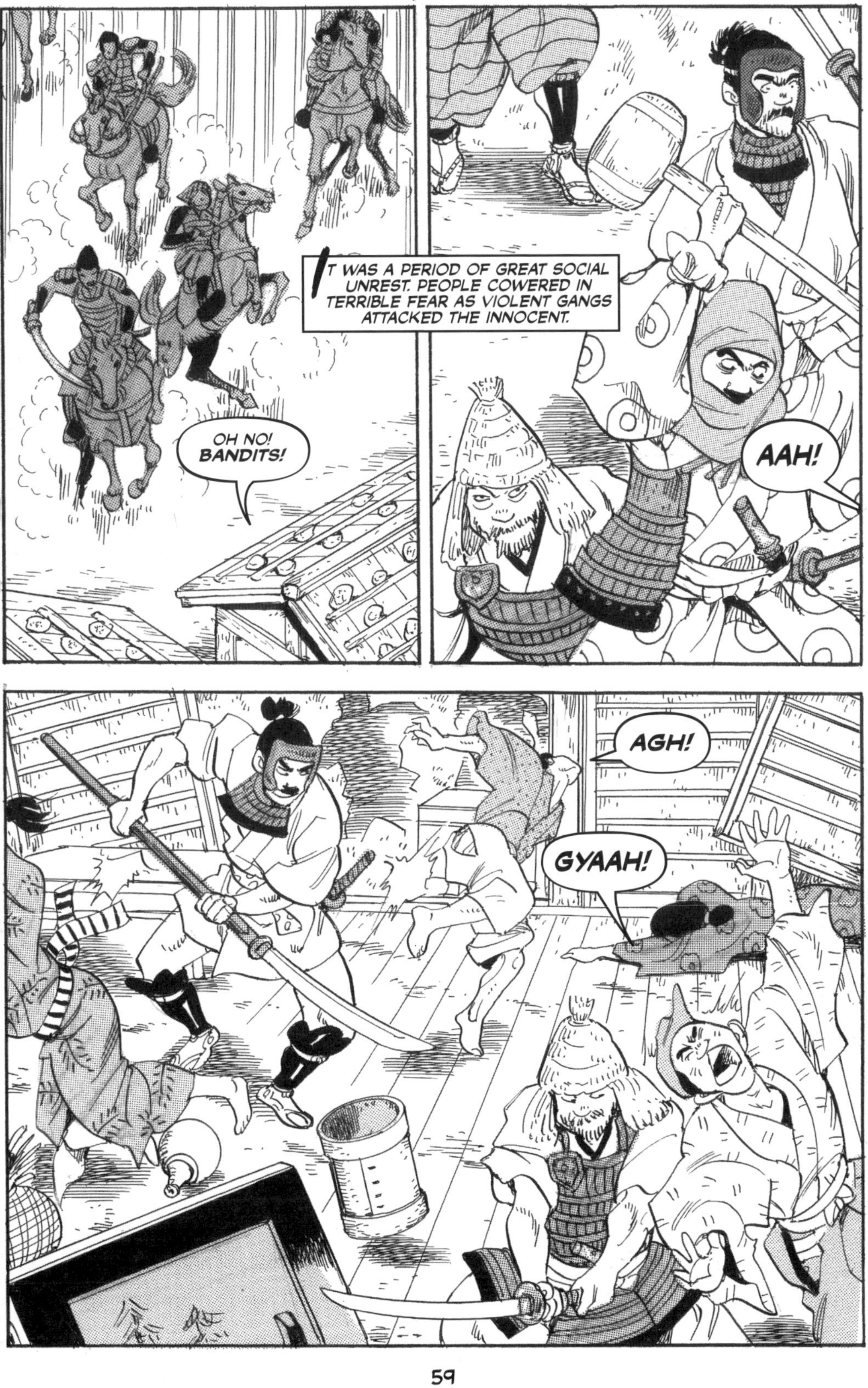
IT WAS A PERIOD OF GREAT SOCIAL UNREST. PEOPLE COWERED IN TERRIBLE FEAR AS VIOLENT GANGS ATTACKED THE INNOCENT.
OH NO! BANDITS!
AAH!
AGH!
GYAAH!

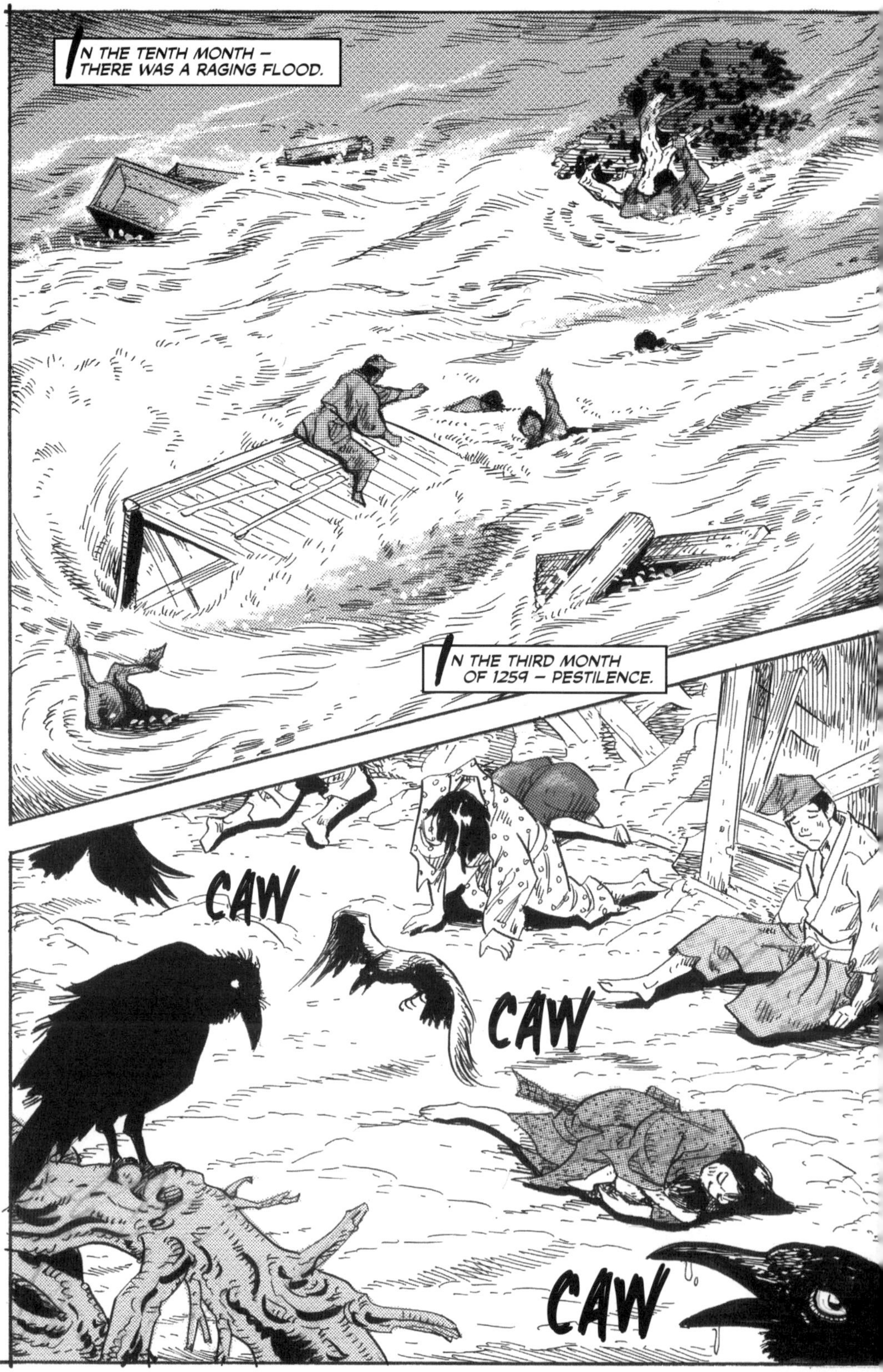
IN THE TENTH MONTH – THERE WAS A RAGING FLOOD.
IN THE THIRD MONTH OF 1259 – PESTILENCE.
CAW
CAW
CAW

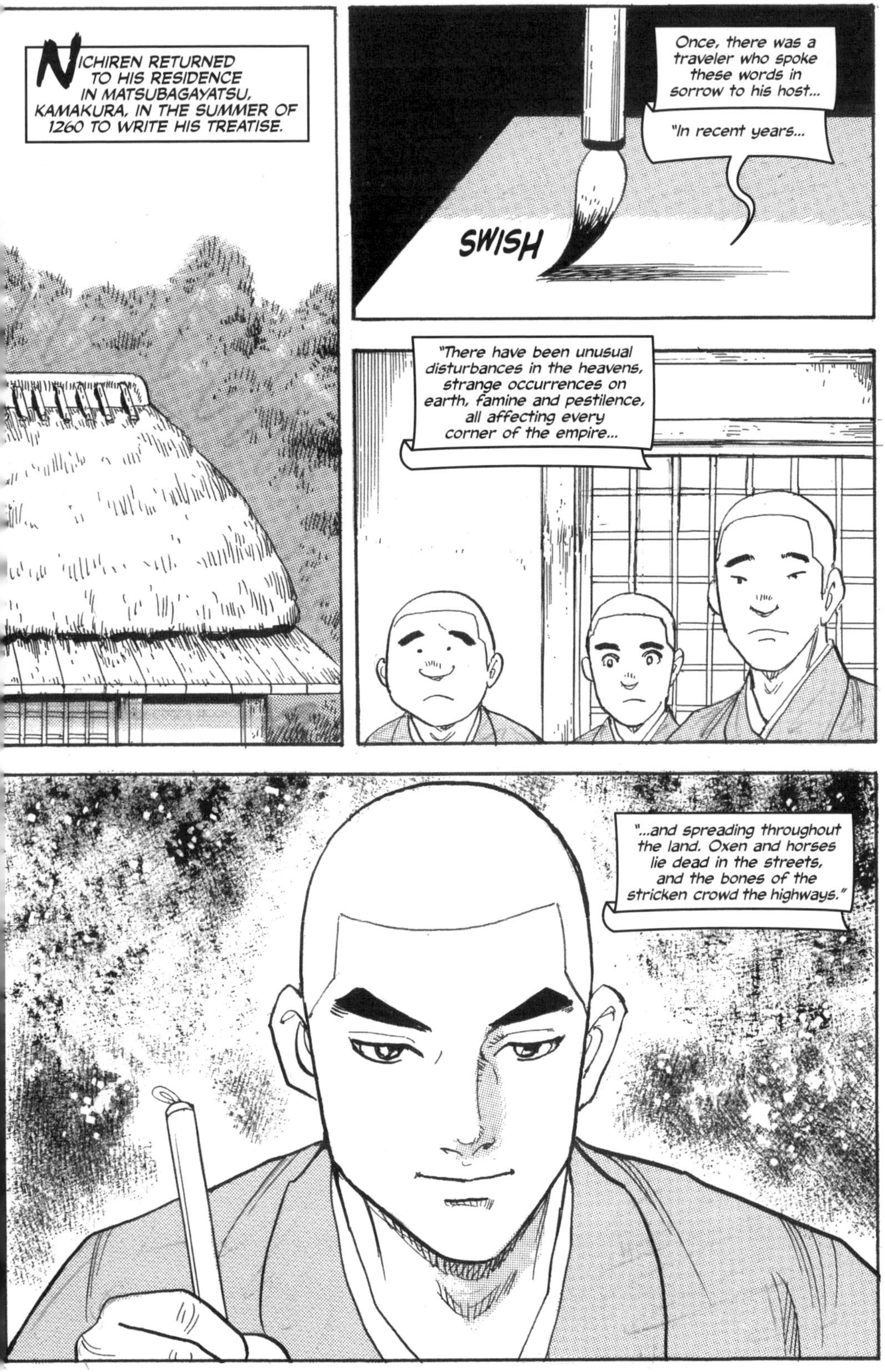
NICHIREN RETURNED TO HIS RESIDENCE IN MATSUBAGAYATSU, KAMAKURA, IN THE SUMMER OF 1260 TO WRITE HIS TREATISE.
Once, there was a traveler who spoke these words in sorrow to his host...
"In recent years...
SWISH
"There have been unusual disturbances in the heavens, strange occurrences on earth, famine and pestilence, all affecting every corner of the empire...
"...and spreading throughout the land. Oxen and horses lie dead in the streets, and the bones of the stricken crowd the highways."

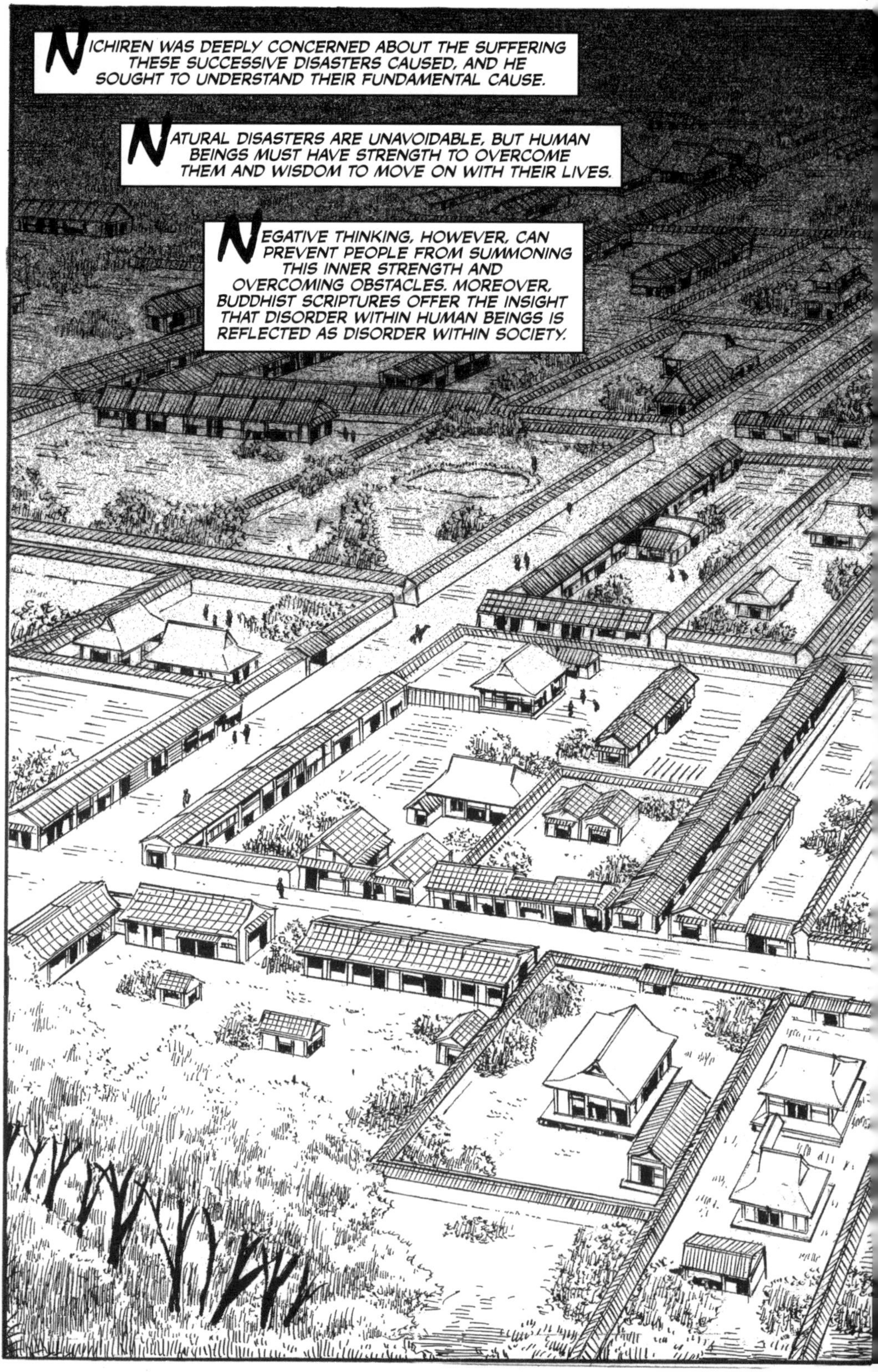
NICHIREN WAS DEEPLY CONCERNED ABOUT THE SUFFERING THESE SUCCESSIVE DISASTERS CAUSED, AND HE SOUGHT TO UNDERSTAND THEIR FUNDAMENTAL CAUSE.
NATURAL DISASTERS ARE UNAVOIDABLE, BUT HUMAN BEINGS MUST HAVE STRENGTH TO OVERCOME THEM AND WISDOM TO MOVE ON WITH THEIR LIVES.
NEGATIVE THINKING, HOWEVER, CAN PREVENT PEOPLE FROM SUMMONING THIS INNER STRENGTH AND OVERCOMING OBSTACLES. MOREOVER, BUDDHIST SCRIPTURES OFFER THE INSIGHT THAT DISORDER WITHIN HUMAN BEINGS IS REFLECTED AS DISORDER WITHIN SOCIETY.

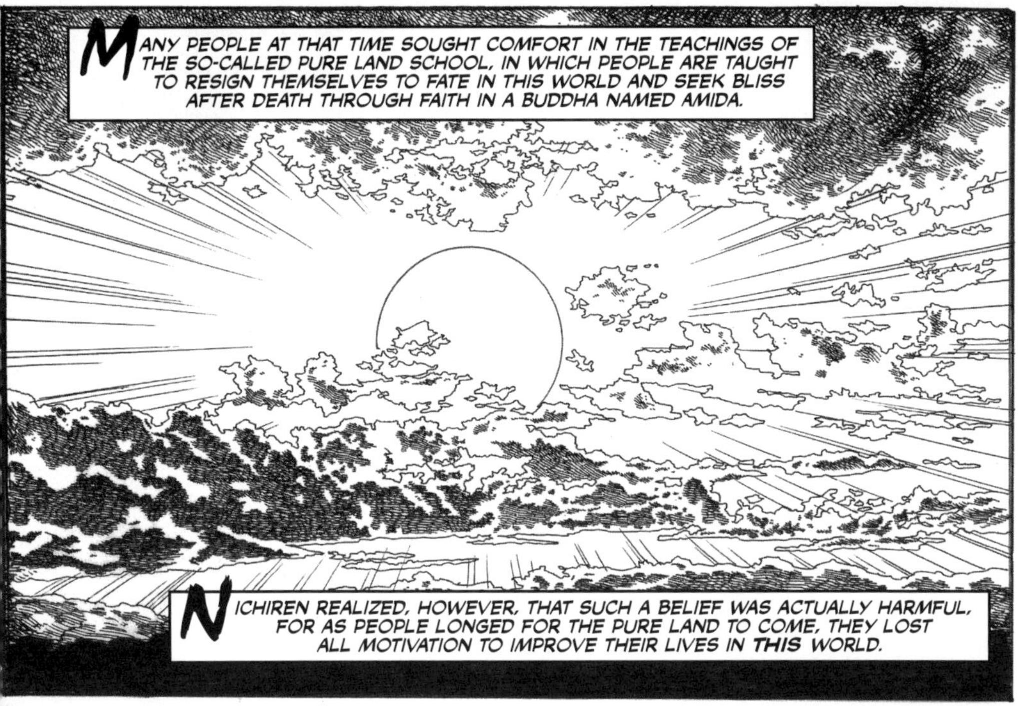
MANY PEOPLE AT THAT TIME SOUGHT COMFORT IN THE TEACHINGS OF THE SO-CALLED PURE LAND SCHOOL, IN WHICH PEOPLE ARE TAUGHT TO RESIGN THEMSELVES TO FATE IN THIS WORLD AND SEEK BLISS AFTER DEATH THROUGH FAITH IN A BUDDHA NAMED AMIDA.
NICHIREN REALIZED, HOWEVER, THAT SUCH A BELIEF WAS ACTUALLY HARMFUL, FOR AS PEOPLE LONGED FOR THE PURE LAND TO COME, THEY LOST ALL MOTIVATION TO IMPROVE THEIR LIVES IN **THIS** WORLD.

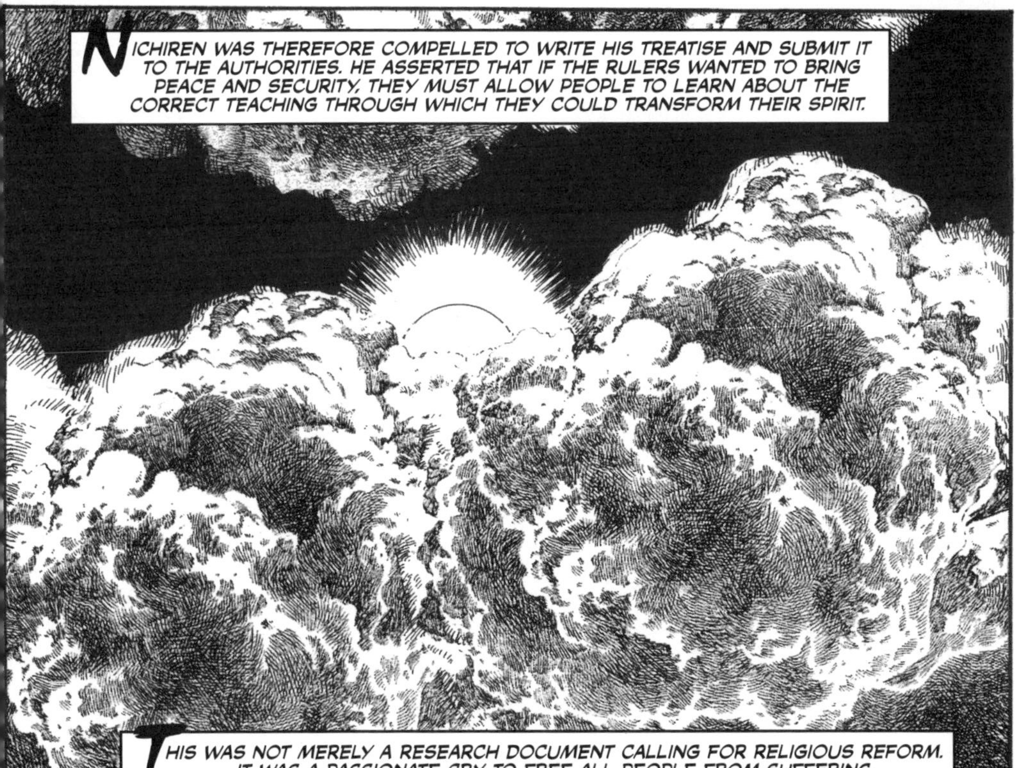
NICHIREN WAS THEREFORE COMPELLED TO WRITE HIS TREATISE AND SUBMIT IT TO THE AUTHORITIES. HE ASSERTED THAT IF THE RULERS WANTED TO BRING PEACE AND SECURITY, THEY MUST ALLOW PEOPLE TO LEARN ABOUT THE CORRECT TEACHING THROUGH WHICH THEY COULD TRANSFORM THEIR SPIRIT.
THIS WAS NOT MERELY A RESEARCH DOCUMENT CALLING FOR RELIGIOUS REFORM. IT WAS A PASSIONATE CRY TO FREE ALL PEOPLE FROM SUFFERING, TO HELP THEM CREATE BETTER LIVES AND BUILD A PEACEFUL SOCIETY.

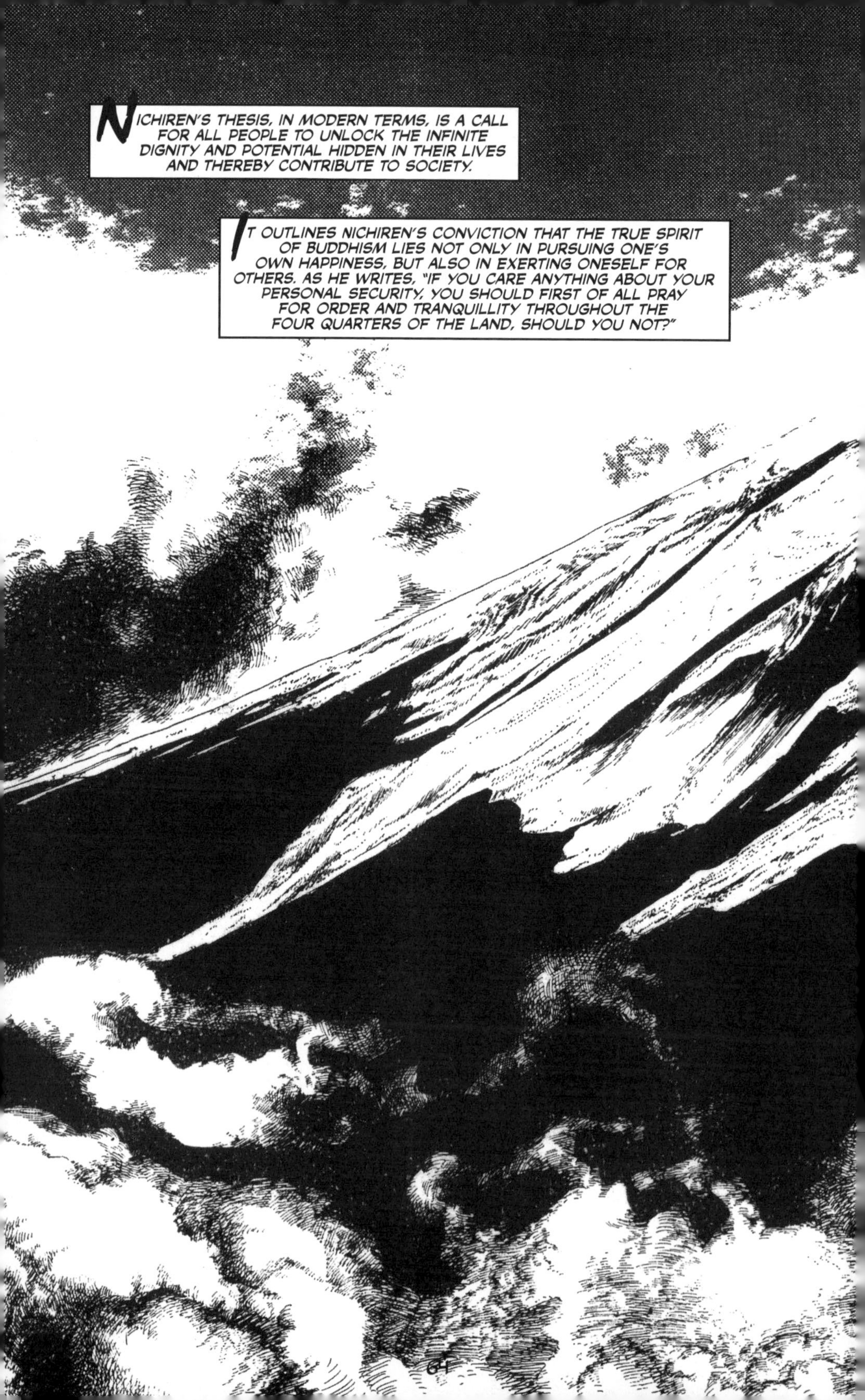
NICHIREN'S THESIS, IN MODERN TERMS, IS A CALL FOR ALL PEOPLE TO UNLOCK THE INFINITE DIGNITY AND POTENTIAL HIDDEN IN THEIR LIVES AND THEREBY CONTRIBUTE TO SOCIETY.
IT OUTLINES NICHIREN'S CONVICTION THAT THE TRUE SPIRIT OF BUDDHISM LIES NOT ONLY IN PURSUING ONE'S OWN HAPPINESS, BUT ALSO IN EXERTING ONESELF FOR OTHERS. AS HE WRITES, "IF YOU CARE ANYTHING ABOUT YOUR PERSONAL SECURITY, YOU SHOULD FIRST OF ALL PRAY FOR ORDER AND TRANQUILLITY THROUGHOUT THE FOUR QUARTERS OF THE LAND, SHOULD YOU NOT?"

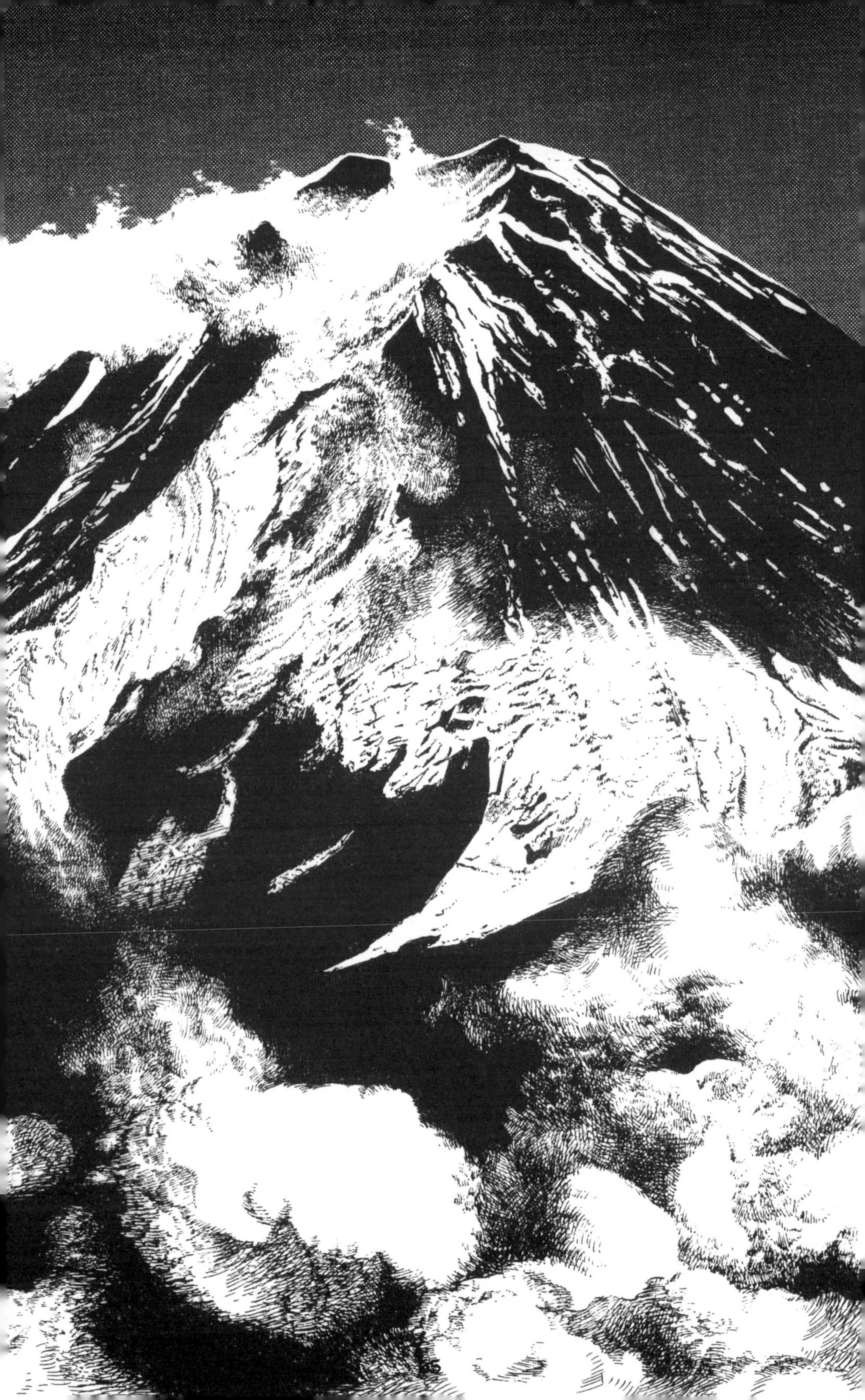

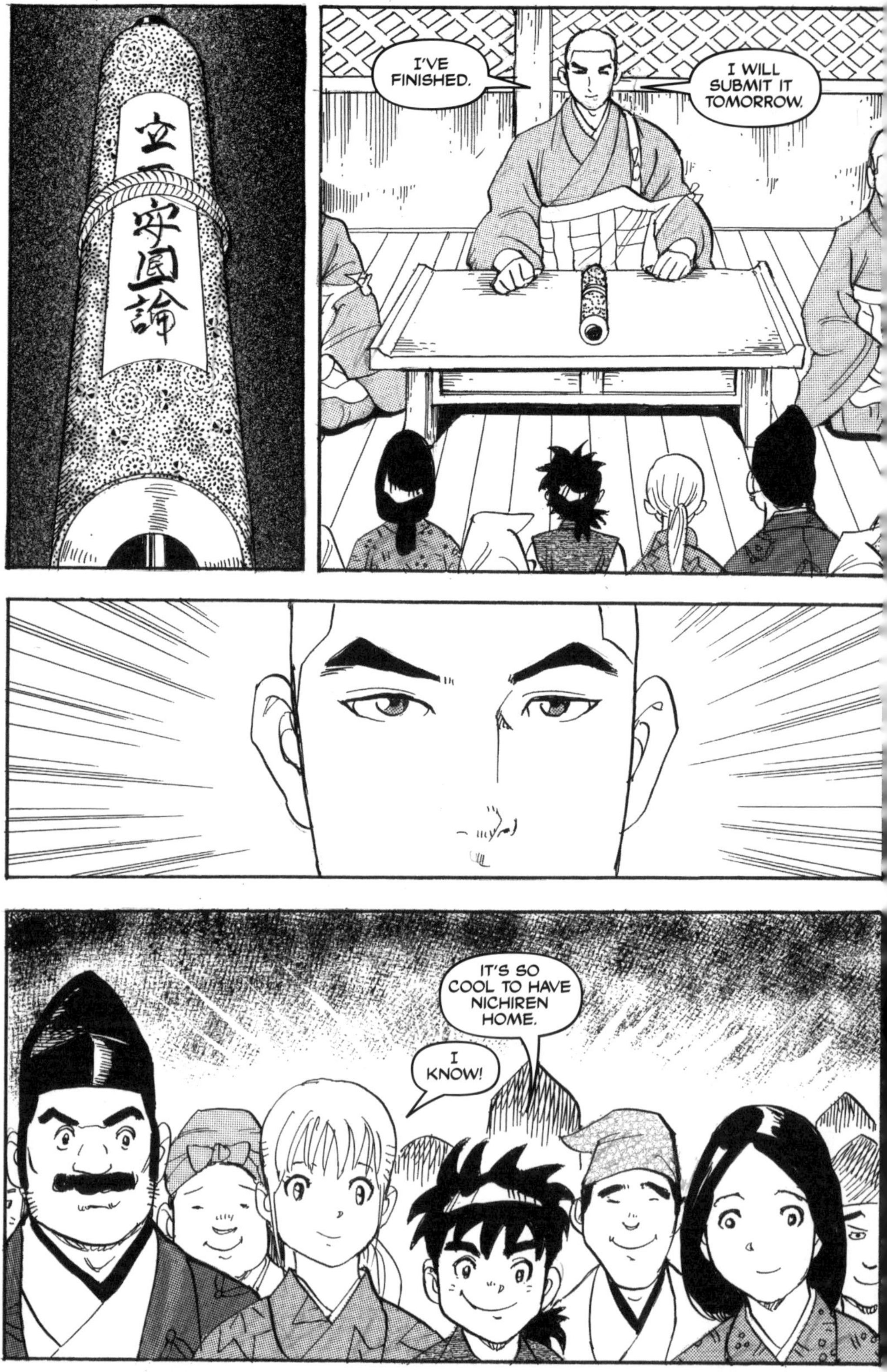

I'VE FINISHED.
I WILL SUBMIT IT TOMORROW.
IT'S SO COOL TO HAVE NICHIREN HOME.
I KNOW!

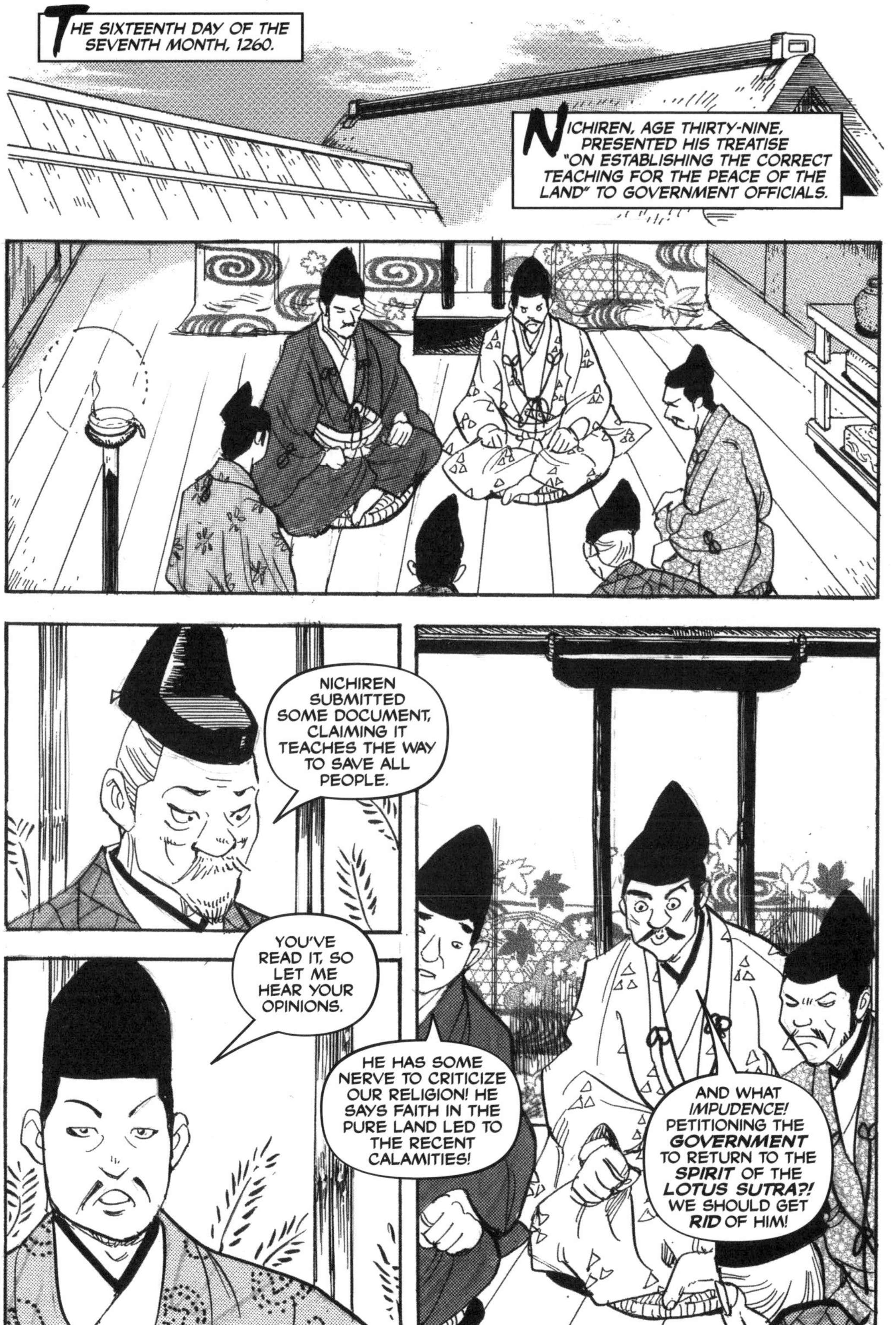
THE SIXTEENTH DAY OF THE SEVENTH MONTH, 1260.
NICHIREN, AGE THIRTY-NINE, PRESENTED HIS TREATISE "ON ESTABLISHING THE CORRECT TEACHING FOR THE PEACE OF THE LAND" TO GOVERNMENT OFFICIALS.
NICHIREN SUBMITTED SOME DOCUMENT, CLAIMING IT TEACHES THE WAY TO SAVE ALL PEOPLE.
YOU'VE READ IT, SO LET ME HEAR YOUR OPINIONS.
HE HAS SOME NERVE TO CRITICIZE OUR RELIGION! HE SAYS FAITH IN THE PURE LAND LED TO THE RECENT CALAMITIES!
AND WHAT *IMPUDENCE!* PETITIONING THE **GOVERNMENT** TO RETURN TO THE **SPIRIT** OF THE **LOTUS SUTRA?!** WE SHOULD GET **RID** OF HIM!

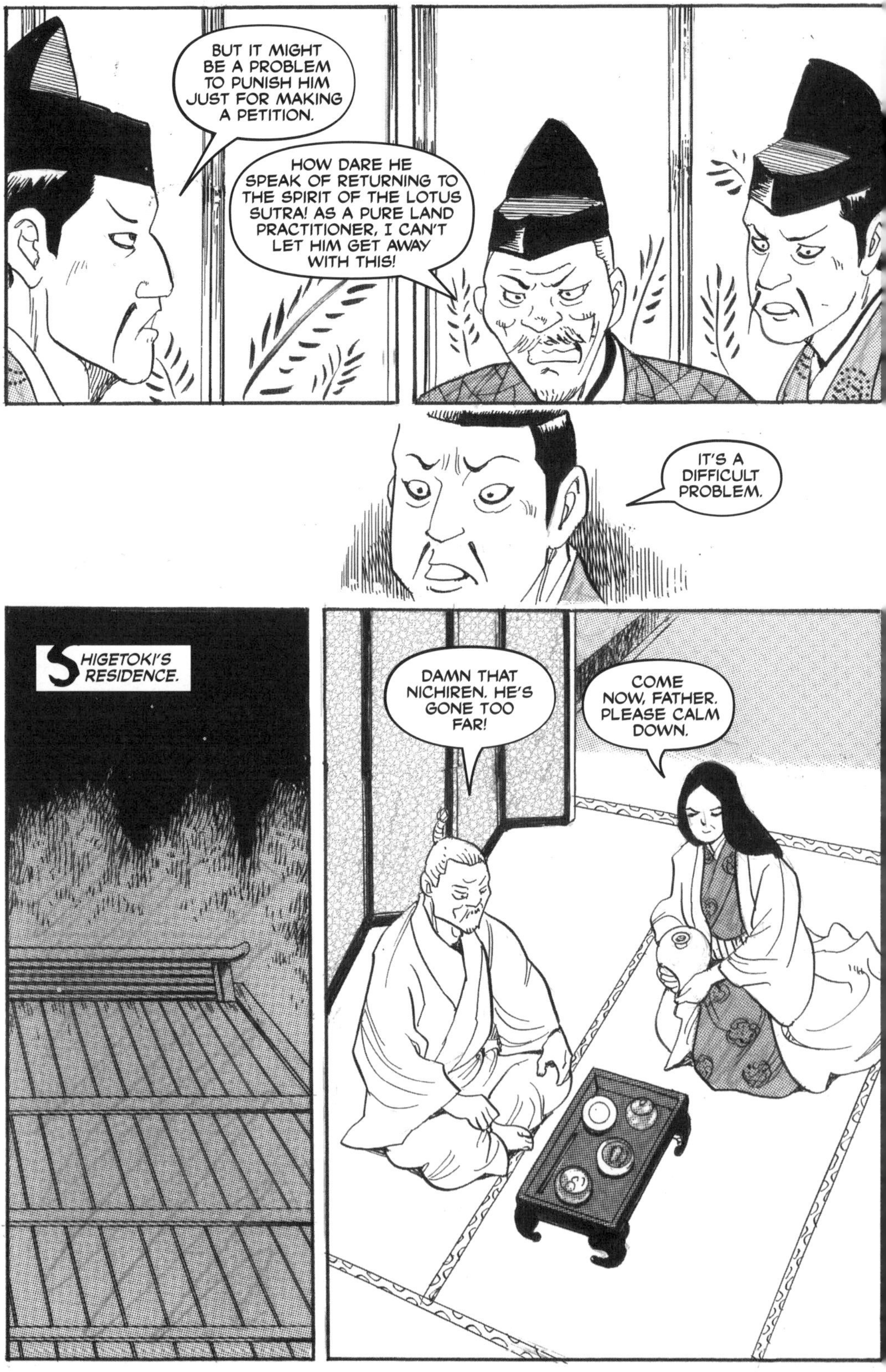

BUT IT MIGHT BE A PROBLEM TO PUNISH HIM JUST FOR MAKING A PETITION.
HOW DARE HE SPEAK OF RETURNING TO THE SPIRIT OF THE LOTUS SUTRA! AS A PURE LAND PRACTITIONER, I CAN'T LET HIM GET AWAY WITH THIS!
IT'S A DIFFICULT PROBLEM.
SHIGETOKI'S RESIDENCE.
DAMN THAT NICHIREN. HE'S GONE TOO FAR!
COME NOW, FATHER. PLEASE CALM DOWN.

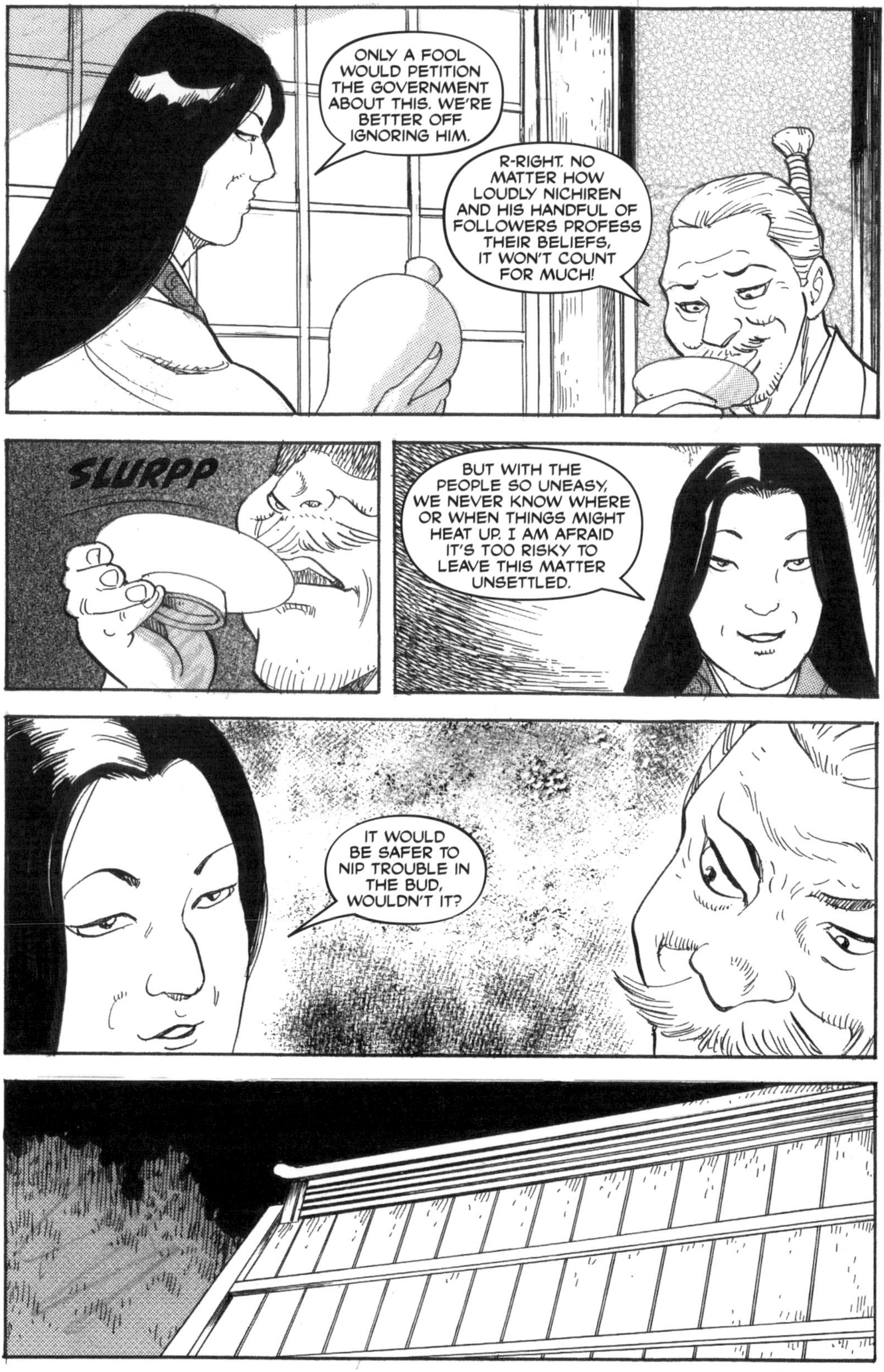
ONLY A FOOL WOULD PETITION THE GOVERNMENT ABOUT THIS. WE'RE BETTER OFF IGNORING HIM.
R-RIGHT. NO MATTER HOW LOUDLY NICHIREN AND HIS HANDFUL OF FOLLOWERS PROFESS THEIR BELIEFS, IT WON'T COUNT FOR MUCH!
SLURPP
BUT WITH THE PEOPLE SO UNEASY, WE NEVER KNOW WHERE OR WHEN THINGS MIGHT HEAT UP. I AM AFRAID IT'S TOO RISKY TO LEAVE THIS MATTER UNSETTLED.
IT WOULD BE SAFER TO NIP TROUBLE IN THE BUD, WOULDN'T IT?

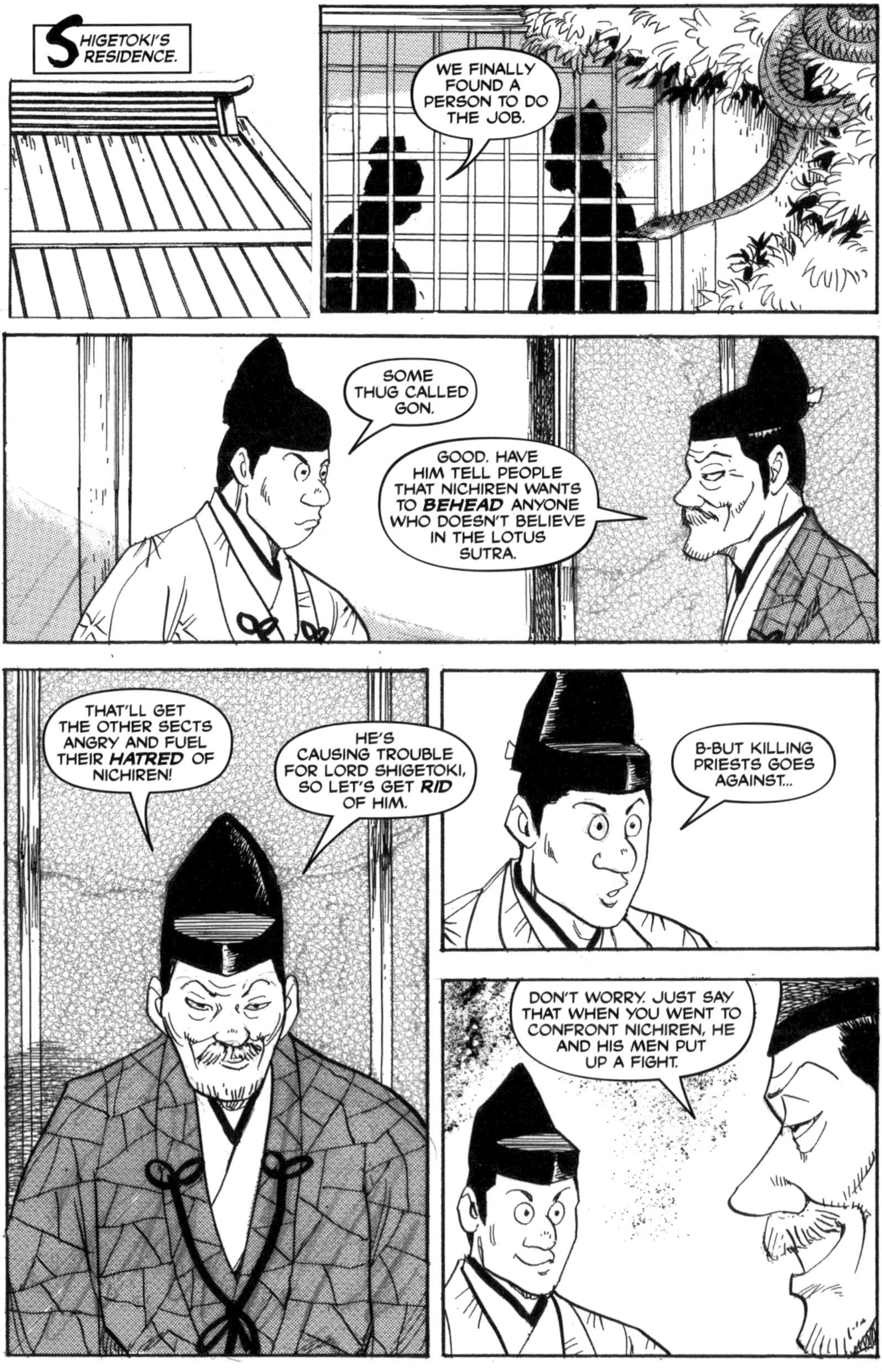
SHIGETOKI'S RESIDENCE.
WE FINALLY FOUND A PERSON TO DO THE JOB.
SOME THUG CALLED GON.
GOOD. HAVE HIM TELL PEOPLE THAT NICHIREN WANTS TO BEHEAD ANYONE WHO DOESN'T BELIEVE IN THE LOTUS SUTRA.
THAT'LL GET THE OTHER SECTS ANGRY AND FUEL THEIR HATRED OF NICHIREN!
HE'S CAUSING TROUBLE FOR LORD SHIGETOKI, SO LET'S GET RID OF HIM.
B-BUT KILLING PRIESTS GOES AGAINST...
DON'T WORRY. JUST SAY THAT WHEN YOU WENT TO CONFRONT NICHIREN, HE AND HIS MEN PUT UP A FIGHT.

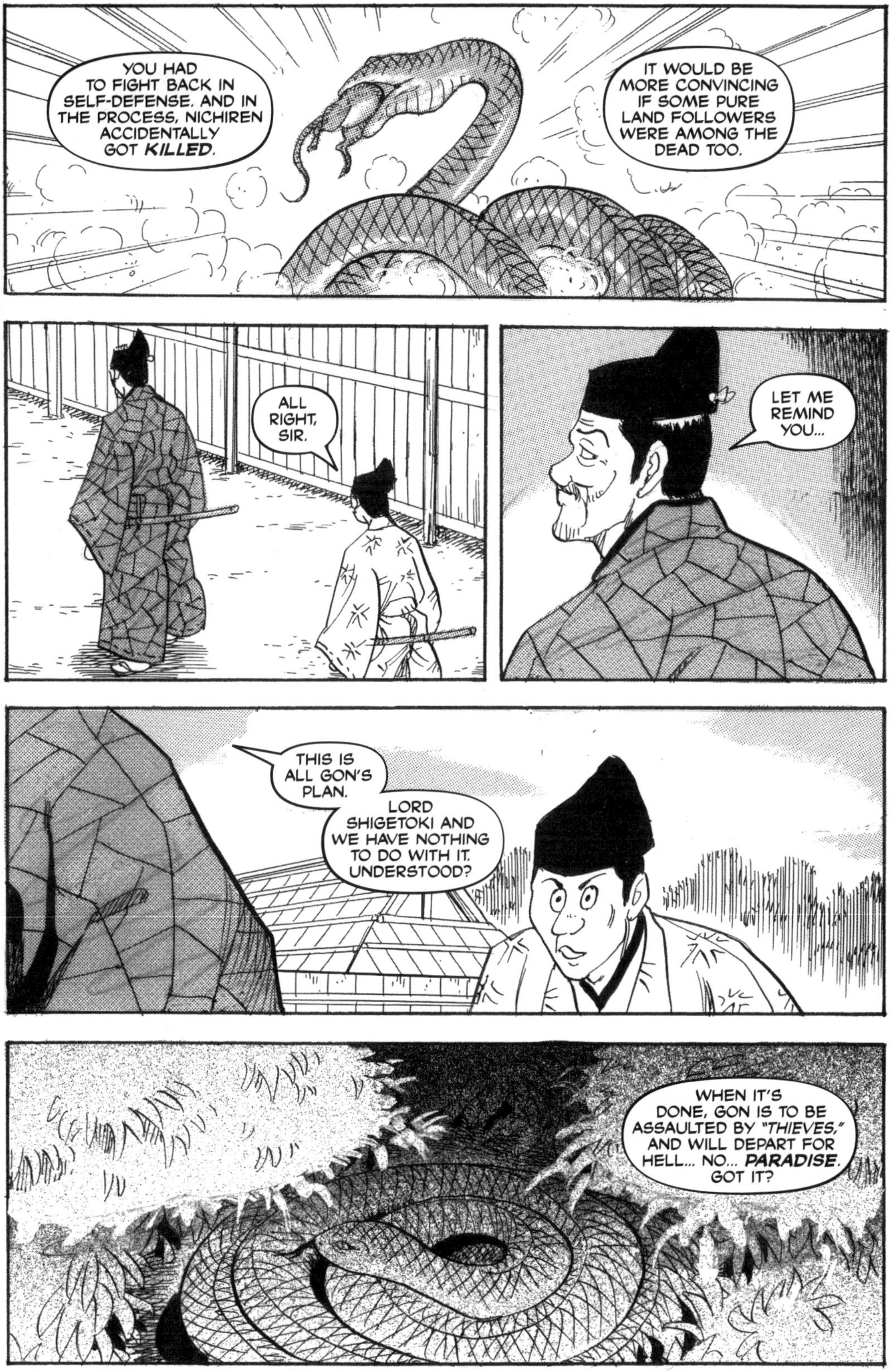
YOU HAD TO FIGHT BACK IN SELF-DEFENSE. AND IN THE PROCESS, NICHIREN ACCIDENTALLY GOT **KILLED**.
IT WOULD BE MORE CONVINCING IF SOME PURE LAND FOLLOWERS WERE AMONG THE DEAD TOO.
ALL RIGHT, SIR.
LET ME REMIND YOU...
THIS IS ALL GON'S PLAN.
LORD SHIGETOKI AND WE HAVE NOTHING TO DO WITH IT. UNDERSTOOD?
WHEN IT'S DONE, GON IS TO BE ASSAULTED BY *"THIEVES,"* AND WILL DEPART FOR HELL... NO... ***PARADISE***. GOT IT?

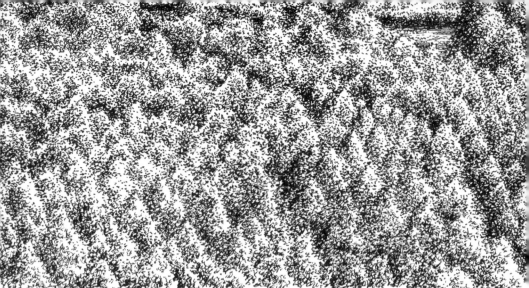

NOW EVERYONE'S HERE.

MY NAME'S GON.

JUST FOLLOW MY LEAD, GOT IT?

UH-HUH. YOU WANT US TO ROUGH UP A PRIEST CALLED NICHIREN, RIGHT?

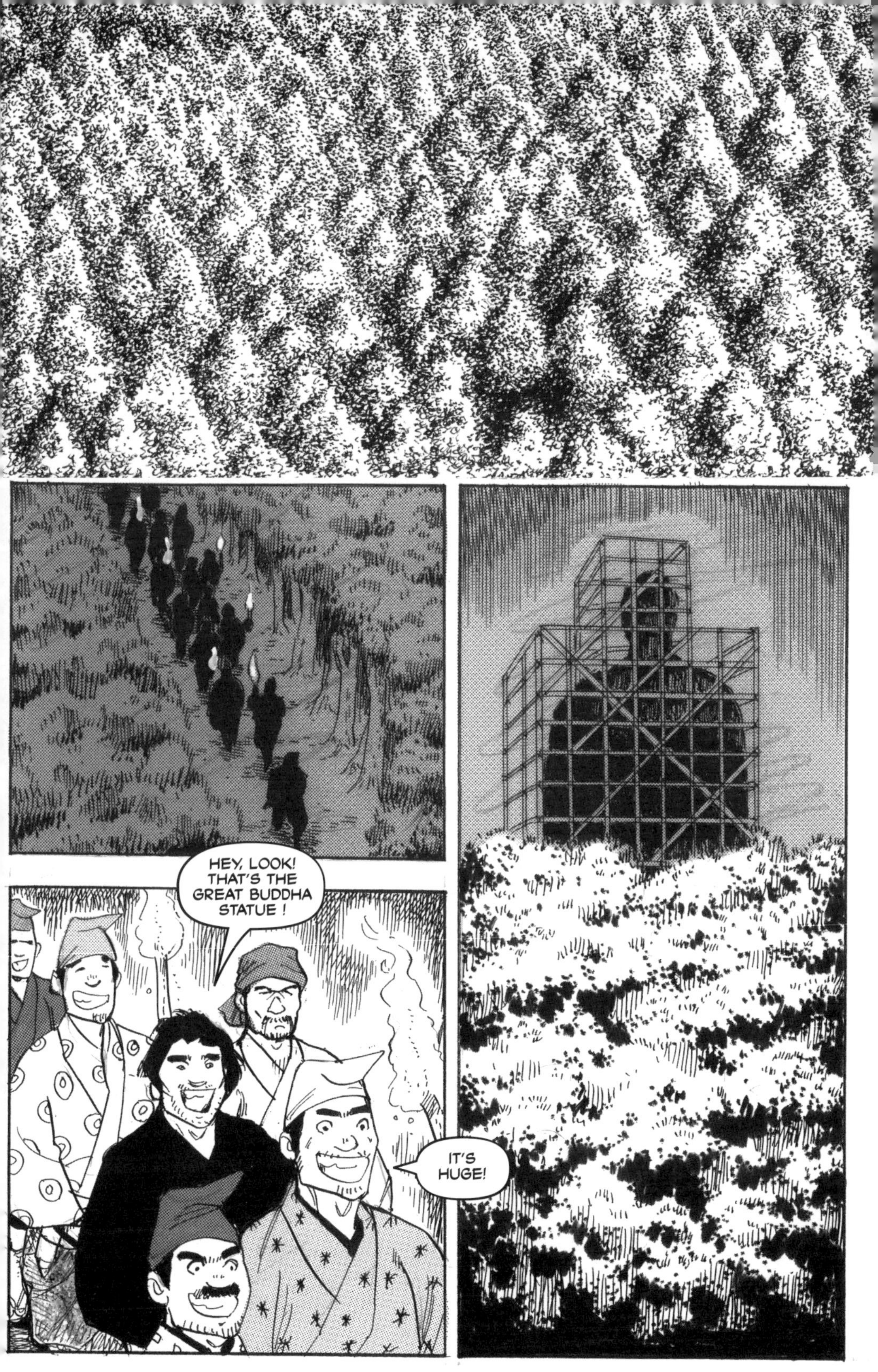
HEY, LOOK! THAT'S THE GREAT BUDDHA STATUE !
IT'S HUGE!

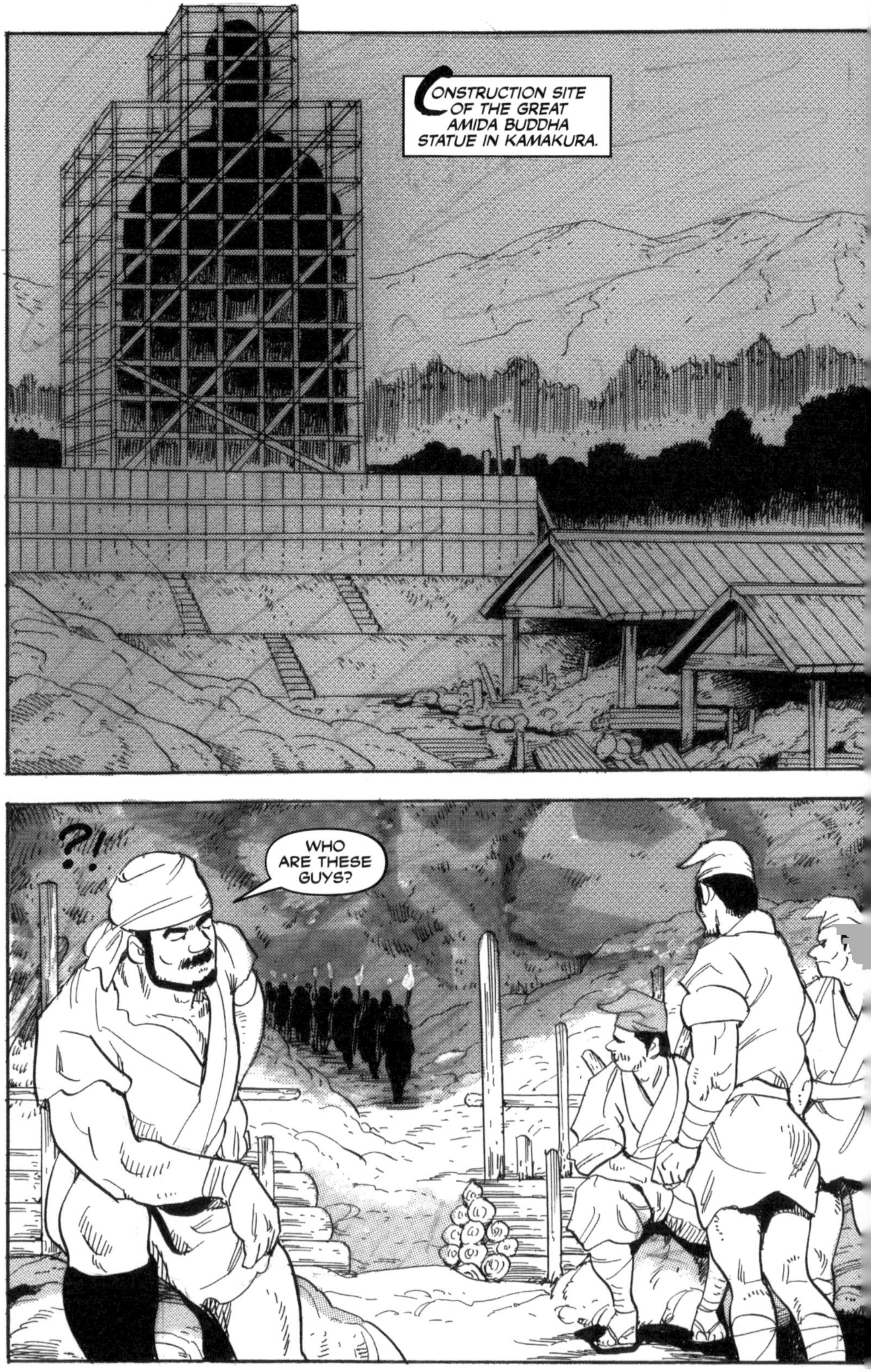
CONSTRUCTION SITE OF THE GREAT AMIDA BUDDHA STATUE IN KAMAKURA.
?!
WHO ARE THESE GUYS?

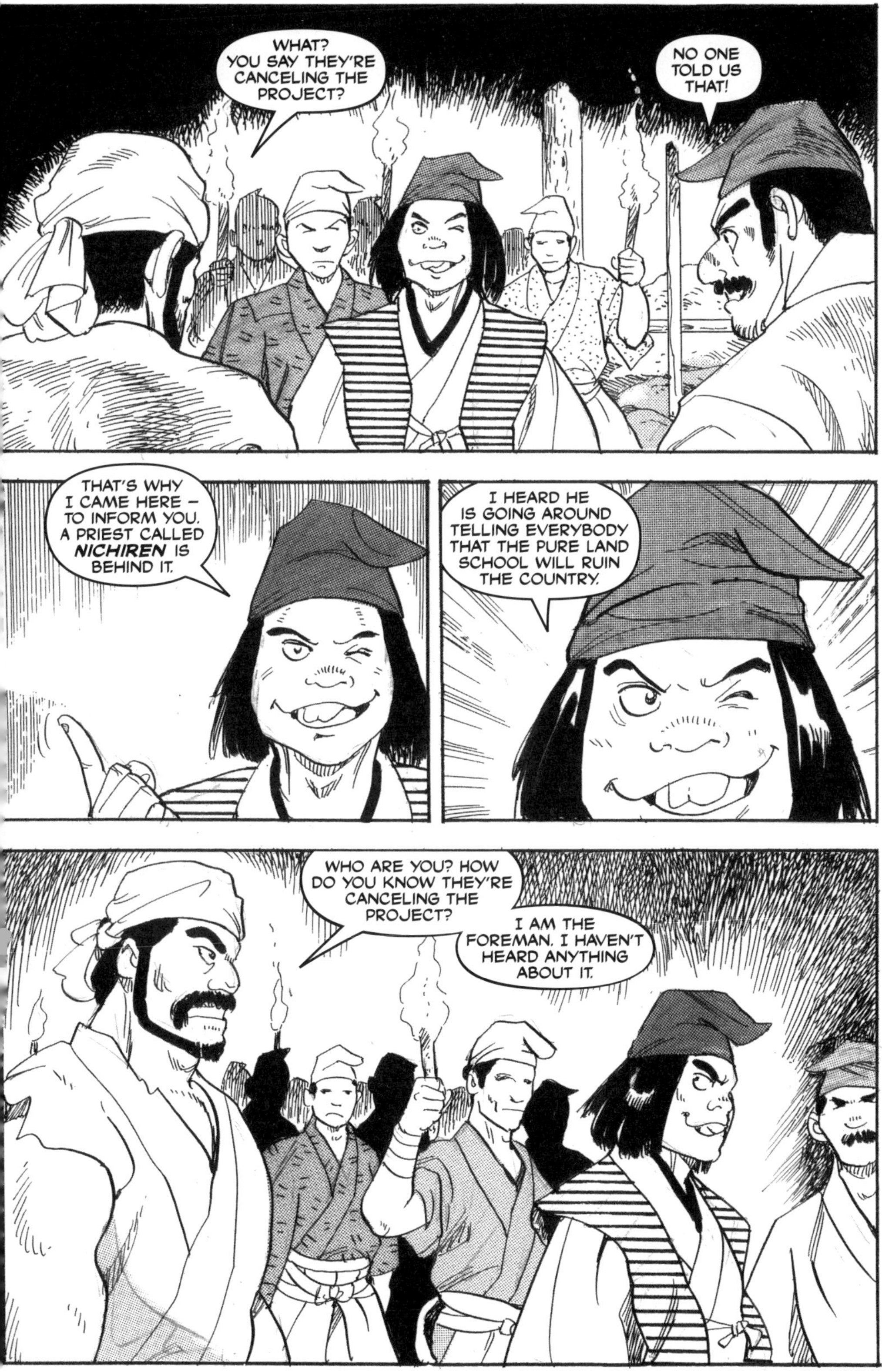
WHAT? YOU SAY THEY'RE CANCELING THE PROJECT?
NO ONE TOLD US THAT!
THAT'S WHY I CAME HERE – TO INFORM YOU. A PRIEST CALLED ***NICHIREN*** IS BEHIND IT.
I HEARD HE IS GOING AROUND TELLING EVERYBODY THAT THE PURE LAND SCHOOL WILL RUIN THE COUNTRY.
WHO ARE YOU? HOW DO YOU KNOW THEY'RE CANCELING THE PROJECT?
I AM THE FOREMAN. I HAVEN'T HEARD ANYTHING ABOUT IT.

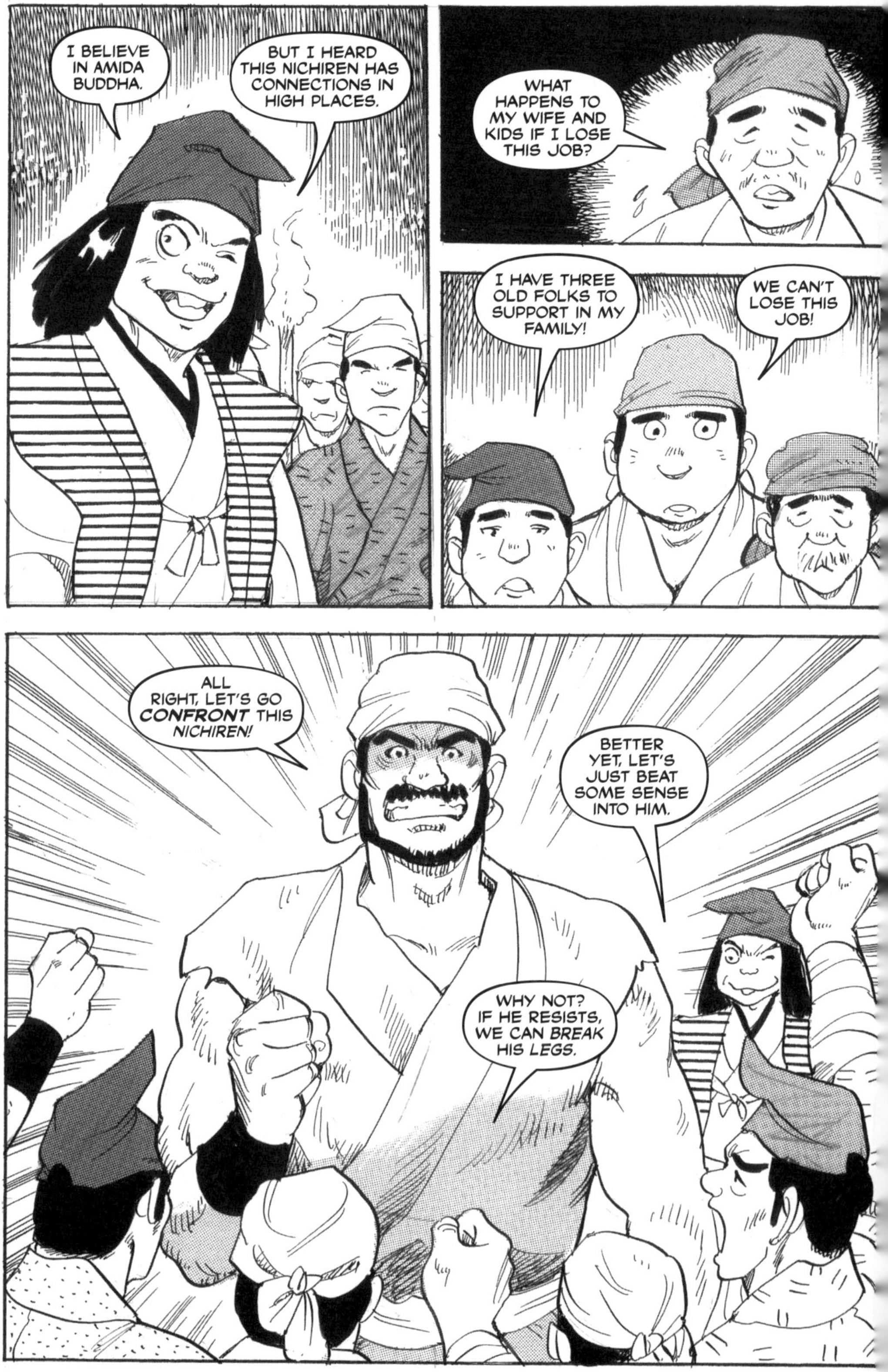
I BELIEVE IN AMIDA BUDDHA.
BUT I HEARD THIS NICHIREN HAS CONNECTIONS IN HIGH PLACES.
WHAT HAPPENS TO MY WIFE AND KIDS IF I LOSE THIS JOB?
I HAVE THREE OLD FOLKS TO SUPPORT IN MY FAMILY!
WE CAN'T LOSE THIS JOB!
ALL RIGHT, LET'S GO ***CONFRONT*** THIS *NICHIREN!*
BETTER YET, LET'S JUST BEAT SOME SENSE INTO HIM.
WHY NOT? IF HE RESISTS, WE CAN *BREAK* HIS *LEGS.*

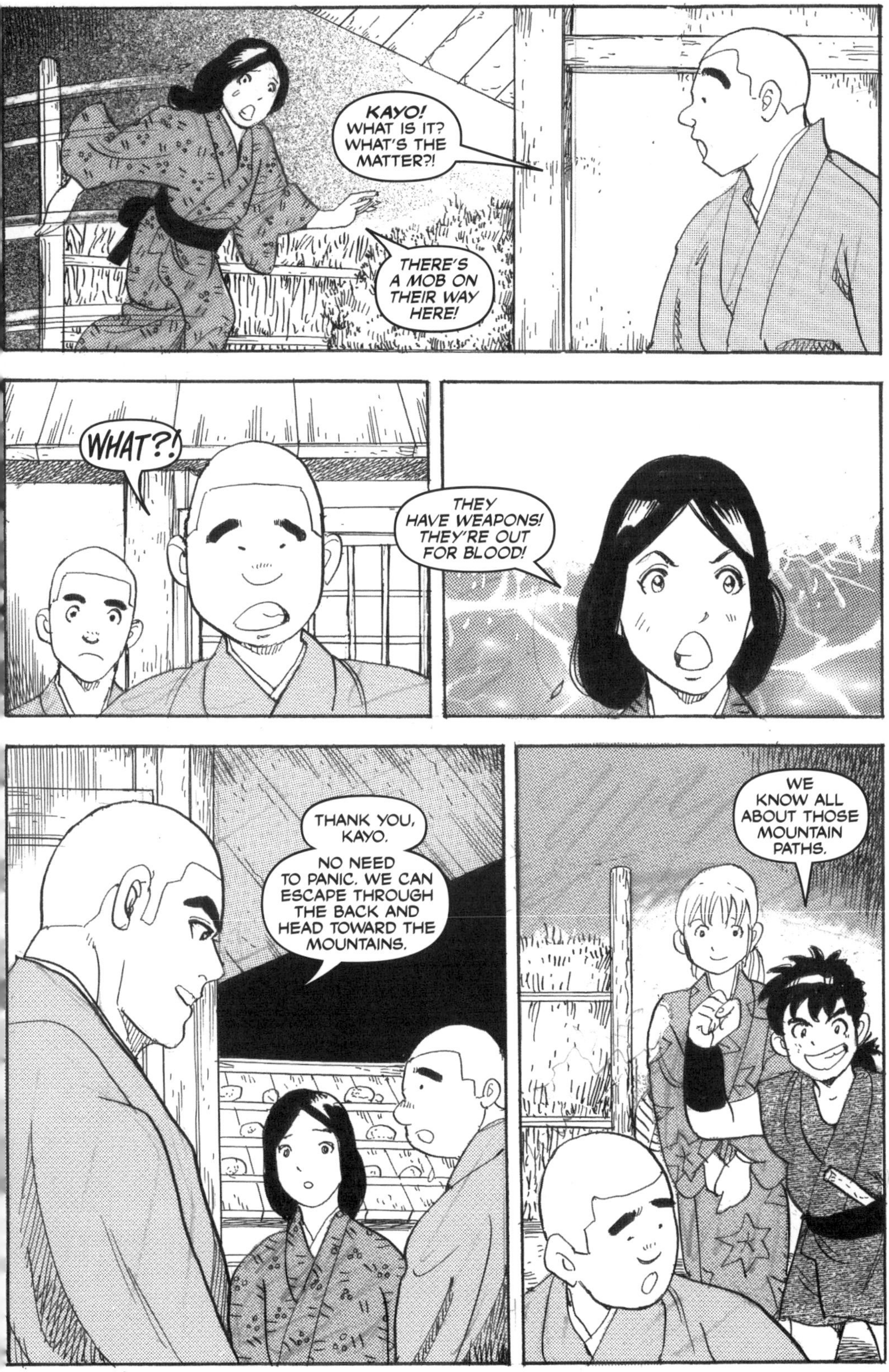

KAYO! WHAT IS IT? WHAT'S THE MATTER?!
THERE'S A MOB ON THEIR WAY HERE!
WHAT?!
THEY HAVE WEAPONS! THEY'RE OUT FOR BLOOD!
THANK YOU, KAYO.
NO NEED TO PANIC. WE CAN ESCAPE THROUGH THE BACK AND HEAD TOWARD THE MOUNTAINS.
WE KNOW ALL ABOUT THOSE MOUNTAIN PATHS.

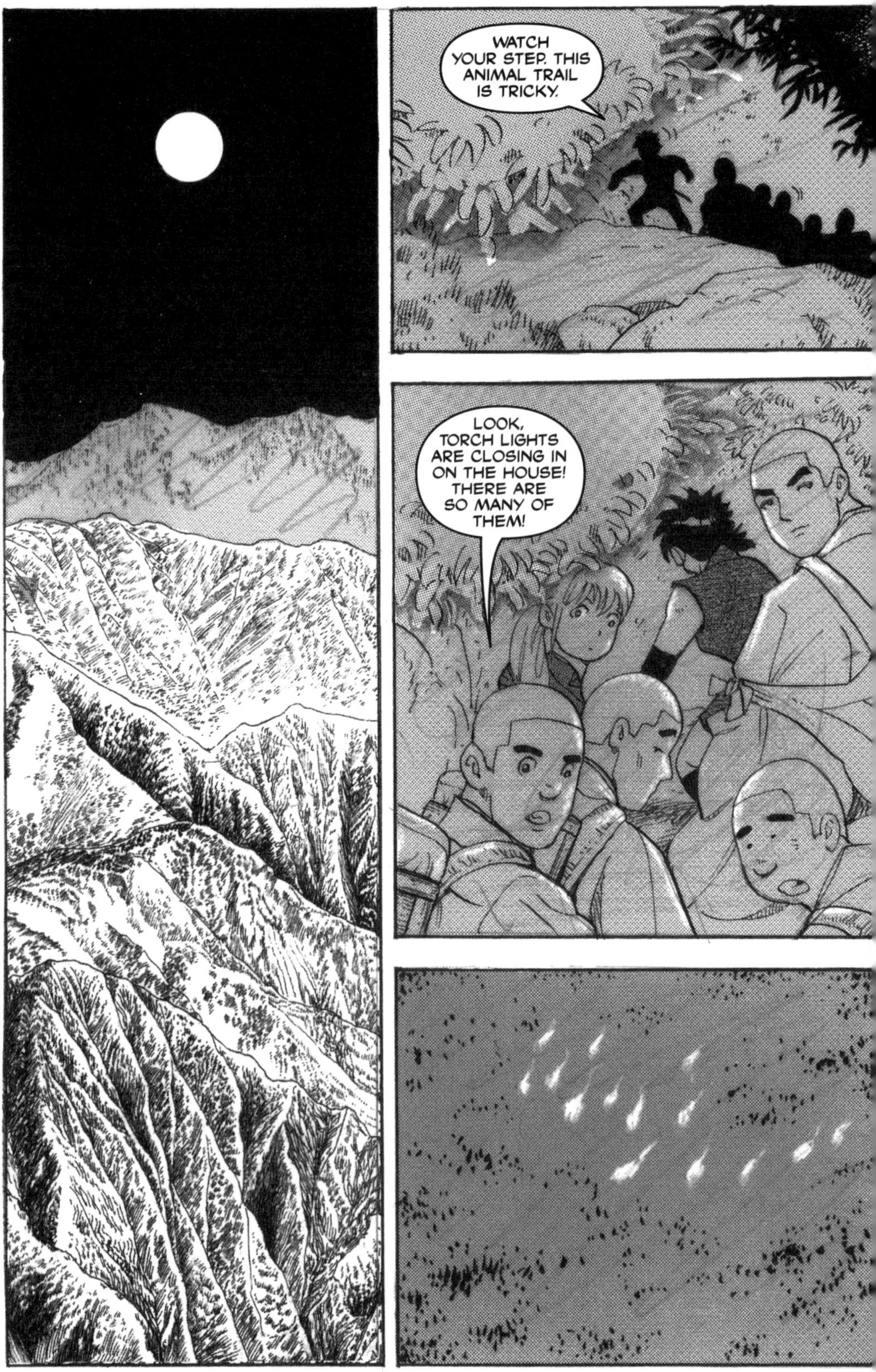
WATCH YOUR STEP. THIS ANIMAL TRAIL IS TRICKY.
LOOK, TORCH LIGHTS ARE CLOSING IN ON THE HOUSE! THERE ARE SO MANY OF THEM!

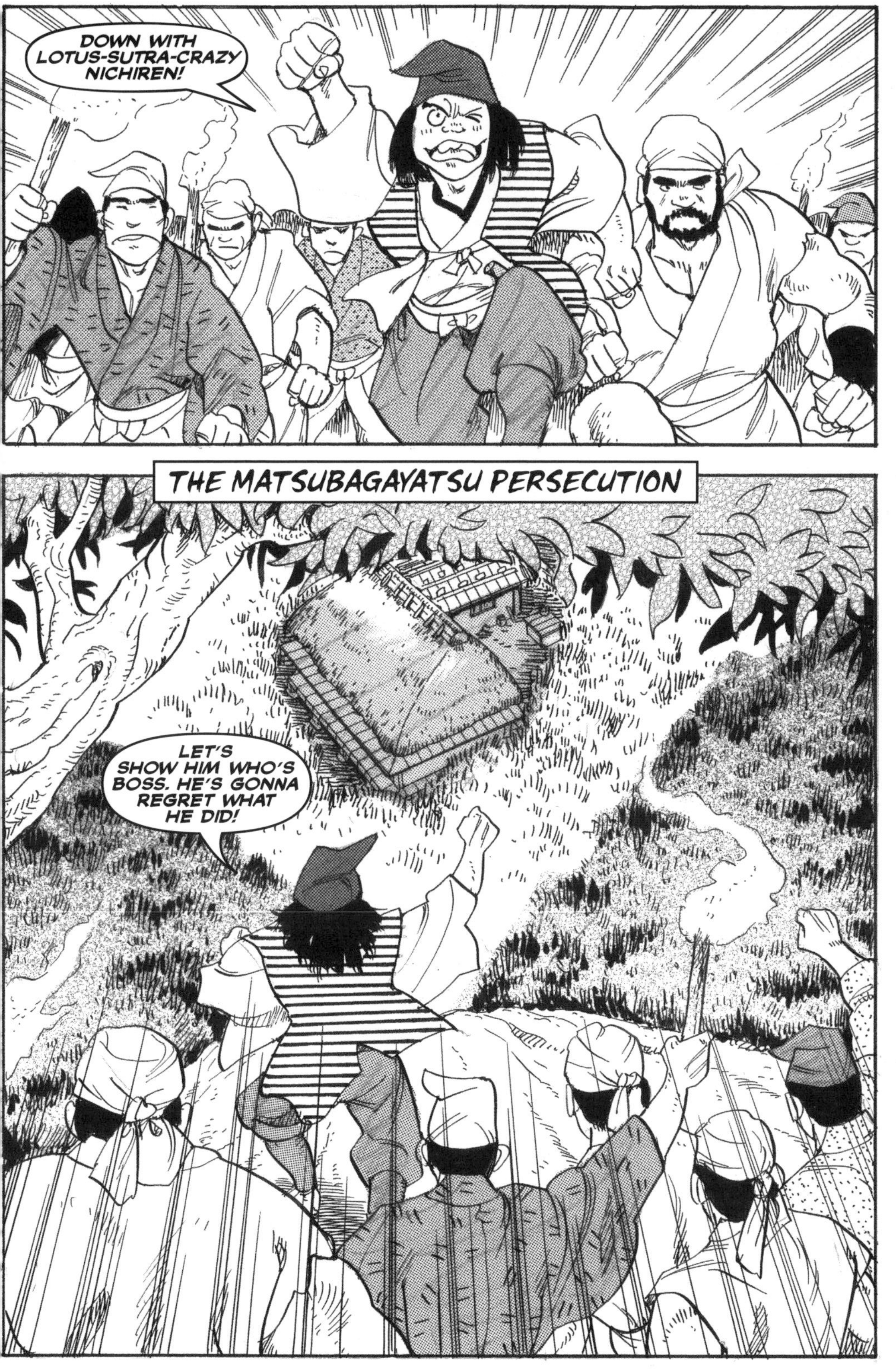
DOWN WITH LOTUS-SUTRA-CRAZY NICHIREN!
THE MATSUBAGAYATSU PERSECUTION
LET'S SHOW HIM WHO'S BOSS. HE'S GONNA REGRET WHAT HE DID!

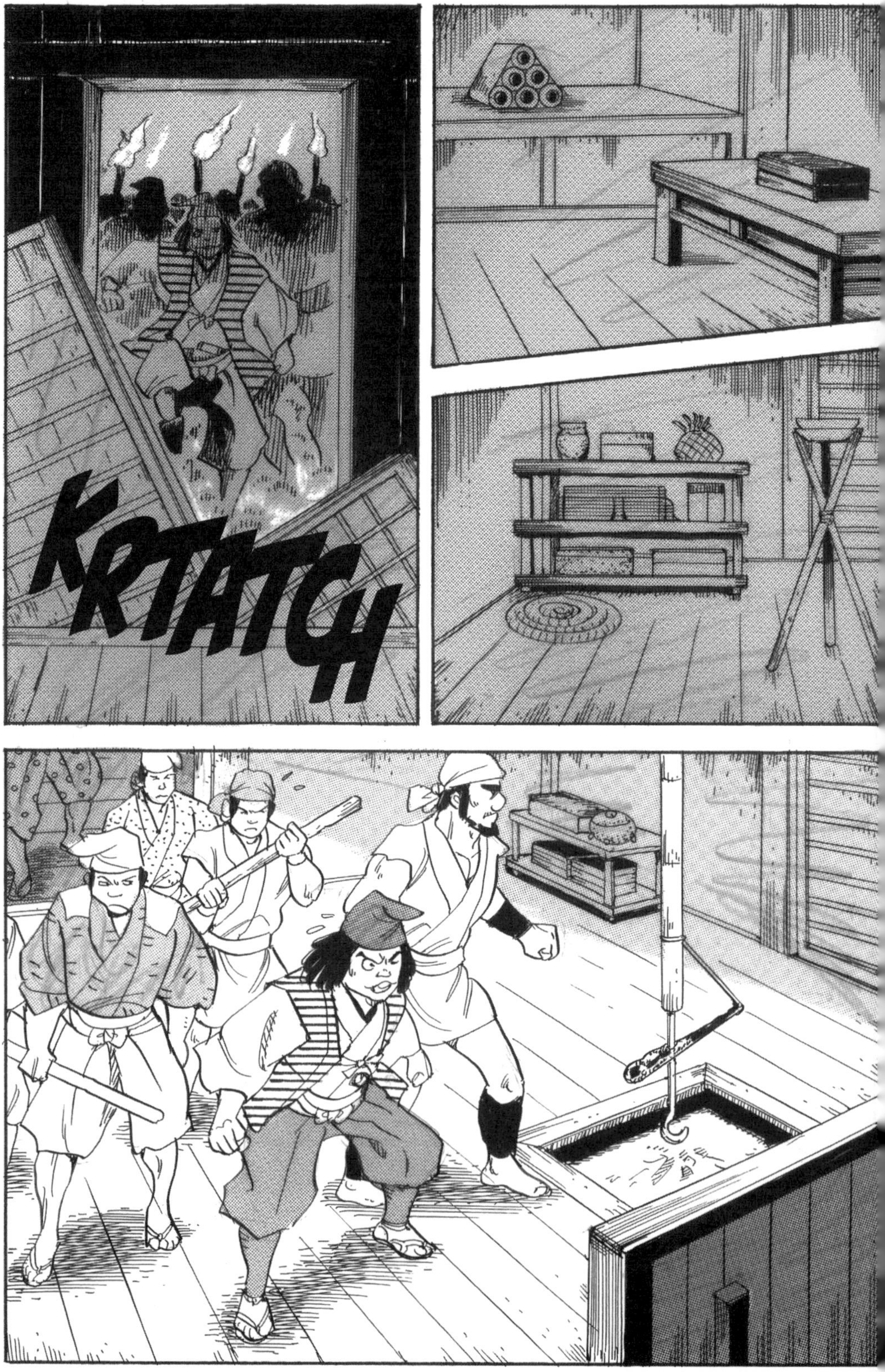
KRTATCH

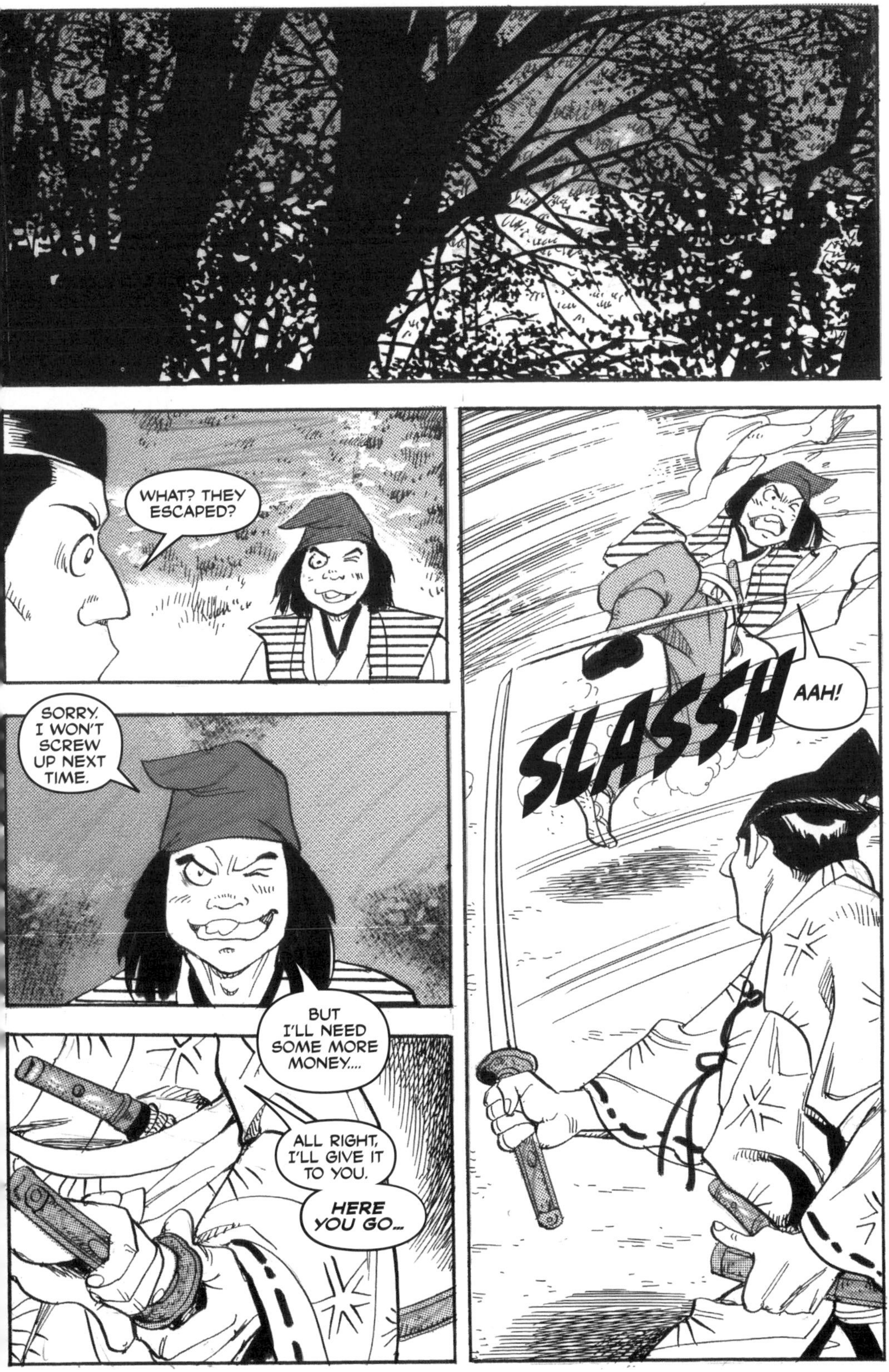

WHAT? THEY ESCAPED?
SORRY. I WON'T SCREW UP NEXT TIME.
BUT I'LL NEED SOME MORE MONEY....
ALL RIGHT, I'LL GIVE IT TO YOU.
HERE YOU GO...
SLASSH
AAH!

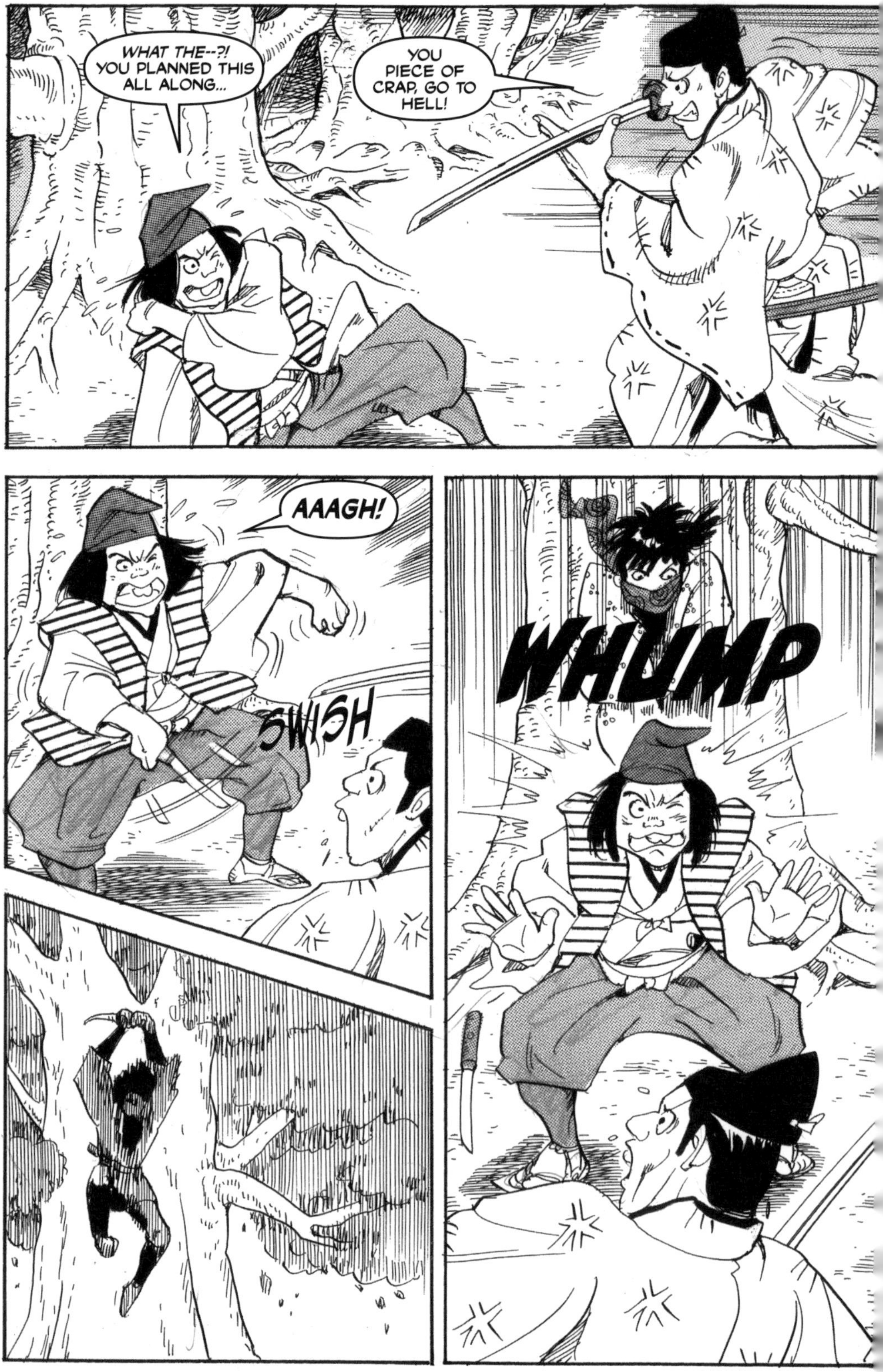
WHAT THE--?! YOU PLANNED THIS ALL ALONG...
YOU PIECE OF CRAP, GO TO HELL!
AAAGH!
SWISH
WHUMP

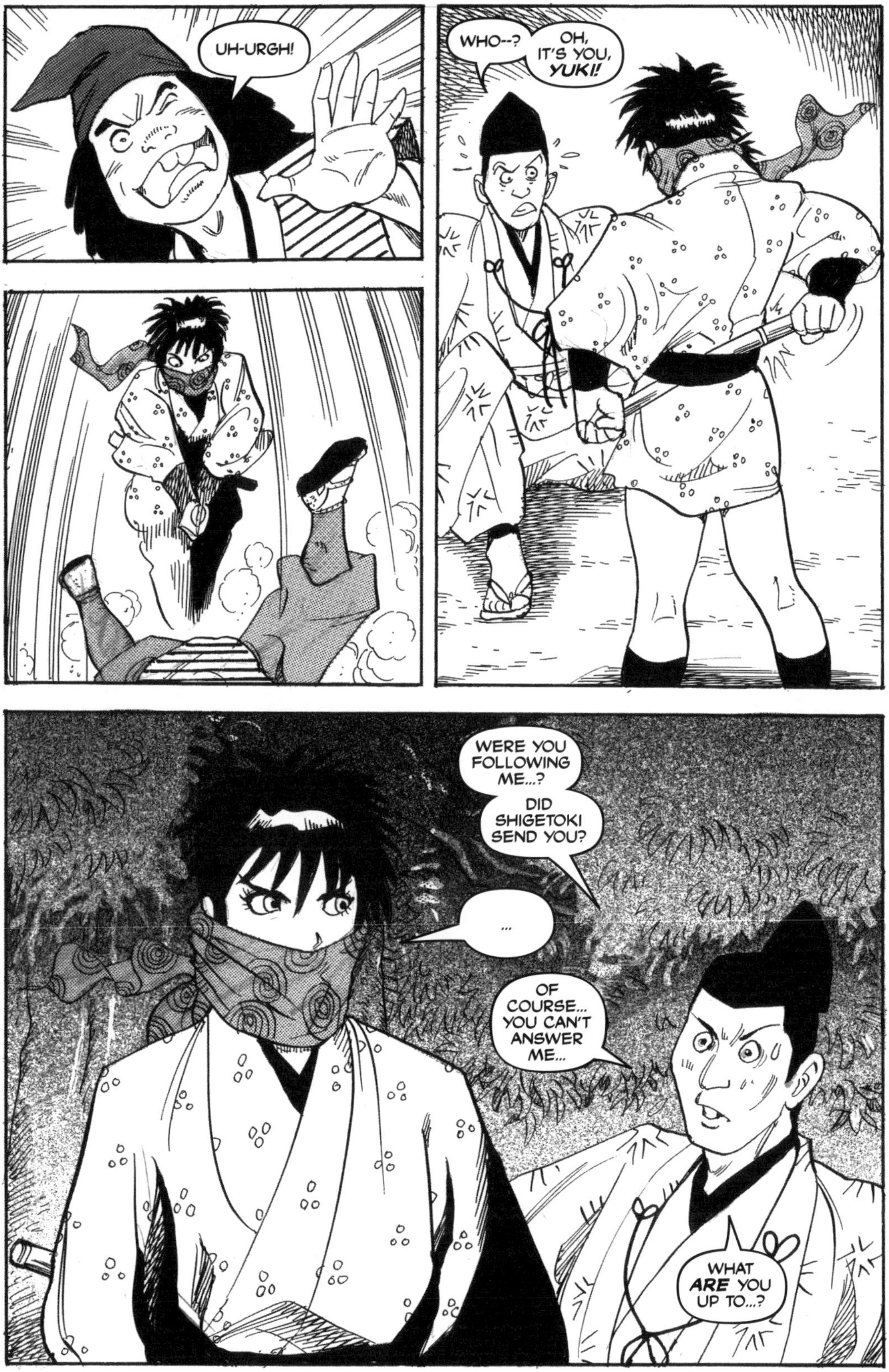
UH-URGH!
WHO--?
OH, IT'S YOU, *YUKI!*
WERE YOU FOLLOWING ME...?
DID SHIGETOKI SEND YOU?
...
OF COURSE... YOU CAN'T ANSWER ME...
WHAT *ARE* YOU UP TO...?

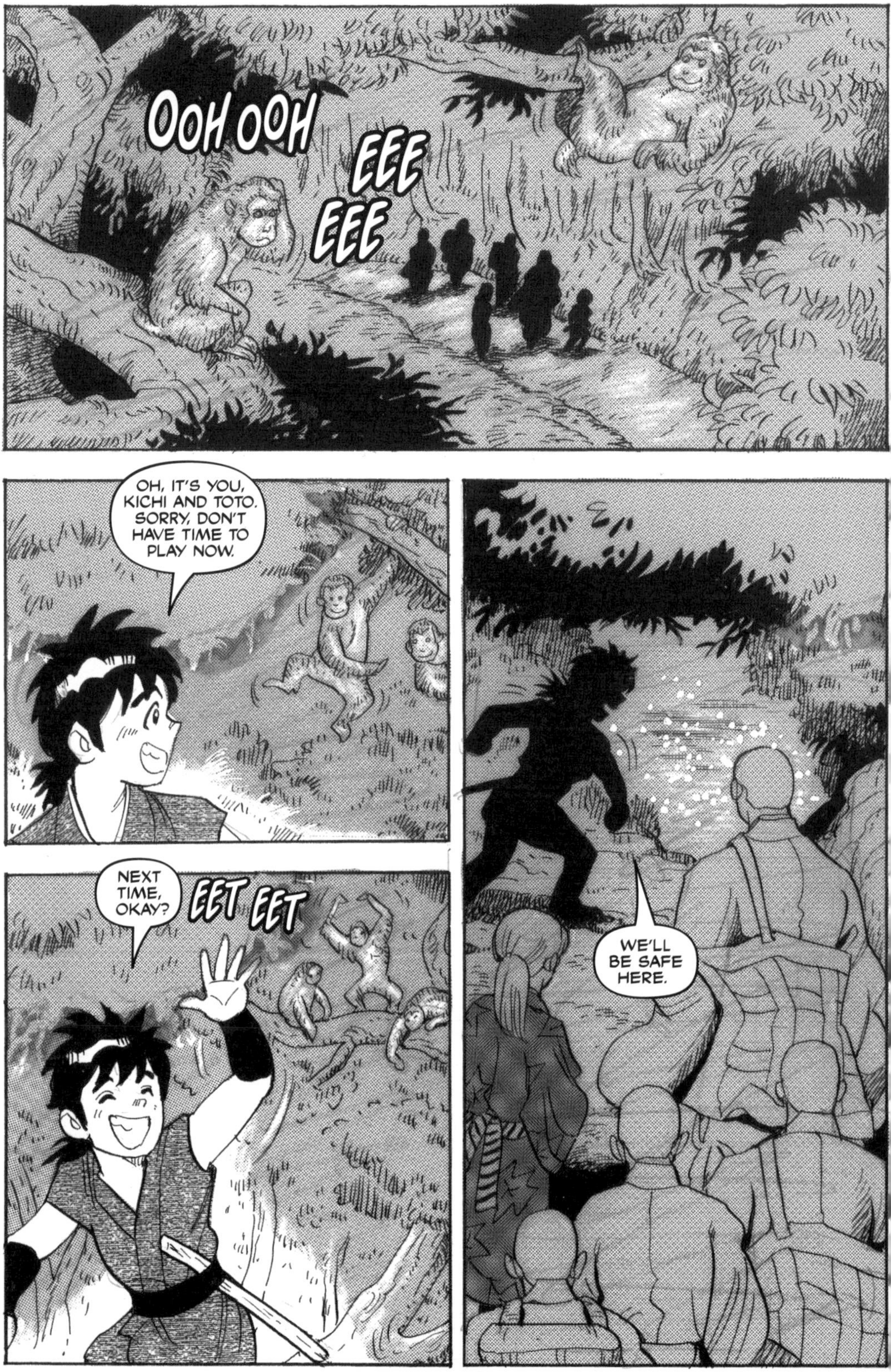
OOH OOH
EEE EEE
OH, IT'S YOU, KICHI AND TOTO. SORRY, DON'T HAVE TIME TO PLAY NOW.
NEXT TIME, OKAY?
EET EET
WE'LL BE SAFE HERE.

Chapter 2

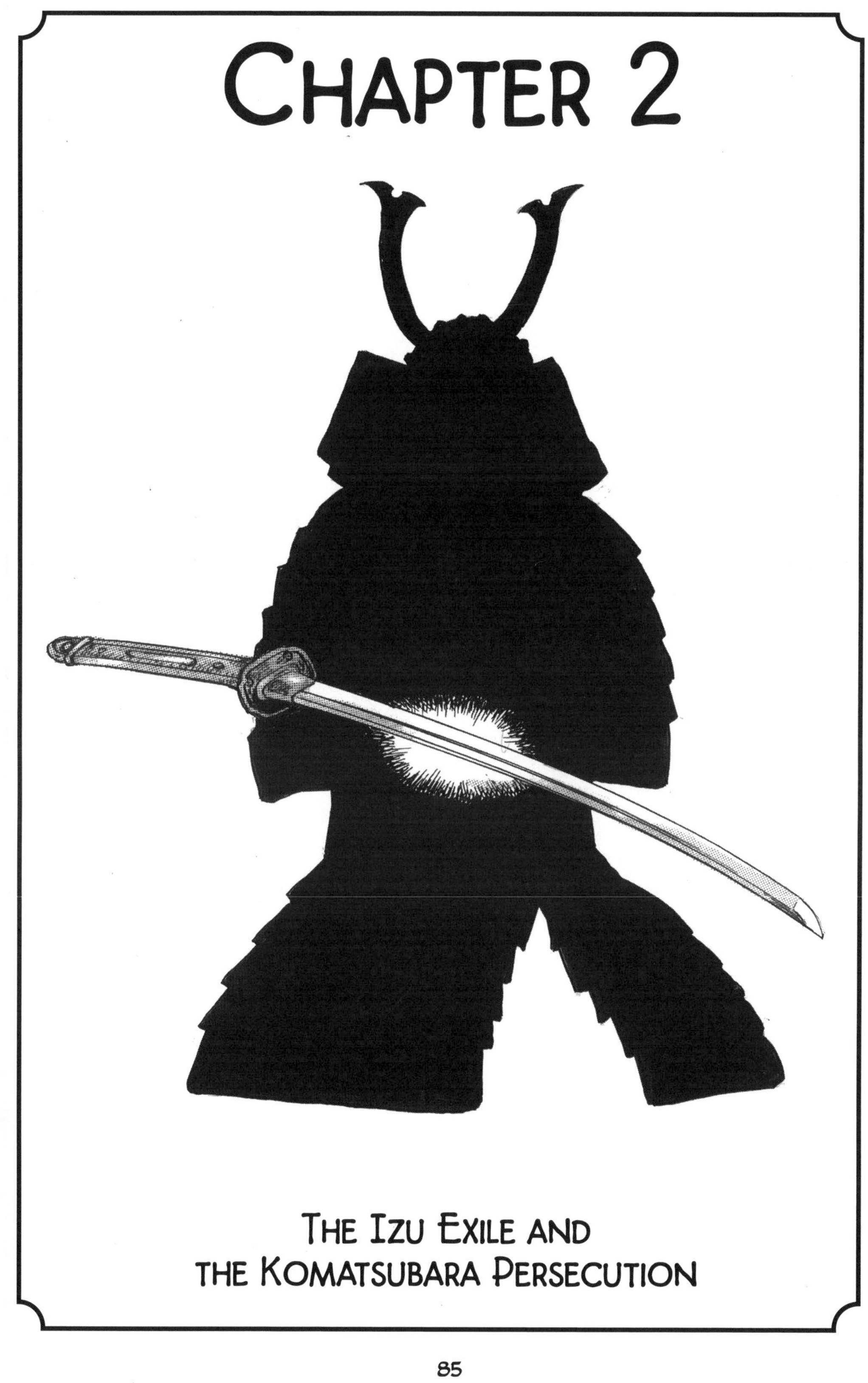

The Izu Exile and the Komatsubara Persecution

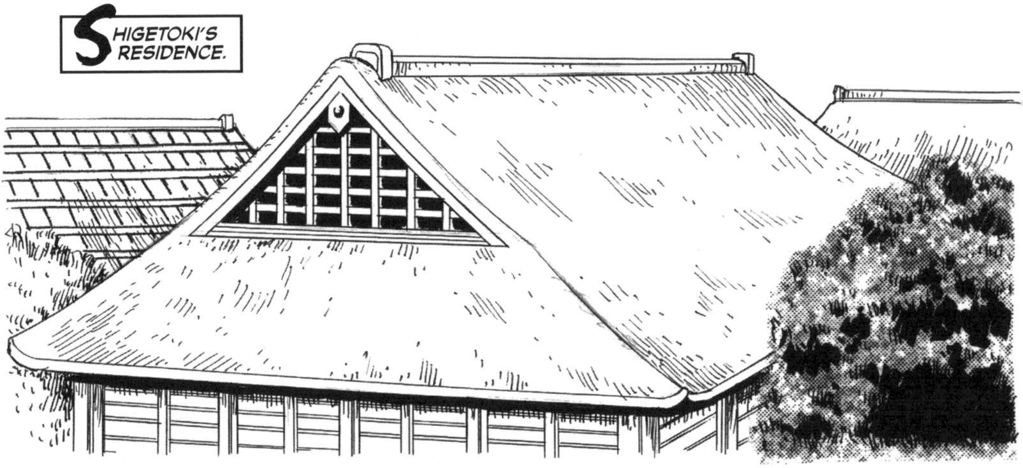
SHIGETOKI'S RESIDENCE.

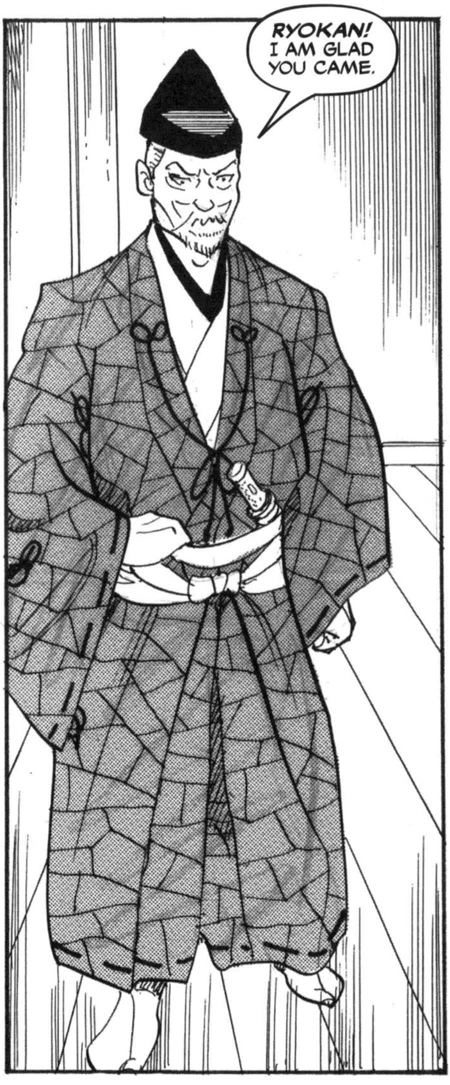
RYOKAN! I AM GLAD YOU CAME.

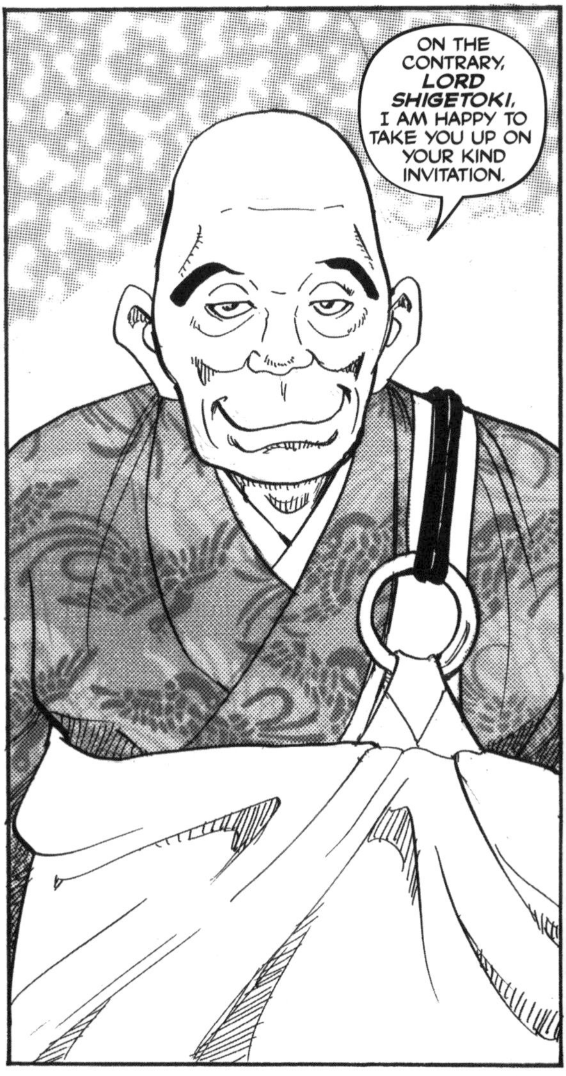
ON THE CONTRARY, LORD SHIGETOKI, I AM HAPPY TO TAKE YOU UP ON YOUR KIND INVITATION.

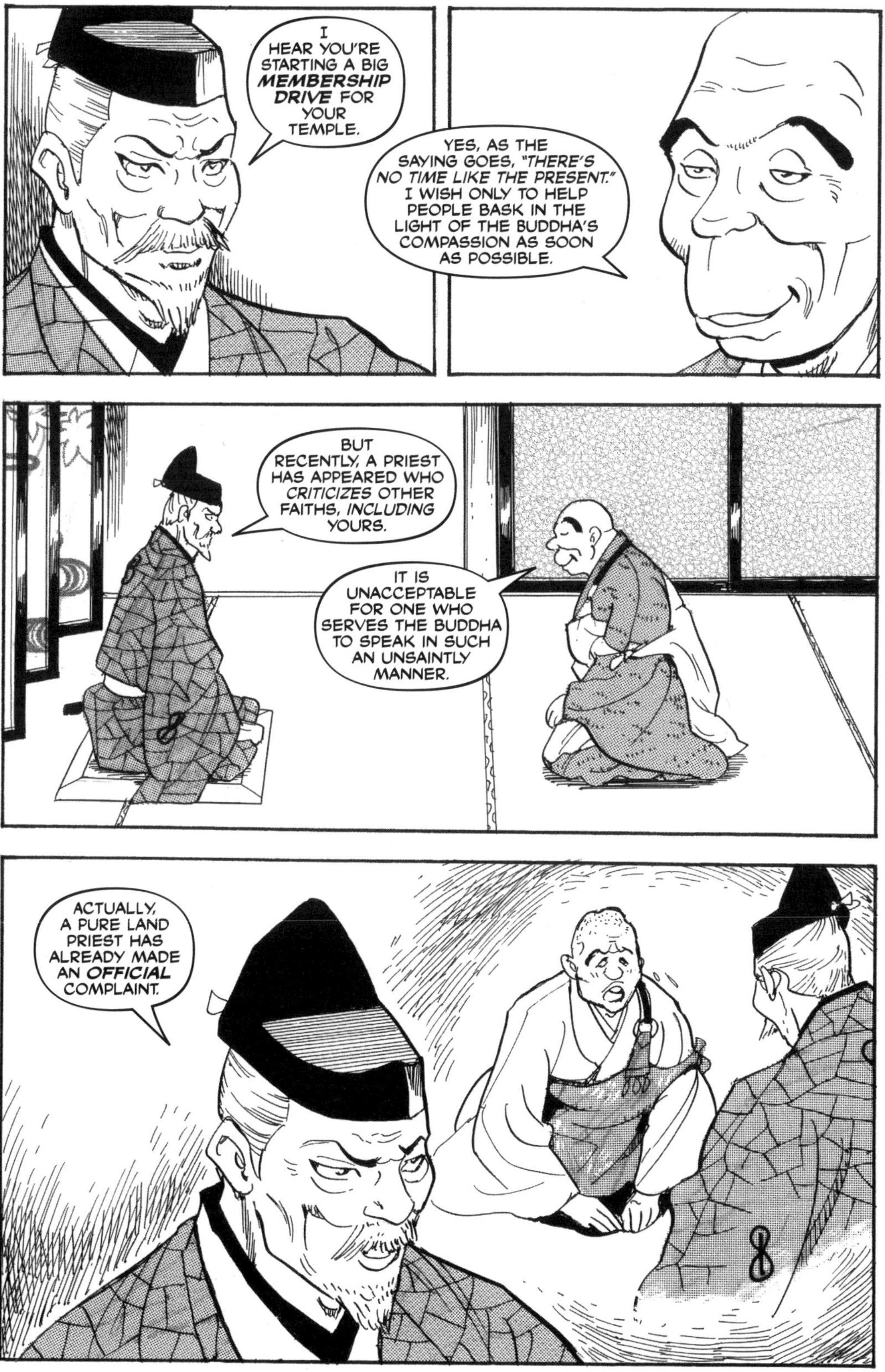
I HEAR YOU'RE STARTING A BIG ***MEMBERSHIP DRIVE*** FOR YOUR TEMPLE.
YES, AS THE SAYING GOES, *"THERE'S NO TIME LIKE THE PRESENT."* I WISH ONLY TO HELP PEOPLE BASK IN THE LIGHT OF THE BUDDHA'S COMPASSION AS SOON AS POSSIBLE.
BUT RECENTLY, A PRIEST HAS APPEARED WHO *CRITICIZES* OTHER FAITHS, *INCLUDING* YOURS.
IT IS UNACCEPTABLE FOR ONE WHO SERVES THE BUDDHA TO SPEAK IN SUCH AN UNSAINTLY MANNER.
ACTUALLY, A PURE LAND PRIEST HAS ALREADY MADE AN ***OFFICIAL*** COMPLAINT.

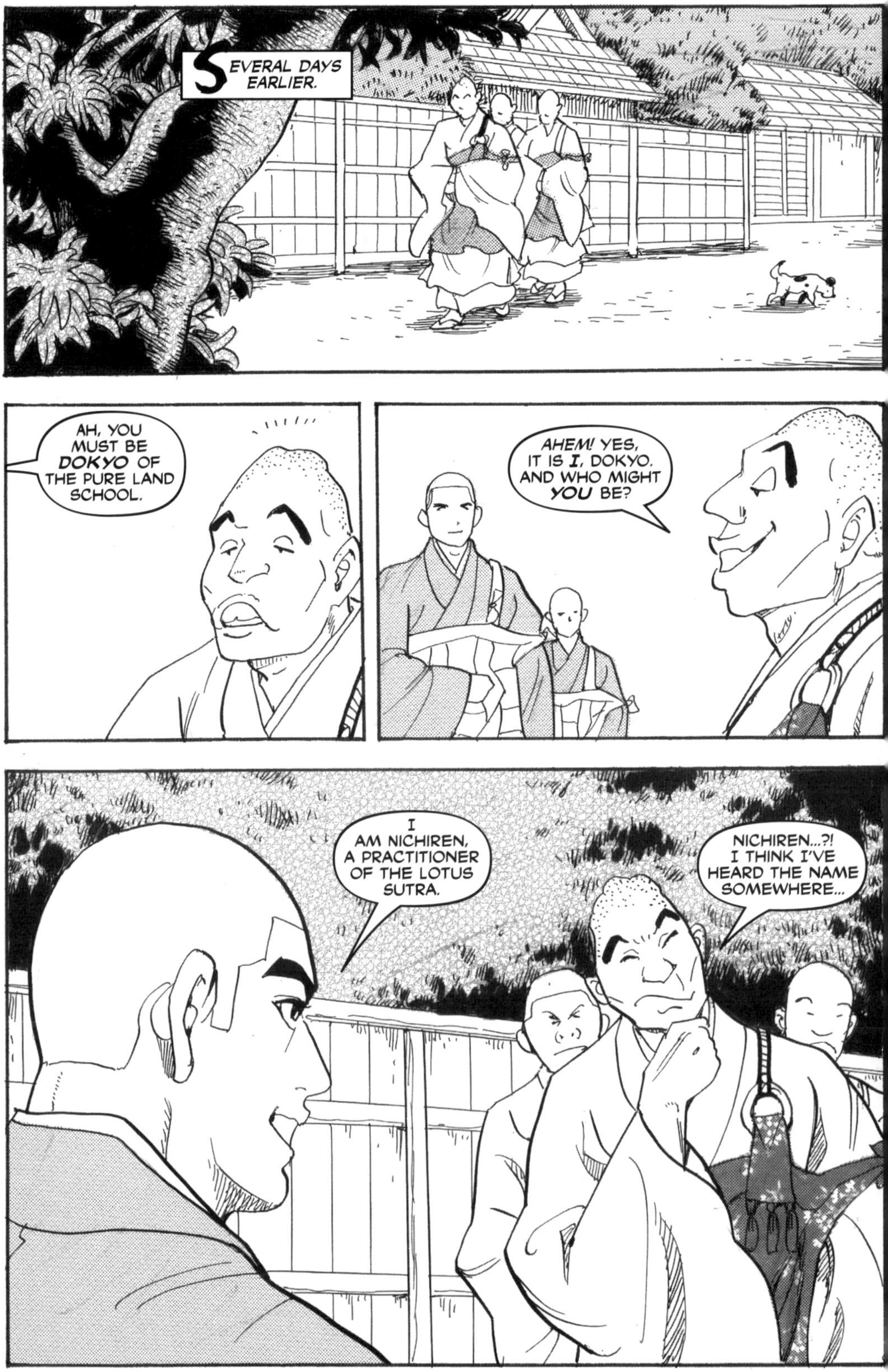
SEVERAL DAYS EARLIER.
AH, YOU MUST BE DOKYO OF THE PURE LAND SCHOOL.
AHEM! YES, IT IS I, DOKYO. AND WHO MIGHT YOU BE?
I AM NICHIREN, A PRACTITIONER OF THE LOTUS SUTRA.
NICHIREN...?! I THINK I'VE HEARD THE NAME SOMEWHERE...

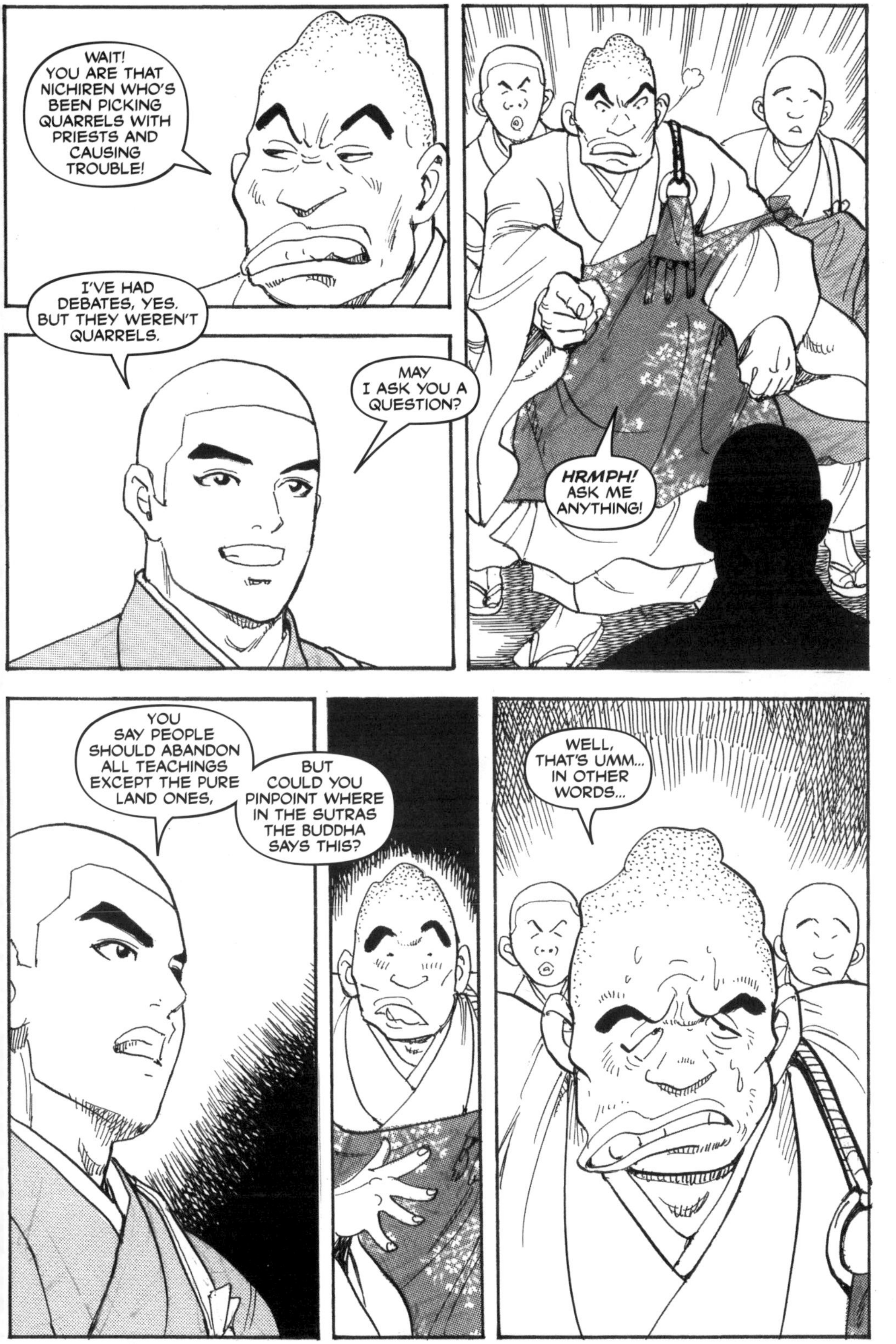
WAIT! YOU ARE THAT NICHIREN WHO'S BEEN PICKING QUARRELS WITH PRIESTS AND CAUSING TROUBLE!
I'VE HAD DEBATES, YES. BUT THEY WEREN'T QUARRELS.
MAY I ASK YOU A QUESTION?
HRMPH! ASK ME ANYTHING!
YOU SAY PEOPLE SHOULD ABANDON ALL TEACHINGS EXCEPT THE PURE LAND ONES,
BUT COULD YOU PINPOINT WHERE IN THE SUTRAS THE BUDDHA SAYS THIS?
WELL, THAT'S UMM... IN OTHER WORDS...

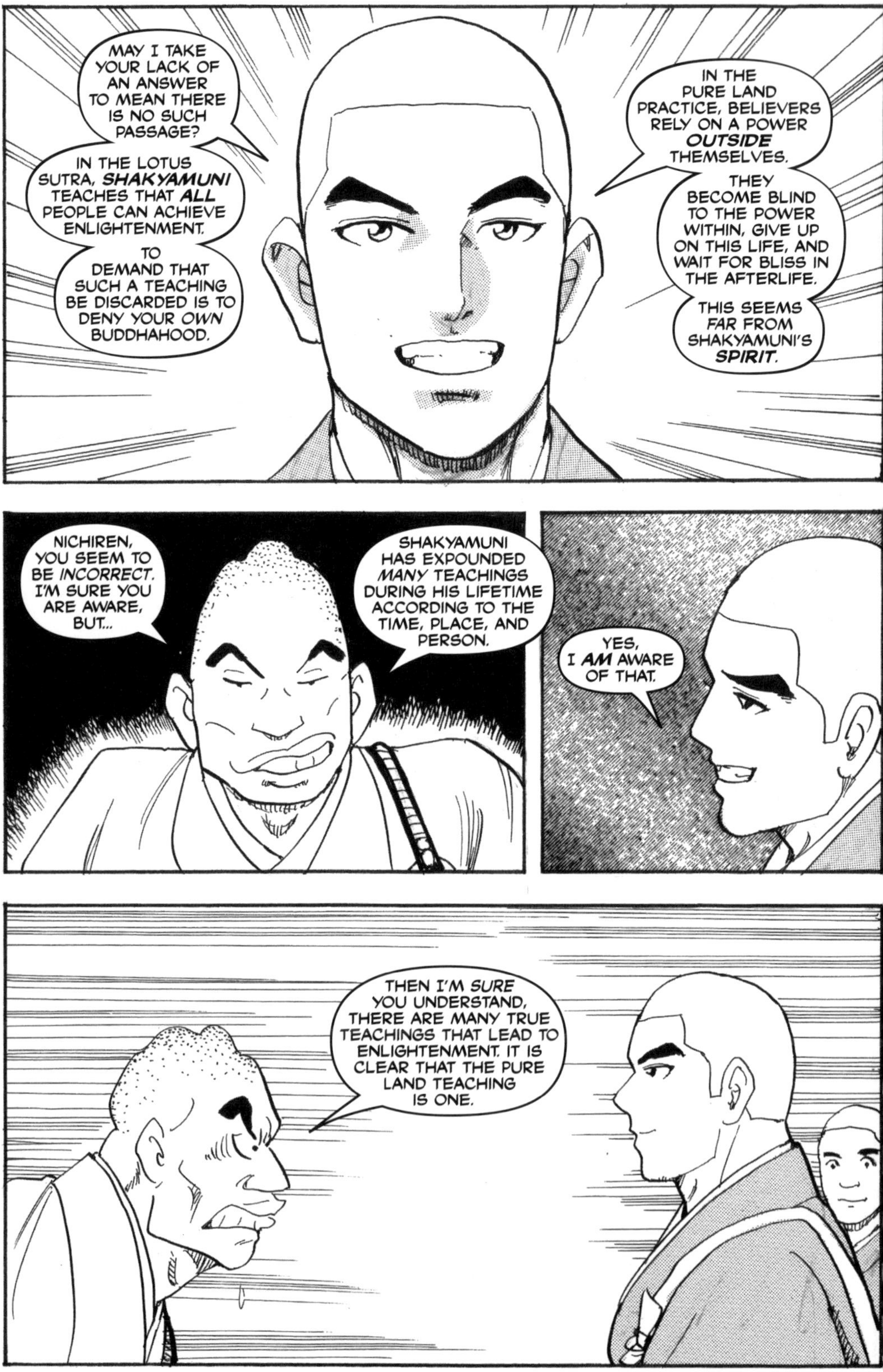
MAY I TAKE YOUR LACK OF AN ANSWER TO MEAN THERE IS NO SUCH PASSAGE?
IN THE LOTUS SUTRA, *SHAKYAMUNI* TEACHES THAT *ALL* PEOPLE CAN ACHIEVE ENLIGHTENMENT.
TO DEMAND THAT SUCH A TEACHING BE DISCARDED IS TO DENY YOUR *OWN* BUDDHAHOOD.
IN THE PURE LAND PRACTICE, BELIEVERS RELY ON A POWER *OUTSIDE* THEMSELVES.
THEY BECOME BLIND TO THE POWER WITHIN, GIVE UP ON THIS LIFE, AND WAIT FOR BLISS IN THE AFTERLIFE.
THIS SEEMS *FAR* FROM SHAKYAMUNI'S *SPIRIT*.
NICHIREN, YOU SEEM TO BE *INCORRECT*. I'M SURE YOU ARE AWARE, BUT...
SHAKYAMUNI HAS EXPOUNDED *MANY* TEACHINGS DURING HIS LIFETIME ACCORDING TO THE TIME, PLACE, AND PERSON.
YES, I *AM* AWARE OF THAT.
THEN I'M *SURE* YOU UNDERSTAND, THERE ARE MANY TRUE TEACHINGS THAT LEAD TO ENLIGHTENMENT. IT IS CLEAR THAT THE PURE LAND TEACHING IS ONE.

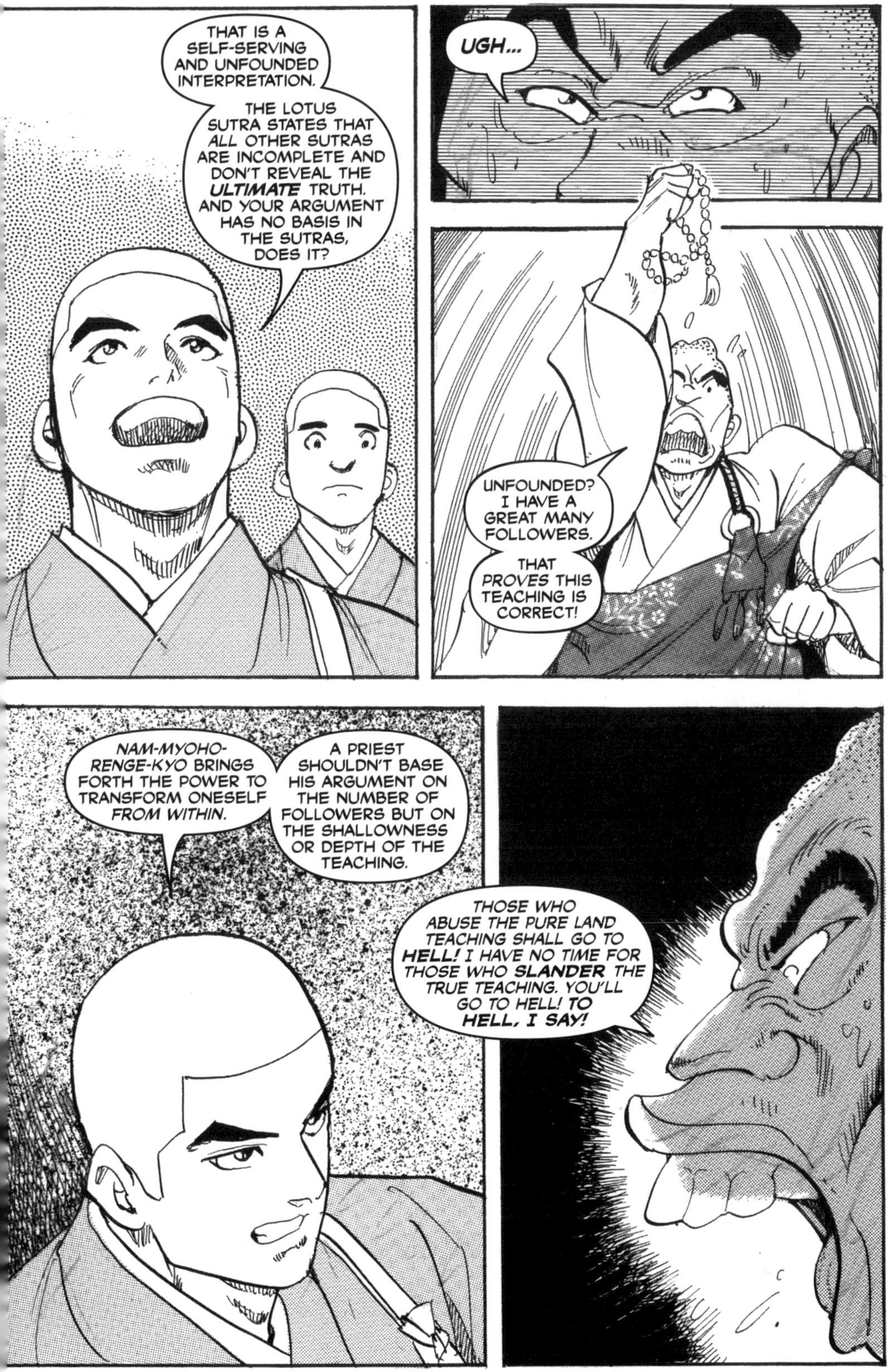
THAT IS A SELF-SERVING AND UNFOUNDED INTERPRETATION.
THE LOTUS SUTRA STATES THAT *ALL* OTHER SUTRAS ARE INCOMPLETE AND DON'T REVEAL THE ***ULTIMATE*** TRUTH. AND YOUR ARGUMENT HAS NO BASIS IN THE SUTRAS, DOES IT?
UGH...
UNFOUNDED? I HAVE A GREAT MANY FOLLOWERS.
THAT *PROVES* THIS TEACHING IS CORRECT!
NAM-MYOHO-RENGE-KYO BRINGS FORTH THE POWER TO TRANSFORM ONESELF *FROM WITHIN.*
A PRIEST SHOULDN'T BASE HIS ARGUMENT ON THE NUMBER OF FOLLOWERS BUT ON THE SHALLOWNESS OR DEPTH OF THE TEACHING.
*THOSE WHO ABUSE THE PURE LAND TEACHING SHALL GO TO **HELL!** I HAVE NO TIME FOR THOSE WHO **SLANDER** THE TRUE TEACHING. YOU'LL GO TO HELL! **TO HELL, I SAY!***

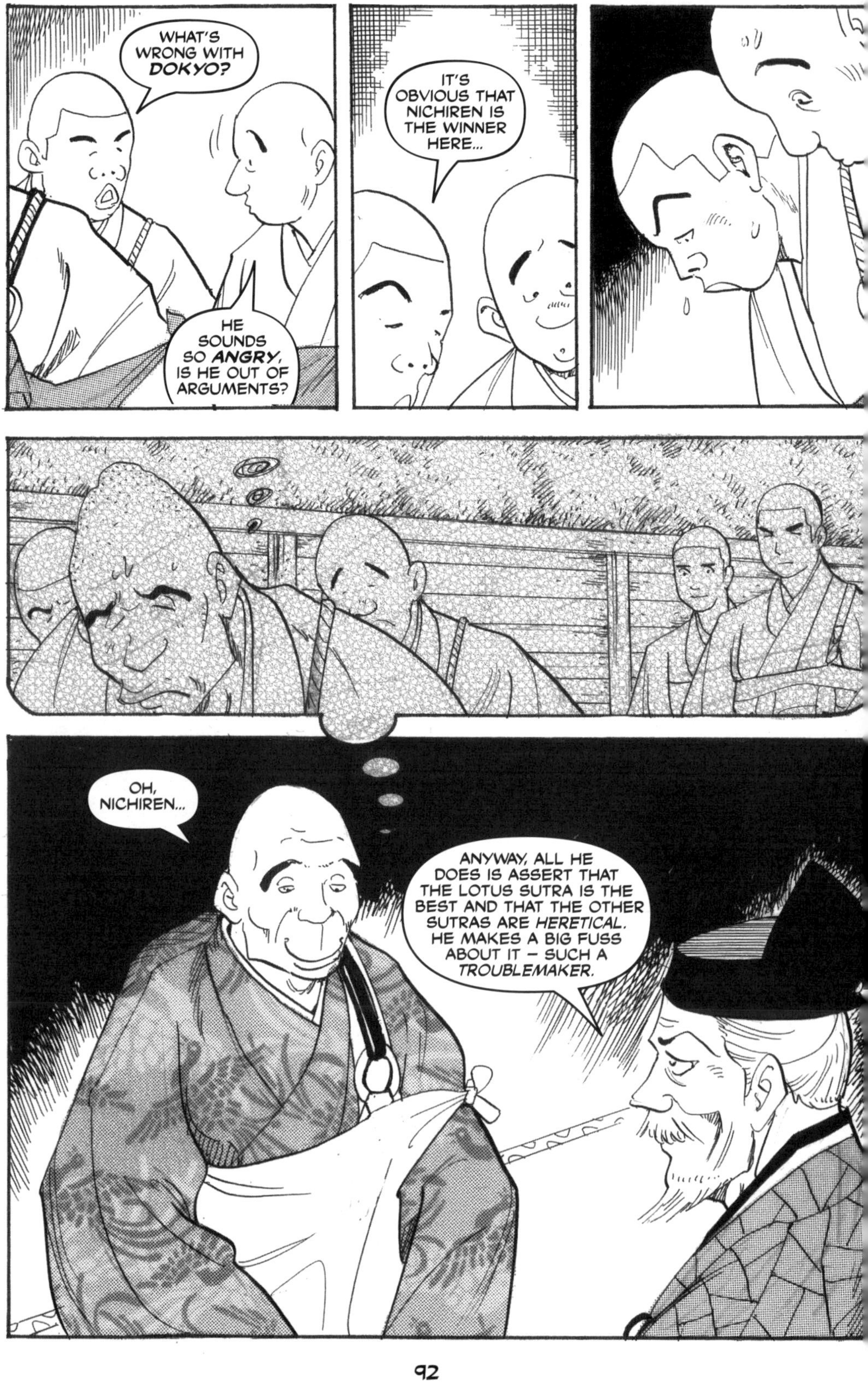
WHAT'S WRONG WITH DOKYO?
HE SOUNDS SO ANGRY, IS HE OUT OF ARGUMENTS?
IT'S OBVIOUS THAT NICHIREN IS THE WINNER HERE...
OH, NICHIREN...
ANYWAY, ALL HE DOES IS ASSERT THAT THE LOTUS SUTRA IS THE BEST AND THAT THE OTHER SUTRAS ARE HERETICAL. HE MAKES A BIG FUSS ABOUT IT – SUCH A TROUBLEMAKER.

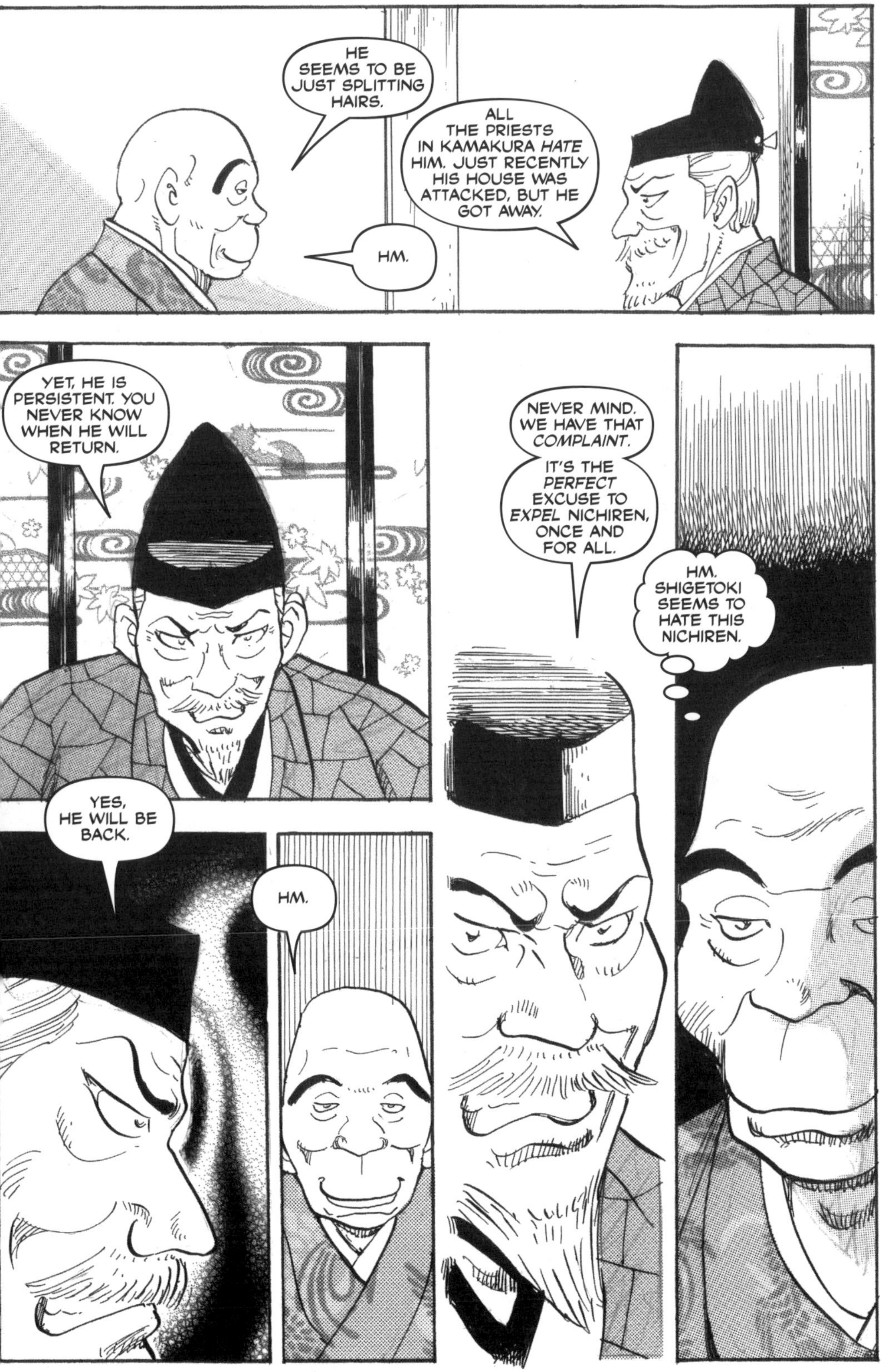
HE SEEMS TO BE JUST SPLITTING HAIRS.
ALL THE PRIESTS IN KAMAKURA *HATE* HIM. JUST RECENTLY HIS HOUSE WAS ATTACKED, BUT HE GOT AWAY.
HM.
YET, HE IS PERSISTENT. YOU NEVER KNOW WHEN HE WILL RETURN.
NEVER MIND. WE HAVE THAT *COMPLAINT*.
IT'S THE *PERFECT* EXCUSE TO *EXPEL* NICHIREN, ONCE AND FOR ALL.
HM. SHIGETOKI SEEMS TO HATE THIS NICHIREN.
YES, HE WILL BE BACK.
HM.

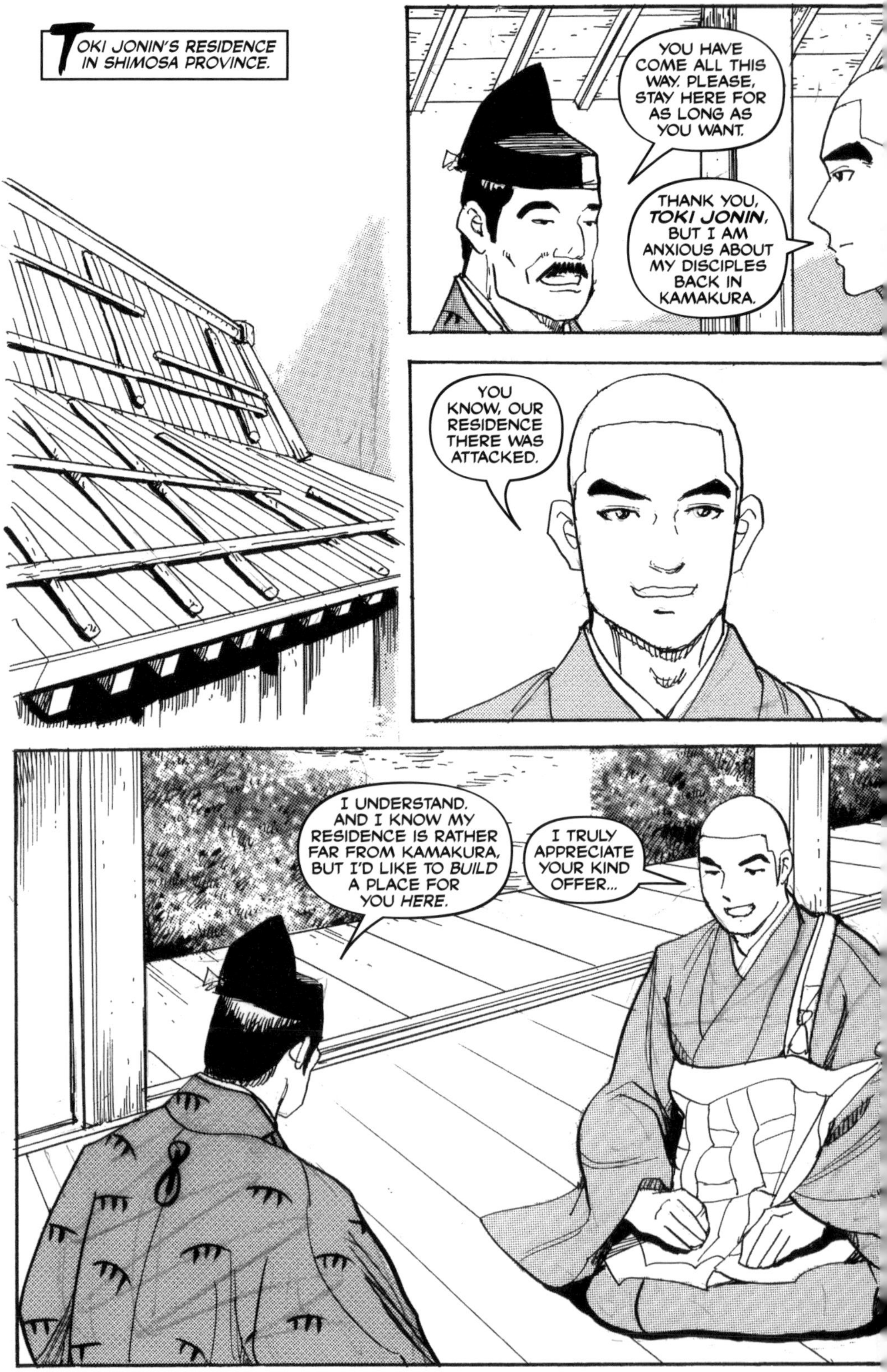
TOKI JONIN'S RESIDENCE IN SHIMOSA PROVINCE.
YOU HAVE COME ALL THIS WAY. PLEASE, STAY HERE FOR AS LONG AS YOU WANT.
THANK YOU, TOKI JONIN, BUT I AM ANXIOUS ABOUT MY DISCIPLES BACK IN KAMAKURA.
YOU KNOW, OUR RESIDENCE THERE WAS ATTACKED.
I UNDERSTAND. AND I KNOW MY RESIDENCE IS RATHER FAR FROM KAMAKURA, BUT I'D LIKE TO BUILD A PLACE FOR YOU HERE.
I TRULY APPRECIATE YOUR KIND OFFER...

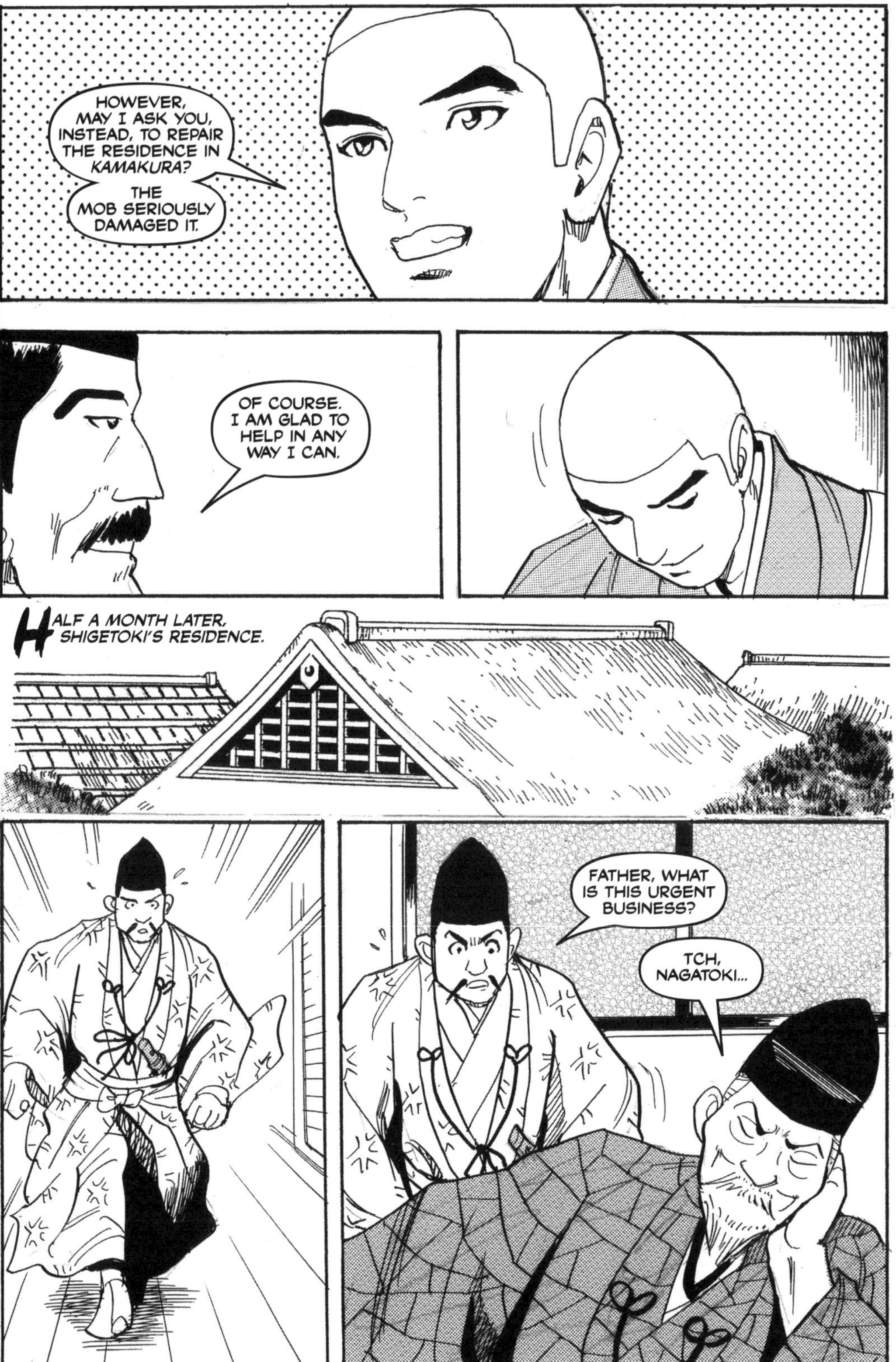
HOWEVER, MAY I ASK YOU, INSTEAD, TO REPAIR THE RESIDENCE IN *KAMAKURA?*
THE MOB SERIOUSLY DAMAGED IT.
OF COURSE. I AM GLAD TO HELP IN ANY WAY I CAN.
HALF A MONTH LATER, SHIGETOKI'S RESIDENCE.
FATHER, WHAT IS THIS URGENT BUSINESS?
TCH, NAGATOKI...

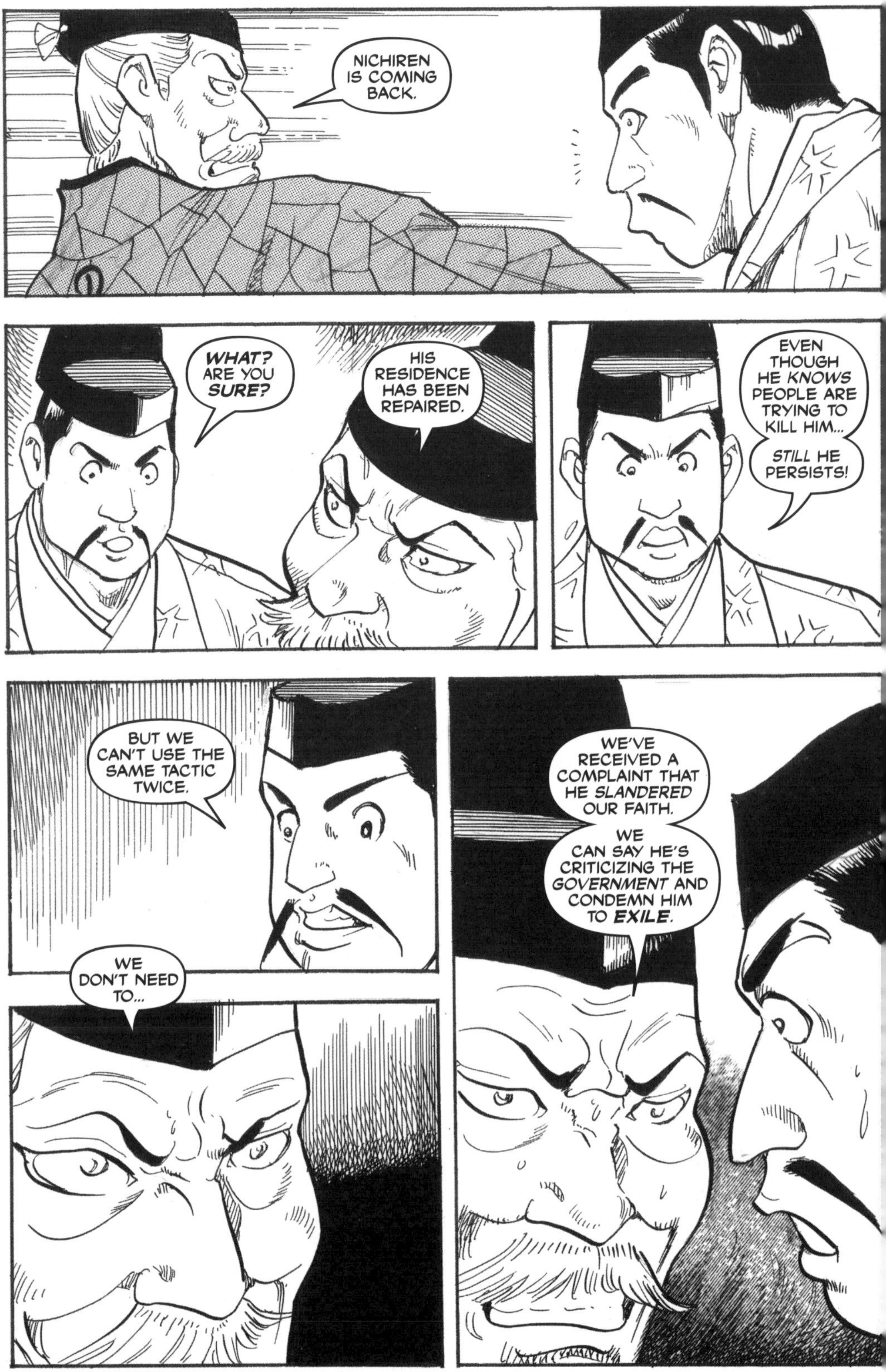
NICHIREN IS COMING BACK.
WHAT? ARE YOU *SURE?*
HIS RESIDENCE HAS BEEN REPAIRED.
EVEN THOUGH HE *KNOWS* PEOPLE ARE TRYING TO KILL HIM...
STILL HE PERSISTS!
BUT WE CAN'T USE THE SAME TACTIC TWICE.
WE DON'T NEED TO...
WE'VE RECEIVED A COMPLAINT THAT HE *SLANDERED* OUR FAITH.
WE CAN SAY HE'S CRITICIZING THE *GOVERNMENT* AND CONDEMN HIM TO ***EXILE***.

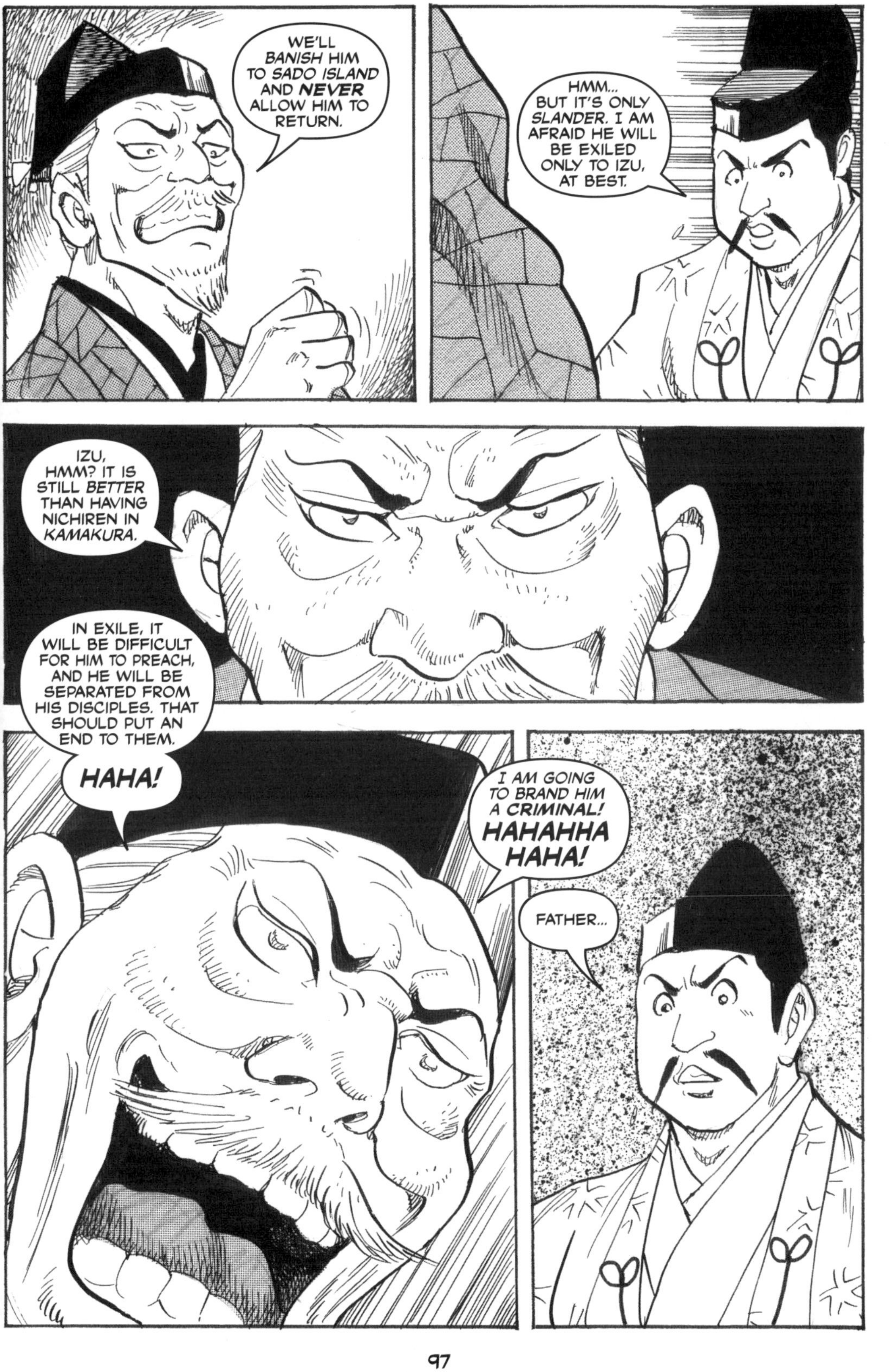
WE'LL BANISH HIM TO SADO ISLAND AND NEVER ALLOW HIM TO RETURN.
HMM... BUT IT'S ONLY SLANDER. I AM AFRAID HE WILL BE EXILED ONLY TO IZU, AT BEST.
IZU, HMM? IT IS STILL BETTER THAN HAVING NICHIREN IN KAMAKURA.
IN EXILE, IT WILL BE DIFFICULT FOR HIM TO PREACH, AND HE WILL BE SEPARATED FROM HIS DISCIPLES. THAT SHOULD PUT AN END TO THEM.
HAHA!
I AM GOING TO BRAND HIM A CRIMINAL! HAHAHHA HAHA!
FATHER...

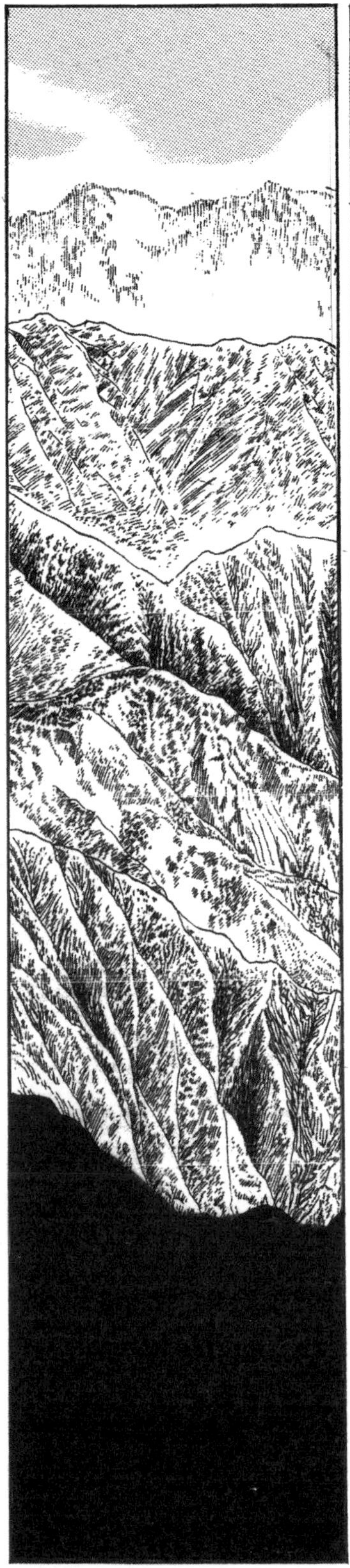

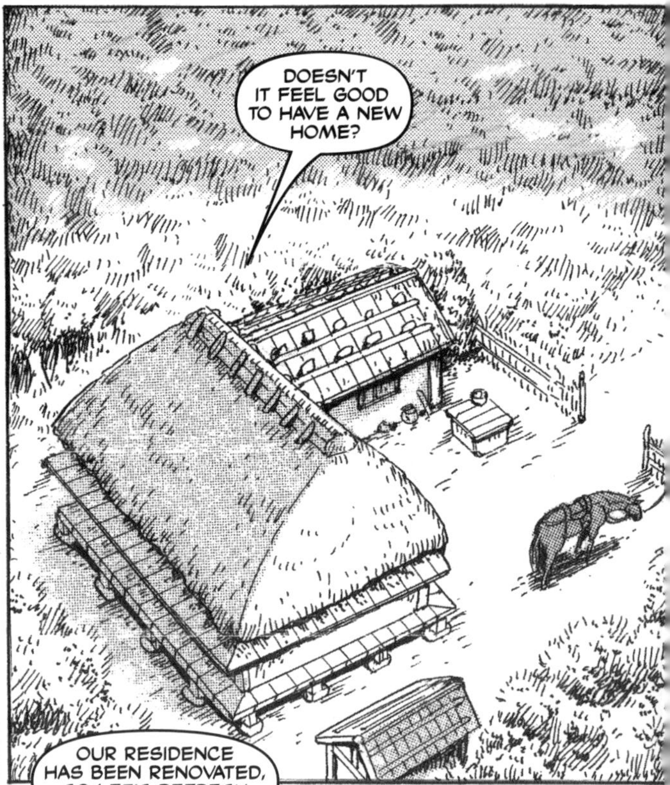
DOESN'T IT FEEL GOOD TO HAVE A NEW HOME?

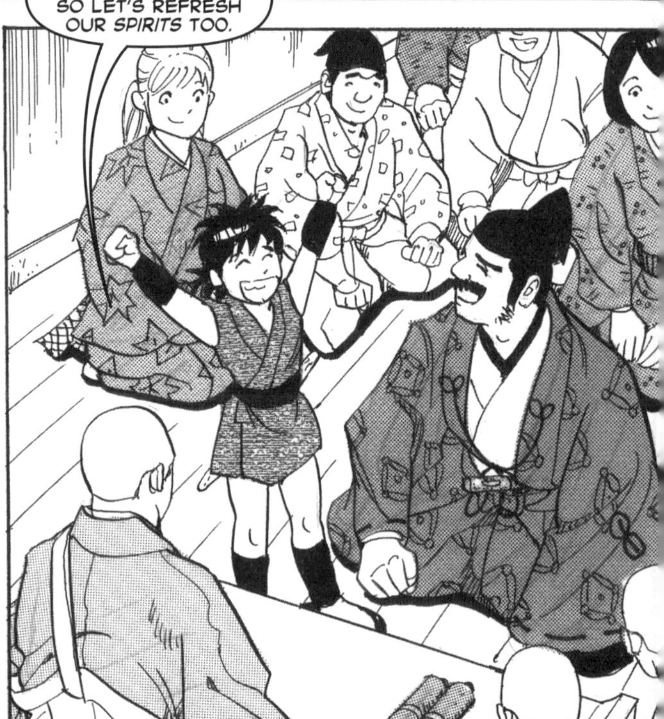
OUR RESIDENCE HAS BEEN RENOVATED, SO LET'S REFRESH OUR *SPIRITS* TOO.

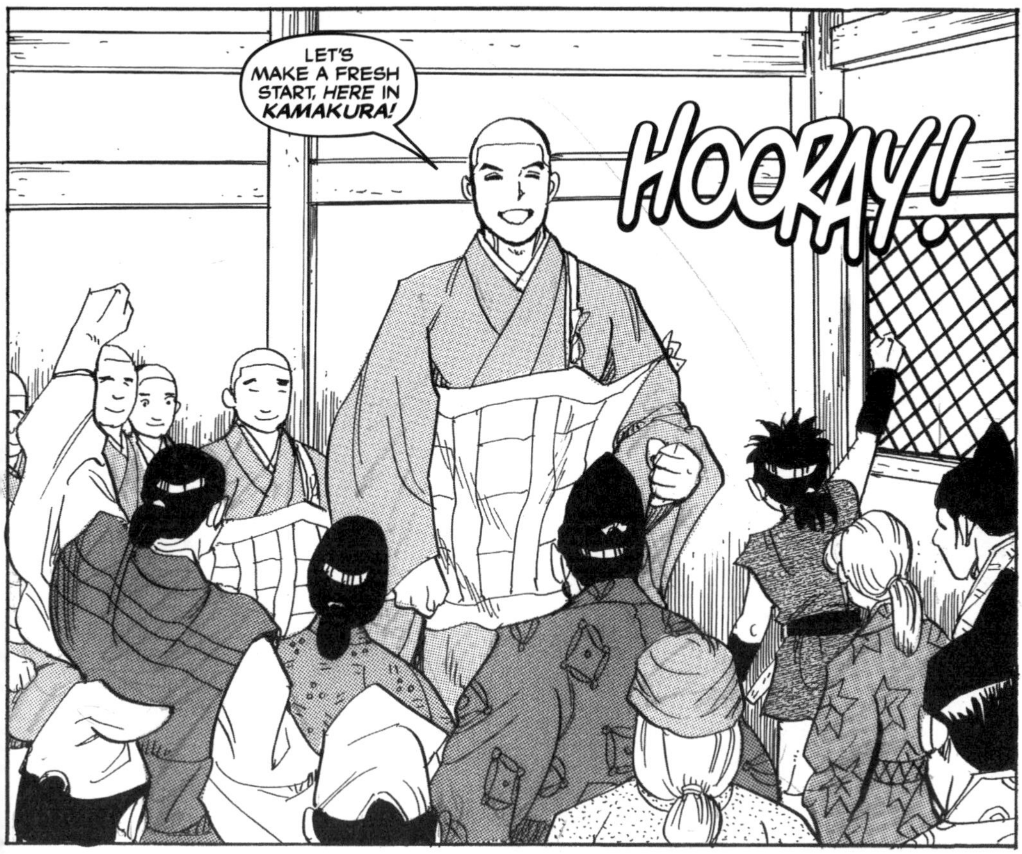
LET'S MAKE A FRESH START, HERE IN KAMAKURA!
HOORAY!

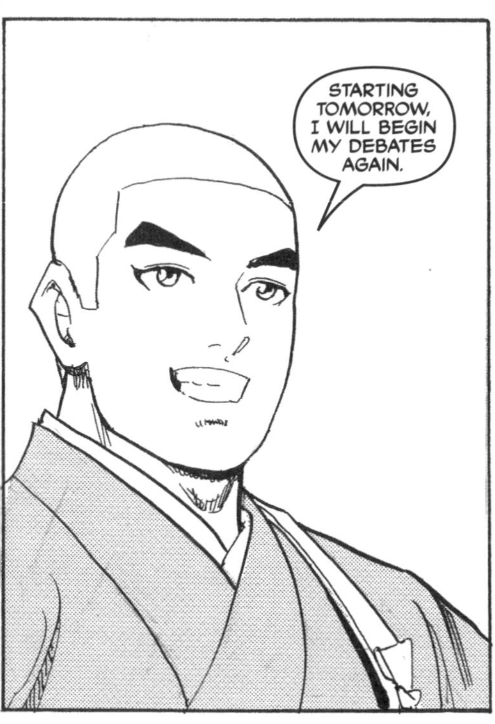
STARTING TOMORROW, I WILL BEGIN MY DEBATES AGAIN.

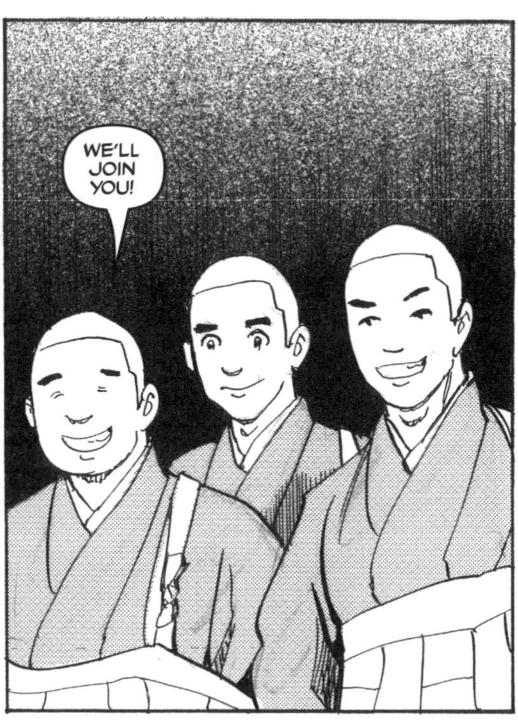
WE'LL JOIN YOU!

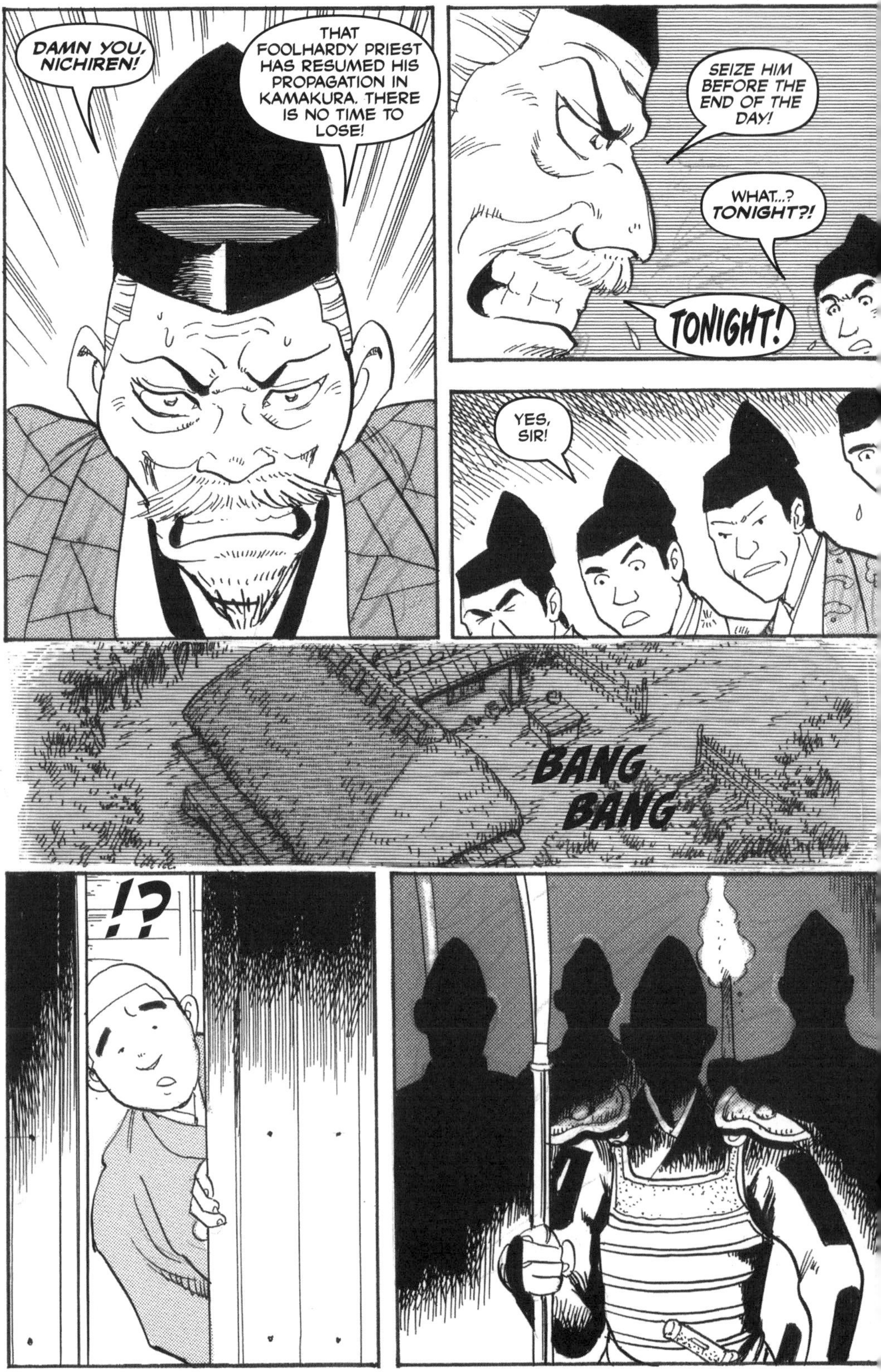
DAMN YOU, NICHIREN!
THAT FOOLHARDY PRIEST HAS RESUMED HIS PROPAGATION IN KAMAKURA. THERE IS NO TIME TO LOSE!
SEIZE HIM BEFORE THE END OF THE DAY!
WHAT...? TONIGHT?!
TONIGHT!
YES, SIR!
BANG BANG
!?

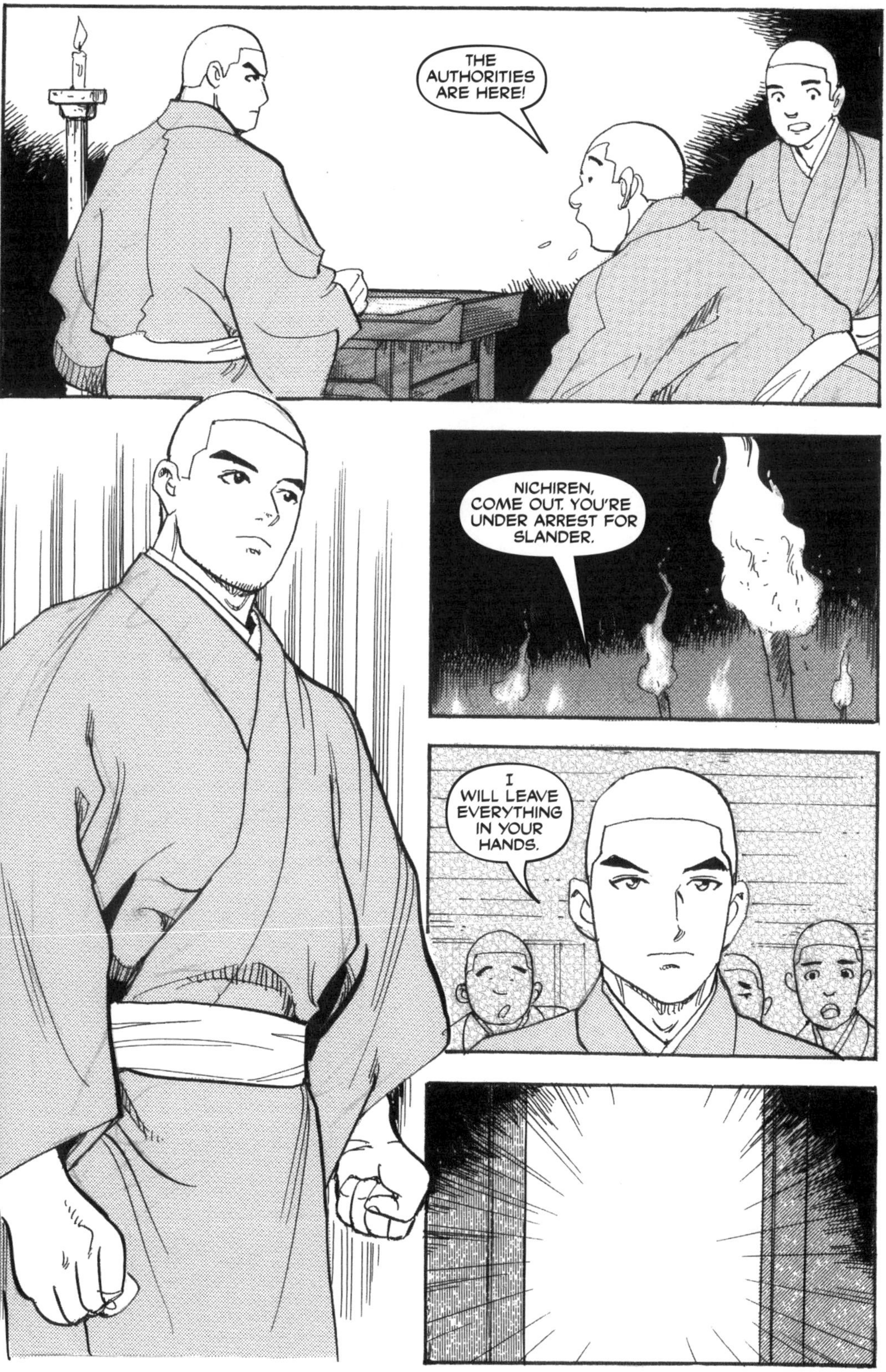
THE AUTHORITIES ARE HERE!
NICHIREN, COME OUT. YOU'RE UNDER ARREST FOR SLANDER.
I WILL LEAVE EVERYTHING IN YOUR HANDS.

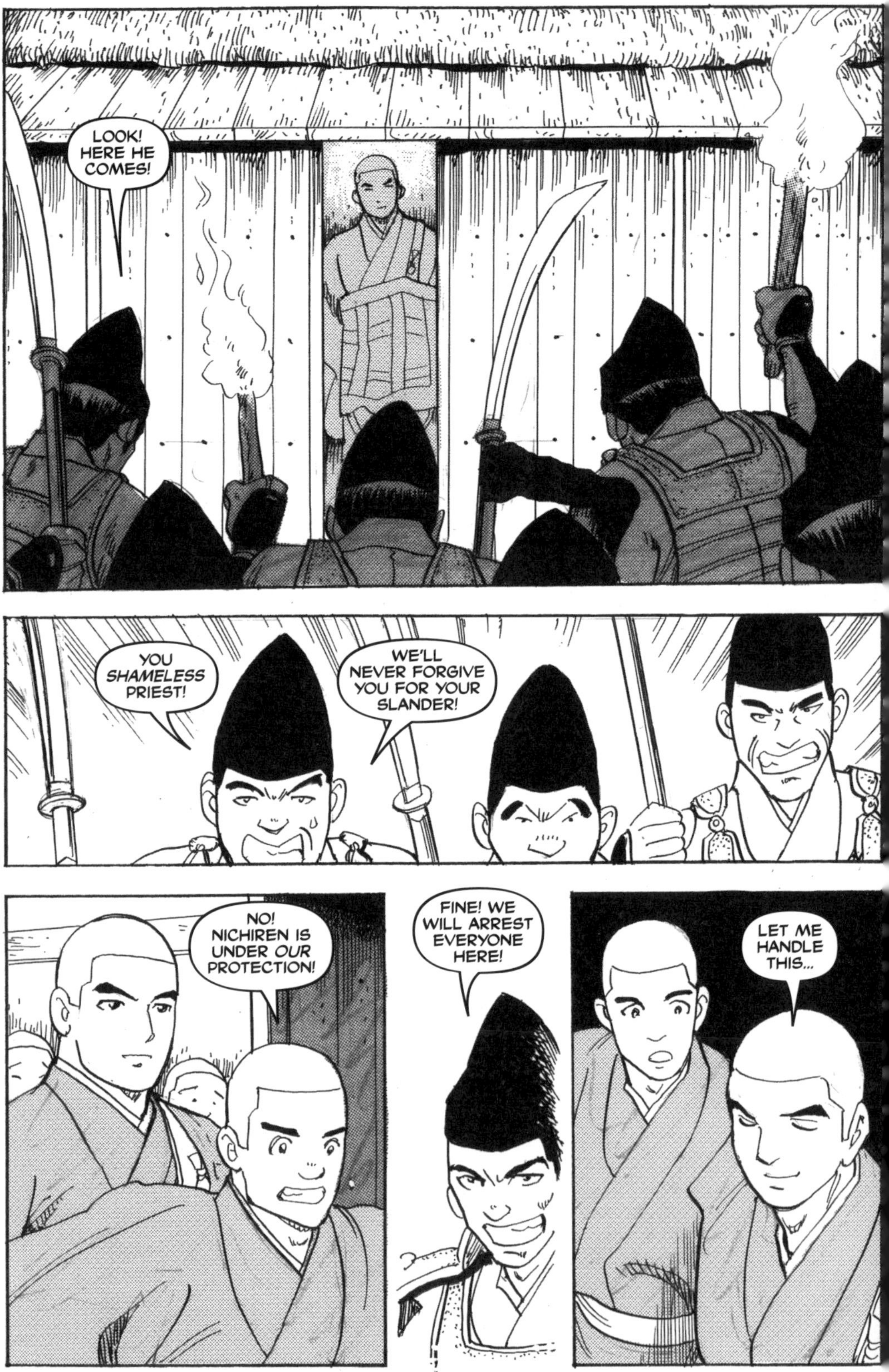
LOOK! HERE HE COMES!
YOU *SHAMELESS* PRIEST!
WE'LL NEVER FORGIVE YOU FOR YOUR SLANDER!
NO! NICHIREN IS UNDER *OUR* PROTECTION!
FINE! WE WILL ARREST EVERYONE HERE!
LET ME HANDLE THIS...

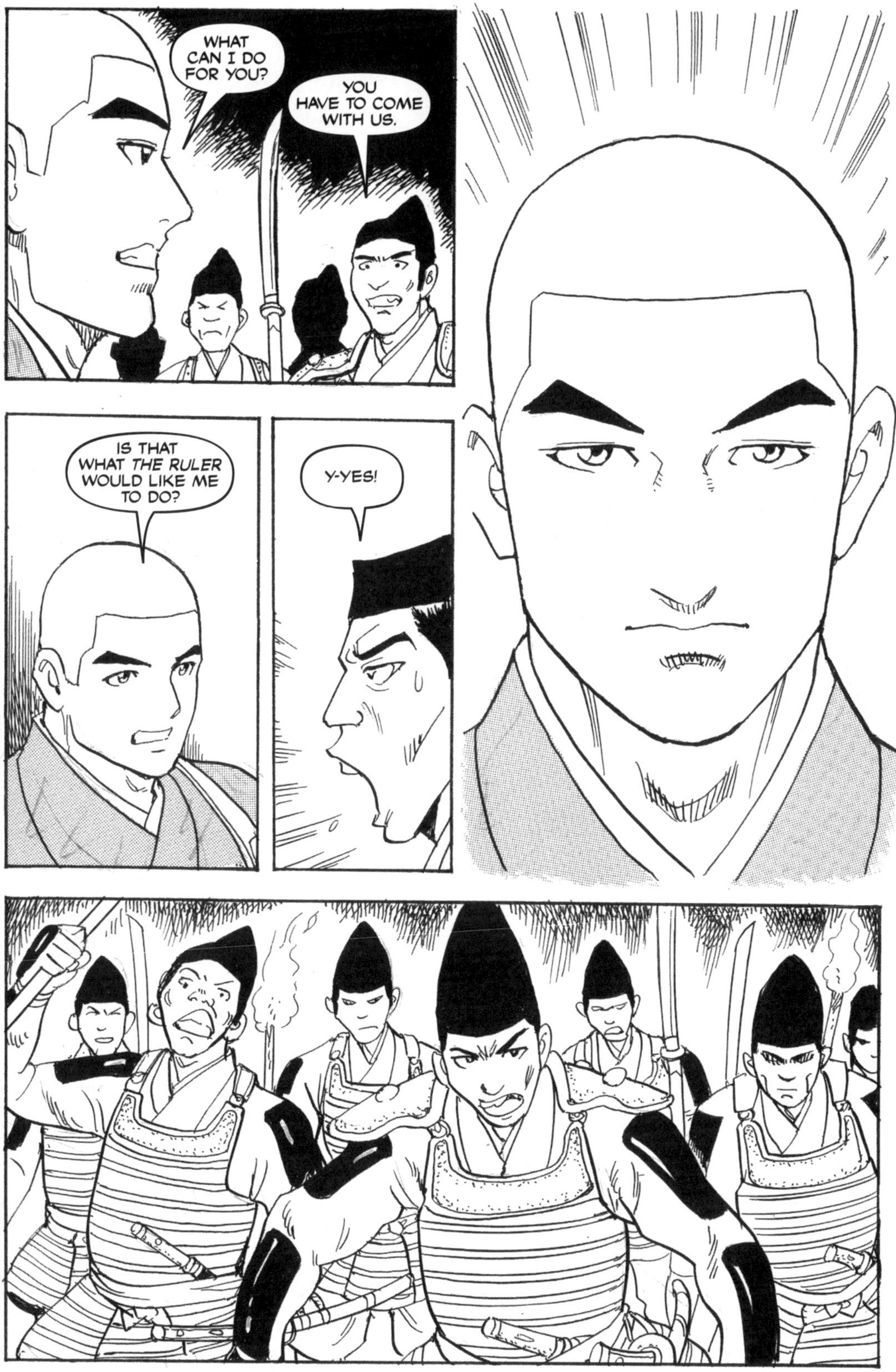
WHAT CAN I DO FOR YOU?
YOU HAVE TO COME WITH US.
IS THAT WHAT *THE RULER* WOULD LIKE ME TO DO?
Y-YES!

WHAT ARE YOU WAITING FOR? TAKE HIM!
MOVE! HURRY IT UP!
I'LL GO PEACEFULLY.
DON'T WORRY, MY FRIENDS. WAIT FOR ME.
NO!
TRUST ME.
THIS IS FOR THE BEST.

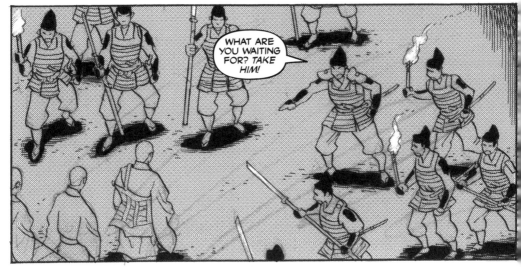

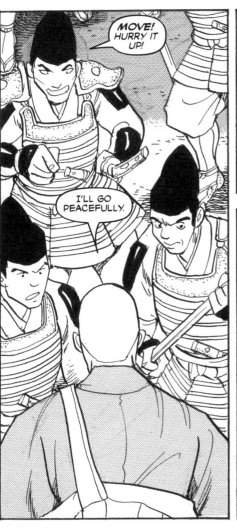

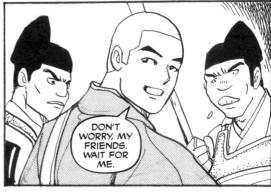

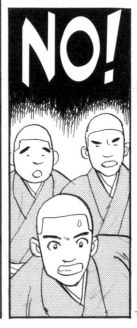

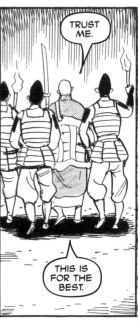

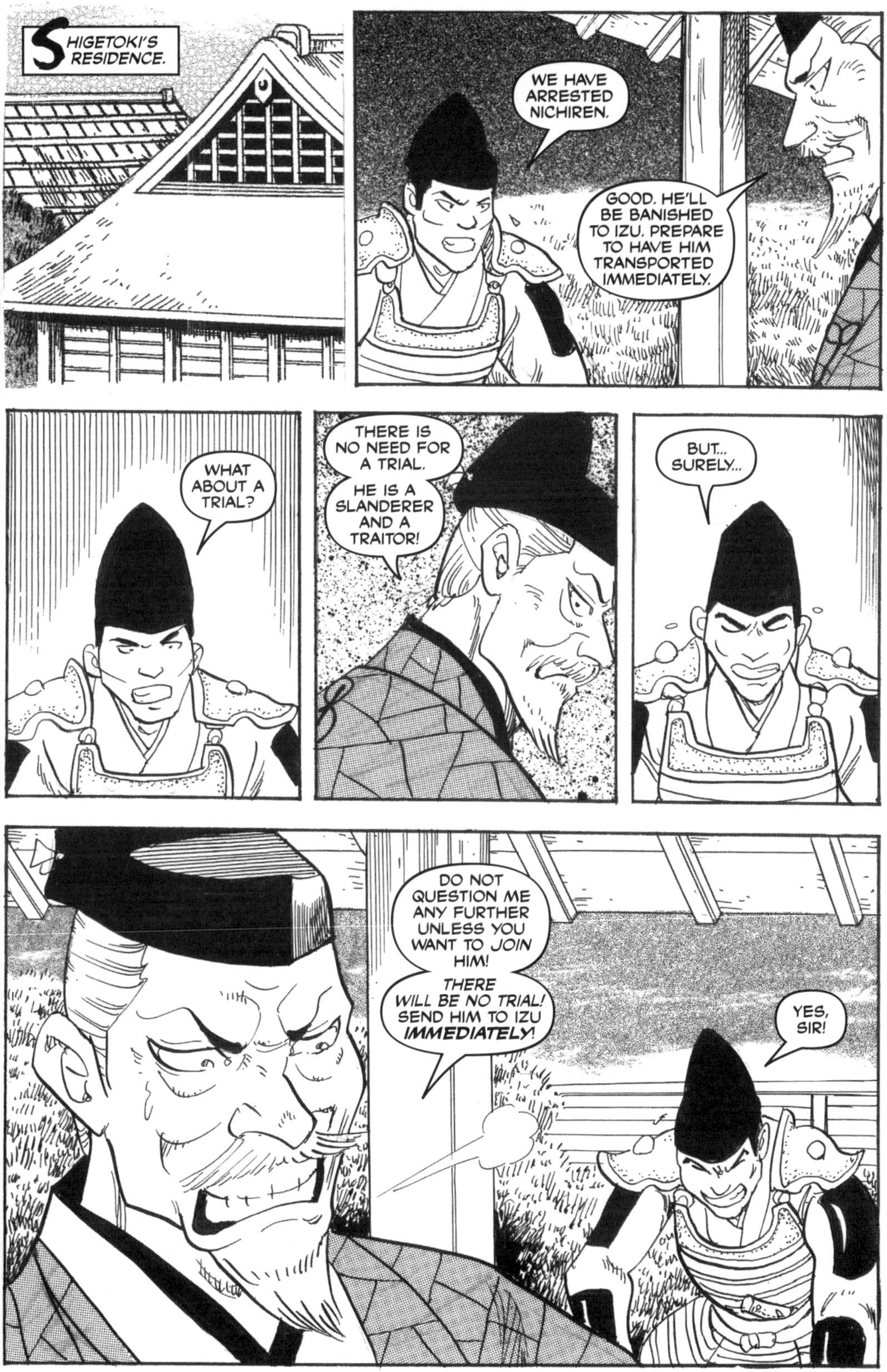
SHIGETOKI'S RESIDENCE.
WE HAVE ARRESTED NICHIREN.
GOOD. HE'LL BE BANISHED TO IZU. PREPARE TO HAVE HIM TRANSPORTED IMMEDIATELY.
WHAT ABOUT A TRIAL?
THERE IS NO NEED FOR A TRIAL.
HE IS A SLANDERER AND A TRAITOR!
BUT... SURELY...
DO NOT QUESTION ME ANY FURTHER UNLESS YOU WANT TO *JOIN* HIM!
THERE WILL BE NO TRIAL! SEND HIM TO IZU ***IMMEDIATELY***!
YES, SIR!

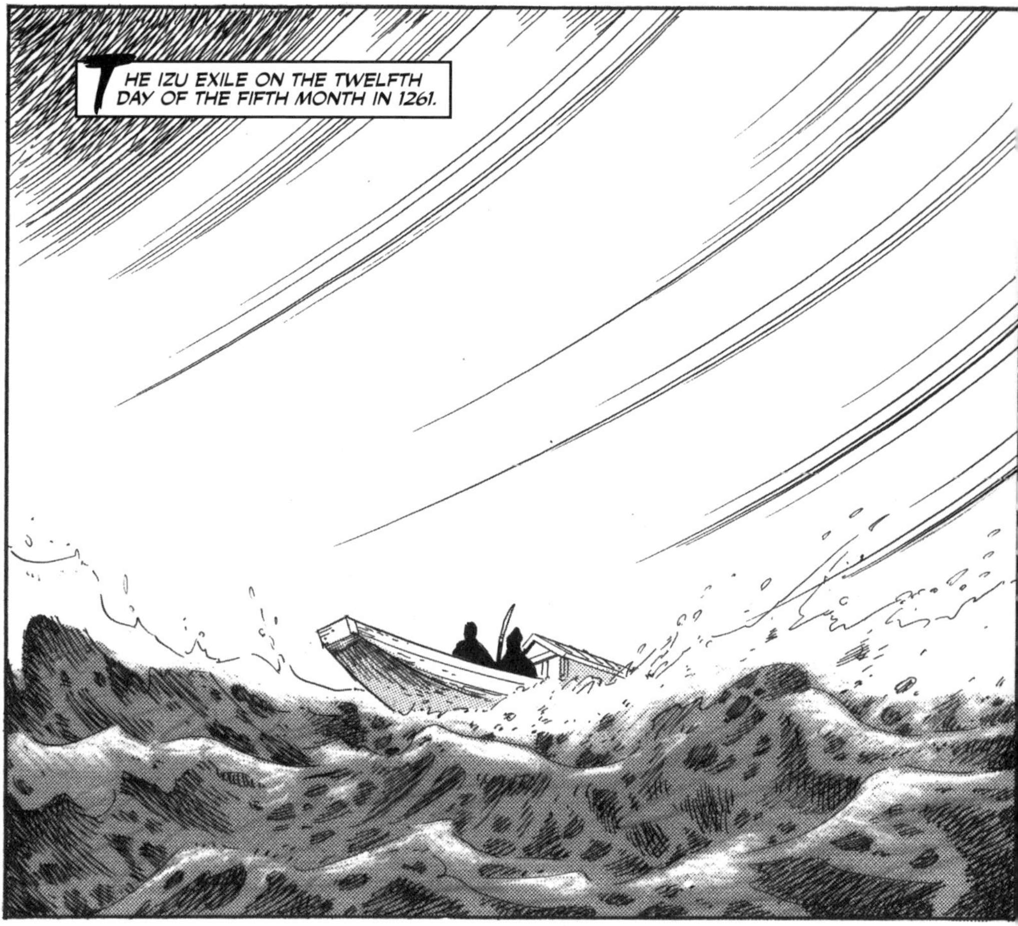
THE IZU EXILE ON THE TWELFTH DAY OF THE FIFTH MONTH IN 1261.

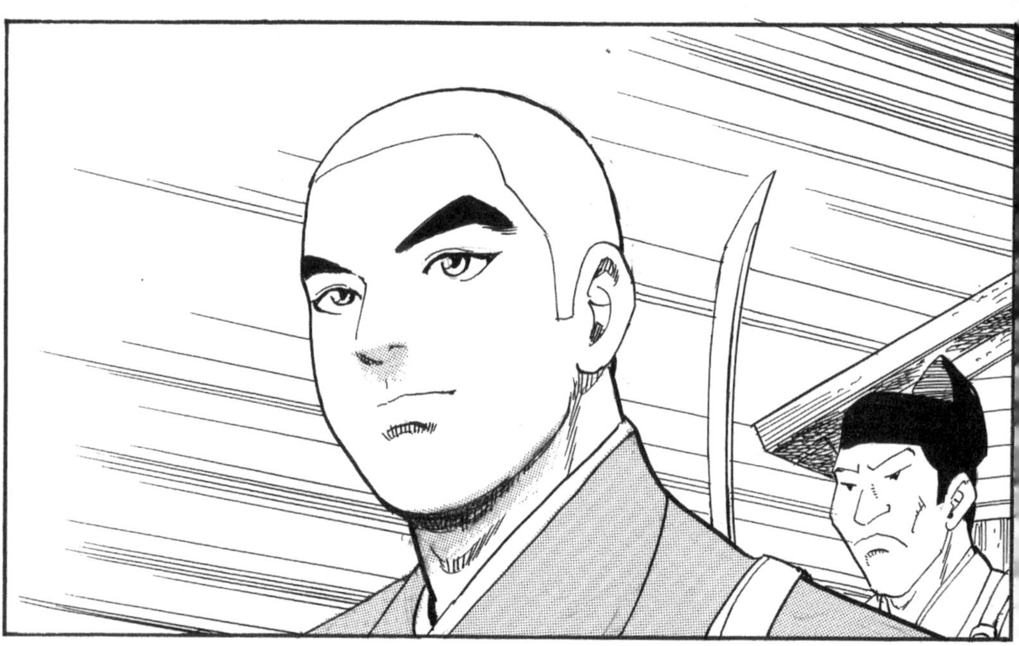

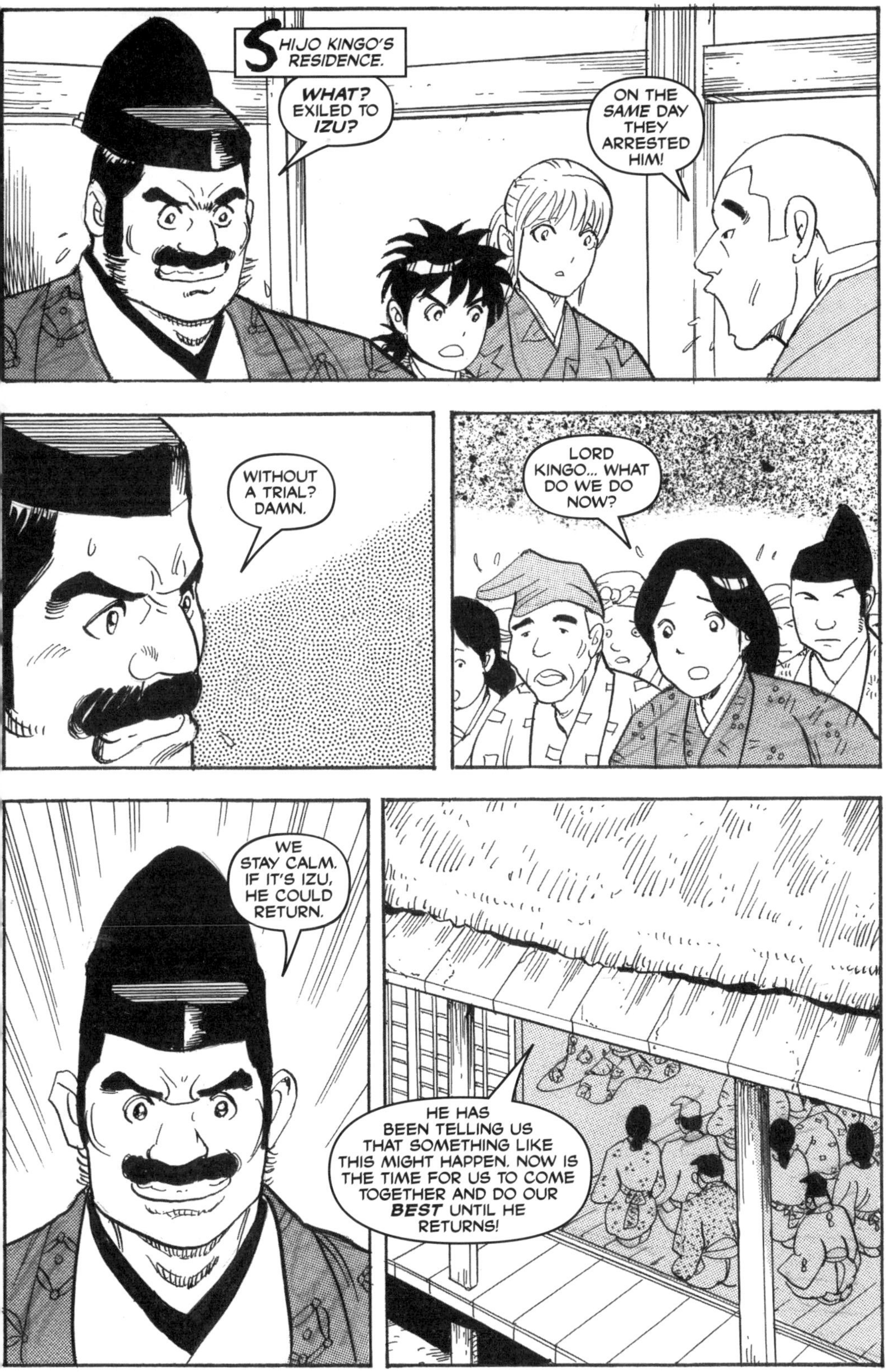
SHIJO KINGO'S RESIDENCE.
WHAT? EXILED TO IZU?
ON THE SAME DAY THEY ARRESTED HIM!
WITHOUT A TRIAL? DAMN.
LORD KINGO... WHAT DO WE DO NOW?
WE STAY CALM. IF IT'S IZU, HE COULD RETURN.
HE HAS BEEN TELLING US THAT SOMETHING LIKE THIS MIGHT HAPPEN. NOW IS THE TIME FOR US TO COME TOGETHER AND DO OUR BEST UNTIL HE RETURNS!

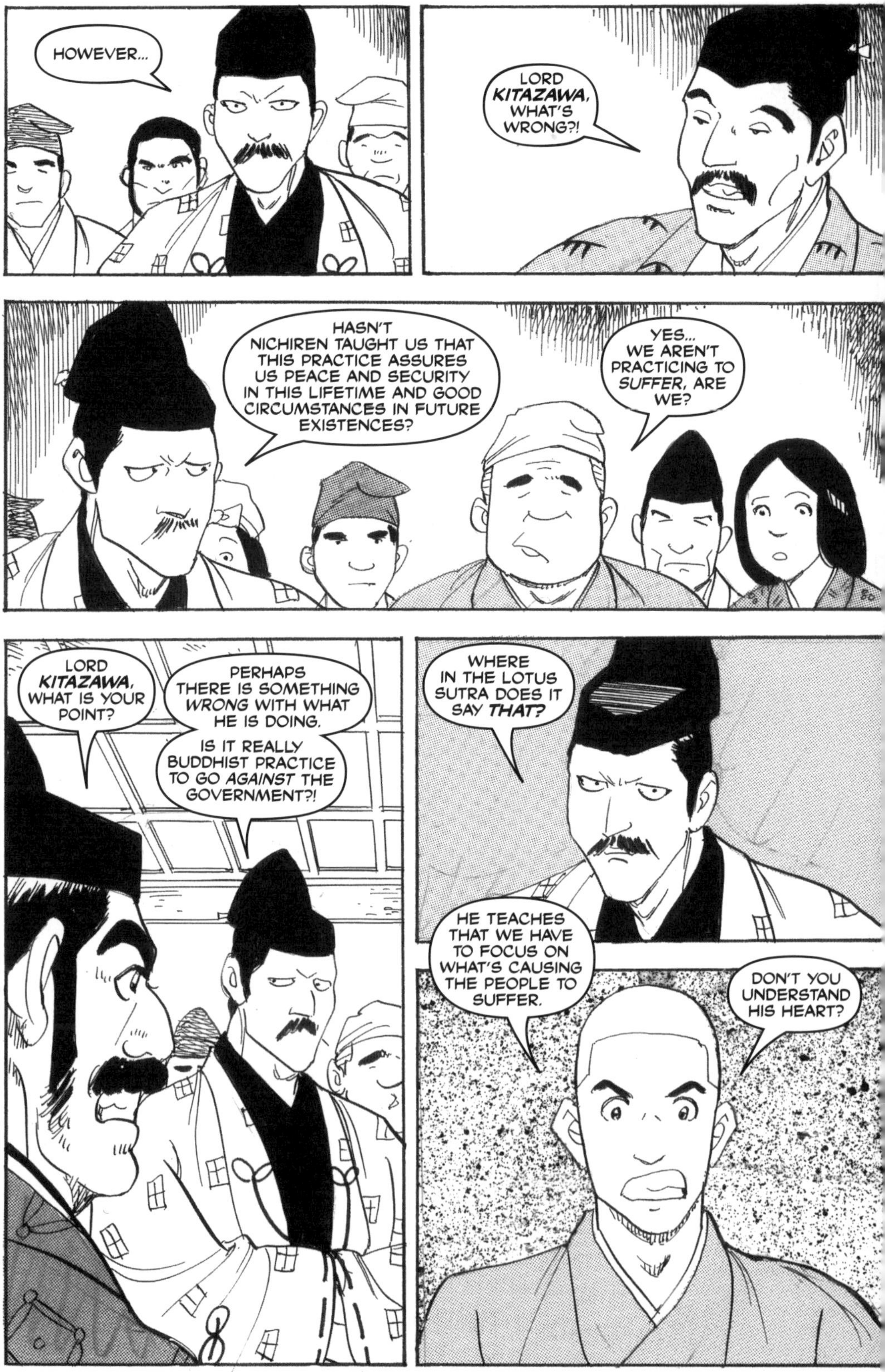
HOWEVER...
LORD *KITAZAWA*, WHAT'S WRONG?!
HASN'T NICHIREN TAUGHT US THAT THIS PRACTICE ASSURES US PEACE AND SECURITY IN THIS LIFETIME AND GOOD CIRCUMSTANCES IN FUTURE EXISTENCES?
YES... WE AREN'T PRACTICING TO *SUFFER*, ARE WE?
LORD *KITAZAWA*, WHAT IS YOUR POINT?
PERHAPS THERE IS SOMETHING *WRONG* WITH WHAT HE IS DOING.
IS IT REALLY BUDDHIST PRACTICE TO GO *AGAINST* THE GOVERNMENT?!
WHERE IN THE LOTUS SUTRA DOES IT SAY ***THAT?***
HE TEACHES THAT WE HAVE TO FOCUS ON WHAT'S CAUSING THE PEOPLE TO SUFFER.
DON'T YOU UNDERSTAND HIS HEART?

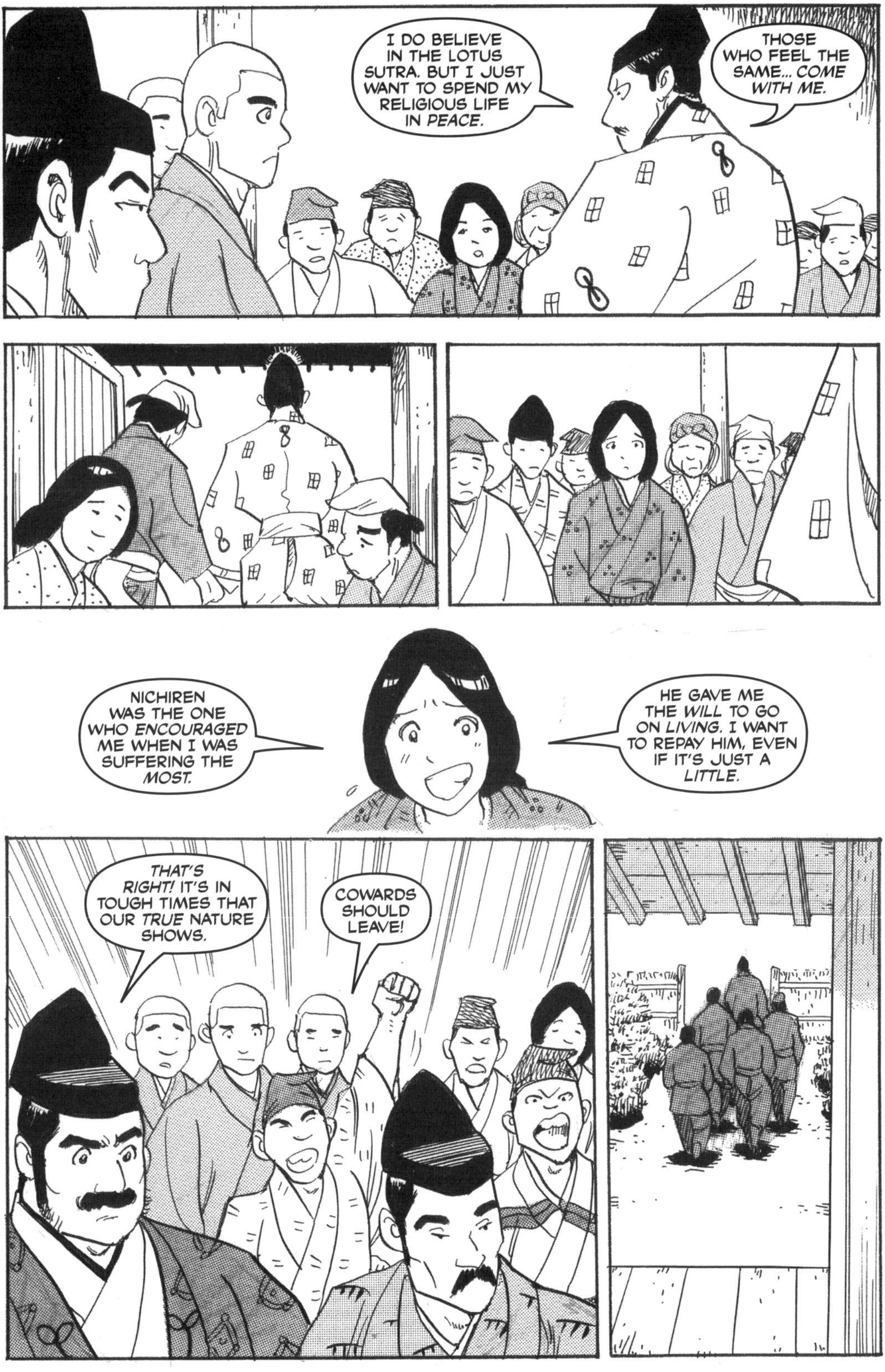
I DO BELIEVE IN THE LOTUS SUTRA. BUT I JUST WANT TO SPEND MY RELIGIOUS LIFE IN *PEACE*.
THOSE WHO FEEL THE SAME... *COME WITH ME*.
NICHIREN WAS THE ONE WHO *ENCOURAGED* ME WHEN I WAS SUFFERING THE *MOST*.
HE GAVE ME THE *WILL* TO GO ON *LIVING*. I WANT TO REPAY HIM, EVEN IF IT'S JUST A *LITTLE*.
THAT'S RIGHT! IT'S IN TOUGH TIMES THAT OUR *TRUE* NATURE SHOWS.
COWARDS SHOULD LEAVE!

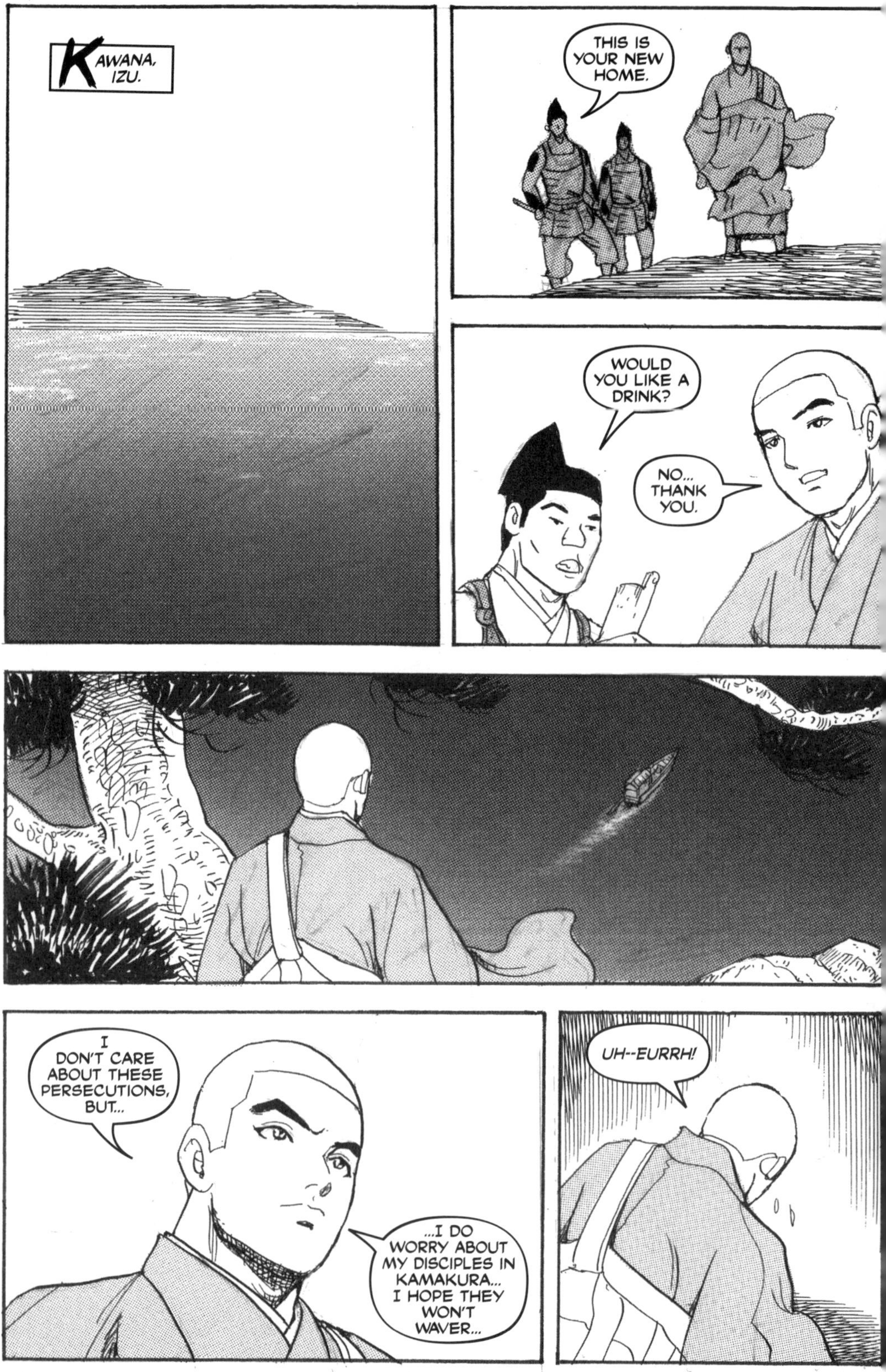
KAWANA, IZU.
THIS IS YOUR NEW HOME.
WOULD YOU LIKE A DRINK?
NO... THANK YOU.
I DON'T CARE ABOUT THESE PERSECUTIONS, BUT...
...I DO WORRY ABOUT MY DISCIPLES IN KAMAKURA... I HOPE THEY WON'T WAVER...
UH--EURRH!

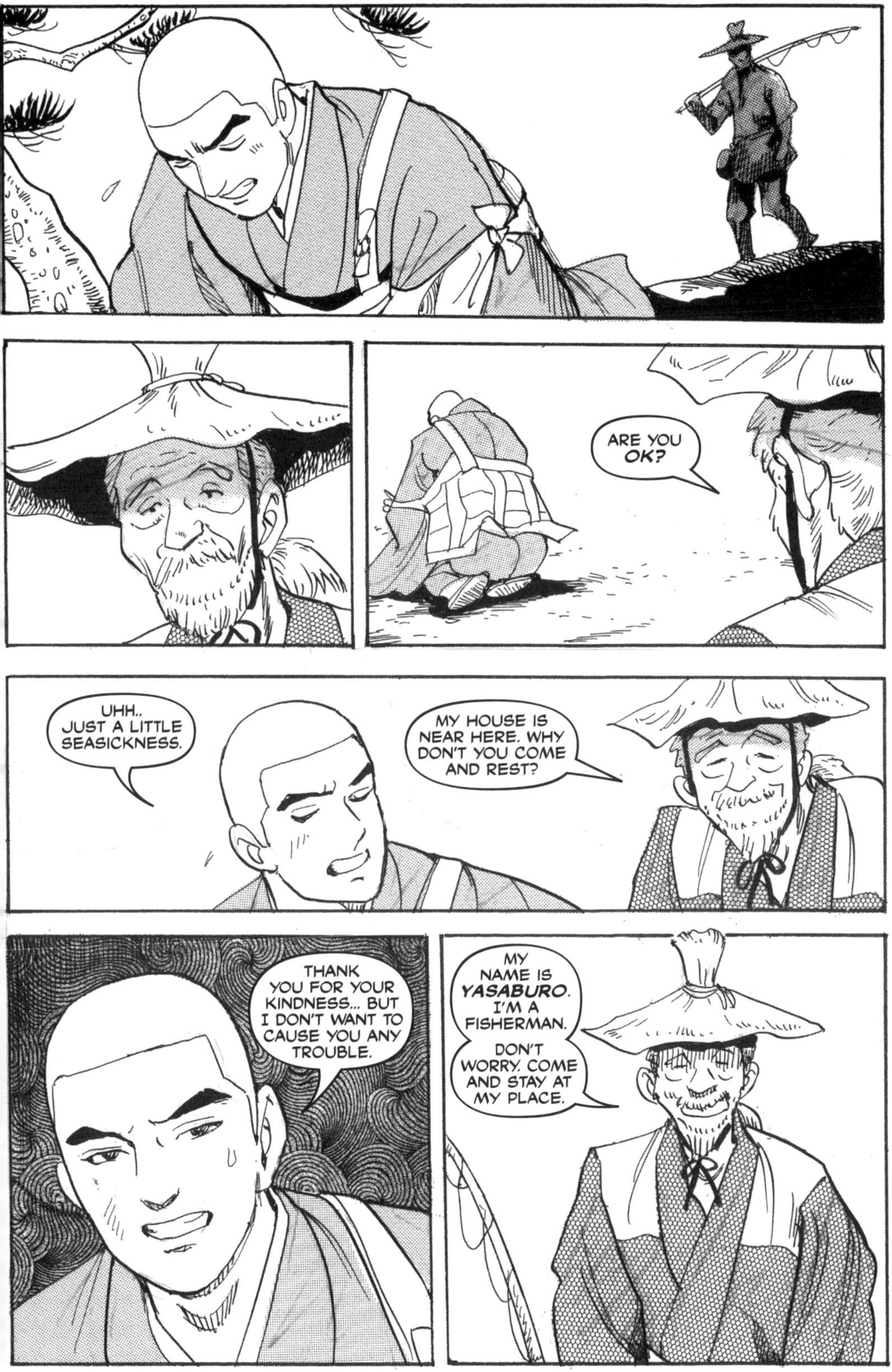
ARE YOU OK?
UHH.. JUST A LITTLE SEASICKNESS.
MY HOUSE IS NEAR HERE. WHY DON'T YOU COME AND REST?
THANK YOU FOR YOUR KINDNESS... BUT I DON'T WANT TO CAUSE YOU ANY TROUBLE.
MY NAME IS YASABURO. I'M A FISHERMAN.
DON'T WORRY. COME AND STAY AT MY PLACE.

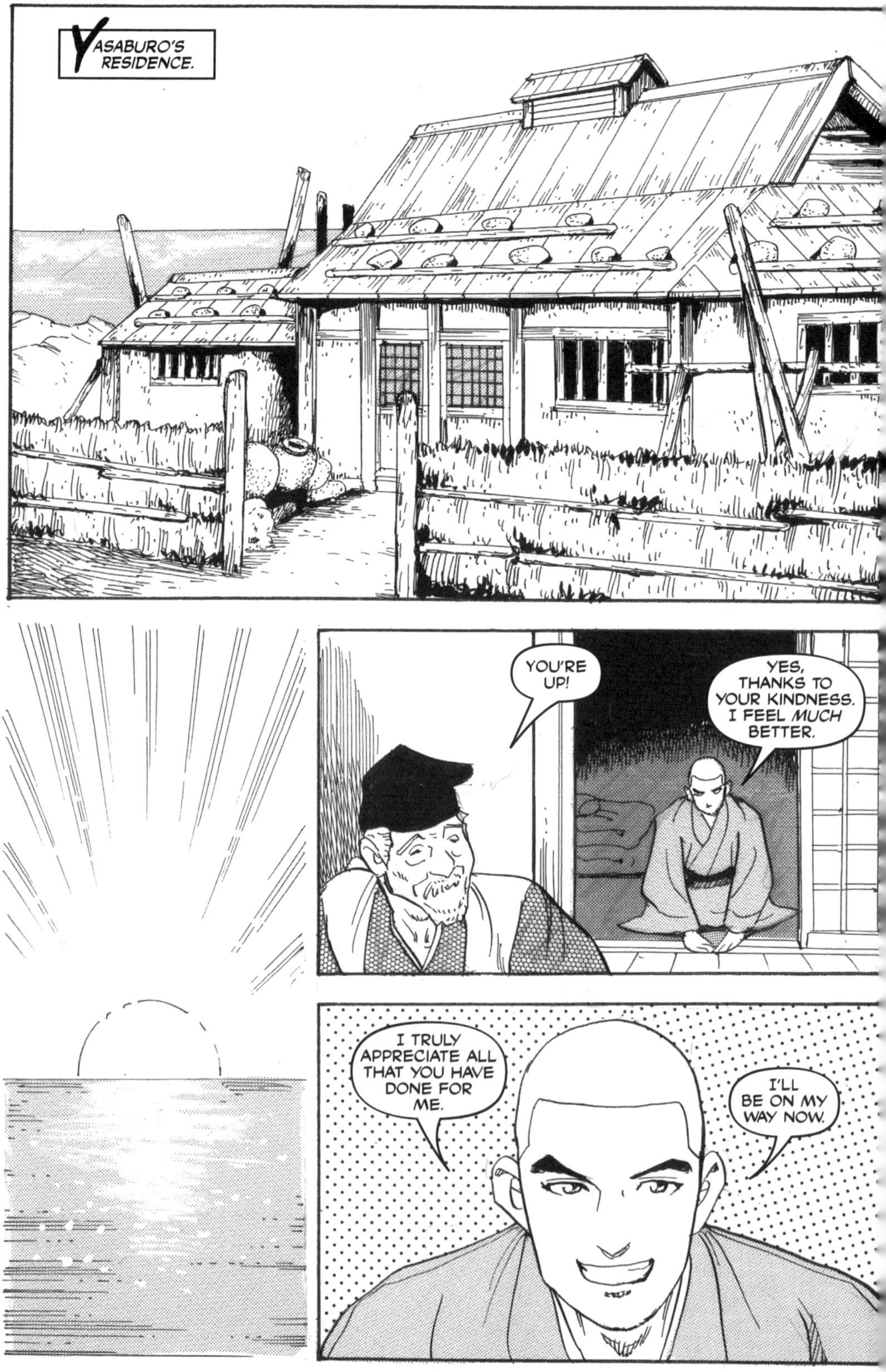
YASABURO'S RESIDENCE.
YOU'RE UP!
YES, THANKS TO YOUR KINDNESS. I FEEL *MUCH* BETTER.
I TRULY APPRECIATE ALL THAT YOU HAVE DONE FOR ME.
I'LL BE ON MY WAY NOW.

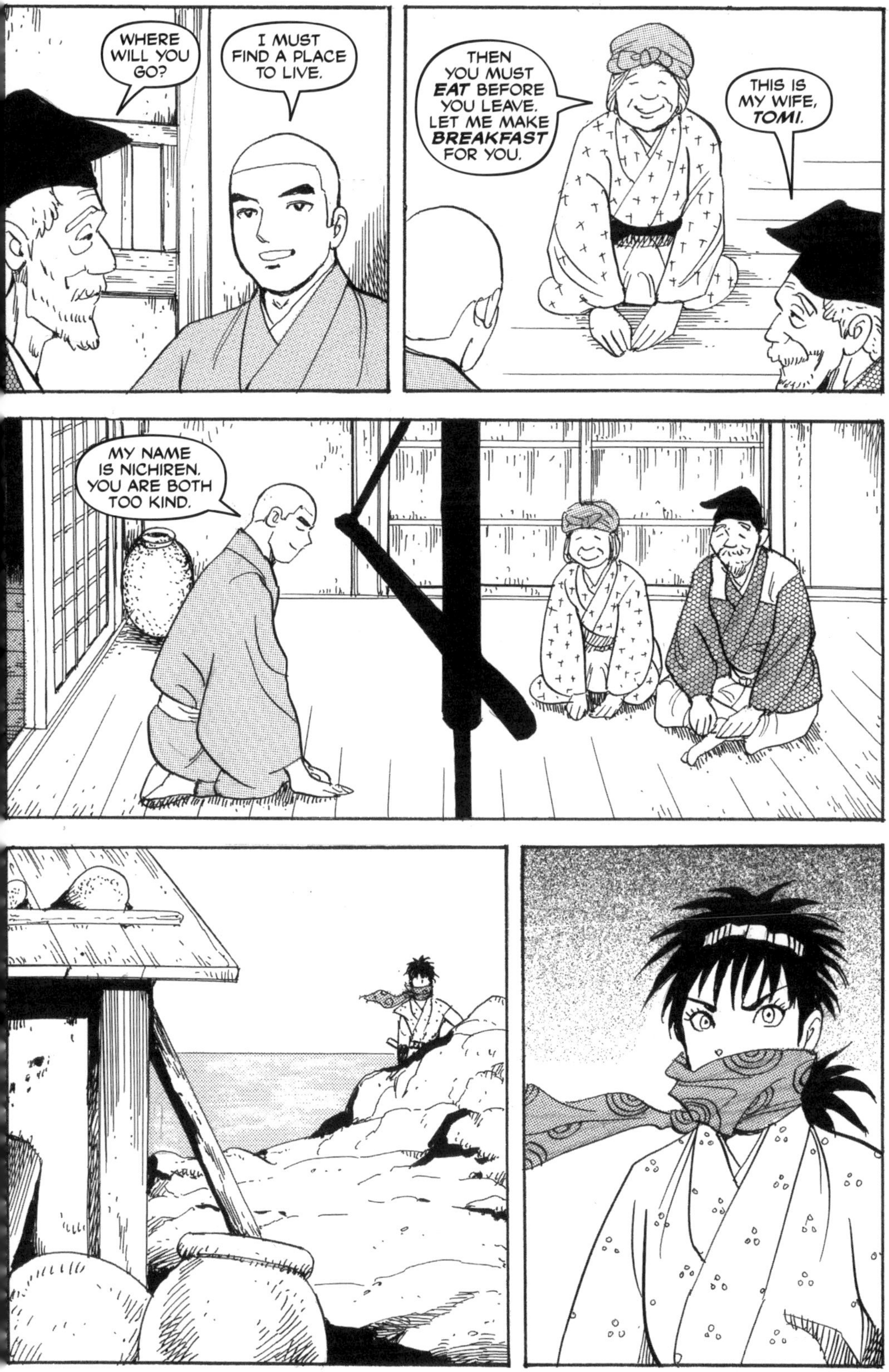
WHERE WILL YOU GO?
I MUST FIND A PLACE TO LIVE.
THEN YOU MUST **EAT** BEFORE YOU LEAVE. LET ME MAKE **BREAKFAST** FOR YOU.
THIS IS MY WIFE, **TOMI**.
MY NAME IS NICHIREN. YOU ARE BOTH TOO KIND.

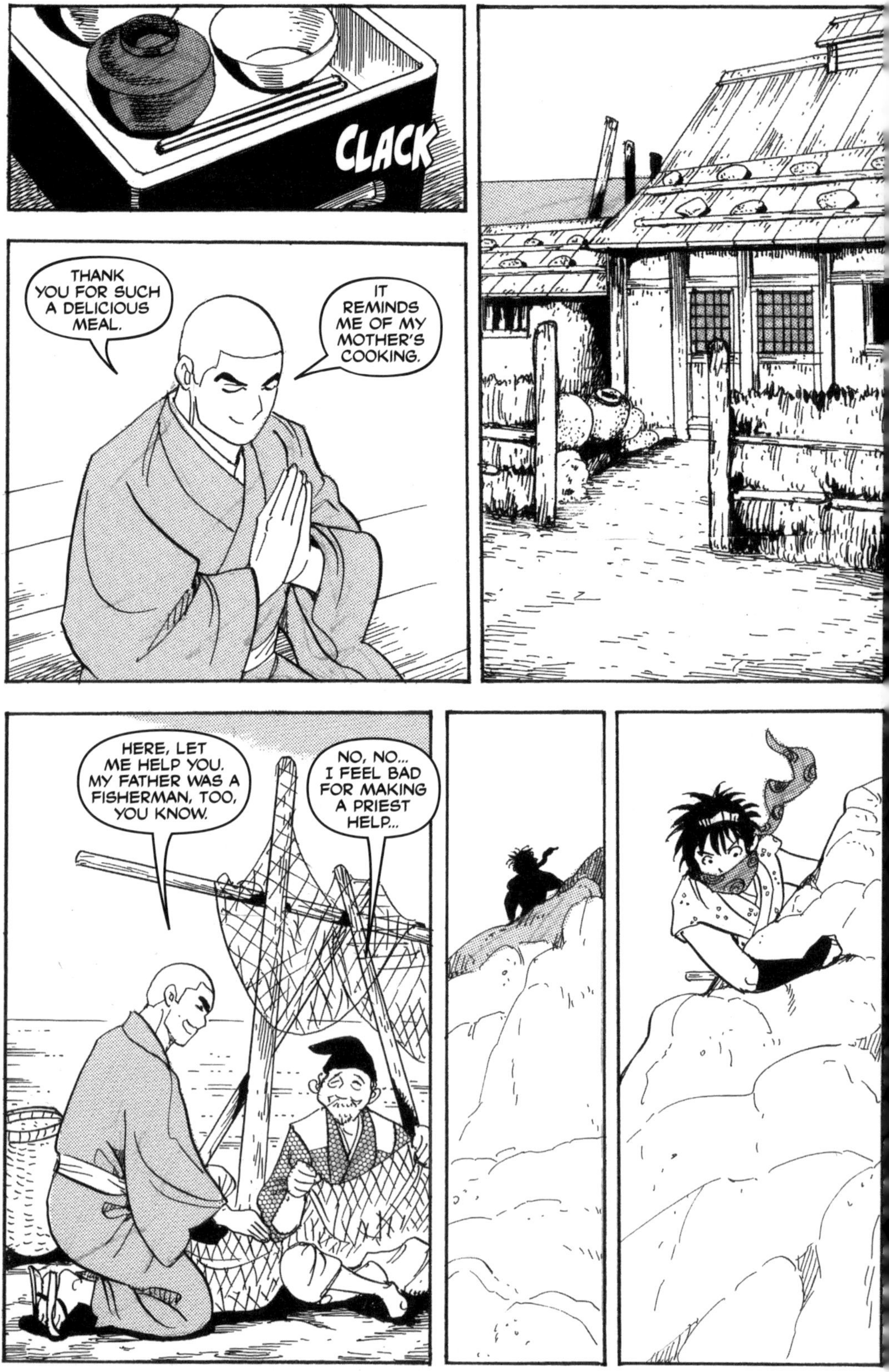
CLACK
THANK YOU FOR SUCH A DELICIOUS MEAL.
IT REMINDS ME OF MY MOTHER'S COOKING.
HERE, LET ME HELP YOU. MY FATHER WAS A FISHERMAN, TOO, YOU KNOW.
NO, NO... I FEEL BAD FOR MAKING A PRIEST HELP...

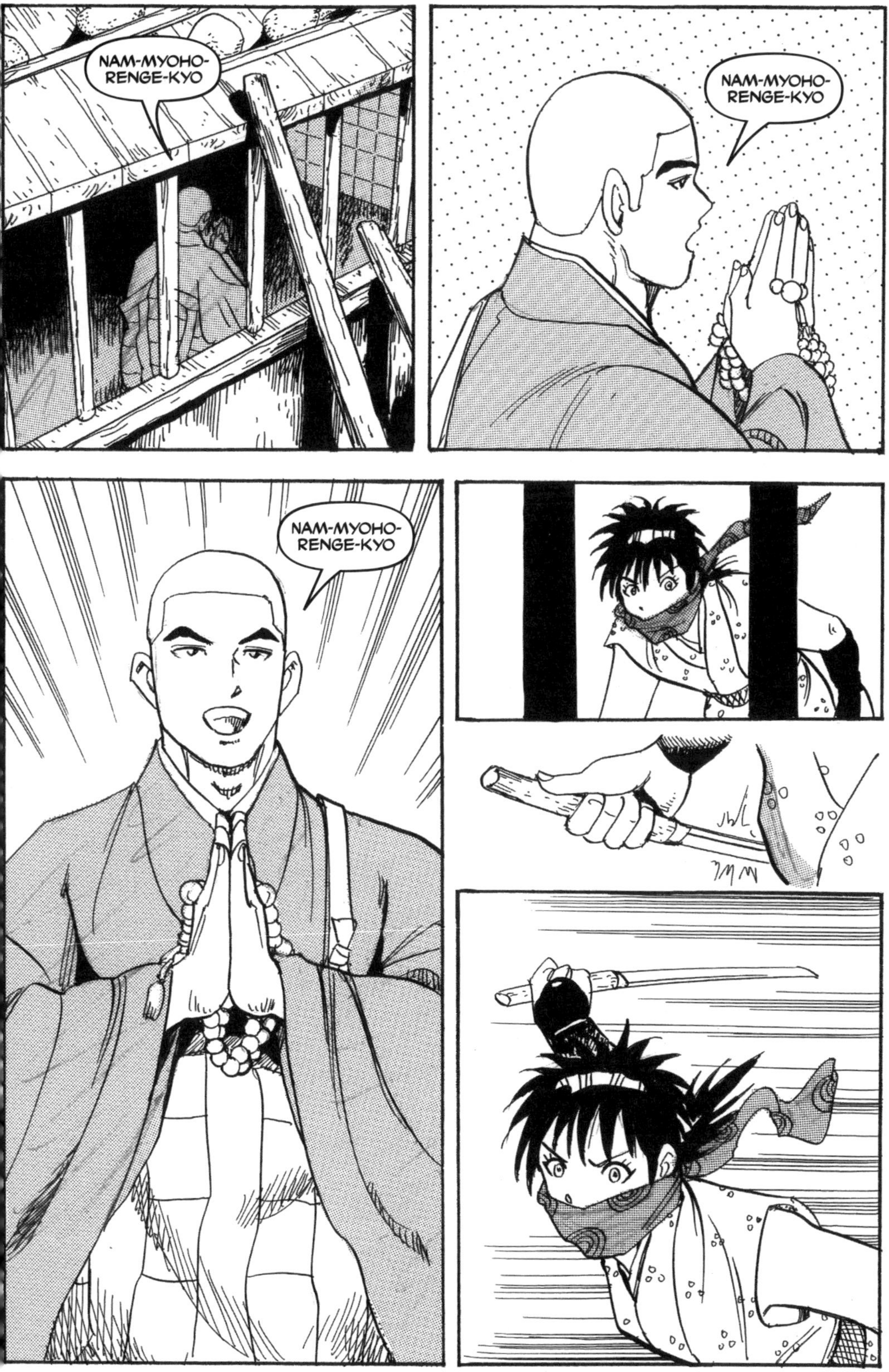
NAM-MYOHO-RENGE-KYO
NAM-MYOHO-RENGE-KYO
NAM-MYOHO-RENGE-KYO

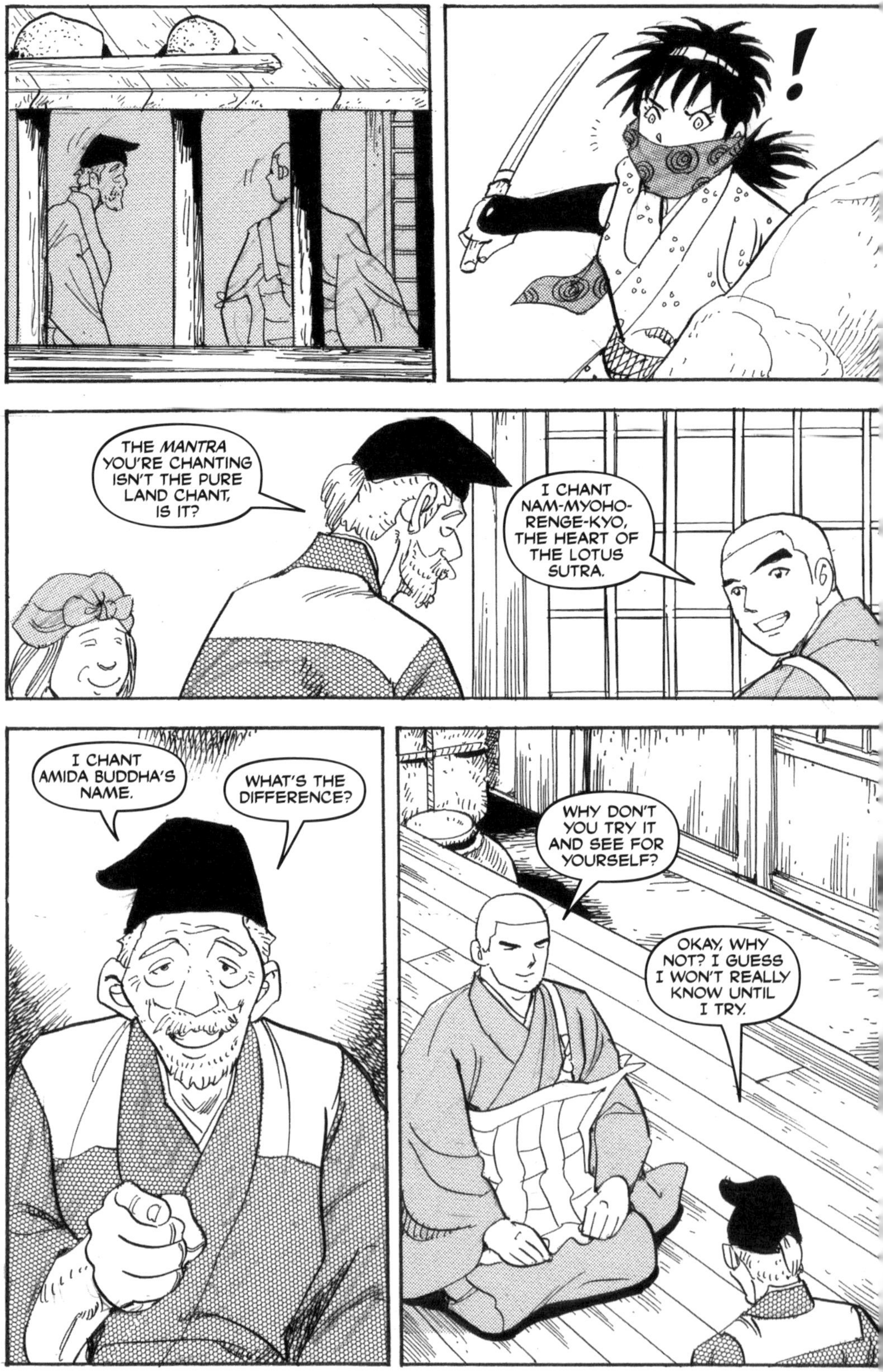

!
THE *MANTRA* YOU'RE CHANTING ISN'T THE PURE LAND CHANT, IS IT?
I CHANT NAM-MYOHO-RENGE-KYO, THE HEART OF THE LOTUS SUTRA.
I CHANT AMIDA BUDDHA'S NAME.
WHAT'S THE DIFFERENCE?
WHY DON'T YOU TRY IT AND SEE FOR YOURSELF?
OKAY, WHY NOT? I GUESS I WON'T REALLY KNOW UNTIL I TRY.

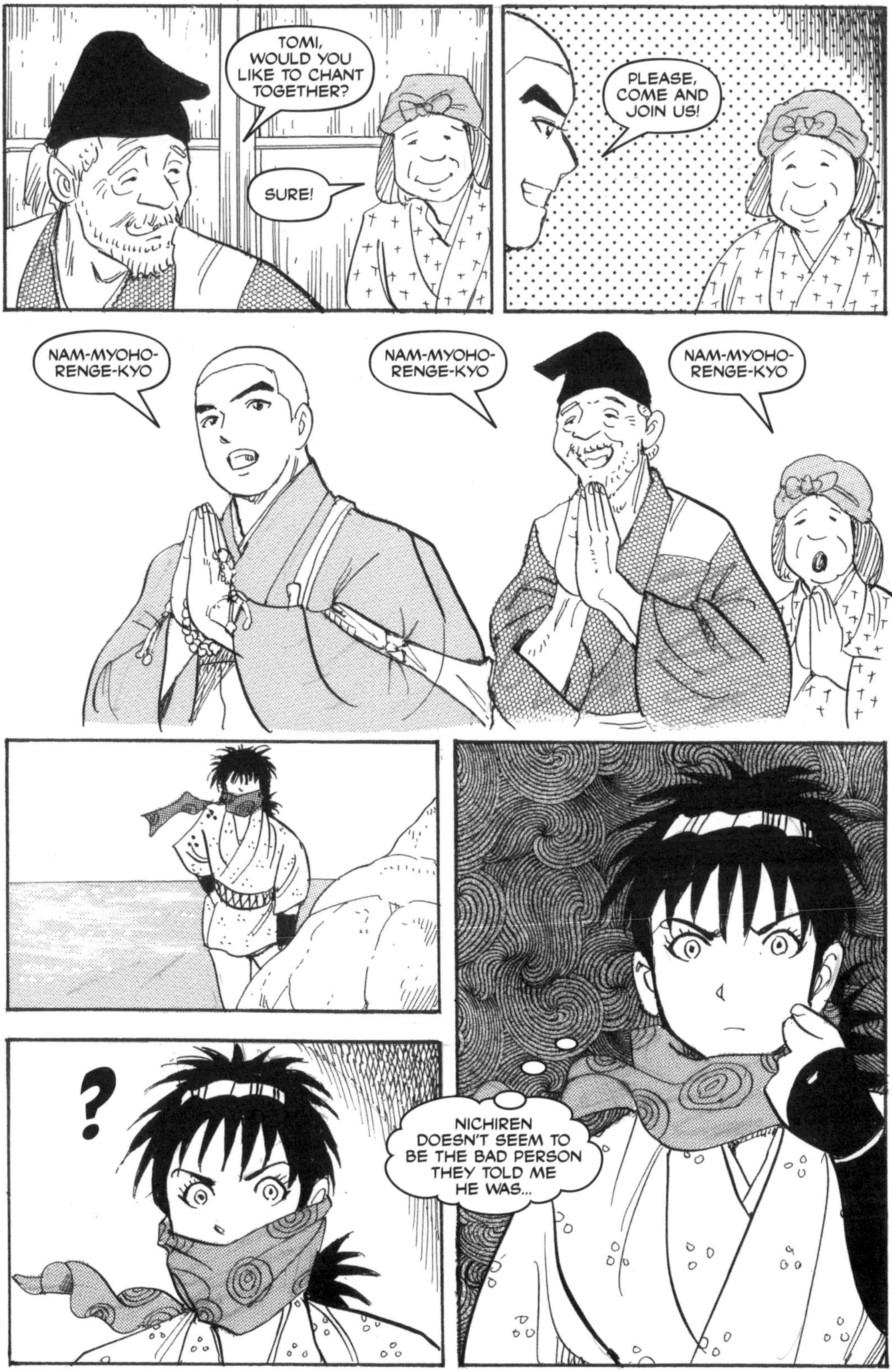
TOMI, WOULD YOU LIKE TO CHANT TOGETHER?
SURE!
PLEASE, COME AND JOIN US!
NAM-MYOHO-RENGE-KYO
NAM-MYOHO-RENGE-KYO
NAM-MYOHO-RENGE-KYO
?
NICHIREN DOESN'T SEEM TO BE THE BAD PERSON THEY TOLD ME HE WAS...

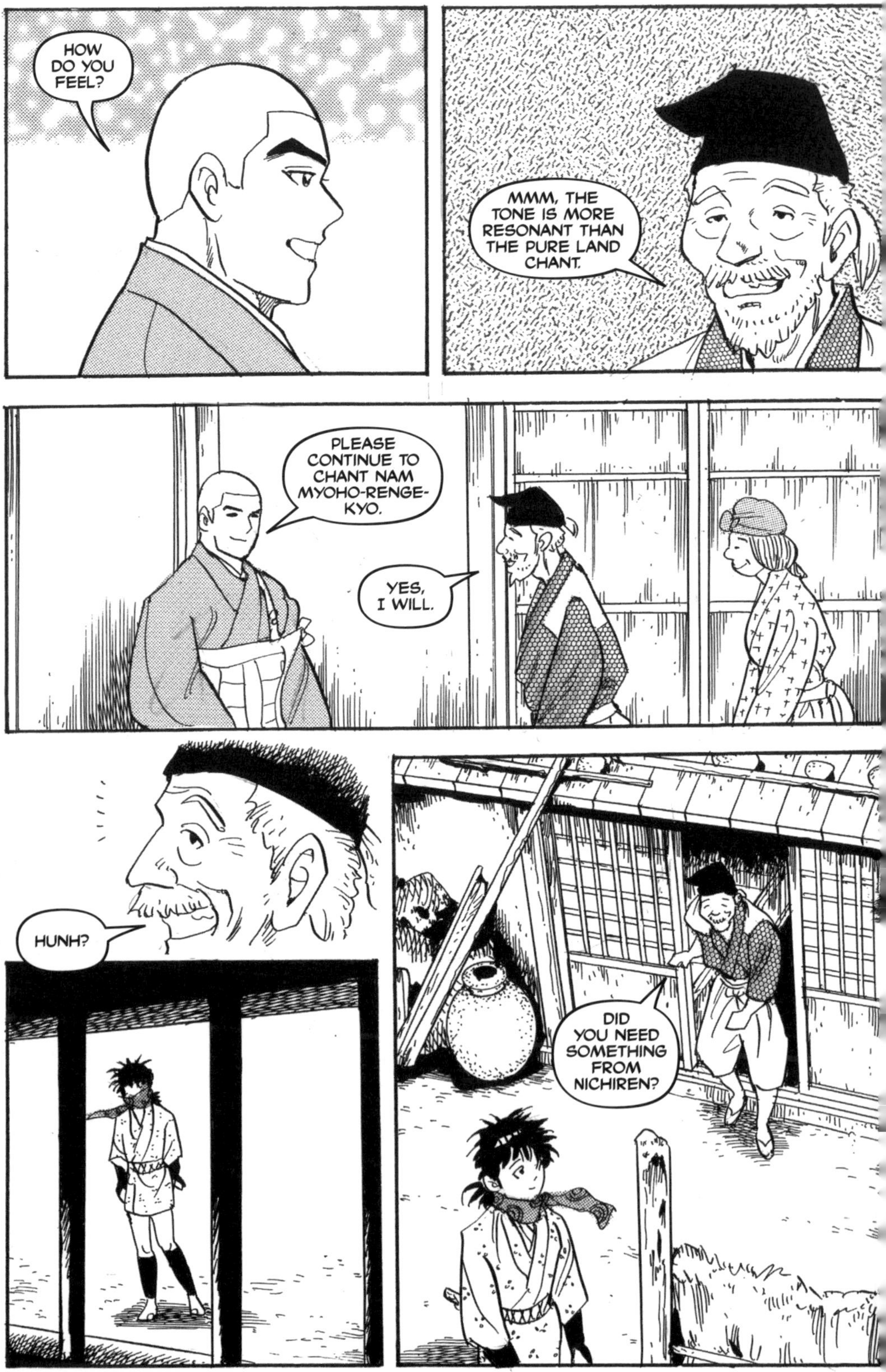
HOW DO YOU FEEL?
MMM, THE TONE IS MORE RESONANT THAN THE PURE LAND CHANT.
PLEASE CONTINUE TO CHANT NAM MYOHO-RENGE-KYO.
YES, I WILL.
HUNH?
DID YOU NEED SOMETHING FROM NICHIREN?

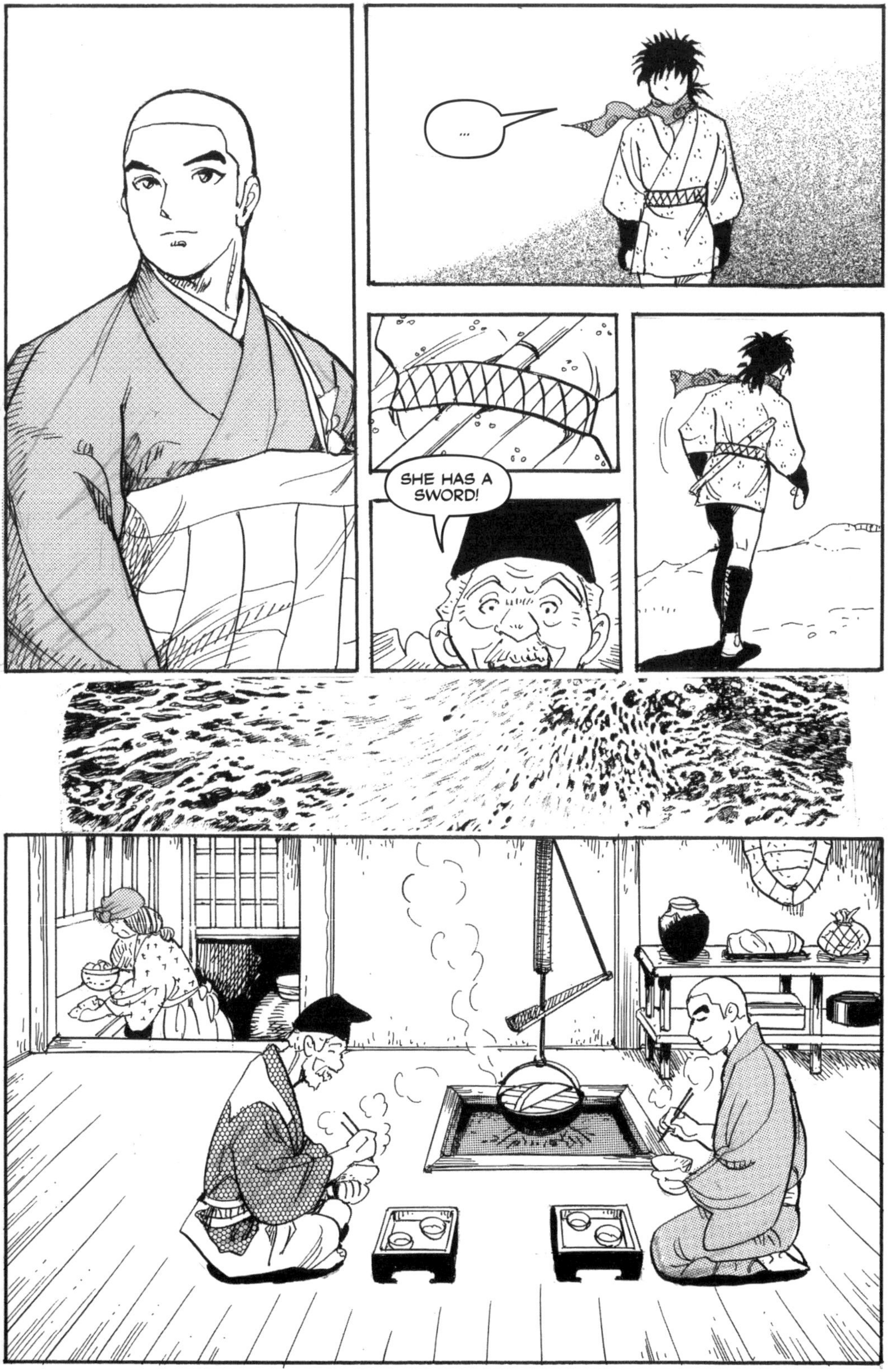
...
SHE HAS A SWORD!

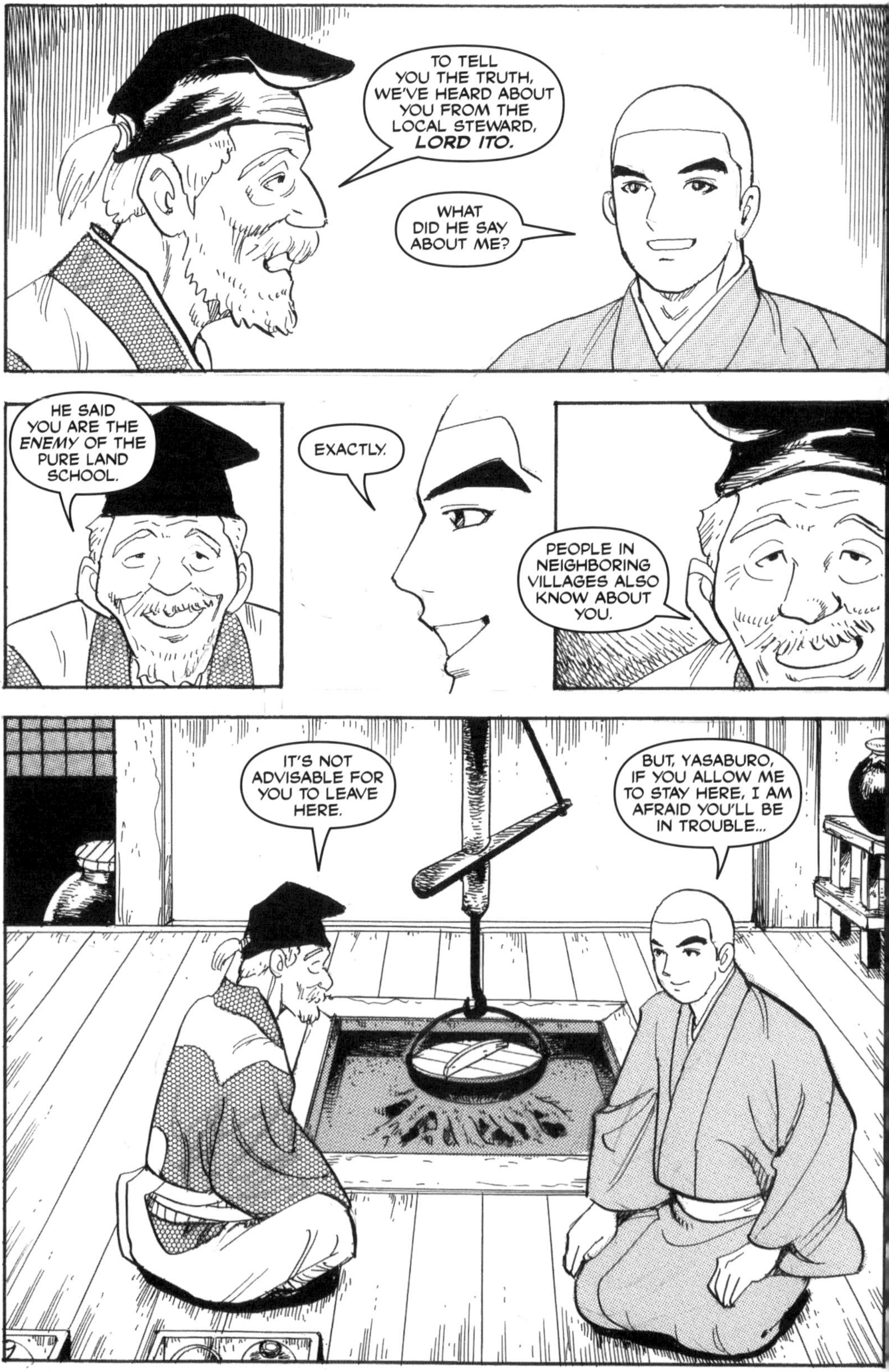

TO TELL YOU THE TRUTH, WE'VE HEARD ABOUT YOU FROM THE LOCAL STEWARD, **LORD ITO.**
WHAT DID HE SAY ABOUT ME?
HE SAID YOU ARE THE *ENEMY* OF THE PURE LAND SCHOOL.
EXACTLY.
PEOPLE IN NEIGHBORING VILLAGES ALSO KNOW ABOUT YOU.
IT'S NOT ADVISABLE FOR YOU TO LEAVE HERE.
BUT, YASABURO, IF YOU ALLOW ME TO STAY HERE, I AM AFRAID YOU'LL BE IN TROUBLE...

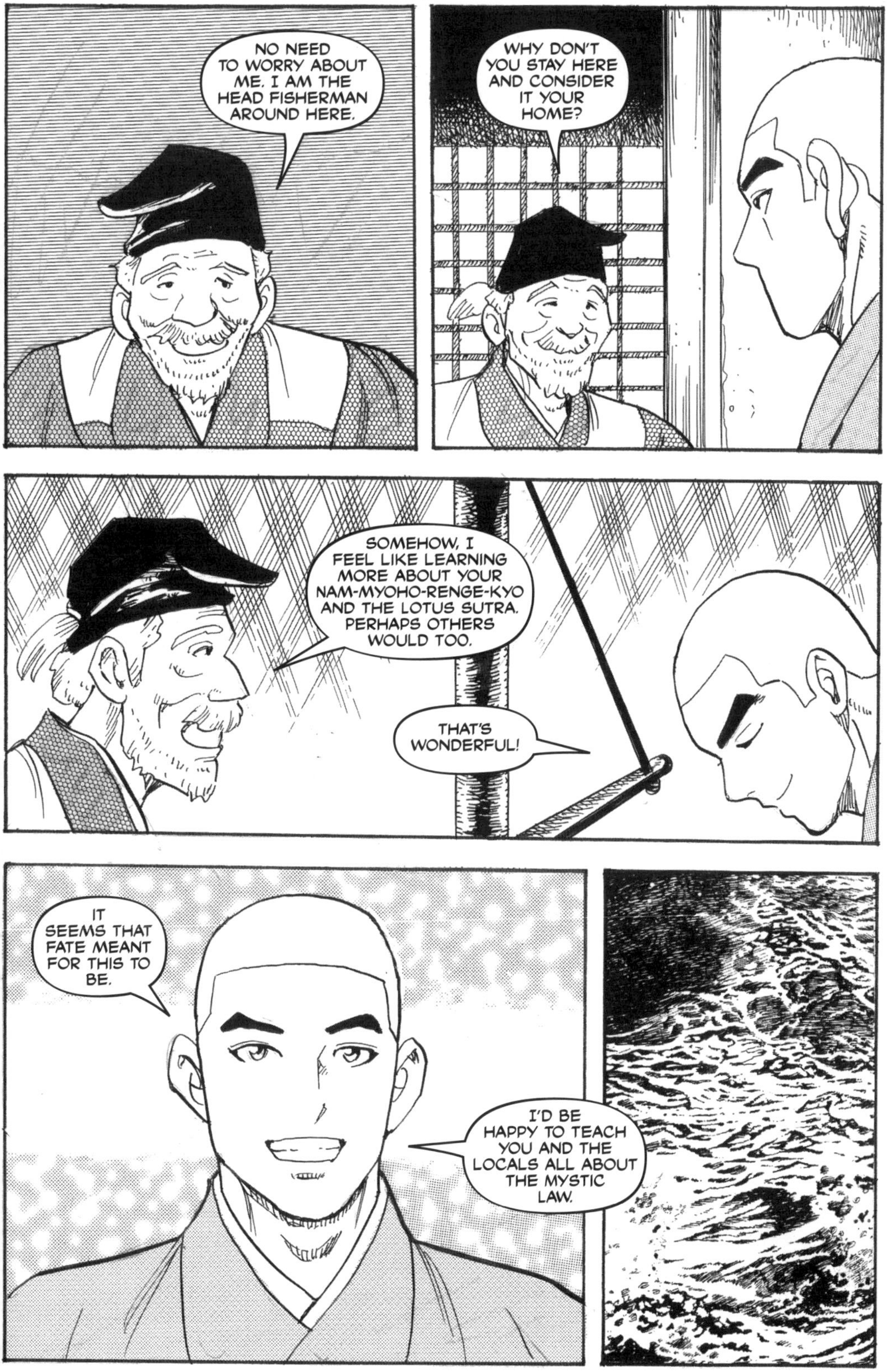
NO NEED TO WORRY ABOUT ME. I AM THE HEAD FISHERMAN AROUND HERE.
WHY DON'T YOU STAY HERE AND CONSIDER IT YOUR HOME?
SOMEHOW, I FEEL LIKE LEARNING MORE ABOUT YOUR NAM-MYOHO-RENGE-KYO AND THE LOTUS SUTRA. PERHAPS OTHERS WOULD TOO.
THAT'S WONDERFUL!
IT SEEMS THAT FATE MEANT FOR THIS TO BE.
I'D BE HAPPY TO TEACH YOU AND THE LOCALS ALL ABOUT THE MYSTIC LAW.

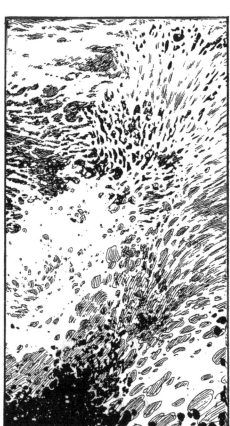

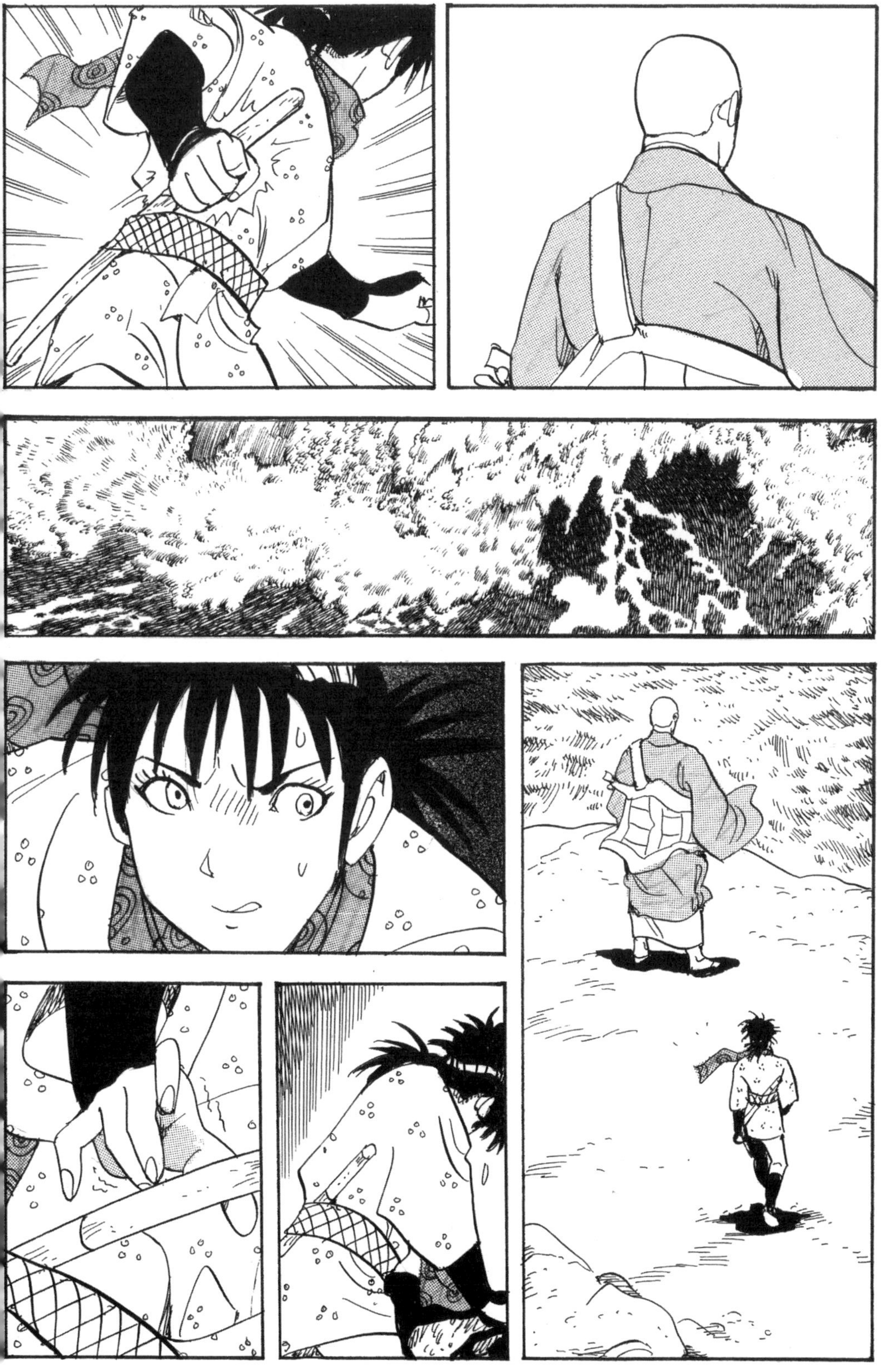

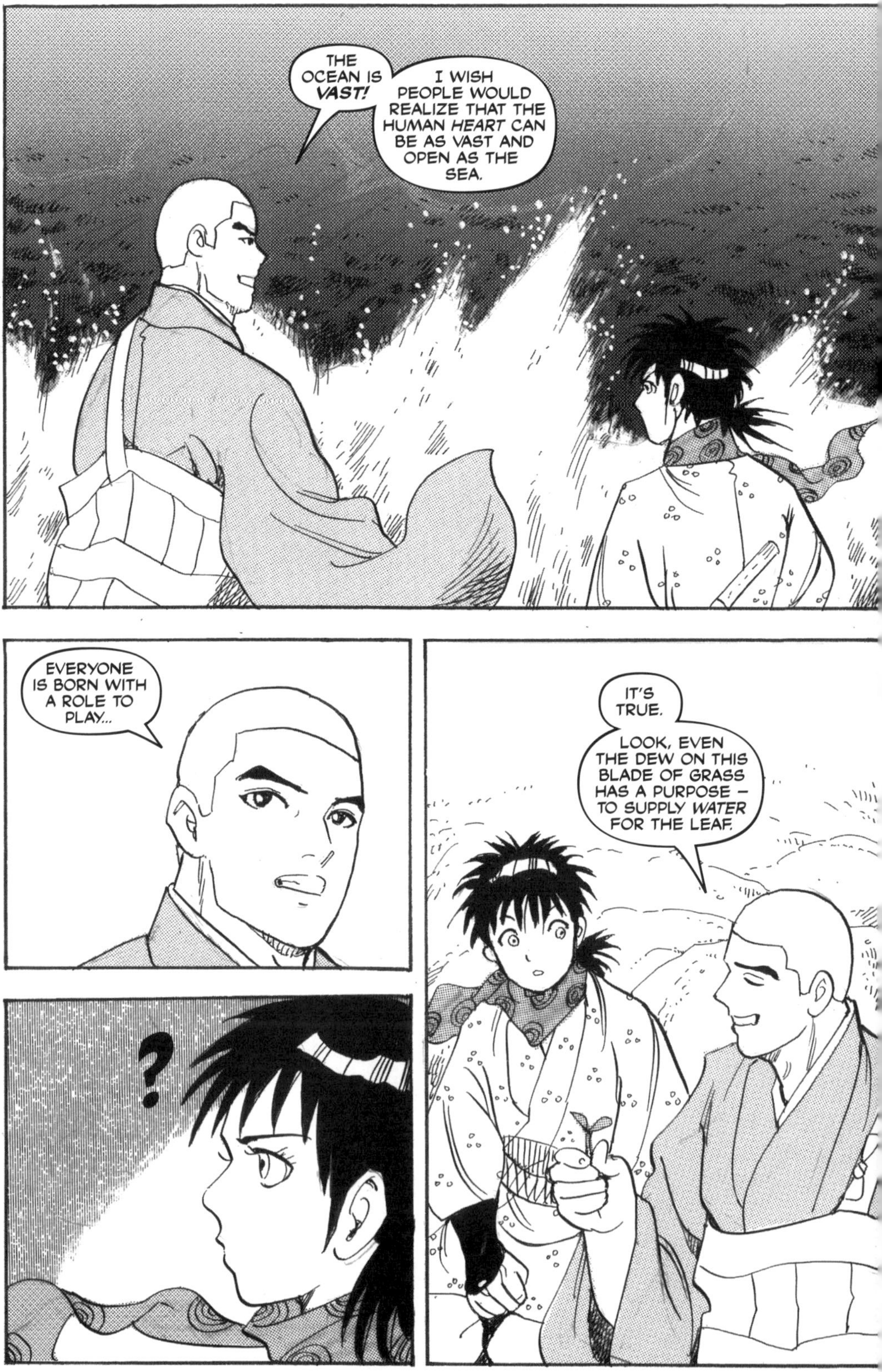
THE OCEAN IS VAST!
I WISH PEOPLE WOULD REALIZE THAT THE HUMAN HEART CAN BE AS VAST AND OPEN AS THE SEA.
EVERYONE IS BORN WITH A ROLE TO PLAY...
?
IT'S TRUE.
LOOK, EVEN THE DEW ON THIS BLADE OF GRASS HAS A PURPOSE – TO SUPPLY WATER FOR THE LEAF.

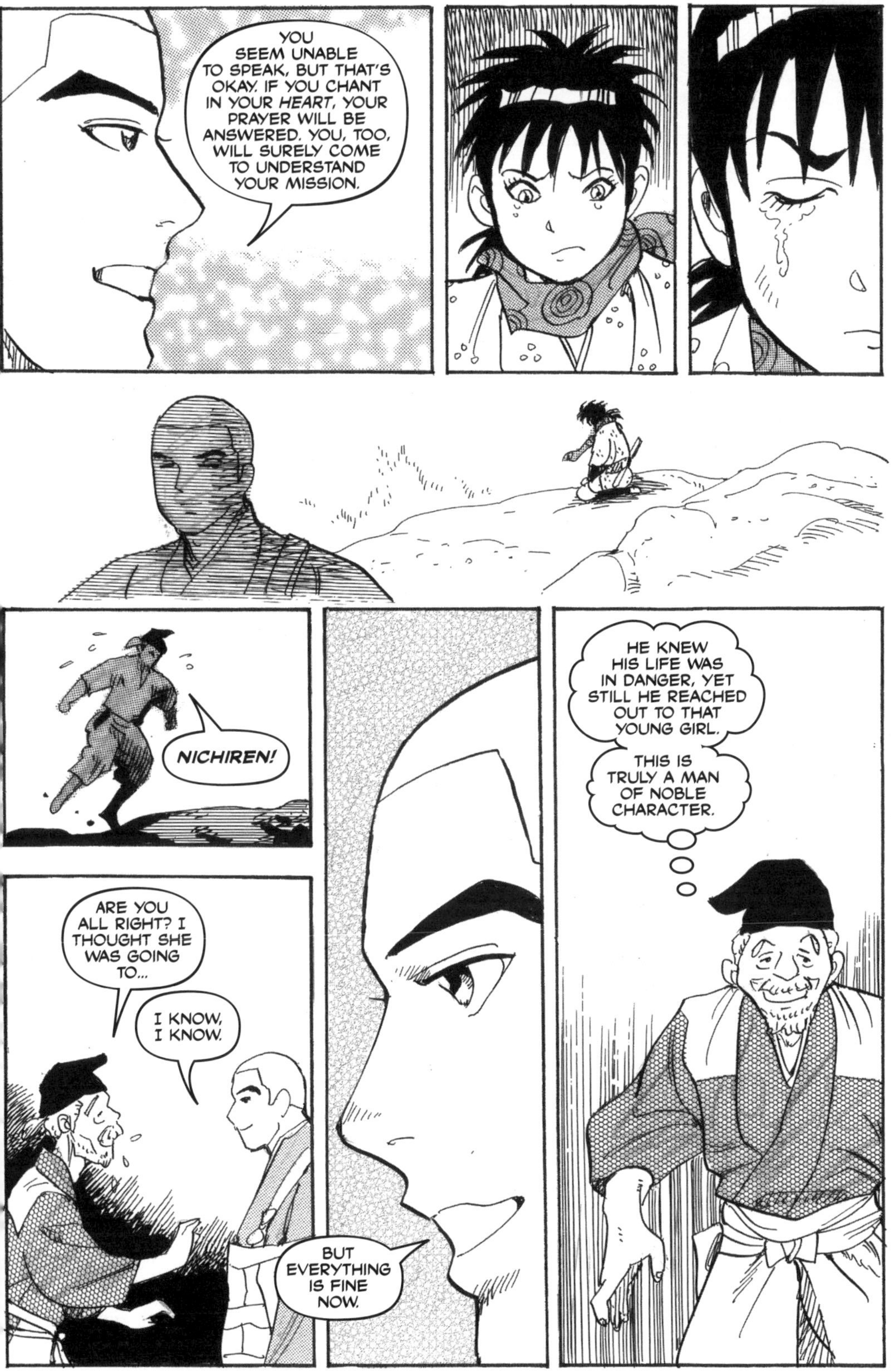
YOU SEEM UNABLE TO SPEAK, BUT THAT'S OKAY. IF YOU CHANT IN YOUR *HEART*, YOUR PRAYER WILL BE ANSWERED. YOU, TOO, WILL SURELY COME TO UNDERSTAND YOUR MISSION.
NICHIREN!
HE KNEW HIS LIFE WAS IN DANGER, YET STILL HE REACHED OUT TO THAT YOUNG GIRL.
THIS IS TRULY A MAN OF NOBLE CHARACTER.
ARE YOU ALL RIGHT? I THOUGHT SHE WAS GOING TO...
I KNOW, I KNOW.
BUT EVERYTHING IS FINE NOW.

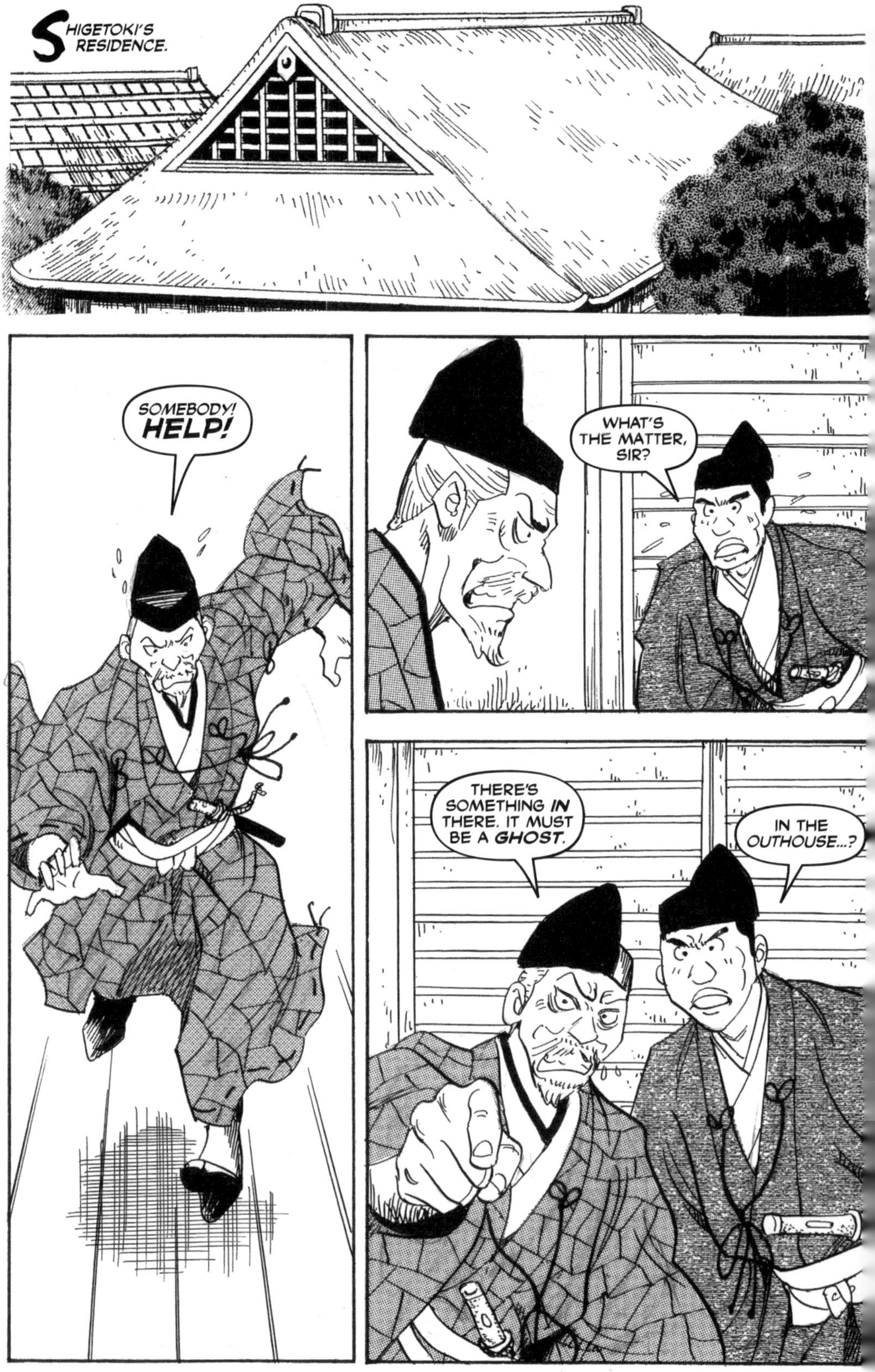
SHIGETOKI'S RESIDENCE.
SOMEBODY! **HELP!**
WHAT'S THE MATTER, SIR?
THERE'S SOMETHING *IN* THERE. IT MUST BE A *GHOST*.
IN THE OUTHOUSE...?

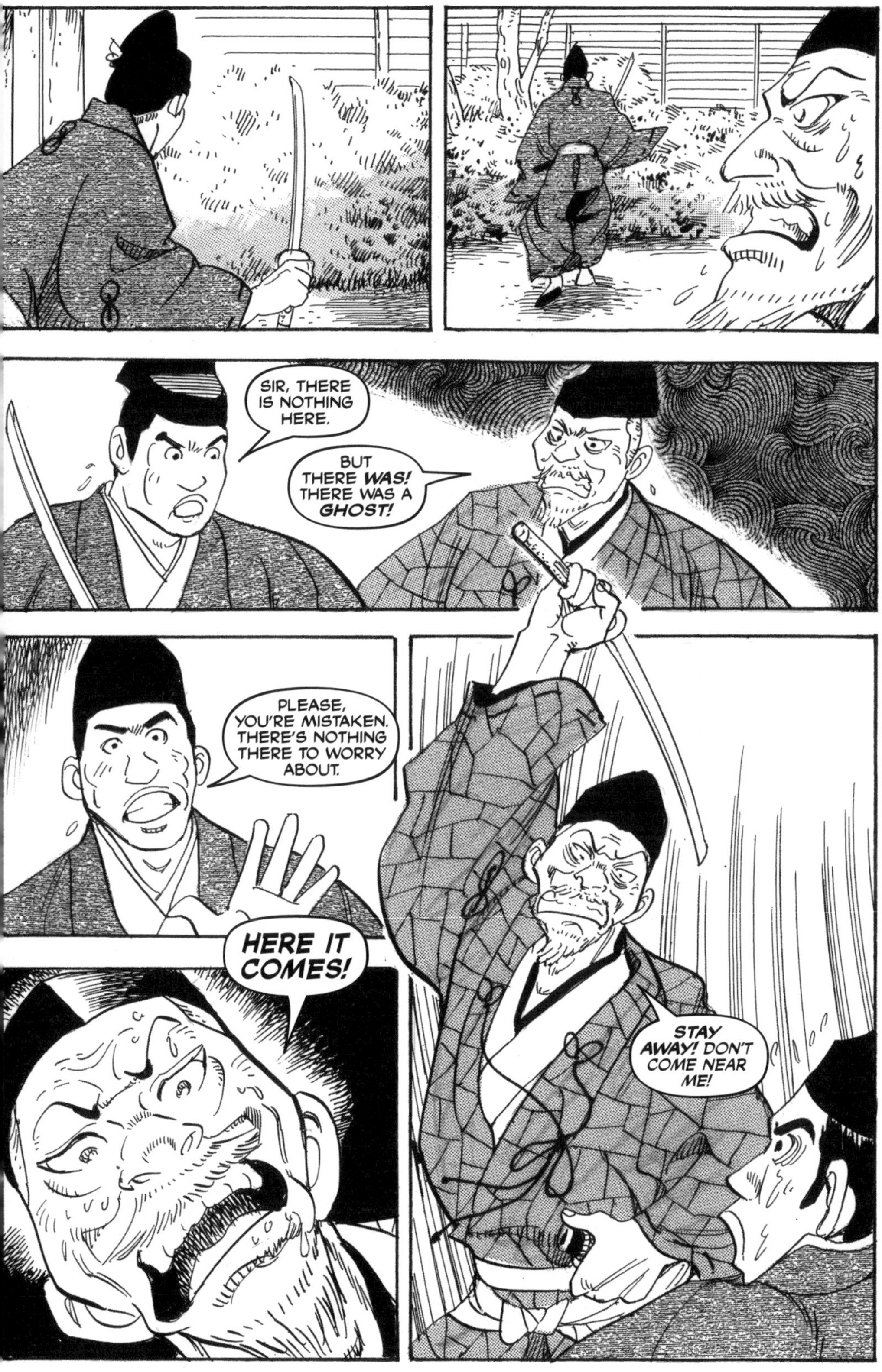
SIR, THERE IS NOTHING HERE.
BUT THERE **WAS!** THERE WAS A **GHOST!**
PLEASE, YOU'RE MISTAKEN. THERE'S NOTHING THERE TO WORRY ABOUT.
HERE IT COMES!
STAY AWAY! DON'T COME NEAR ME!

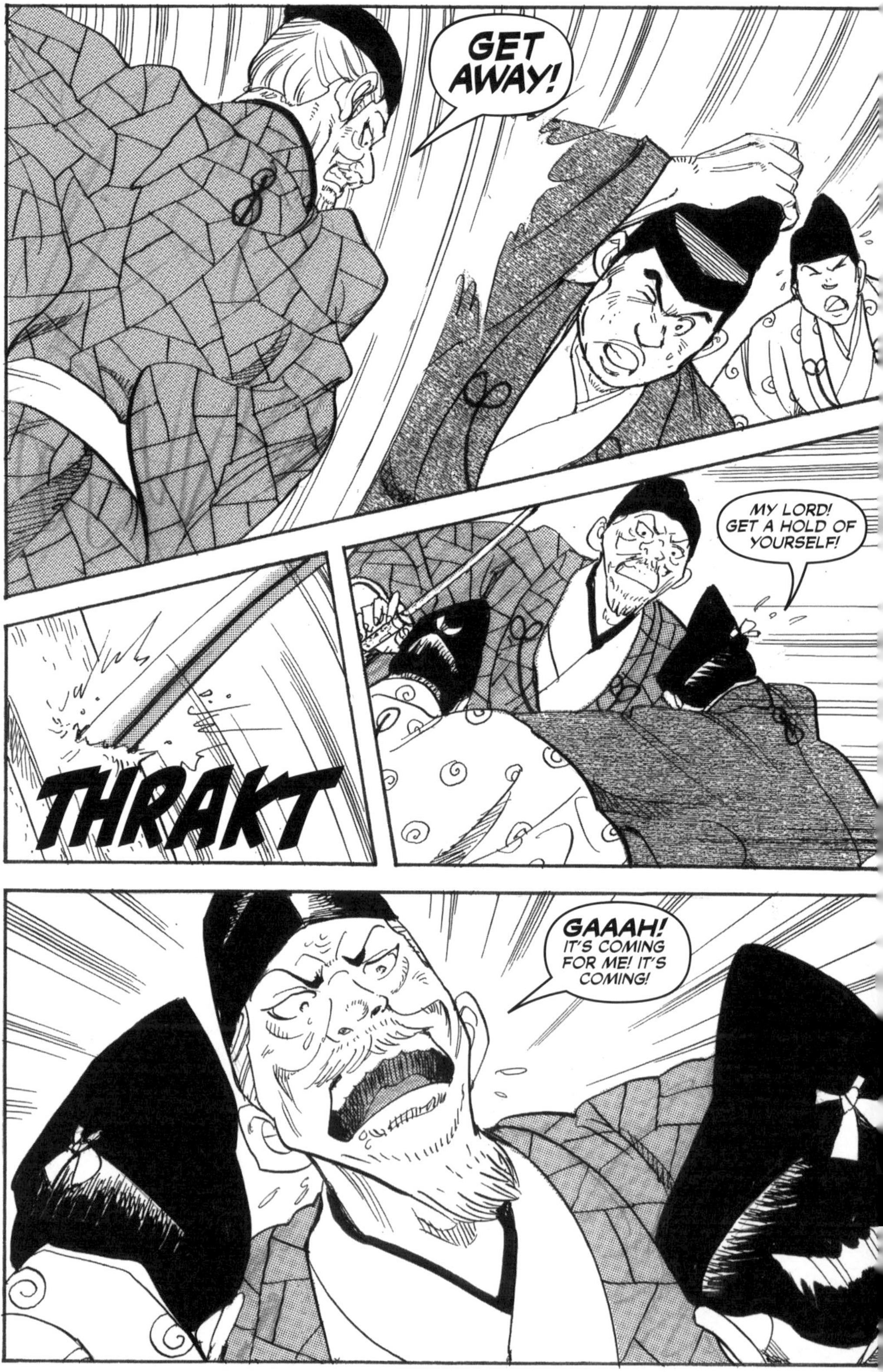
GET AWAY!
THRAKT
MY LORD! GET A HOLD OF YOURSELF!
GAAAH! IT'S COMING FOR ME! IT'S COMING!

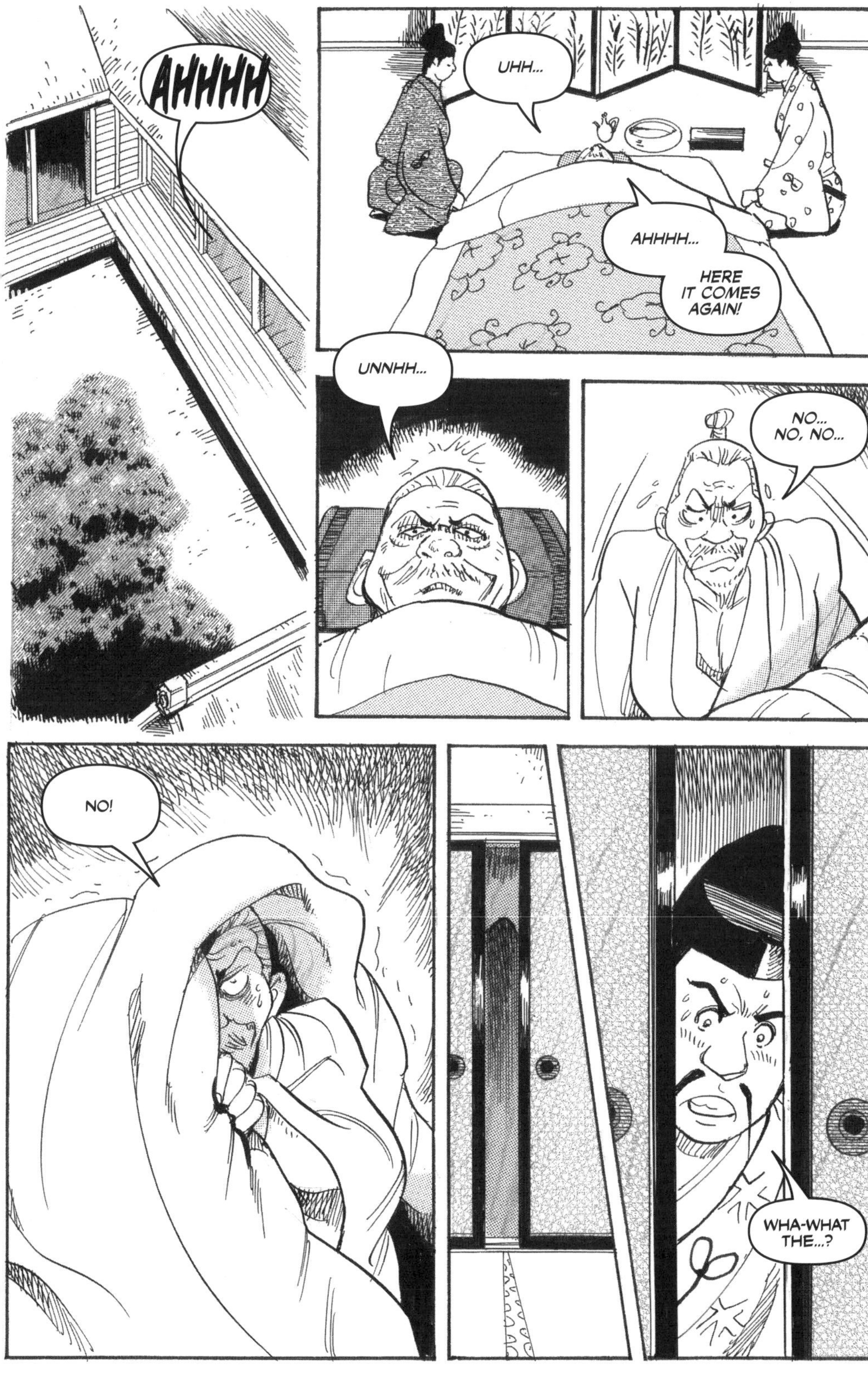
AHHHH
UHH...
AHHHH...
HERE IT COMES AGAIN!
UNNHH...
NO... NO, NO...
NO!
WHA-WHAT THE...?

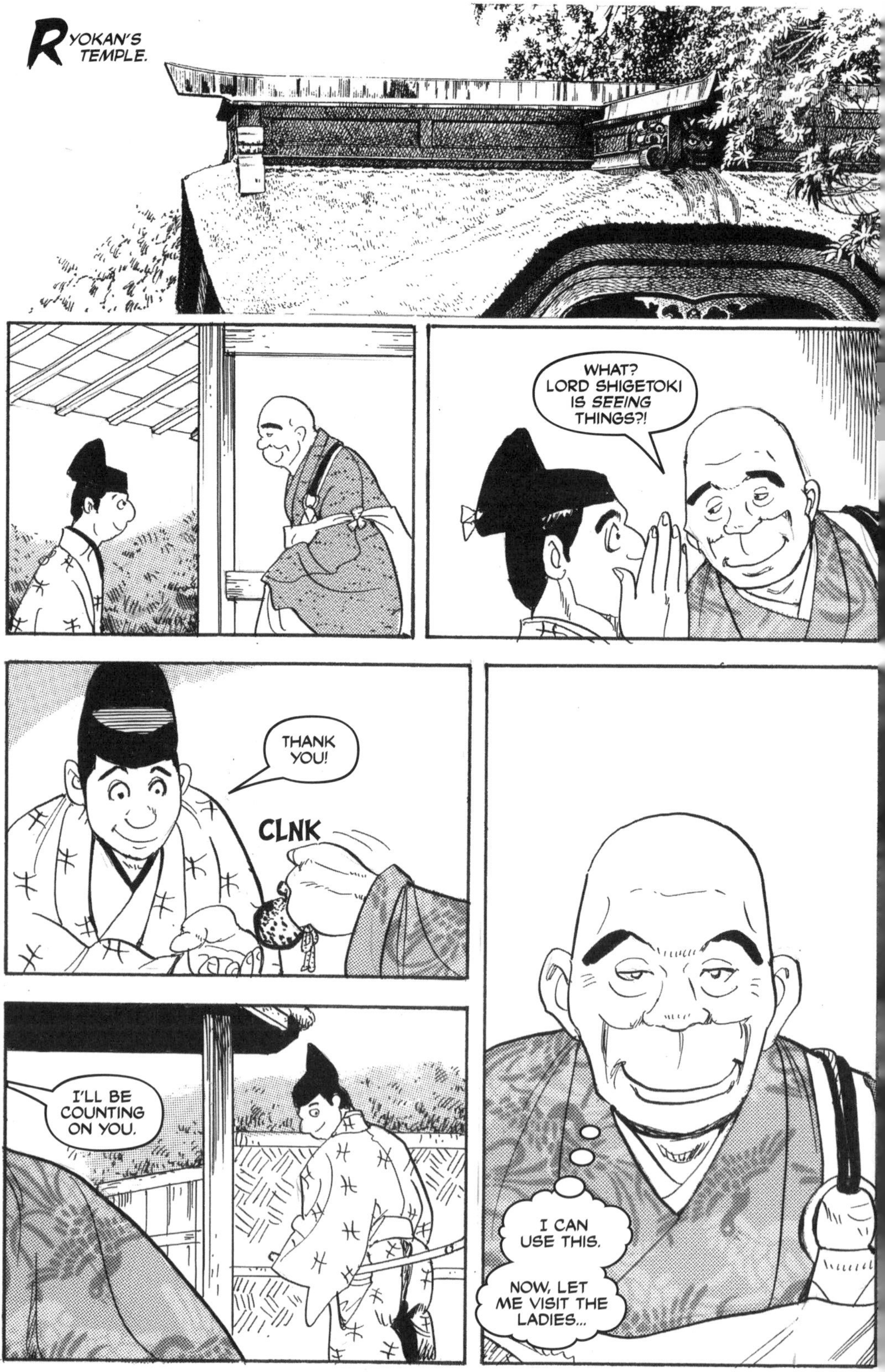
RYOKAN'S TEMPLE.
WHAT? LORD SHIGETOKI IS *SEEING* THINGS?!
THANK YOU!
CLNK
I'LL BE COUNTING ON YOU.
I CAN USE THIS.
NOW, LET ME VISIT THE LADIES...

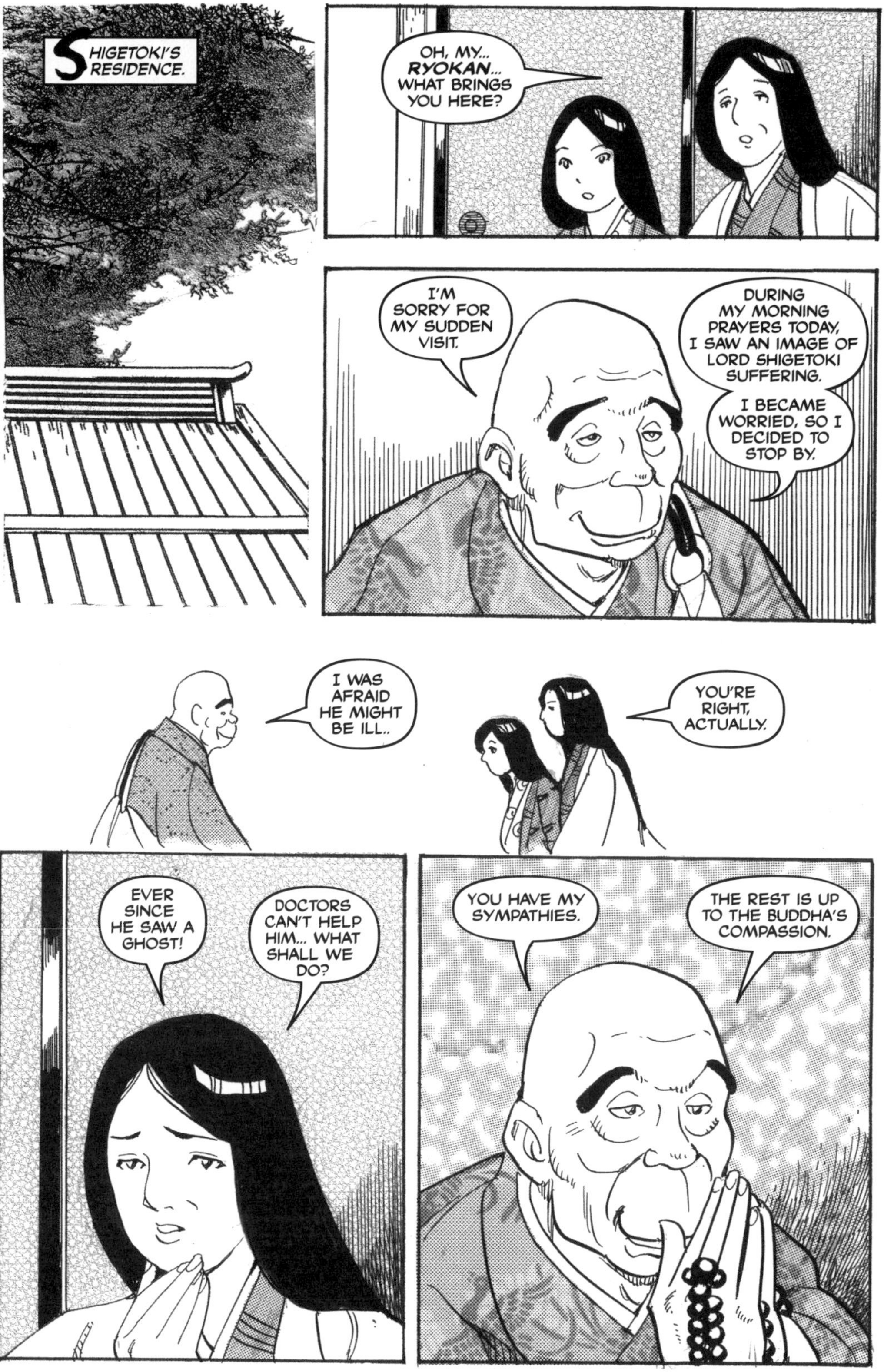
SHIGETOKI'S RESIDENCE.
OH, MY... RYOKAN... WHAT BRINGS YOU HERE?
I'M SORRY FOR MY SUDDEN VISIT.
DURING MY MORNING PRAYERS TODAY, I SAW AN IMAGE OF LORD SHIGETOKI SUFFERING.
I BECAME WORRIED, SO I DECIDED TO STOP BY.
I WAS AFRAID HE MIGHT BE ILL..
YOU'RE RIGHT, ACTUALLY.
EVER SINCE HE SAW A GHOST!
DOCTORS CAN'T HELP HIM... WHAT SHALL WE DO?
YOU HAVE MY SYMPATHIES.
THE REST IS UP TO THE BUDDHA'S COMPASSION.

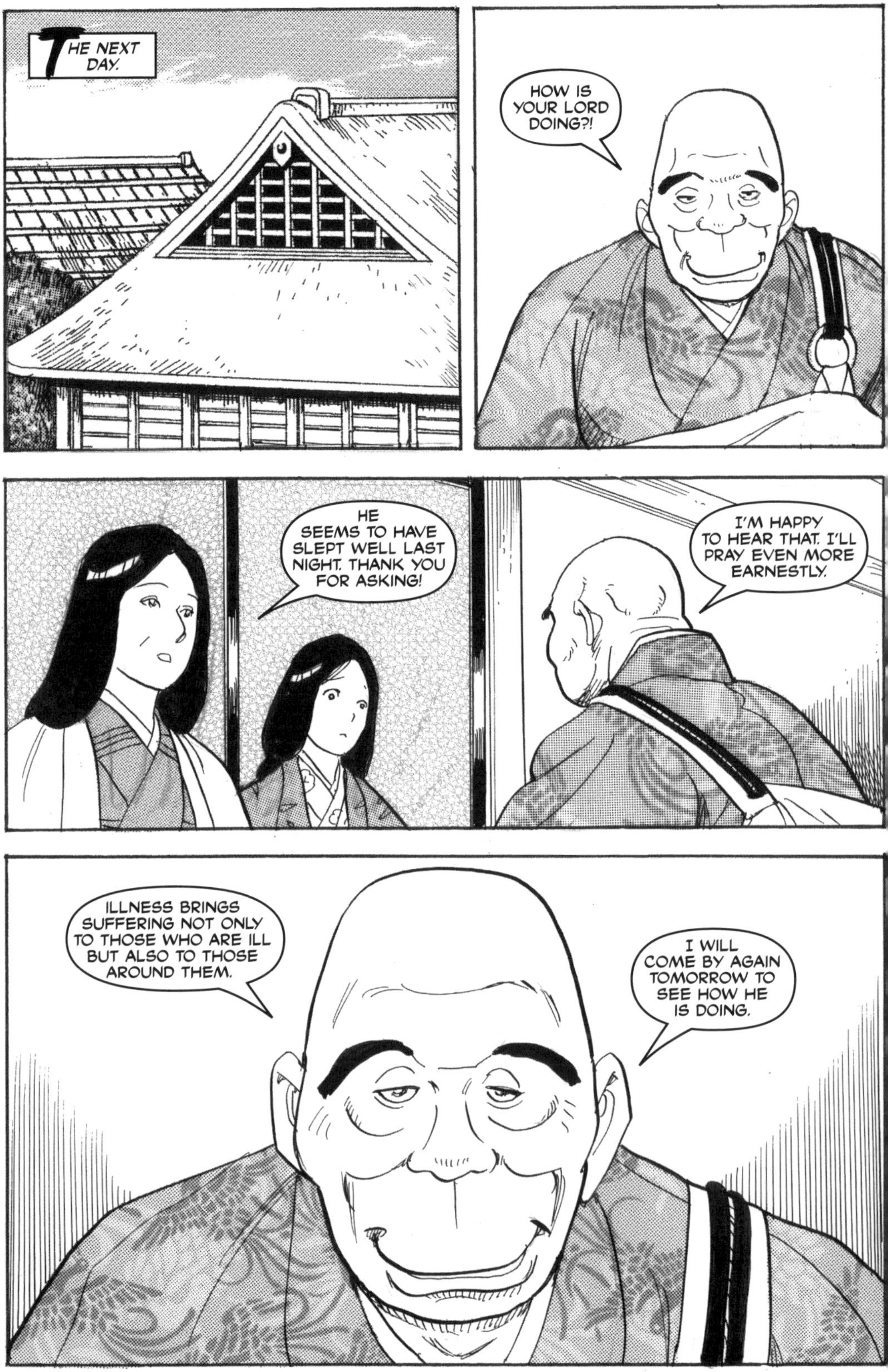

THE NEXT DAY.
HOW IS YOUR LORD DOING?!
HE SEEMS TO HAVE SLEPT WELL LAST NIGHT. THANK YOU FOR ASKING!
I'M HAPPY TO HEAR THAT. I'LL PRAY EVEN MORE EARNESTLY.
ILLNESS BRINGS SUFFERING NOT ONLY TO THOSE WHO ARE ILL BUT ALSO TO THOSE AROUND THEM.
I WILL COME BY AGAIN TOMORROW TO SEE HOW HE IS DOING.

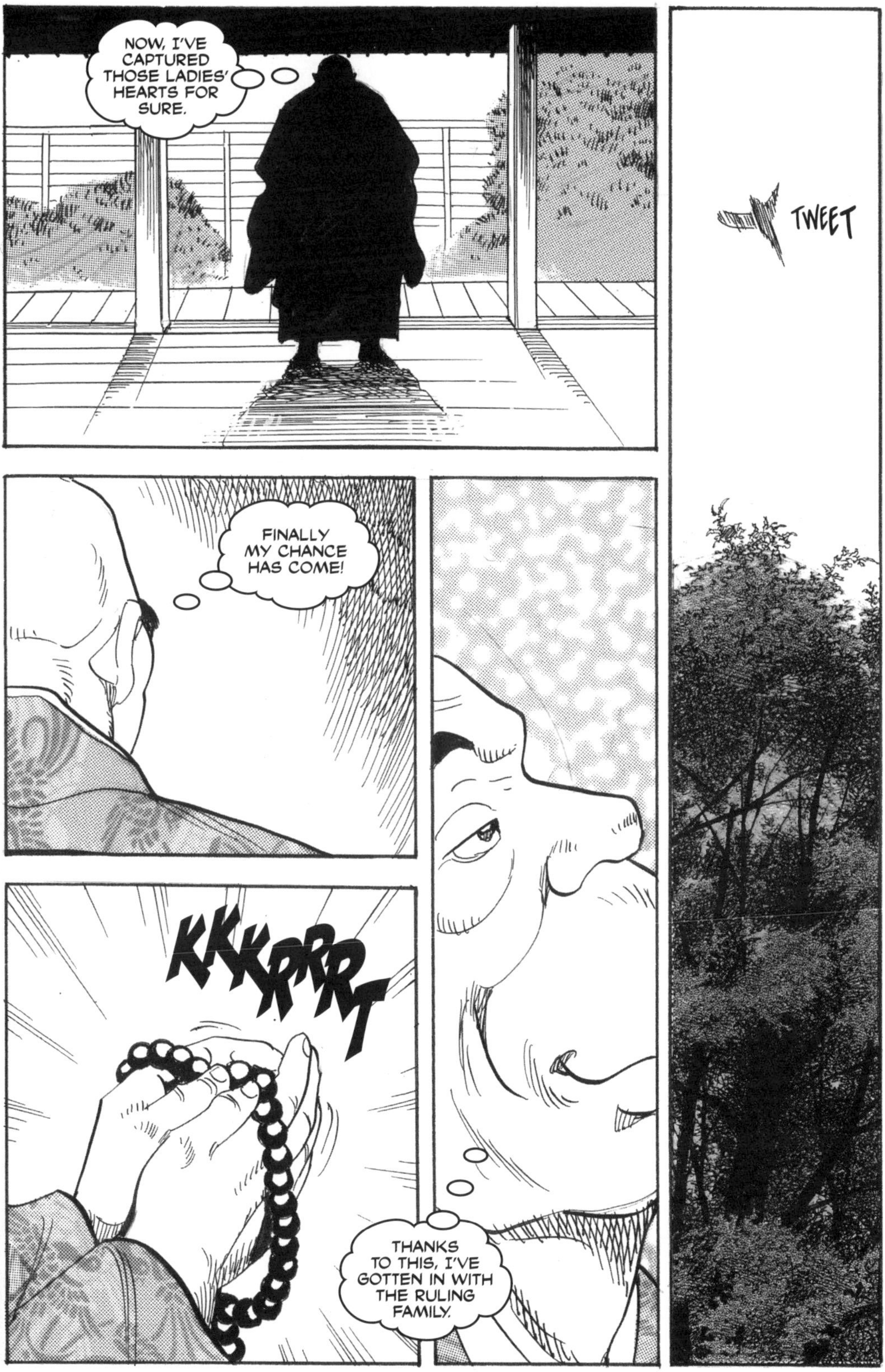
NOW, I'VE CAPTURED THOSE LADIES' HEARTS FOR SURE.
TWEET
FINALLY MY CHANCE HAS COME!
KKKRRRT
THANKS TO THIS, I'VE GOTTEN IN WITH THE RULING FAMILY.

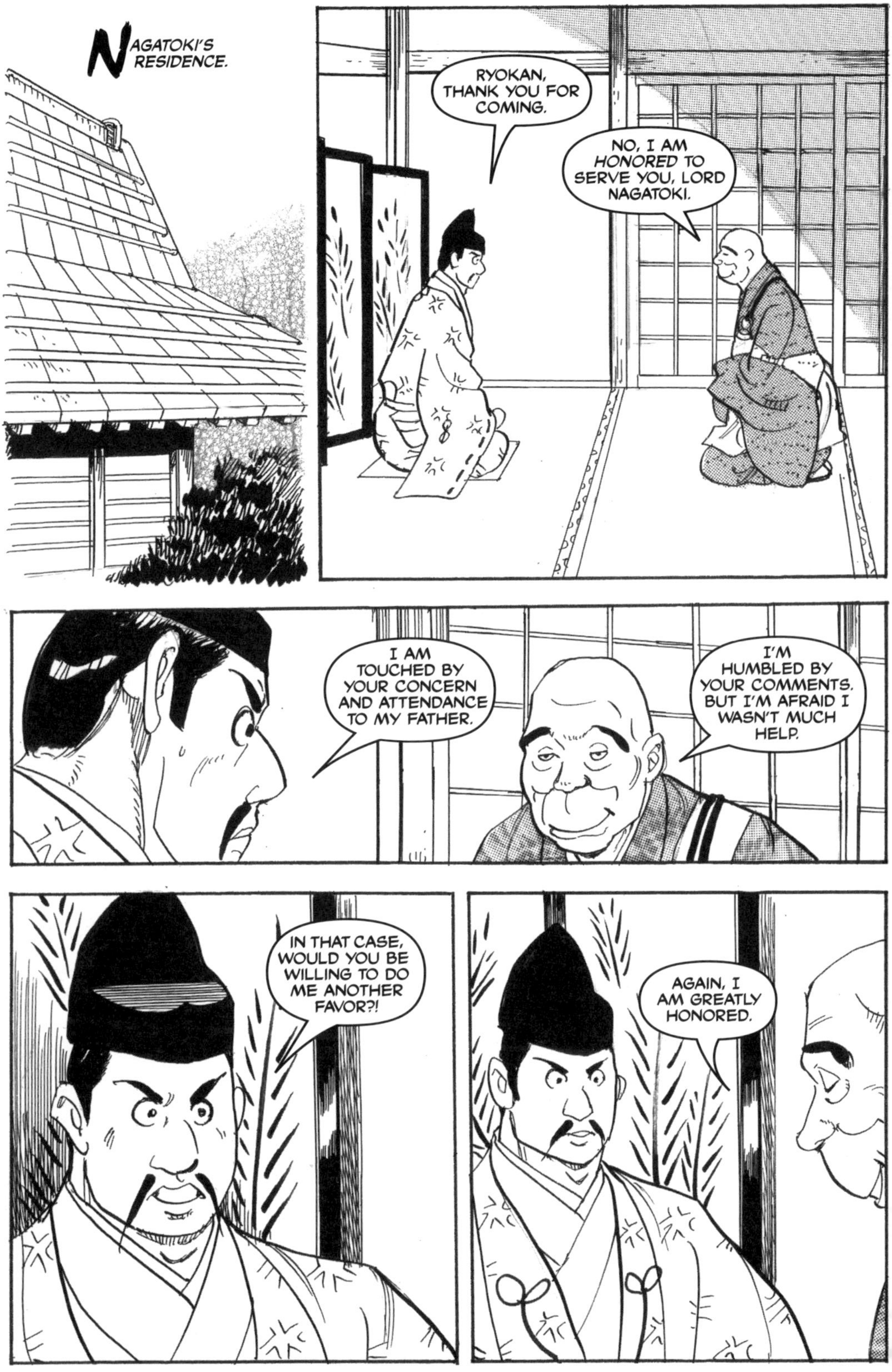
NAGATOKI'S RESIDENCE.
RYOKAN, THANK YOU FOR COMING.
NO, I AM *HONORED* TO SERVE YOU, LORD NAGATOKI.
I AM TOUCHED BY YOUR CONCERN AND ATTENDANCE TO MY FATHER.
I'M HUMBLED BY YOUR COMMENTS. BUT I'M AFRAID I WASN'T MUCH HELP.
IN THAT CASE, WOULD YOU BE WILLING TO DO ME ANOTHER FAVOR?!
AGAIN, I AM GREATLY HONORED.

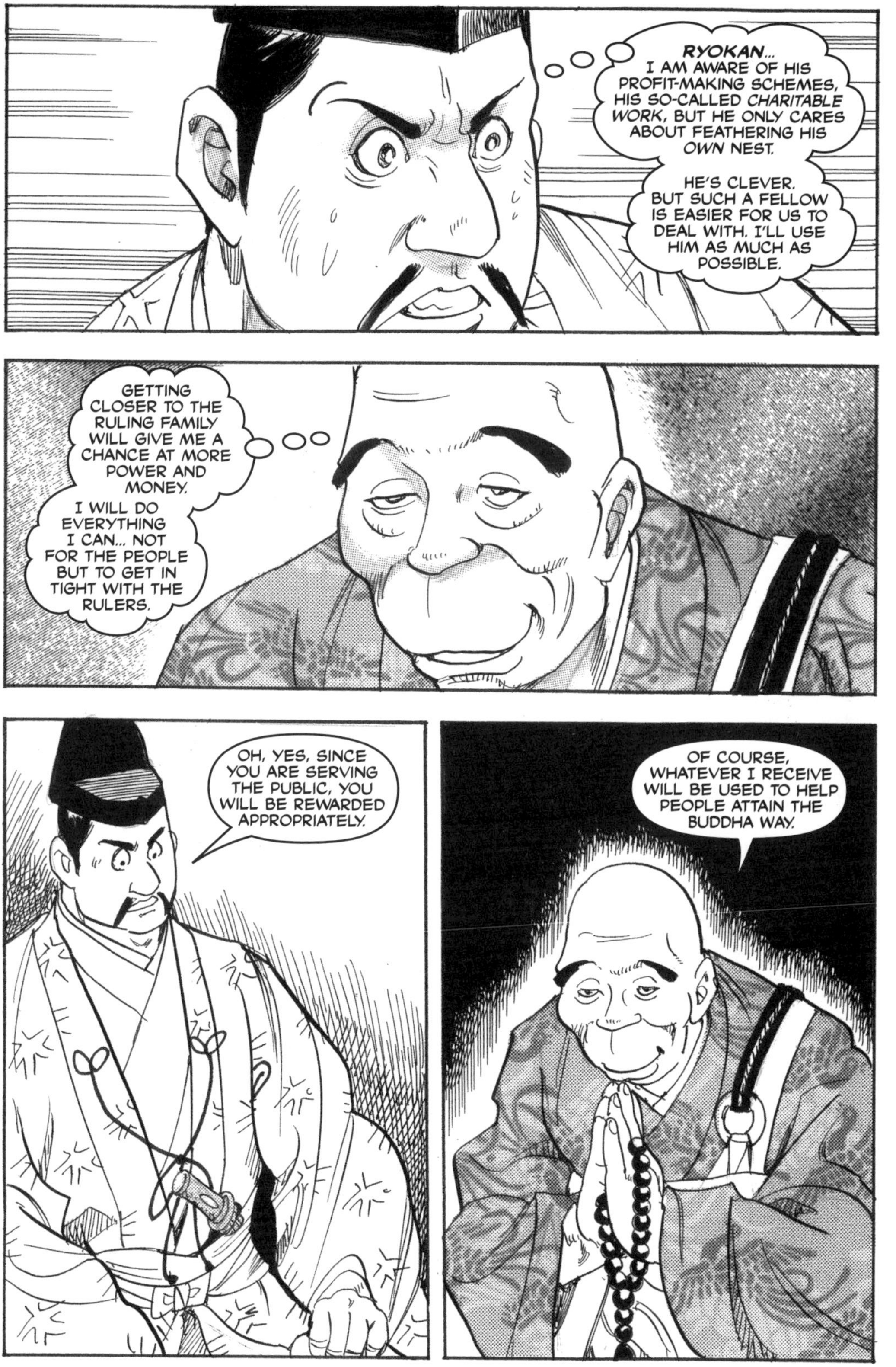
RYOKAN... I AM AWARE OF HIS PROFIT-MAKING SCHEMES, HIS SO-CALLED *CHARITABLE WORK*, BUT HE ONLY CARES ABOUT FEATHERING HIS *OWN* NEST.
HE'S CLEVER. BUT SUCH A FELLOW IS EASIER FOR US TO DEAL WITH. I'LL USE HIM AS MUCH AS POSSIBLE.
GETTING CLOSER TO THE RULING FAMILY WILL GIVE ME A CHANCE AT MORE POWER AND MONEY.
I WILL DO EVERYTHING I CAN... NOT FOR THE PEOPLE BUT TO GET IN TIGHT WITH THE RULERS.
OH, YES, SINCE YOU ARE SERVING THE PUBLIC, YOU WILL BE REWARDED APPROPRIATELY.
OF COURSE, WHATEVER I RECEIVE WILL BE USED TO HELP PEOPLE ATTAIN THE BUDDHA WAY.

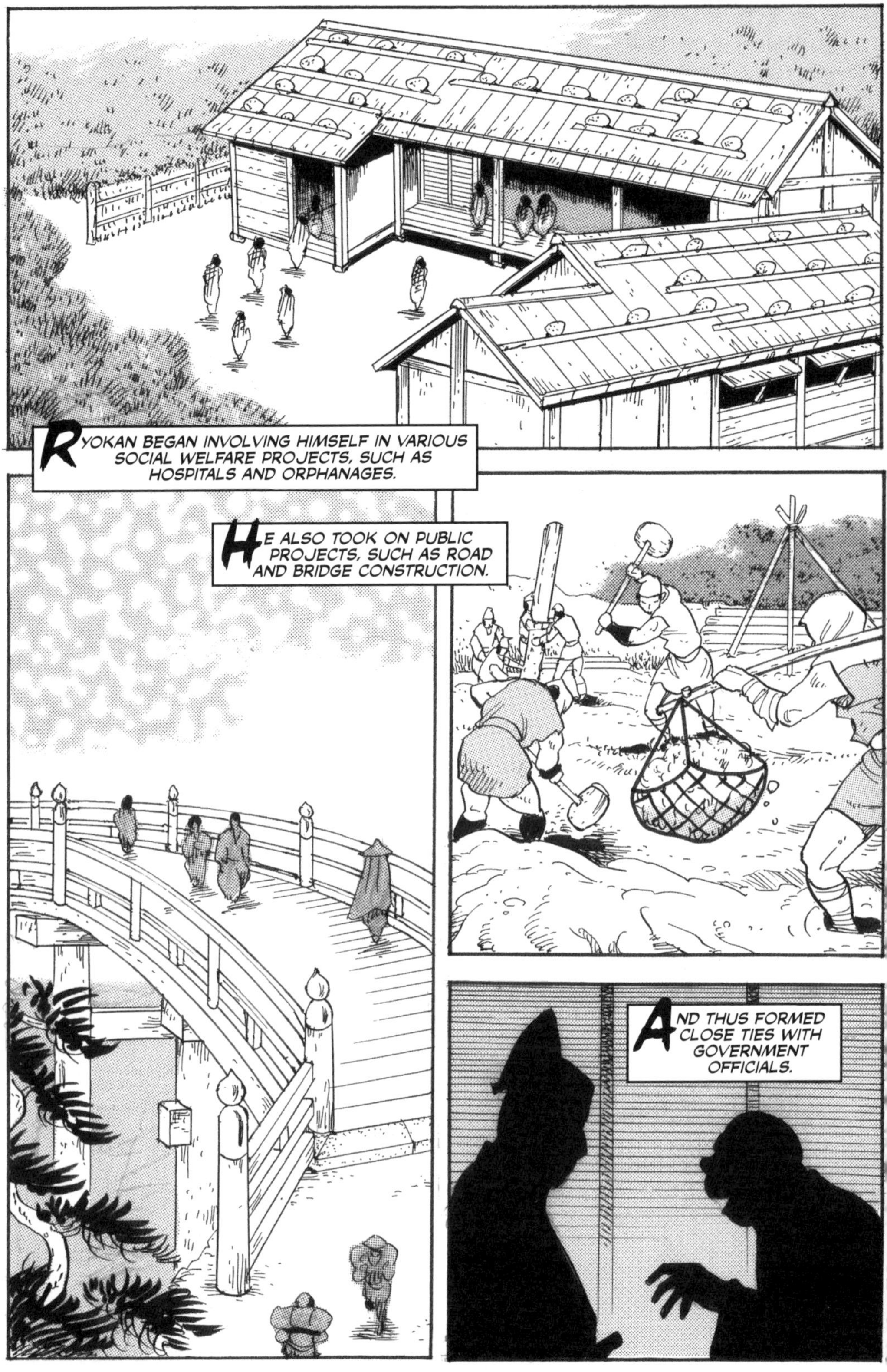
RYOKAN BEGAN INVOLVING HIMSELF IN VARIOUS SOCIAL WELFARE PROJECTS, SUCH AS HOSPITALS AND ORPHANAGES.
HE ALSO TOOK ON PUBLIC PROJECTS, SUCH AS ROAD AND BRIDGE CONSTRUCTION.
AND THUS FORMED CLOSE TIES WITH GOVERNMENT OFFICIALS.

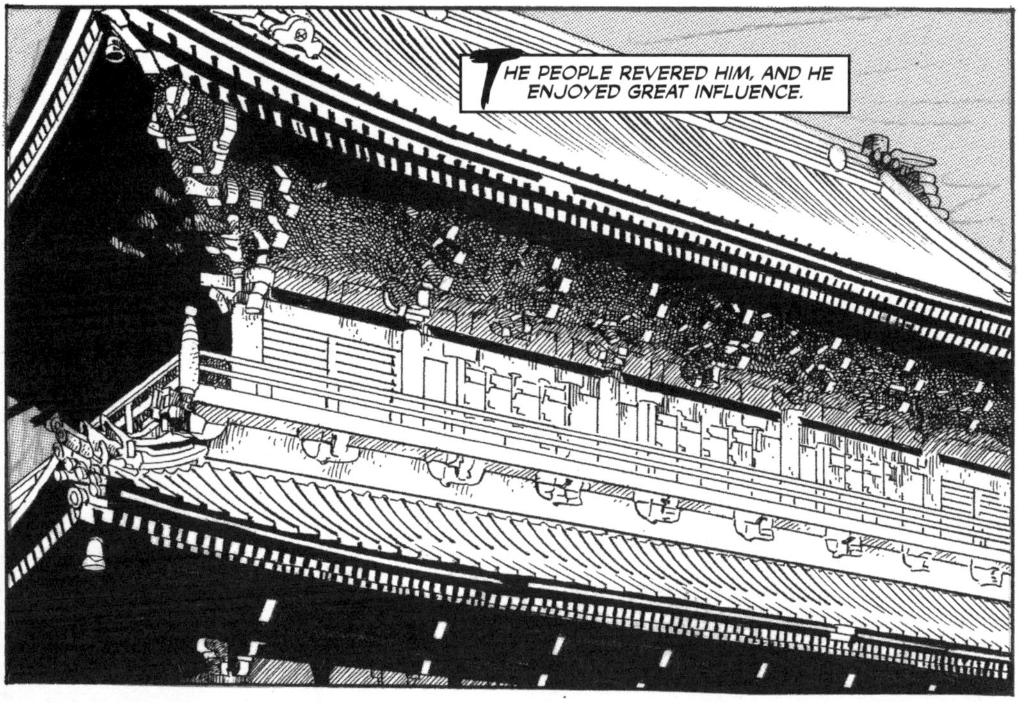
THE PEOPLE REVERED HIM, AND HE ENJOYED GREAT INFLUENCE.

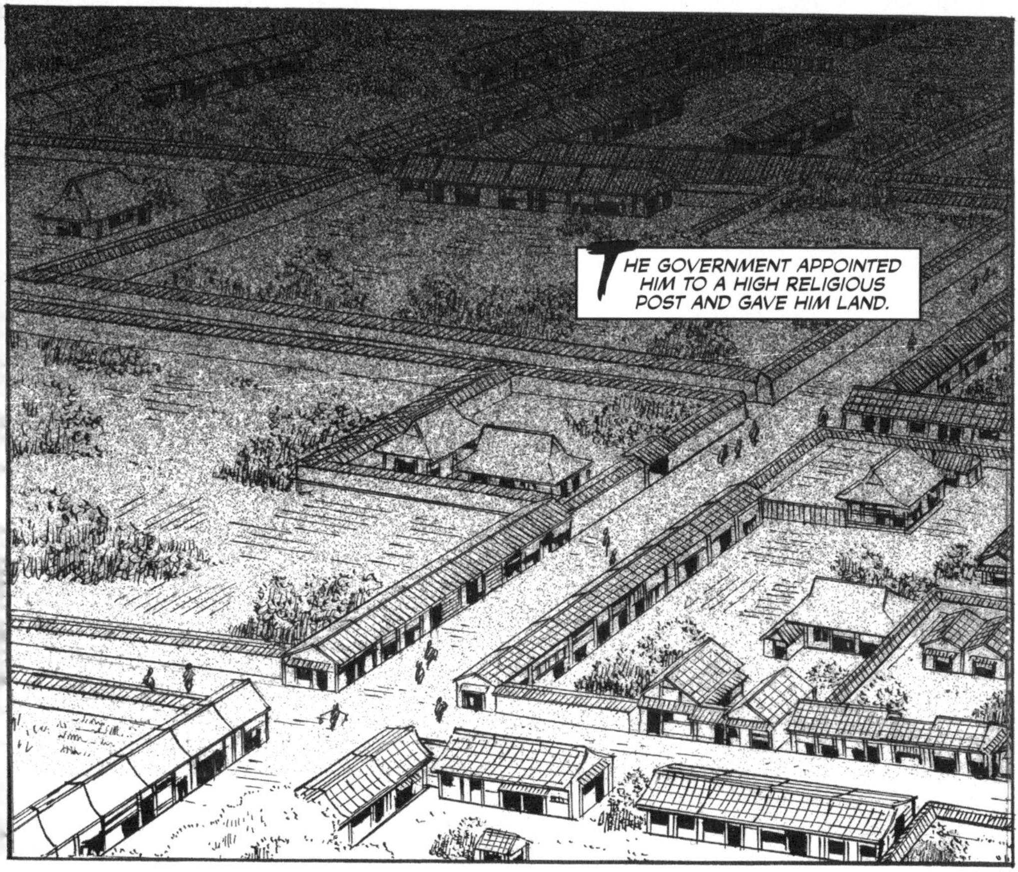
THE GOVERNMENT APPOINTED HIM TO A HIGH RELIGIOUS POST AND GAVE HIM LAND.

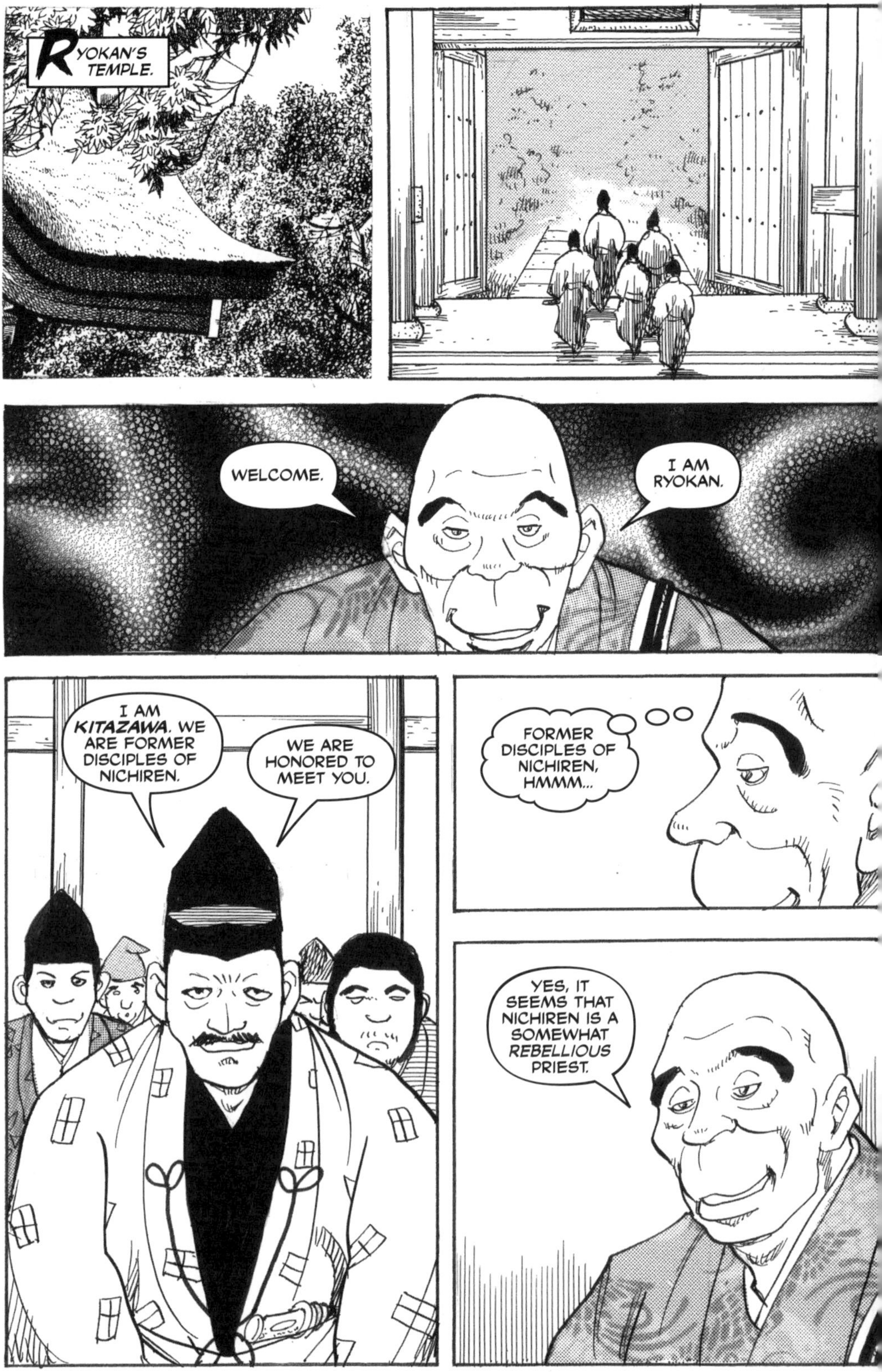
RYOKAN'S TEMPLE.
WELCOME.
I AM RYOKAN.
I AM *KITAZAWA*. WE ARE FORMER DISCIPLES OF NICHIREN.
WE ARE HONORED TO MEET YOU.
FORMER DISCIPLES OF NICHIREN, HMMM...
YES, IT SEEMS THAT NICHIREN IS A SOMEWHAT *REBELLIOUS* PRIEST.

BUT WHAT BRINGS YOU ALL HERE?

WE DON'T LIKE NICHIREN'S AGGRESSIVENESS AND WE HAVE DECIDED TO LEAVE HIM.

WE WOULD LIKE TO FOLLOW YOU FROM NOW ON. PLEASE ACCEPT US AS YOUR DISCIPLES.

BESIDES, WE KNOW NICHIREN'S WAYS VERY WELL.

WE THOUGHT WE COULD HELP.

I SEE...

THIS IS GETTING INTERESTING...

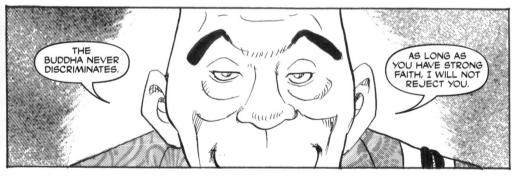

THE BUDDHA NEVER DISCRIMINATES.

AS LONG AS YOU HAVE STRONG FAITH, I WILL NOT REJECT YOU.

THANK YOU VERY MUCH.

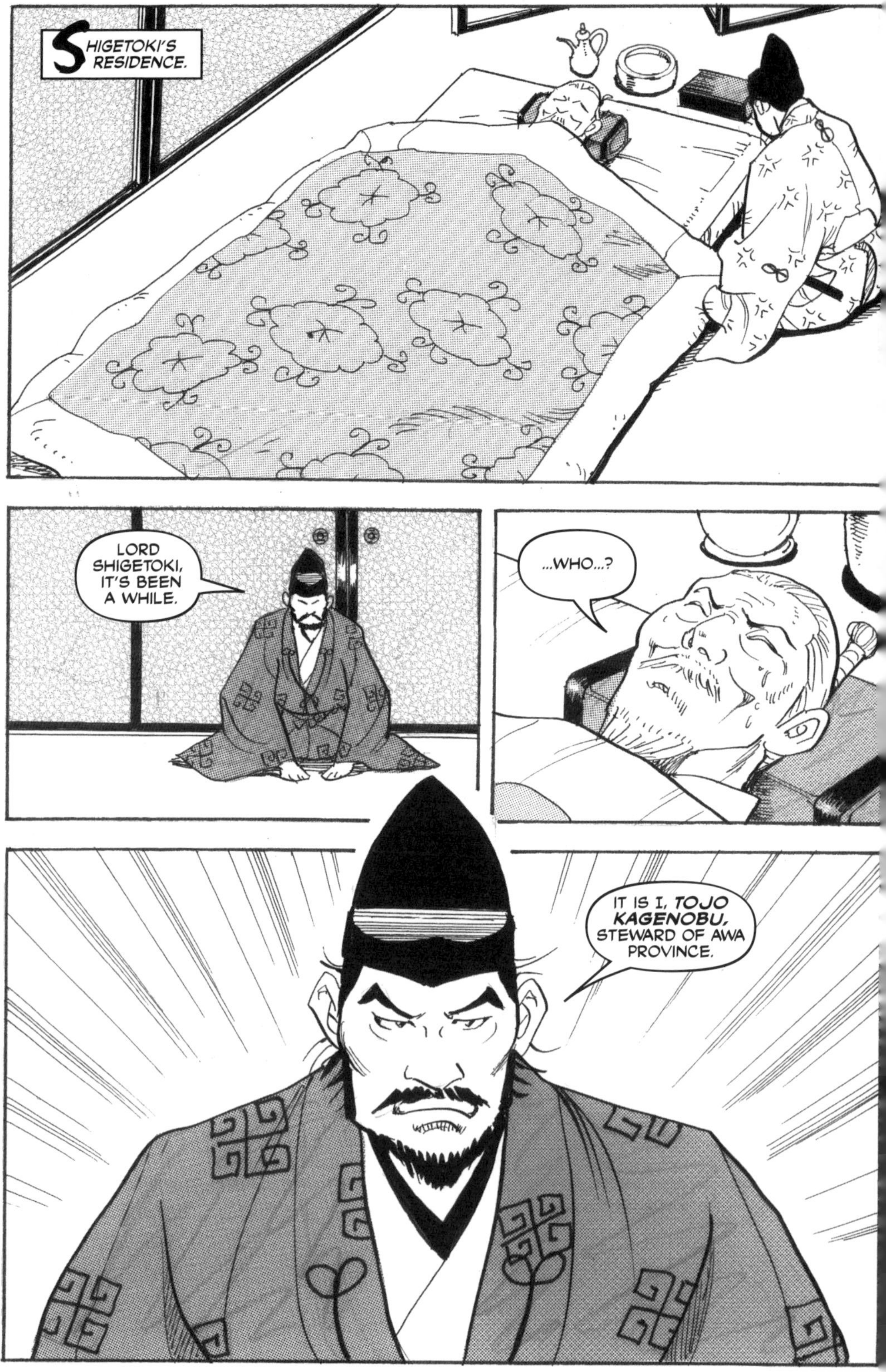
SHIGETOKI'S RESIDENCE.
LORD SHIGETOKI, IT'S BEEN A WHILE.
...WHO...?
IT IS I, TOJO KAGENOBU, STEWARD OF AWA PROVINCE.

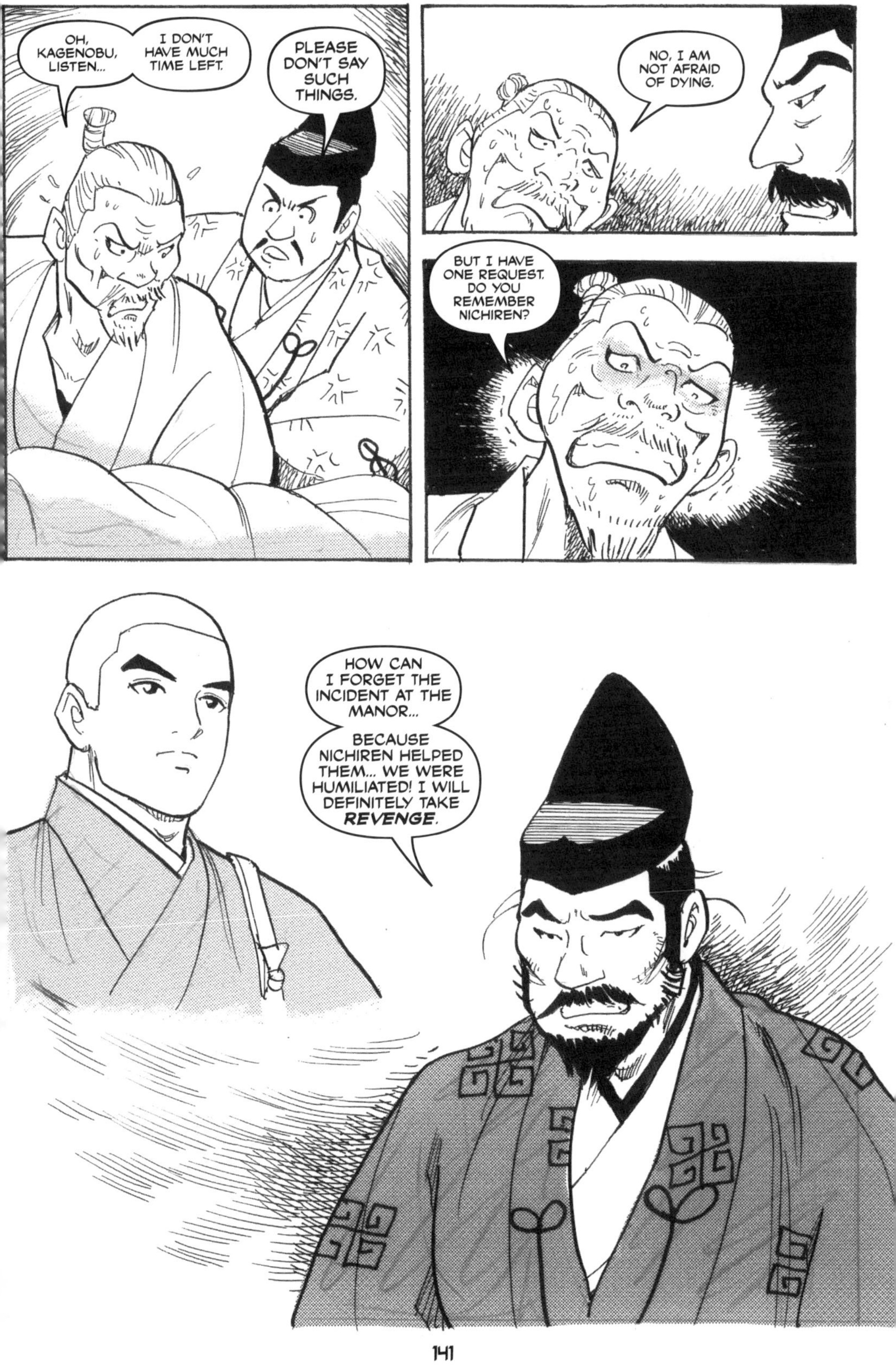
OH, KAGENOBU, LISTEN...
I DON'T HAVE MUCH TIME LEFT.
PLEASE DON'T SAY SUCH THINGS.
NO, I AM NOT AFRAID OF DYING.
BUT I HAVE ONE REQUEST. DO YOU REMEMBER NICHIREN?
HOW CAN I FORGET THE INCIDENT AT THE MANOR...
BECAUSE NICHIREN HELPED THEM... WE WERE HUMILIATED! I WILL DEFINITELY TAKE ***REVENGE***.

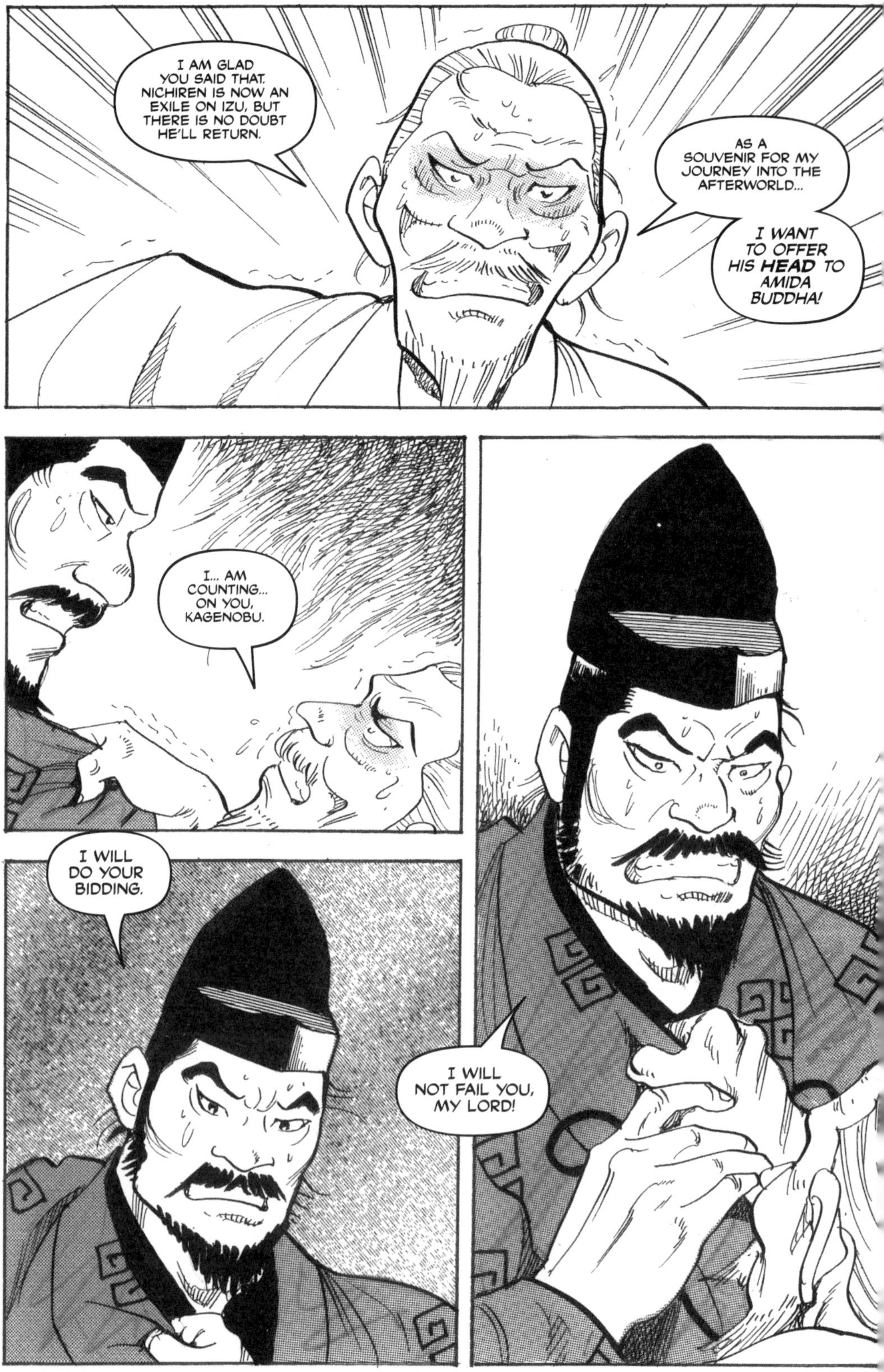
I AM GLAD YOU SAID THAT. NICHIREN IS NOW AN EXILE ON IZU, BUT THERE IS NO DOUBT HE'LL RETURN.
AS A SOUVENIR FOR MY JOURNEY INTO THE AFTERWORLD...
I WANT TO OFFER HIS **HEAD** TO AMIDA BUDDHA!
I... AM COUNTING... ON YOU, KAGENOBU.
I WILL DO YOUR BIDDING.
I WILL NOT FAIL YOU, MY LORD!

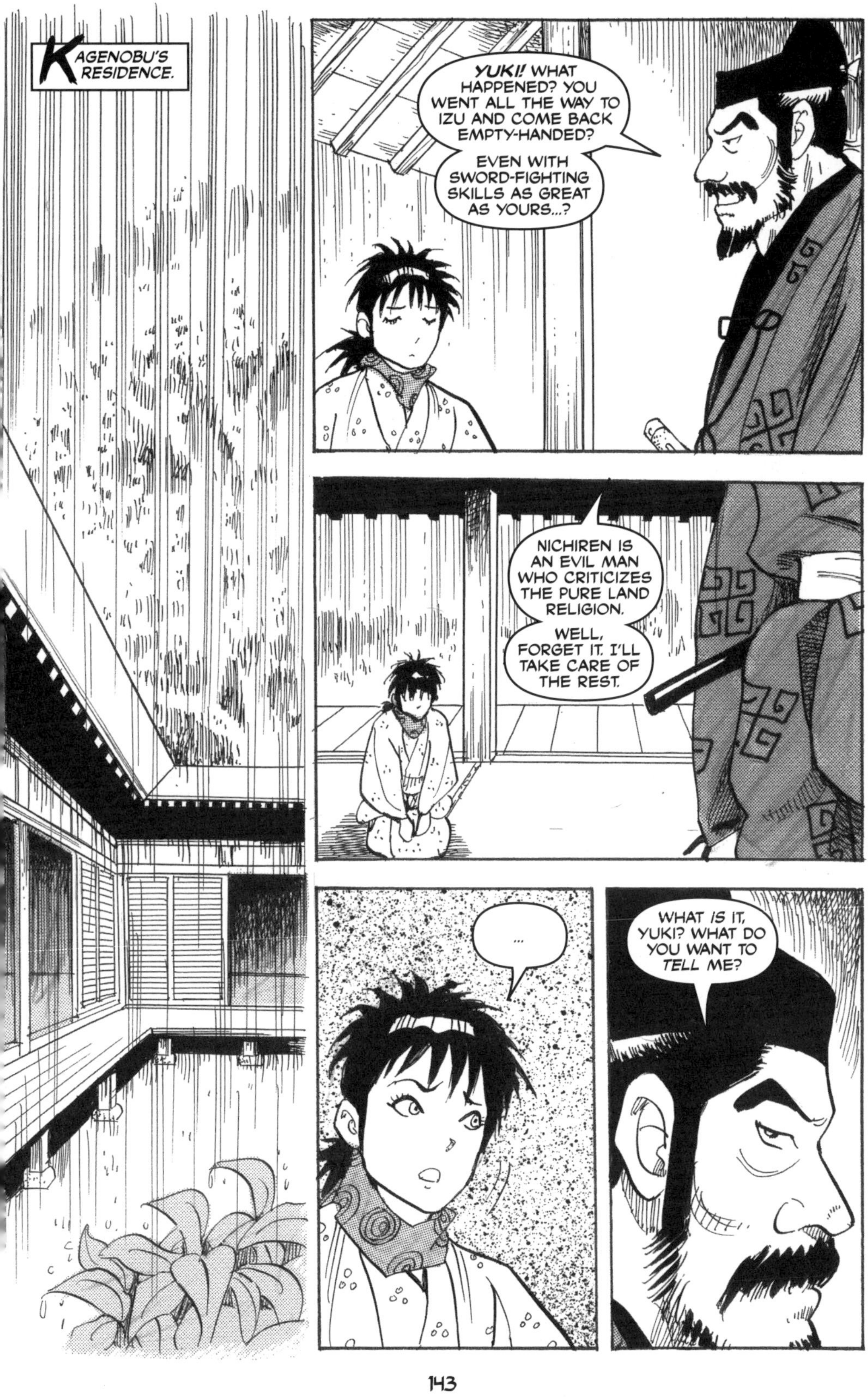
KAGENOBU'S RESIDENCE.
YUKI! WHAT HAPPENED? YOU WENT ALL THE WAY TO IZU AND COME BACK EMPTY-HANDED?
EVEN WITH SWORD-FIGHTING SKILLS AS GREAT AS YOURS...?
NICHIREN IS AN EVIL MAN WHO CRITICIZES THE PURE LAND RELIGION.
WELL, FORGET IT. I'LL TAKE CARE OF THE REST.
...
WHAT IS IT, YUKI? WHAT DO YOU WANT TO TELL ME?

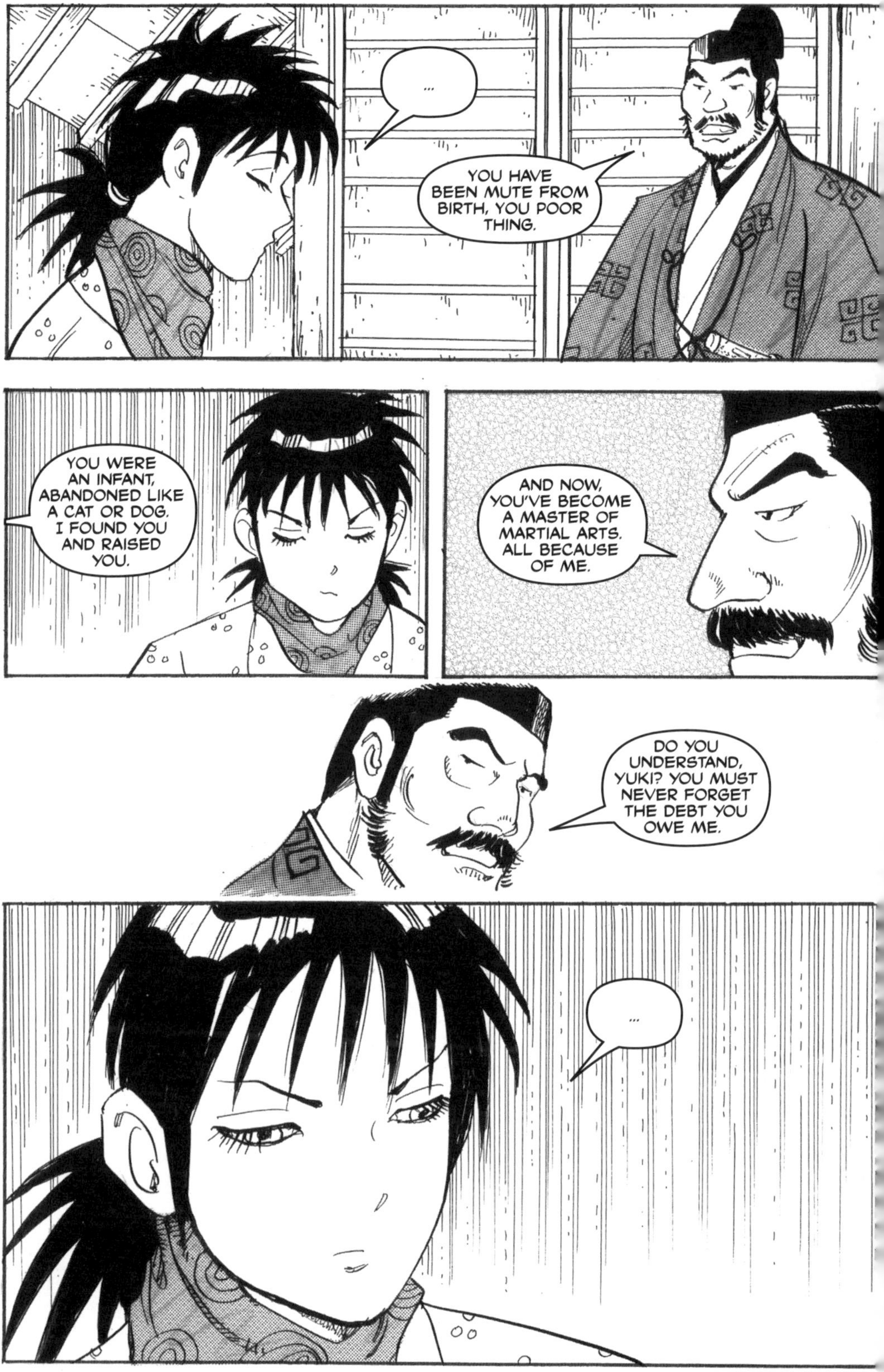
...
YOU HAVE BEEN MUTE FROM BIRTH, YOU POOR THING.
YOU WERE AN INFANT, ABANDONED LIKE A CAT OR DOG. I FOUND YOU AND RAISED YOU.
AND NOW, YOU'VE BECOME A MASTER OF MARTIAL ARTS. ALL BECAUSE OF ME.
DO YOU UNDERSTAND, YUKI? YOU MUST NEVER FORGET THE DEBT YOU OWE ME.
...

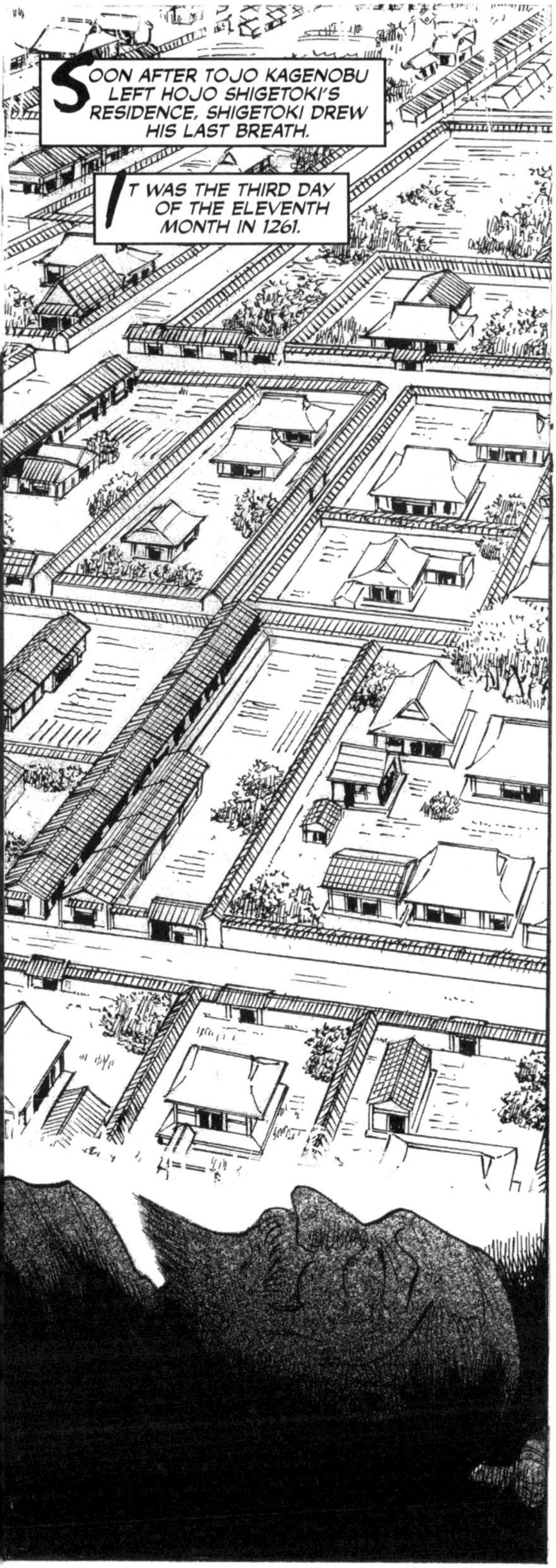
SOON AFTER TOJO KAGENOBU LEFT HOJO SHIGETOKI'S RESIDENCE, SHIGETOKI DREW HIS LAST BREATH.
IT WAS THE THIRD DAY OF THE ELEVENTH MONTH IN 1261.
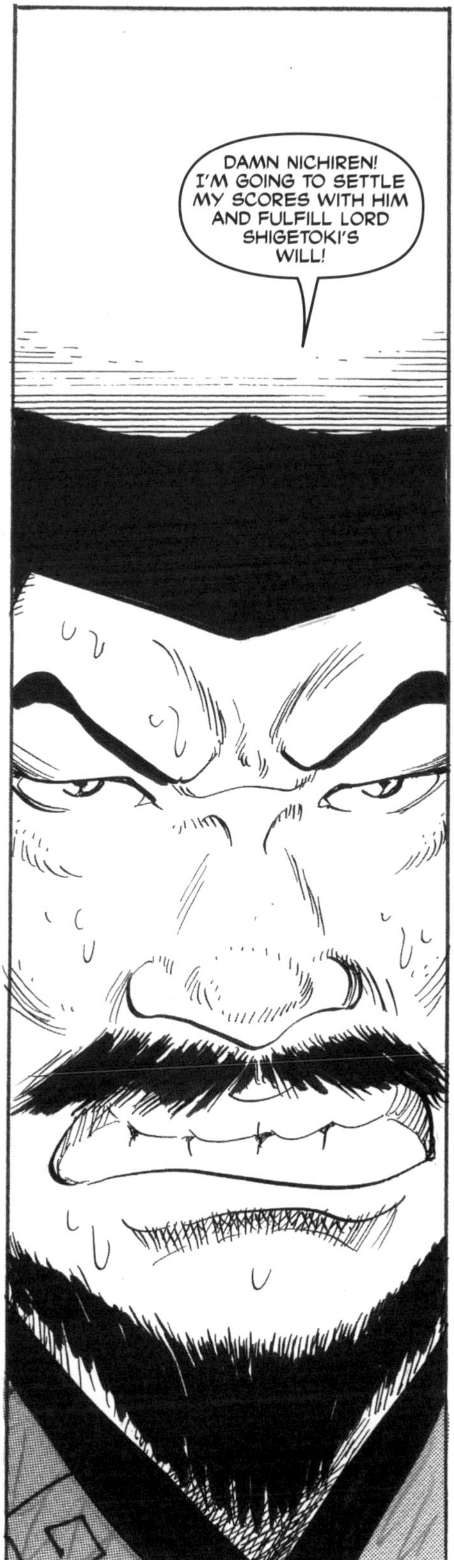
DAMN NICHIREN! I'M GOING TO SETTLE MY SCORES WITH HIM AND FULFILL LORD SHIGETOKI'S WILL!

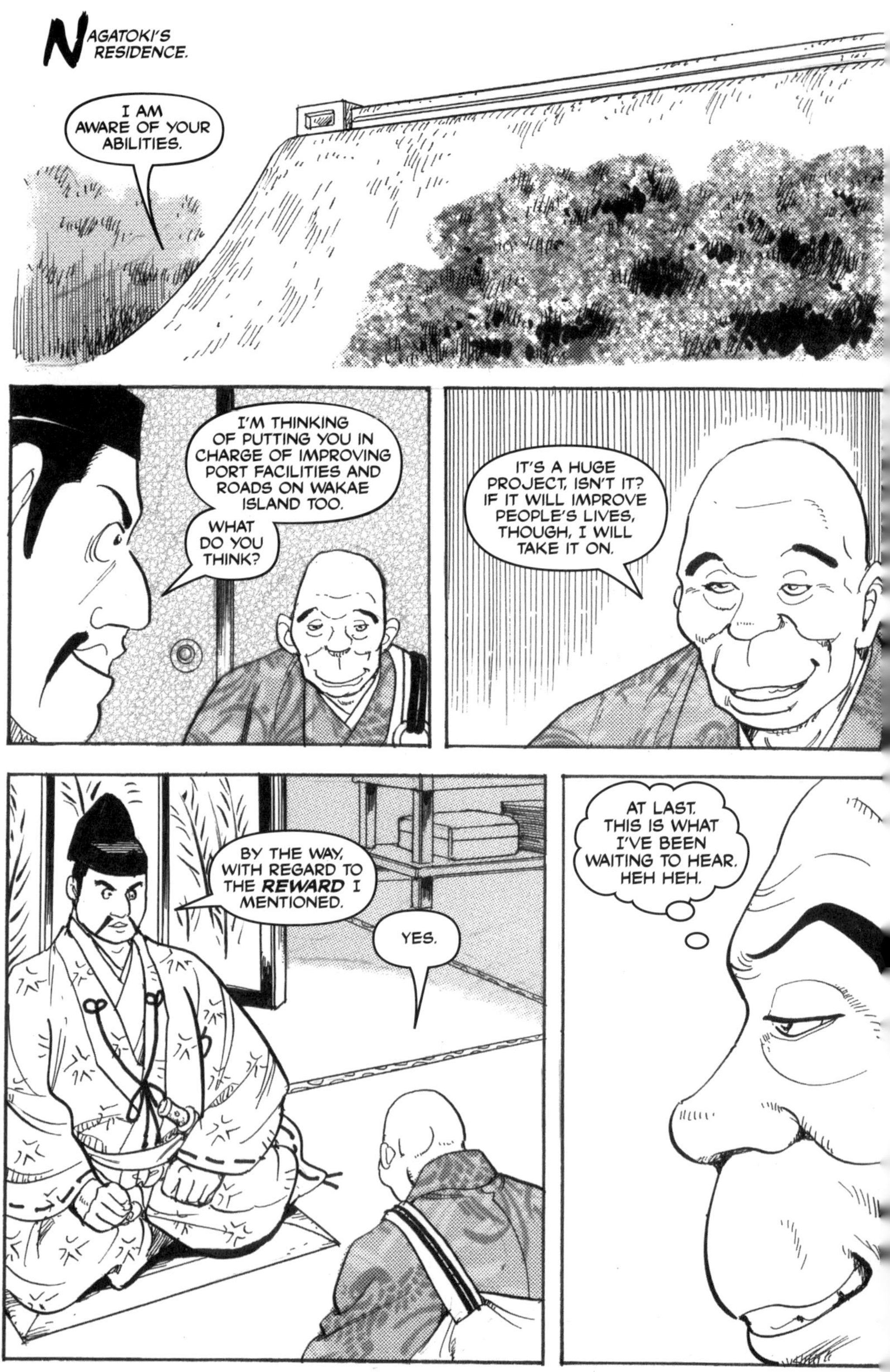
NAGATOKI'S RESIDENCE.
I AM AWARE OF YOUR ABILITIES.
I'M THINKING OF PUTTING YOU IN CHARGE OF IMPROVING PORT FACILITIES AND ROADS ON WAKAE ISLAND TOO.
WHAT DO YOU THINK?
IT'S A HUGE PROJECT, ISN'T IT? IF IT WILL IMPROVE PEOPLE'S LIVES, THOUGH, I WILL TAKE IT ON.
BY THE WAY, WITH REGARD TO THE REWARD I MENTIONED.
YES.
AT LAST. THIS IS WHAT I'VE BEEN WAITING TO HEAR. HEH HEH.

I'M THINKING ABOUT GRANTING YOU AUTHORITY TO COLLECT TOLLS. HOW DO YOU LIKE THAT?

IT'S MUCH MORE THAN I DESERVE. BUT I WILL ACCEPT THIS PRIVILEGE AS THE BUDDHA'S WILL.

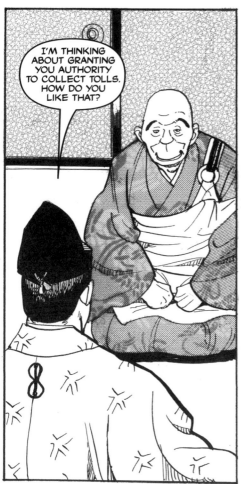

HMPH, YOU CONNIVING MONK.

BY THE WAY, WHAT HAPPENED TO THAT PRIEST CALLED NICHIREN?

HE WAS EXILED TO IZU. THANKS TO THAT, KAMAKURA IS CALM AGAIN.

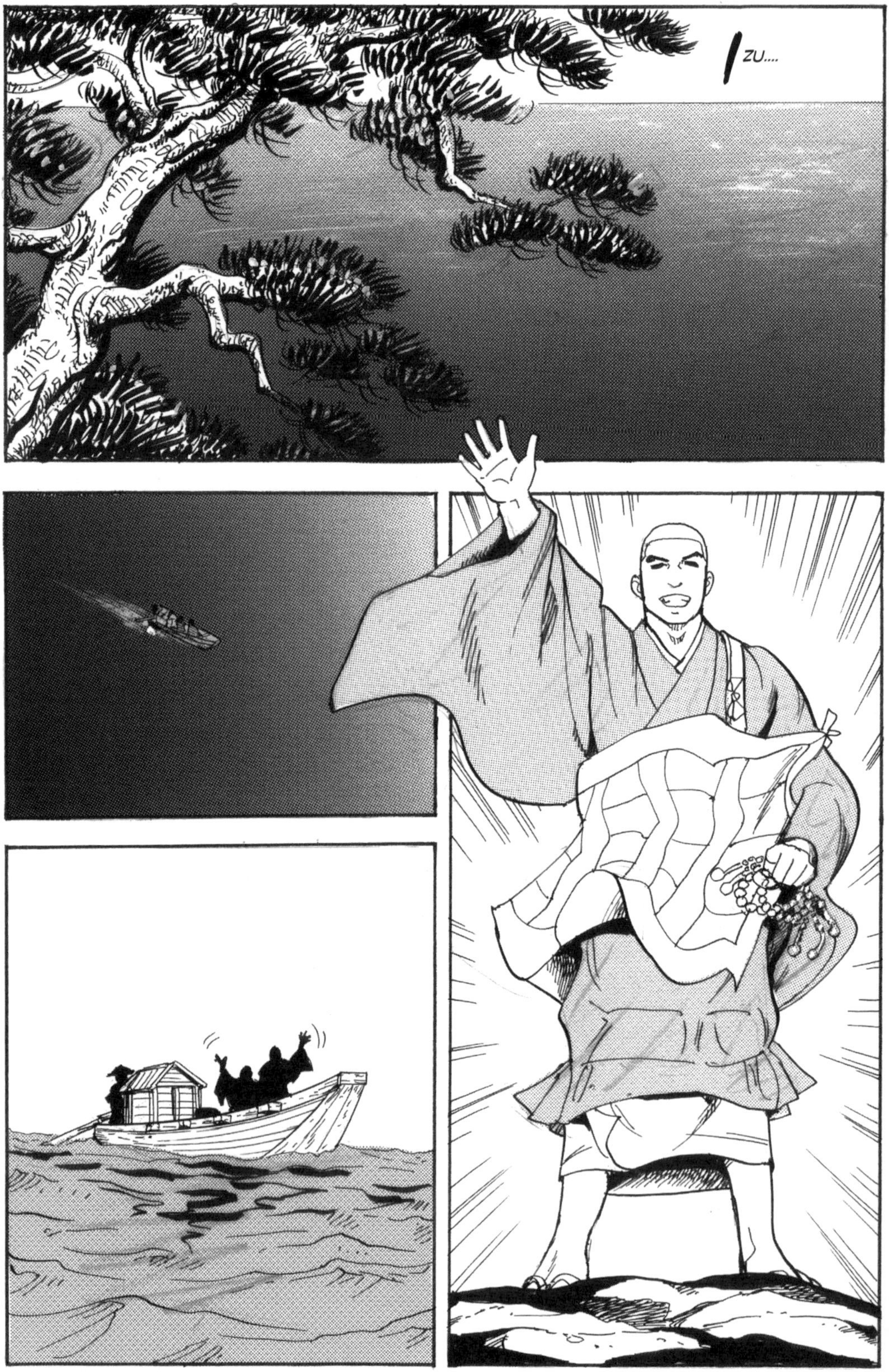
IZU....

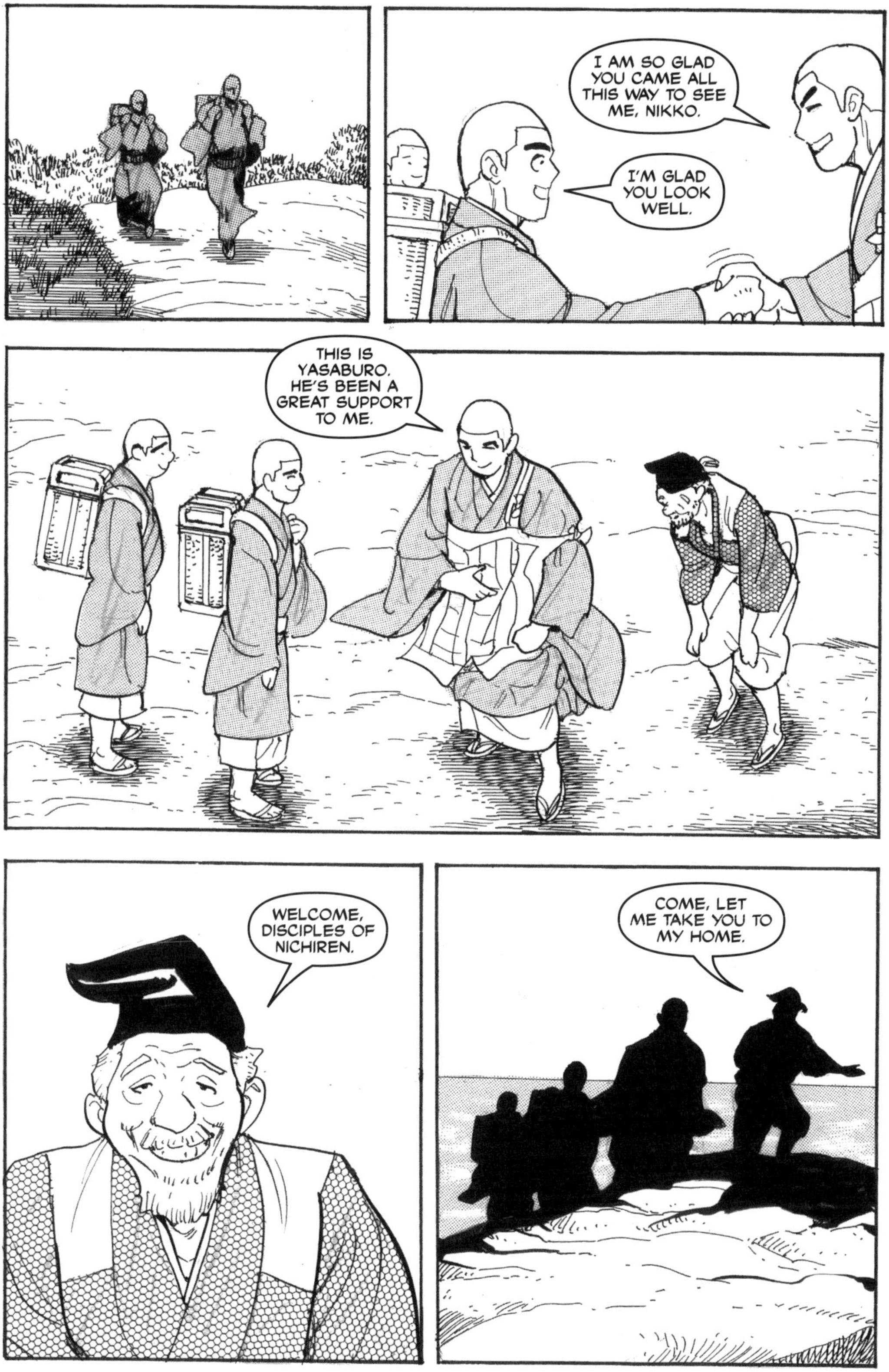
I AM SO GLAD YOU CAME ALL THIS WAY TO SEE ME, NIKKO.
I'M GLAD YOU LOOK WELL.
THIS IS YASABURO. HE'S BEEN A GREAT SUPPORT TO ME.
WELCOME, DISCIPLES OF NICHIREN.
COME, LET ME TAKE YOU TO MY HOME.

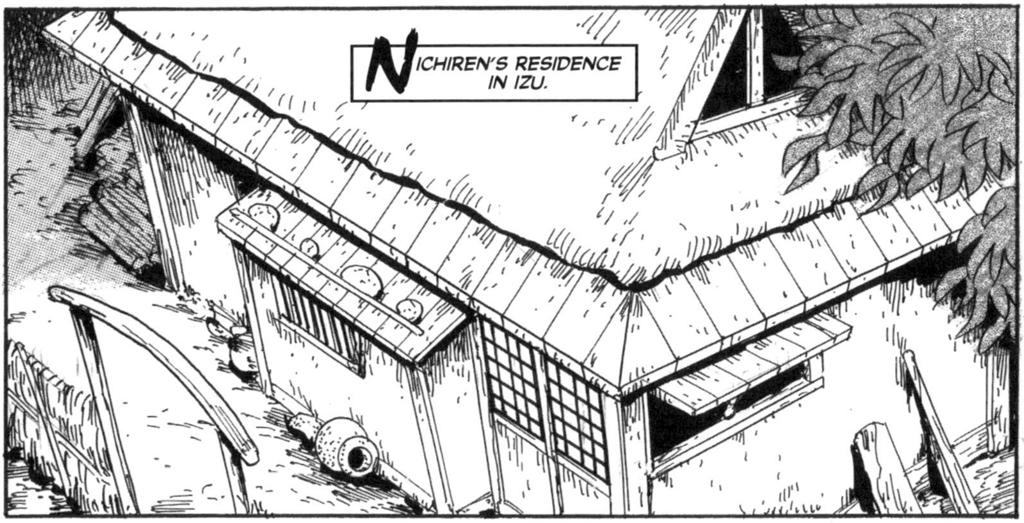
NICHIREN'S RESIDENCE IN IZU.

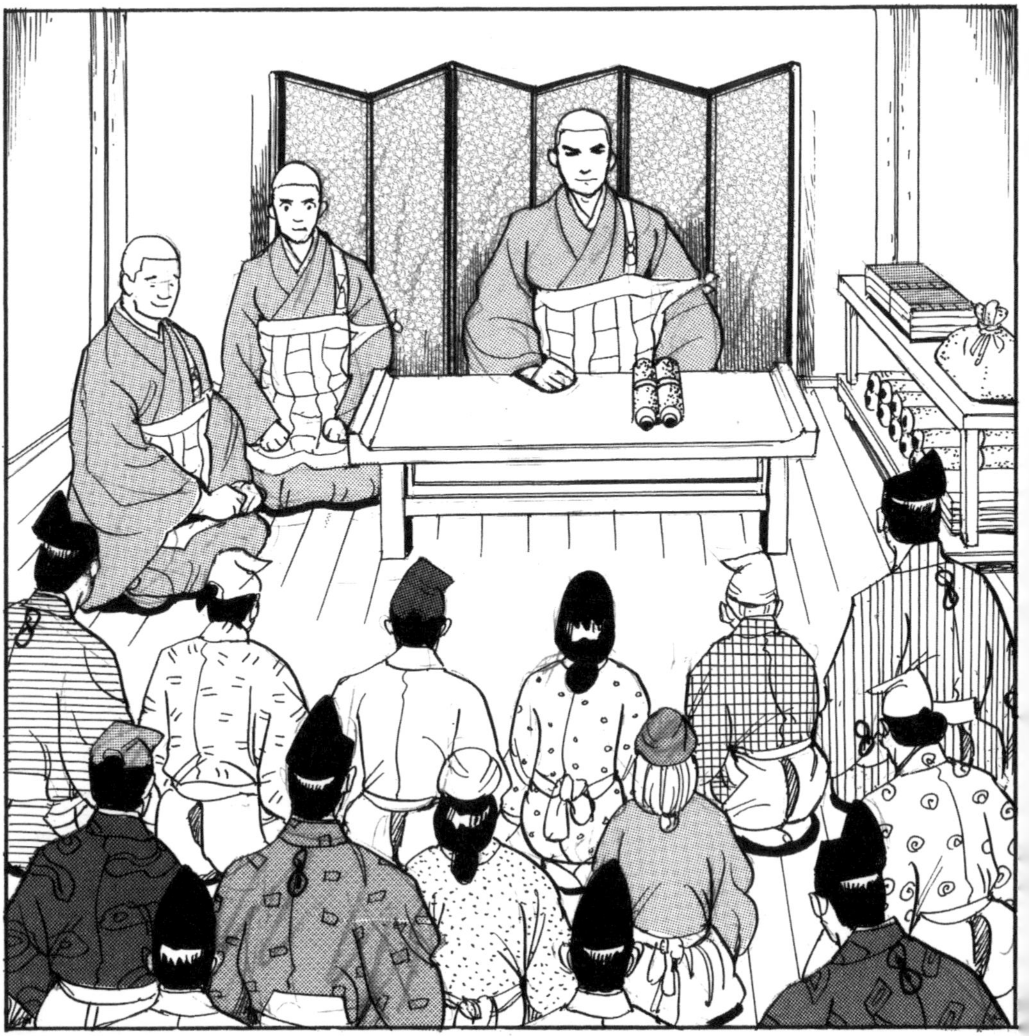

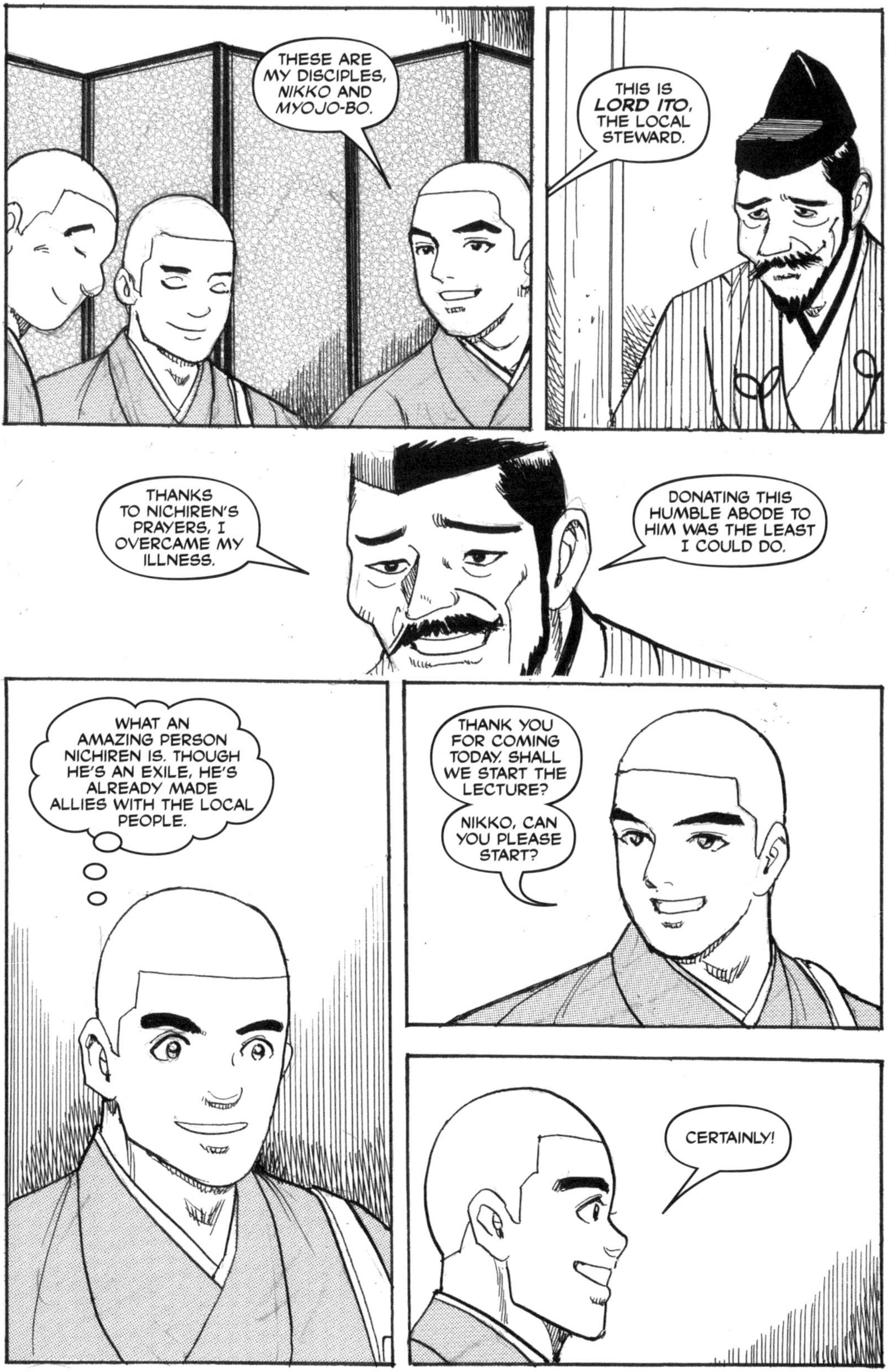
THESE ARE MY DISCIPLES, *NIKKO* AND *MYOJO-BO*.
THIS IS ***LORD ITO***, THE LOCAL STEWARD.
THANKS TO NICHIREN'S PRAYERS, I OVERCAME MY ILLNESS.
DONATING THIS HUMBLE ABODE TO HIM WAS THE LEAST I COULD DO.
WHAT AN AMAZING PERSON NICHIREN IS. THOUGH HE'S AN EXILE, HE'S ALREADY MADE ALLIES WITH THE LOCAL PEOPLE.
THANK YOU FOR COMING TODAY. SHALL WE START THE LECTURE?
NIKKO, CAN YOU PLEASE START?
CERTAINLY!

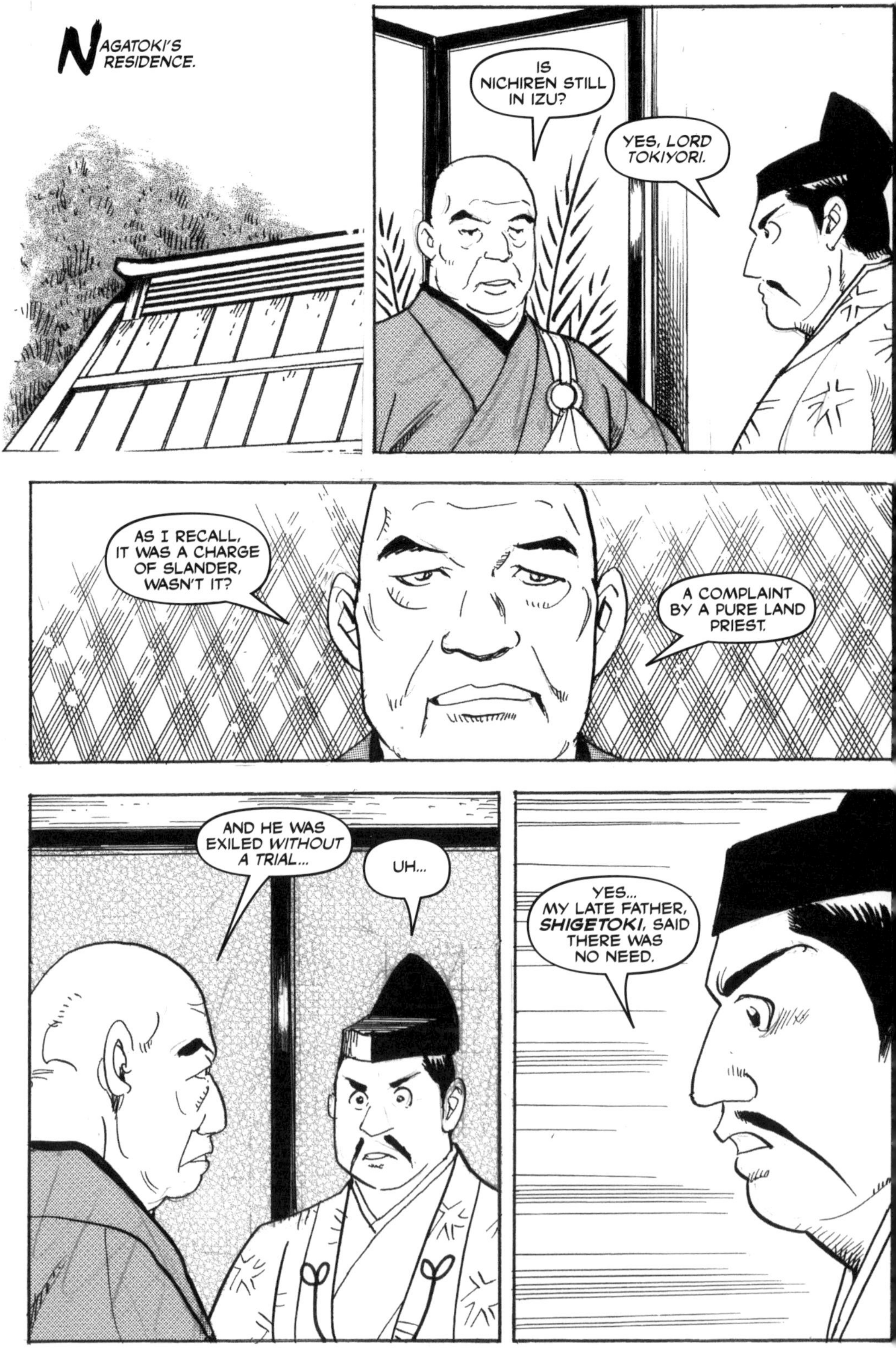
NAGATOKI'S RESIDENCE.
IS NICHIREN STILL IN IZU?
YES, LORD TOKIYORI.
AS I RECALL, IT WAS A CHARGE OF SLANDER, WASN'T IT?
A COMPLAINT BY A PURE LAND PRIEST.
AND HE WAS EXILED *WITHOUT* A TRIAL...
UH...
YES... MY LATE FATHER, **SHIGETOKI**, SAID THERE WAS NO NEED.

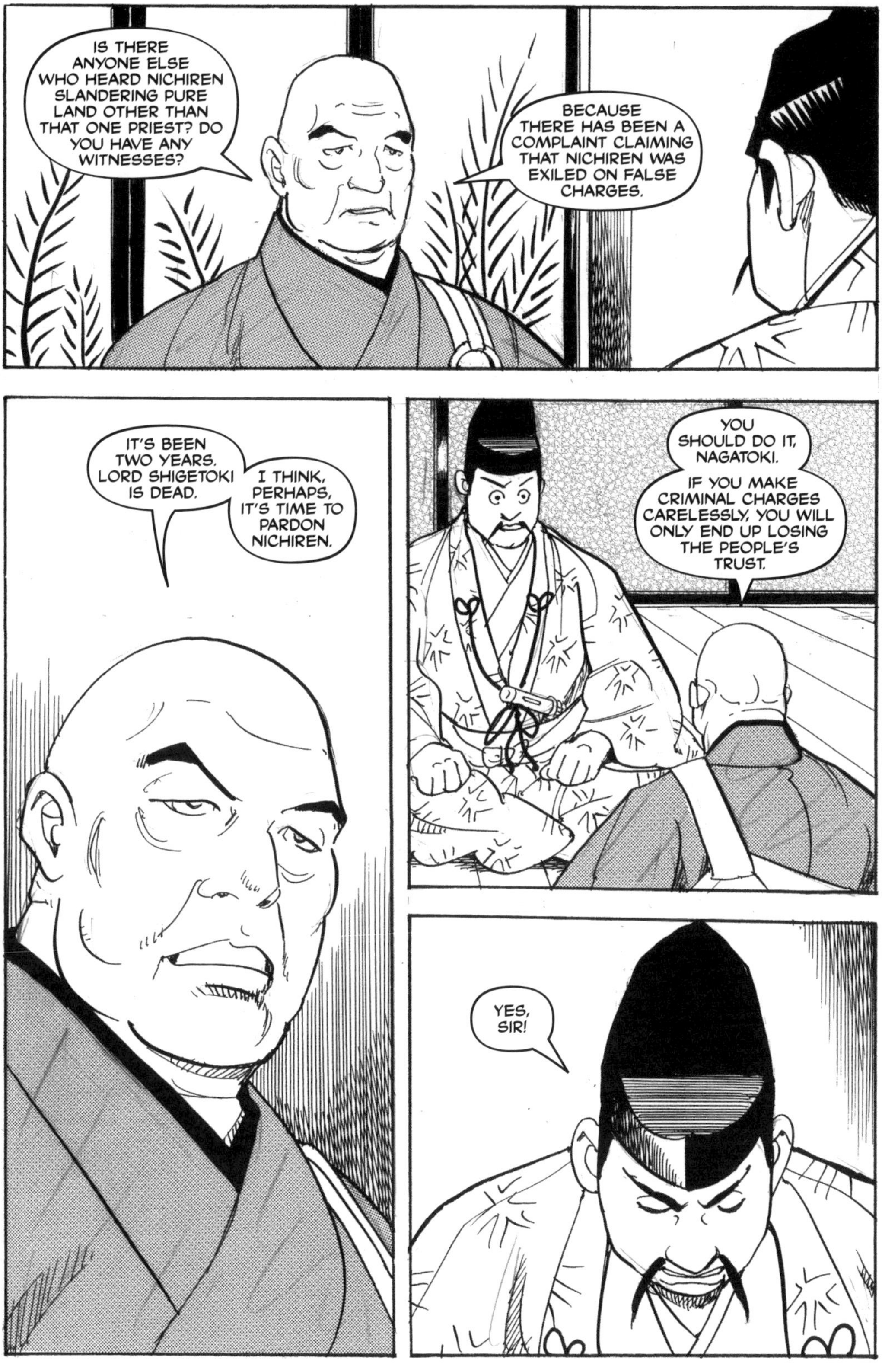
IS THERE ANYONE ELSE WHO HEARD NICHIREN SLANDERING PURE LAND OTHER THAN THAT ONE PRIEST? DO YOU HAVE ANY WITNESSES?
BECAUSE THERE HAS BEEN A COMPLAINT CLAIMING THAT NICHIREN WAS EXILED ON FALSE CHARGES.
IT'S BEEN TWO YEARS. LORD SHIGETOKI IS DEAD.
I THINK, PERHAPS, IT'S TIME TO PARDON NICHIREN.
YOU SHOULD DO IT, NAGATOKI.
IF YOU MAKE CRIMINAL CHARGES CARELESSLY, YOU WILL ONLY END UP LOSING THE PEOPLE'S TRUST.
YES, SIR!

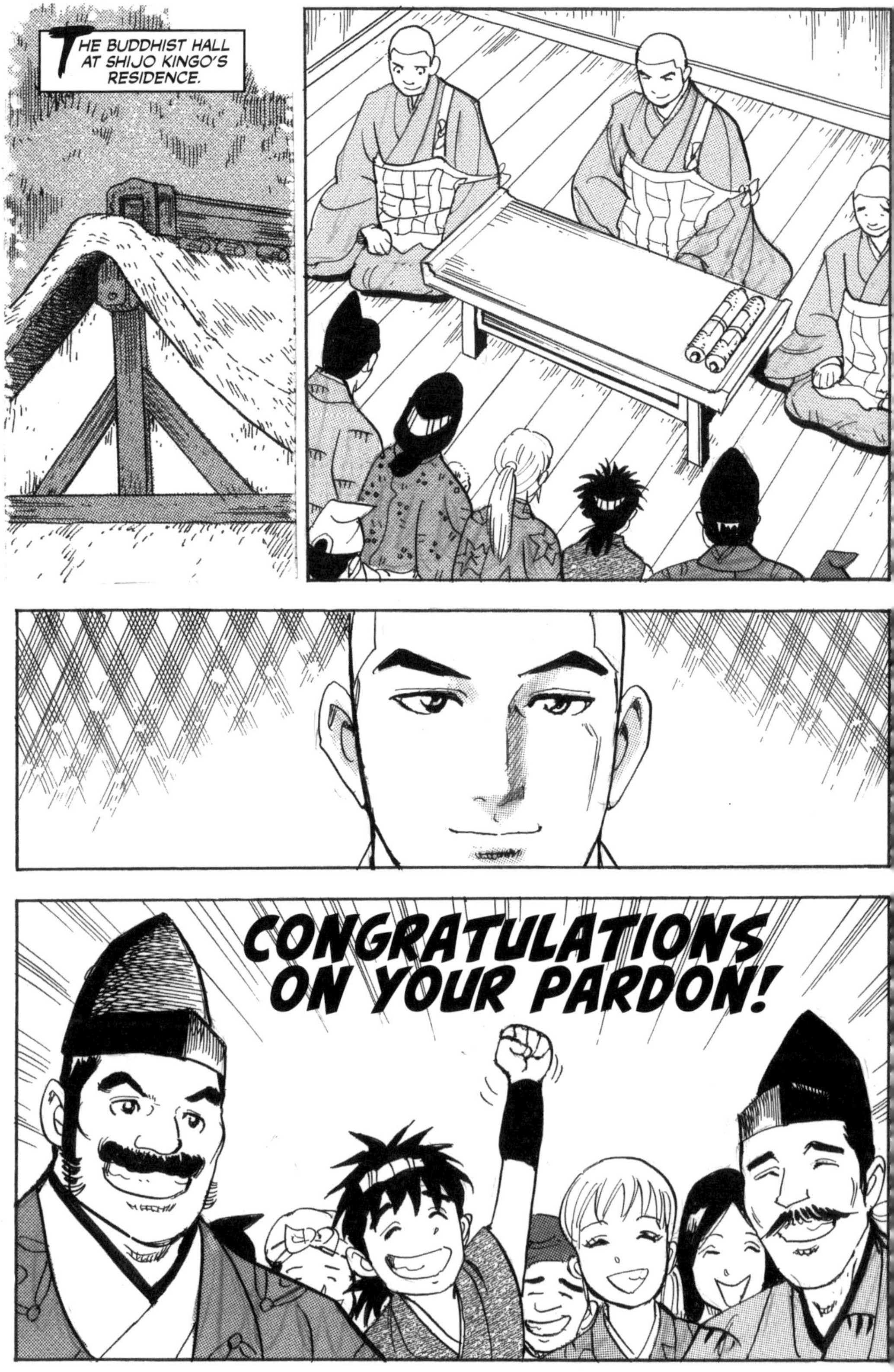
THE BUDDHIST HALL AT SHIJO KINGO'S RESIDENCE.
CONGRATULATIONS ON YOUR PARDON!

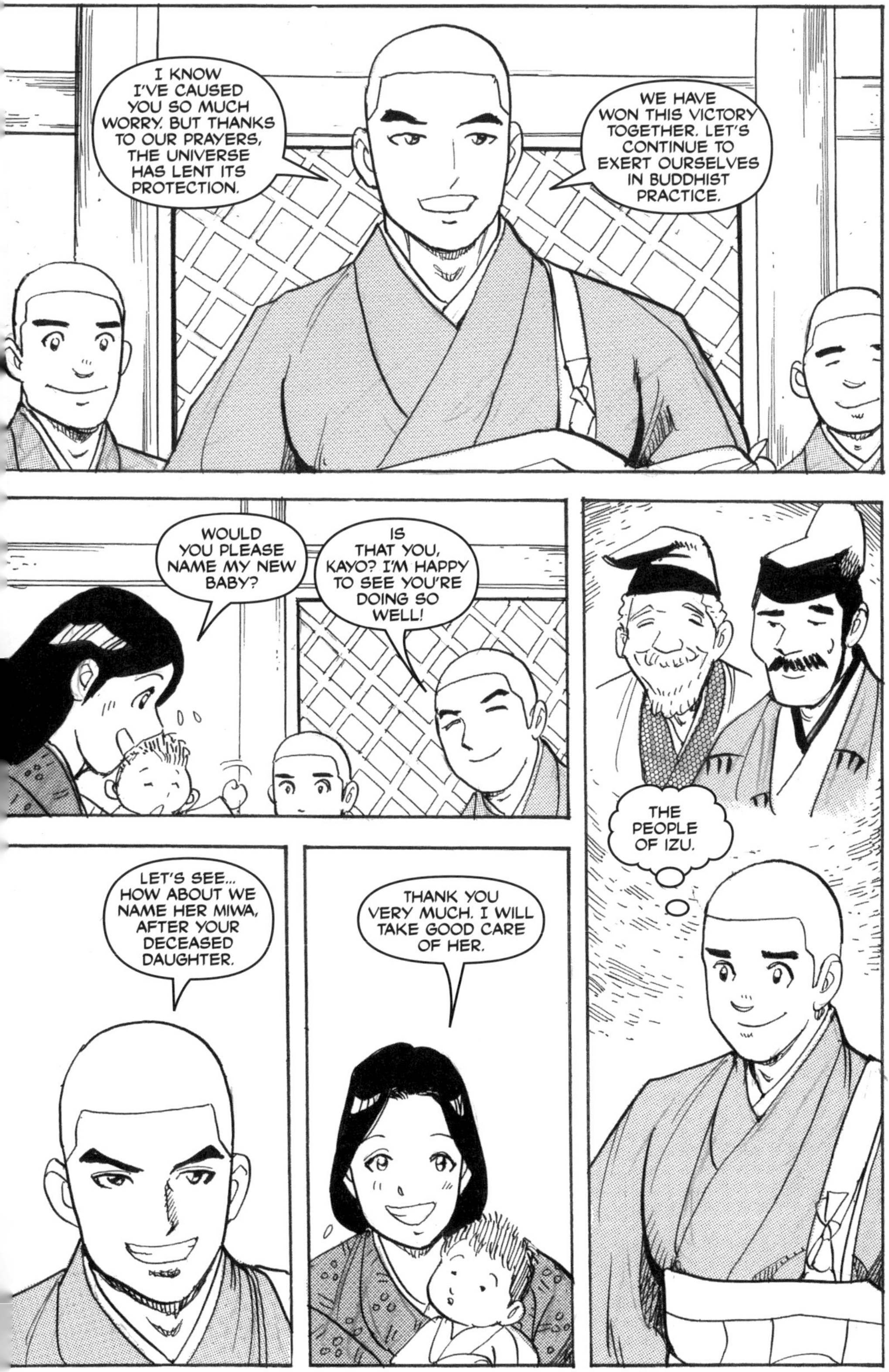
I KNOW I'VE CAUSED YOU SO MUCH WORRY. BUT THANKS TO OUR PRAYERS, THE UNIVERSE HAS LENT ITS PROTECTION.
WE HAVE WON THIS VICTORY TOGETHER. LET'S CONTINUE TO EXERT OURSELVES IN BUDDHIST PRACTICE.
WOULD YOU PLEASE NAME MY NEW BABY?
IS THAT YOU, KAYO? I'M HAPPY TO SEE YOU'RE DOING SO WELL!
THE PEOPLE OF IZU.
LET'S SEE... HOW ABOUT WE NAME HER MIWA, AFTER YOUR DECEASED DAUGHTER.
THANK YOU VERY MUCH. I WILL TAKE GOOD CARE OF HER.

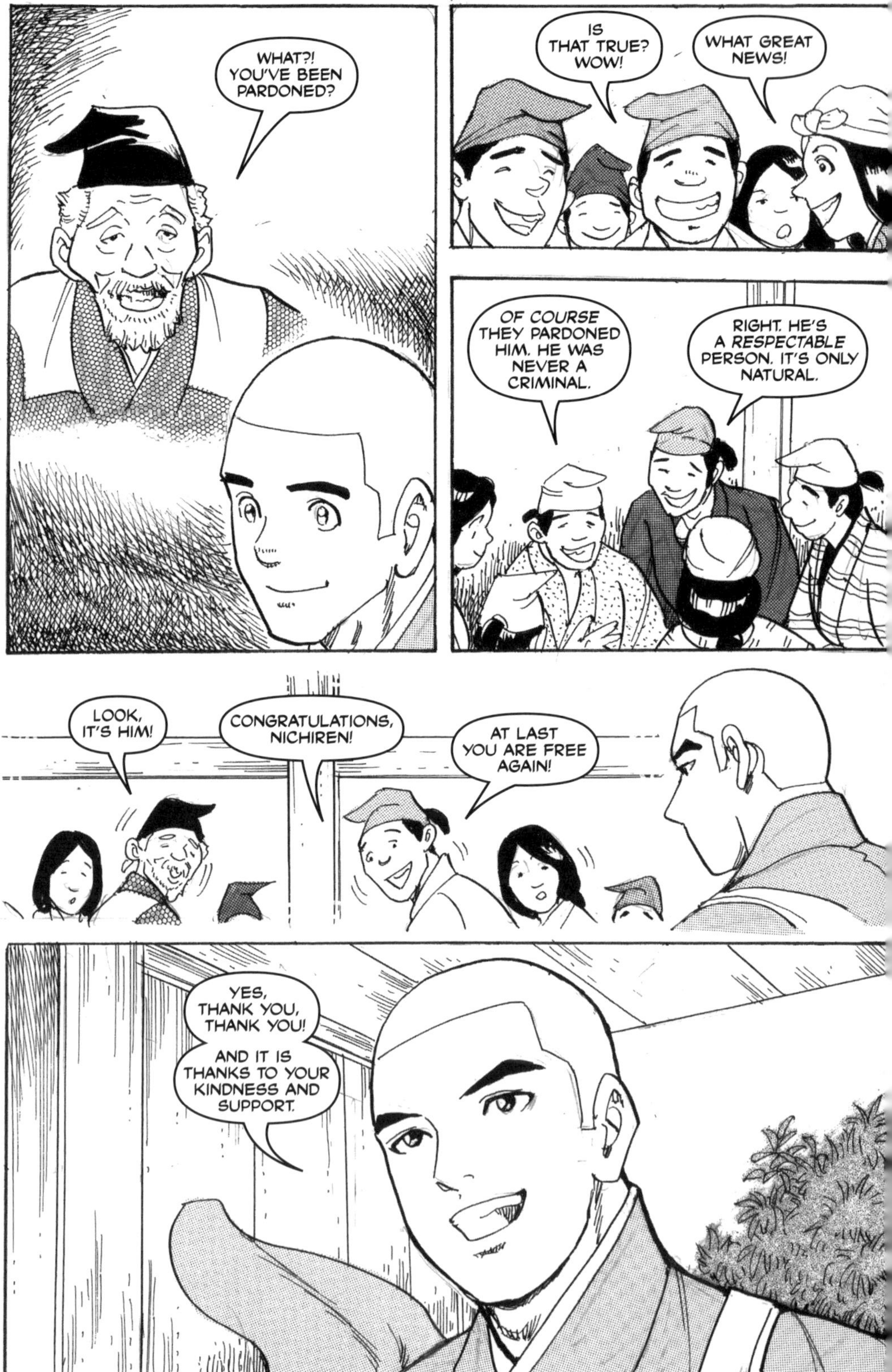
WHAT?! YOU'VE BEEN PARDONED?
IS THAT TRUE? WOW!
WHAT GREAT NEWS!
OF COURSE THEY PARDONED HIM. HE WAS NEVER A CRIMINAL.
RIGHT. HE'S A *RESPECTABLE* PERSON. IT'S ONLY NATURAL.
LOOK, IT'S HIM!
CONGRATULATIONS, NICHIREN!
AT LAST YOU ARE FREE AGAIN!
YES, THANK YOU, THANK YOU!
AND IT IS THANKS TO YOUR KINDNESS AND SUPPORT.

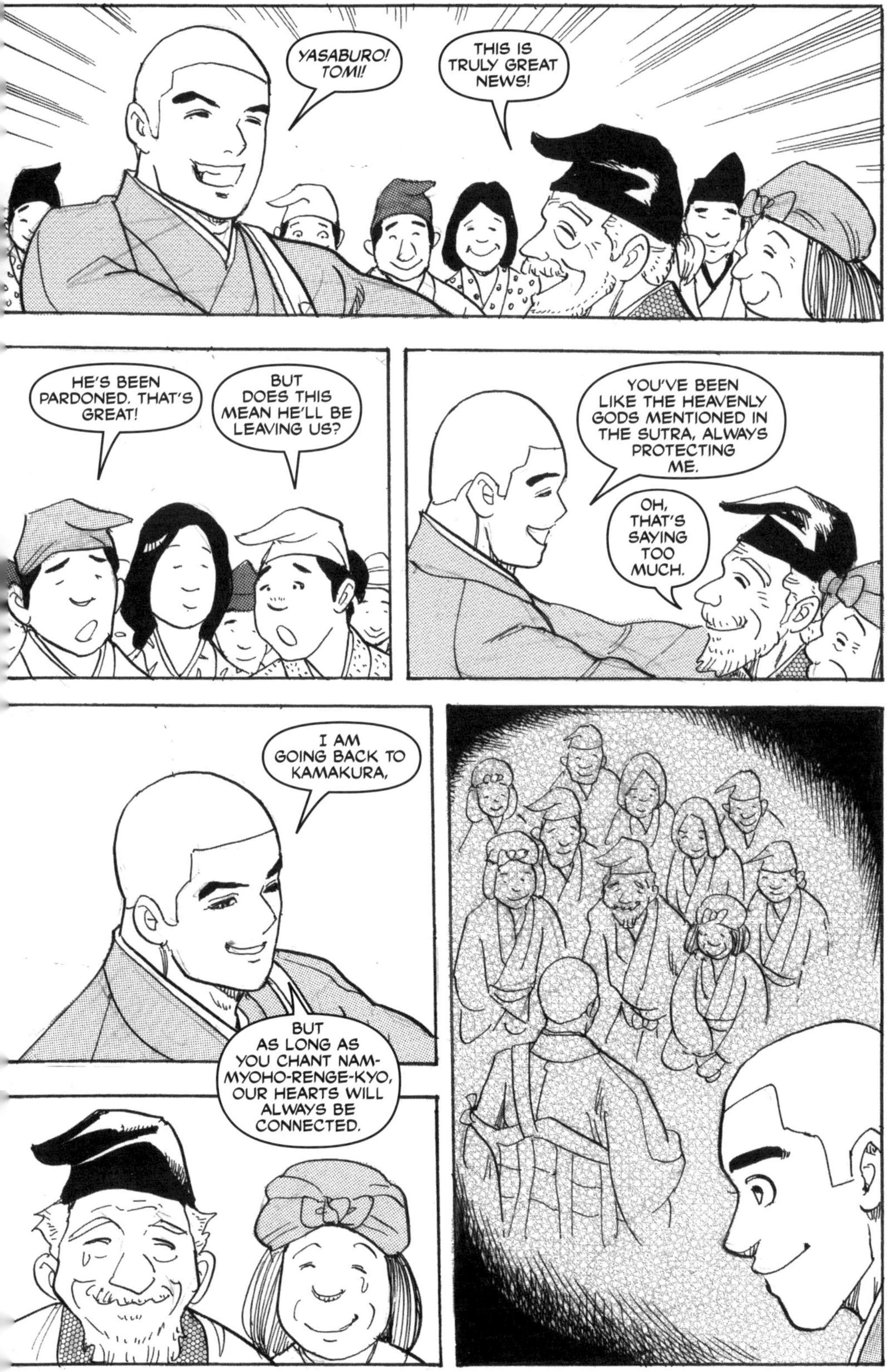
YASABURO! TOMI!
THIS IS TRULY GREAT NEWS!
HE'S BEEN PARDONED. THAT'S GREAT!
BUT DOES THIS MEAN HE'LL BE LEAVING US?
YOU'VE BEEN LIKE THE HEAVENLY GODS MENTIONED IN THE SUTRA, ALWAYS PROTECTING ME.
OH, THAT'S SAYING TOO MUCH.
I AM GOING BACK TO KAMAKURA,
BUT AS LONG AS YOU CHANT NAM-MYOHO-RENGE-KYO, OUR HEARTS WILL ALWAYS BE CONNECTED.

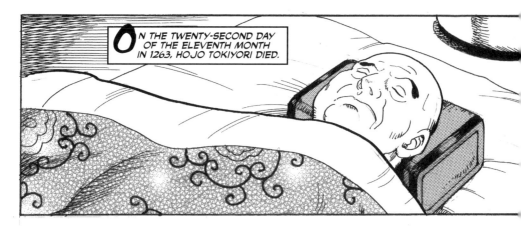

ON THE TWENTY-SECOND DAY OF THE ELEVENTH MONTH IN 1263, HOJO TOKIYORI DIED.

WHAT A BIG SHOOTING STAR THAT IS...

I HOPE IT'S NOT A BAD OMEN.

ON THE TWENTY-FIRST DAY OF THE EIGHTH MONTH OF THE FOLLOWING YEAR, IN 1264, HOJO NAGATOKI DIED.

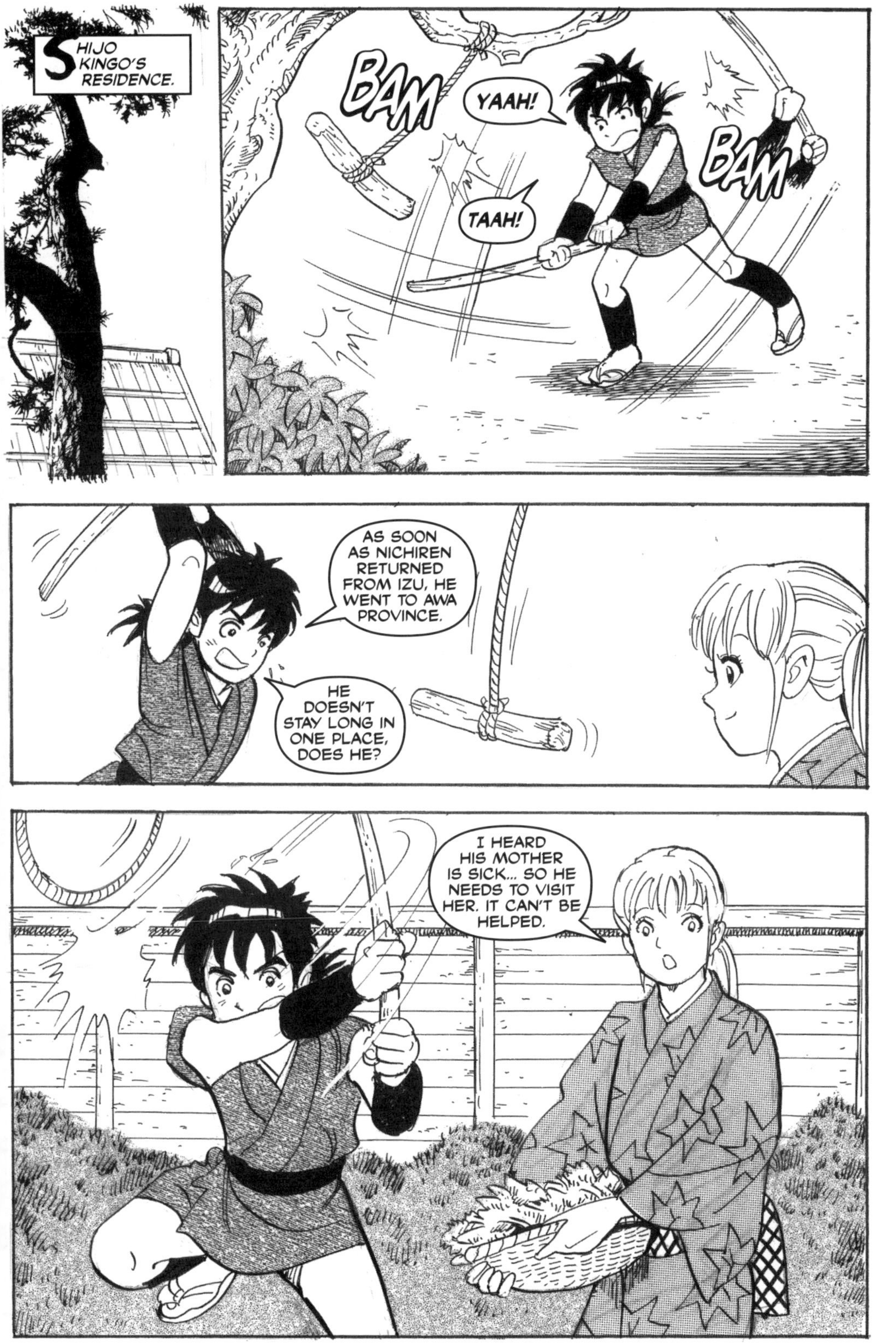
SHIJO KINGO'S RESIDENCE.
BAM
YAAH!
BAM
TAAH!
AS SOON AS NICHIREN RETURNED FROM IZU, HE WENT TO AWA PROVINCE.
HE DOESN'T STAY LONG IN ONE PLACE, DOES HE?
I HEARD HIS MOTHER IS SICK... SO HE NEEDS TO VISIT HER. IT CAN'T BE HELPED.

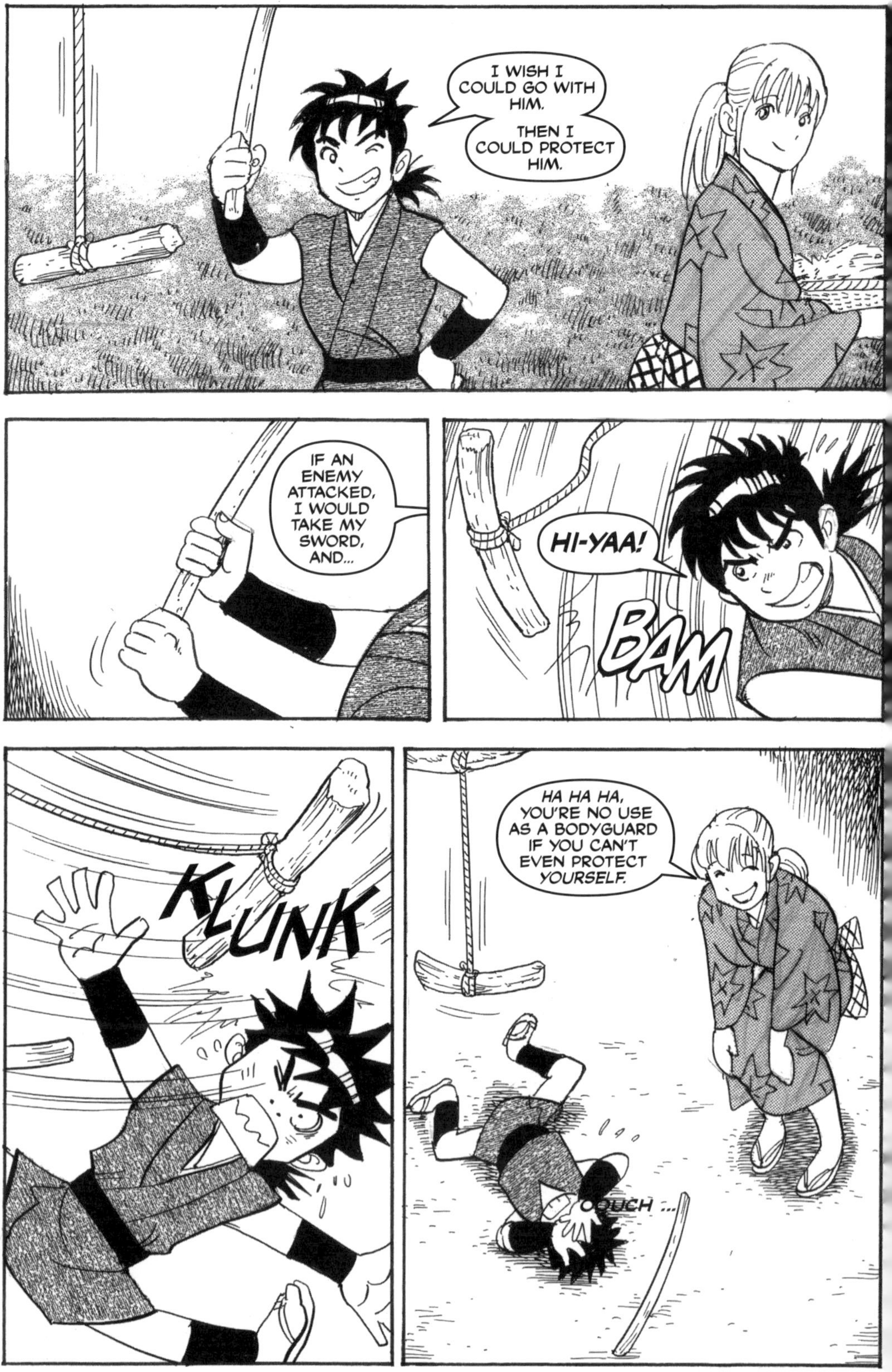
I WISH I COULD GO WITH HIM.
THEN I COULD PROTECT HIM.
IF AN ENEMY ATTACKED, I WOULD TAKE MY SWORD, AND...
HI-YAA!
BAM
KLUNK
HA HA HA, YOU'RE NO USE AS A BODYGUARD IF YOU CAN'T EVEN PROTECT *YOURSELF*.
OOUCH ...

AWA PROVINCE.

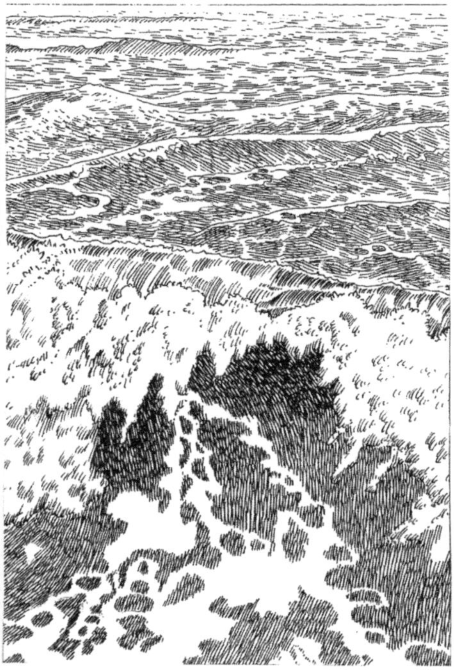

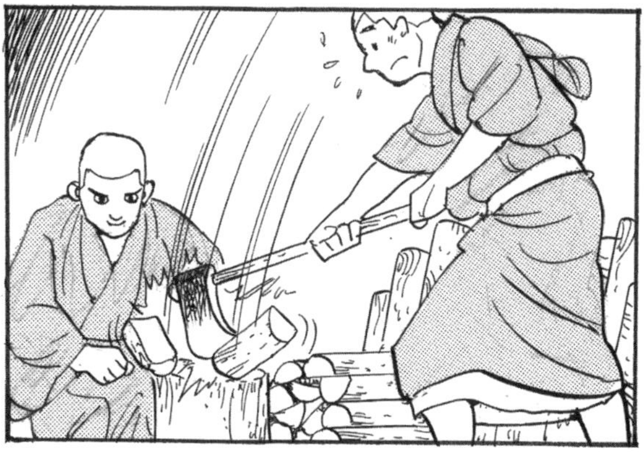

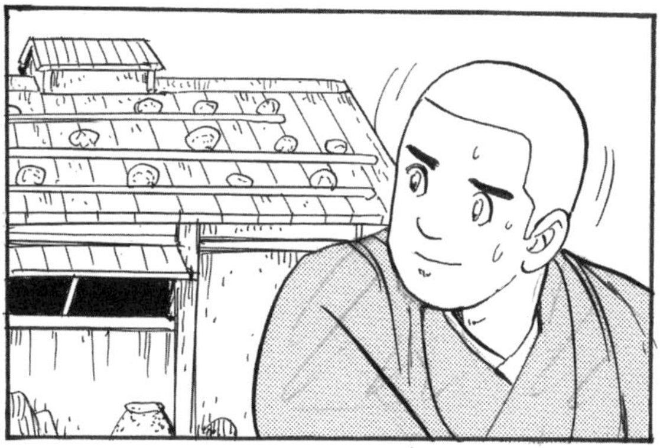

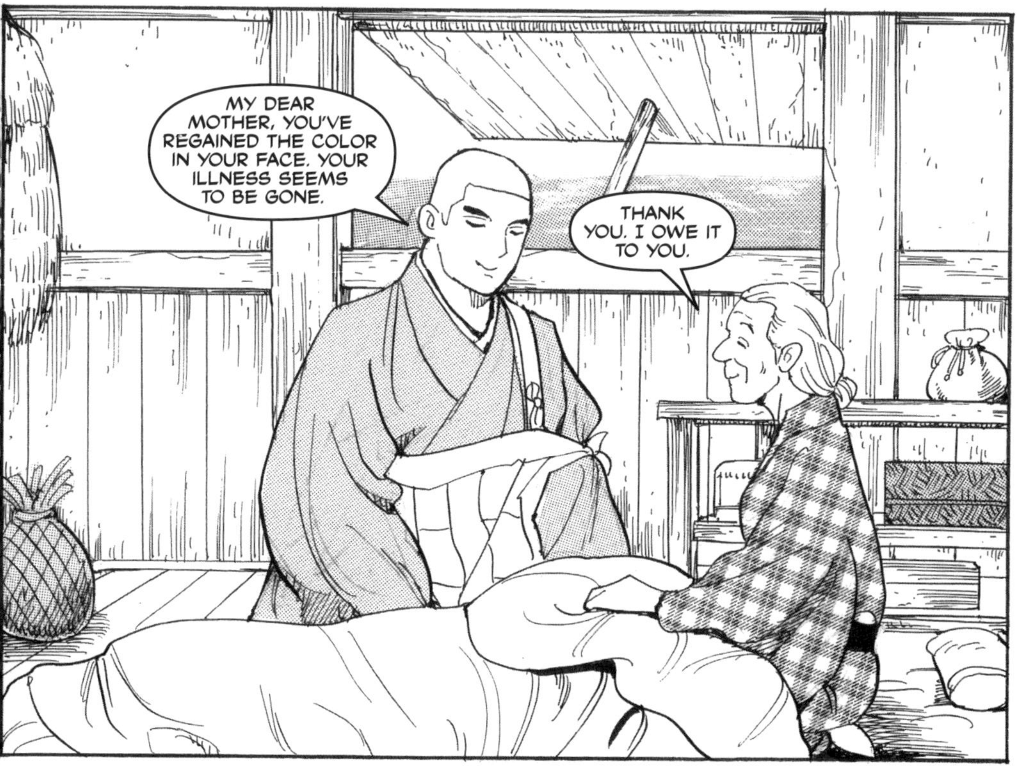
MY DEAR MOTHER, YOU'VE REGAINED THE COLOR IN YOUR FACE. YOUR ILLNESS SEEMS TO BE GONE.
THANK YOU. I OWE IT TO YOU.

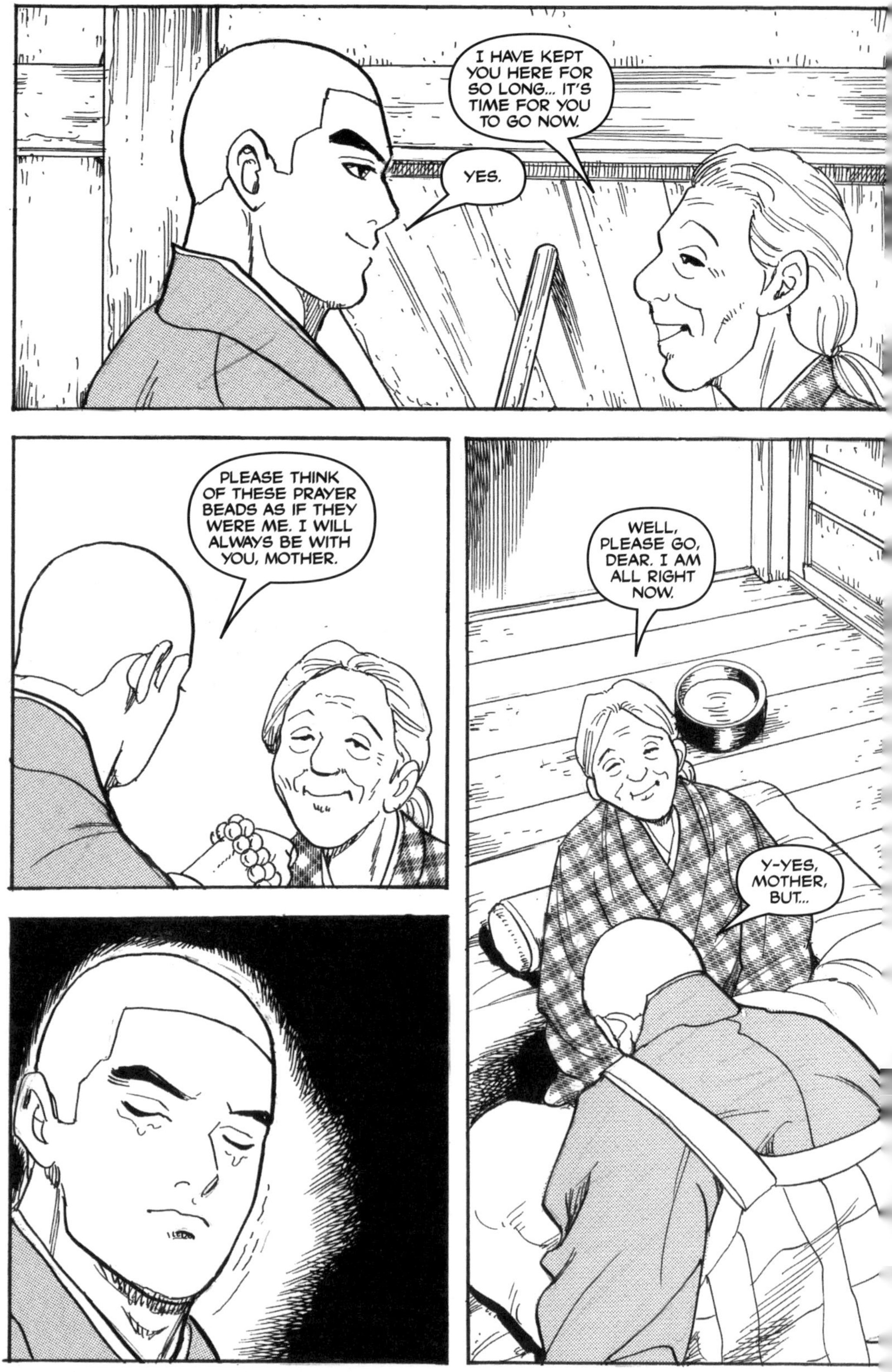
I HAVE KEPT YOU HERE FOR SO LONG... IT'S TIME FOR YOU TO GO NOW.
YES.
PLEASE THINK OF THESE PRAYER BEADS AS IF THEY WERE ME. I WILL ALWAYS BE WITH YOU, MOTHER.
WELL, PLEASE GO, DEAR. I AM ALL RIGHT NOW.
Y-YES, MOTHER, BUT...

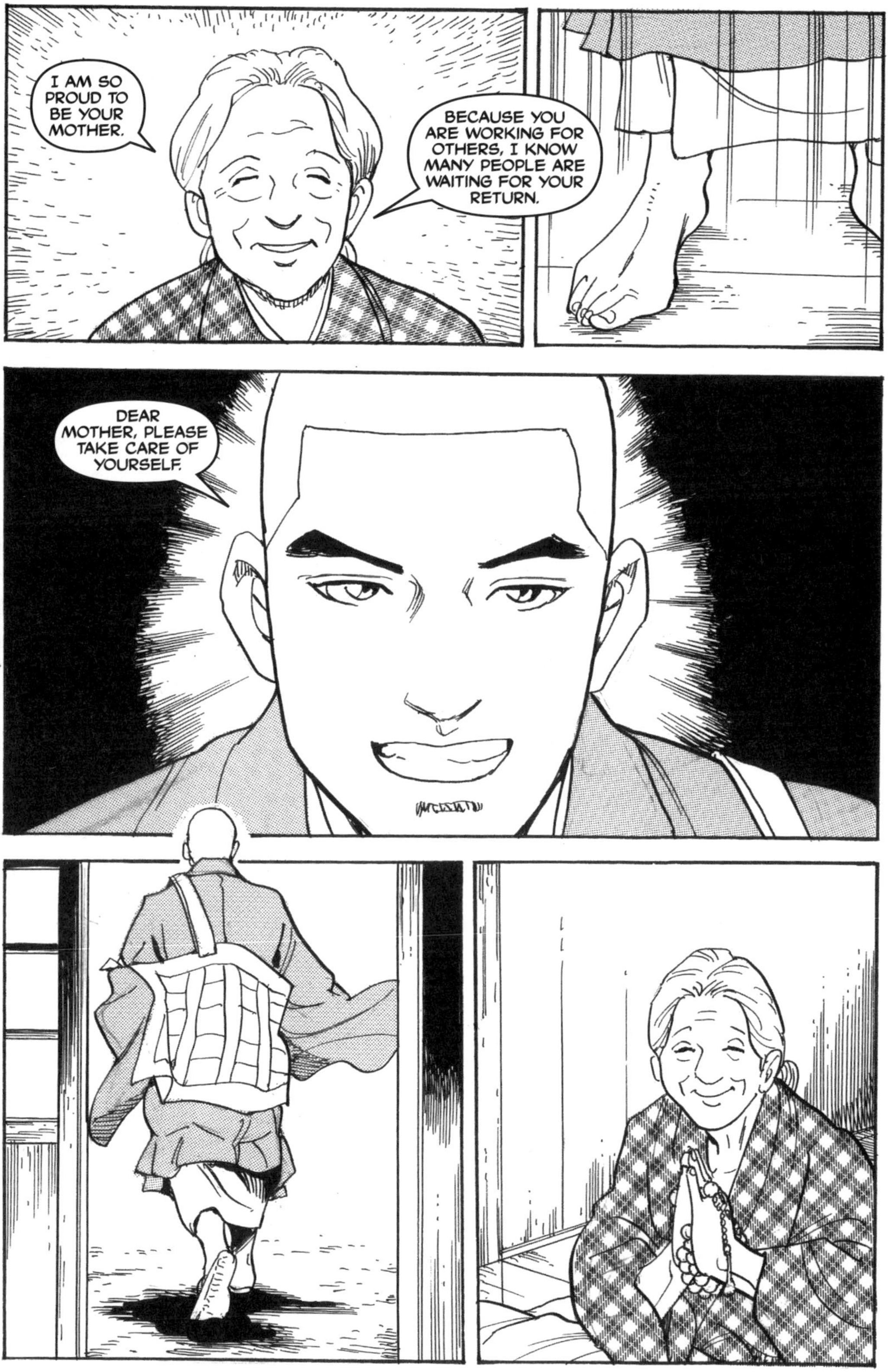
I AM SO PROUD TO BE YOUR MOTHER.
BECAUSE YOU ARE WORKING FOR OTHERS, I KNOW MANY PEOPLE ARE WAITING FOR YOUR RETURN.
DEAR MOTHER, PLEASE TAKE CARE OF YOURSELF.

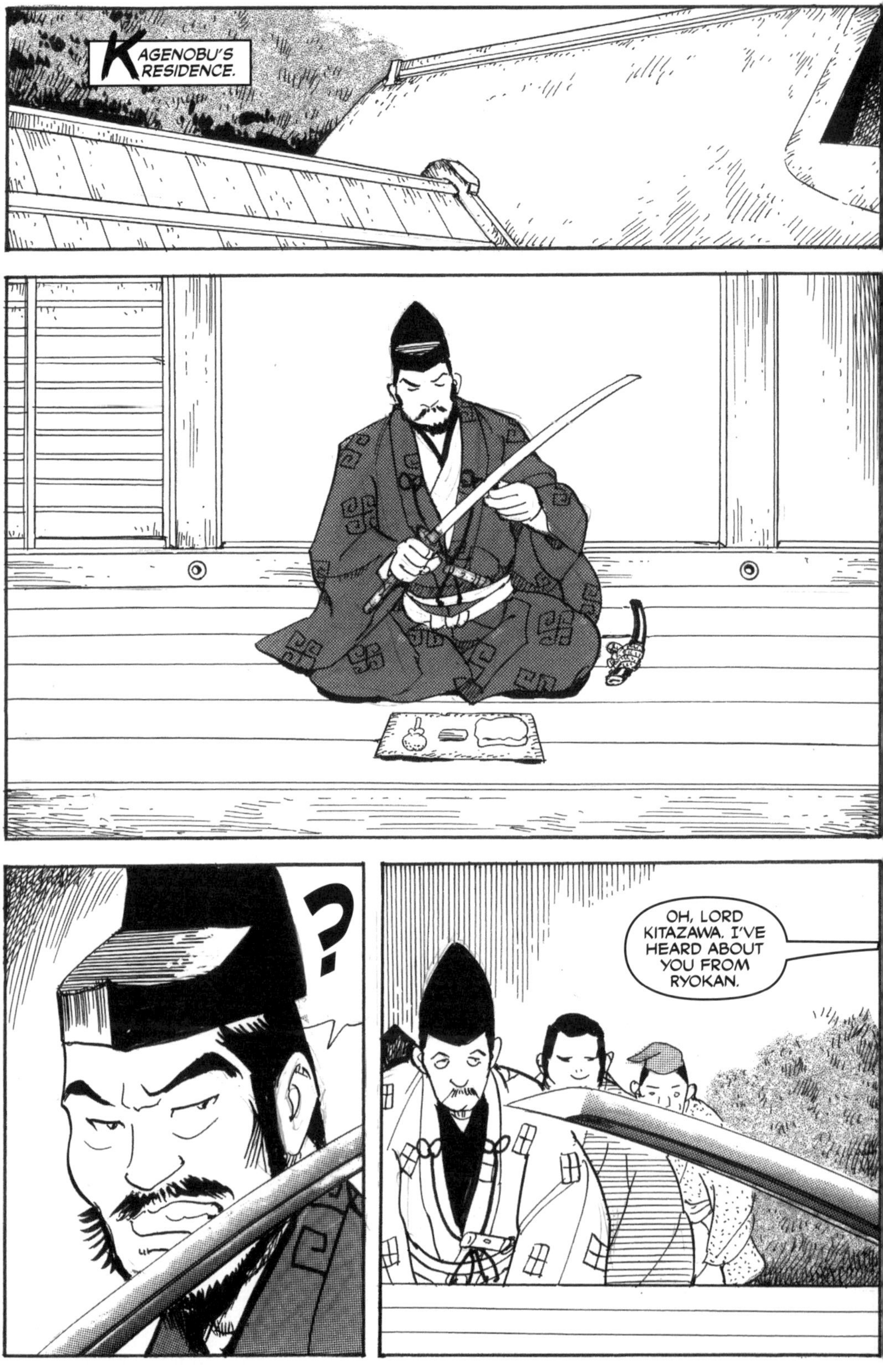
KAGENOBU'S RESIDENCE.
?
OH, LORD KITAZAWA. I'VE HEARD ABOUT YOU FROM RYOKAN.

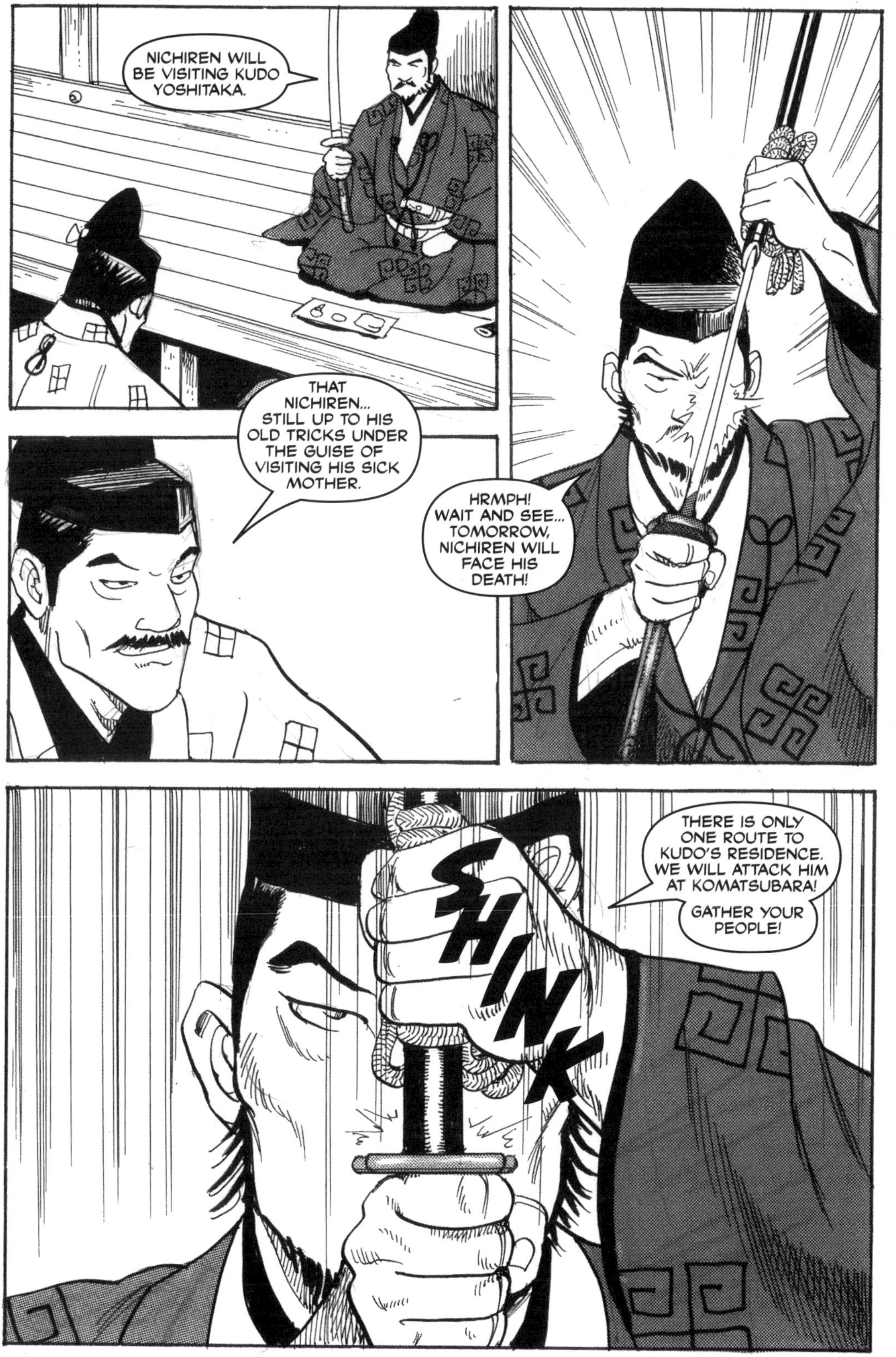
NICHIREN WILL BE VISITING KUDO YOSHITAKA.
THAT NICHIREN... STILL UP TO HIS OLD TRICKS UNDER THE GUISE OF VISITING HIS SICK MOTHER.
HRMPH! WAIT AND SEE... TOMORROW, NICHIREN WILL FACE HIS DEATH!
SHINK
THERE IS ONLY ONE ROUTE TO KUDO'S RESIDENCE. WE WILL ATTACK HIM AT KOMATSUBARA!
GATHER YOUR PEOPLE!

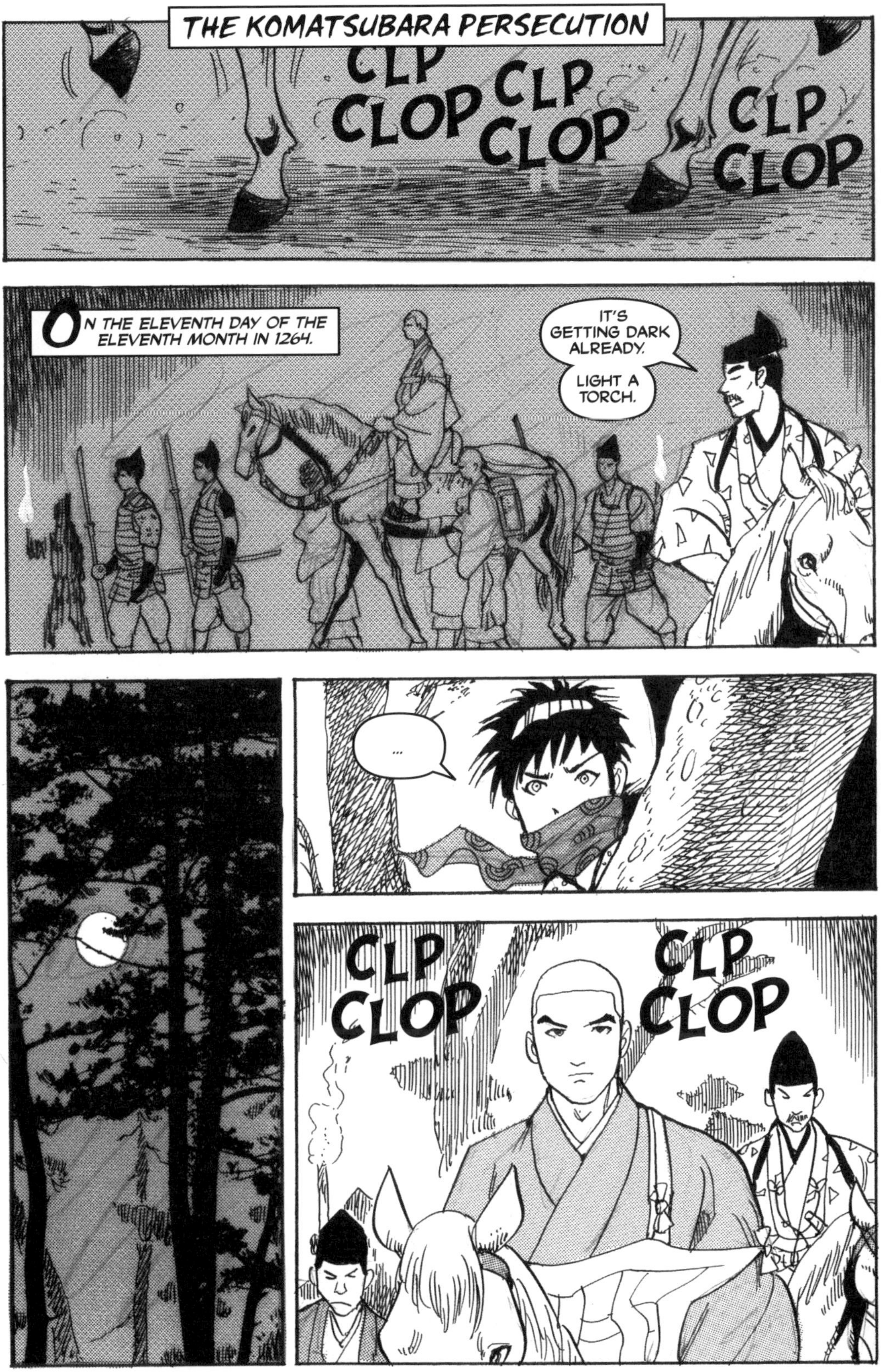
THE KOMATSUBARA PERSECUTION
CLP CLOP
CLP CLOP
CLP CLOP
ON THE ELEVENTH DAY OF THE ELEVENTH MONTH IN 1264.
IT'S GETTING DARK ALREADY.
LIGHT A TORCH.
...
CLP CLOP
CLP CLOP

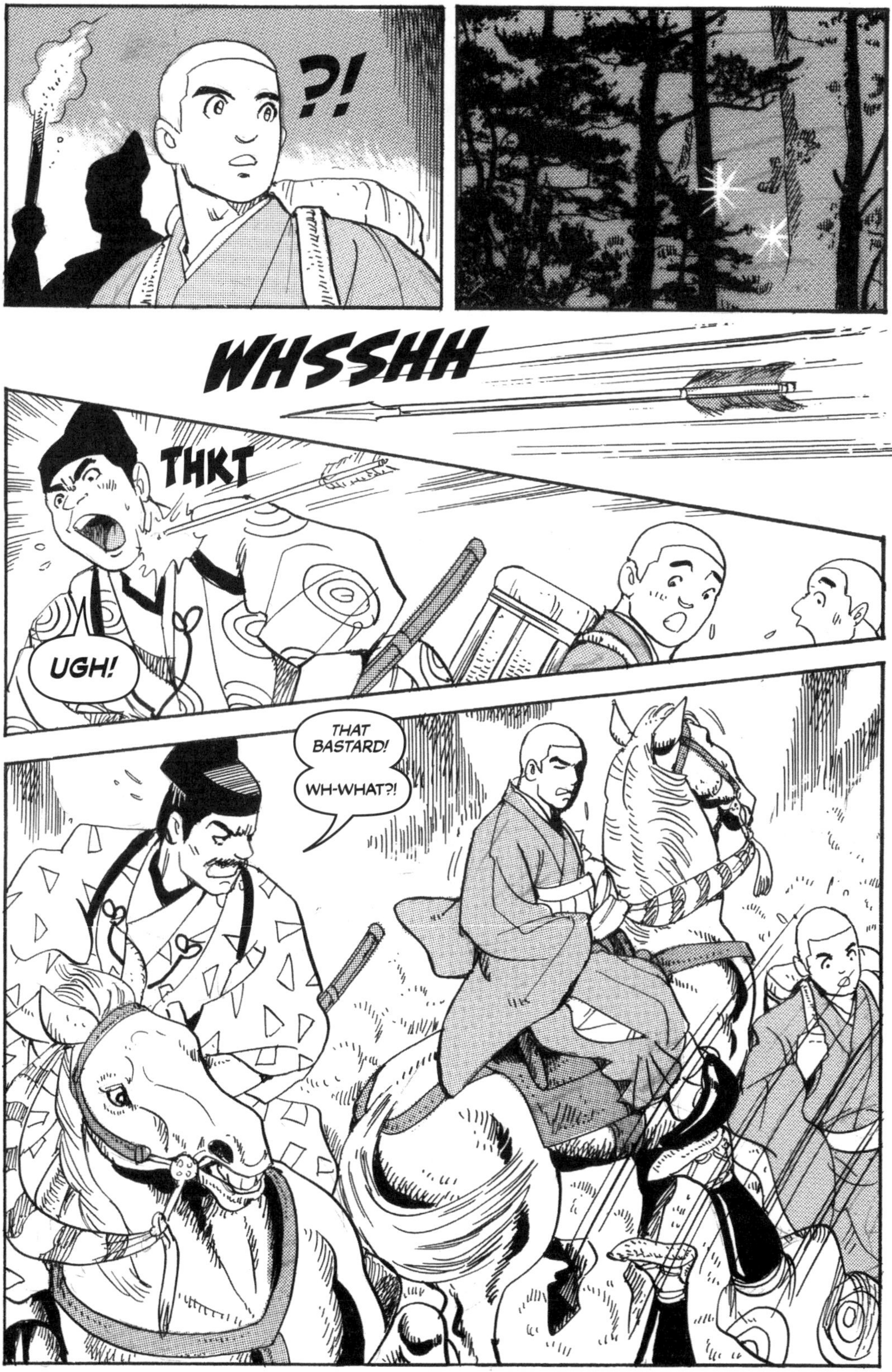
?!
WHSSHH
THKT
UGH!
THAT BASTARD!
WH-WHAT?!

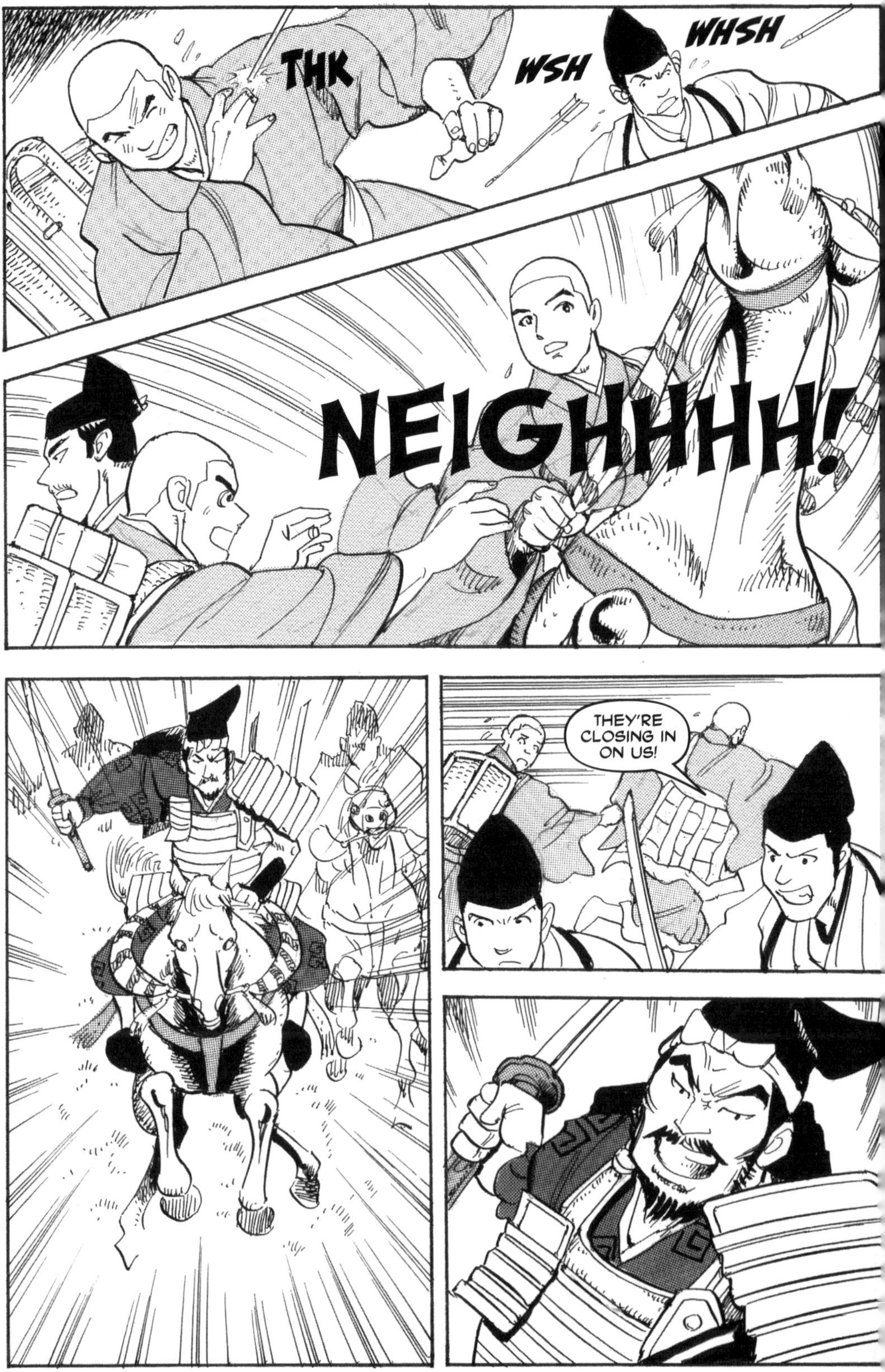
THK
WSH
WHSH
NEIGHHHH!
THEY'RE CLOSING IN ON US!

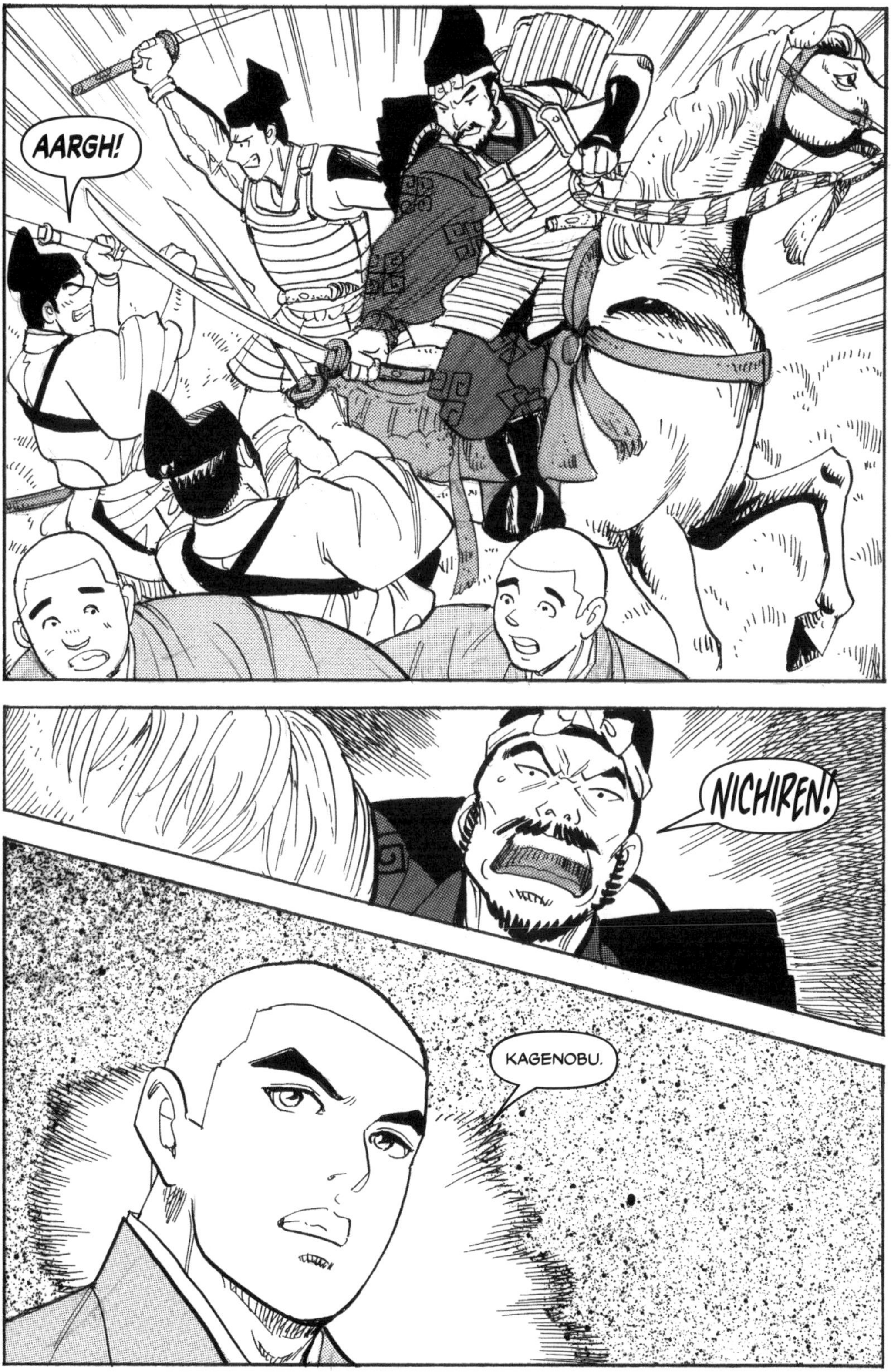
AARGH!
NICHIREN!
KAGENOBU.

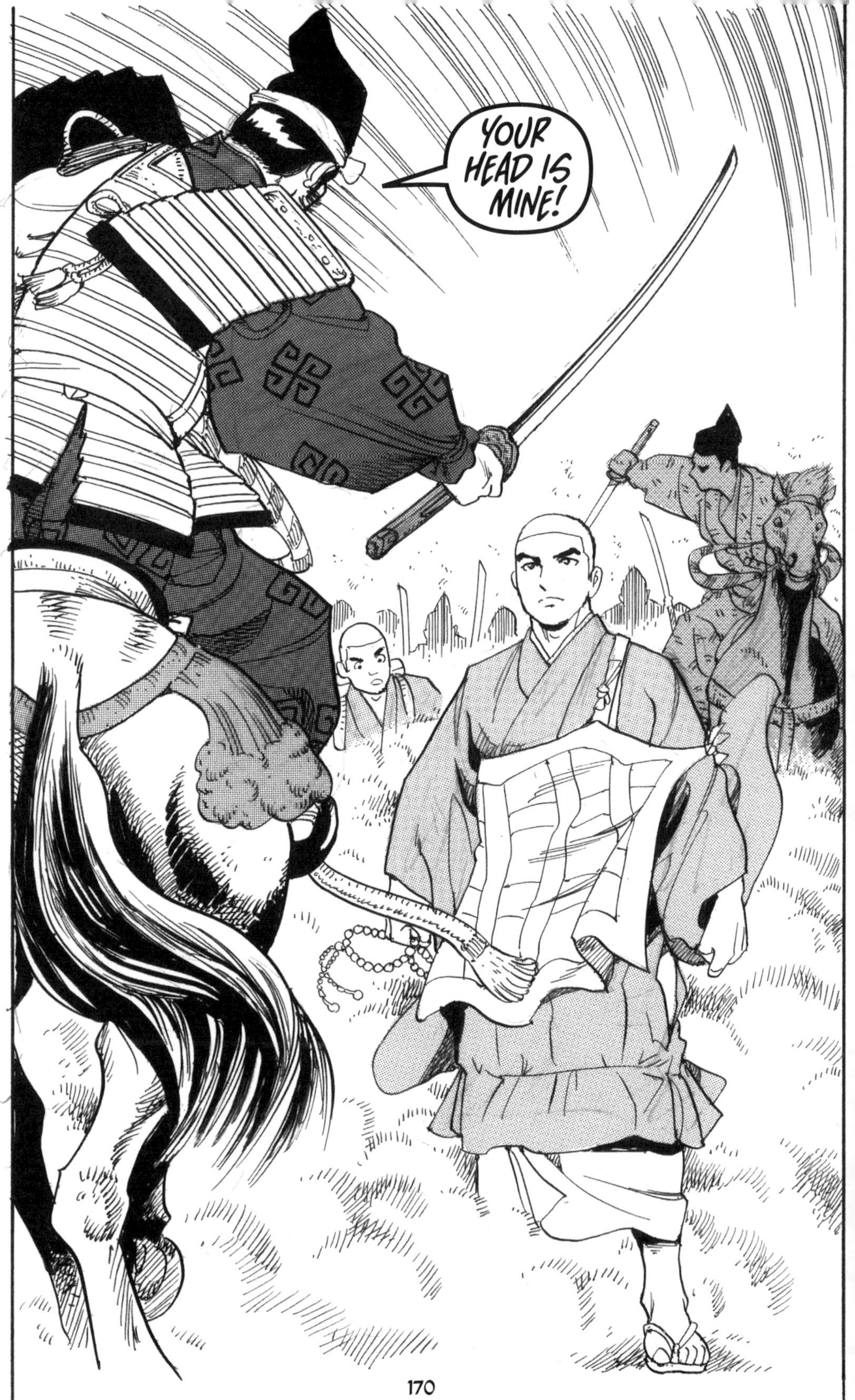
YOUR HEAD IS MINE!

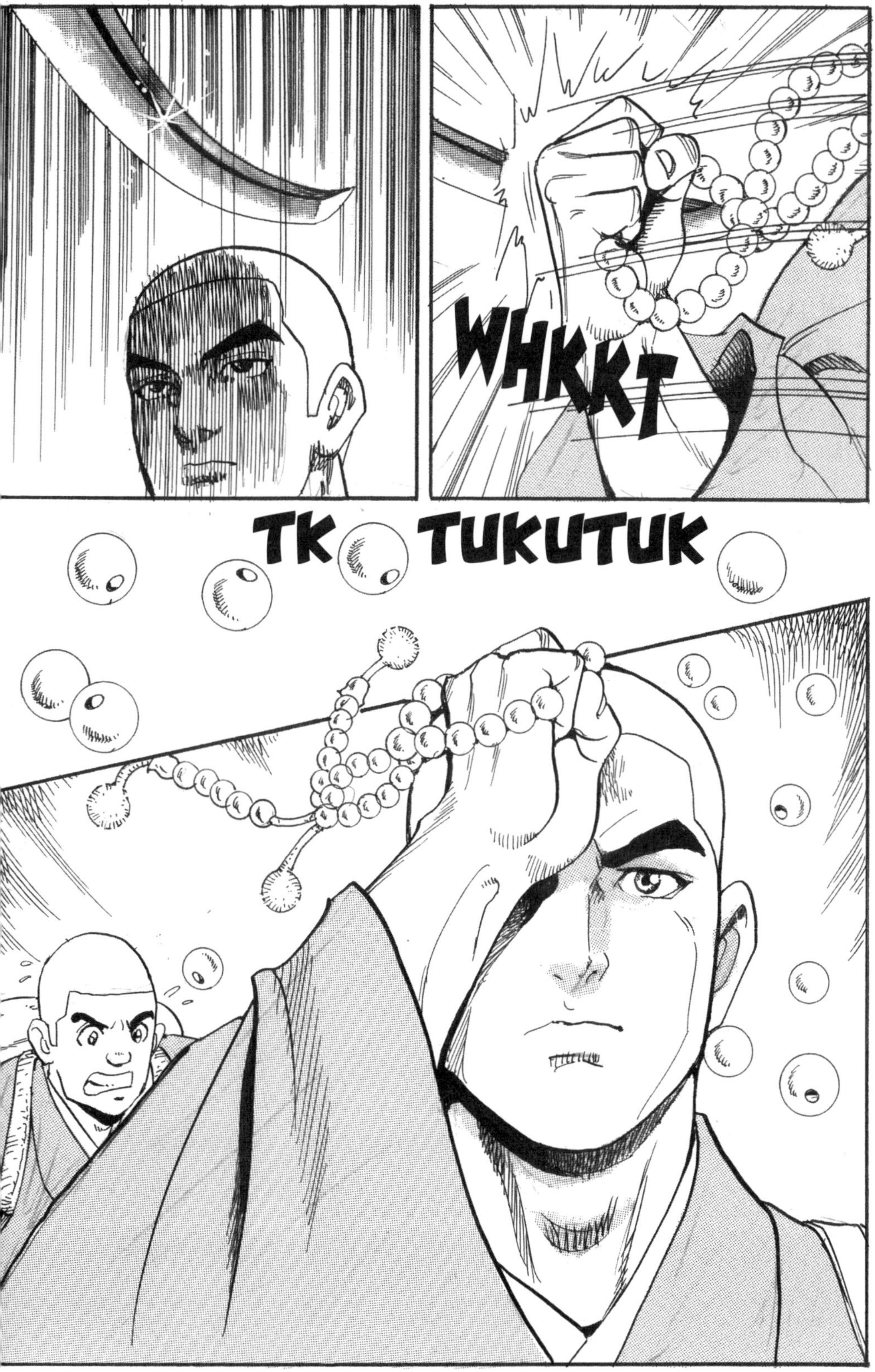
WHKKT
TK
TUKUTUK

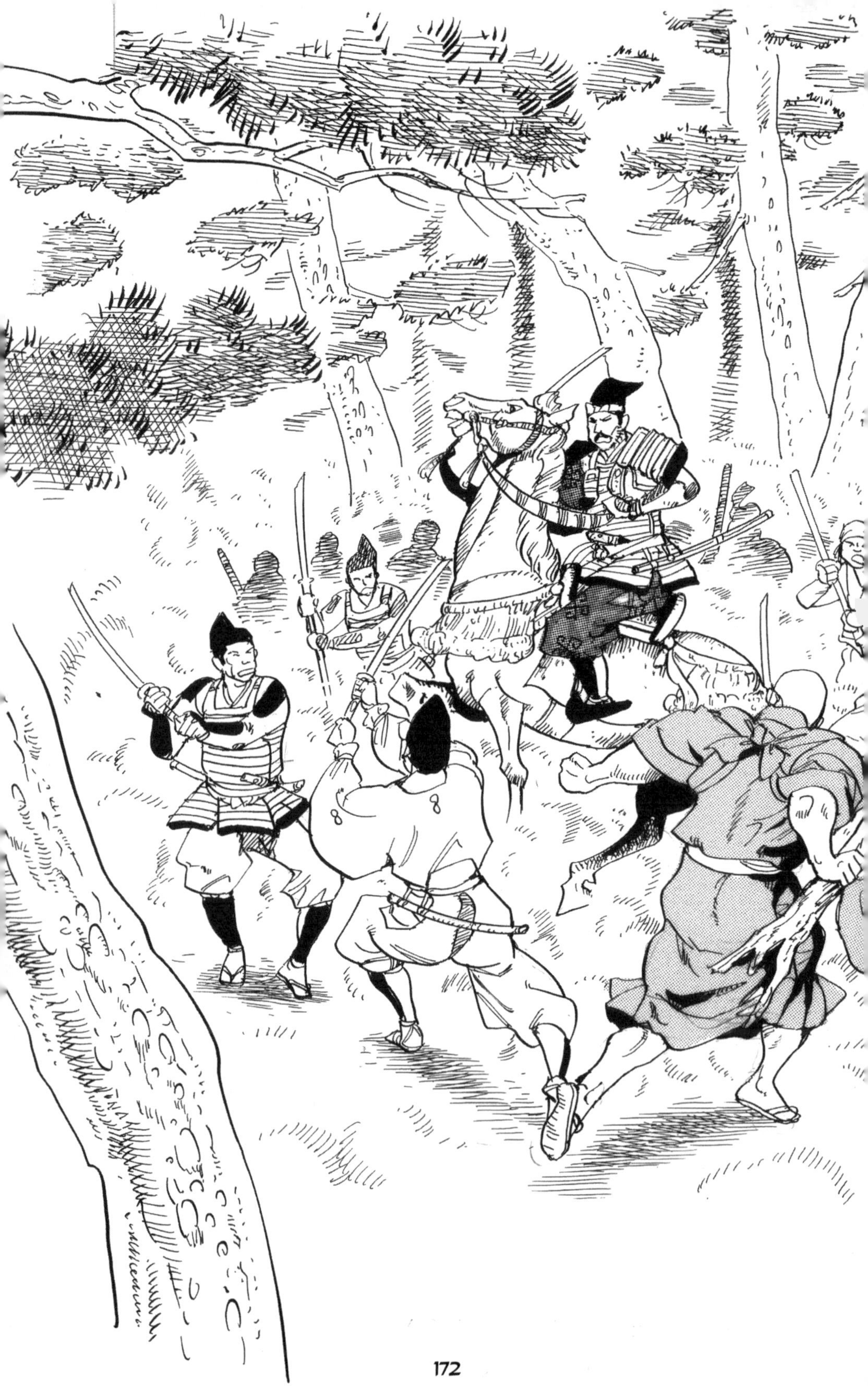

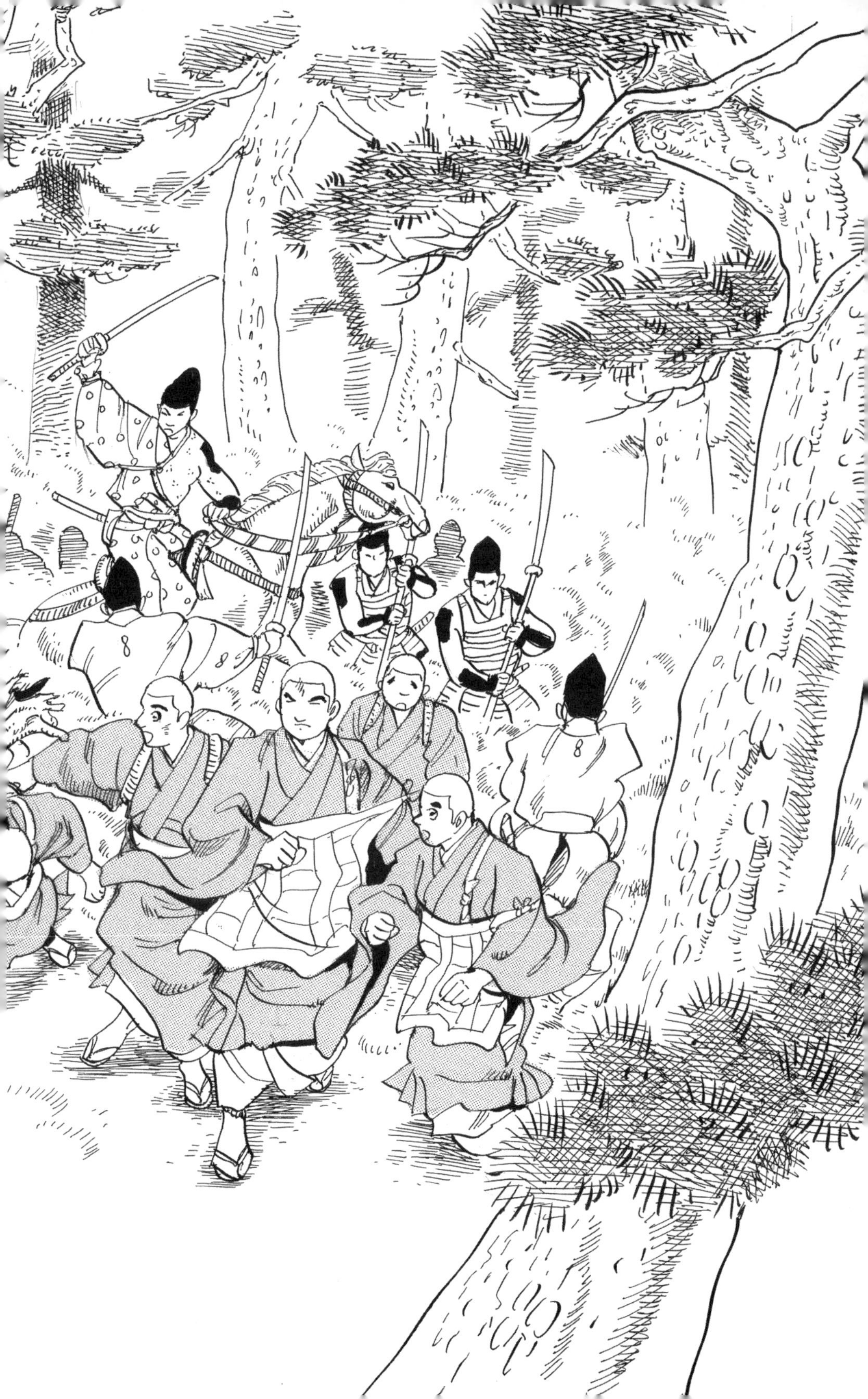

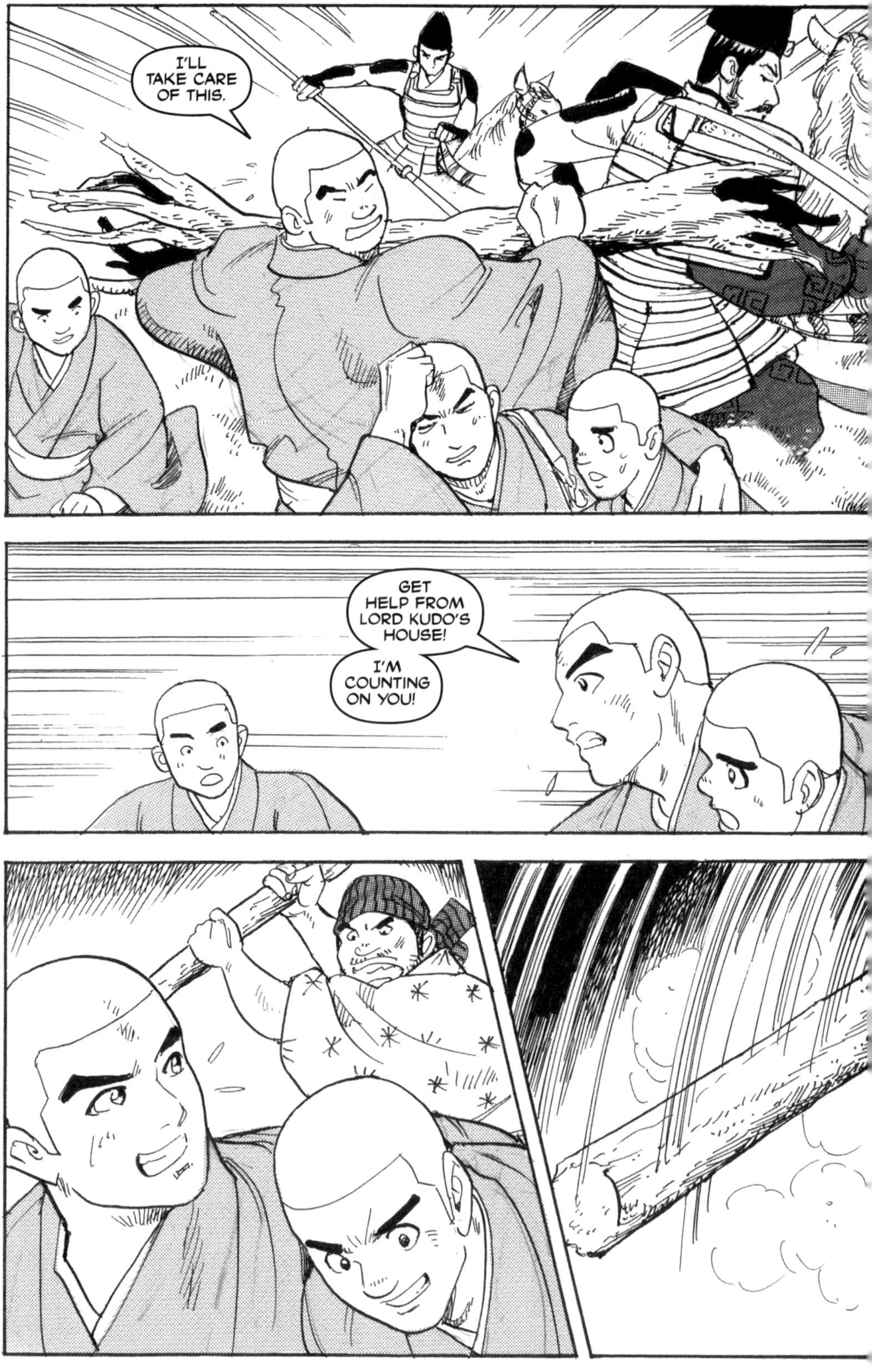
I'LL TAKE CARE OF THIS.
GET HELP FROM LORD KUDO'S HOUSE!
I'M COUNTING ON YOU!

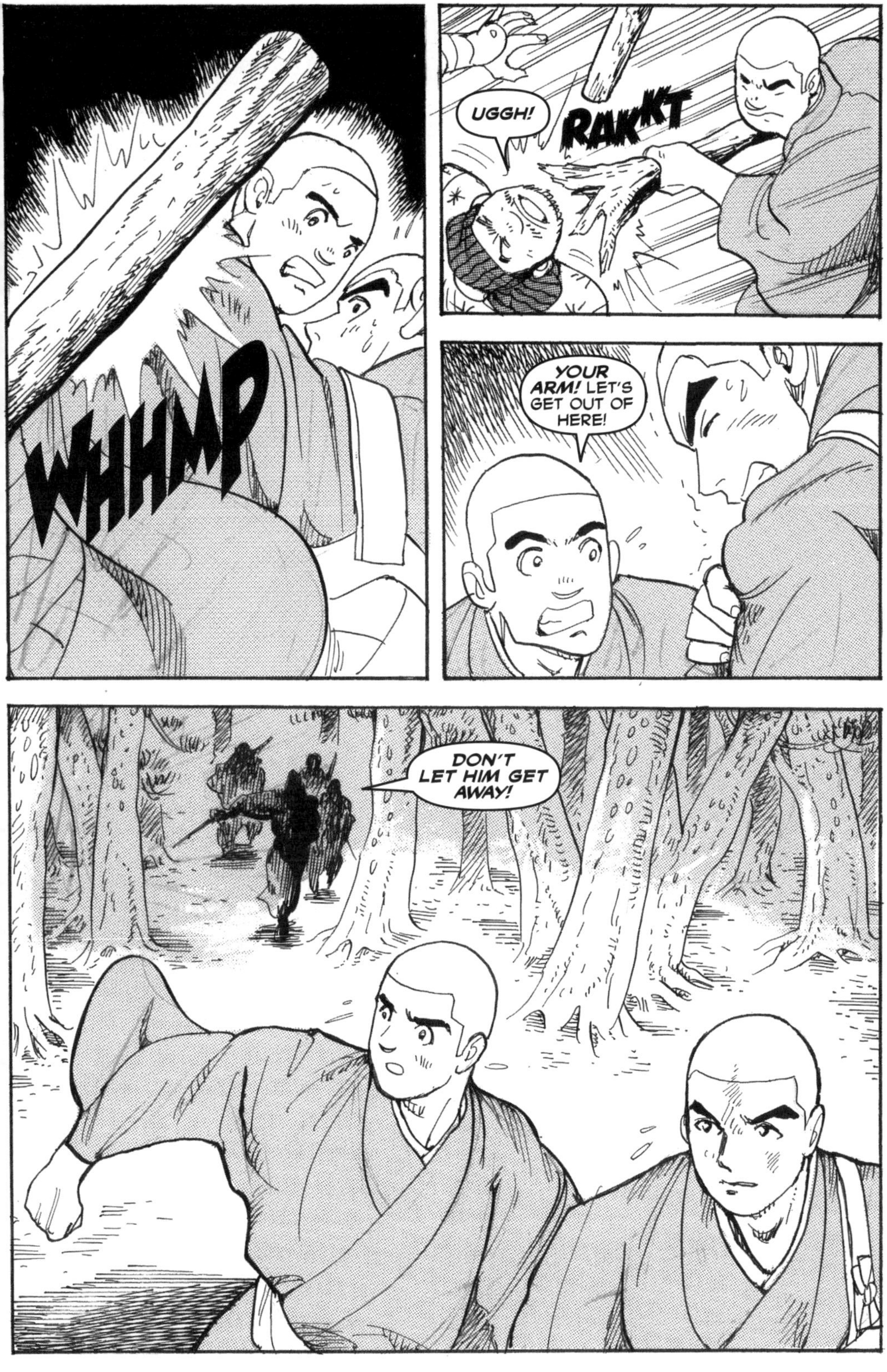
WHHMP
UGGH!
RAKKT
YOUR ARM! LET'S GET OUT OF HERE!
DON'T LET HIM GET AWAY!

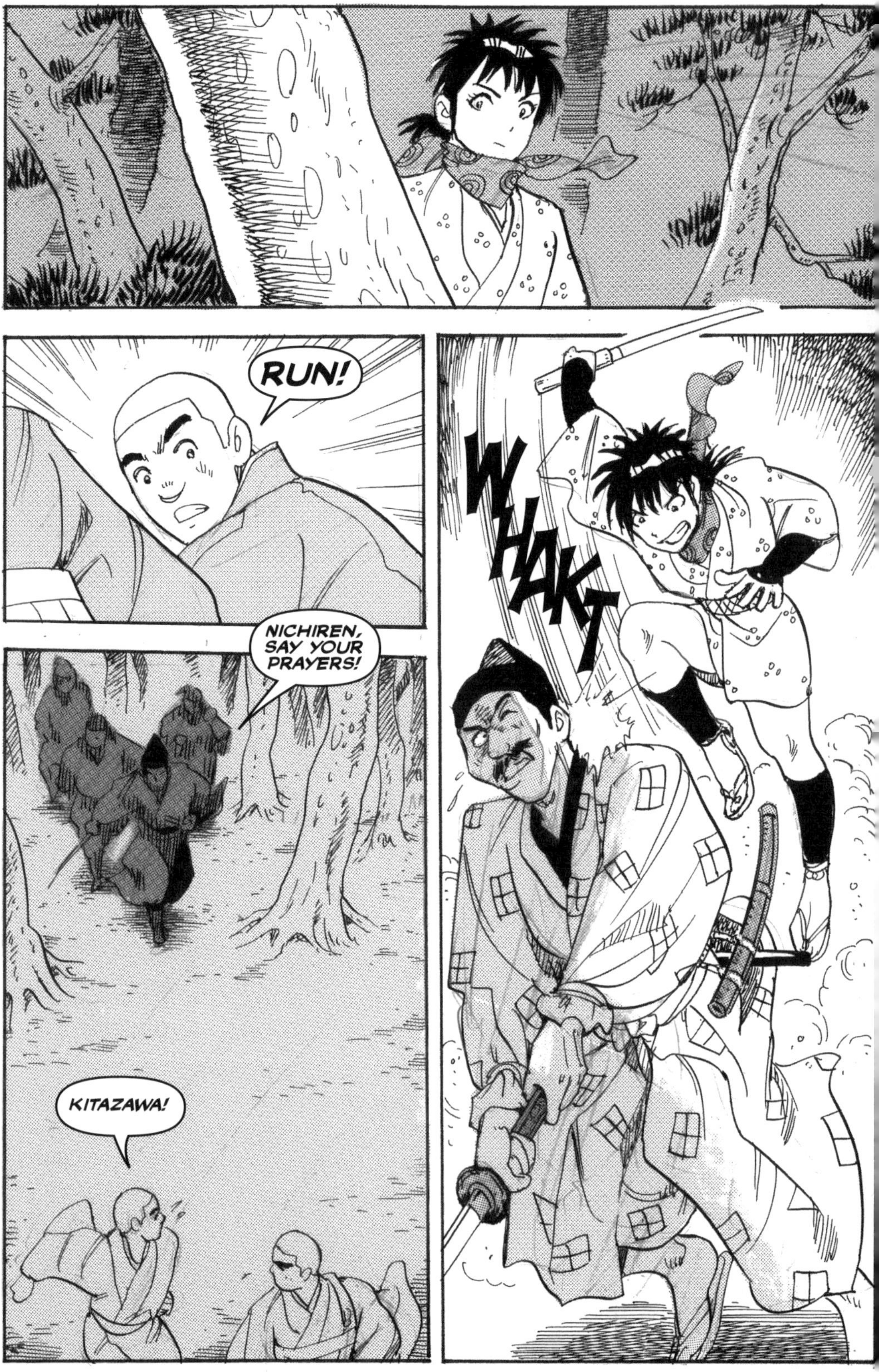
RUN!
NICHIREN, SAY YOUR PRAYERS!
KITAZAWA!
WHAKT

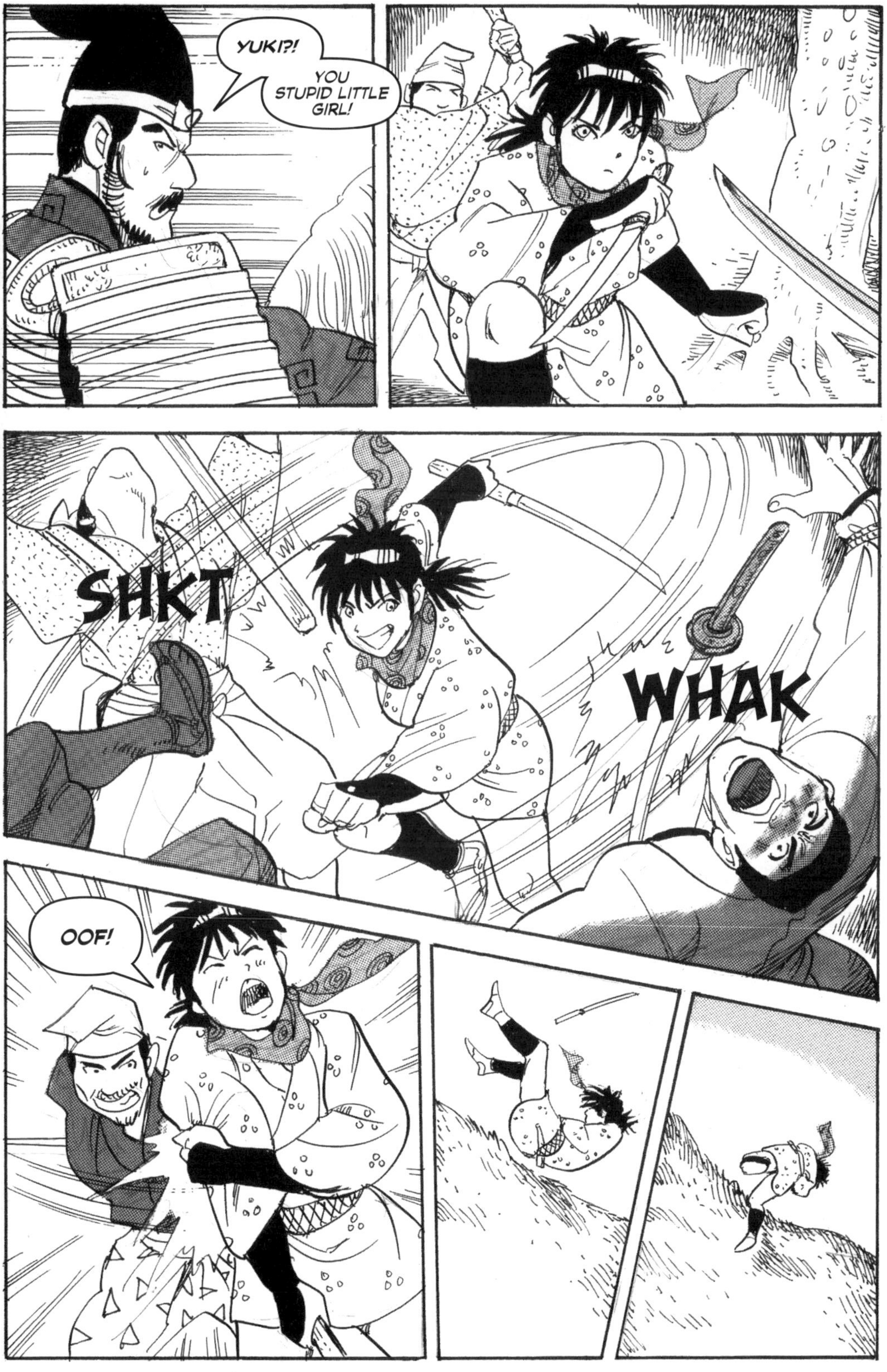
YUKI?!
YOU STUPID LITTLE GIRL!
SHKT
WHAK
OOF!

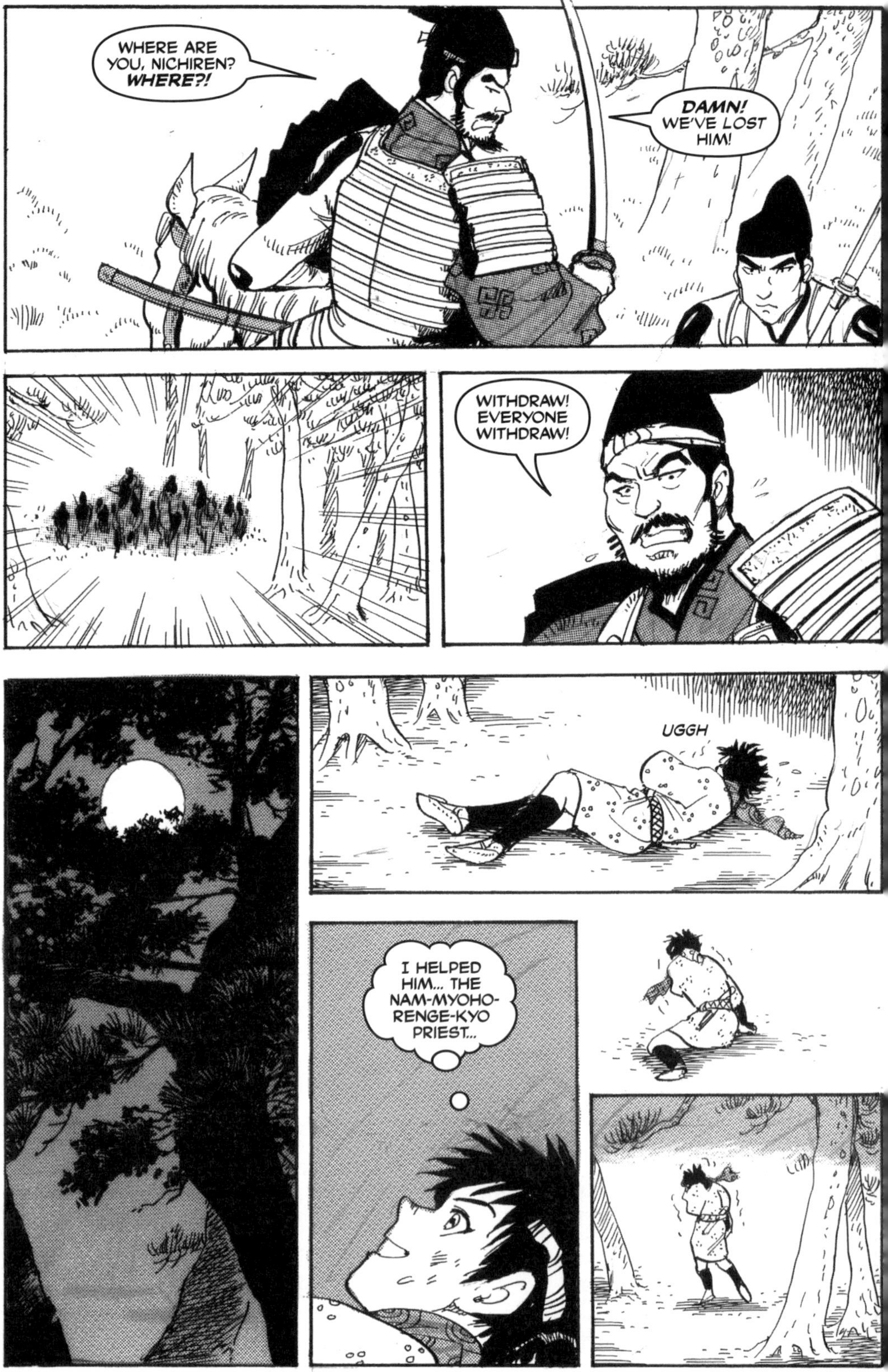
WHERE ARE YOU, NICHIREN? ***WHERE?!***
DAMN! WE'VE LOST HIM!
WITHDRAW! EVERYONE WITHDRAW!
UGGH
I HELPED HIM... THE NAM-MYOHO-RENGE-KYO PRIEST...

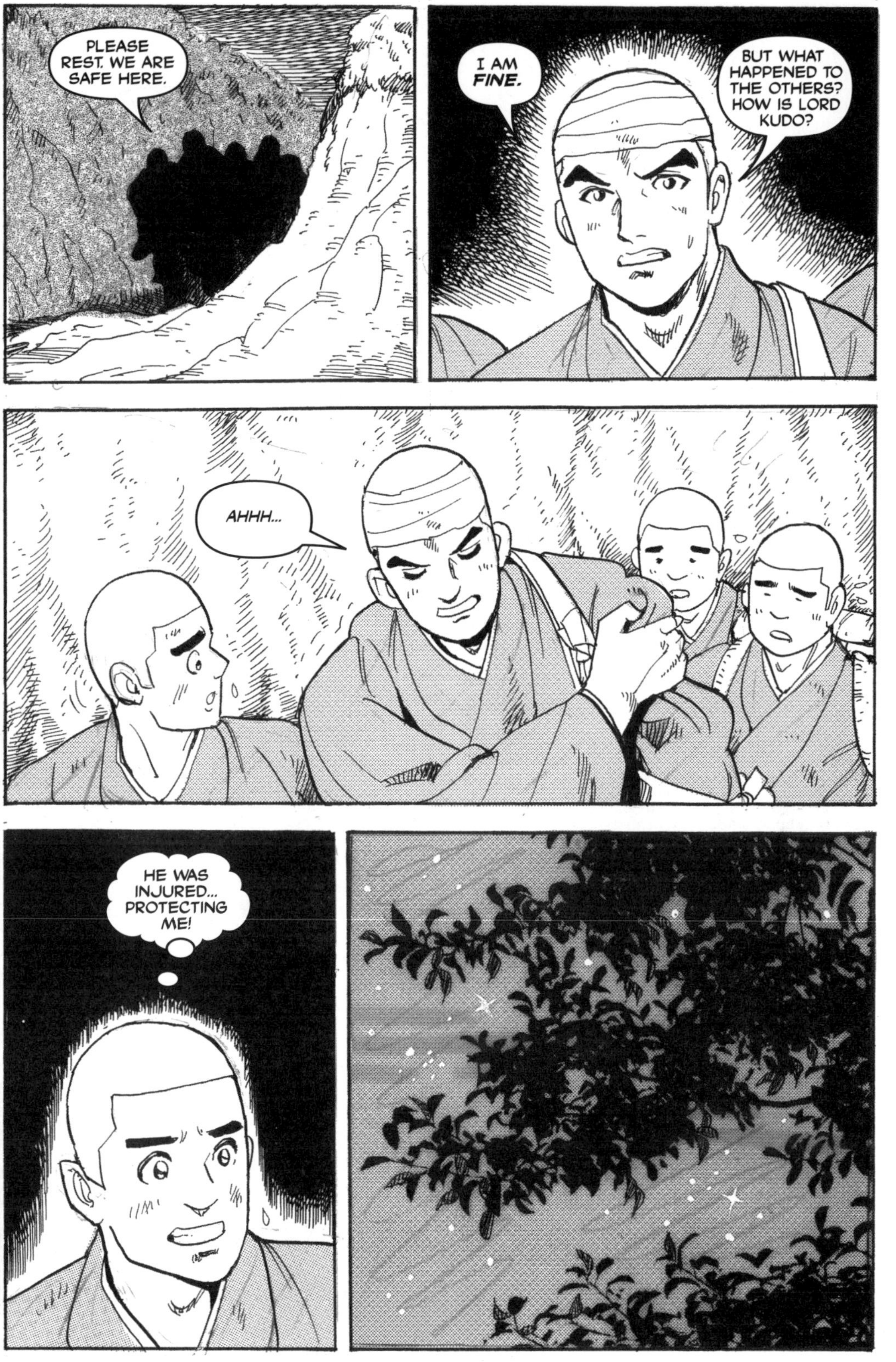
PLEASE REST. WE ARE SAFE HERE.
I AM *FINE.*
BUT WHAT HAPPENED TO THE OTHERS? HOW IS LORD KUDO?
AHHH...
HE WAS INJURED... PROTECTING ME!

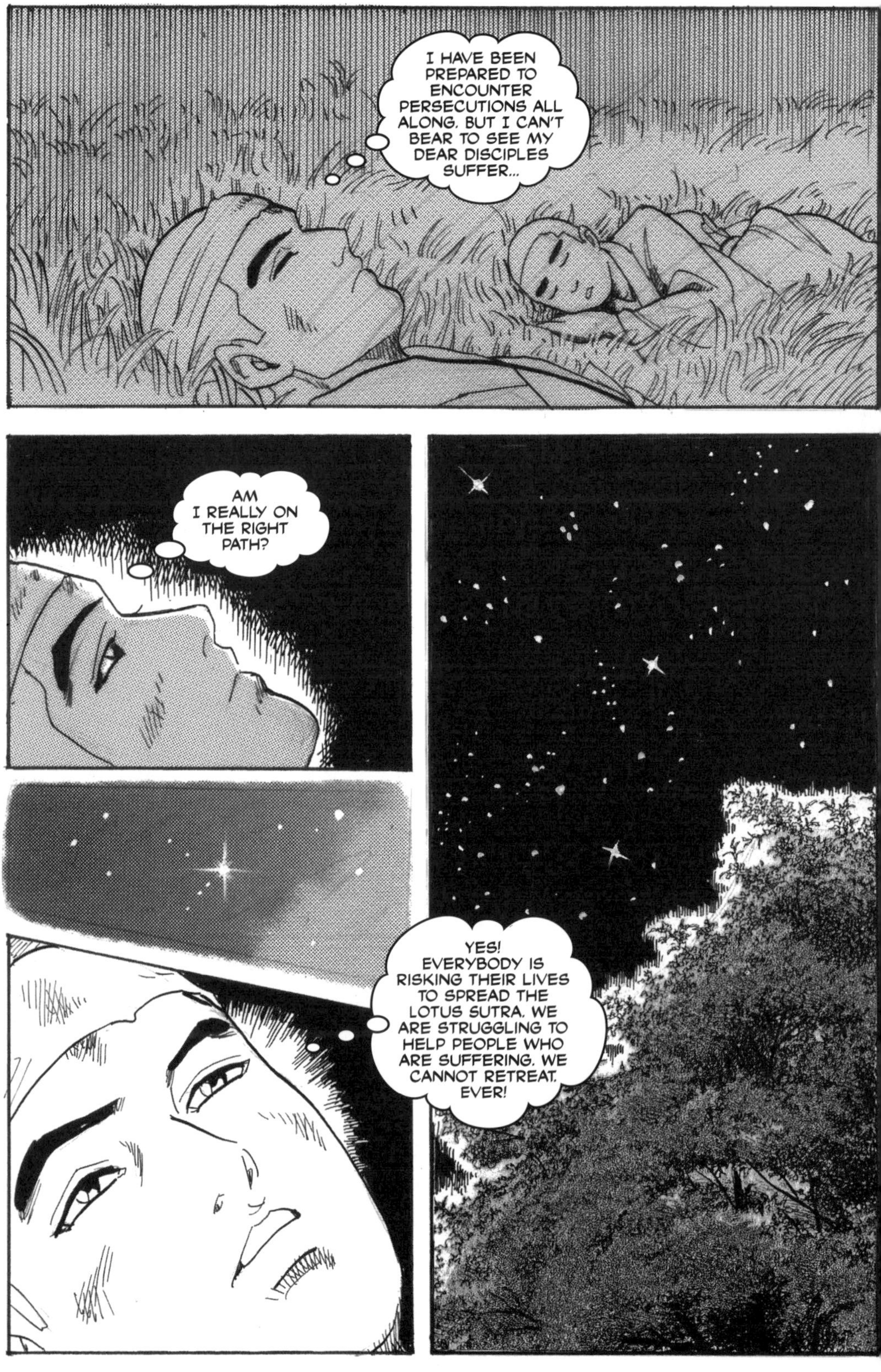
I HAVE BEEN PREPARED TO ENCOUNTER PERSECUTIONS ALL ALONG. BUT I CAN'T BEAR TO SEE MY DEAR DISCIPLES SUFFER...
AM I REALLY ON THE RIGHT PATH?
YES! EVERYBODY IS RISKING THEIR LIVES TO SPREAD THE LOTUS SUTRA. WE ARE STRUGGLING TO HELP PEOPLE WHO ARE SUFFERING. WE CANNOT RETREAT. EVER!

Chapter 3

The Tatsunokuchi Persecution

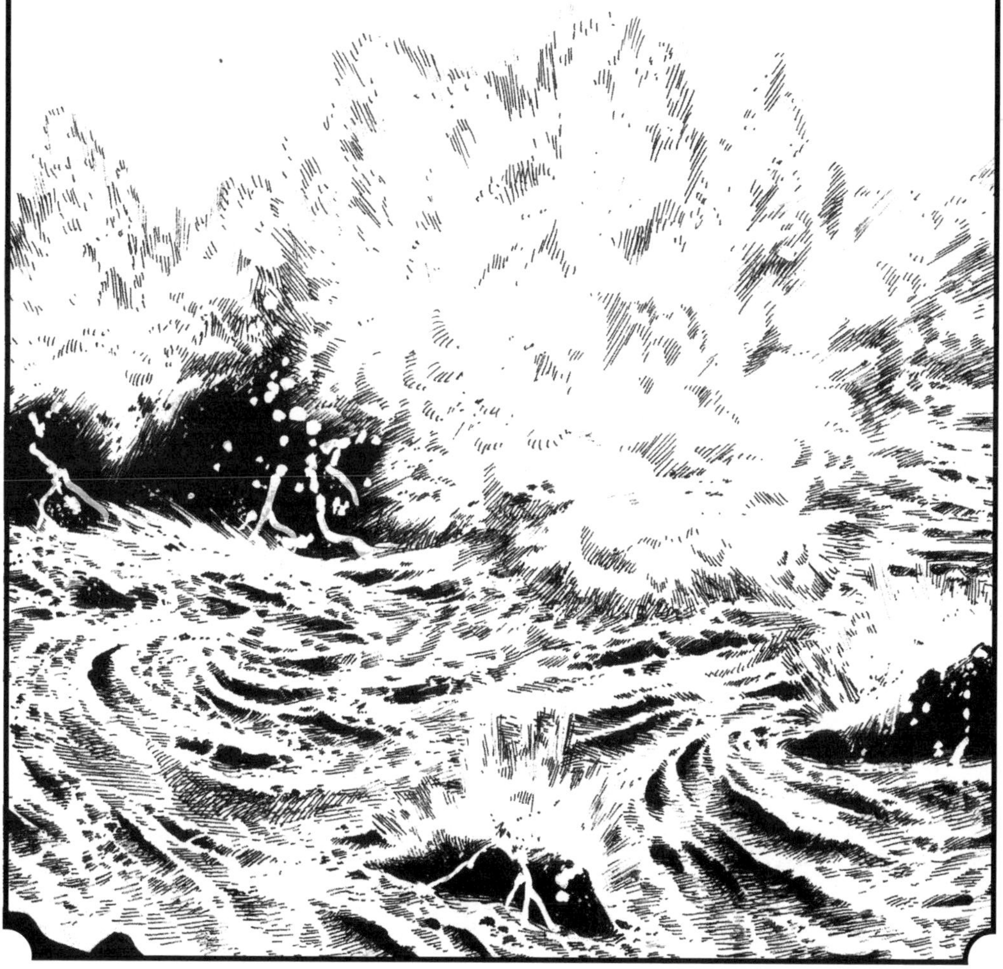

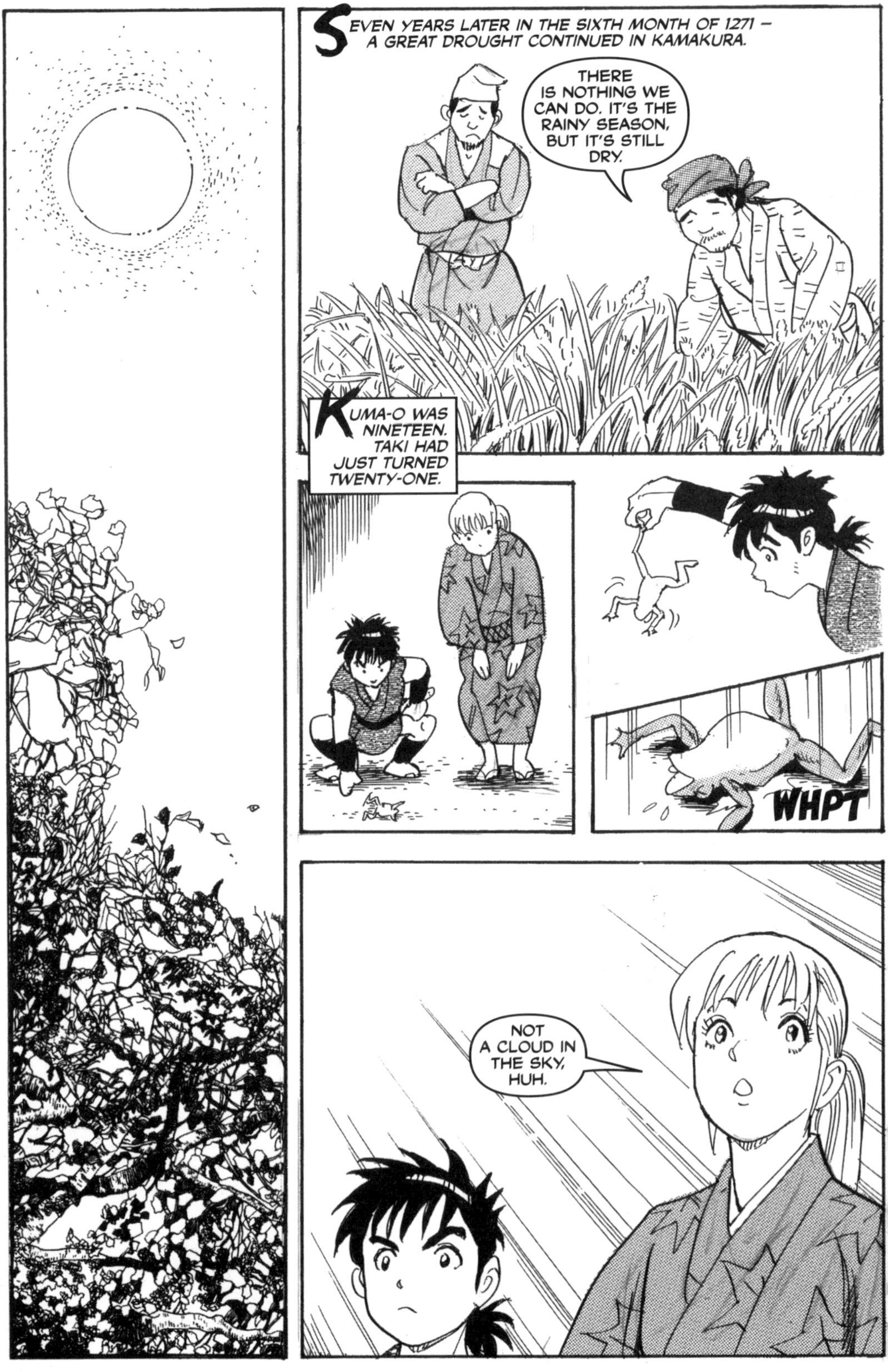
SEVEN YEARS LATER IN THE SIXTH MONTH OF 1271 – A GREAT DROUGHT CONTINUED IN KAMAKURA.
THERE IS NOTHING WE CAN DO. IT'S THE RAINY SEASON, BUT IT'S STILL DRY.
KUMA-O WAS NINETEEN. TAKI HAD JUST TURNED TWENTY-ONE.
WHPT
NOT A CLOUD IN THE SKY, HUH.

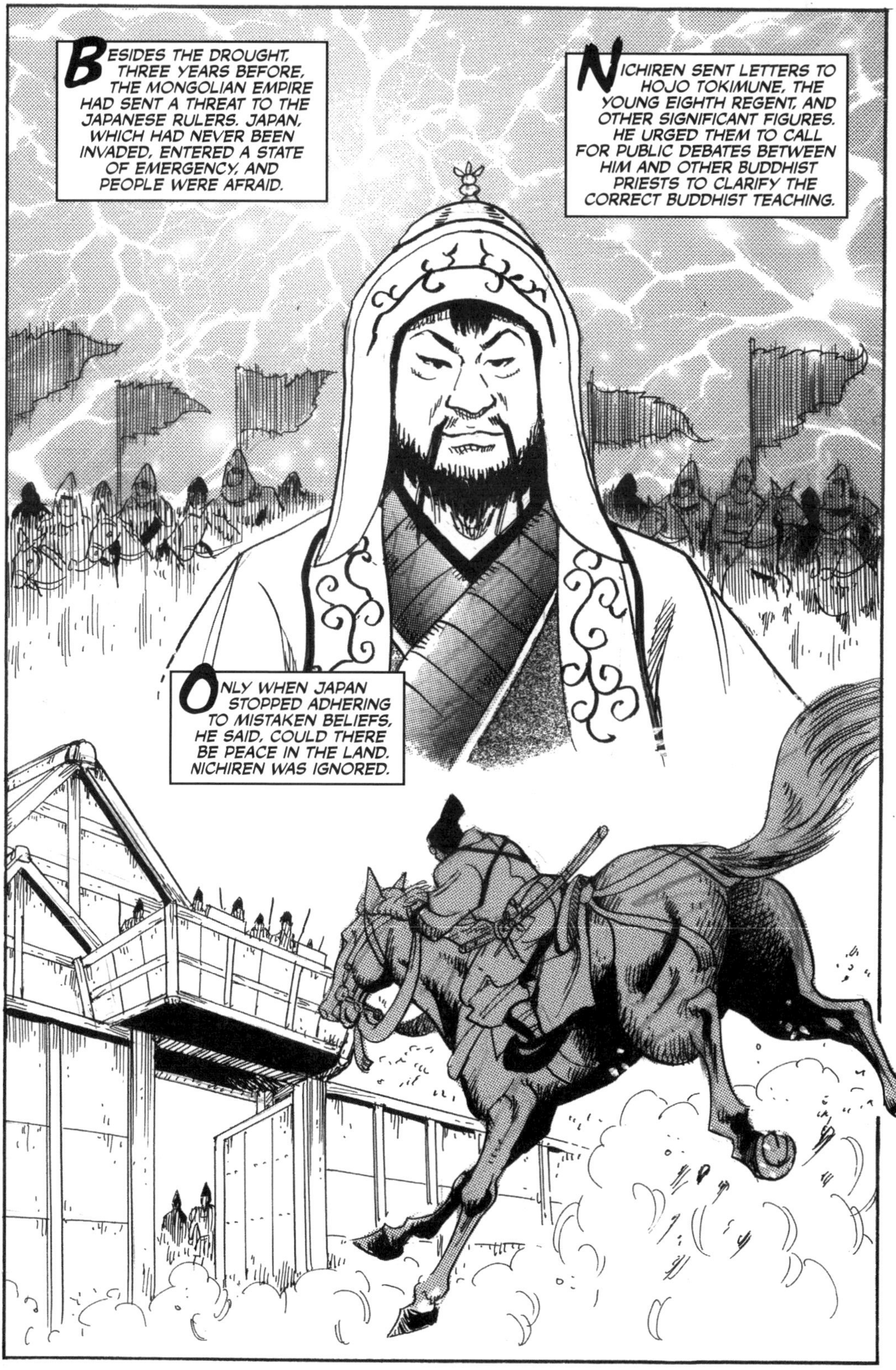
BESIDES THE DROUGHT, THREE YEARS BEFORE, THE MONGOLIAN EMPIRE HAD SENT A THREAT TO THE JAPANESE RULERS. JAPAN, WHICH HAD NEVER BEEN INVADED, ENTERED A STATE OF EMERGENCY, AND PEOPLE WERE AFRAID.
NICHIREN SENT LETTERS TO HOJO TOKIMUNE, THE YOUNG EIGHTH REGENT, AND OTHER SIGNIFICANT FIGURES. HE URGED THEM TO CALL FOR PUBLIC DEBATES BETWEEN HIM AND OTHER BUDDHIST PRIESTS TO CLARIFY THE CORRECT BUDDHIST TEACHING.
ONLY WHEN JAPAN STOPPED ADHERING TO MISTAKEN BELIEFS, HE SAID, COULD THERE BE PEACE IN THE LAND. NICHIREN WAS IGNORED.

NICHIREN'S RESIDENCE IN MATSUBAGAYATSU.

NICHIREN WAS NOW FIFTY.

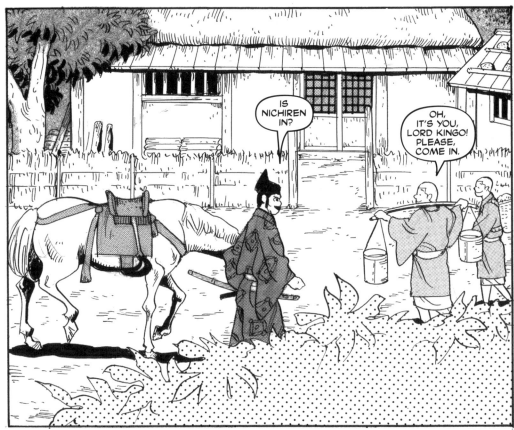

IS NICHIREN IN?

OH, IT'S YOU, LORD KINGO! PLEASE, COME IN.

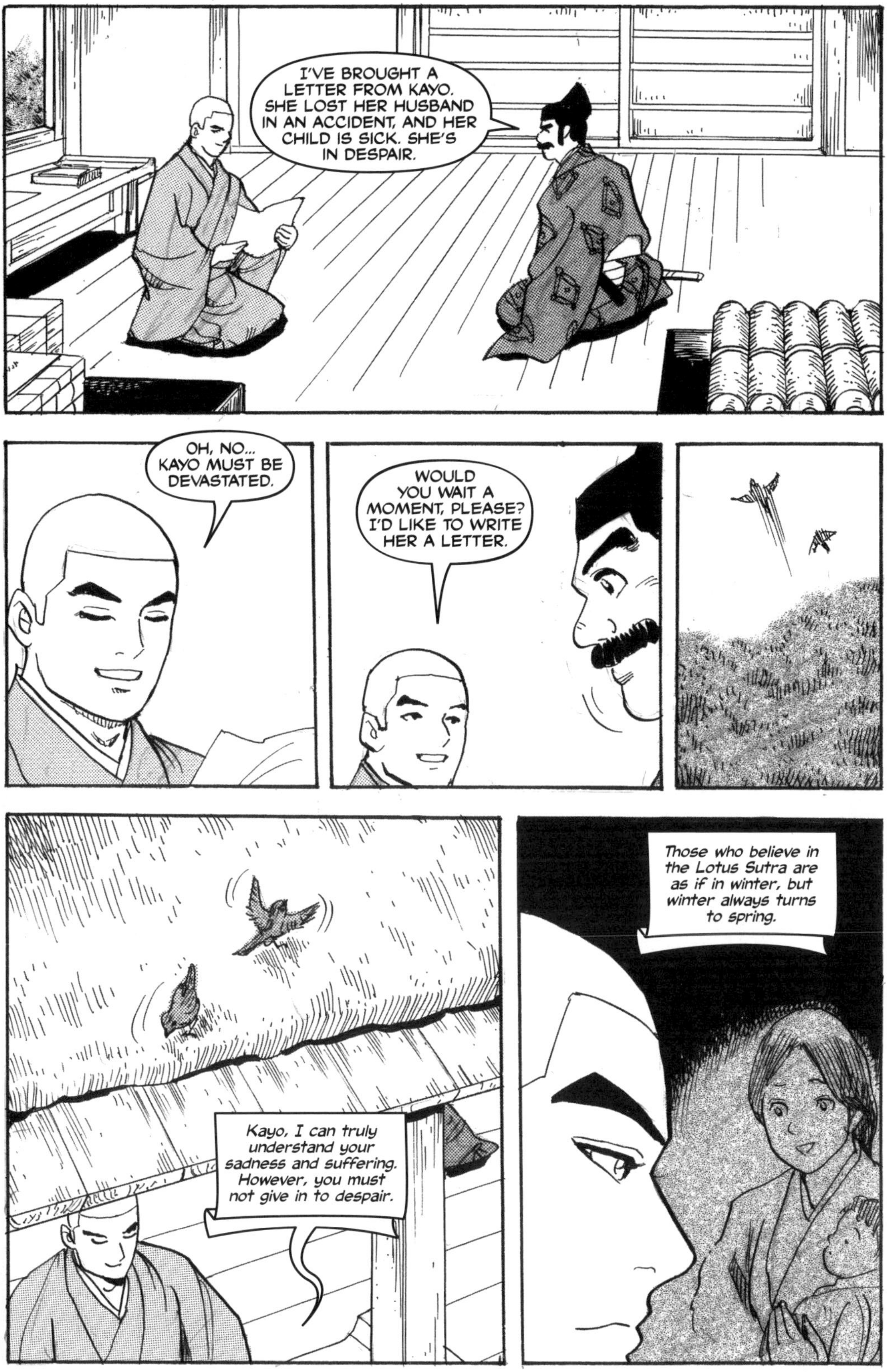
I'VE BROUGHT A LETTER FROM KAYO. SHE LOST HER HUSBAND IN AN ACCIDENT, AND HER CHILD IS SICK. SHE'S IN DESPAIR.
OH, NO... KAYO MUST BE DEVASTATED.
WOULD YOU WAIT A MOMENT, PLEASE? I'D LIKE TO WRITE HER A LETTER.
Kayo, I can truly understand your sadness and suffering. However, you must not give in to despair.
Those who believe in the Lotus Sutra are as if in winter, but winter always turns to spring.

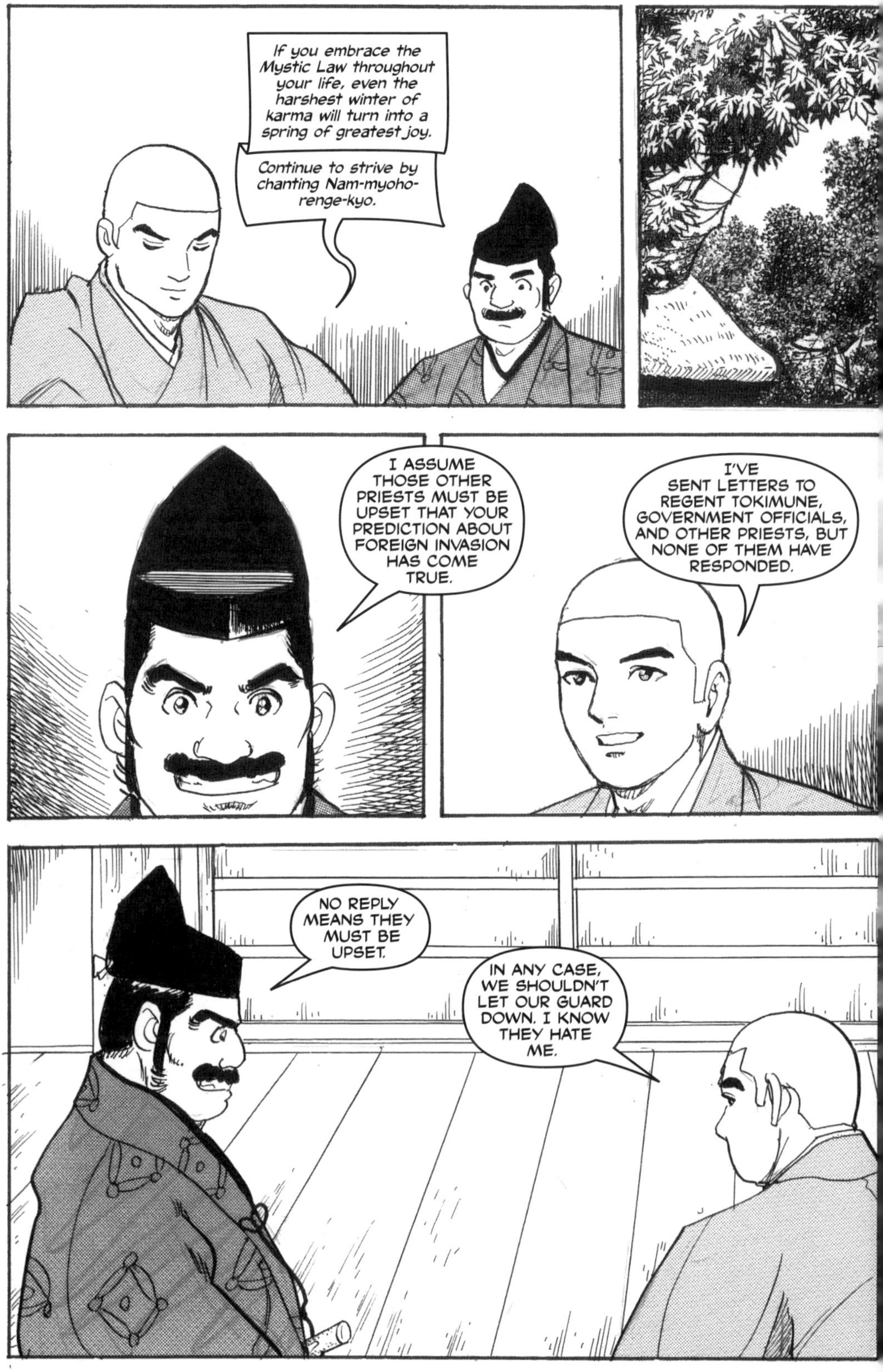

If you embrace the Mystic Law throughout your life, even the harshest winter of karma will turn into a spring of greatest joy.
Continue to strive by chanting Nam-myoho-renge-kyo.
I ASSUME THOSE OTHER PRIESTS MUST BE UPSET THAT YOUR PREDICTION ABOUT FOREIGN INVASION HAS COME TRUE.
I'VE SENT LETTERS TO REGENT TOKIMUNE, GOVERNMENT OFFICIALS, AND OTHER PRIESTS, BUT NONE OF THEM HAVE RESPONDED.
NO REPLY MEANS THEY MUST BE UPSET.
IN ANY CASE, WE SHOULDN'T LET OUR GUARD DOWN. I KNOW THEY HATE ME.

GOKURAKU-JI,
A TEMPLE IN
KAMAKURA.

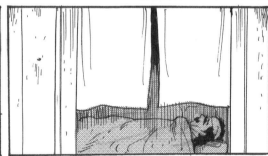

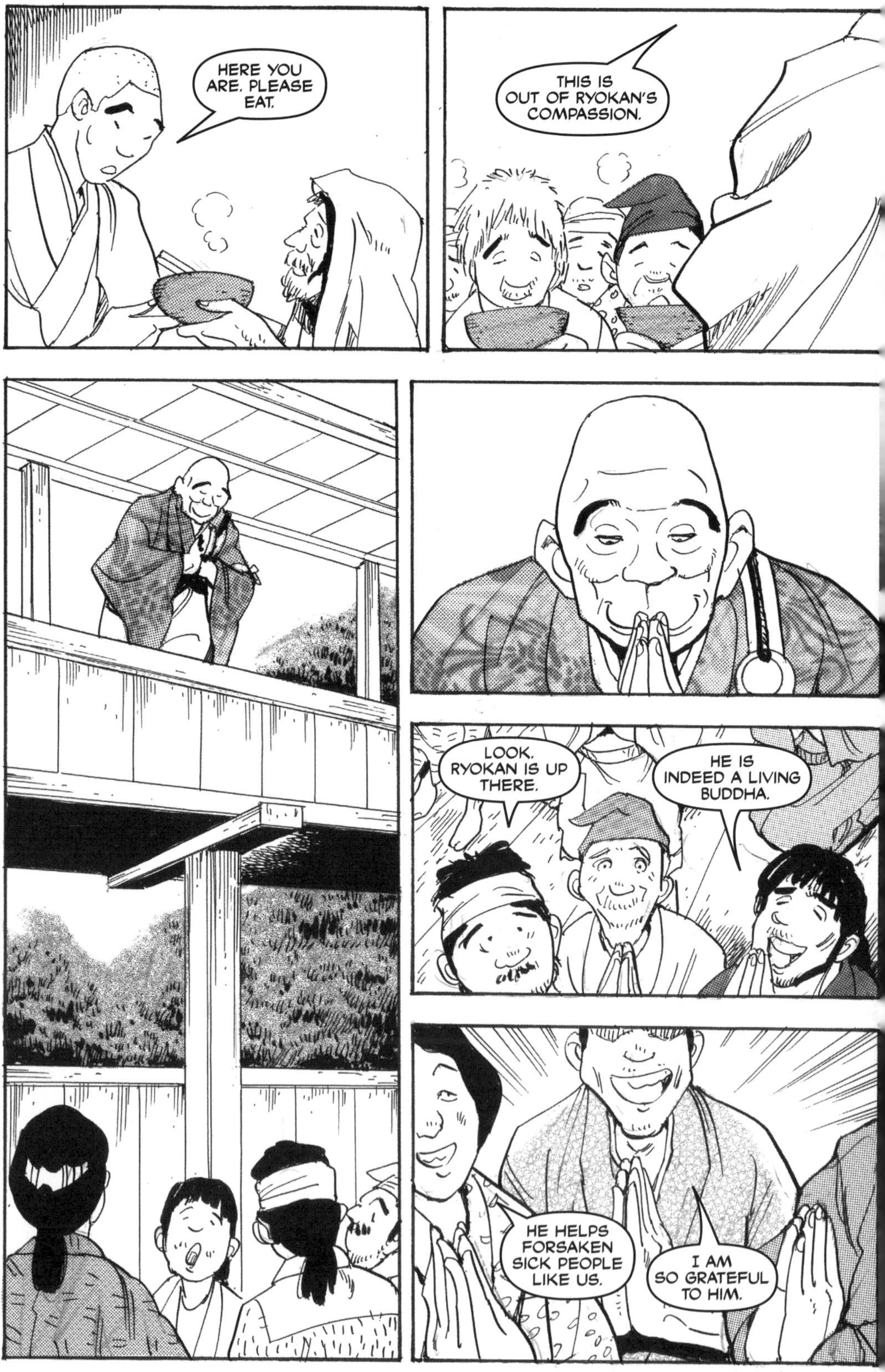
HERE YOU ARE. PLEASE EAT.
THIS IS OUT OF RYOKAN'S COMPASSION.
LOOK. RYOKAN IS UP THERE.
HE IS INDEED A LIVING BUDDHA.
HE HELPS FORSAKEN SICK PEOPLE LIKE US.
I AM SO GRATEFUL TO HIM.

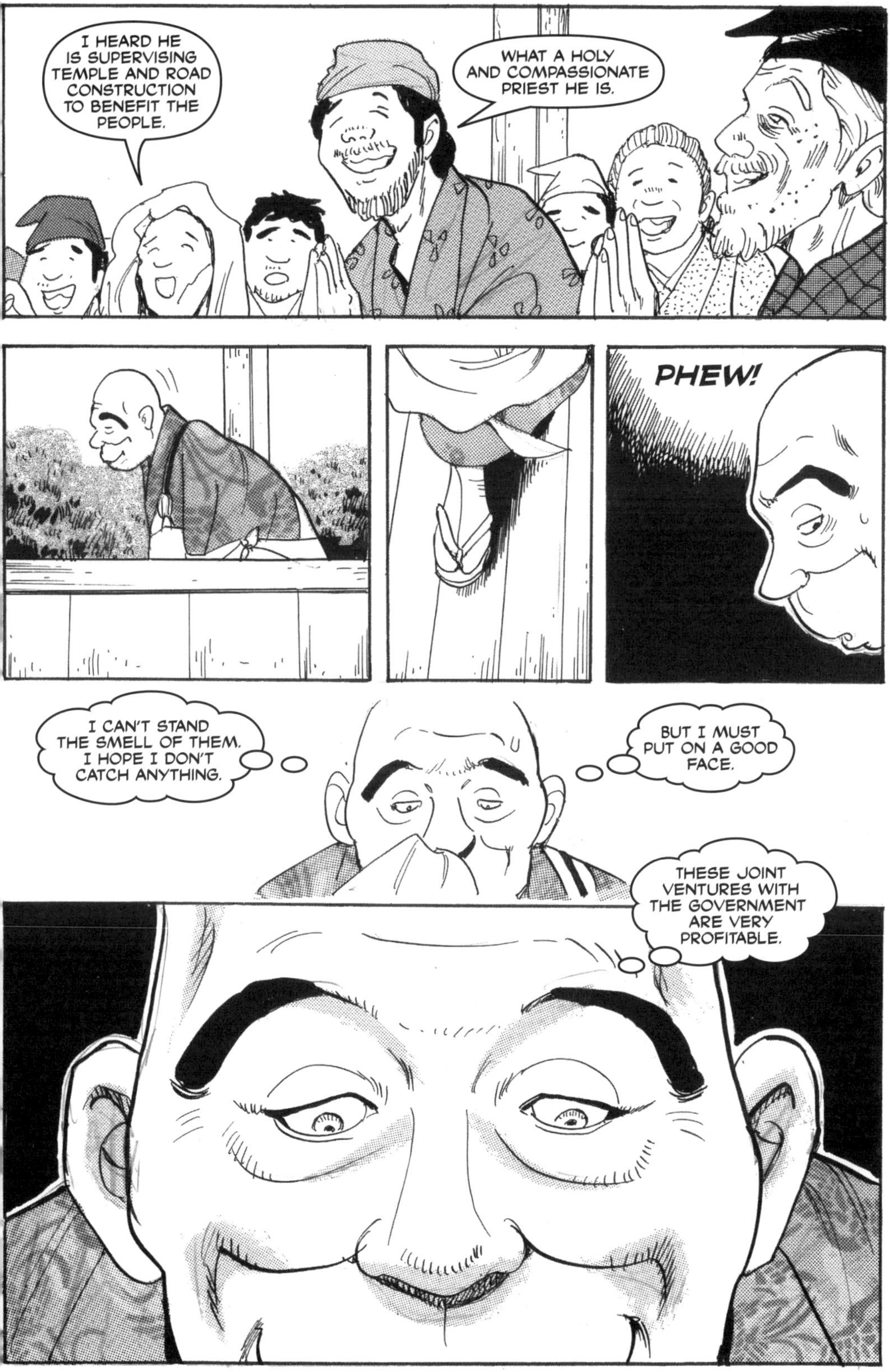
I HEARD HE IS SUPERVISING TEMPLE AND ROAD CONSTRUCTION TO BENEFIT THE PEOPLE.
WHAT A HOLY AND COMPASSIONATE PRIEST HE IS.
PHEW!
I CAN'T STAND THE SMELL OF THEM. I HOPE I DON'T CATCH ANYTHING.
BUT I MUST PUT ON A GOOD FACE.
THESE JOINT VENTURES WITH THE GOVERNMENT ARE VERY PROFITABLE.

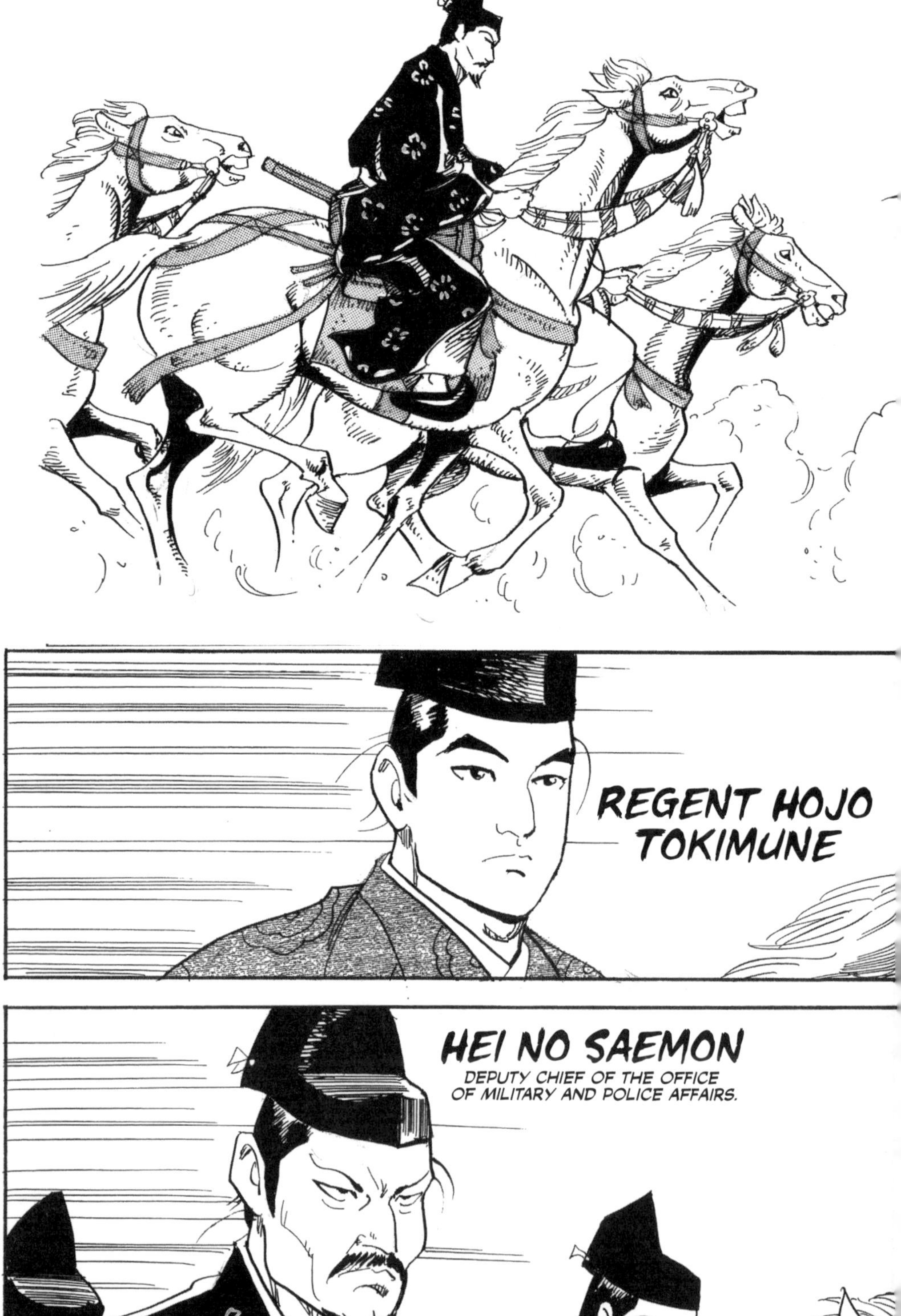
REGENT HOJO TOKIMUNE
HEI NO SAEMON
DEPUTY CHIEF OF THE OFFICE OF MILITARY AND POLICE AFFAIRS.

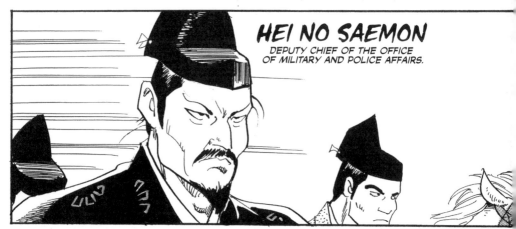

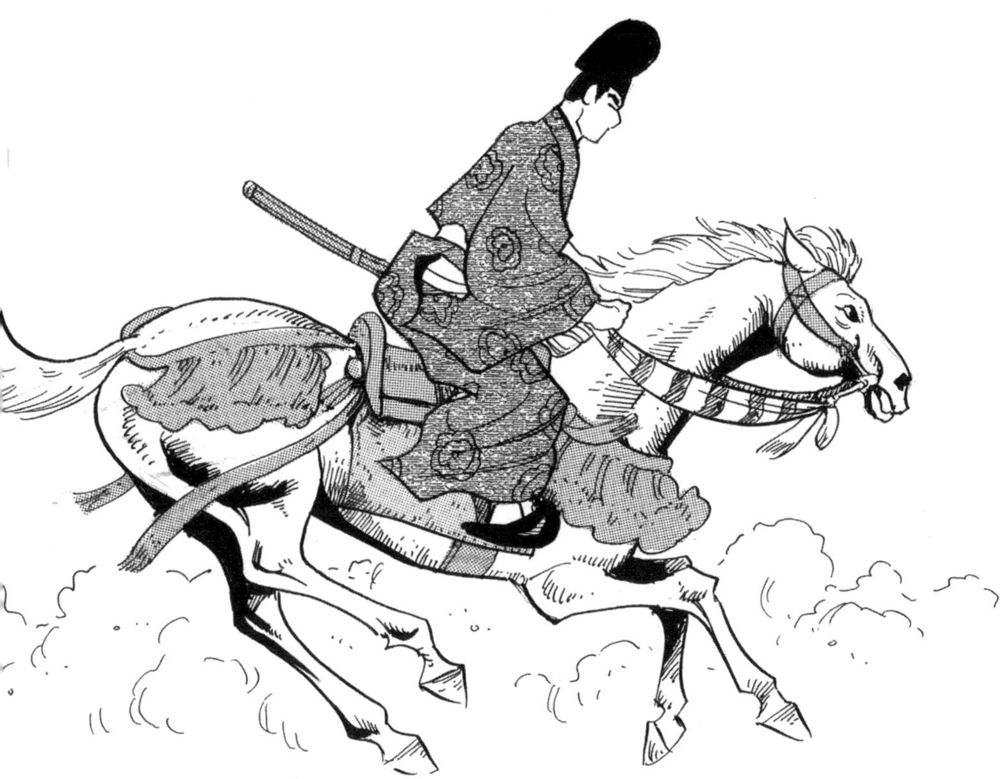

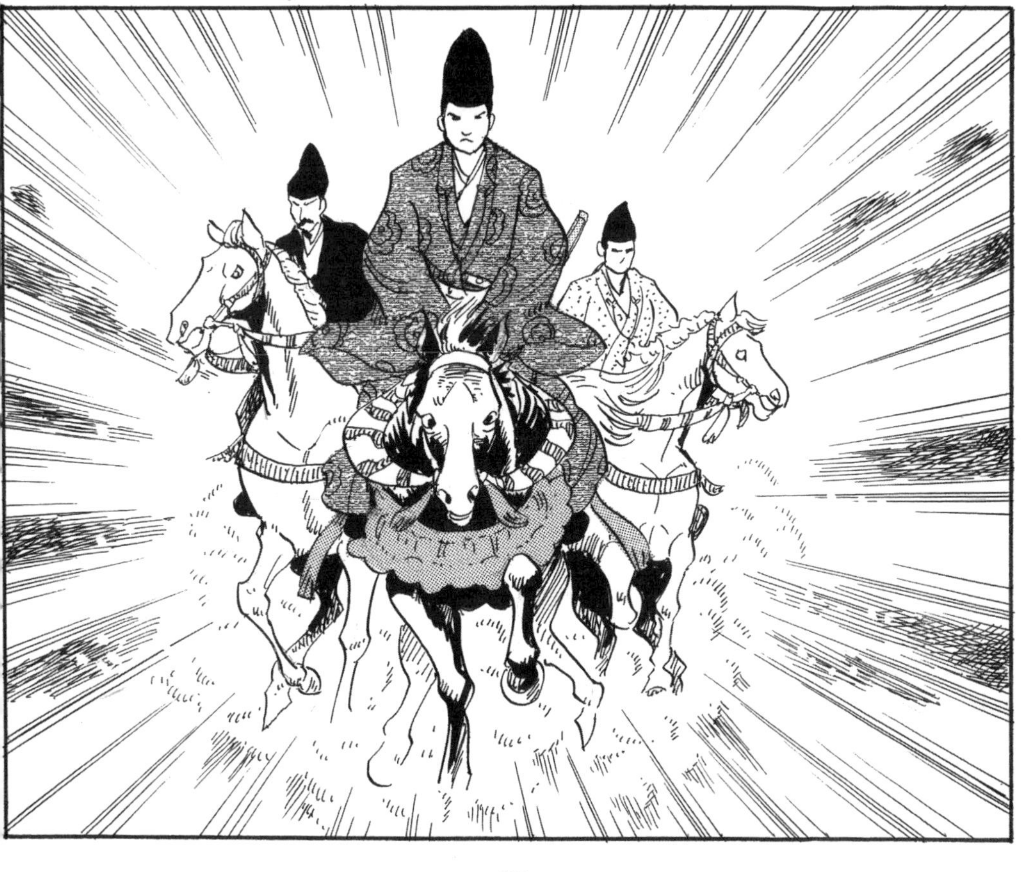

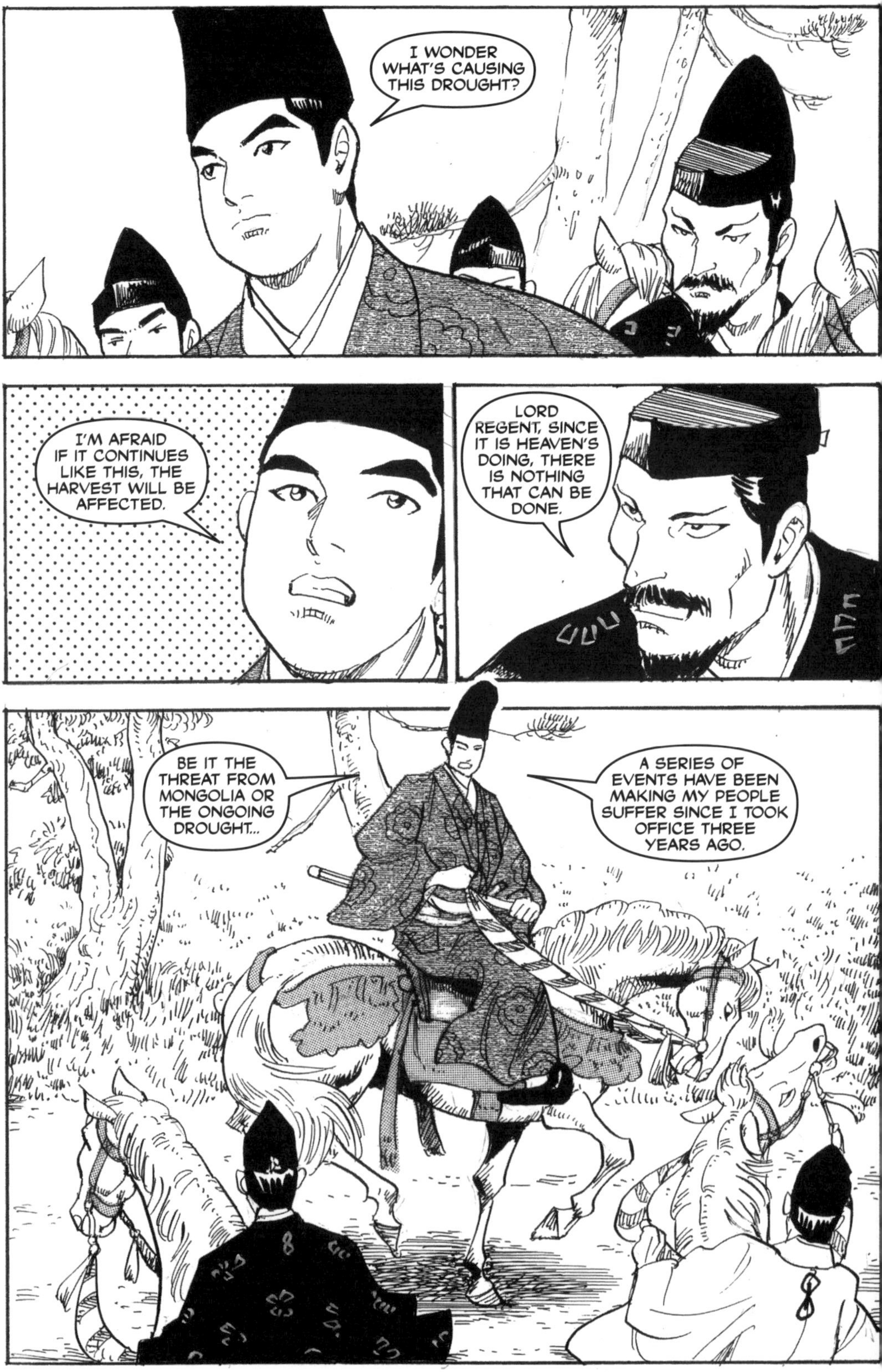
I WONDER WHAT'S CAUSING THIS DROUGHT?
I'M AFRAID IF IT CONTINUES LIKE THIS, THE HARVEST WILL BE AFFECTED.
LORD REGENT, SINCE IT IS HEAVEN'S DOING, THERE IS NOTHING THAT CAN BE DONE.
BE IT THE THREAT FROM MONGOLIA OR THE ONGOING DROUGHT...
A SERIES OF EVENTS HAVE BEEN MAKING MY PEOPLE SUFFER SINCE I TOOK OFFICE THREE YEARS AGO.

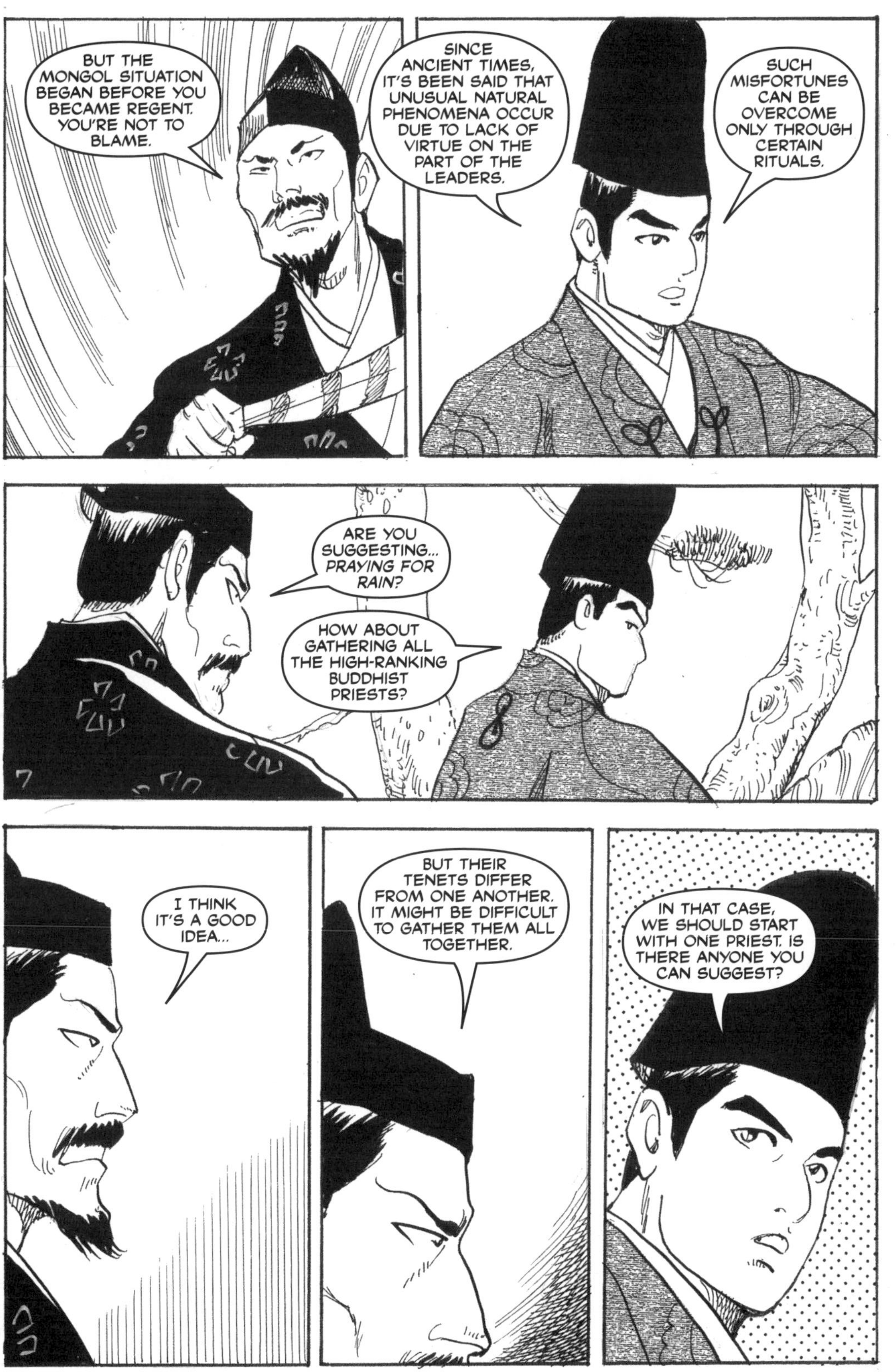

BUT THE MONGOL SITUATION BEGAN BEFORE YOU BECAME REGENT. YOU'RE NOT TO BLAME.
SINCE ANCIENT TIMES, IT'S BEEN SAID THAT UNUSUAL NATURAL PHENOMENA OCCUR DUE TO LACK OF VIRTUE ON THE PART OF THE LEADERS.
SUCH MISFORTUNES CAN BE OVERCOME ONLY THROUGH CERTAIN RITUALS.
ARE YOU SUGGESTING... *PRAYING FOR RAIN?*
HOW ABOUT GATHERING ALL THE HIGH-RANKING BUDDHIST PRIESTS?
I THINK IT'S A GOOD IDEA...
BUT THEIR TENETS DIFFER FROM ONE ANOTHER. IT MIGHT BE DIFFICULT TO GATHER THEM ALL TOGETHER.
IN THAT CASE, WE SHOULD START WITH ONE PRIEST. IS THERE ANYONE YOU CAN SUGGEST?

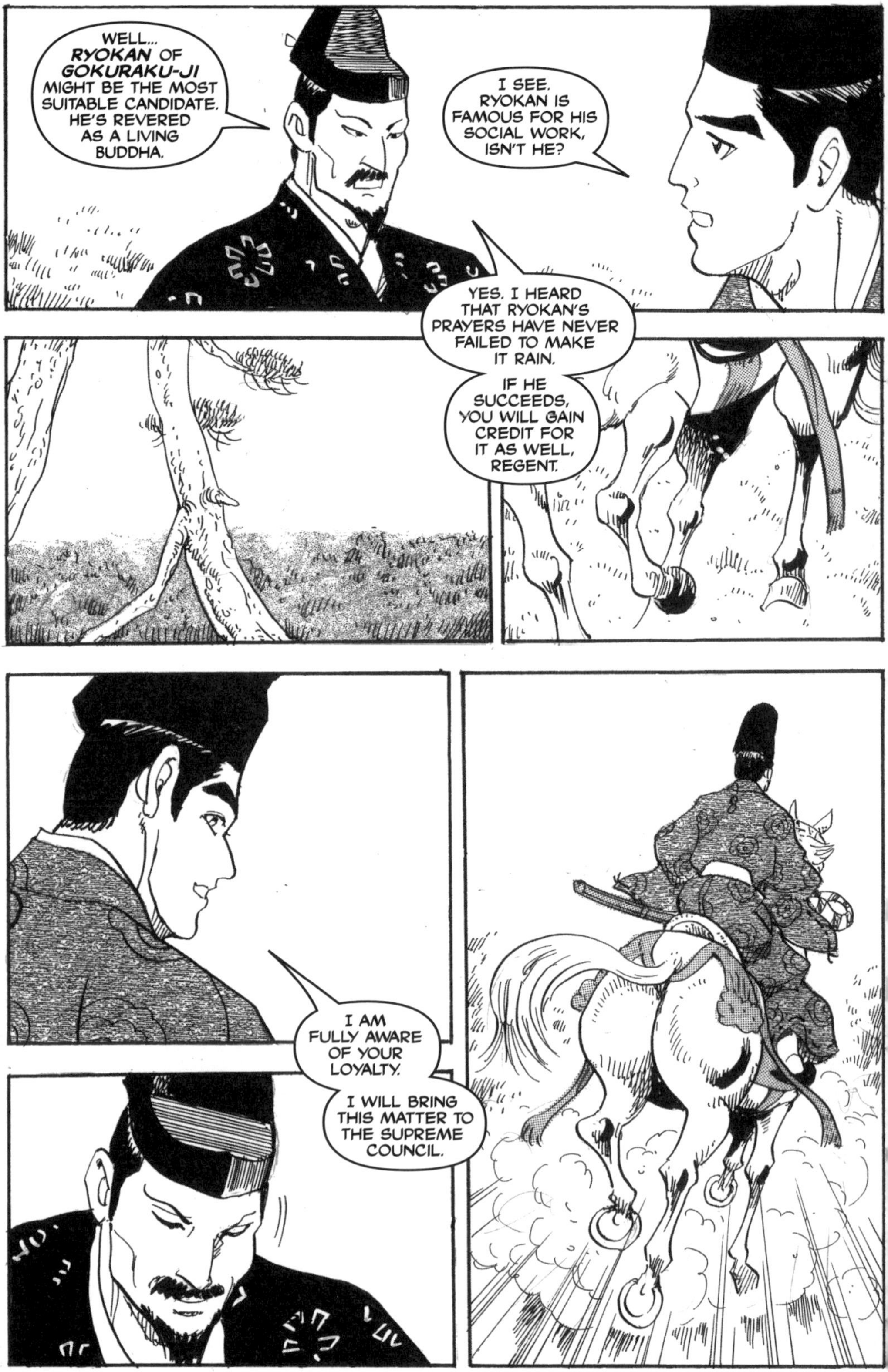
WELL... RYOKAN OF GOKURAKU-JI MIGHT BE THE MOST SUITABLE CANDIDATE. HE'S REVERED AS A LIVING BUDDHA.
I SEE. RYOKAN IS FAMOUS FOR HIS SOCIAL WORK, ISN'T HE?
YES. I HEARD THAT RYOKAN'S PRAYERS HAVE NEVER FAILED TO MAKE IT RAIN.
IF HE SUCCEEDS, YOU WILL GAIN CREDIT FOR IT AS WELL, REGENT.
I AM FULLY AWARE OF YOUR LOYALTY.
I WILL BRING THIS MATTER TO THE SUPREME COUNCIL.

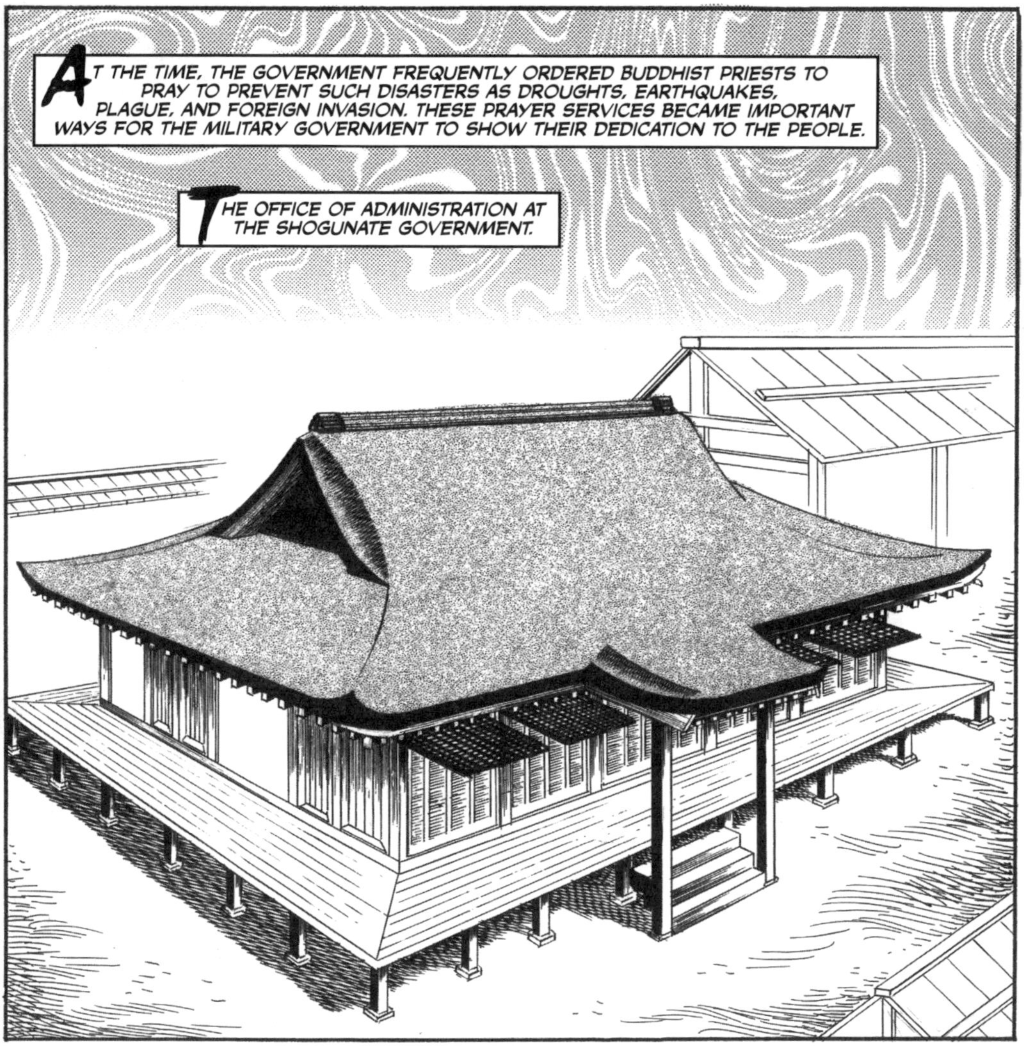
AT THE TIME, THE GOVERNMENT FREQUENTLY ORDERED BUDDHIST PRIESTS TO PRAY TO PREVENT SUCH DISASTERS AS DROUGHTS, EARTHQUAKES, PLAGUE, AND FOREIGN INVASION. THESE PRAYER SERVICES BECAME IMPORTANT WAYS FOR THE MILITARY GOVERNMENT TO SHOW THEIR DEDICATION TO THE PEOPLE.
THE OFFICE OF ADMINISTRATION AT THE SHOGUNATE GOVERNMENT.

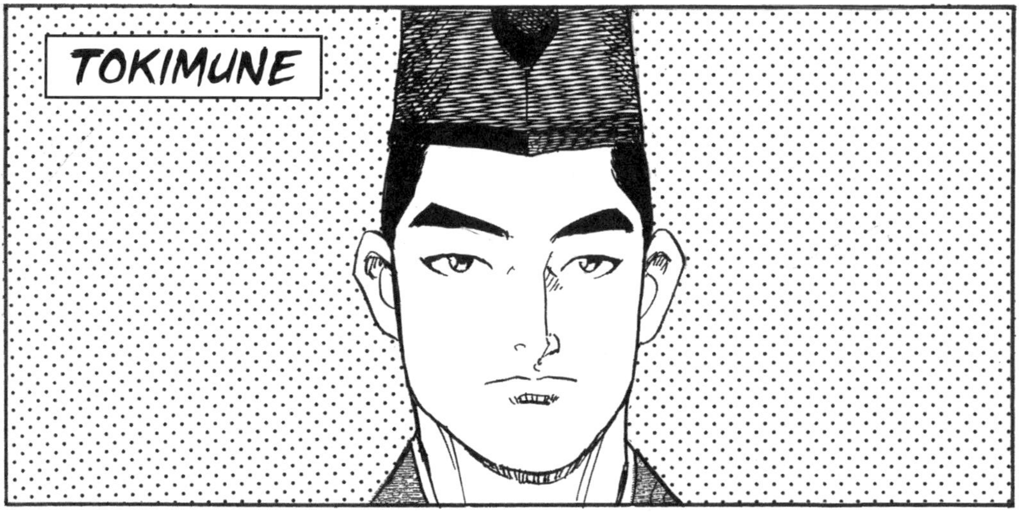
TOKIMUNE

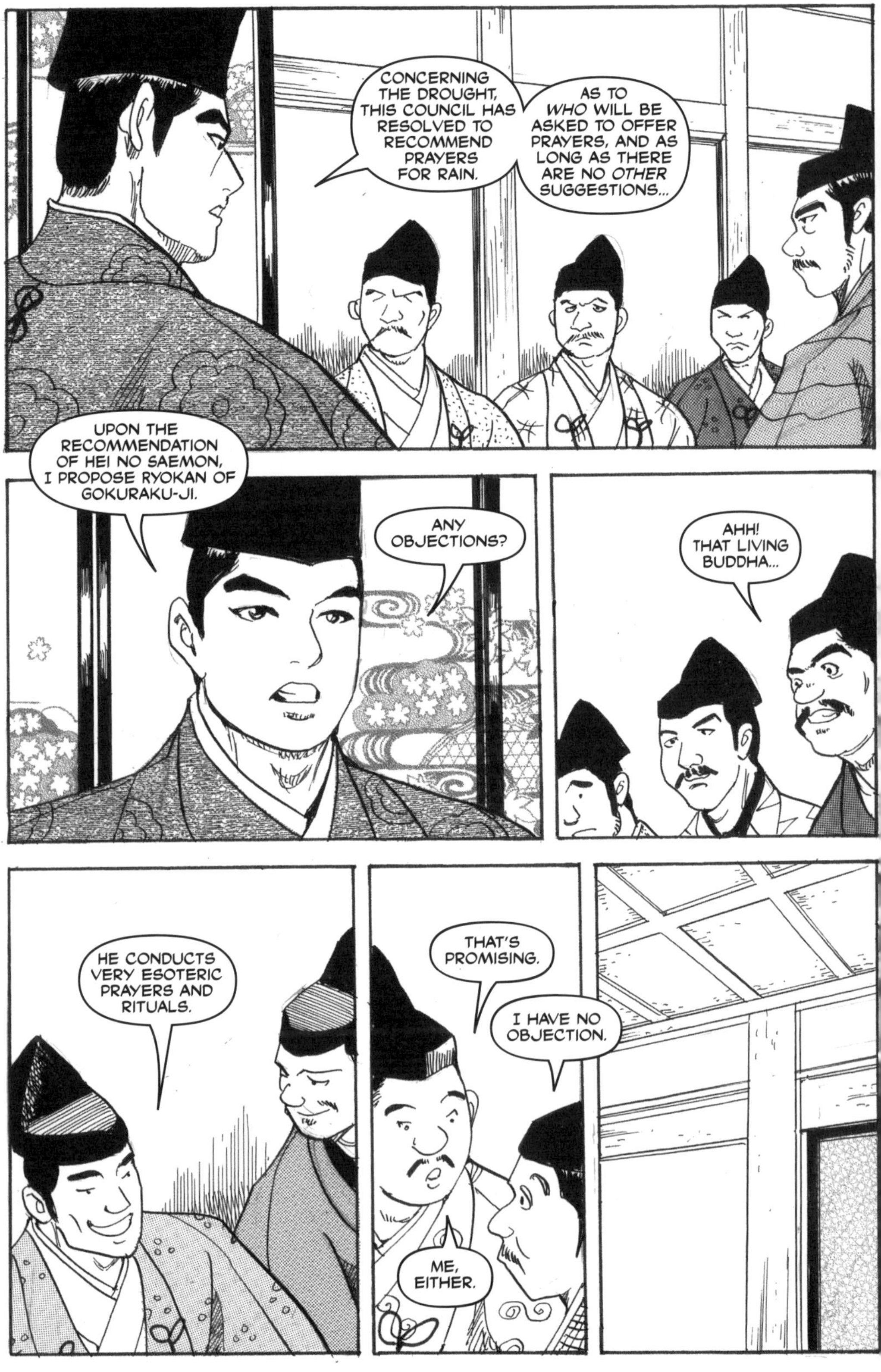
CONCERNING THE DROUGHT, THIS COUNCIL HAS RESOLVED TO RECOMMEND PRAYERS FOR RAIN.
AS TO *WHO* WILL BE ASKED TO OFFER PRAYERS, AND AS LONG AS THERE ARE NO *OTHER* SUGGESTIONS...
UPON THE RECOMMENDATION OF HEI NO SAEMON, I PROPOSE RYOKAN OF GOKURAKU-JI.
ANY OBJECTIONS?
AHH! THAT LIVING BUDDHA...
HE CONDUCTS VERY ESOTERIC PRAYERS AND RITUALS.
THAT'S PROMISING.
I HAVE NO OBJECTION.
ME, EITHER.

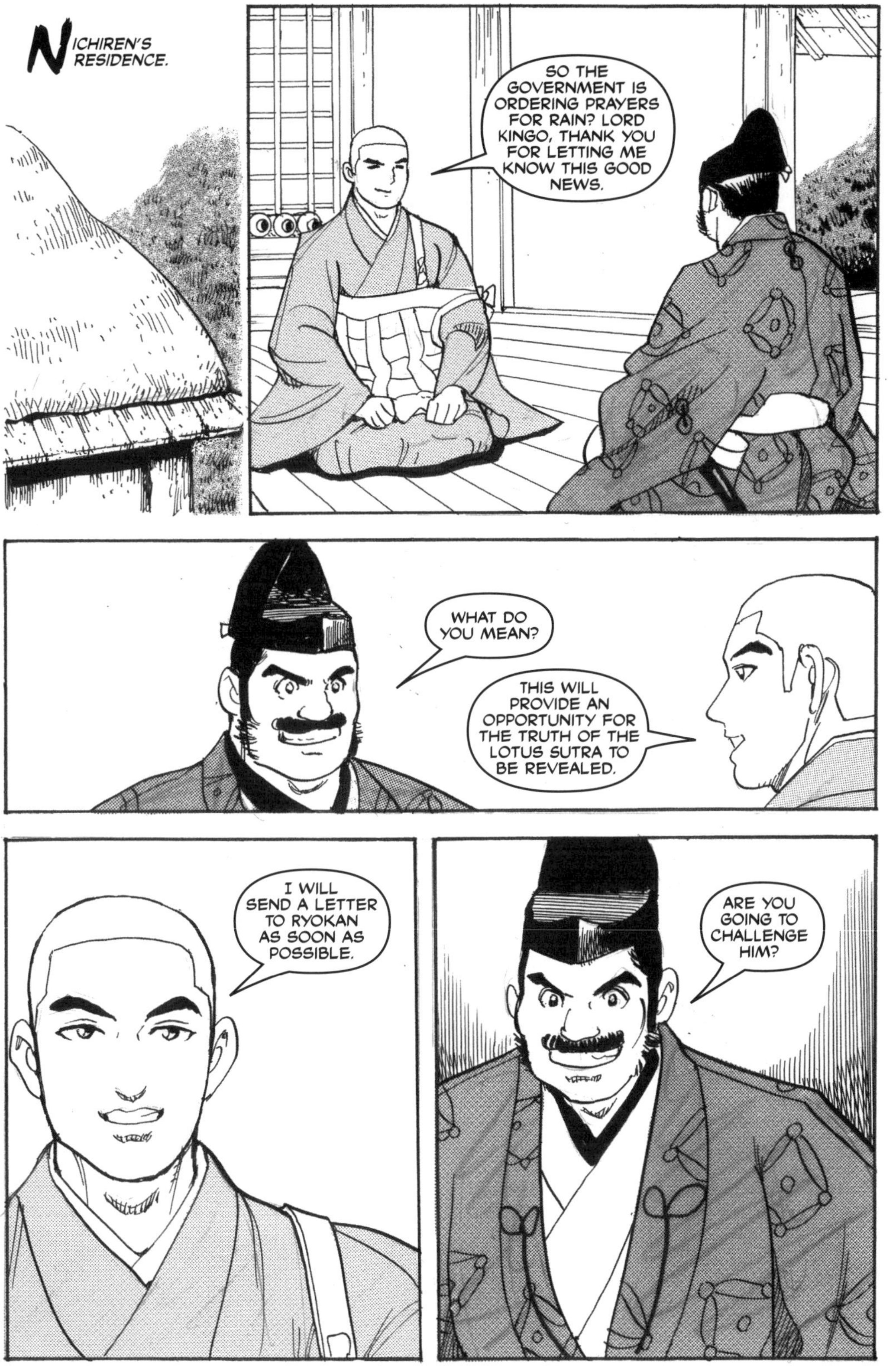
NICHIREN'S RESIDENCE.
SO THE GOVERNMENT IS ORDERING PRAYERS FOR RAIN? LORD KINGO, THANK YOU FOR LETTING ME KNOW THIS GOOD NEWS.
WHAT DO YOU MEAN?
THIS WILL PROVIDE AN OPPORTUNITY FOR THE TRUTH OF THE LOTUS SUTRA TO BE REVEALED.
I WILL SEND A LETTER TO RYOKAN AS SOON AS POSSIBLE.
ARE YOU GOING TO CHALLENGE HIM?

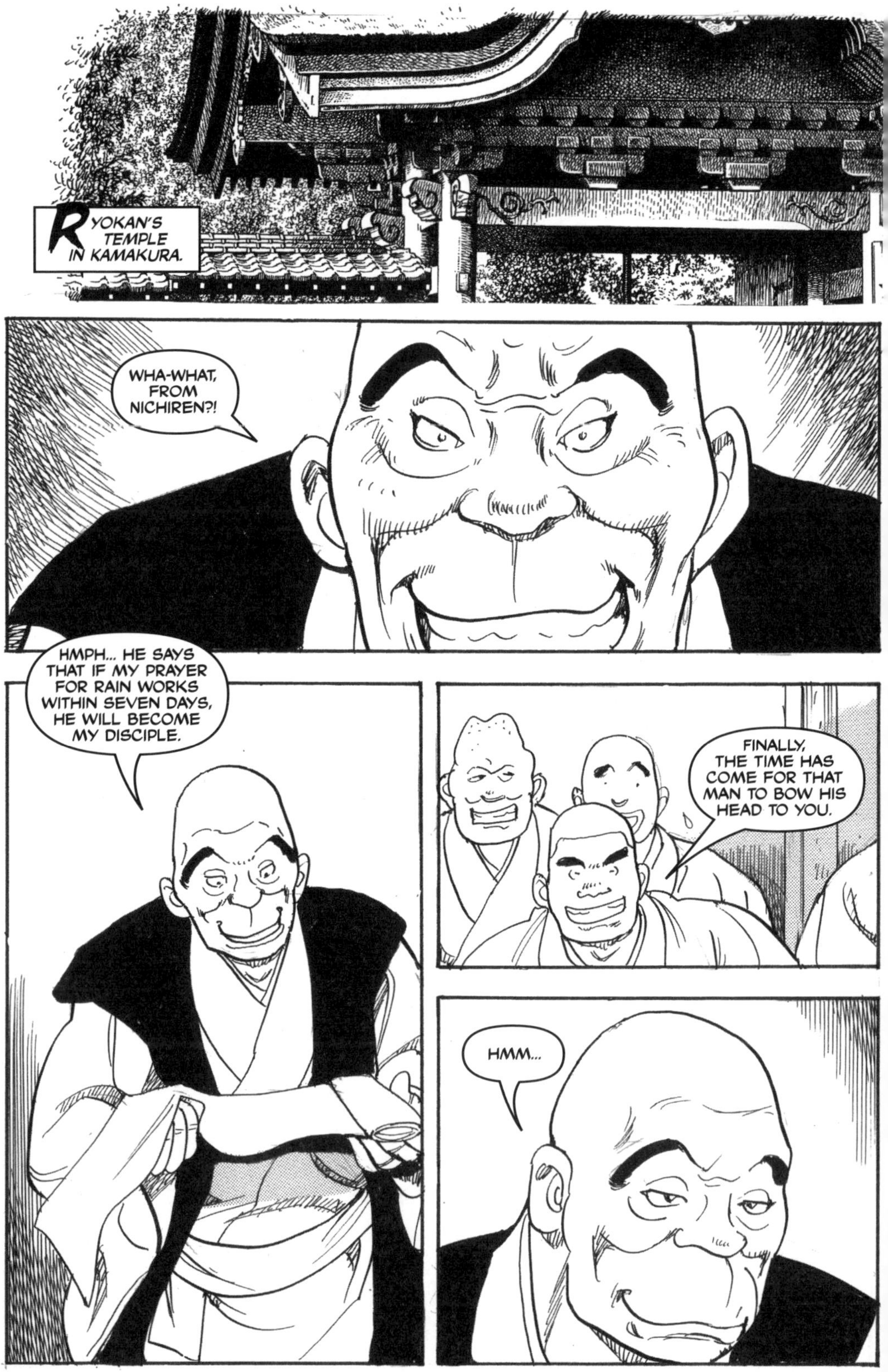
RYOKAN'S TEMPLE IN KAMAKURA.
WHA-WHAT, FROM NICHIREN?!
HMPH... HE SAYS THAT IF MY PRAYER FOR RAIN WORKS WITHIN SEVEN DAYS, HE WILL BECOME MY DISCIPLE.
FINALLY, THE TIME HAS COME FOR THAT MAN TO BOW HIS HEAD TO YOU.
HMM...

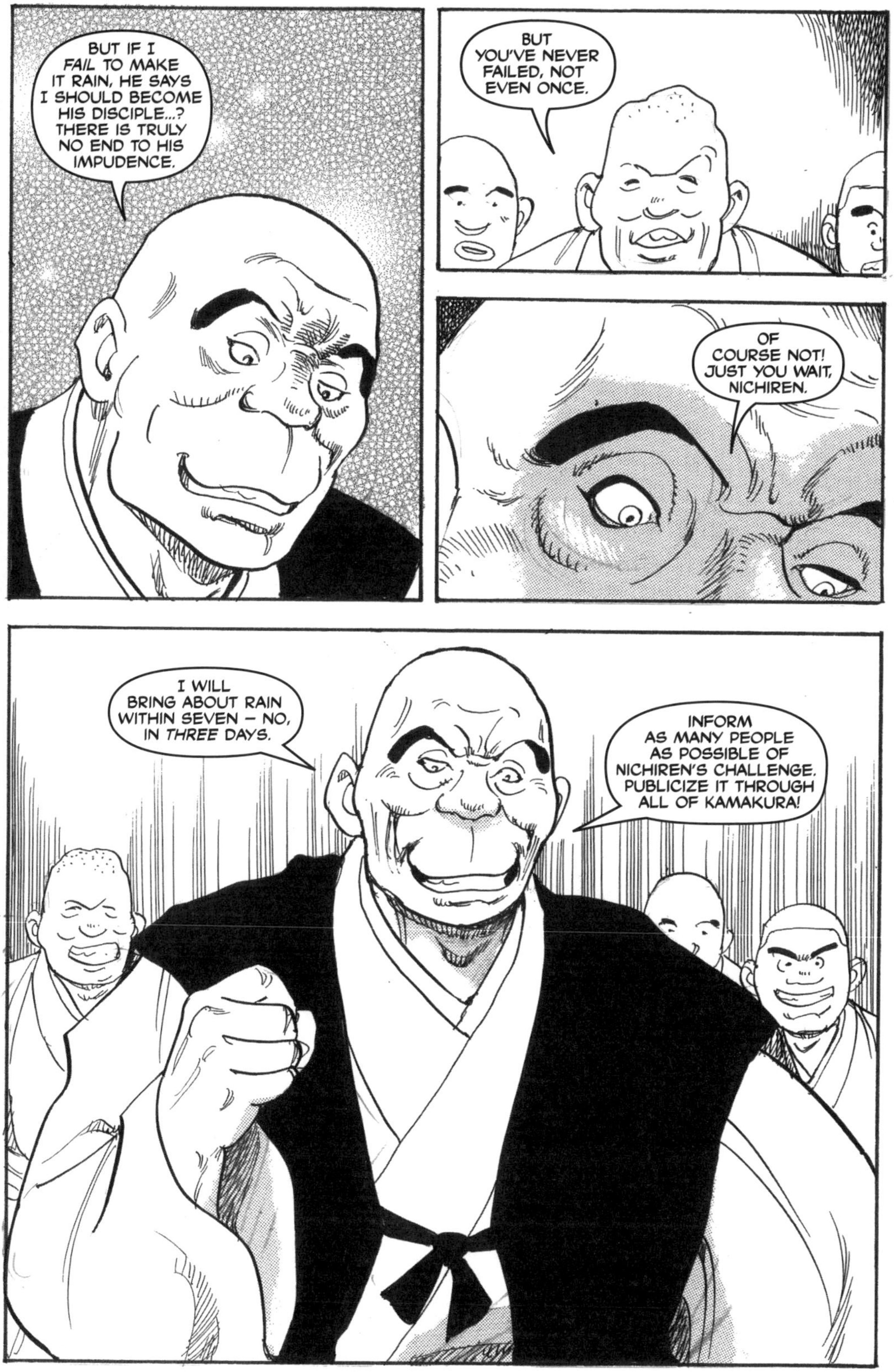
BUT IF I *FAIL* TO MAKE IT RAIN, HE SAYS I SHOULD BECOME HIS DISCIPLE...? THERE IS TRULY NO END TO HIS IMPUDENCE.
BUT YOU'VE NEVER FAILED, NOT EVEN ONCE.
OF COURSE NOT! JUST YOU WAIT, NICHIREN.
I WILL BRING ABOUT RAIN WITHIN SEVEN – NO, IN *THREE* DAYS.
INFORM AS MANY PEOPLE AS POSSIBLE OF NICHIREN'S CHALLENGE. PUBLICIZE IT THROUGH ALL OF KAMAKURA!

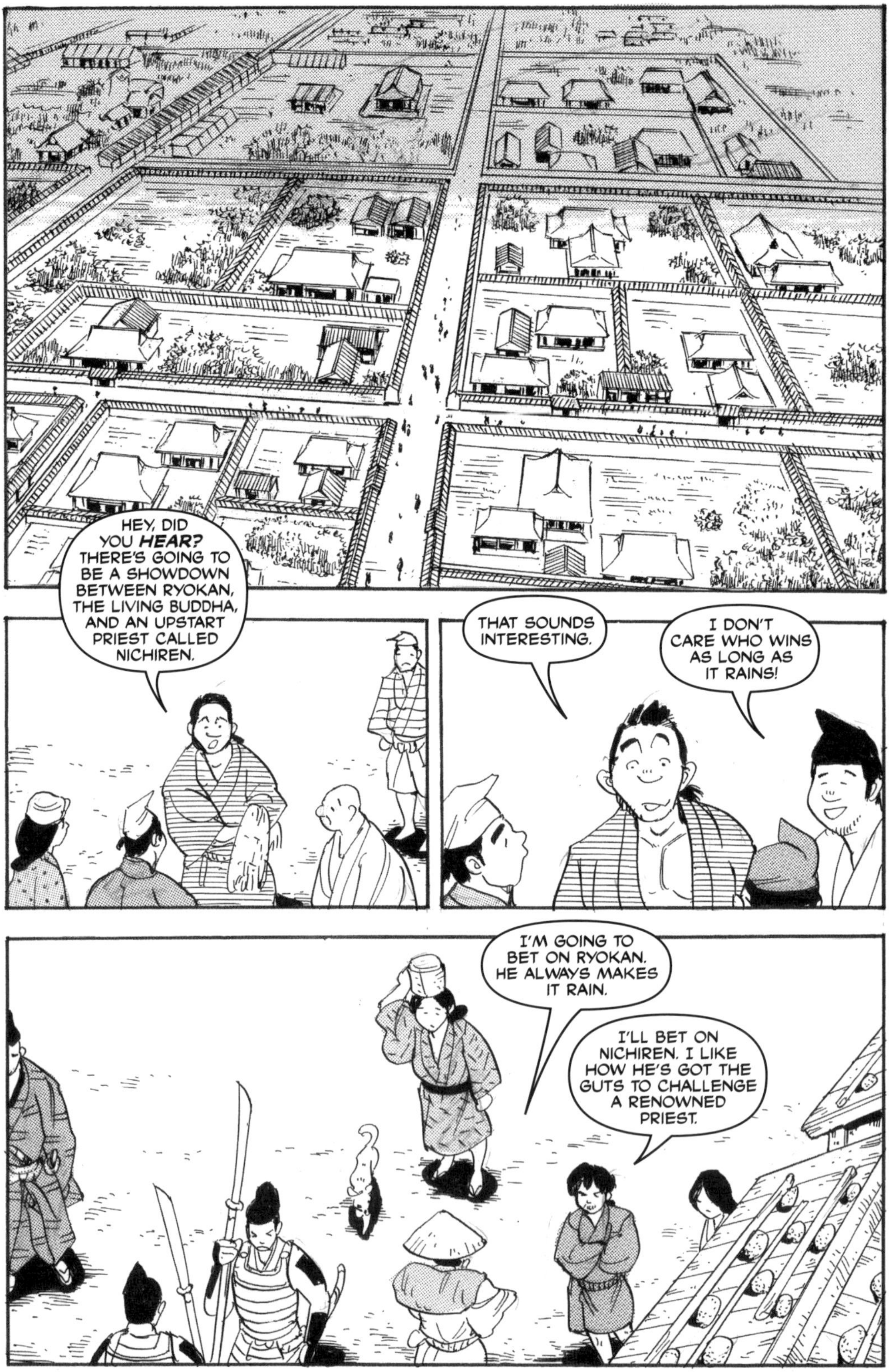
HEY, DID YOU ***HEAR?*** THERE'S GOING TO BE A SHOWDOWN BETWEEN RYOKAN, THE LIVING BUDDHA, AND AN UPSTART PRIEST CALLED NICHIREN.
THAT SOUNDS INTERESTING.
I DON'T CARE WHO WINS AS LONG AS IT RAINS!
I'M GOING TO BET ON RYOKAN. HE ALWAYS MAKES IT RAIN.
I'LL BET ON NICHIREN. I LIKE HOW HE'S GOT THE GUTS TO CHALLENGE A RENOWNED PRIEST.

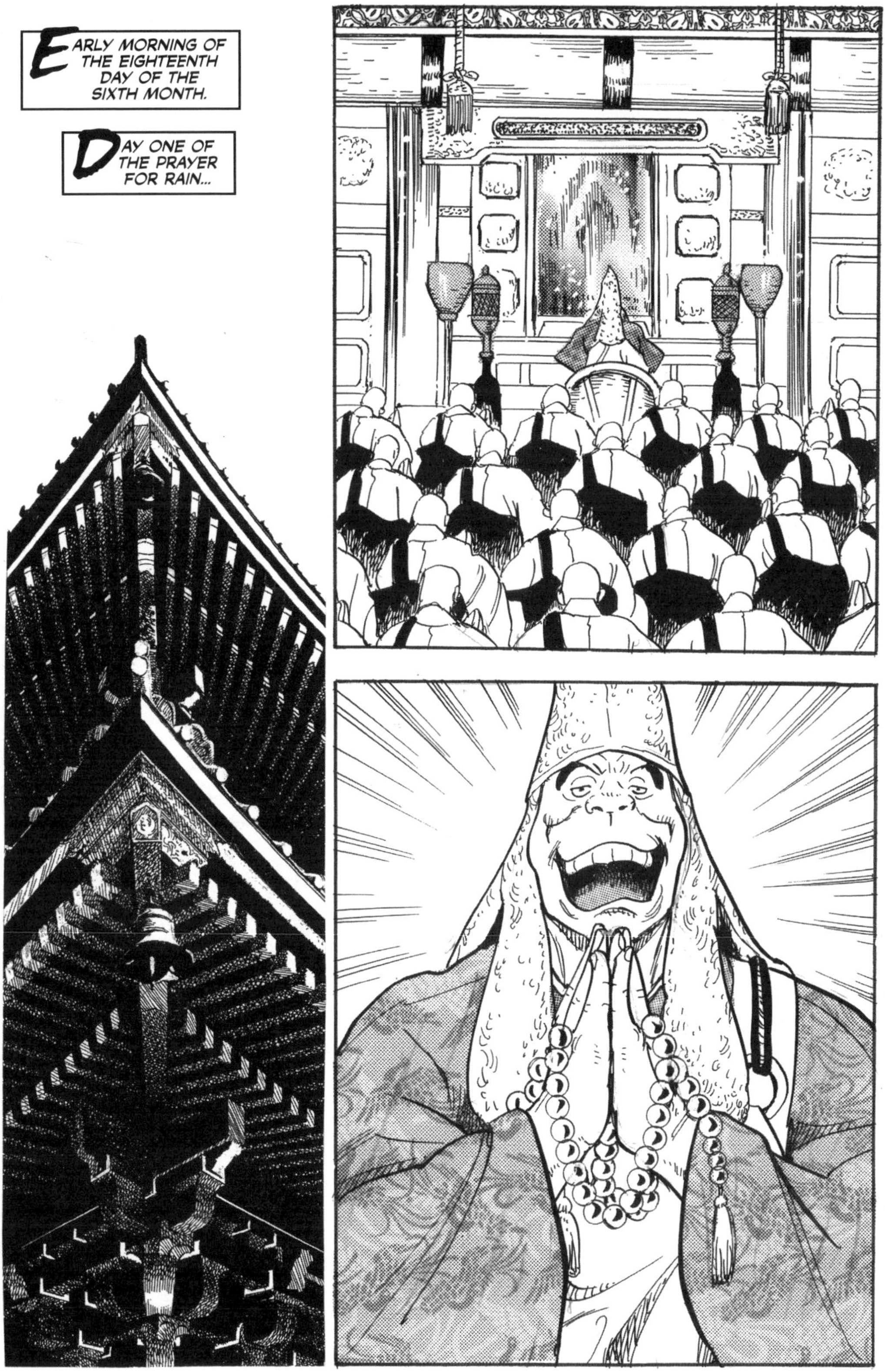
EARLY MORNING OF THE EIGHTEENTH DAY OF THE SIXTH MONTH.
DAY ONE OF THE PRAYER FOR RAIN...

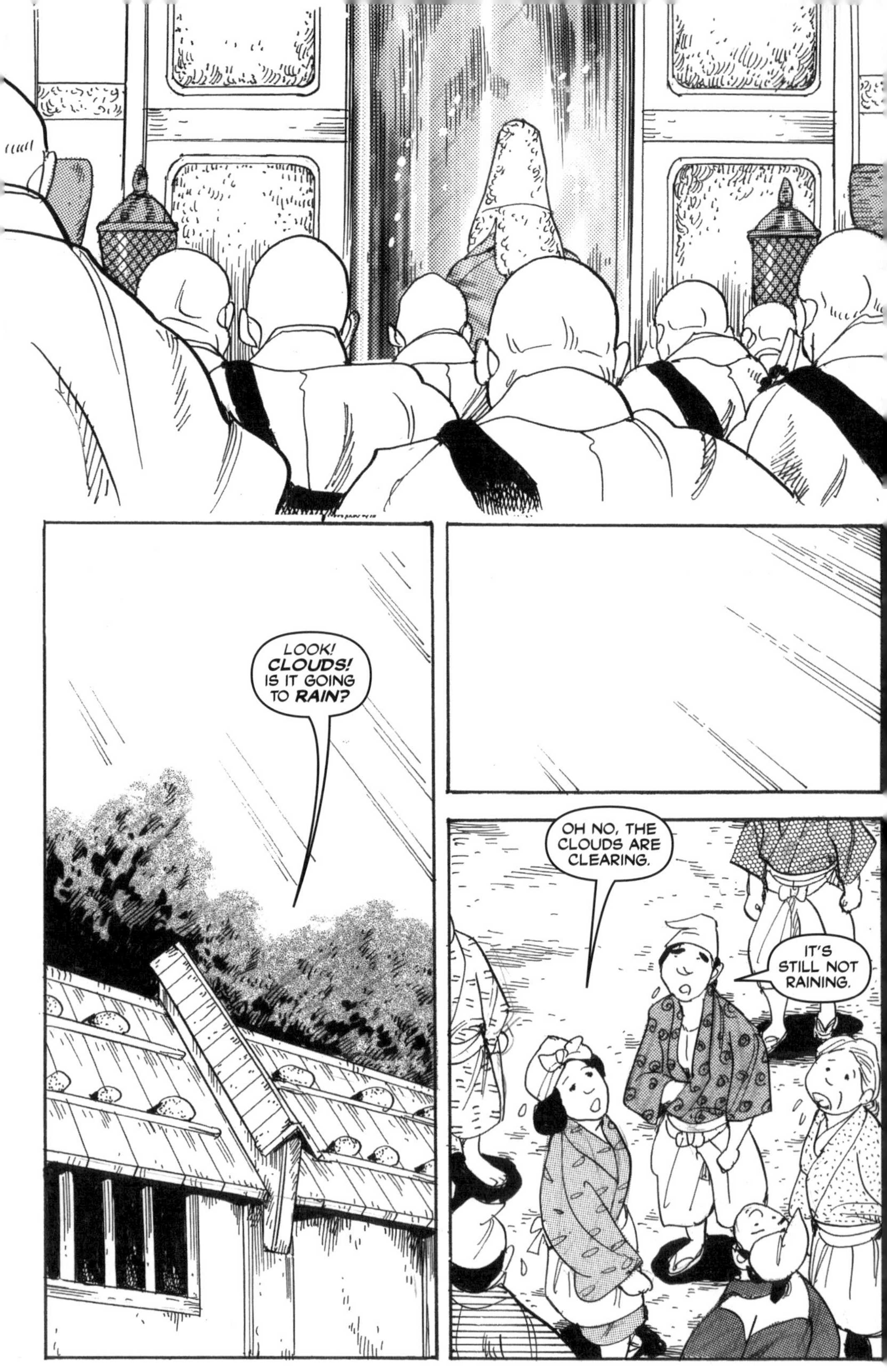
LOOK! CLOUDS! IS IT GOING TO RAIN?
OH NO, THE CLOUDS ARE CLEARING.
IT'S STILL NOT RAINING.

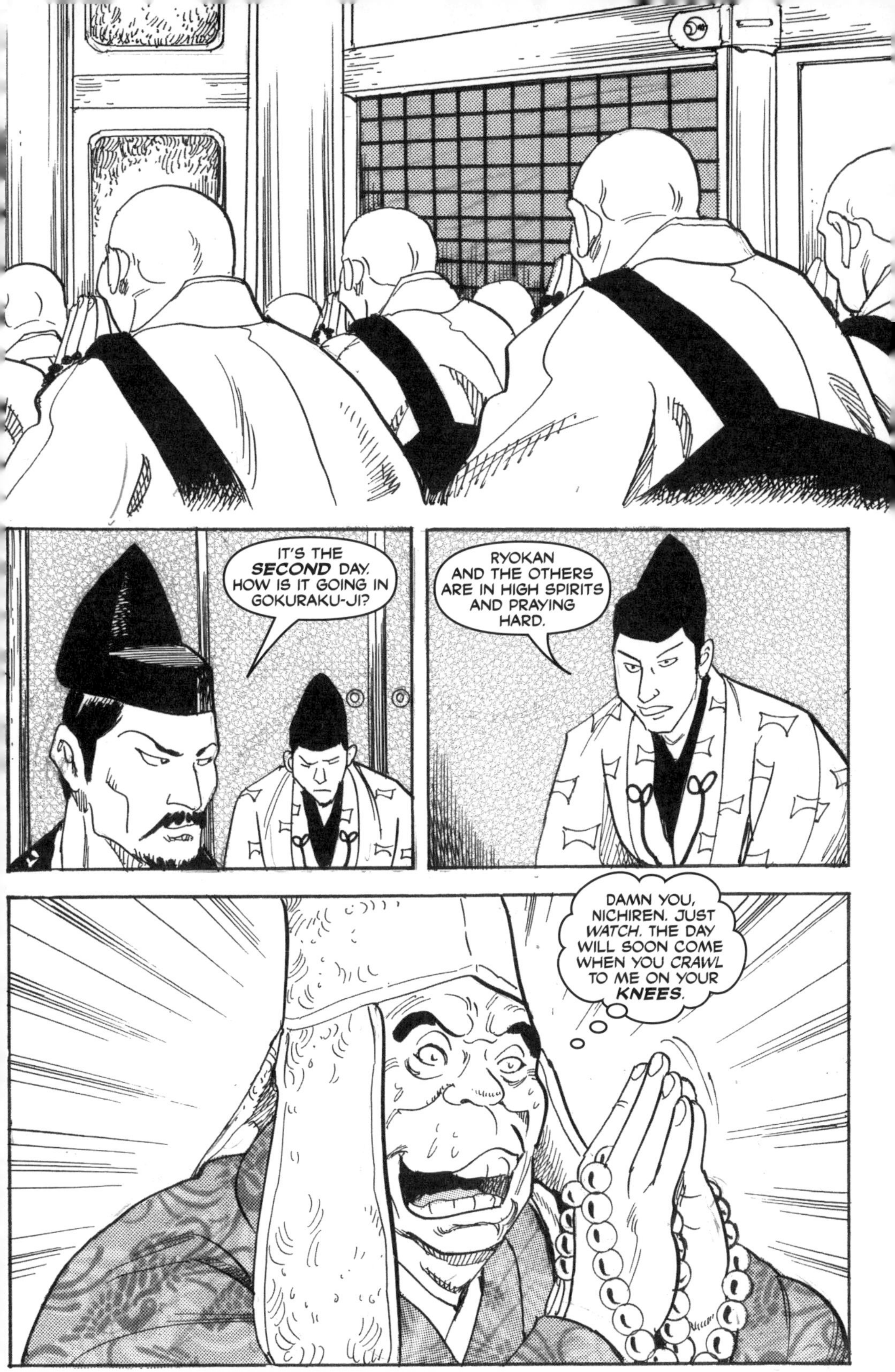
IT'S THE **SECOND** DAY. HOW IS IT GOING IN GOKURAKU-JI?
RYOKAN AND THE OTHERS ARE IN HIGH SPIRITS AND PRAYING HARD.
DAMN YOU, NICHIREN. JUST *WATCH*. THE DAY WILL SOON COME WHEN YOU *CRAWL* TO ME ON YOUR **KNEES**.

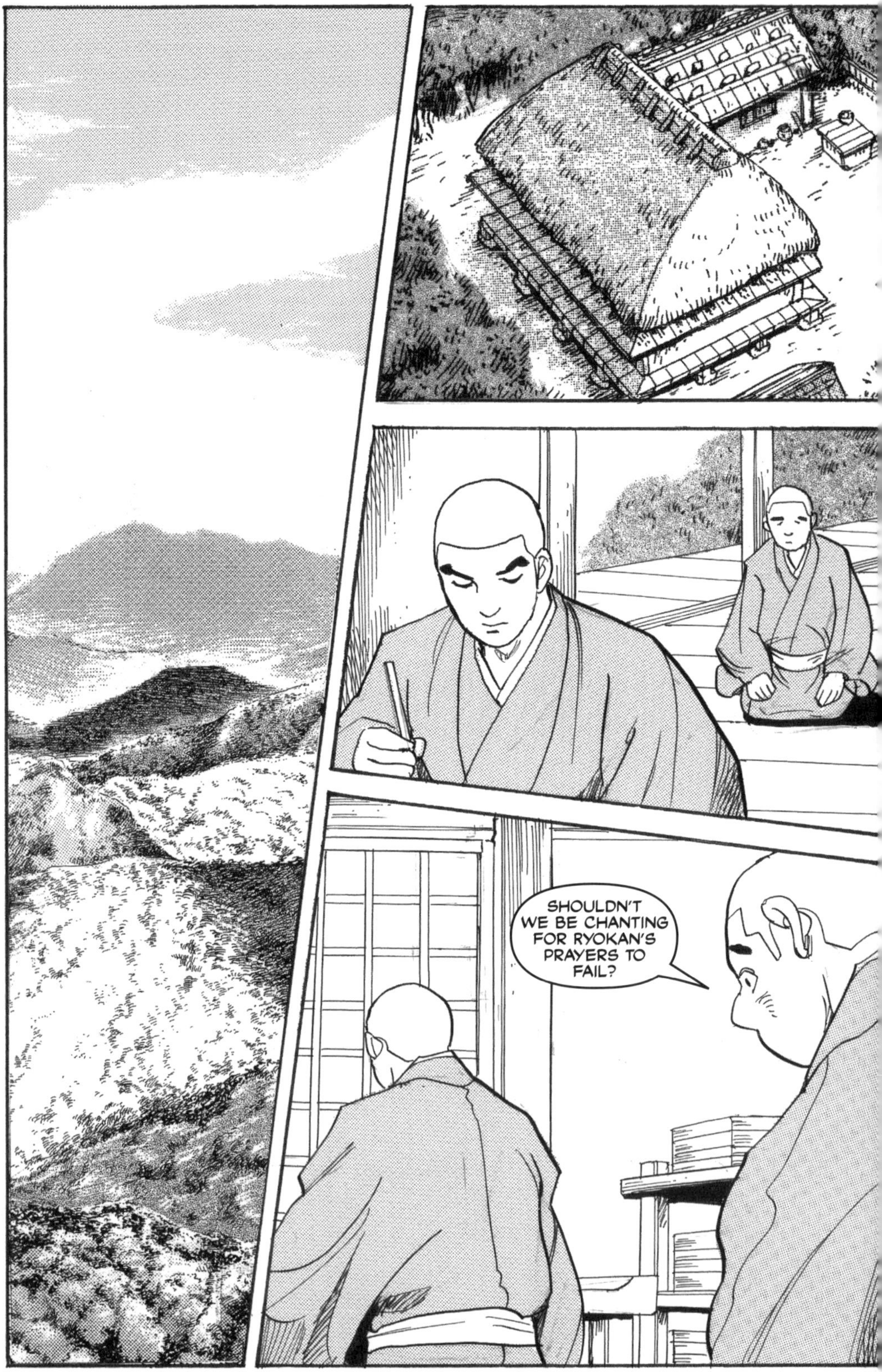
SHOULDN'T WE BE CHANTING FOR RYOKAN'S PRAYERS TO FAIL?

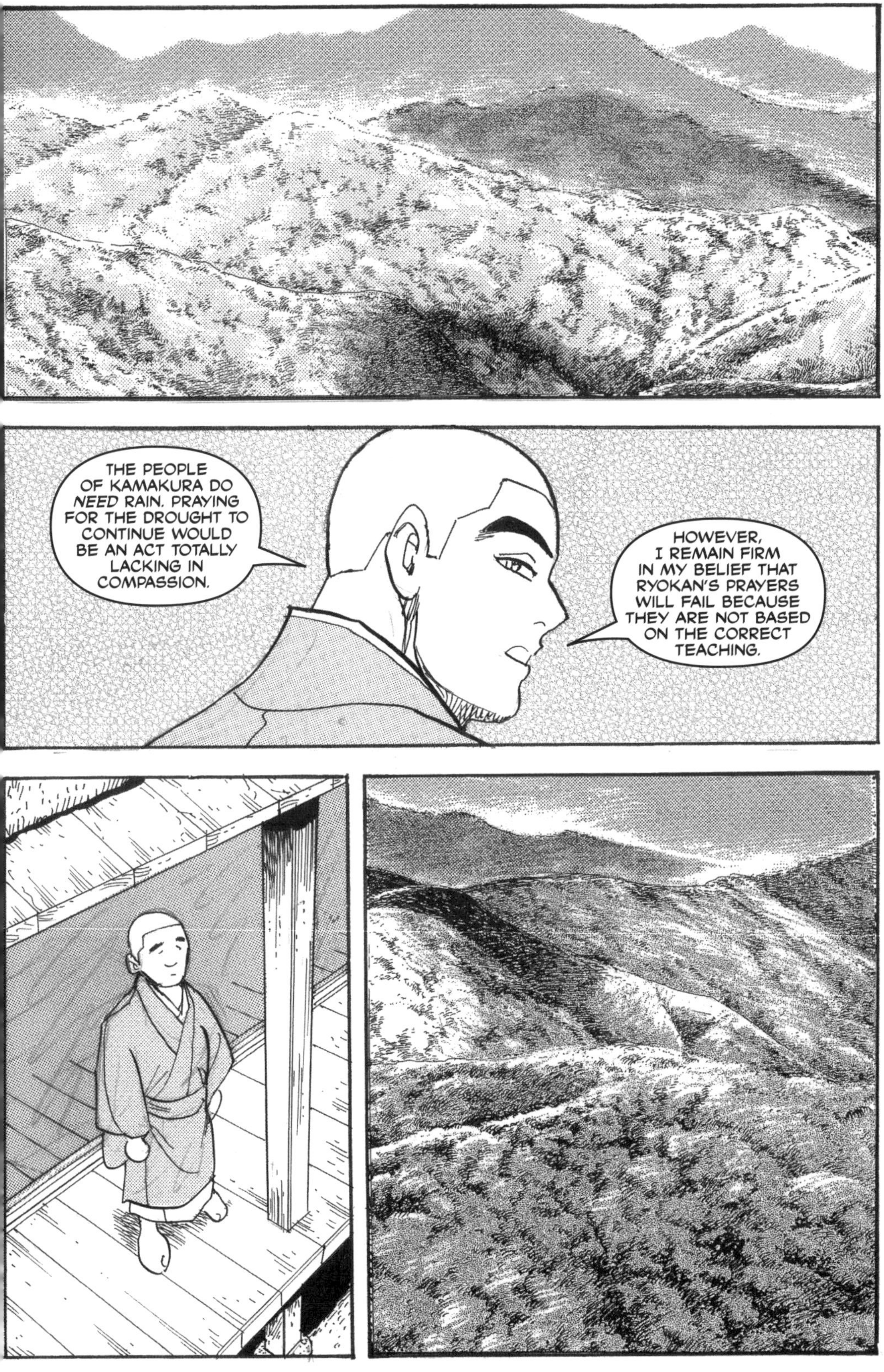
THE PEOPLE OF KAMAKURA DO *NEED* RAIN. PRAYING FOR THE DROUGHT TO CONTINUE WOULD BE AN ACT TOTALLY LACKING IN COMPASSION.
HOWEVER, I REMAIN FIRM IN MY BELIEF THAT RYOKAN'S PRAYERS WILL FAIL BECAUSE THEY ARE NOT BASED ON THE CORRECT TEACHING.

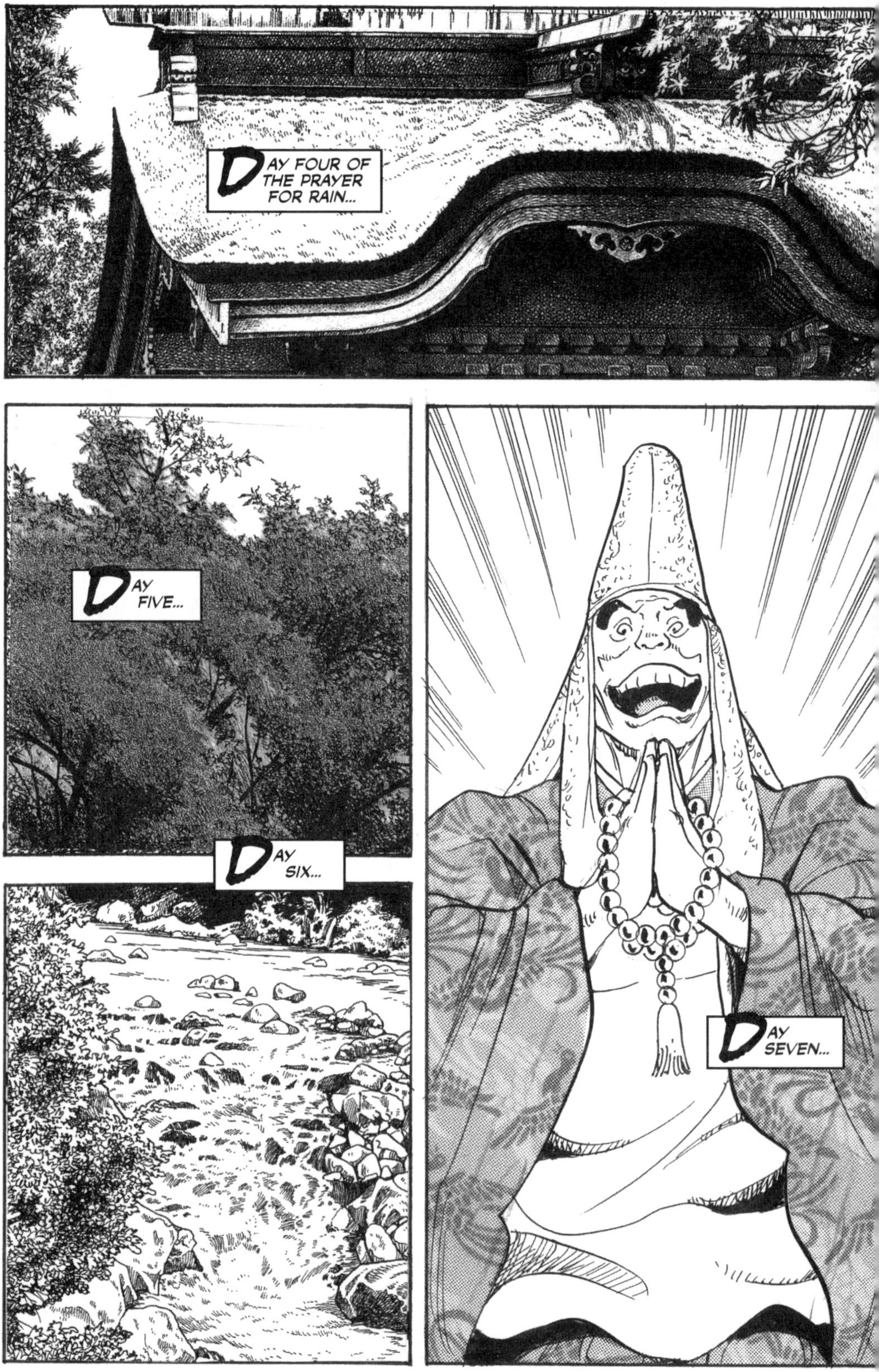
DAY FOUR OF THE PRAYER FOR RAIN...
DAY FIVE...
DAY SIX...
DAY SEVEN...

WELL, IT'S THE *LAST* DAY.

YES... IT SHOULD RAIN BY THE END OF THE DAY.

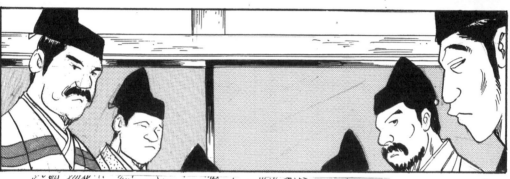

IT LOOKS LIKE NICHIREN WILL WIN.

THE SEVENTH DAY ISN'T OVER YET. I BET IT WILL BE POURING BY MIDNIGHT.

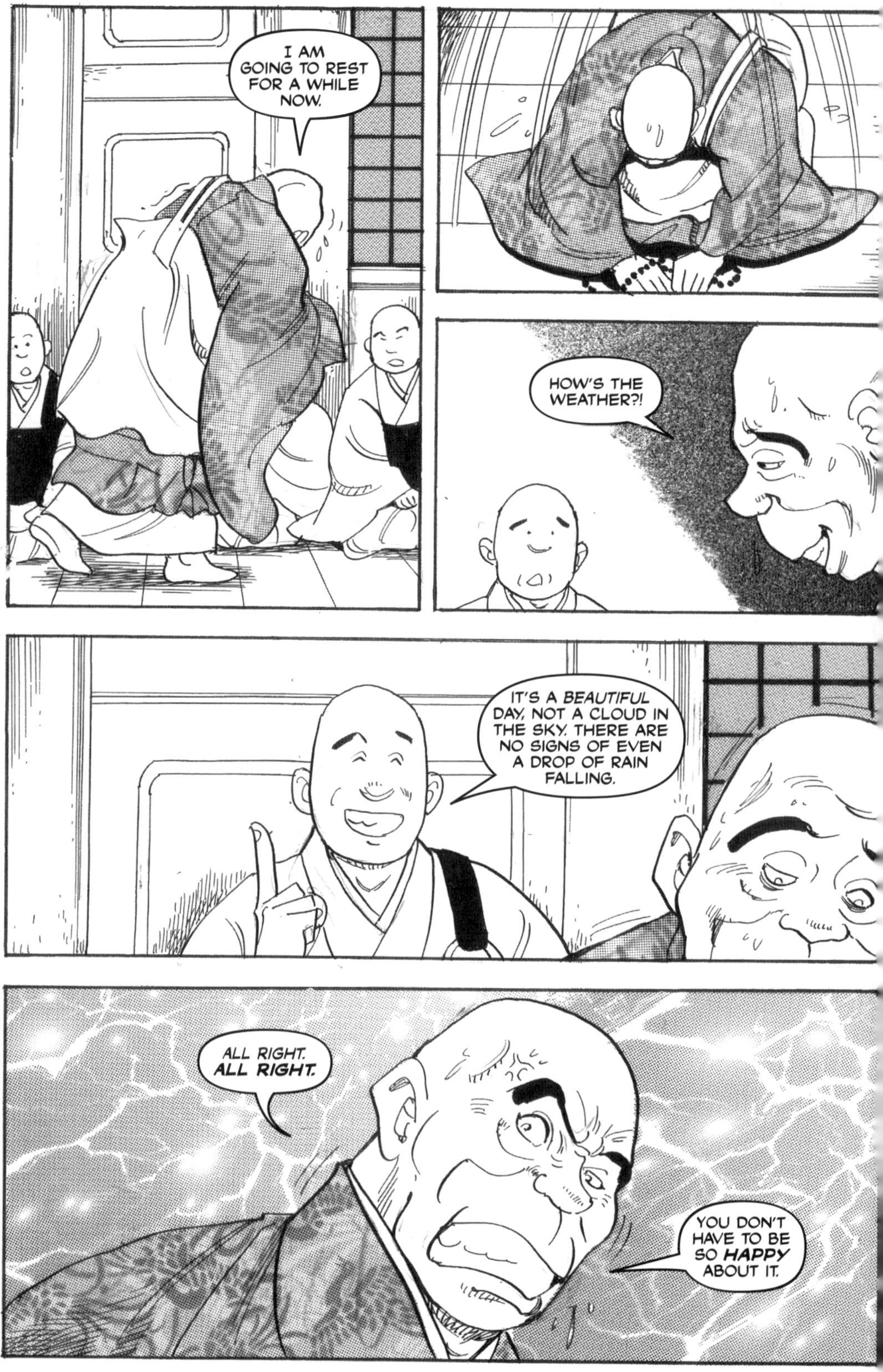
I AM GOING TO REST FOR A WHILE NOW.
HOW'S THE WEATHER?!
IT'S A *BEAUTIFUL* DAY, NOT A CLOUD IN THE SKY. THERE ARE NO SIGNS OF EVEN A DROP OF RAIN FALLING.
ALL RIGHT. **ALL RIGHT.**
YOU DON'T HAVE TO BE SO ***HAPPY*** ABOUT IT.

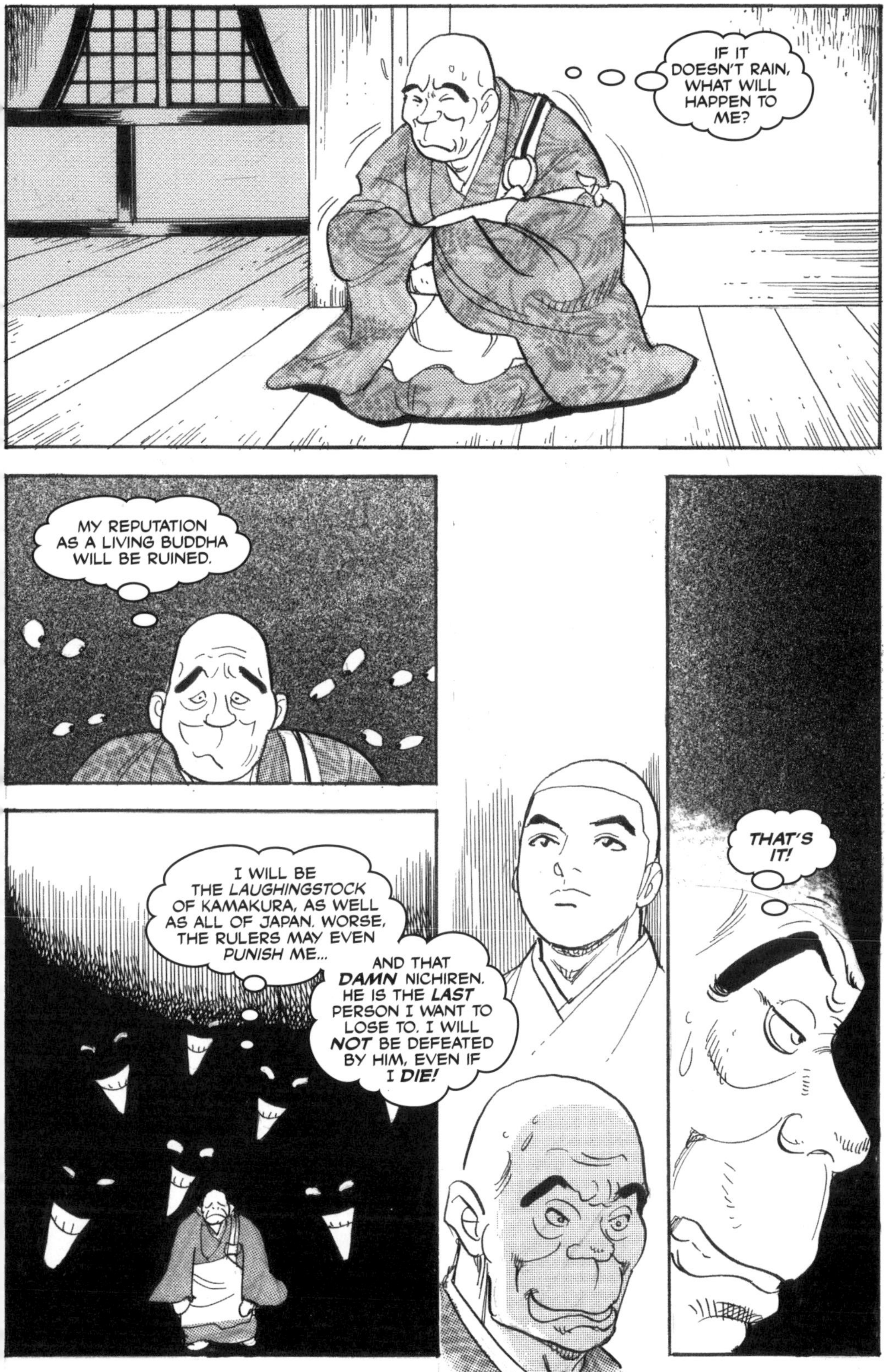
IF IT DOESN'T RAIN, WHAT WILL HAPPEN TO ME?
MY REPUTATION AS A LIVING BUDDHA WILL BE RUINED.
I WILL BE THE *LAUGHINGSTOCK* OF KAMAKURA, AS WELL AS ALL OF JAPAN. WORSE, THE RULERS MAY EVEN *PUNISH* ME...
AND THAT ***DAMN*** NICHIREN. HE IS THE ***LAST*** PERSON I WANT TO LOSE TO. I WILL ***NOT*** BE DEFEATED BY HIM, EVEN IF I ***DIE!***
THAT'S IT!

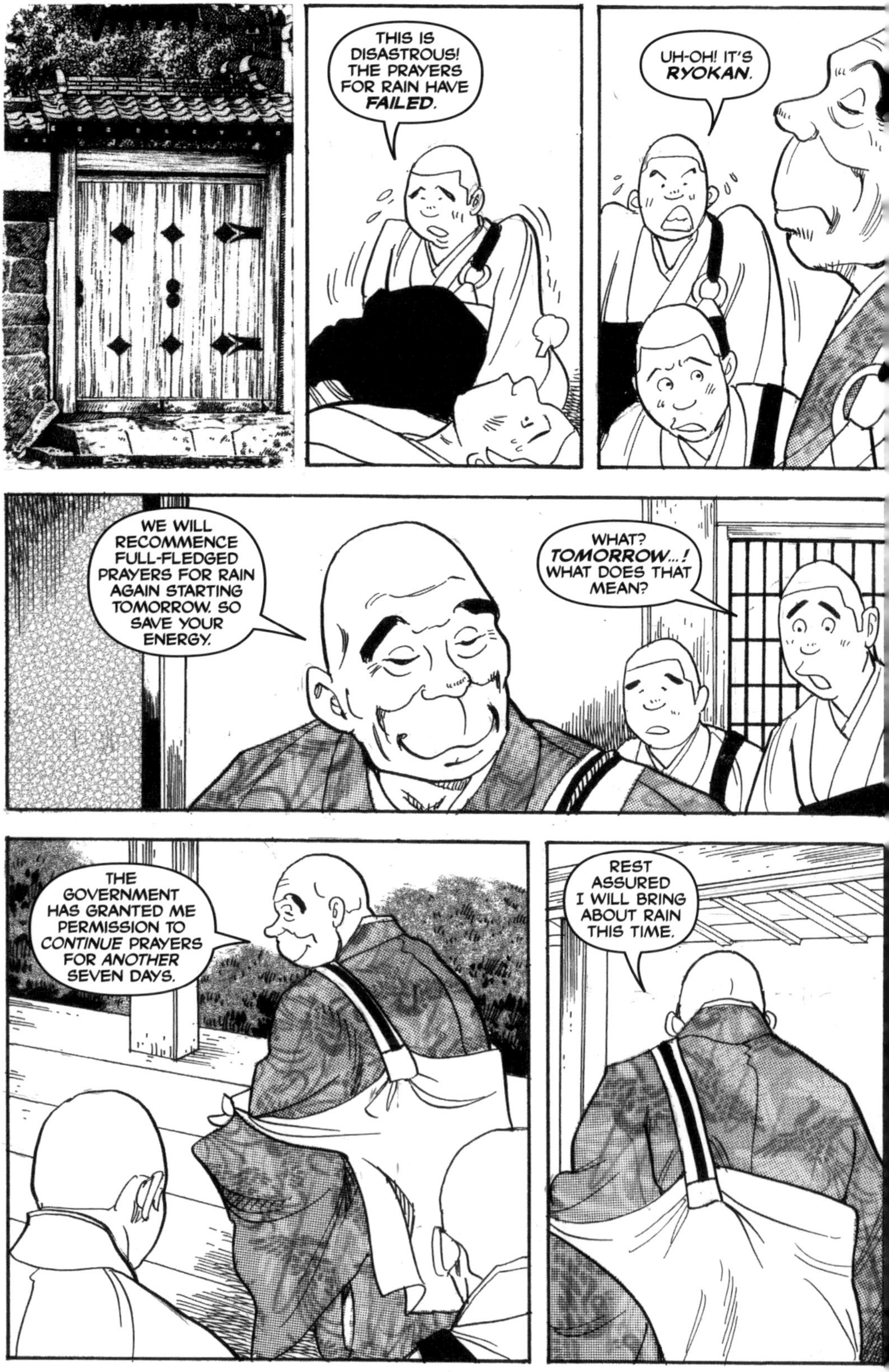
THIS IS DISASTROUS! THE PRAYERS FOR RAIN HAVE *FAILED*.
UH-OH! IT'S *RYOKAN*.
WE WILL RECOMMENCE FULL-FLEDGED PRAYERS FOR RAIN AGAIN STARTING TOMORROW. SO SAVE YOUR ENERGY.
WHAT? *TOMORROW...!* WHAT DOES THAT MEAN?
THE GOVERNMENT HAS GRANTED ME PERMISSION TO *CONTINUE* PRAYERS FOR *ANOTHER* SEVEN DAYS.
REST ASSURED I WILL BRING ABOUT RAIN THIS TIME.

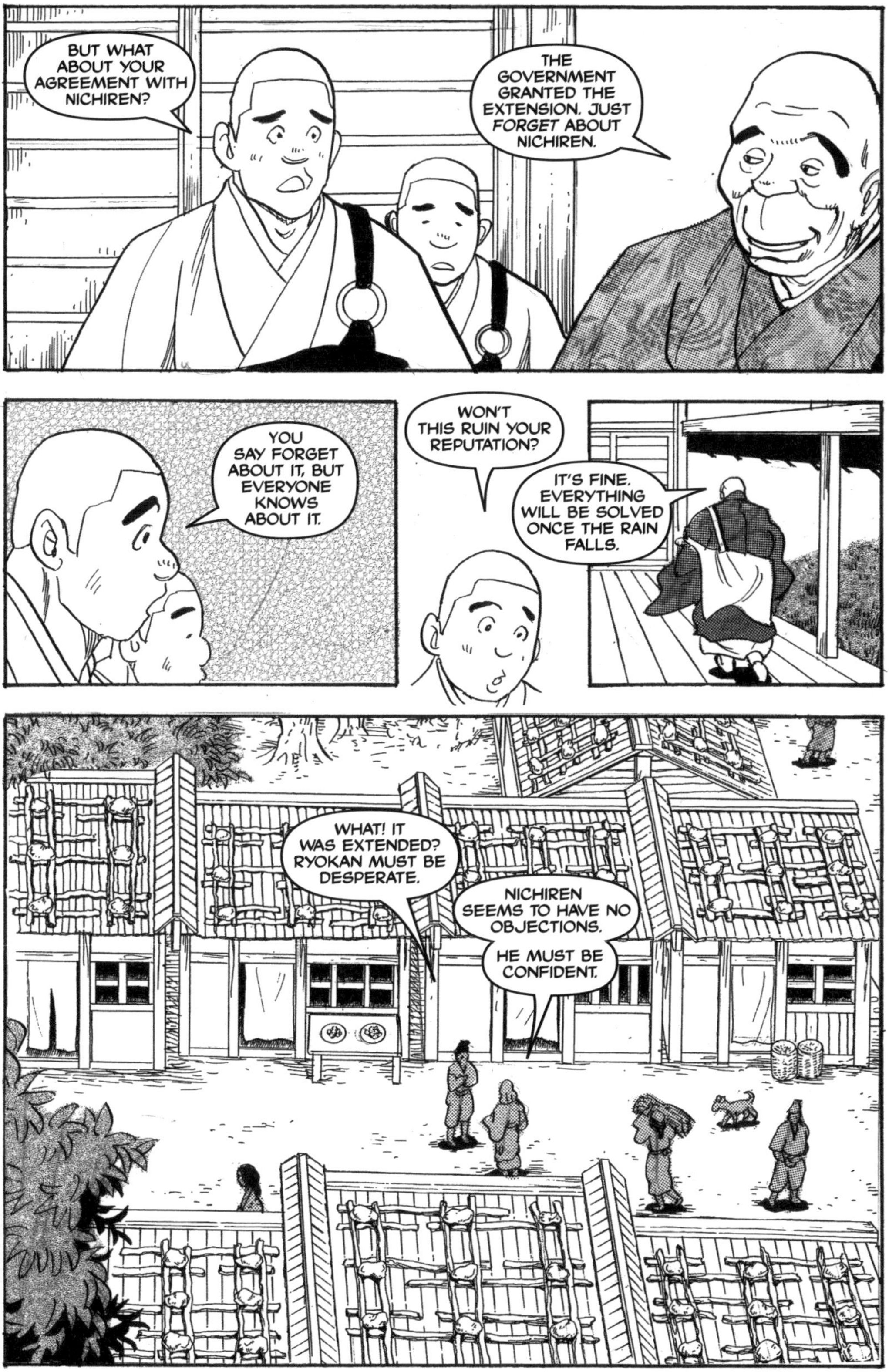
BUT WHAT ABOUT YOUR AGREEMENT WITH NICHIREN?
THE GOVERNMENT GRANTED THE EXTENSION. JUST *FORGET* ABOUT NICHIREN.
YOU SAY FORGET ABOUT IT, BUT EVERYONE KNOWS ABOUT IT.
WON'T THIS RUIN YOUR REPUTATION?
IT'S FINE. EVERYTHING WILL BE SOLVED ONCE THE RAIN FALLS.
WHAT! IT WAS EXTENDED? RYOKAN MUST BE DESPERATE.
NICHIREN SEEMS TO HAVE NO OBJECTIONS.
HE MUST BE CONFIDENT.

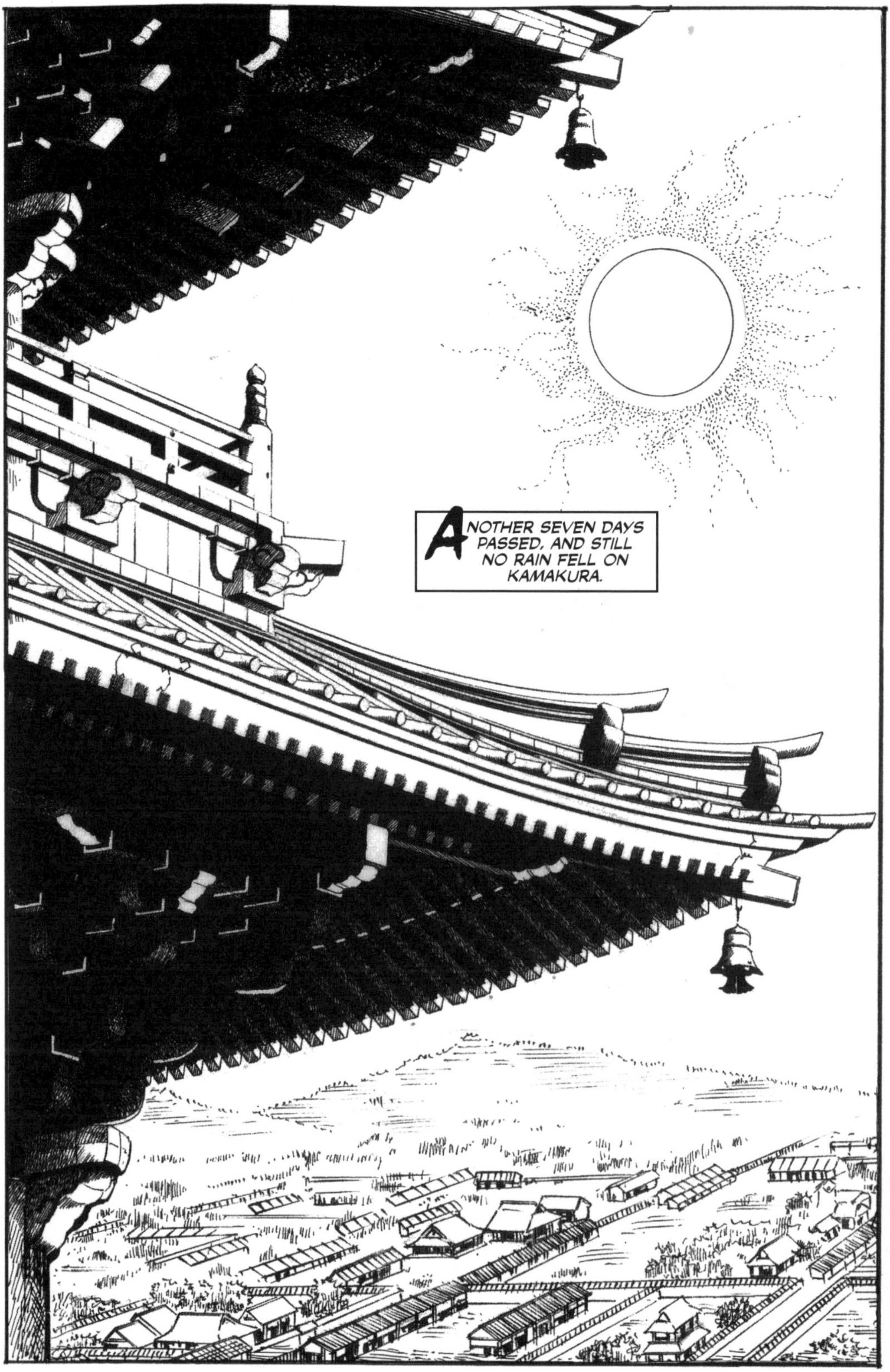
ANOTHER SEVEN DAYS PASSED, AND STILL NO RAIN FELL ON KAMAKURA.

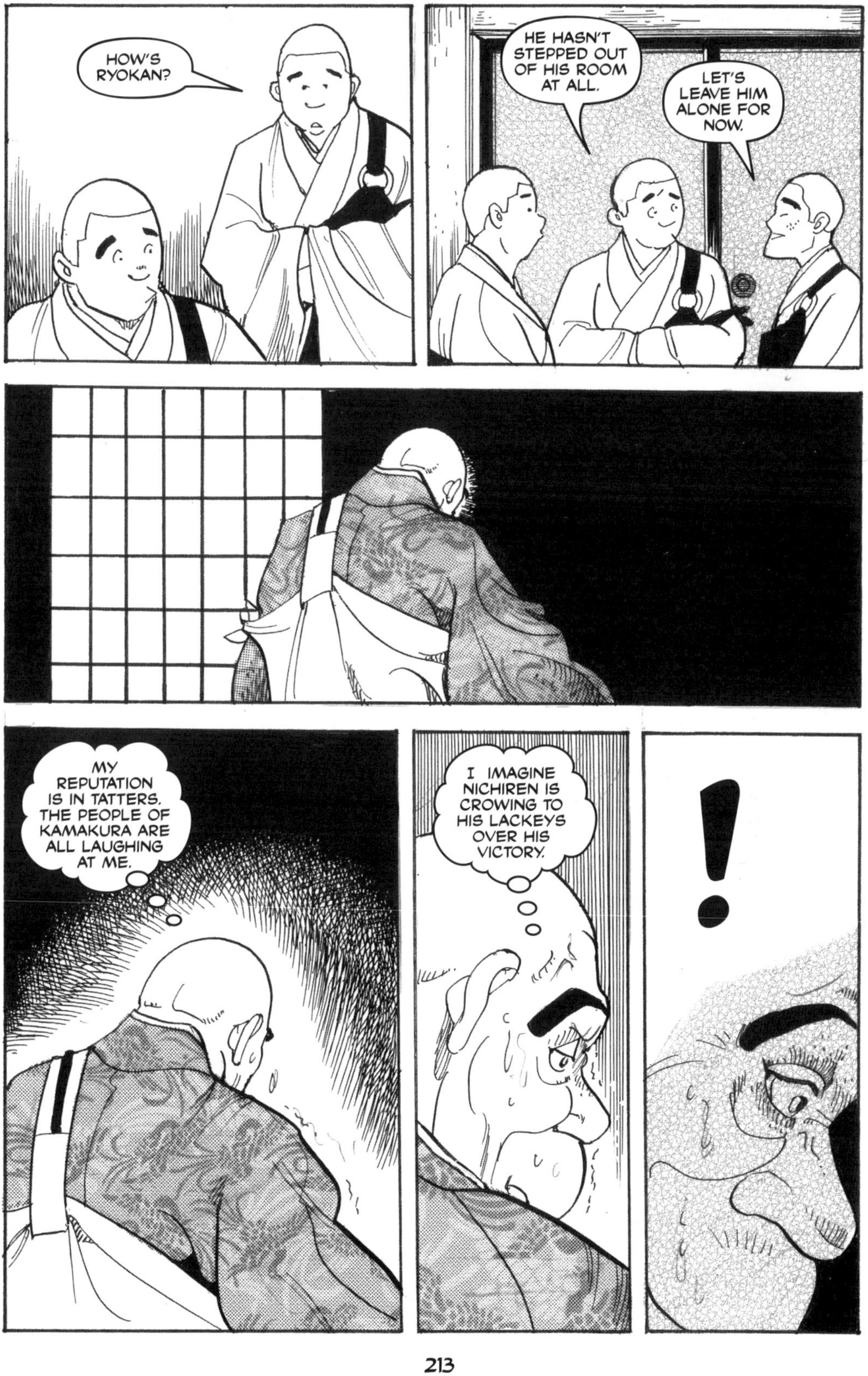
HOW'S RYOKAN?
HE HASN'T STEPPED OUT OF HIS ROOM AT ALL.
LET'S LEAVE HIM ALONE FOR NOW.
MY REPUTATION IS IN TATTERS. THE PEOPLE OF KAMAKURA ARE ALL LAUGHING AT ME.
I IMAGINE NICHIREN IS CROWING TO HIS LACKEYS OVER HIS VICTORY.
!

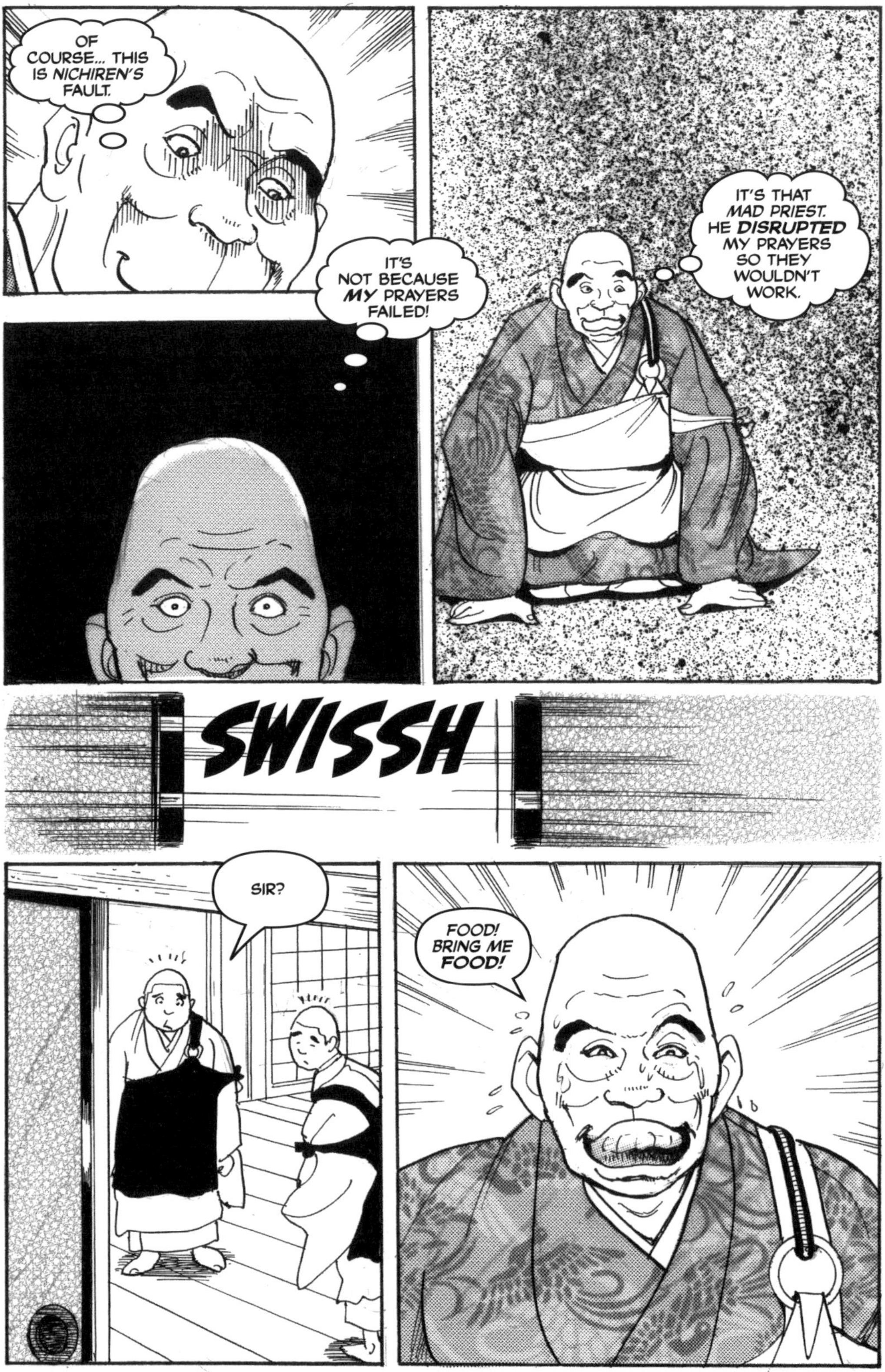
OF COURSE... THIS IS NICHIREN'S FAULT.
IT'S NOT BECAUSE MY PRAYERS FAILED!
IT'S THAT MAD PRIEST. HE DISRUPTED MY PRAYERS SO THEY WOULDN'T WORK.
SWISSH
SIR?
FOOD! BRING ME FOOD!

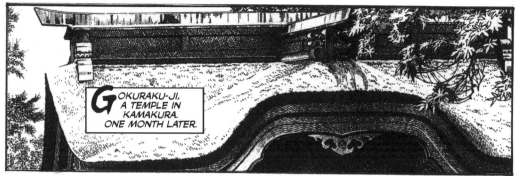

G OKURAKU-JI, A TEMPLE IN KAMAKURA. ONE MONTH LATER.

S HIGETOKI'S DAUGHTER, THE WIDOW OF HOJO TOKIYORI.

I'M MUCH OBLIGED THAT YOU HAVE TRAVELED ALL THIS WAY TO SEE ME.

LET ME SPEAK IN REGARD TO YOUR PRAYERS FOR RAIN:

WHATEVER OTHERS SAY, PLEASE KNOW THAT I BELIEVE THE RECENT DELUGE CAME BECAUSE OF YOU.

BUT THE RAIN FELL A WHOLE MONTH AFTER HIS PRAYERS...

215

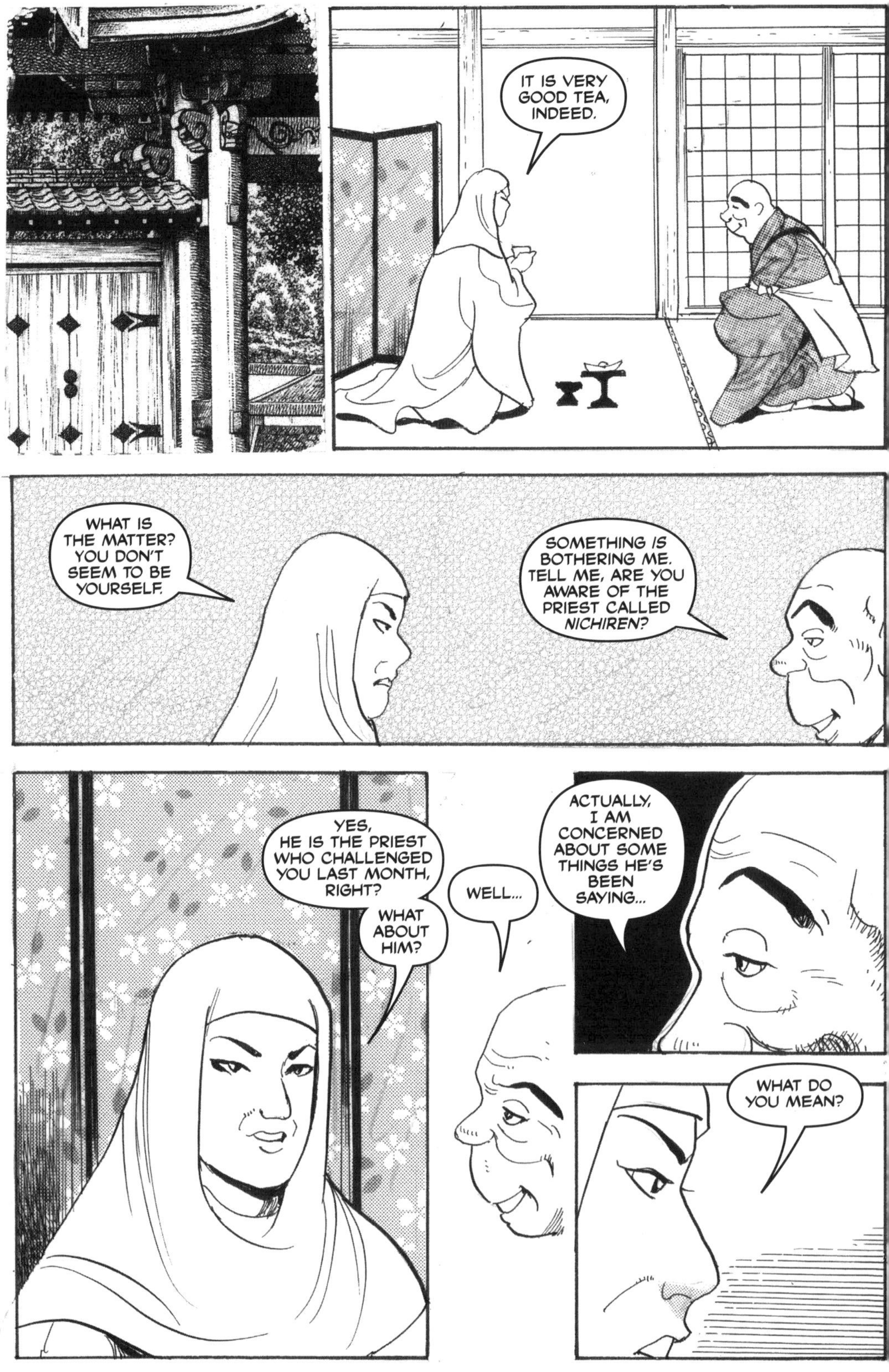
IT IS VERY GOOD TEA, INDEED.
WHAT IS THE MATTER? YOU DON'T SEEM TO BE YOURSELF.
SOMETHING *IS* BOTHERING ME. TELL ME, ARE YOU AWARE OF THE PRIEST CALLED *NICHIREN*?
YES, HE IS THE PRIEST WHO CHALLENGED YOU LAST MONTH, RIGHT?
WHAT ABOUT HIM?
WELL...
ACTUALLY, I AM CONCERNED ABOUT SOME THINGS HE'S BEEN SAYING...
WHAT DO YOU MEAN?

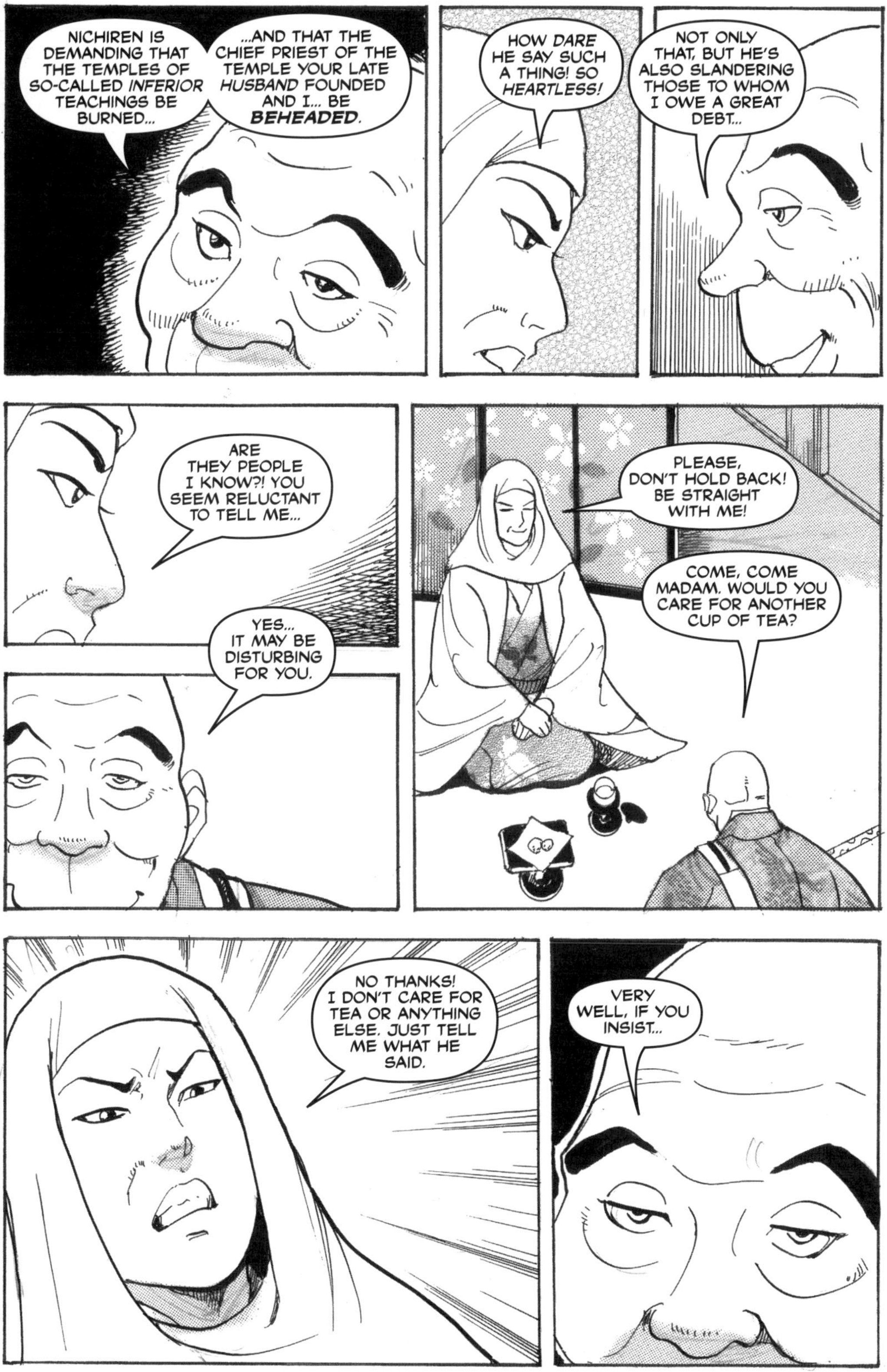

NICHIREN IS DEMANDING THAT THE TEMPLES OF SO-CALLED *INFERIOR* TEACHINGS BE BURNED...
...AND THAT THE CHIEF PRIEST OF THE TEMPLE YOUR LATE *HUSBAND* FOUNDED AND I... BE ***BEHEADED***.
HOW *DARE* HE SAY SUCH A THING! SO *HEARTLESS!*
NOT ONLY THAT, BUT HE'S ALSO SLANDERING THOSE TO WHOM I OWE A GREAT DEBT...
ARE THEY PEOPLE I KNOW?! YOU SEEM RELUCTANT TO TELL ME...
YES... IT MAY BE DISTURBING FOR YOU.
PLEASE, DON'T HOLD BACK! BE STRAIGHT WITH ME!
COME, COME MADAM. WOULD YOU CARE FOR ANOTHER CUP OF TEA?
NO THANKS! I DON'T CARE FOR TEA OR ANYTHING ELSE. JUST TELL ME WHAT HE SAID.
VERY WELL, IF YOU INSIST...

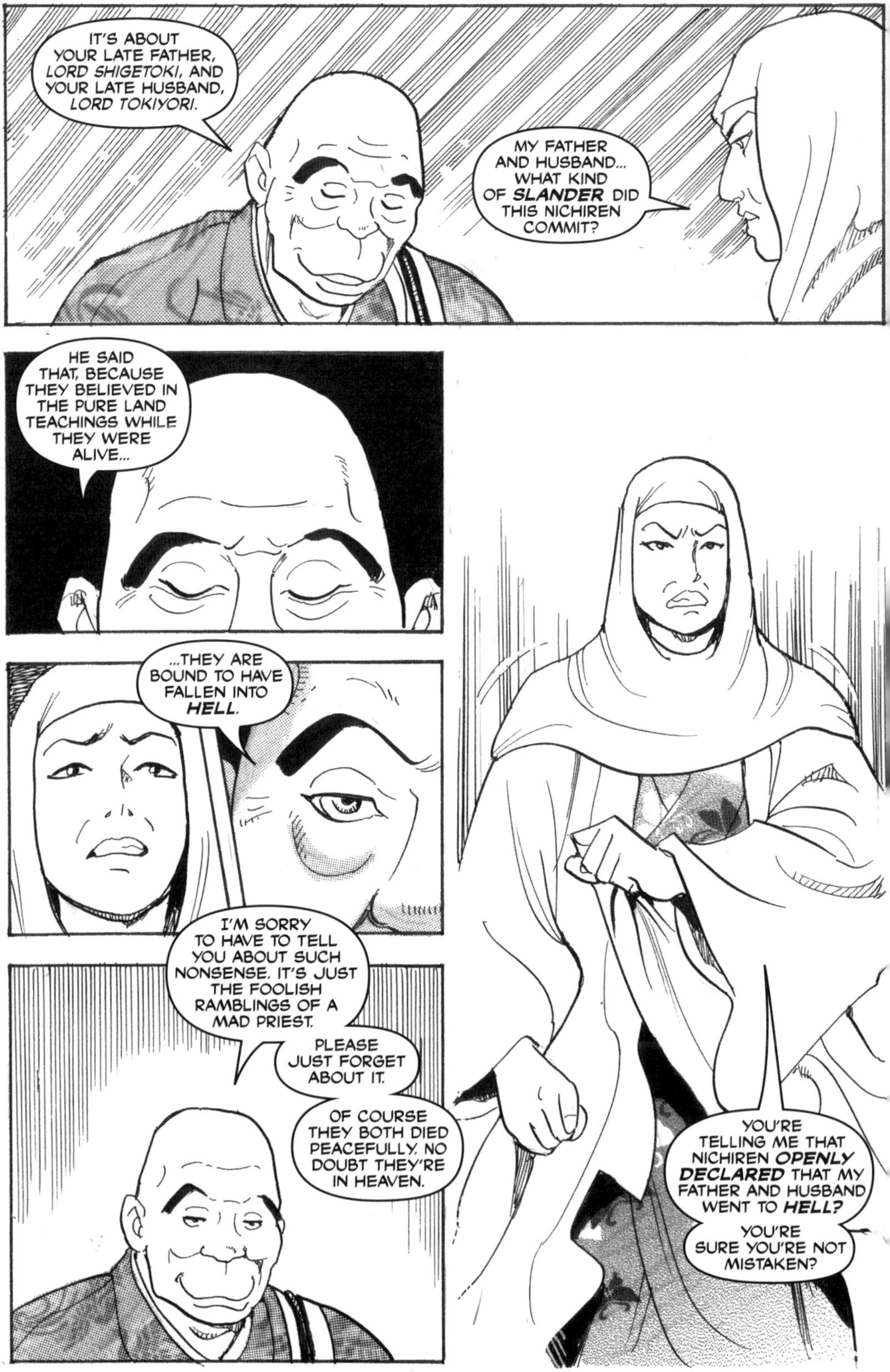

IT'S ABOUT YOUR LATE FATHER, *LORD SHIGETOKI*, AND YOUR LATE HUSBAND, *LORD TOKIYORI*.
MY FATHER AND HUSBAND... WHAT KIND OF ***SLANDER*** DID THIS NICHIREN COMMIT?
HE SAID THAT, BECAUSE THEY BELIEVED IN THE PURE LAND TEACHINGS WHILE THEY WERE ALIVE...
...THEY ARE BOUND TO HAVE FALLEN INTO ***HELL***.
I'M SORRY TO HAVE TO TELL YOU ABOUT SUCH NONSENSE. IT'S JUST THE FOOLISH RAMBLINGS OF A MAD PRIEST.
PLEASE JUST FORGET ABOUT IT.
OF COURSE THEY BOTH DIED PEACEFULLY. NO DOUBT THEY'RE IN HEAVEN.
YOU'RE TELLING ME THAT NICHIREN ***OPENLY DECLARED*** THAT MY FATHER AND HUSBAND WENT TO ***HELL?***
YOU'RE SURE YOU'RE NOT MISTAKEN?

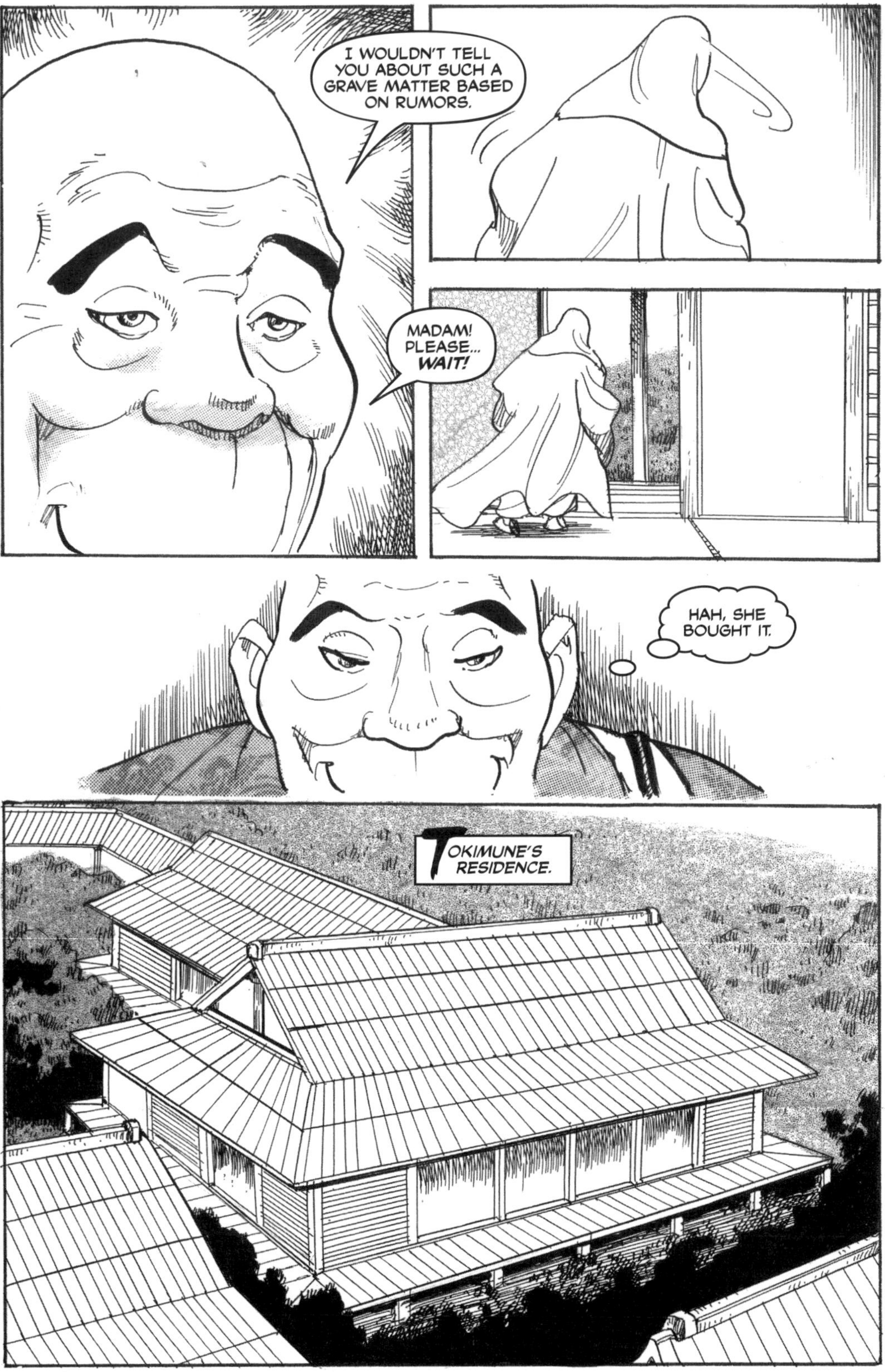
I WOULDN'T TELL YOU ABOUT SUCH A GRAVE MATTER BASED ON RUMORS.
MADAM! PLEASE... WAIT!
HAH, SHE BOUGHT IT.
TOKIMUNE'S RESIDENCE.

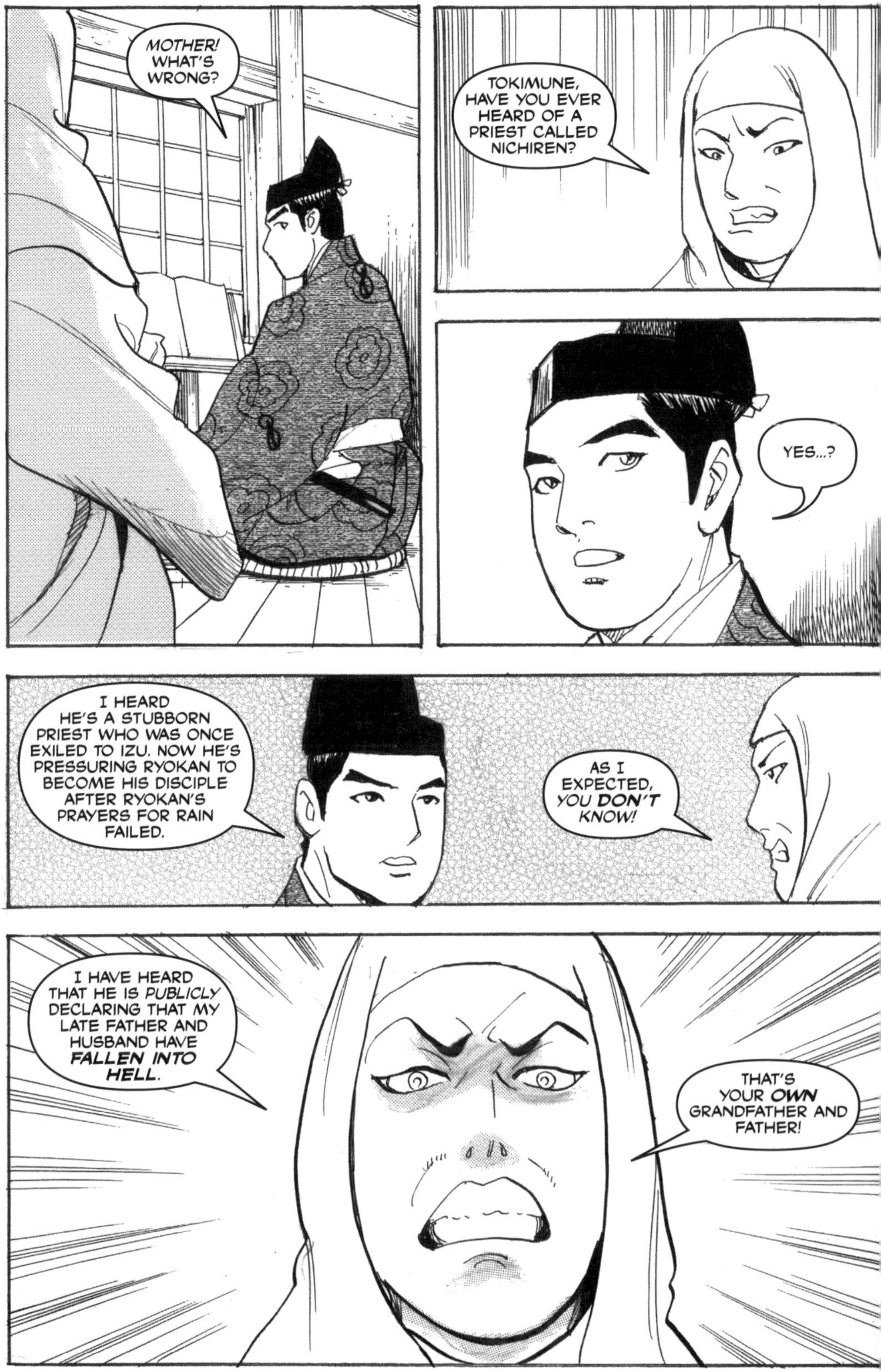
MOTHER! WHAT'S WRONG?
TOKIMUNE, HAVE YOU EVER HEARD OF A PRIEST CALLED NICHIREN?
YES...?
I HEARD HE'S A STUBBORN PRIEST WHO WAS ONCE EXILED TO IZU. NOW HE'S PRESSURING RYOKAN TO BECOME HIS DISCIPLE AFTER RYOKAN'S PRAYERS FOR RAIN FAILED.
AS I EXPECTED, *YOU **DON'T*** KNOW!
I HAVE HEARD THAT HE IS *PUBLICLY* DECLARING THAT MY LATE FATHER AND HUSBAND HAVE ***FALLEN INTO HELL***.
THAT'S YOUR ***OWN*** GRANDFATHER AND FATHER!

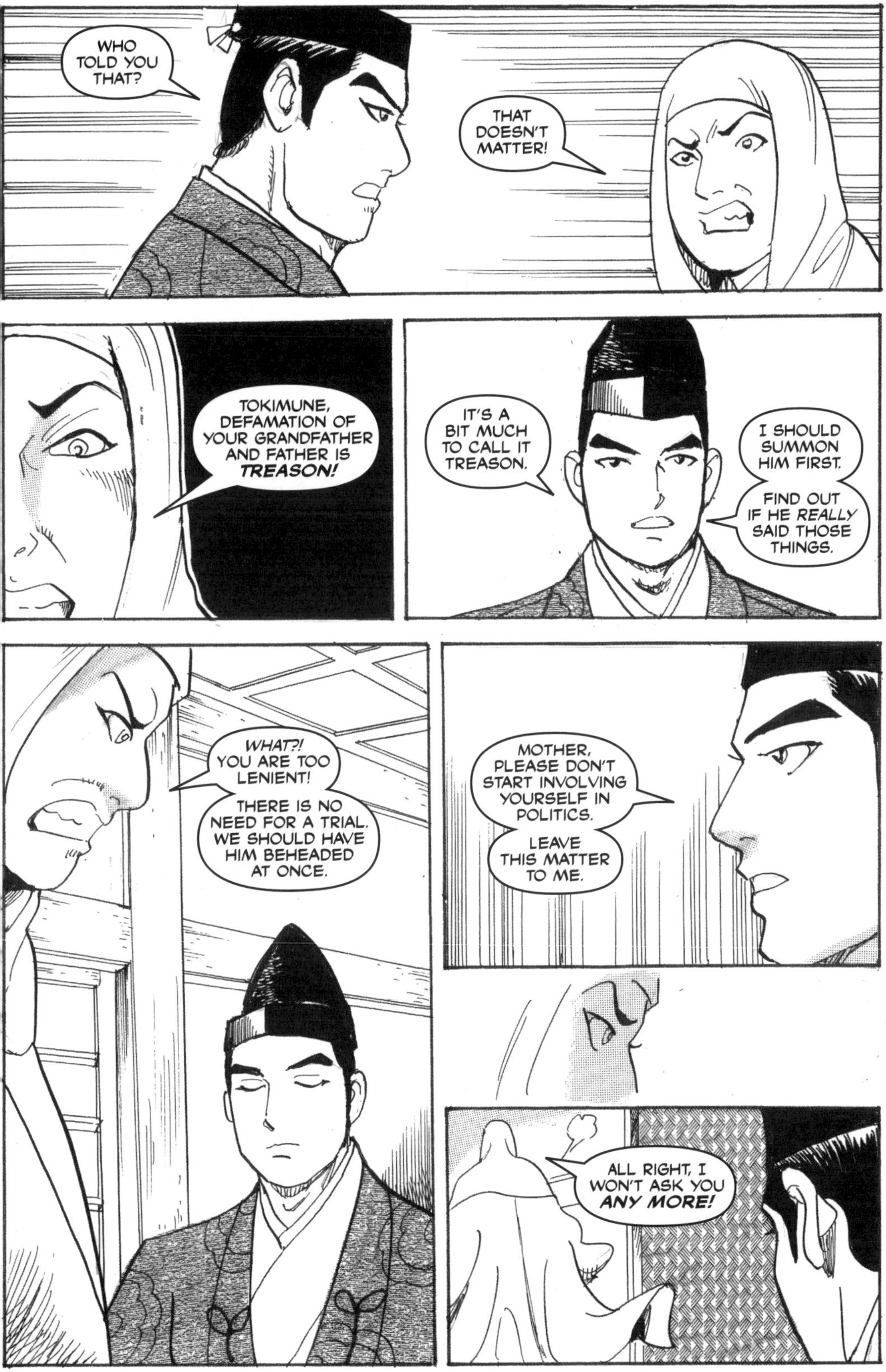
WHO TOLD YOU THAT?
THAT DOESN'T MATTER!
TOKIMUNE, DEFAMATION OF YOUR GRANDFATHER AND FATHER IS *TREASON!*
IT'S A BIT MUCH TO CALL IT TREASON.
I SHOULD SUMMON HIM FIRST.
FIND OUT IF HE *REALLY* SAID THOSE THINGS.
WHAT?! YOU ARE TOO LENIENT!
THERE IS NO NEED FOR A TRIAL. WE SHOULD HAVE HIM BEHEADED AT ONCE.
MOTHER, PLEASE DON'T START INVOLVING YOURSELF IN POLITICS.
LEAVE THIS MATTER TO ME.
ALL RIGHT, I WON'T ASK YOU *ANY MORE!*

THE HOME OF SHIGETOKI'S WIDOW.

WHAT? NICHIREN SAID THAT!?

YES, BUT TOKIMUNE ISN'T DOING ANYTHING ABOUT IT.

THEN *WE* SHOULD.

NOW THAT IT'S COME TO THIS, I WILL SPEAK WITH THE *SUPREME COUNCIL* AND PERSUADE THEM TO *CONVICT* NICHIREN.

HEI NO SAEMON IS ALSO ON OUR SIDE.

CAW

CAW CAW

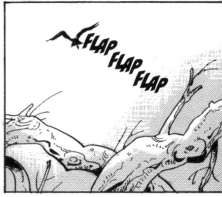

FLAP FLAP FLAP

222

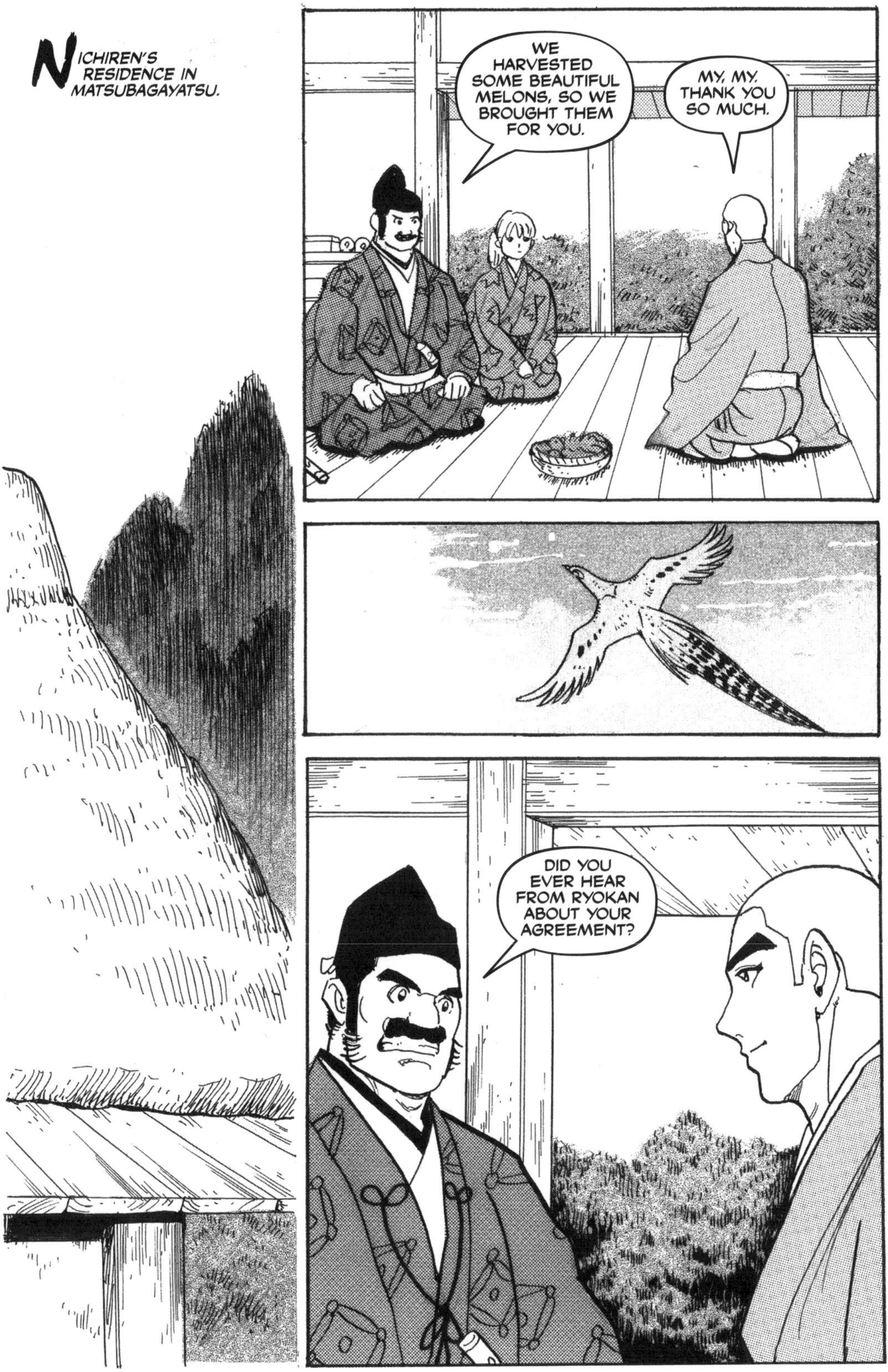
NICHIREN'S RESIDENCE IN MATSUBAGAYATSU.
WE HARVESTED SOME BEAUTIFUL MELONS, SO WE BROUGHT THEM FOR YOU.
MY, MY. THANK YOU SO MUCH.
DID YOU EVER HEAR FROM RYOKAN ABOUT YOUR AGREEMENT?

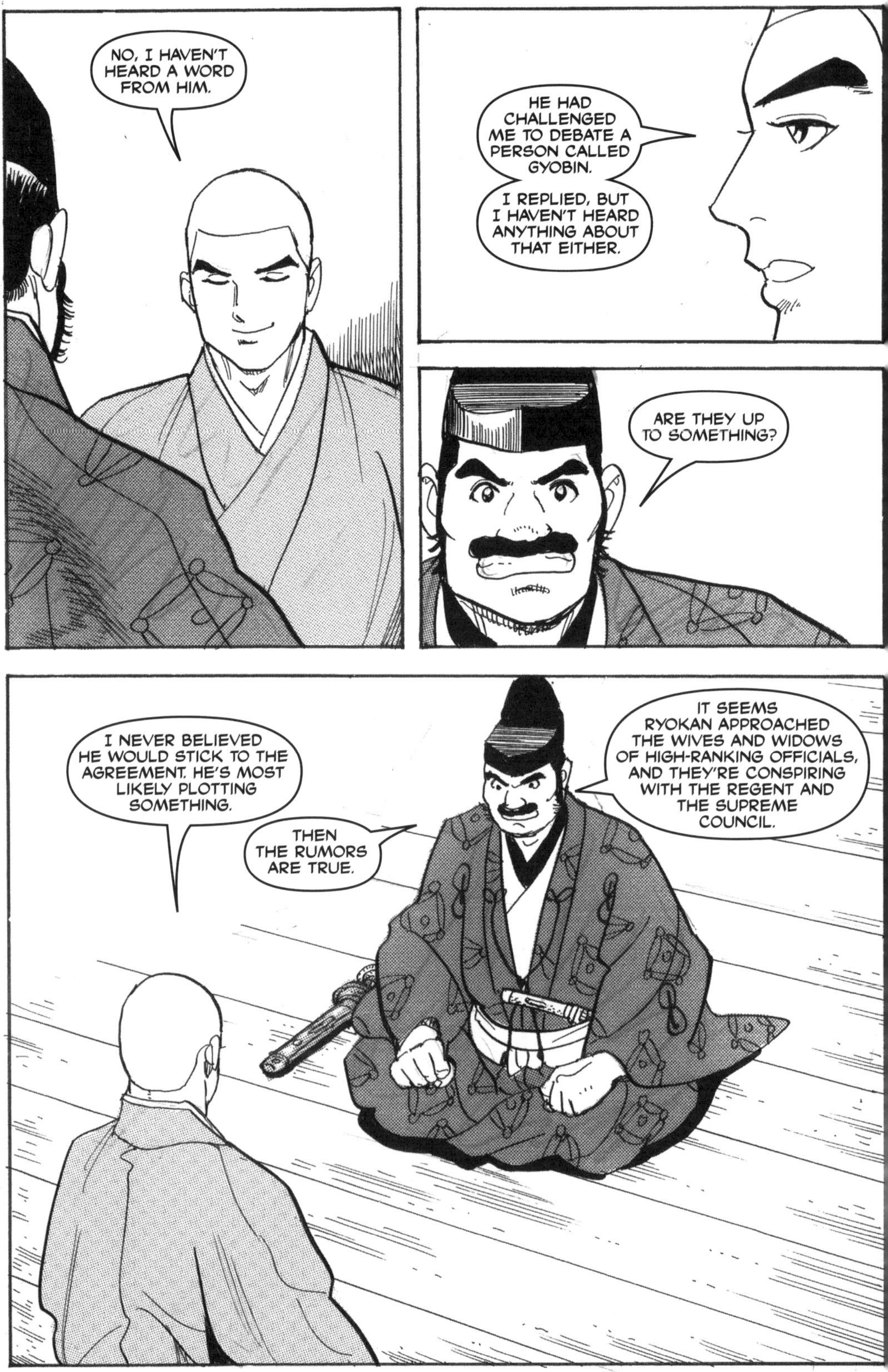
NO, I HAVEN'T HEARD A WORD FROM HIM.
HE HAD CHALLENGED ME TO DEBATE A PERSON CALLED GYOBIN.
I REPLIED, BUT I HAVEN'T HEARD ANYTHING ABOUT THAT EITHER.
ARE THEY UP TO SOMETHING?
I NEVER BELIEVED HE WOULD STICK TO THE AGREEMENT. HE'S MOST LIKELY PLOTTING SOMETHING.
THEN THE RUMORS ARE TRUE.
IT SEEMS RYOKAN APPROACHED THE WIVES AND WIDOWS OF HIGH-RANKING OFFICIALS, AND THEY'RE CONSPIRING WITH THE REGENT AND THE SUPREME COUNCIL.

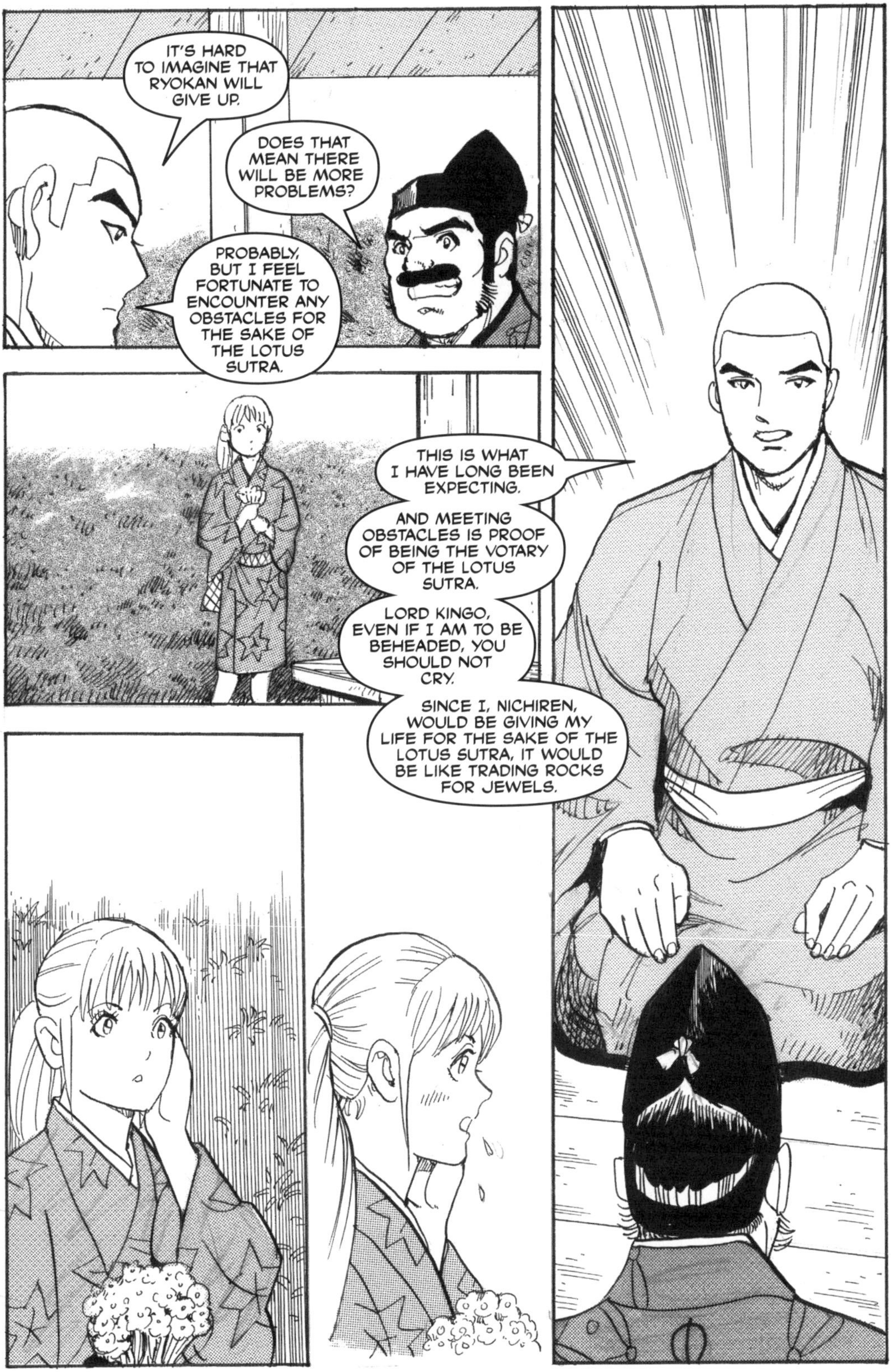
IT'S HARD TO IMAGINE THAT RYOKAN WILL GIVE UP.
DOES THAT MEAN THERE WILL BE MORE PROBLEMS?
PROBABLY, BUT I FEEL FORTUNATE TO ENCOUNTER ANY OBSTACLES FOR THE SAKE OF THE LOTUS SUTRA.
THIS IS WHAT I HAVE LONG BEEN EXPECTING.
AND MEETING OBSTACLES IS PROOF OF BEING THE VOTARY OF THE LOTUS SUTRA.
LORD KINGO, EVEN IF I AM TO BE BEHEADED, YOU SHOULD NOT CRY.
SINCE I, NICHIREN, WOULD BE GIVING MY LIFE FOR THE SAKE OF THE LOTUS SUTRA, IT WOULD BE LIKE TRADING ROCKS FOR JEWELS.

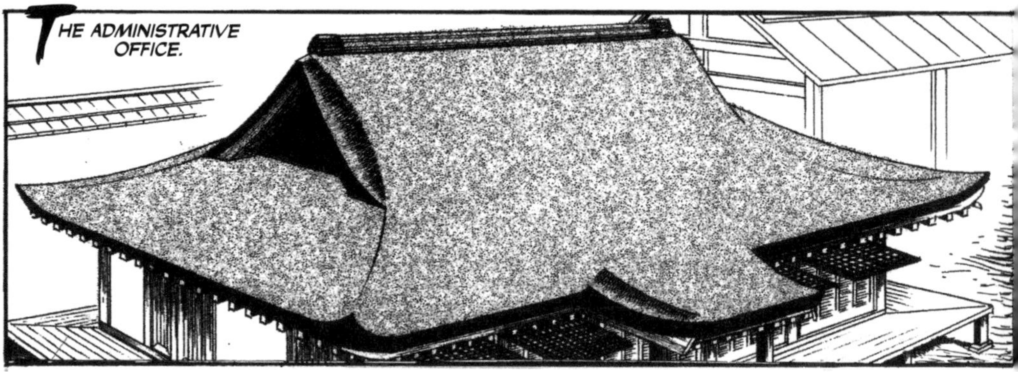
THE ADMINISTRATIVE OFFICE.
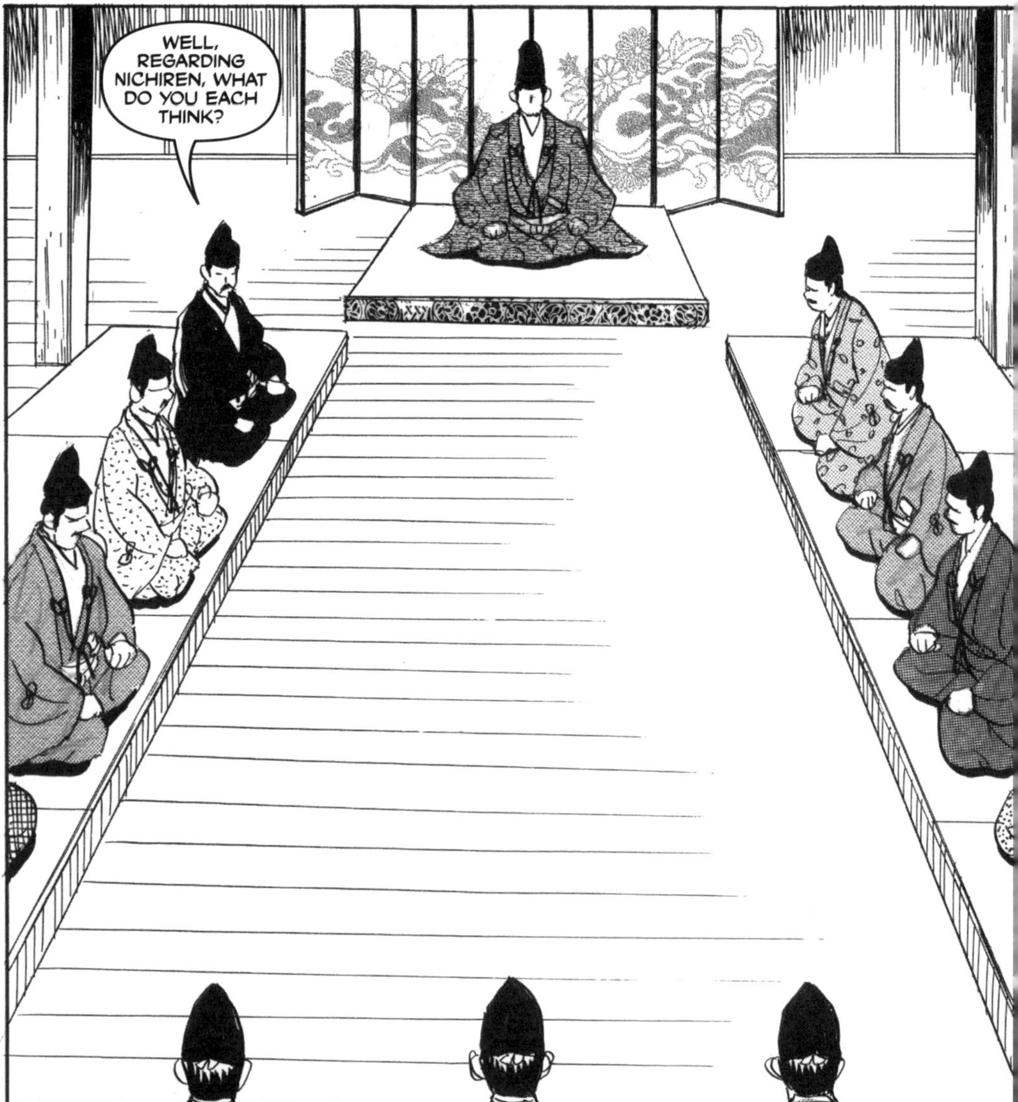
WELL, REGARDING NICHIREN, WHAT DO YOU EACH THINK?

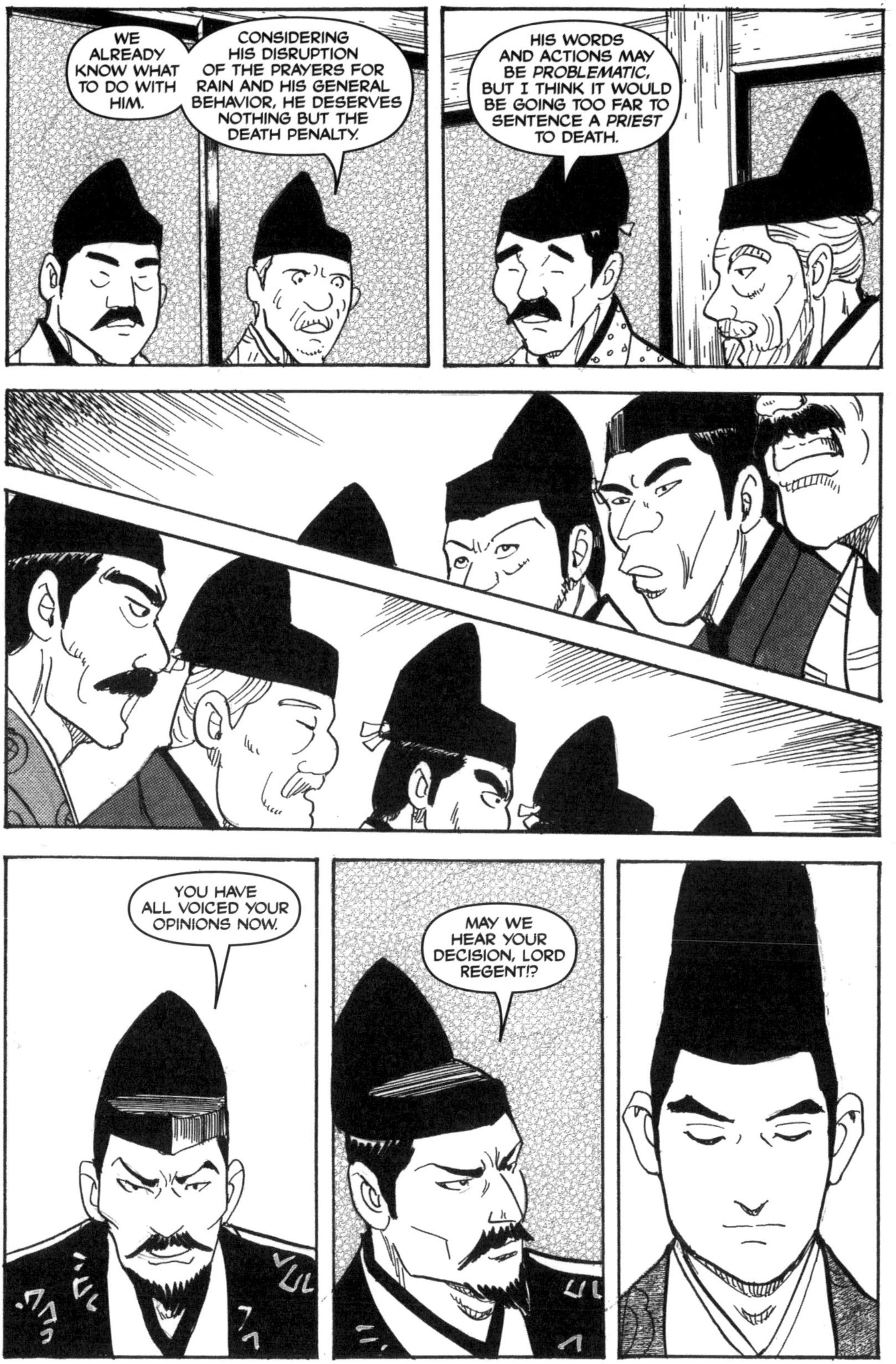

WE ALREADY KNOW WHAT TO DO WITH HIM.
CONSIDERING HIS DISRUPTION OF THE PRAYERS FOR RAIN AND HIS GENERAL BEHAVIOR, HE DESERVES NOTHING BUT THE DEATH PENALTY.
HIS WORDS AND ACTIONS MAY BE *PROBLEMATIC*, BUT I THINK IT WOULD BE GOING TOO FAR TO SENTENCE A *PRIEST* TO DEATH.
YOU HAVE ALL VOICED YOUR OPINIONS NOW.
MAY WE HEAR YOUR DECISION, LORD REGENT!?

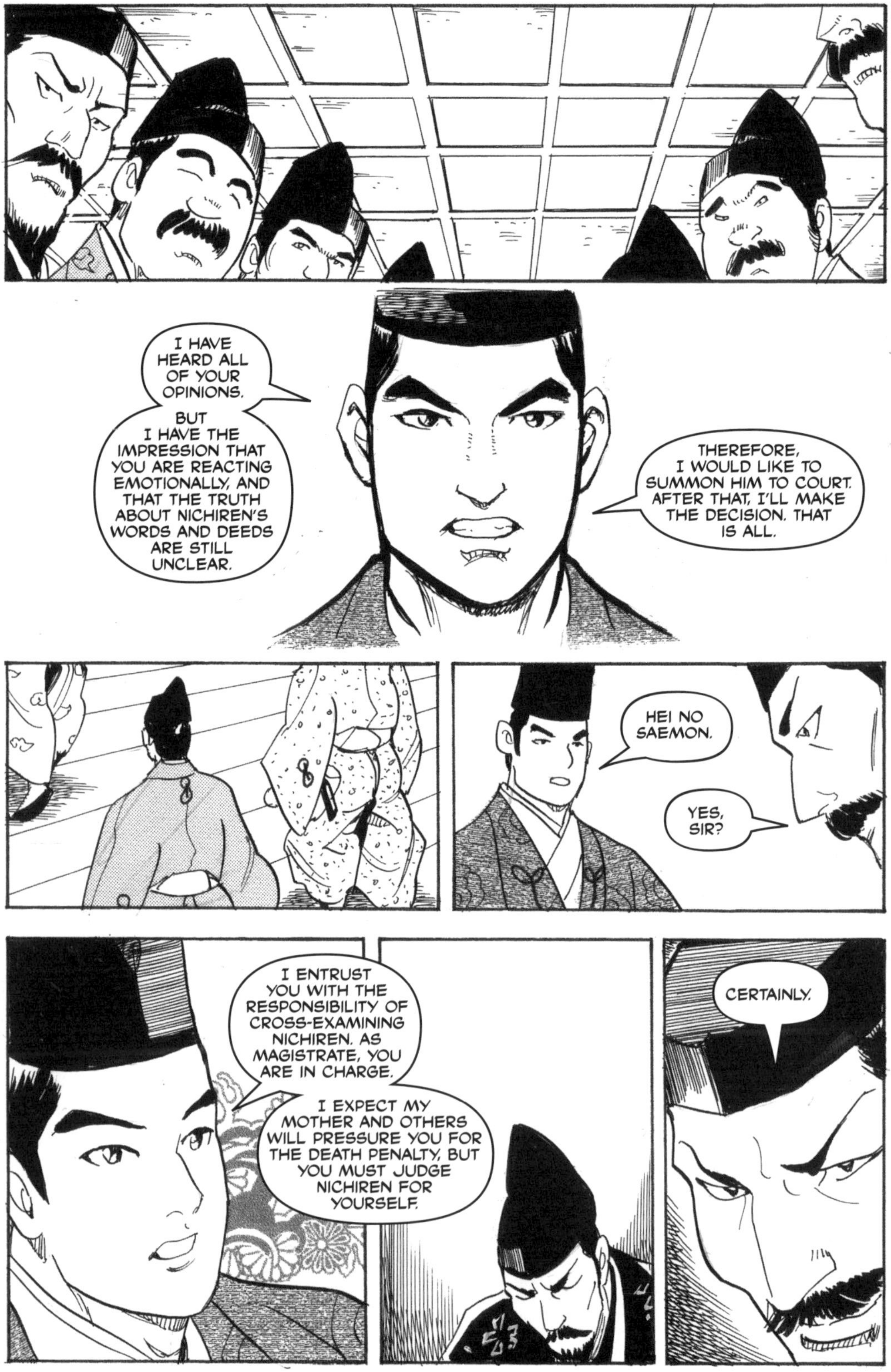
I HAVE HEARD ALL OF YOUR OPINIONS.
BUT I HAVE THE IMPRESSION THAT YOU ARE REACTING EMOTIONALLY, AND THAT THE TRUTH ABOUT NICHIREN'S WORDS AND DEEDS ARE STILL UNCLEAR.
THEREFORE, I WOULD LIKE TO SUMMON HIM TO COURT. AFTER THAT, I'LL MAKE THE DECISION. THAT IS ALL.
HEI NO SAEMON.
YES, SIR?
I ENTRUST YOU WITH THE RESPONSIBILITY OF CROSS-EXAMINING NICHIREN. AS MAGISTRATE, YOU ARE IN CHARGE.
I EXPECT MY MOTHER AND OTHERS WILL PRESSURE YOU FOR THE DEATH PENALTY, BUT YOU MUST JUDGE NICHIREN FOR YOURSELF.
CERTAINLY.

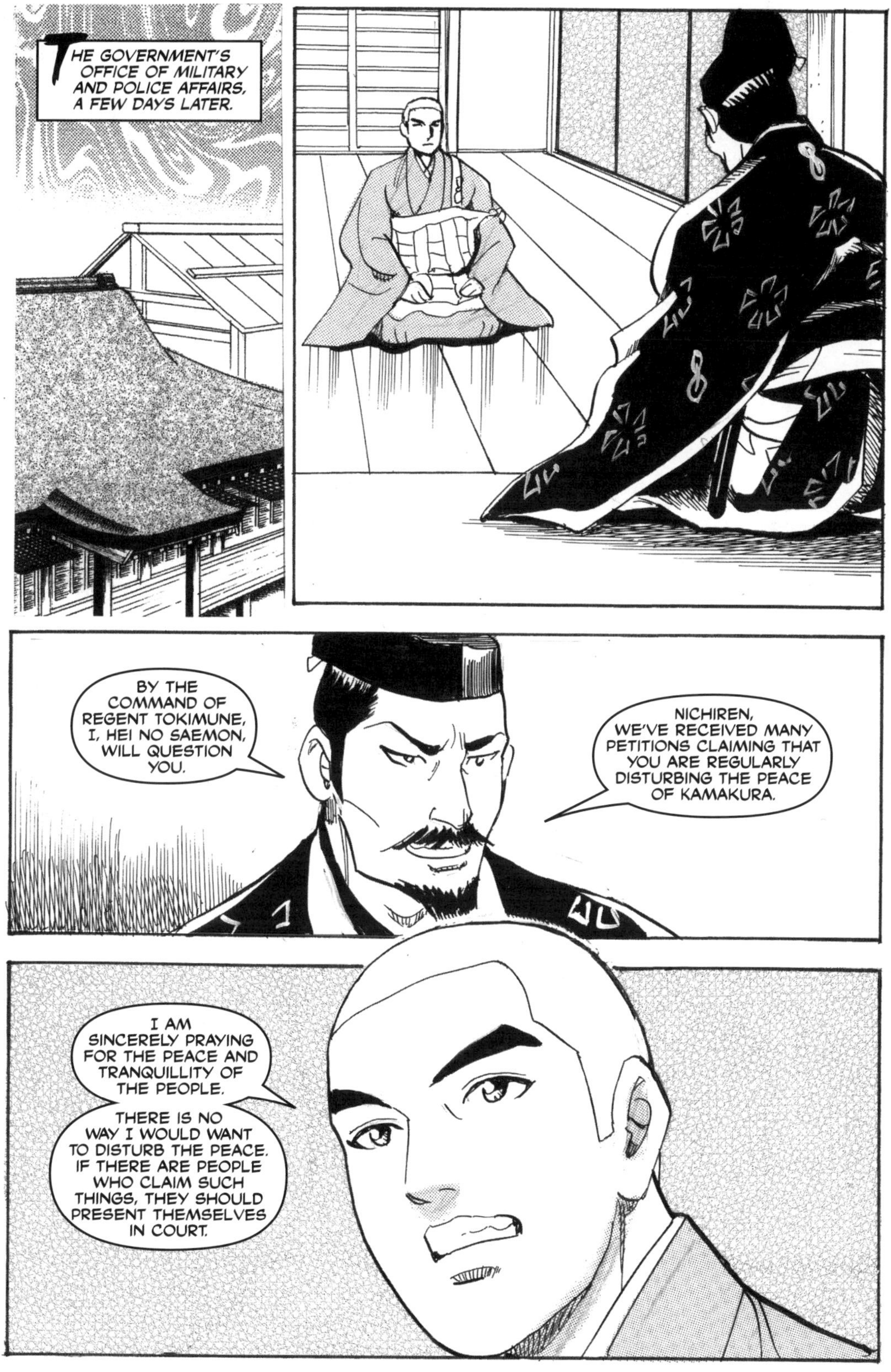
THE GOVERNMENT'S OFFICE OF MILITARY AND POLICE AFFAIRS, A FEW DAYS LATER.
BY THE COMMAND OF REGENT TOKIMUNE, I, HEI NO SAEMON, WILL QUESTION YOU.
NICHIREN, WE'VE RECEIVED MANY PETITIONS CLAIMING THAT YOU ARE REGULARLY DISTURBING THE PEACE OF KAMAKURA.
I AM SINCERELY PRAYING FOR THE PEACE AND TRANQUILLITY OF THE PEOPLE.
THERE IS NO WAY I WOULD WANT TO DISTURB THE PEACE. IF THERE ARE PEOPLE WHO CLAIM SUCH THINGS, THEY SHOULD PRESENT THEMSELVES IN COURT.

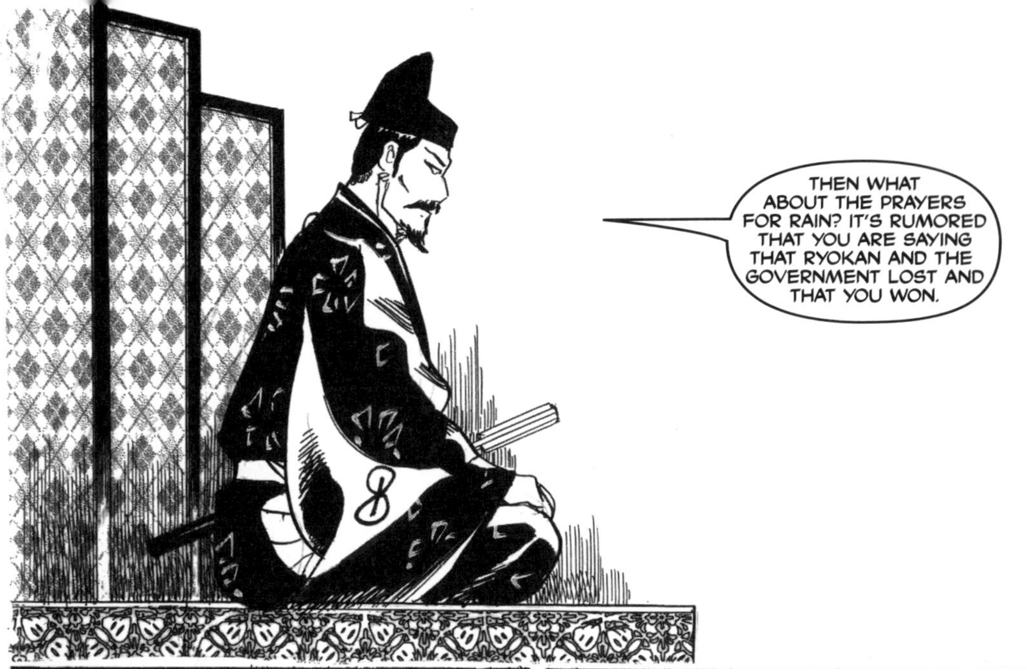
THEN WHAT ABOUT THE PRAYERS FOR RAIN? IT'S RUMORED THAT YOU ARE SAYING THAT RYOKAN AND THE GOVERNMENT LOST AND THAT YOU WON.

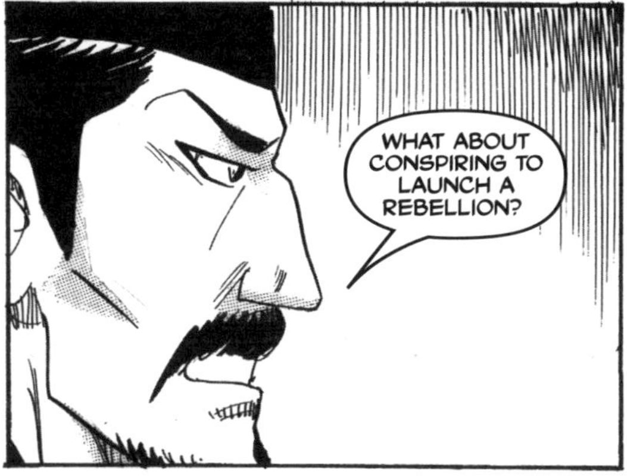
WHAT ABOUT CONSPIRING TO LAUNCH A REBELLION?

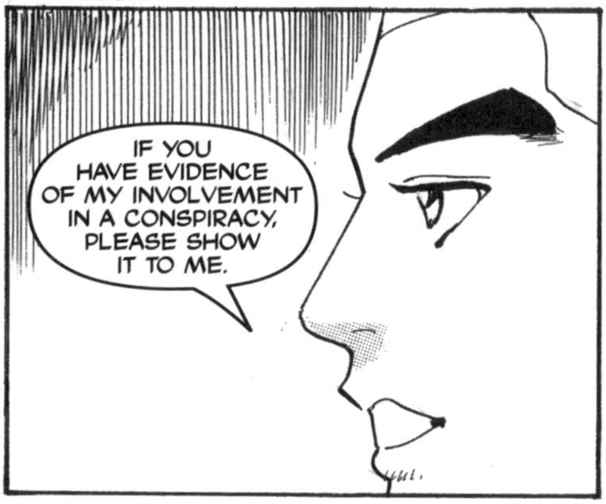
IF YOU HAVE EVIDENCE OF MY INVOLVEMENT IN A CONSPIRACY, PLEASE SHOW IT TO ME.

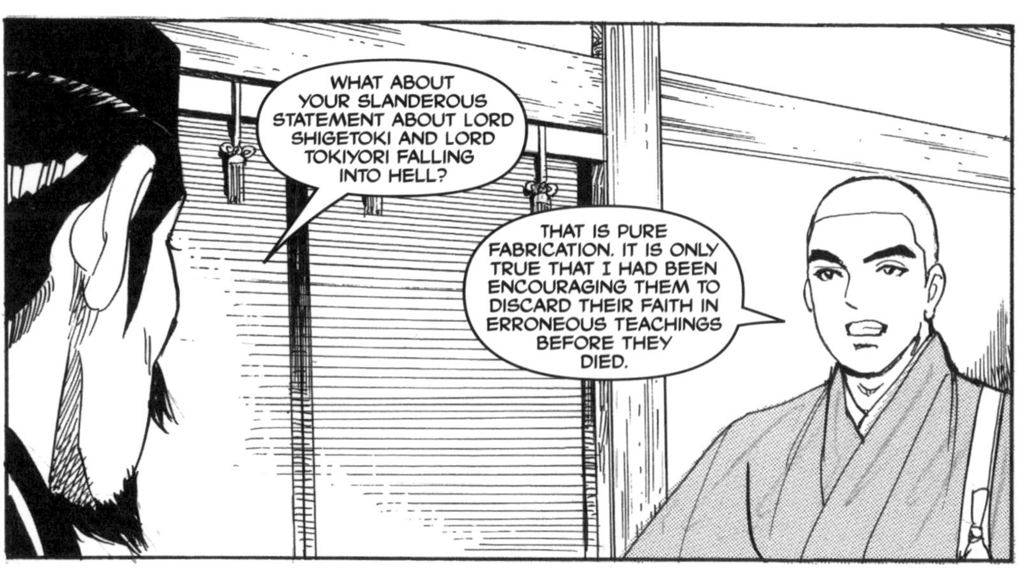
WHAT ABOUT YOUR SLANDEROUS STATEMENT ABOUT LORD SHIGETOKI AND LORD TOKIYORI FALLING INTO HELL?
THAT IS PURE FABRICATION. IT IS ONLY TRUE THAT I HAD BEEN ENCOURAGING THEM TO DISCARD THEIR FAITH IN ERRONEOUS TEACHINGS BEFORE THEY DIED.

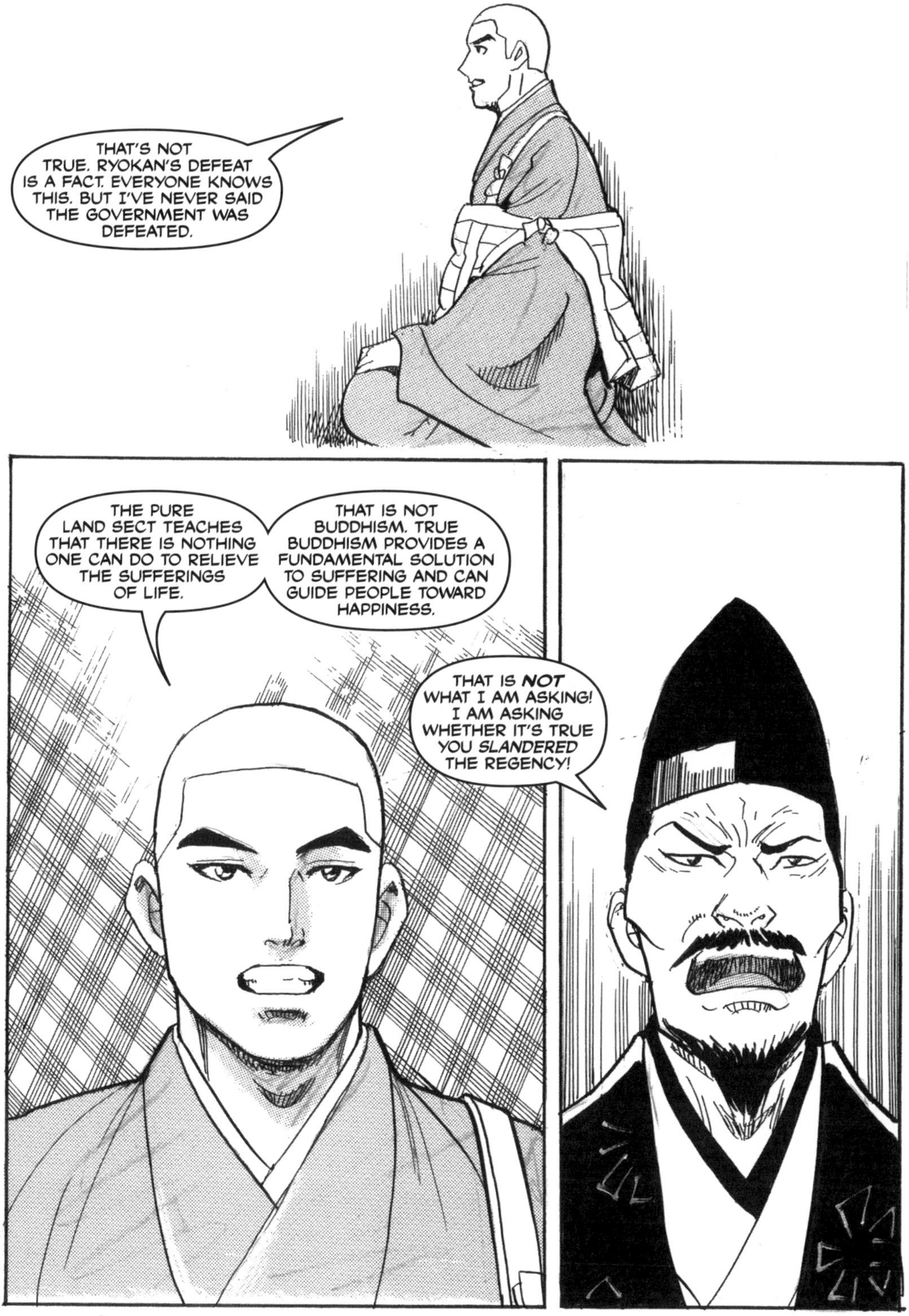

THAT'S NOT TRUE. RYOKAN'S DEFEAT IS A FACT. EVERYONE KNOWS THIS. BUT I'VE NEVER SAID THE GOVERNMENT WAS DEFEATED.
THE PURE LAND SECT TEACHES THAT THERE IS NOTHING ONE CAN DO TO RELIEVE THE SUFFERINGS OF LIFE.
THAT IS NOT BUDDHISM. TRUE BUDDHISM PROVIDES A FUNDAMENTAL SOLUTION TO SUFFERING AND CAN GUIDE PEOPLE TOWARD HAPPINESS.
THAT IS ***NOT*** WHAT I AM ASKING! I AM ASKING WHETHER IT'S TRUE YOU *SLANDERED* THE REGENCY!

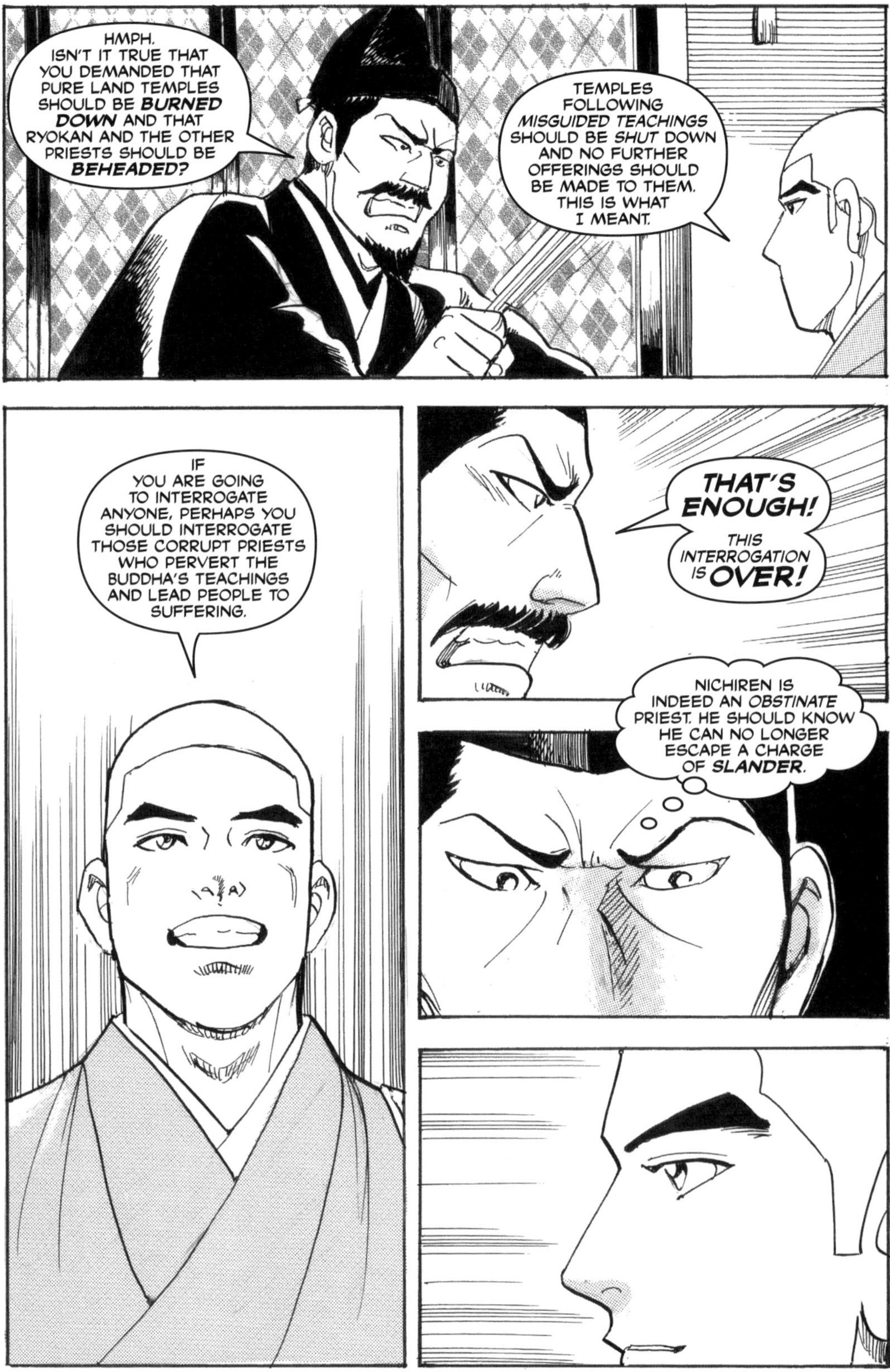
HMPH. ISN'T IT TRUE THAT YOU DEMANDED THAT PURE LAND TEMPLES SHOULD BE **BURNED DOWN** AND THAT RYOKAN AND THE OTHER PRIESTS SHOULD BE **BEHEADED?**
TEMPLES FOLLOWING *MISGUIDED TEACHINGS* SHOULD BE *SHUT* DOWN AND NO FURTHER OFFERINGS SHOULD BE MADE TO THEM. THIS IS WHAT I MEANT.
IF YOU ARE GOING TO INTERROGATE ANYONE, PERHAPS YOU SHOULD INTERROGATE THOSE CORRUPT PRIESTS WHO PERVERT THE BUDDHA'S TEACHINGS AND LEAD PEOPLE TO SUFFERING.
THAT'S ENOUGH! THIS INTERROGATION IS **OVER!**
NICHIREN IS INDEED AN *OBSTINATE* PRIEST. HE SHOULD KNOW HE CAN NO LONGER ESCAPE A CHARGE OF **SLANDER**.

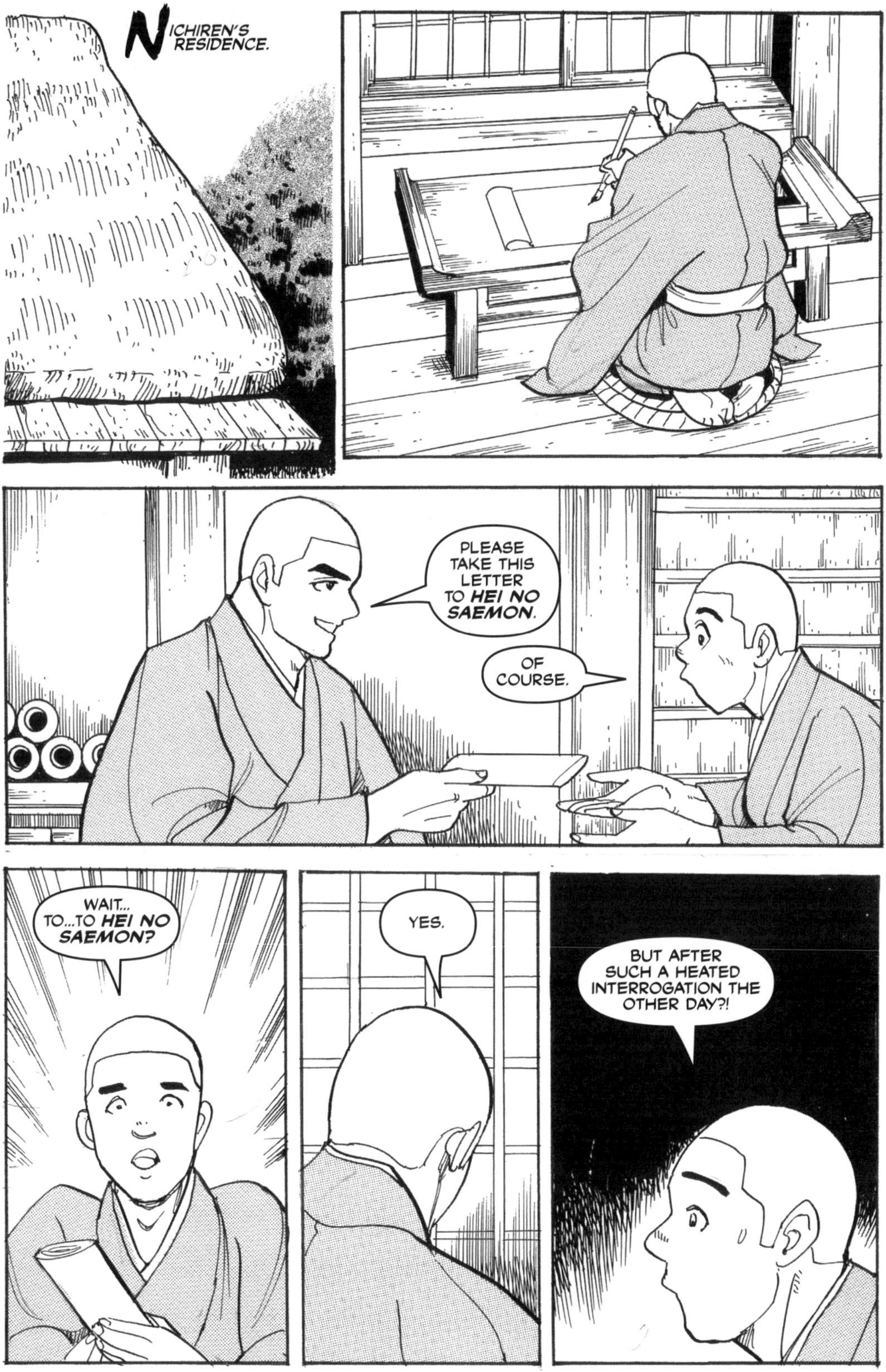
NICHIREN'S RESIDENCE.
PLEASE TAKE THIS LETTER TO HEI NO SAEMON.
OF COURSE.
WAIT... TO...TO HEI NO SAEMON?
YES.
BUT AFTER SUCH A HEATED INTERROGATION THE OTHER DAY?!

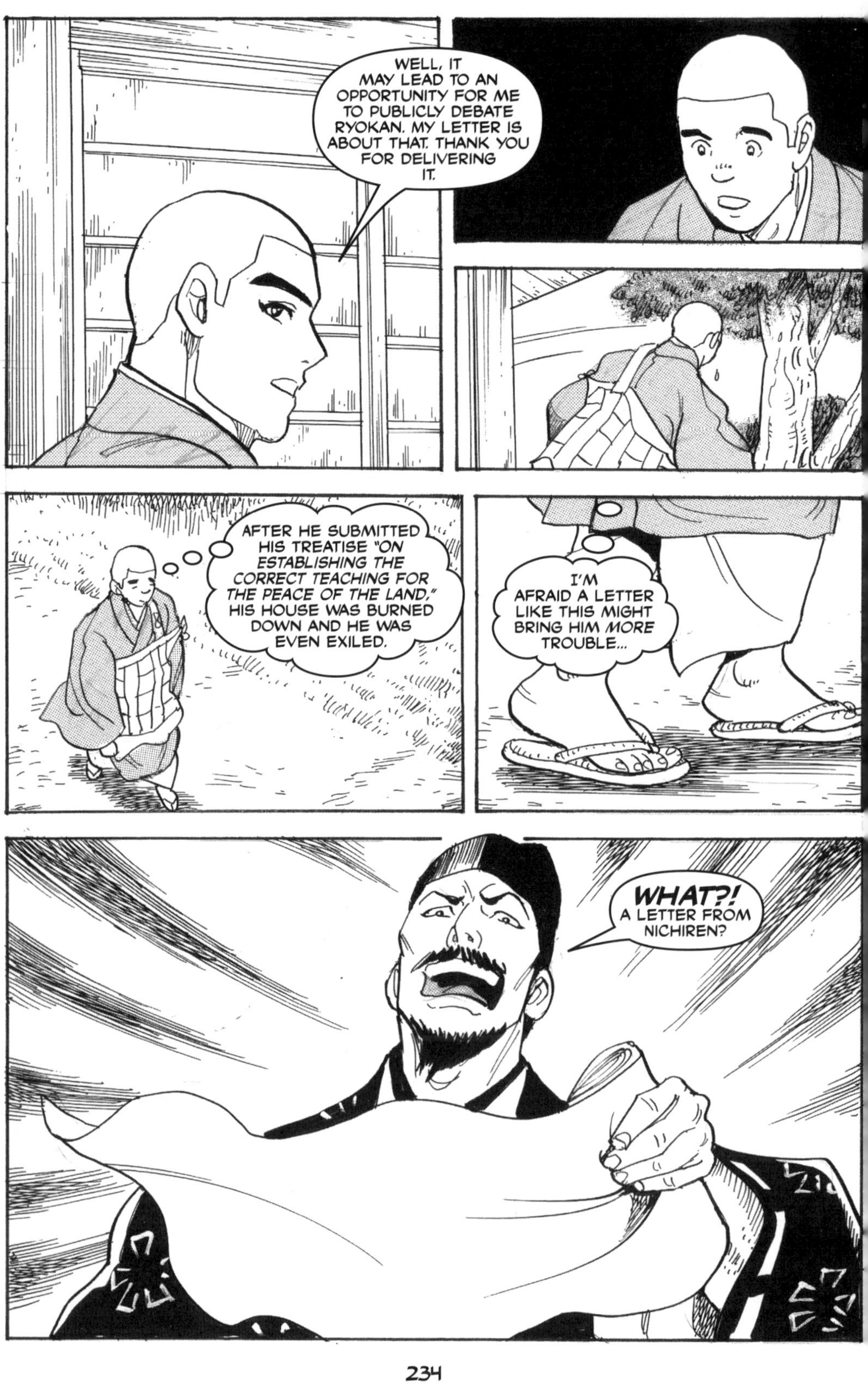
WELL, IT MAY LEAD TO AN OPPORTUNITY FOR ME TO PUBLICLY DEBATE RYOKAN. MY LETTER IS ABOUT THAT. THANK YOU FOR DELIVERING IT.
AFTER HE SUBMITTED HIS TREATISE *"ON ESTABLISHING THE CORRECT TEACHING FOR THE PEACE OF THE LAND,"* HIS HOUSE WAS BURNED DOWN AND HE WAS EVEN EXILED.
I'M AFRAID A LETTER LIKE THIS MIGHT BRING HIM *MORE* TROUBLE...
WHAT?! A LETTER FROM NICHIREN?

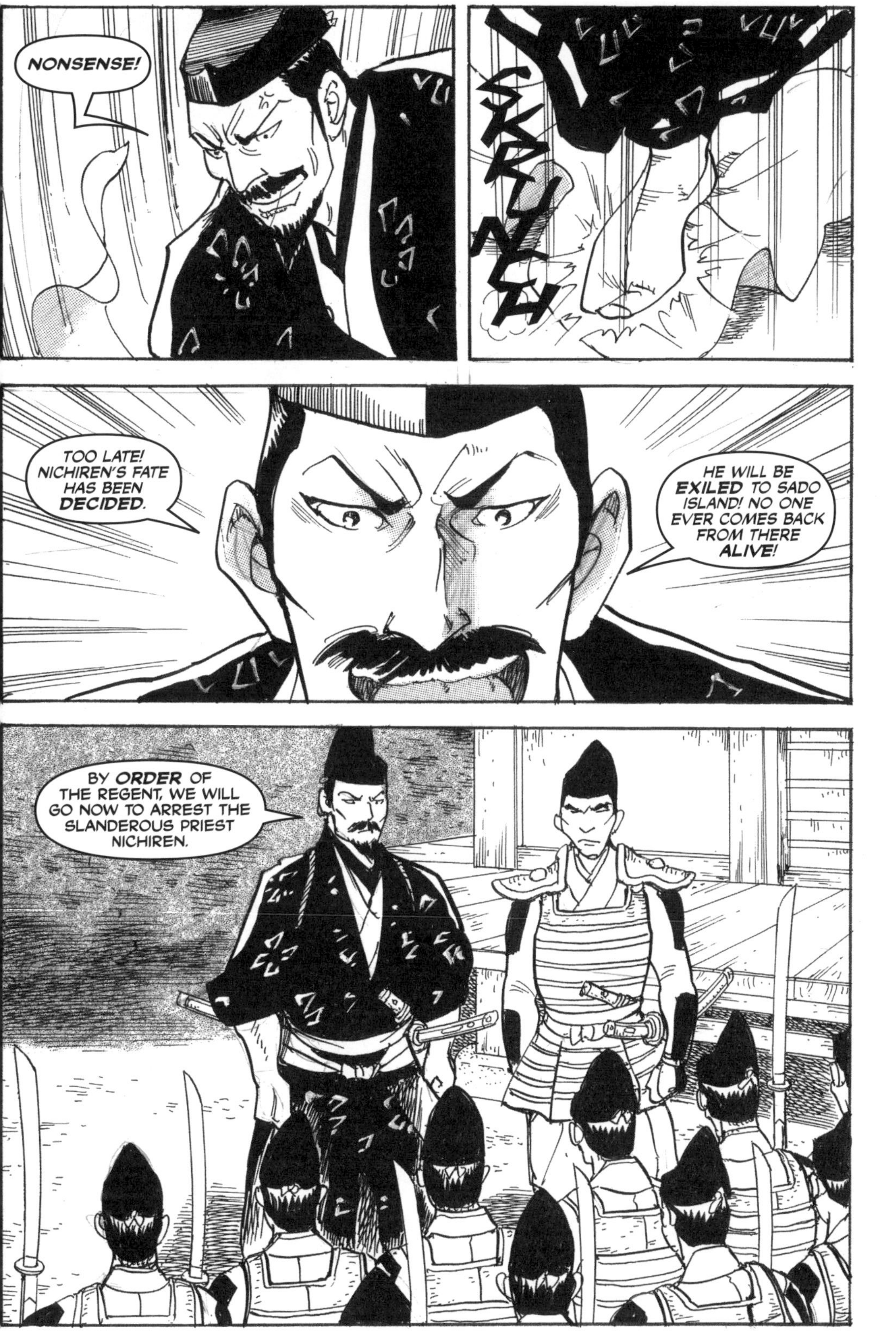
NONSENSE!
SKRUNCH
TOO LATE! NICHIREN'S FATE HAS BEEN DECIDED.
HE WILL BE EXILED TO SADO ISLAND! NO ONE EVER COMES BACK FROM THERE ALIVE!
BY ORDER OF THE REGENT, WE WILL GO NOW TO ARREST THE SLANDEROUS PRIEST NICHIREN.

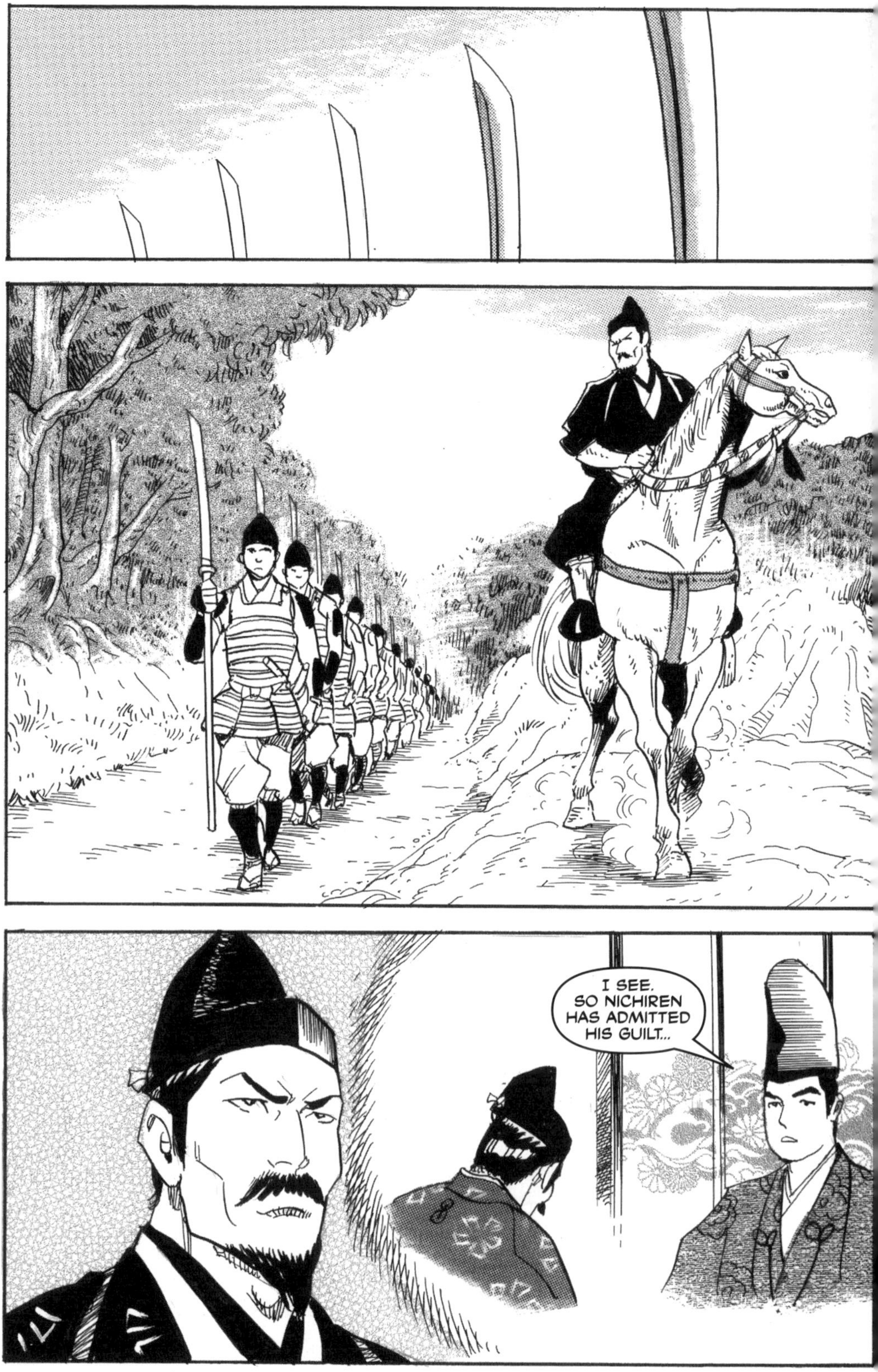
I SEE.
SO NICHIREN
HAS ADMITTED
HIS GUILT...

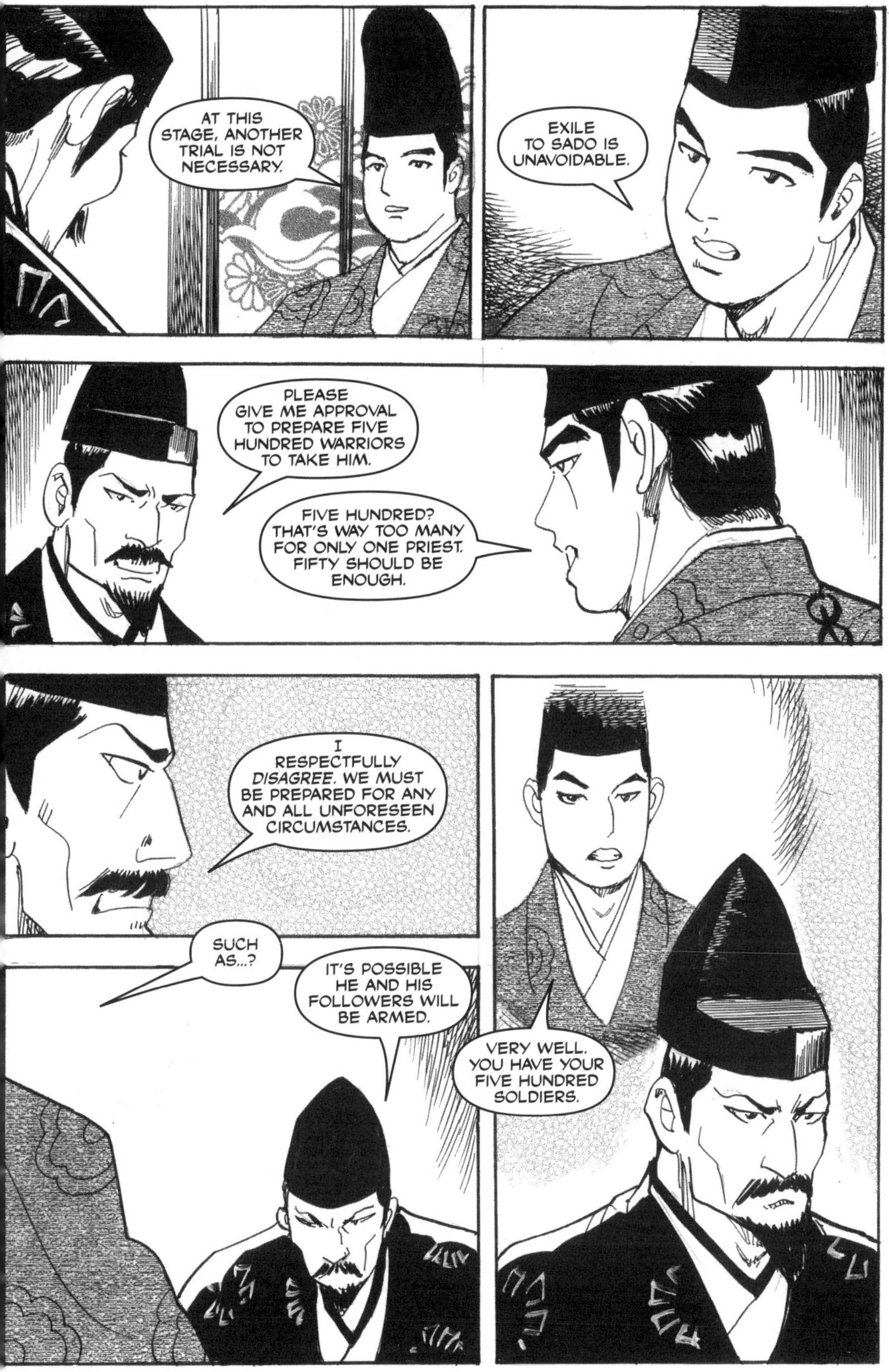
AT THIS STAGE, ANOTHER TRIAL IS NOT NECESSARY.
EXILE TO SADO IS UNAVOIDABLE.
PLEASE GIVE ME APPROVAL TO PREPARE FIVE HUNDRED WARRIORS TO TAKE HIM.
FIVE HUNDRED? THAT'S WAY TOO MANY FOR ONLY ONE PRIEST. FIFTY SHOULD BE ENOUGH.
I RESPECTFULLY *DISAGREE*. WE MUST BE PREPARED FOR ANY AND ALL UNFORESEEN CIRCUMSTANCES.
SUCH AS...?
IT'S POSSIBLE HE AND HIS FOLLOWERS WILL BE ARMED.
VERY WELL. YOU HAVE YOUR FIVE HUNDRED SOLDIERS.

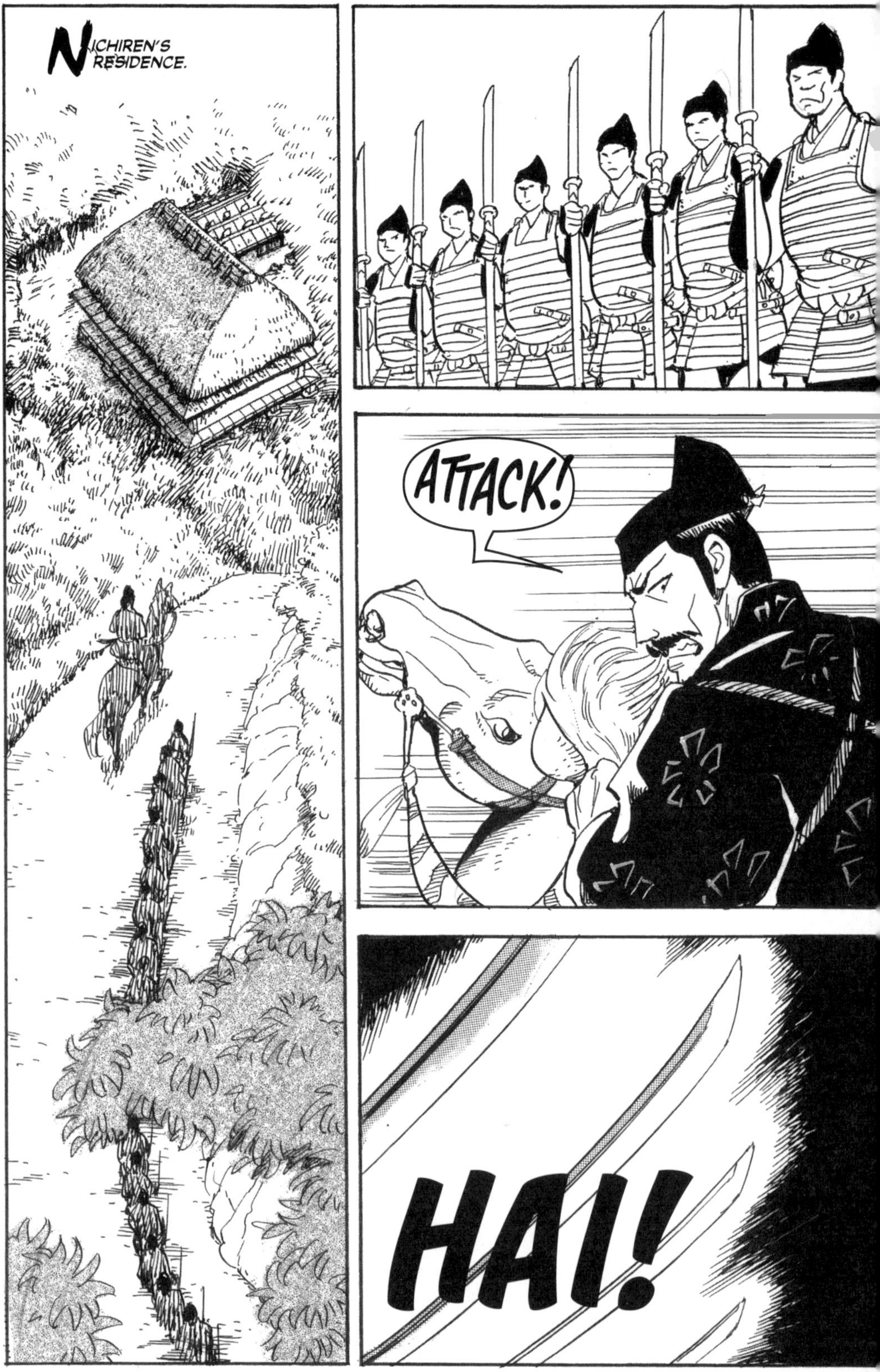
NICHIREN'S RESIDENCE.
ATTACK!
HAI!

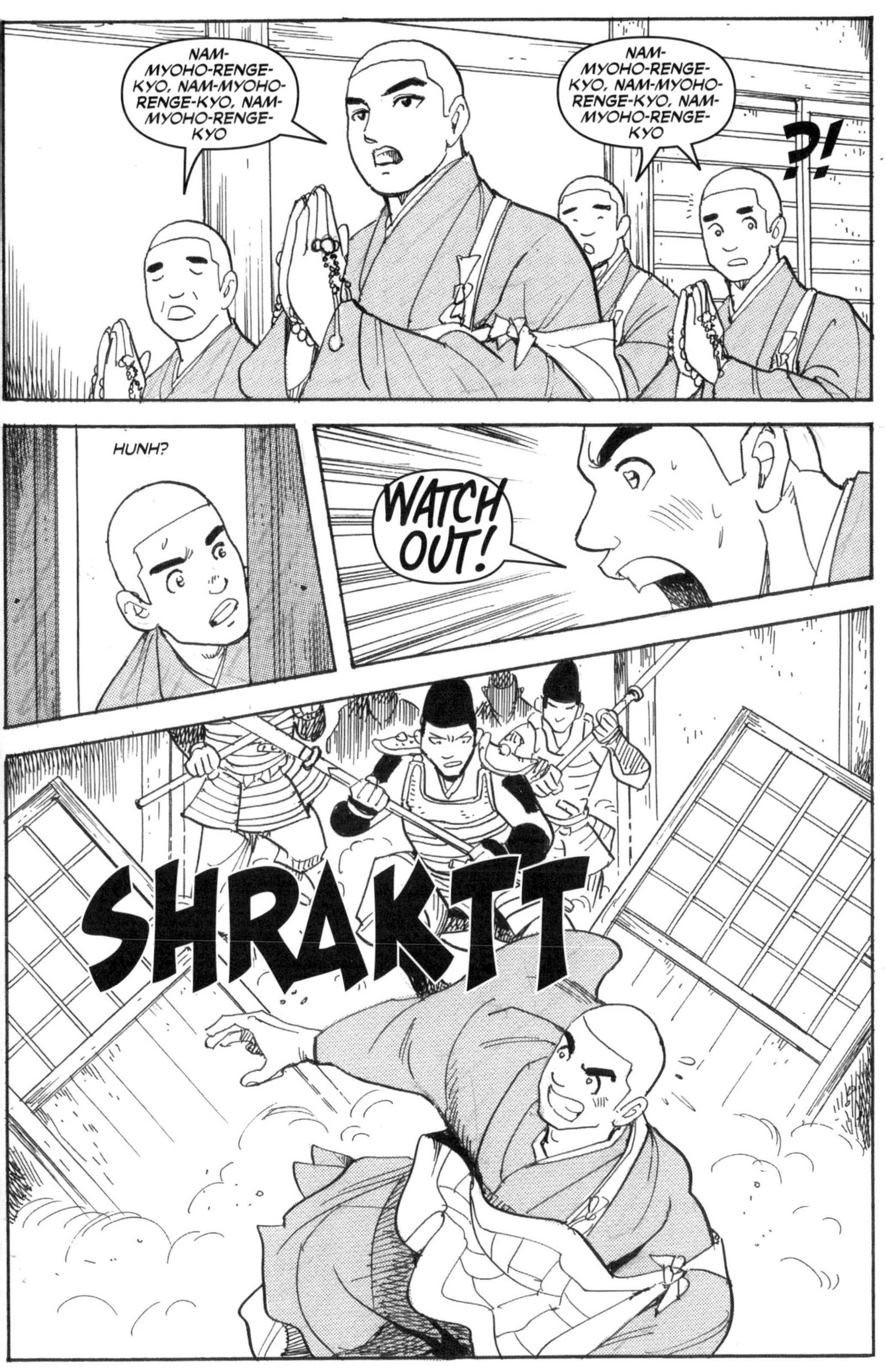
NAM-MYOHO-RENGE-KYO, NAM-MYOHO-RENGE-KYO, NAM-MYOHO-RENGE-KYO
NAM-MYOHO-RENGE-KYO, NAM-MYOHO-RENGE-KYO, NAM-MYOHO-RENGE-KYO
?!
HUNH?
WATCH OUT!
SHRAKTT

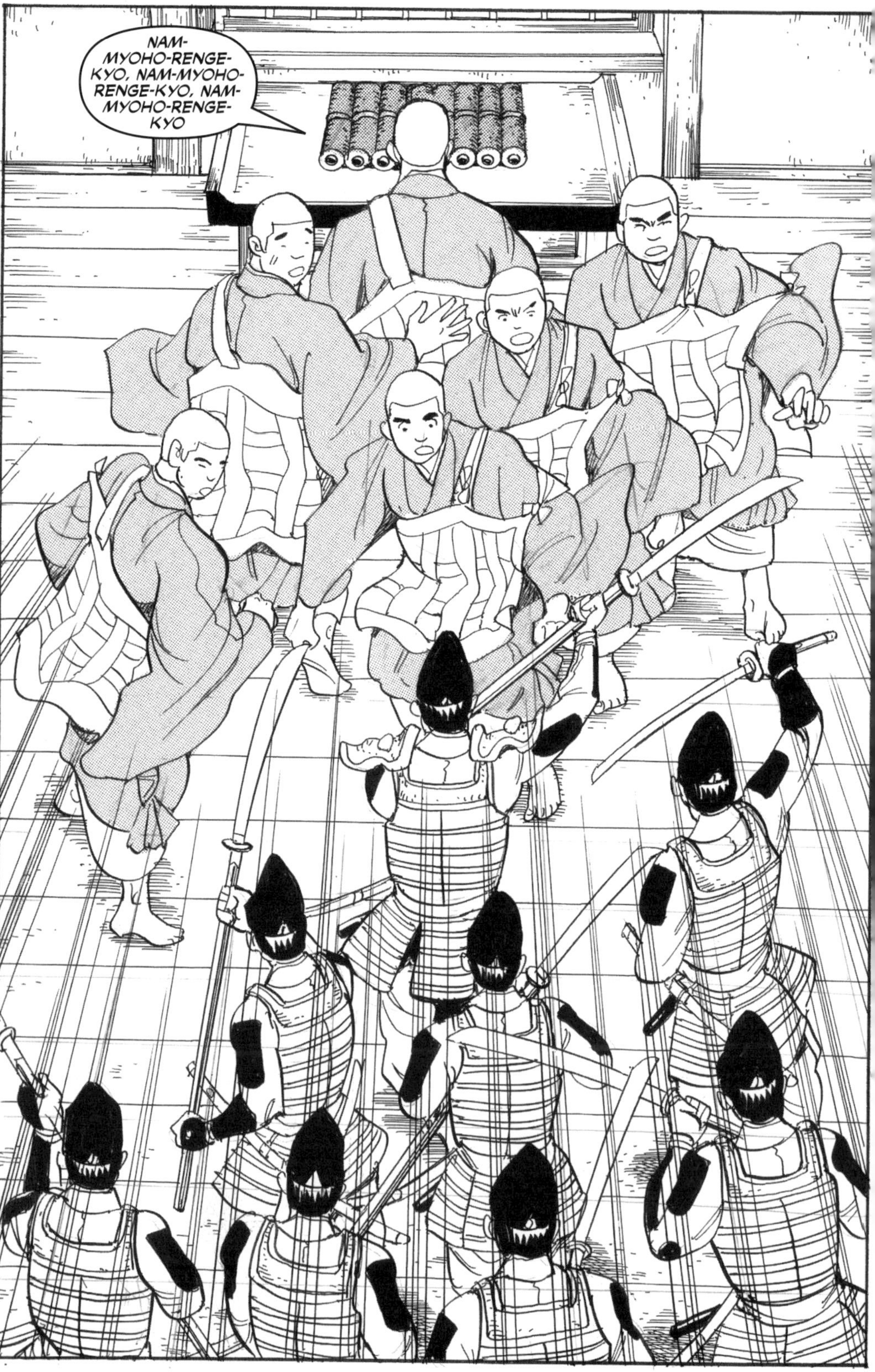
NAM-MYOHO-RENGE-KYO, NAM-MYOHO-RENGE-KYO, NAM-MYOHO-RENGE-KYO

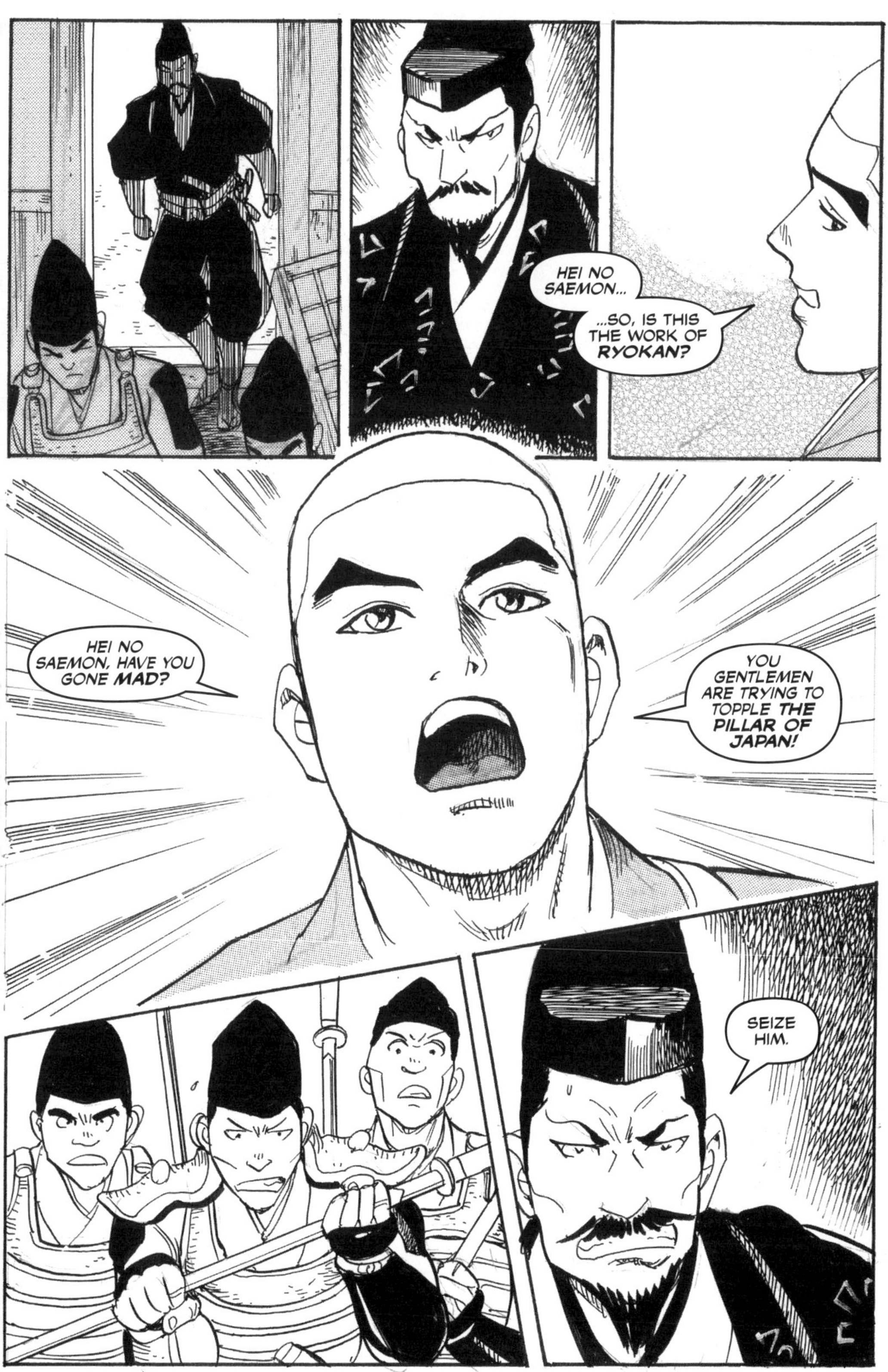
HEI NO SAEMON...
...SO, IS THIS THE WORK OF **RYOKAN?**
HEI NO SAEMON, HAVE YOU GONE **MAD?**
YOU GENTLEMEN ARE TRYING TO TOPPLE **THE PILLAR OF JAPAN!**
SEIZE HIM.

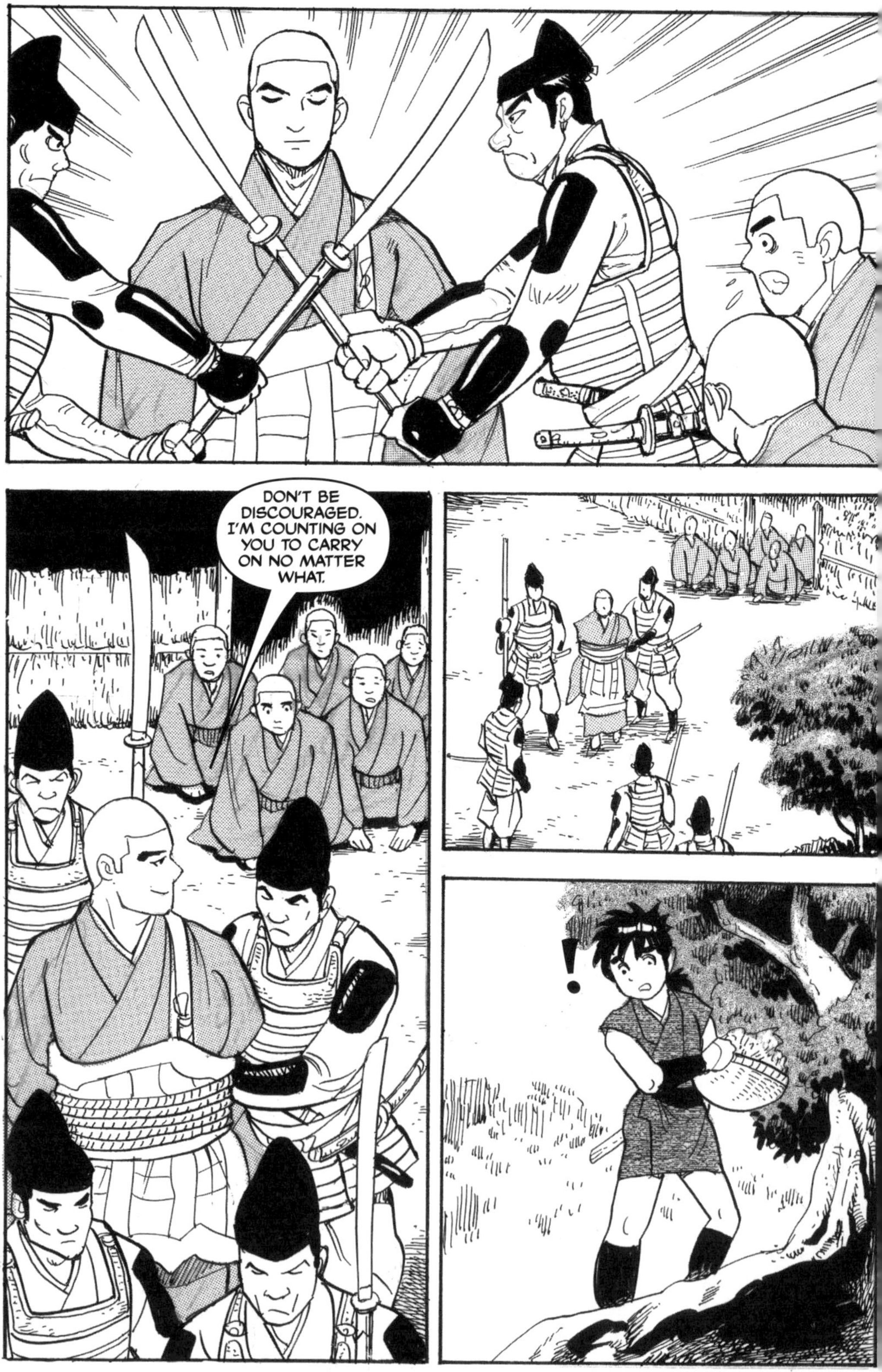
DON'T BE DISCOURAGED. I'M COUNTING ON YOU TO CARRY ON NO MATTER WHAT.
!

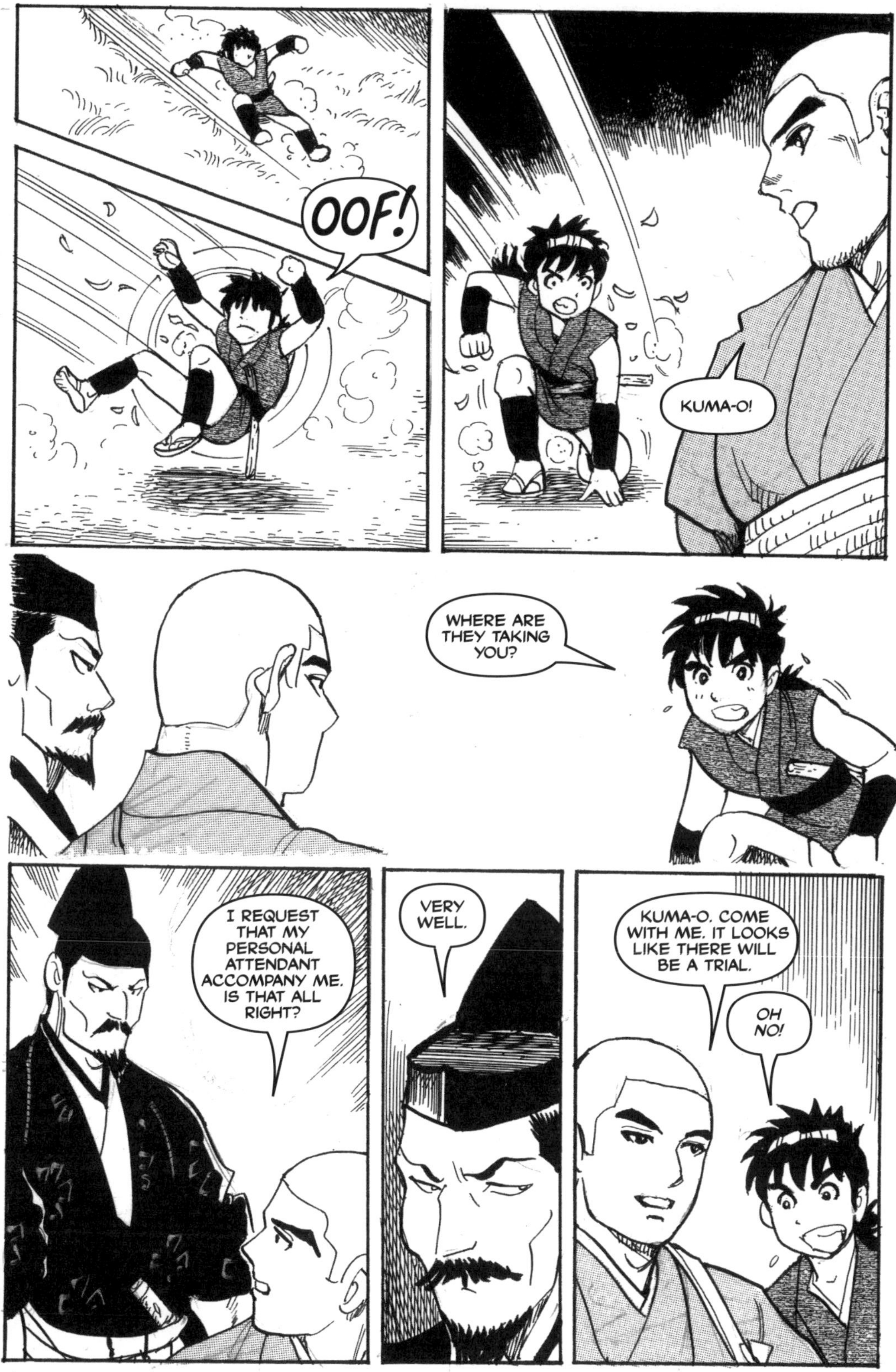
OOF!
KUMA-O!
WHERE ARE THEY TAKING YOU?
I REQUEST THAT MY PERSONAL ATTENDANT ACCOMPANY ME. IS THAT ALL RIGHT?
VERY WELL.
KUMA-O. COME WITH ME. IT LOOKS LIKE THERE WILL BE A TRIAL.
OH NO!

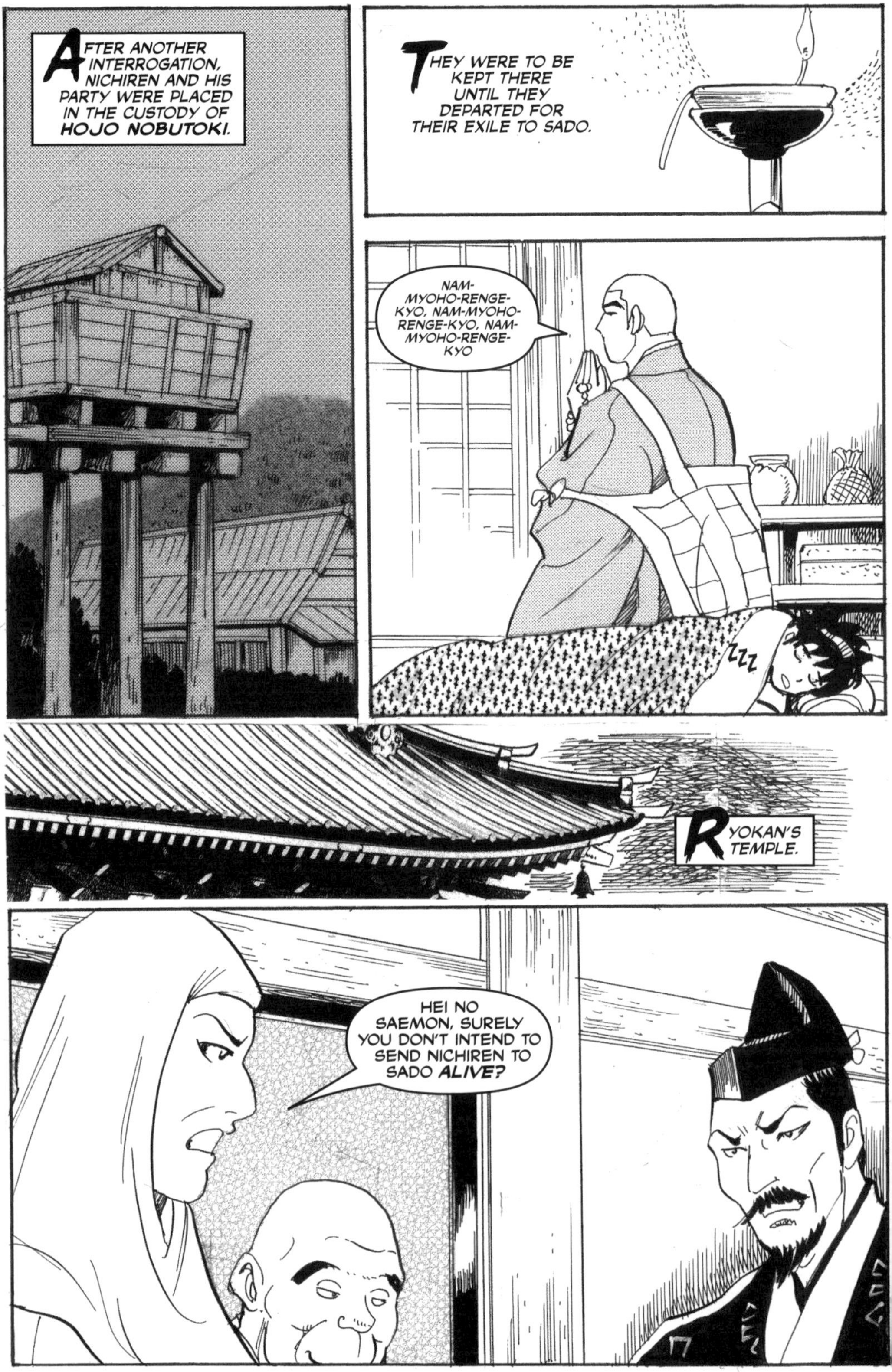
AFTER ANOTHER INTERROGATION, NICHIREN AND HIS PARTY WERE PLACED IN THE CUSTODY OF HOJO NOBUTOKI.
THEY WERE TO BE KEPT THERE UNTIL THEY DEPARTED FOR THEIR EXILE TO SADO.
NAM-MYOHO-RENGE-KYO, NAM-MYOHO-RENGE-KYO, NAM-MYOHO-RENGE-KYO
ZZZ
RYOKAN'S TEMPLE.
HEI NO SAEMON, SURELY YOU DON'T INTEND TO SEND NICHIREN TO SADO ALIVE?

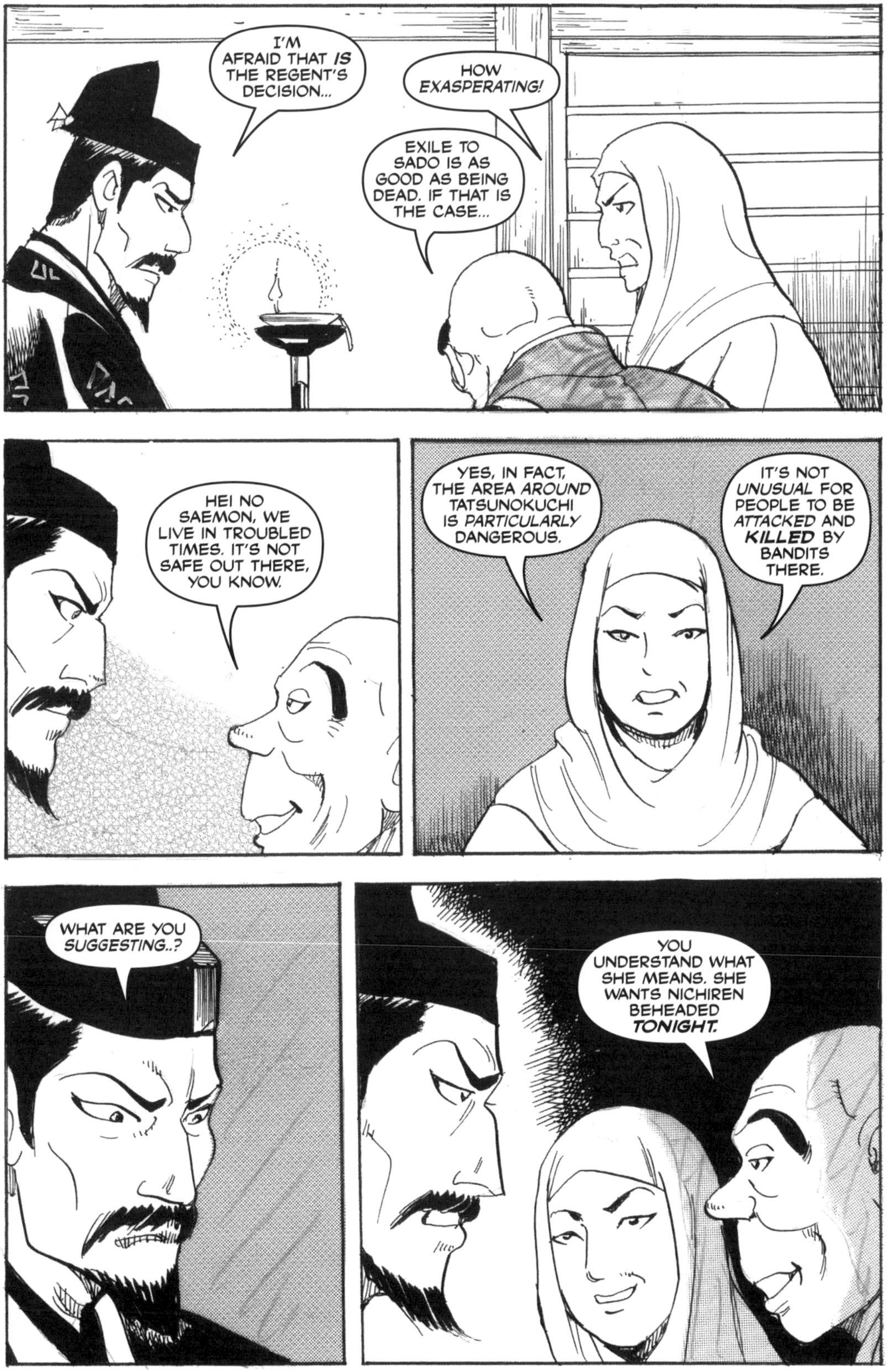
I'M AFRAID THAT *IS* THE REGENT'S DECISION...
HOW *EXASPERATING!*
EXILE TO SADO IS AS GOOD AS BEING DEAD. IF THAT IS THE CASE...
HEI NO SAEMON, WE LIVE IN TROUBLED TIMES. IT'S NOT SAFE OUT THERE, YOU KNOW.
YES, IN FACT, THE AREA *AROUND* TATSUNOKUCHI IS *PARTICULARLY* DANGEROUS.
IT'S NOT *UNUSUAL* FOR PEOPLE TO BE *ATTACKED* AND ***KILLED*** BY BANDITS THERE.
WHAT ARE YOU *SUGGESTING..?*
YOU UNDERSTAND WHAT SHE MEANS. SHE WANTS NICHIREN BEHEADED ***TONIGHT.***

NICHIREN.

I KNOW THIS IS SHORT NOTICE, BUT YOU WILL DEPART FOR SADO NOW. PLEASE GET READY.

VERY WELL... KUMA-O... WAKE UP!

HUNH? WHA...? I'M SLEEPY.

SORRY, KUMA-O.

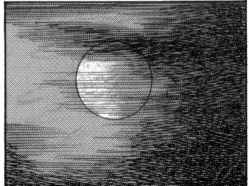

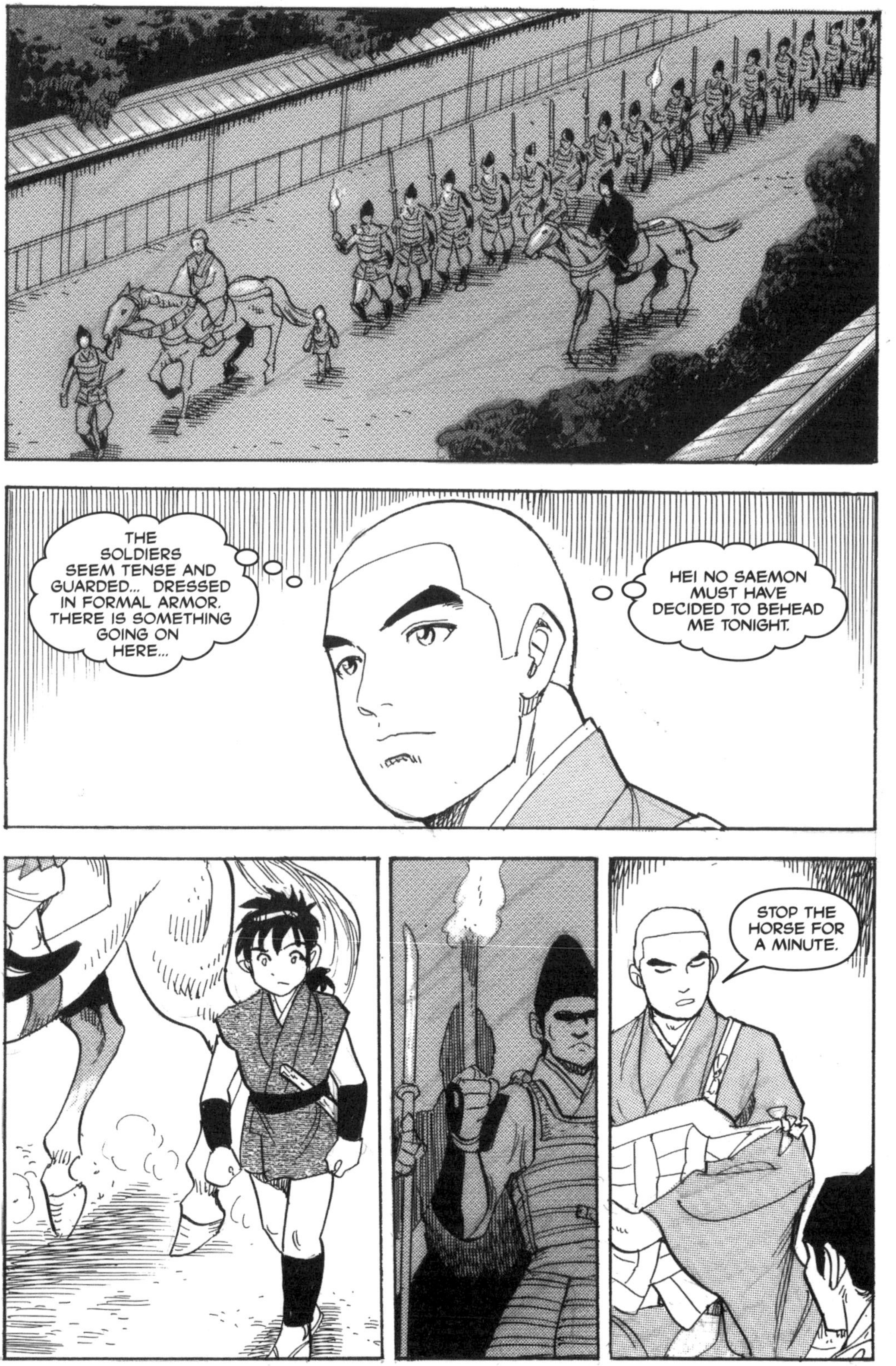
THE SOLDIERS SEEM TENSE AND GUARDED... DRESSED IN FORMAL ARMOR. THERE IS SOMETHING GOING ON HERE...
HEI NO SAEMON MUST HAVE DECIDED TO BEHEAD ME TONIGHT.
STOP THE HORSE FOR A MINUTE.

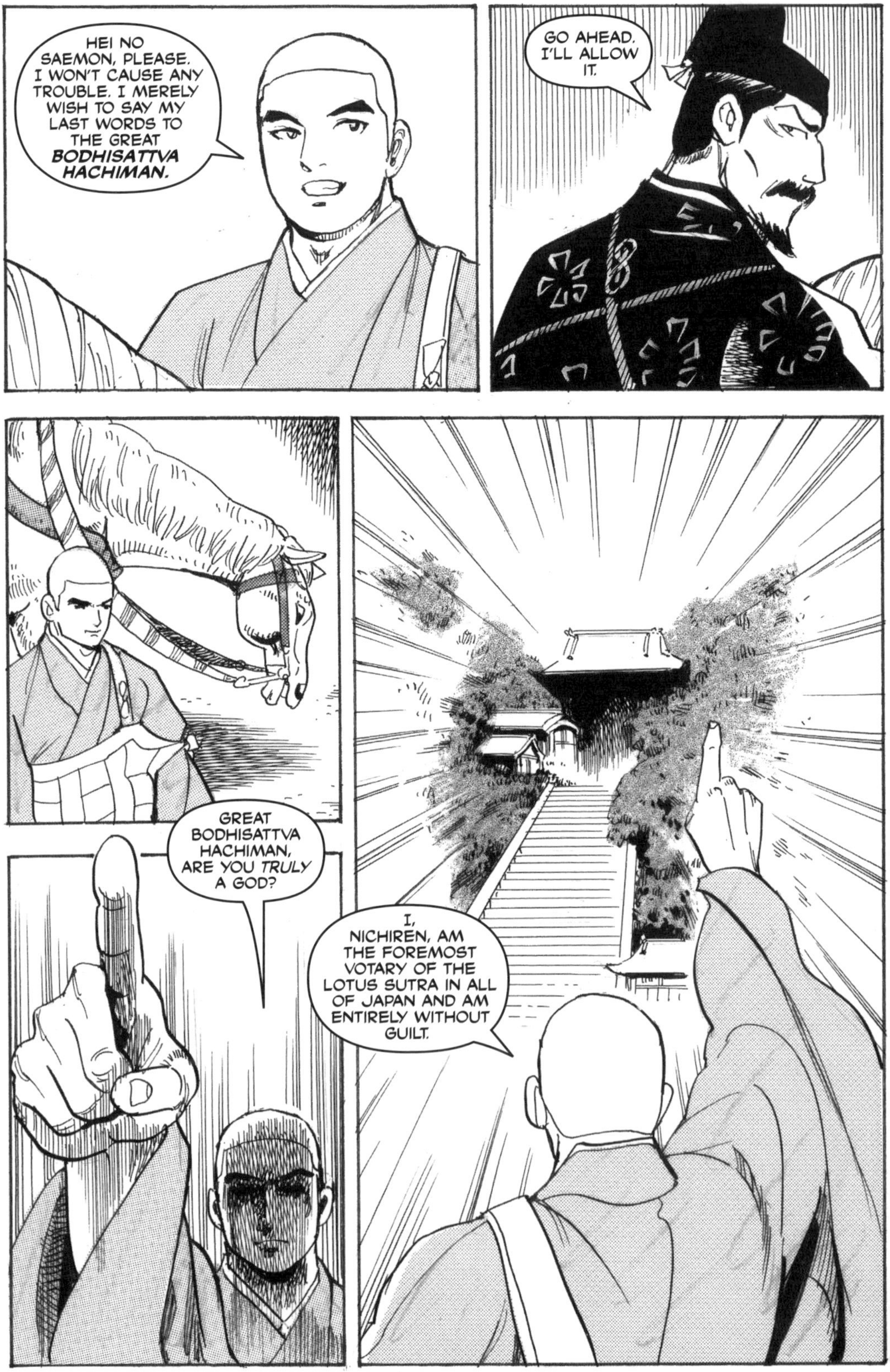
HEI NO SAEMON, PLEASE. I WON'T CAUSE ANY TROUBLE. I MERELY WISH TO SAY MY LAST WORDS TO THE GREAT ***BODHISATTVA HACHIMAN.***
GO AHEAD. I'LL ALLOW IT.
GREAT BODHISATTVA HACHIMAN, ARE YOU *TRULY* A GOD?
I, NICHIREN, AM THE FOREMOST VOTARY OF THE LOTUS SUTRA IN ALL OF JAPAN AND AM ENTIRELY WITHOUT GUILT.

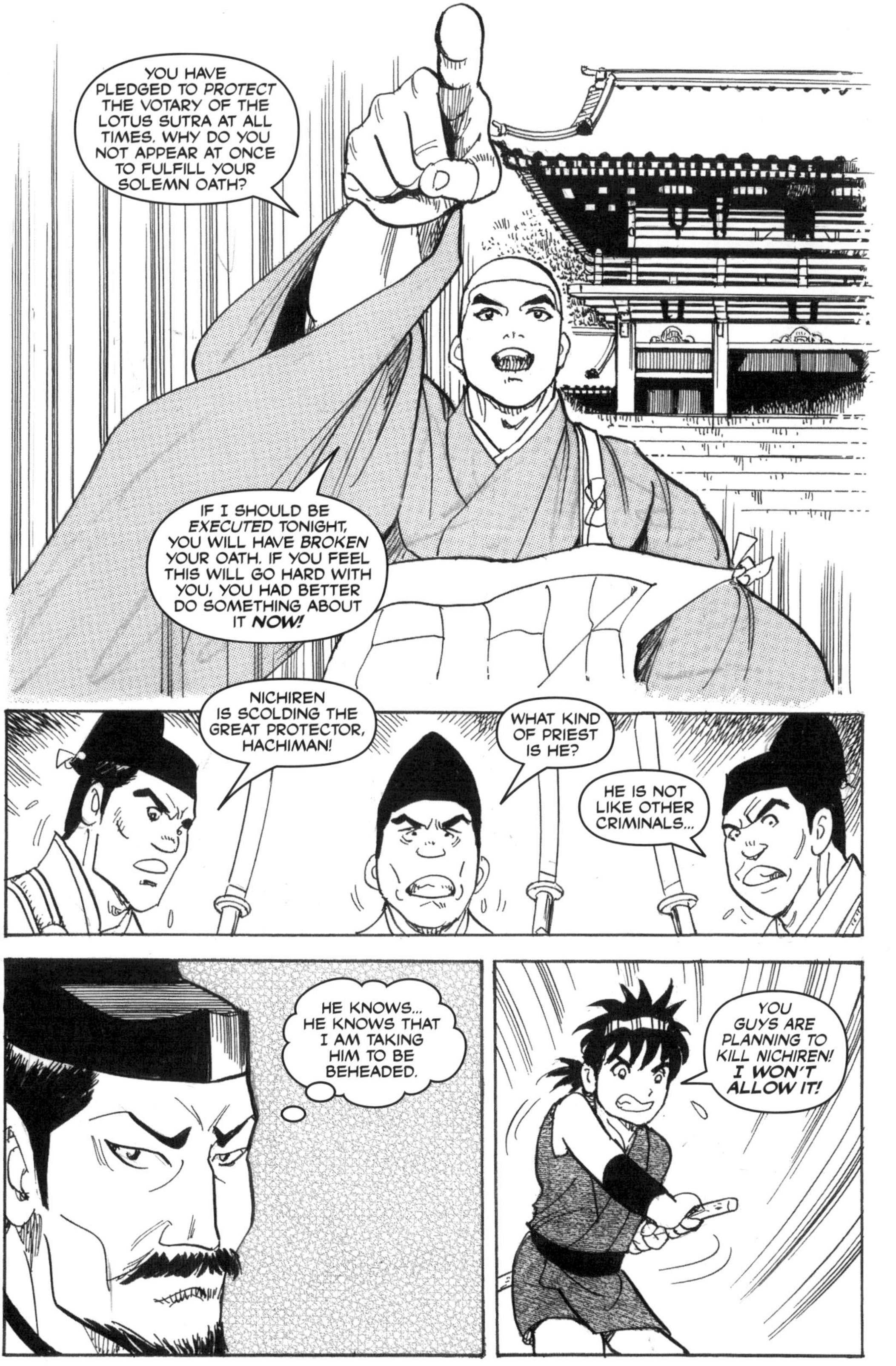
YOU HAVE PLEDGED TO *PROTECT* THE VOTARY OF THE LOTUS SUTRA AT ALL TIMES. WHY DO YOU NOT APPEAR AT ONCE TO FULFILL YOUR SOLEMN OATH?
IF I SHOULD BE *EXECUTED* TONIGHT, YOU WILL HAVE *BROKEN* YOUR OATH. IF YOU FEEL THIS WILL GO HARD WITH YOU, YOU HAD BETTER DO SOMETHING ABOUT IT ***NOW!***
NICHIREN IS SCOLDING THE GREAT PROTECTOR, HACHIMAN!
WHAT KIND OF PRIEST IS HE?
HE IS NOT LIKE OTHER CRIMINALS...
HE KNOWS... HE KNOWS THAT I AM TAKING HIM TO BE BEHEADED.
YOU GUYS ARE PLANNING TO KILL NICHIREN! ***I WON'T ALLOW IT!***

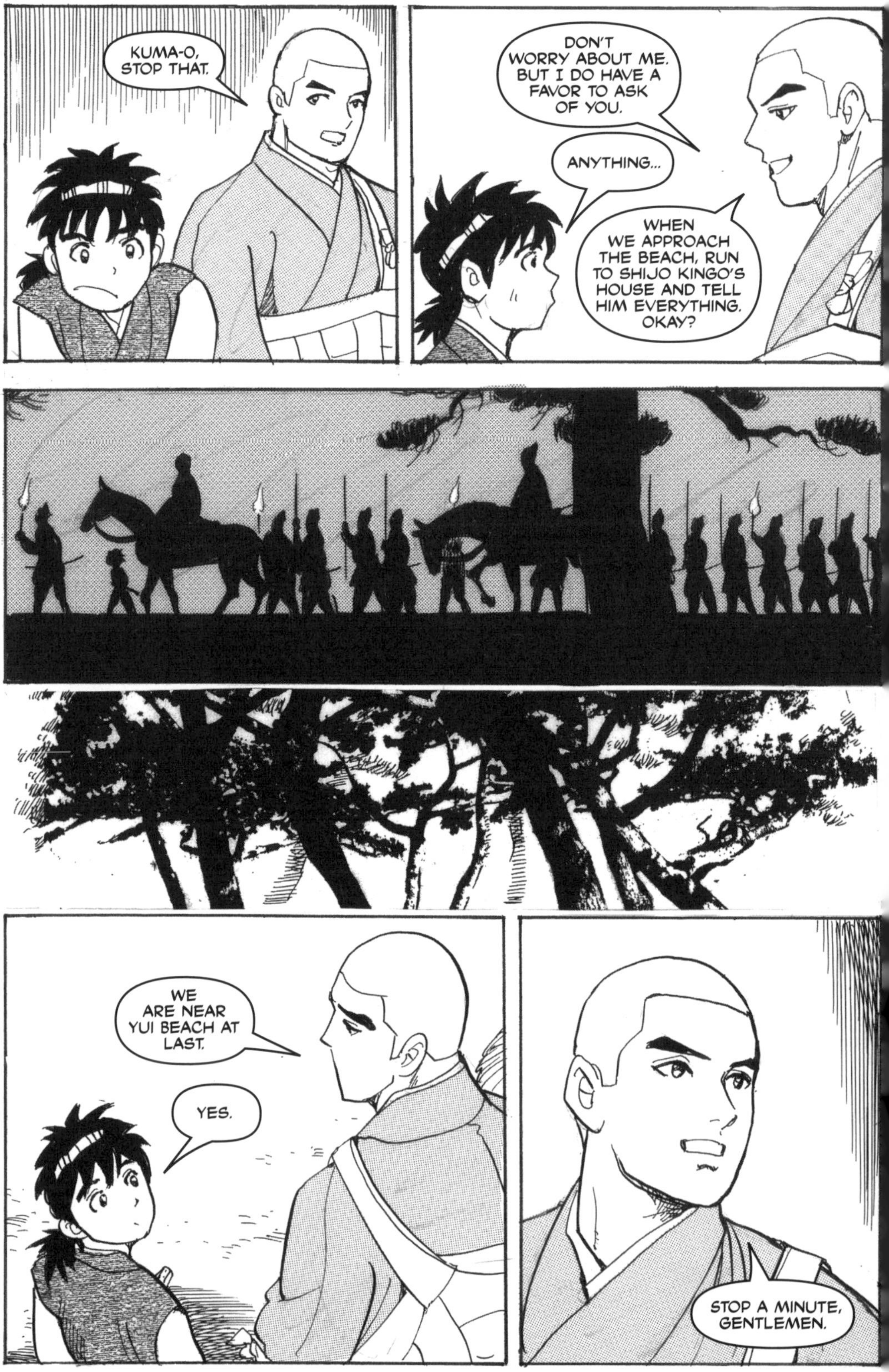
KUMA-O, STOP THAT.
DON'T WORRY ABOUT ME. BUT I DO HAVE A FAVOR TO ASK OF YOU.
ANYTHING...
WHEN WE APPROACH THE BEACH, RUN TO SHIJO KINGO'S HOUSE AND TELL HIM EVERYTHING. OKAY?
WE ARE NEAR YUI BEACH AT LAST.
YES.
STOP A MINUTE, GENTLEMEN.

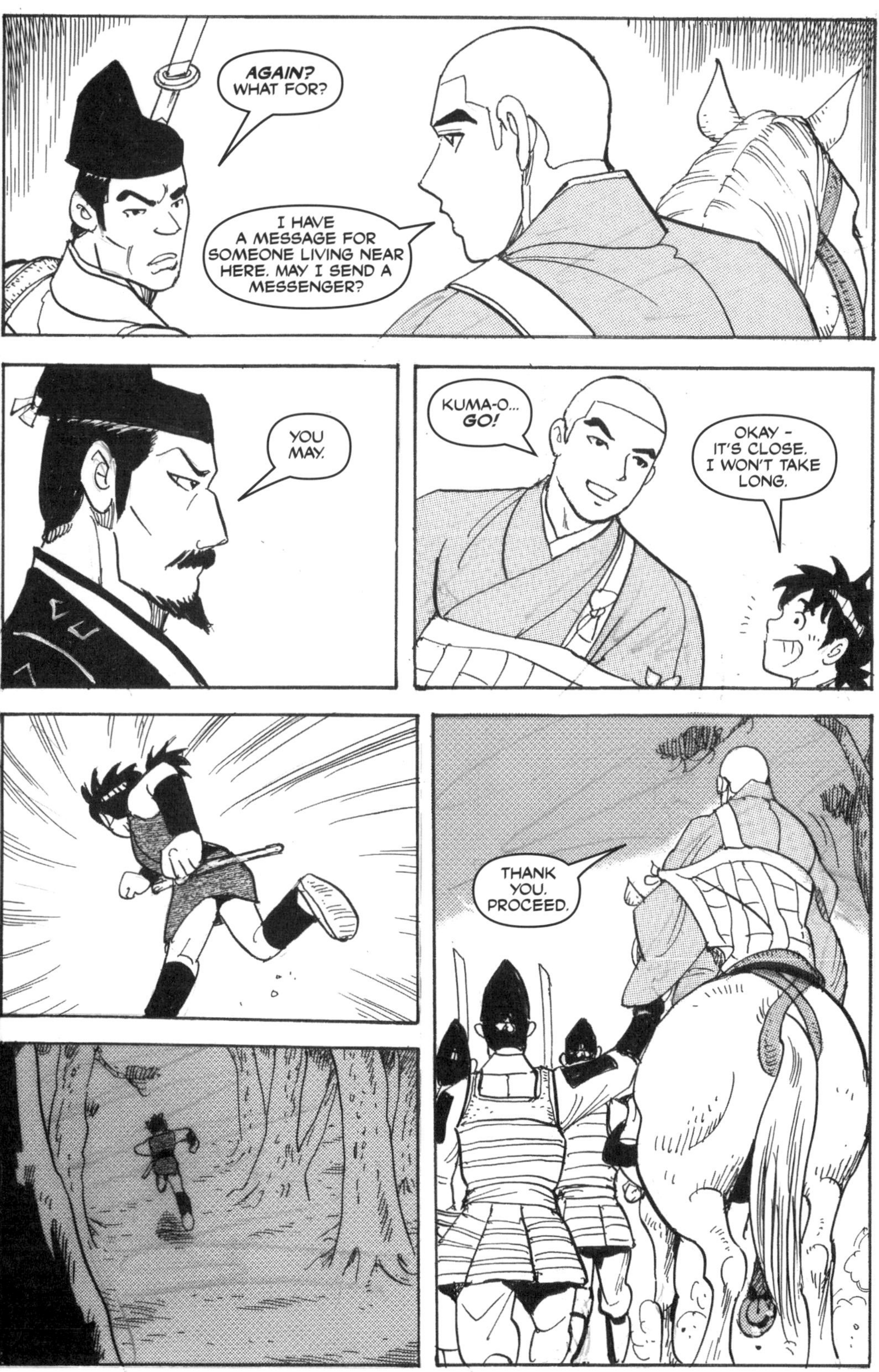

AGAIN? WHAT FOR?
I HAVE A MESSAGE FOR SOMEONE LIVING NEAR HERE. MAY I SEND A MESSENGER?
YOU MAY.
KUMA-O... ***GO!***
OKAY - IT'S CLOSE. I WON'T TAKE LONG.
THANK YOU. PROCEED.

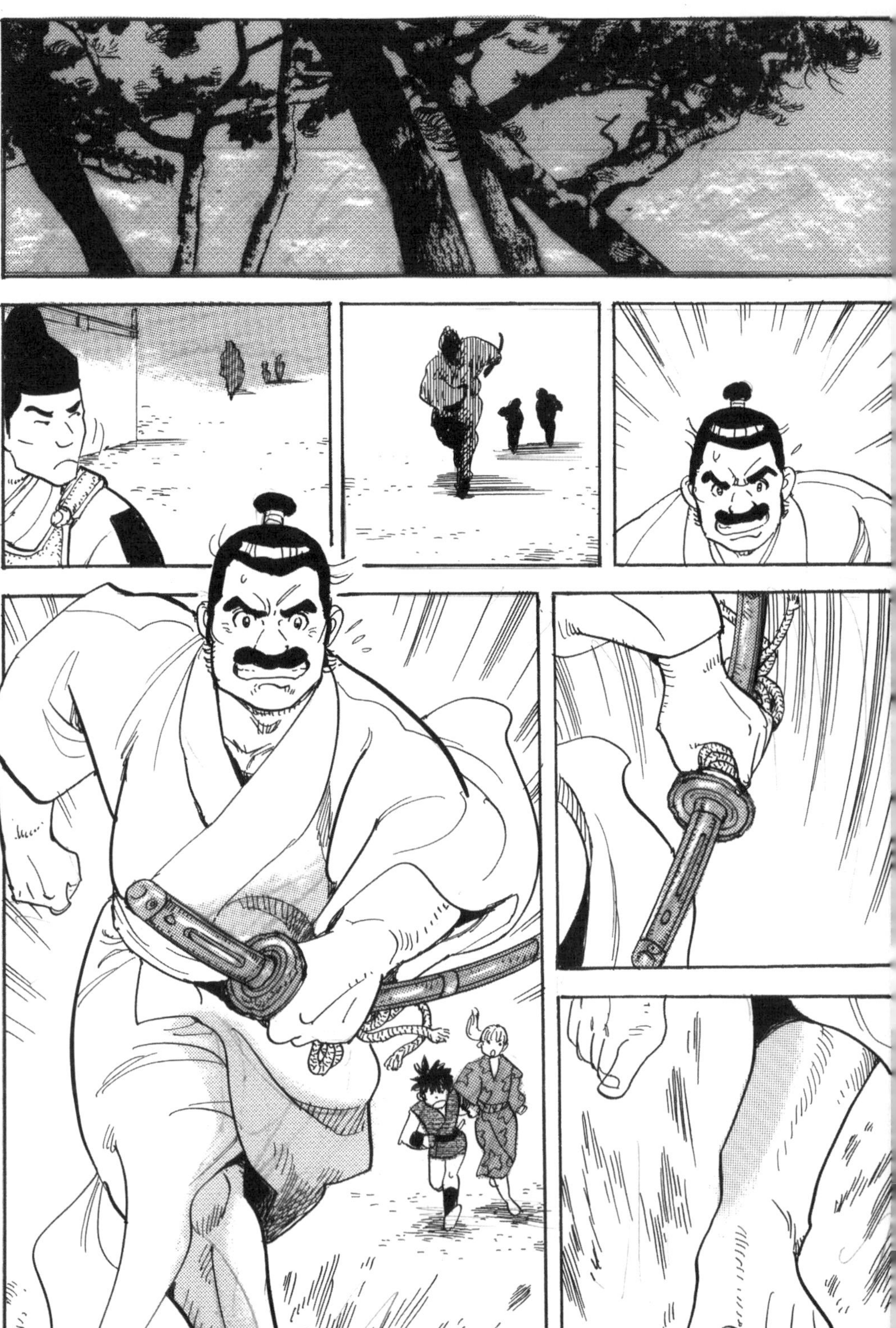

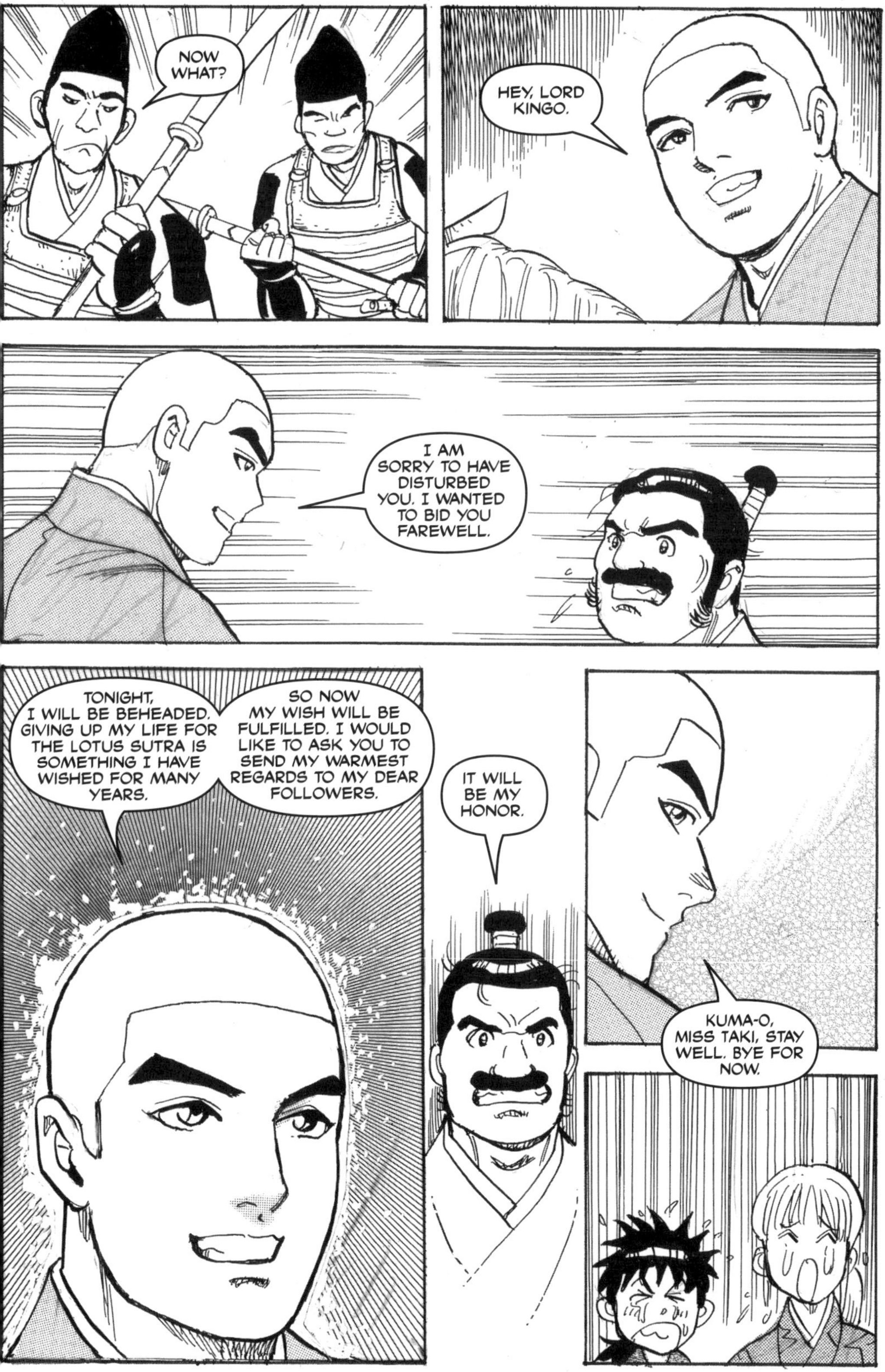
NOW WHAT?
HEY, LORD KINGO.
I AM SORRY TO HAVE DISTURBED YOU. I WANTED TO BID YOU FAREWELL.
TONIGHT, I WILL BE BEHEADED. GIVING UP MY LIFE FOR THE LOTUS SUTRA IS SOMETHING I HAVE WISHED FOR MANY YEARS.
SO NOW MY WISH WILL BE FULFILLED. I WOULD LIKE TO ASK YOU TO SEND MY WARMEST REGARDS TO MY DEAR FOLLOWERS.
IT WILL BE MY HONOR.
KUMA-O, MISS TAKI, STAY WELL. BYE FOR NOW.

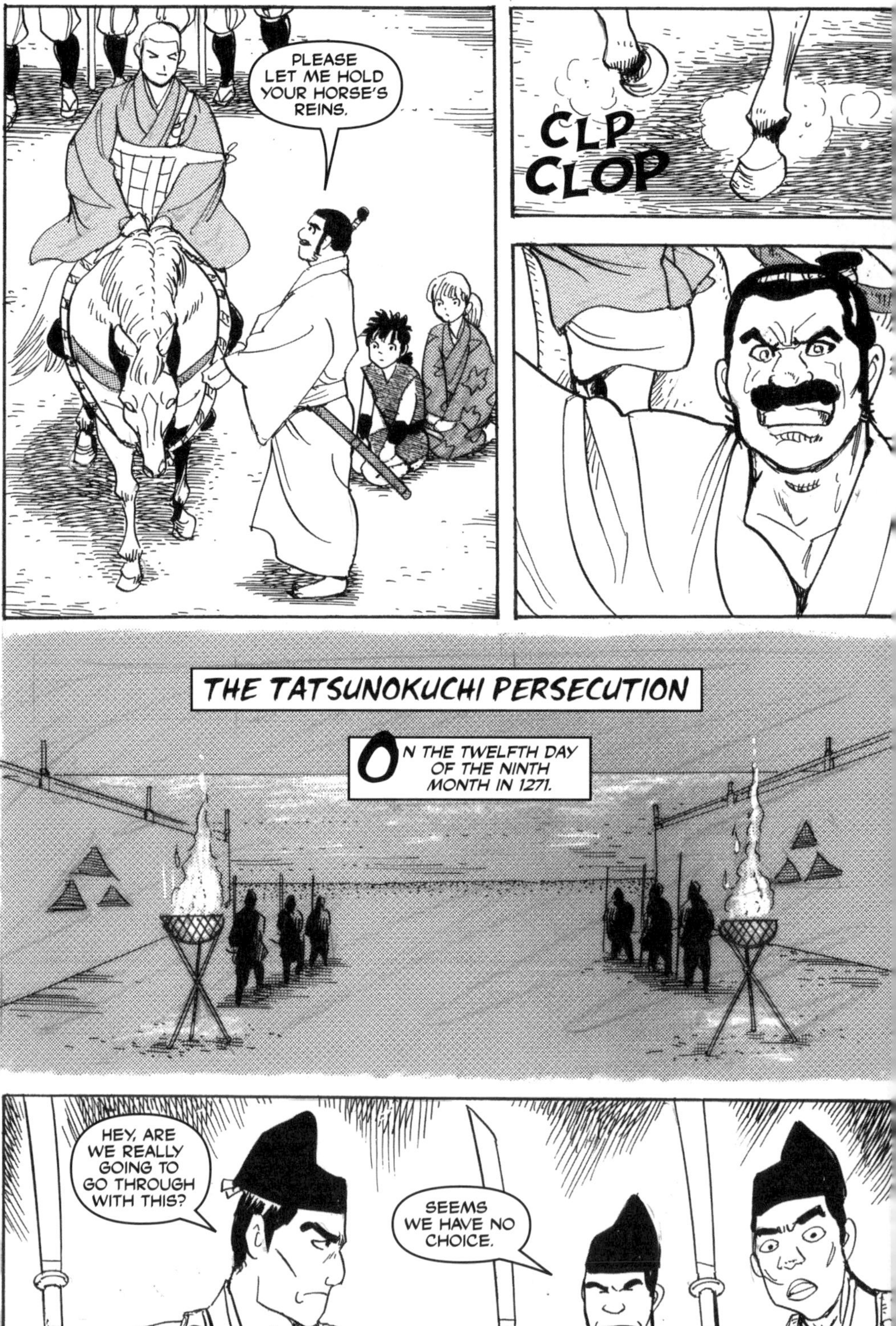
PLEASE LET ME HOLD YOUR HORSE'S REINS.
CLP CLOP
THE TATSUNOKUCHI PERSECUTION
ON THE TWELFTH DAY OF THE NINTH MONTH IN 1271.
HEY, ARE WE REALLY GOING TO GO THROUGH WITH THIS?
SEEMS WE HAVE NO CHOICE.

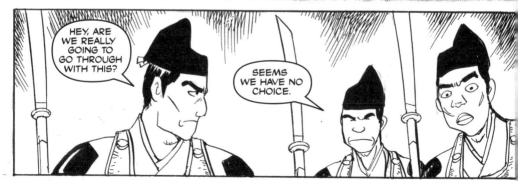

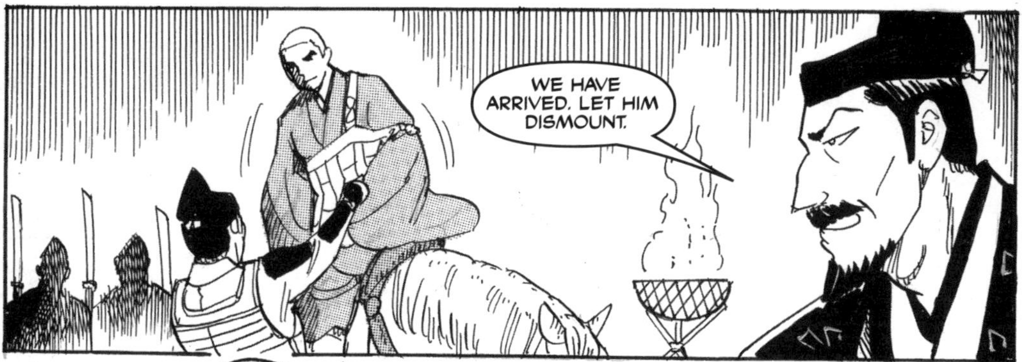
WE HAVE ARRIVED. LET HIM DISMOUNT.

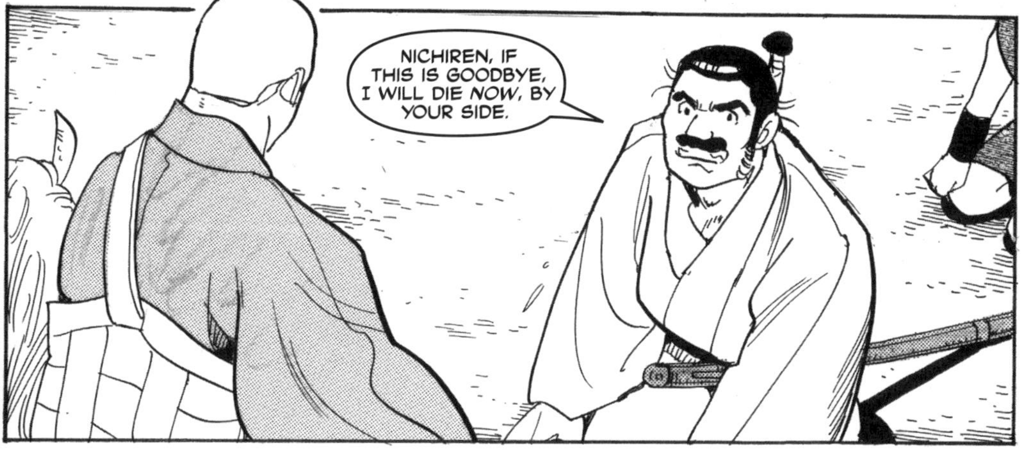
NICHIREN, IF THIS IS GOODBYE, I WILL DIE *NOW*, BY YOUR SIDE.

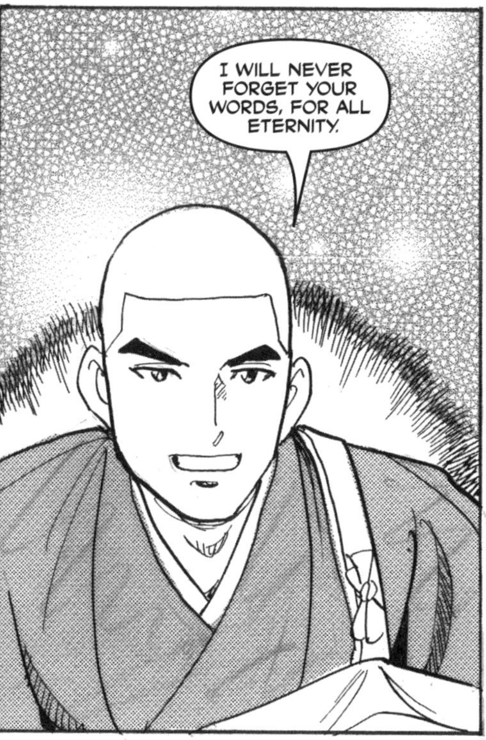
I WILL NEVER FORGET YOUR WORDS, FOR ALL ETERNITY.

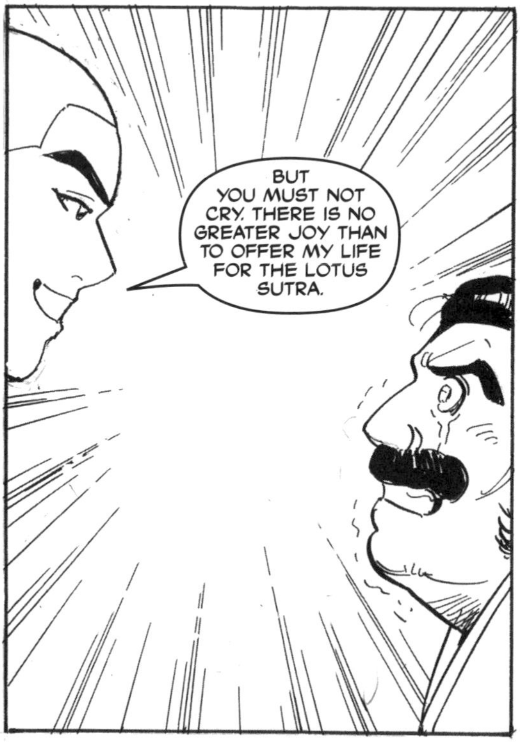
BUT YOU MUST NOT CRY. THERE IS NO GREATER JOY THAN TO OFFER MY LIFE FOR THE LOTUS SUTRA.

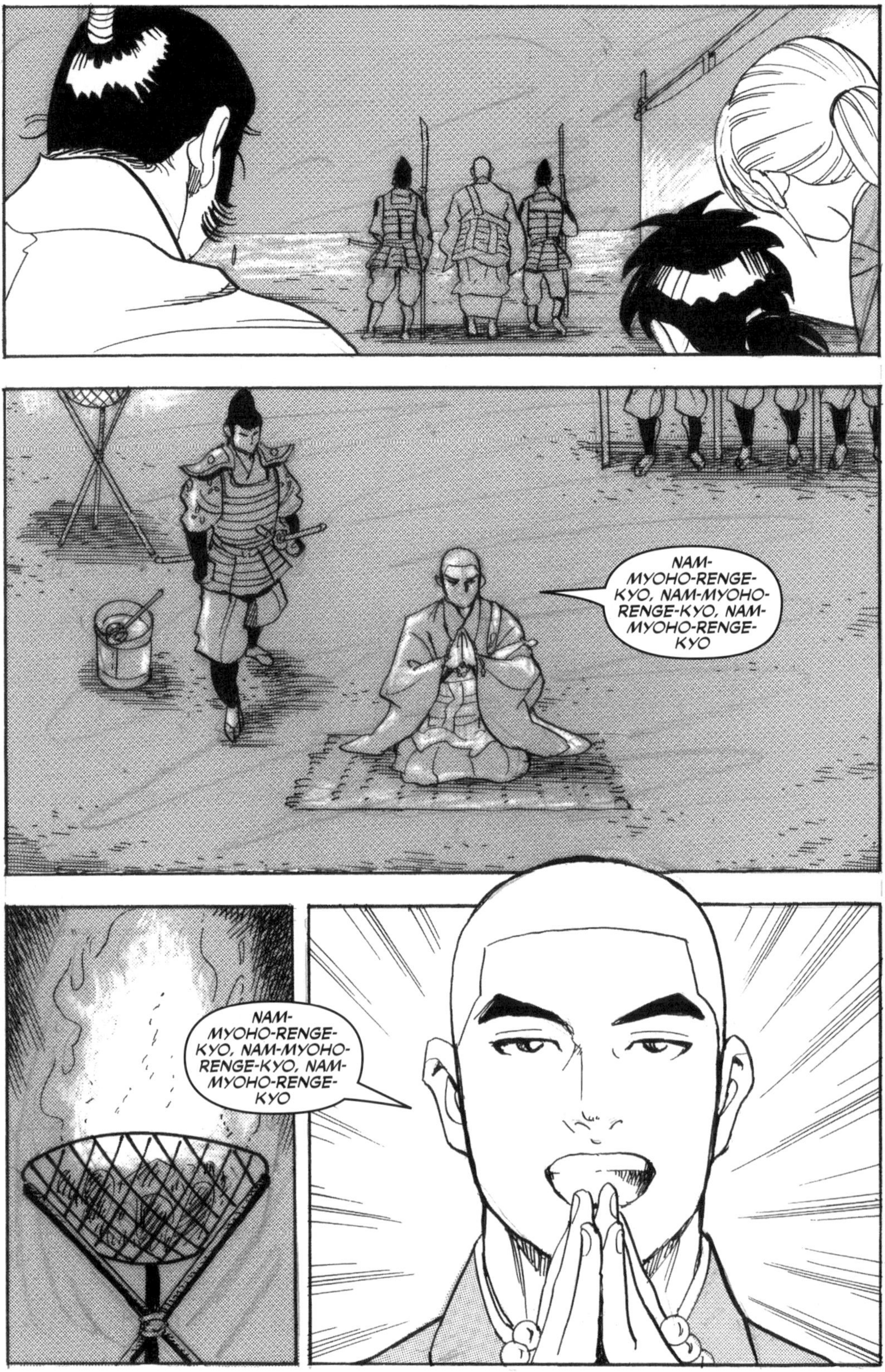
NAM-MYOHO-RENGE-KYO, NAM-MYOHO-RENGE-KYO, NAM-MYOHO-RENGE-KYO
NAM-MYOHO-RENGE-KYO, NAM-MYOHO-RENGE-KYO, NAM-MYOHO-RENGE-KYO

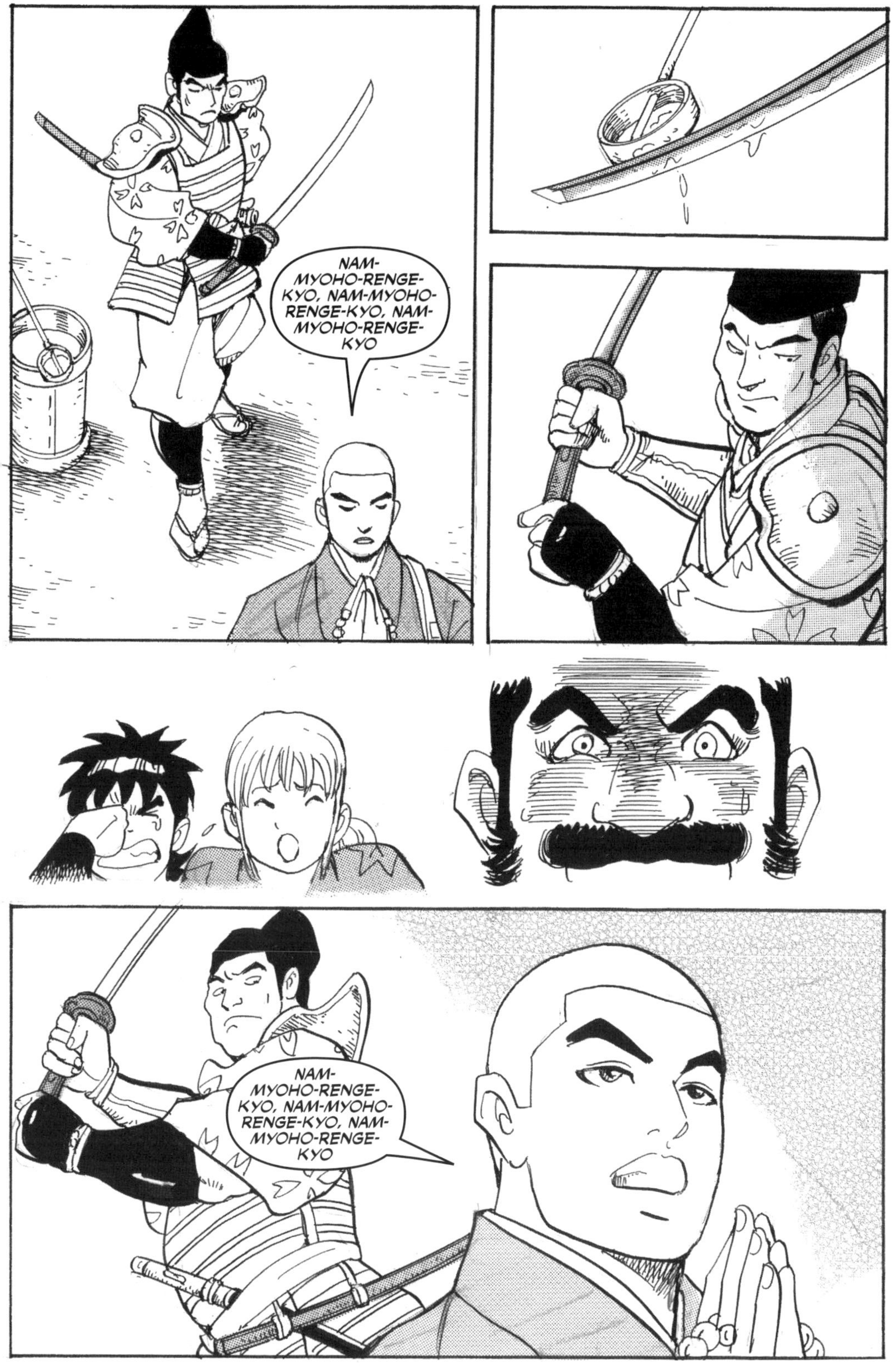
NAM-MYOHO-RENGE-KYO, NAM-MYOHO-RENGE-KYO, NAM-MYOHO-RENGE-KYO
NAM-MYOHO-RENGE-KYO, NAM-MYOHO-RENGE-KYO, NAM-MYOHO-RENGE-KYO

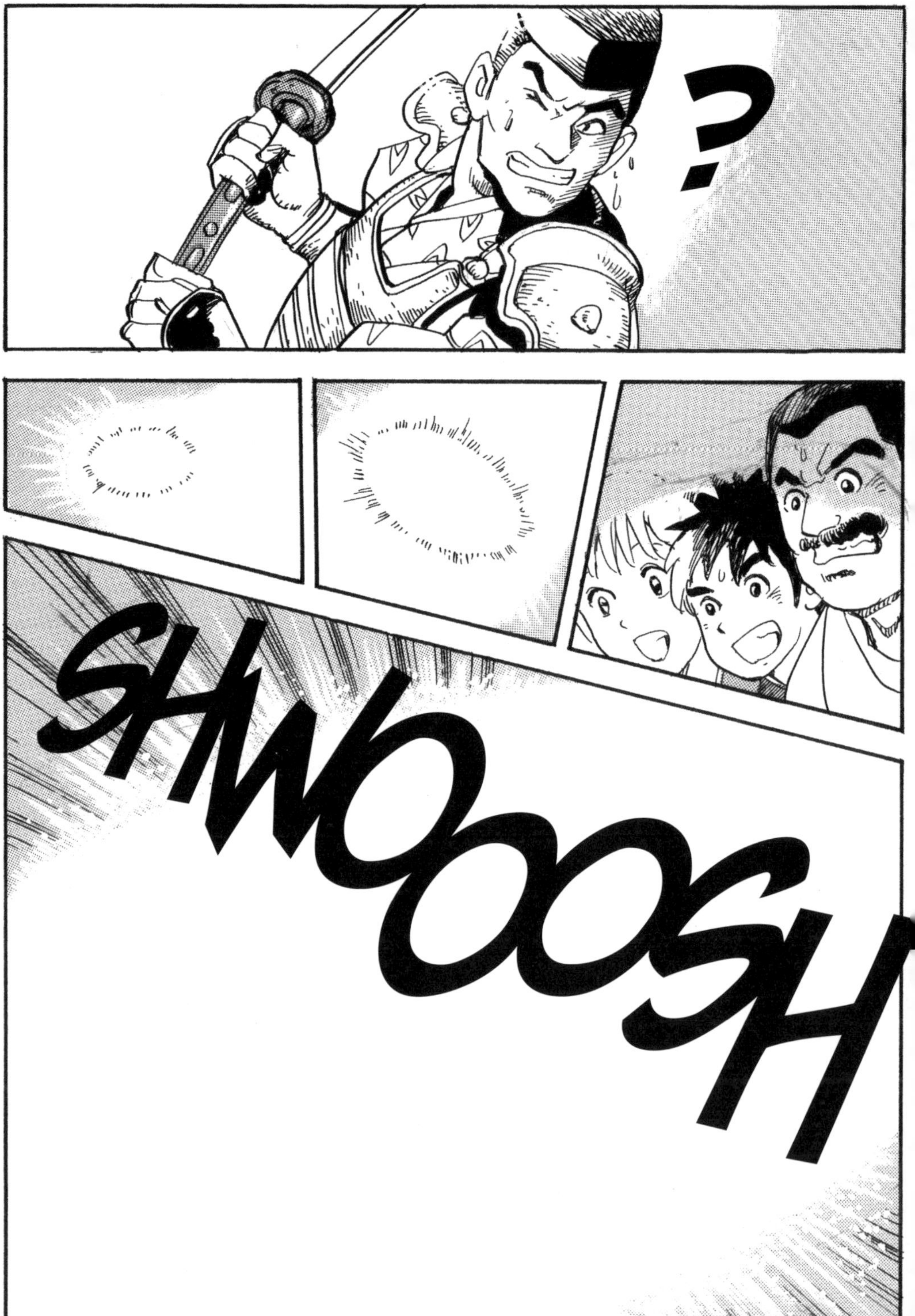
?
SHWOOOSH

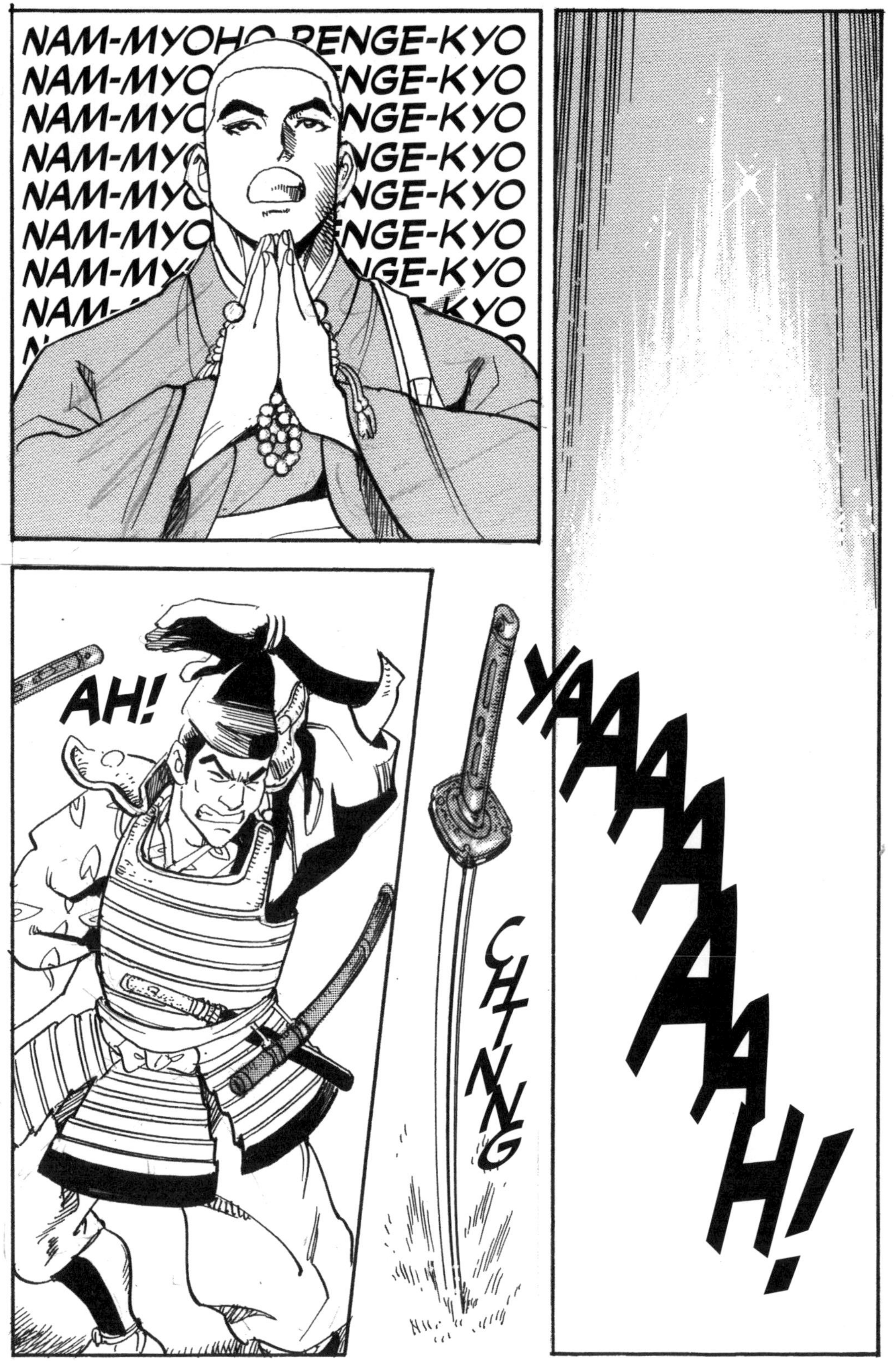
NAM-MYOHO RENGE-KYO
NAM-MYO ENGE-KYO
NAM-MYO NGE-KYO
NAM-MYO NGE-KYO
NAM-MYO NGE-KYO
NAM-MYO ENGE-KYO
NAM-MY GE-KYO
NAM- KYO
AH!
CHTINNG
YAAAAAAAAH!

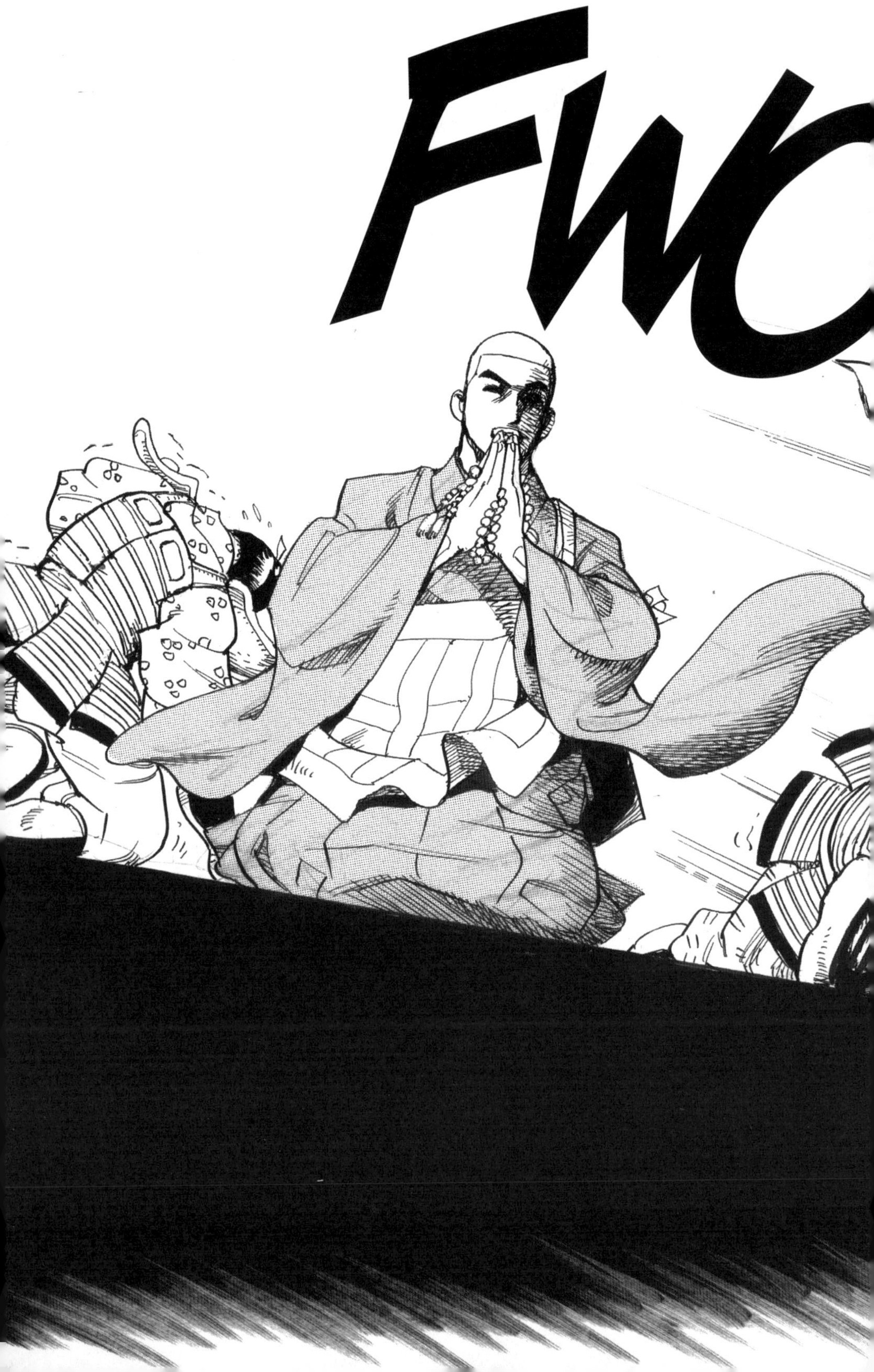
FWO

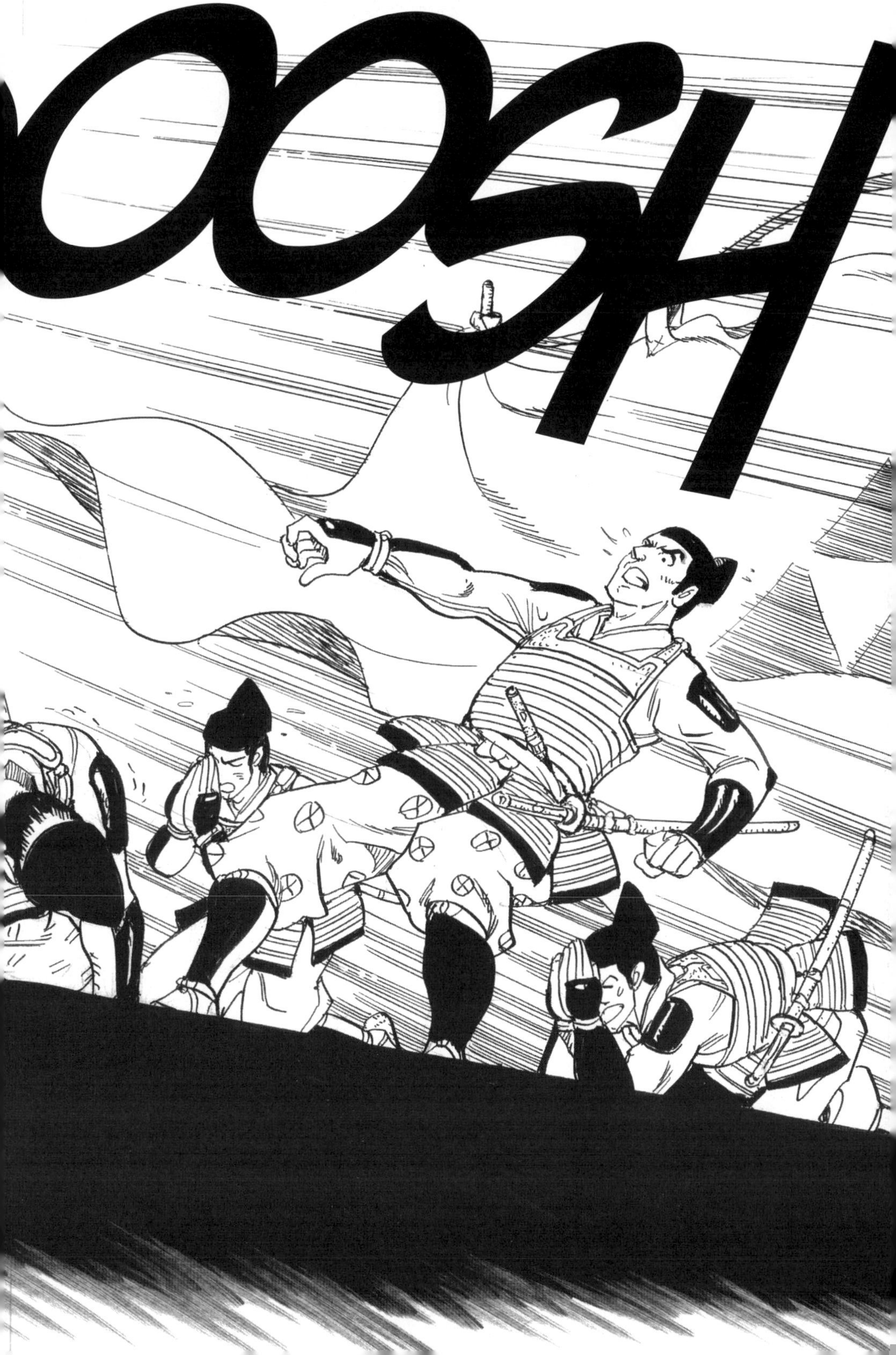
OOSH

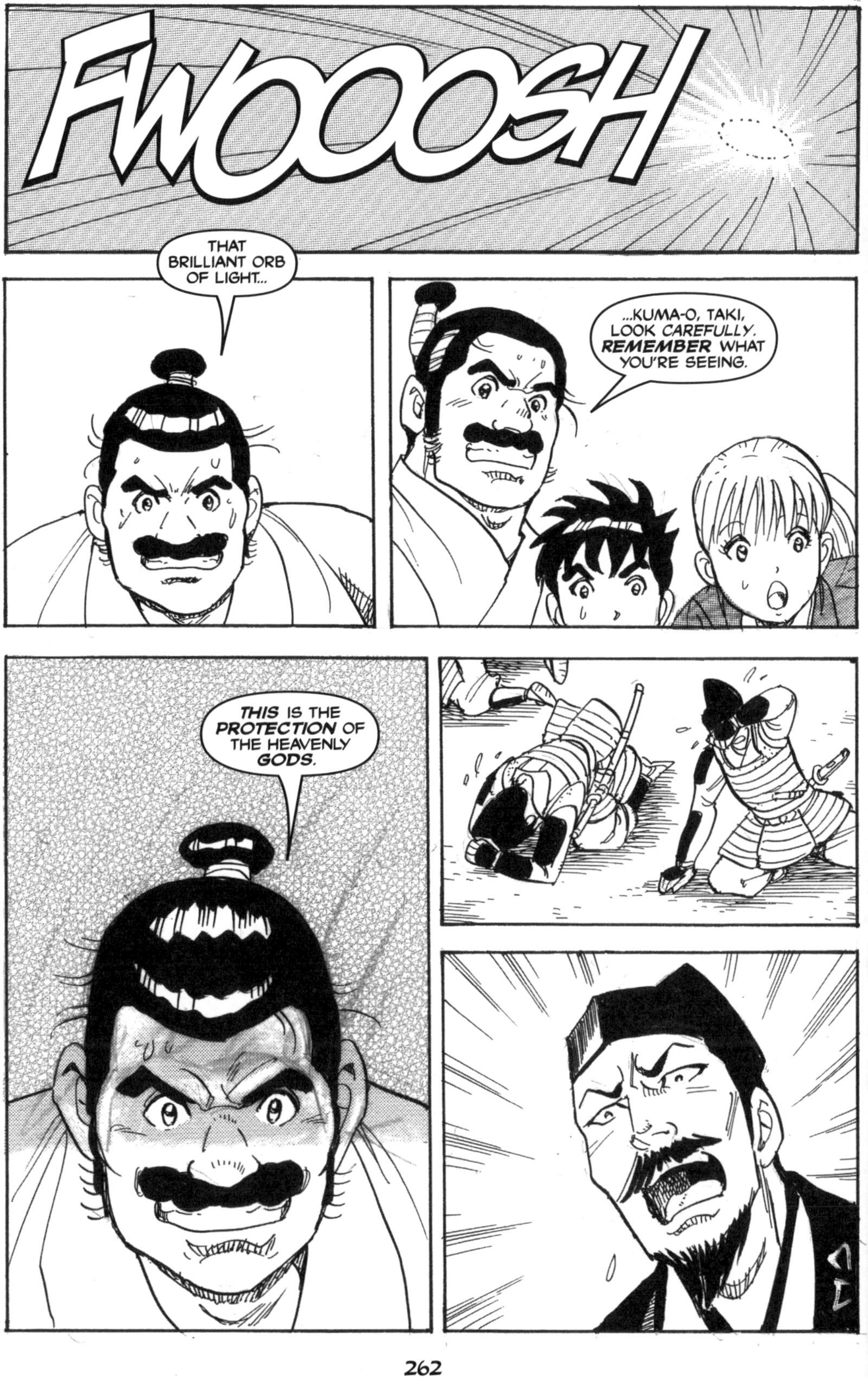
FWOOOSH
THAT BRILLIANT ORB OF LIGHT...
...KUMA-O, TAKI, LOOK CAREFULLY. REMEMBER WHAT YOU'RE SEEING.
THIS IS THE PROTECTION OF THE HEAVENLY GODS.

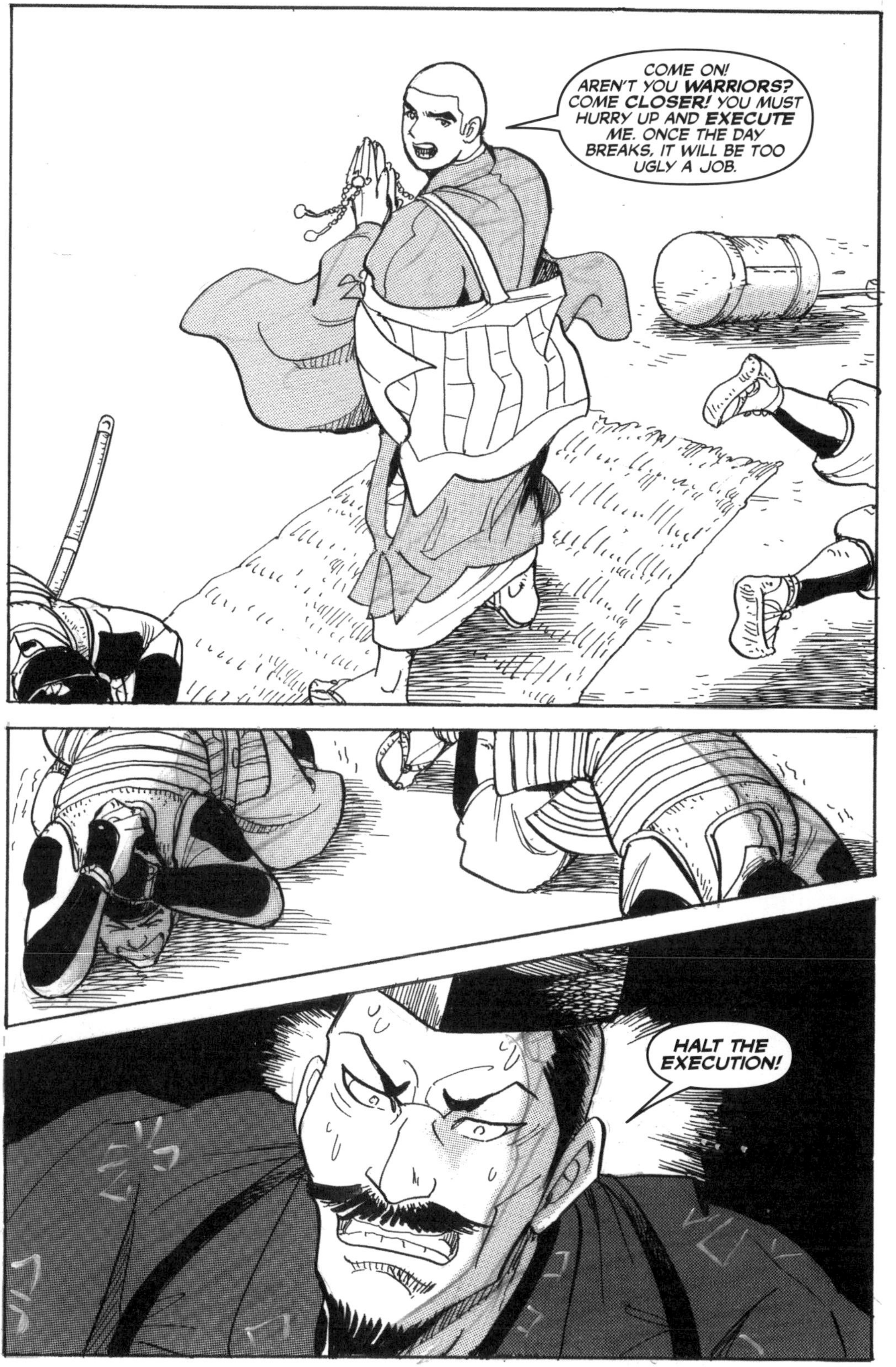
COME ON! AREN'T YOU WARRIORS? COME CLOSER! YOU MUST HURRY UP AND EXECUTE ME. ONCE THE DAY BREAKS, IT WILL BE TOO UGLY A JOB.
HALT THE EXECUTION!

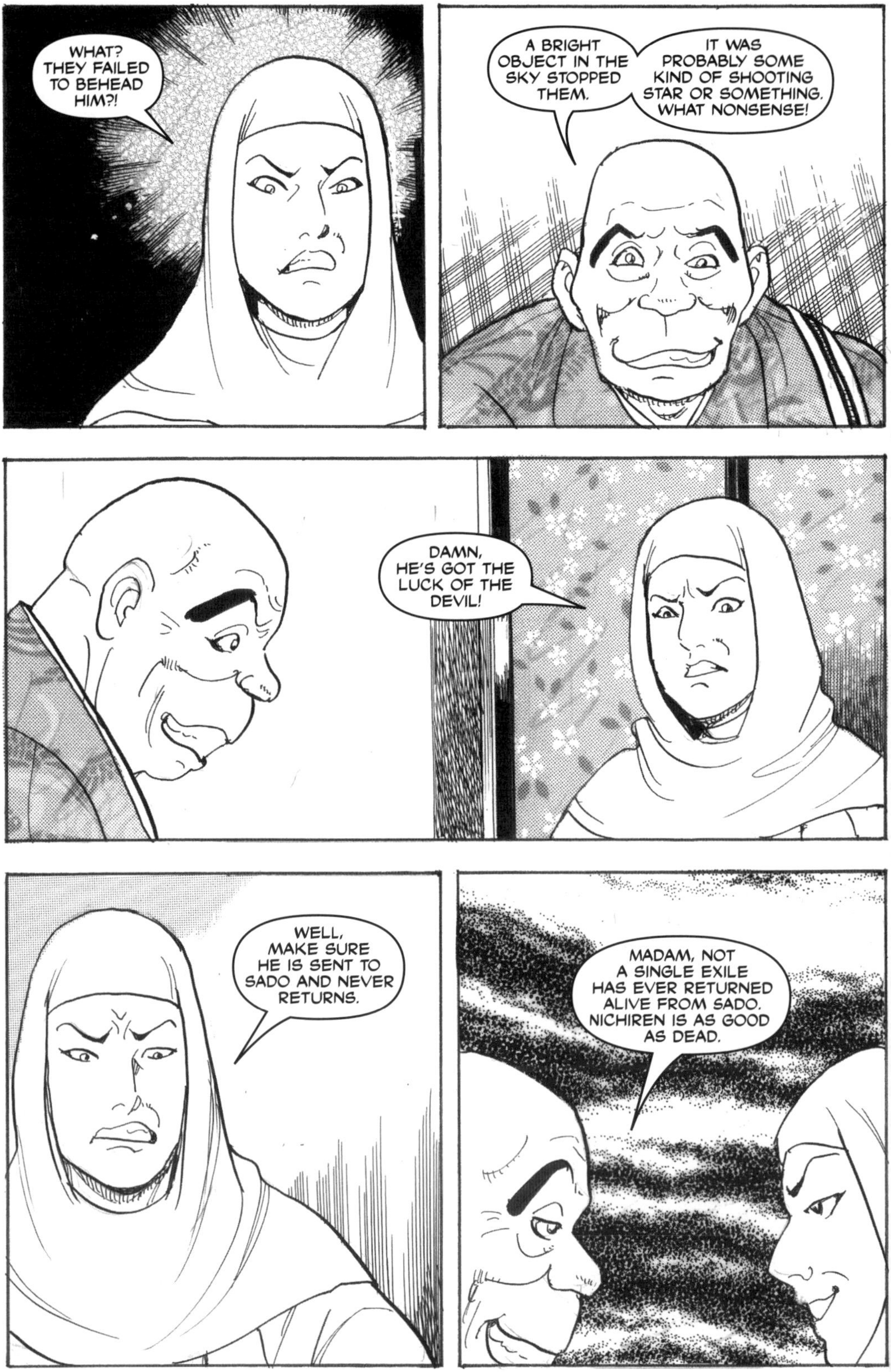
WHAT? THEY FAILED TO BEHEAD HIM?!
A BRIGHT OBJECT IN THE SKY STOPPED THEM.
IT WAS PROBABLY SOME KIND OF SHOOTING STAR OR SOMETHING. WHAT NONSENSE!
DAMN, HE'S GOT THE LUCK OF THE DEVIL!
WELL, MAKE SURE HE IS SENT TO SADO AND NEVER RETURNS.
MADAM, NOT A SINGLE EXILE HAS EVER RETURNED ALIVE FROM SADO. NICHIREN IS AS GOOD AS DEAD.

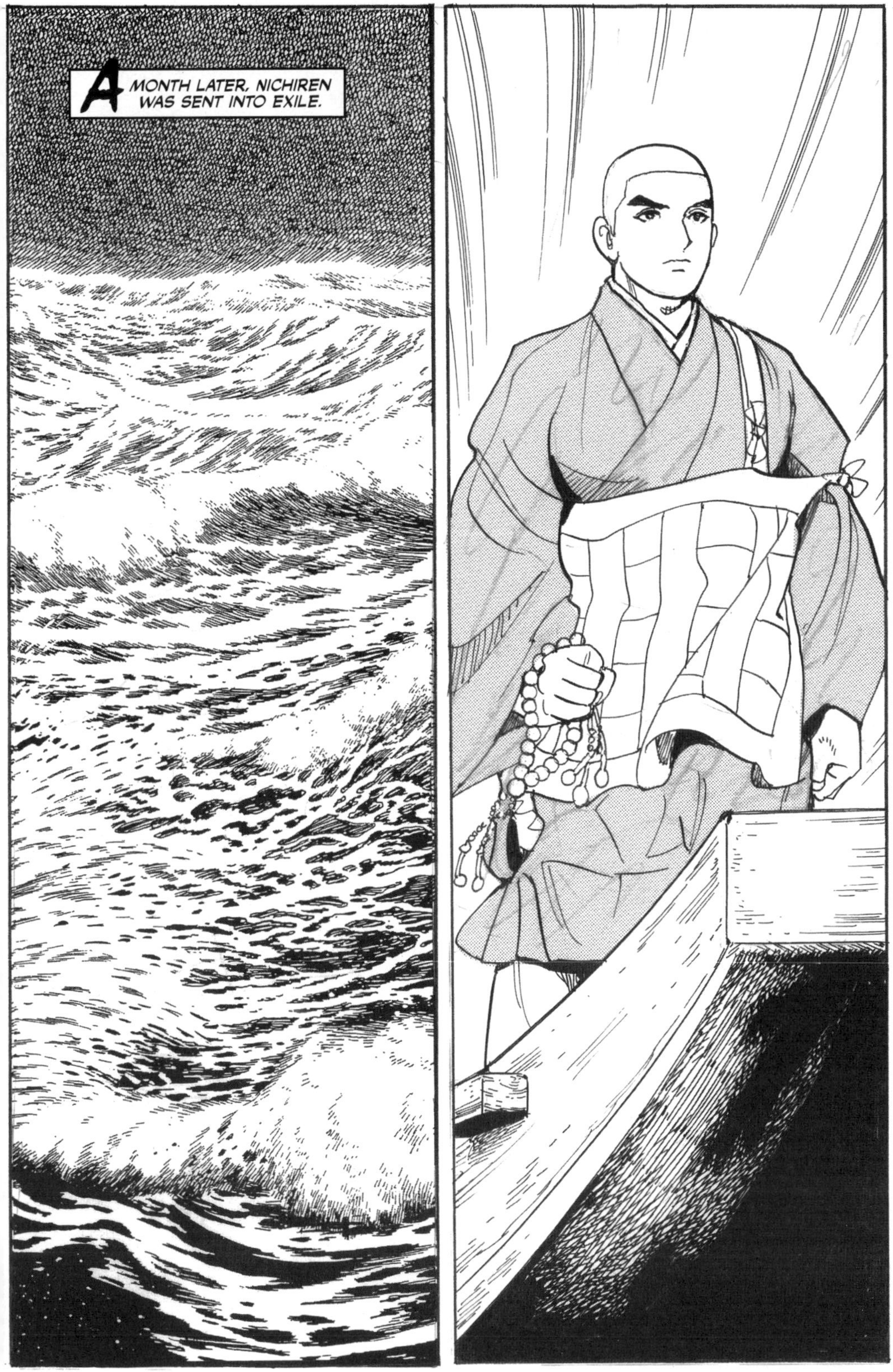
A MONTH LATER, NICHIREN WAS SENT INTO EXILE.

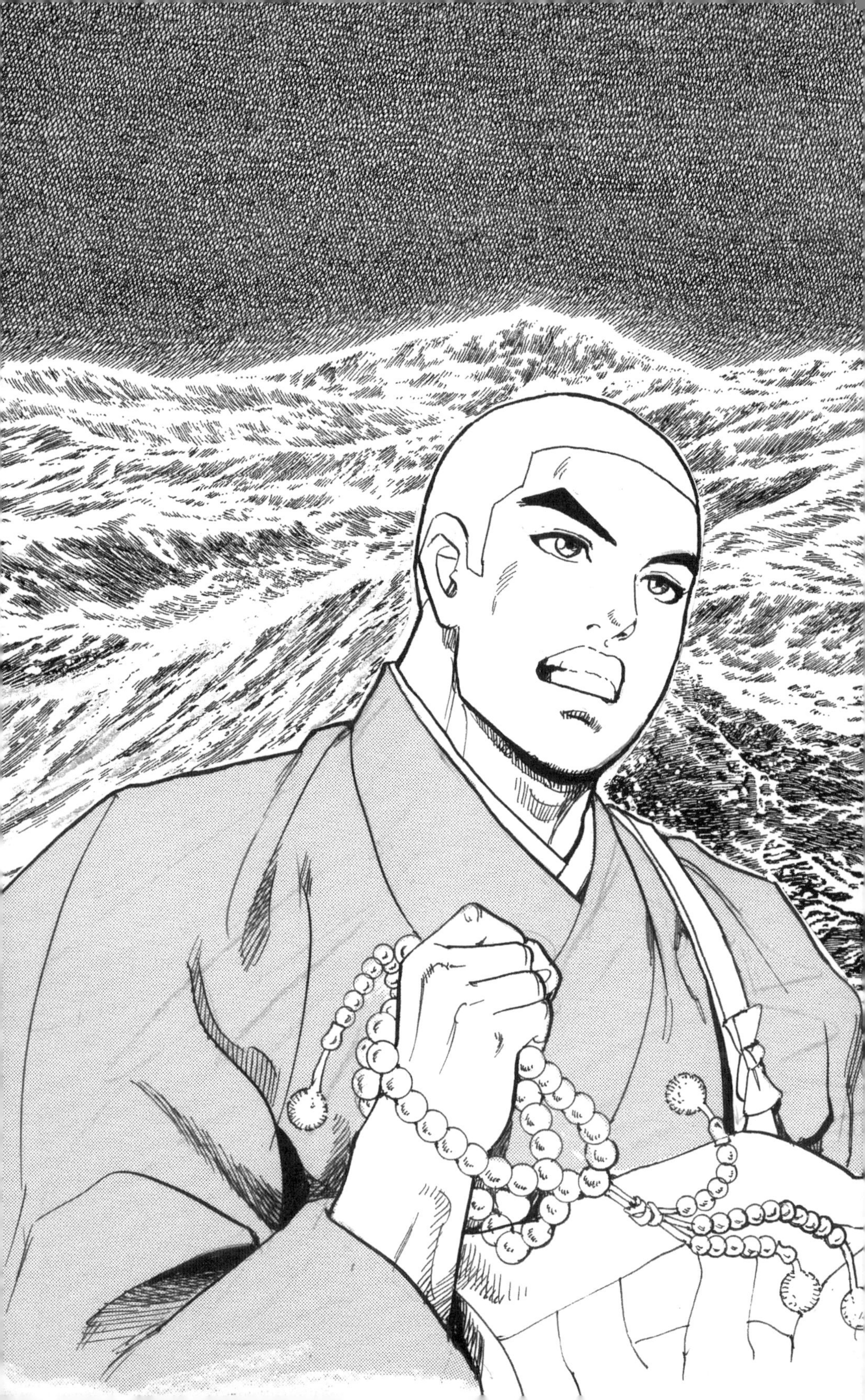

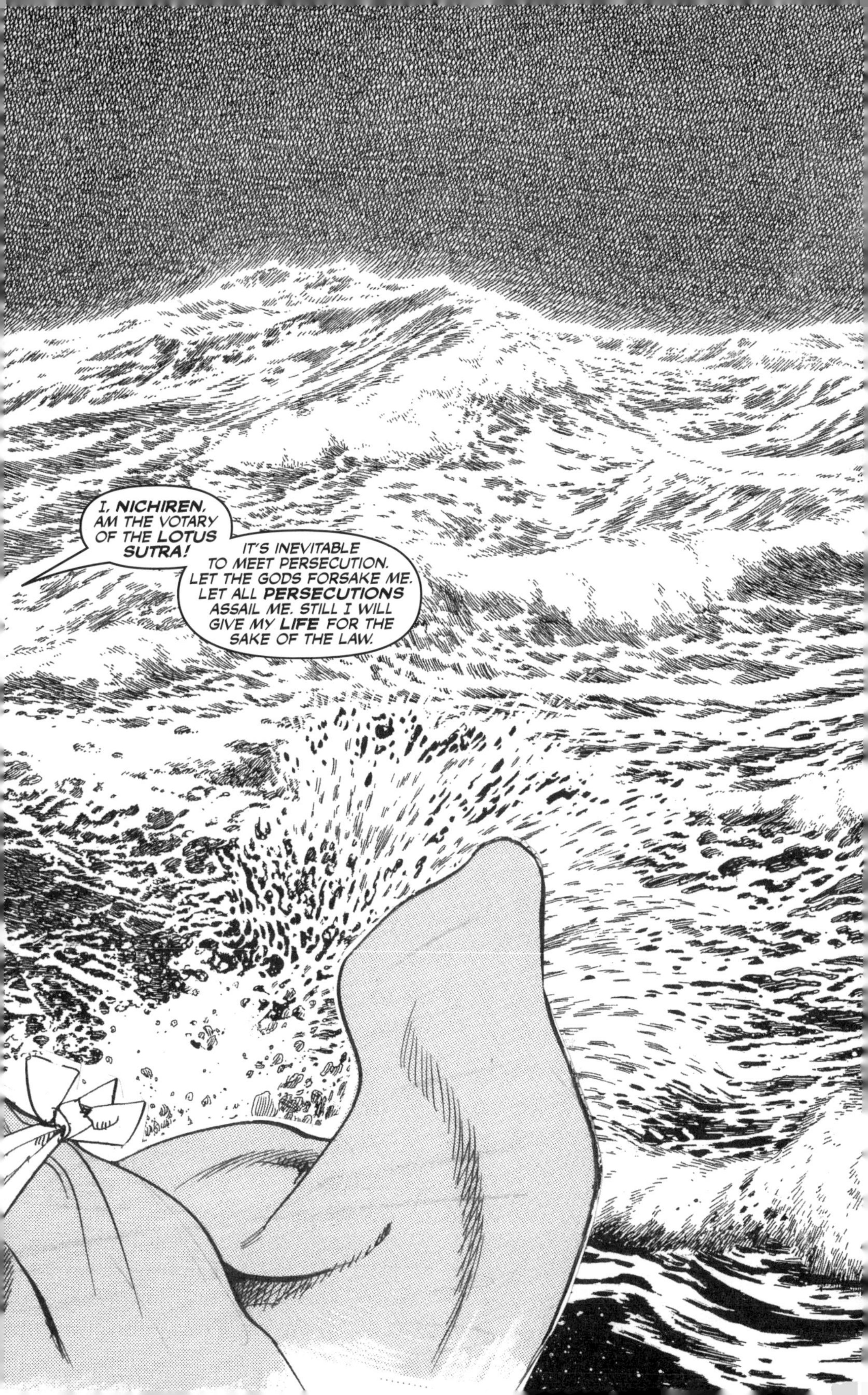
I, NICHIREN, AM THE VOTARY OF THE LOTUS SUTRA!
IT'S INEVITABLE TO MEET PERSECUTION. LET THE GODS FORSAKE ME. LET ALL PERSECUTIONS ASSAIL ME. STILL I WILL GIVE MY LIFE FOR THE SAKE OF THE LAW.

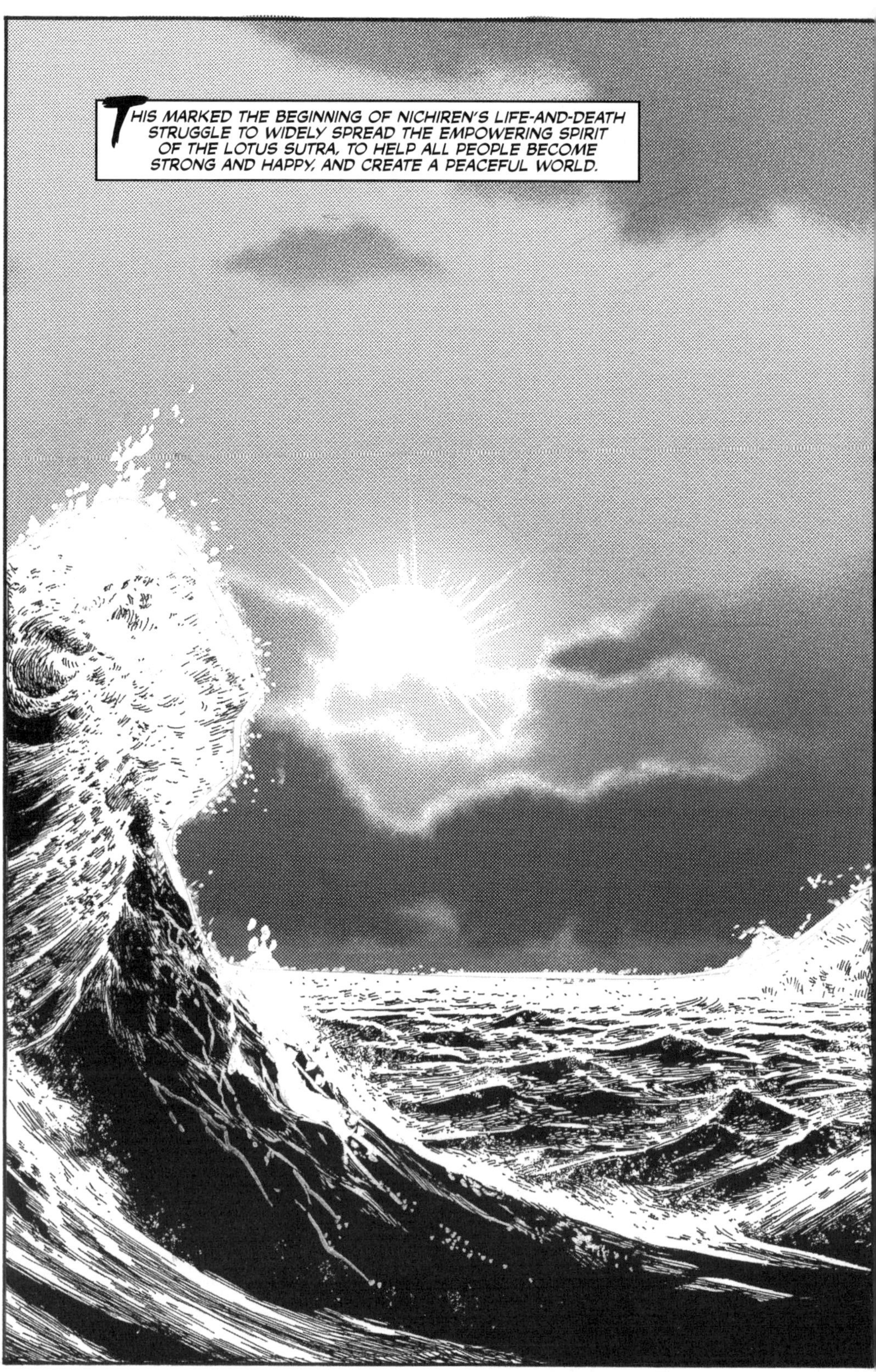
THIS MARKED THE BEGINNING OF NICHIREN'S LIFE-AND-DEATH STRUGGLE TO WIDELY SPREAD THE EMPOWERING SPIRIT OF THE LOTUS SUTRA, TO HELP ALL PEOPLE BECOME STRONG AND HAPPY, AND CREATE A PEACEFUL WORLD.

NICHIREN'S LATER YEARS

On Sado, Nichiren faced one difficulty after another. His quarters were a dilapidated hut in a graveyard, exposed to wind and snow. He often lacked adequate food and was forced to withstand attacks from hostile locals. Yet he overcame each challenge, eventually winning new friends and followers. All the while, he sent letters of encouragement to his disciples who lived far away. In fact, during this period, he authored some of his most important works.

Meanwhile, the Kamakura government faced a series of crises, including a revolt within the ruling clan and the escalating threat of invasion by the Mongol Empire. Nichiren had long before predicted just such social and political unrest, and as these events unfolded, the authorities could no longer ignore him. Two and a half years after sentencing him to what was to be a lifelong exile, the government pardoned him.

After returning to Kamakura a free man, Nichiren was summoned to meet a third time with Hei No Saemon, the official who attempted to behead him. More deferential now, Hei No Saemon asked his opinion about the impending Mongol invasion. Nichiren reiterated his warning that only by practicing the correct Buddhist teaching could this calamity be avoided and peace and happiness brought to the people. His advice was ignored yet again.

Nichiren therefore decided to move the base of his activities from Kamakura to the mountainous region of Minobu. Wanting to transmit the teachings of the Lotus Sutra to future generations, Nichiren inscribed mandalas, objects of devotion, for his followers. The object of devotion, or Gohonzon, embodies the law to which Nichiren had awakened and serves as the basis for believers' faith. Also on Minobu, he wrote treatises detailing the principles of his teaching and letters encouraging his followers throughout Japan. He also poured his energies into lecturing on the Lotus Sutra and training his disciples to succeed him. He died in 1282 at age sixty-one.

Beginning in the latter part of the twentieth century, Nichiren's writings were translated into various languages. Now, people around the world know of his ideas and philosophy, his warm encounters with his followers, and the courageous and compassionate example he set as a Buddhist practitioner.

Learn more about Nichiren's teachings on our website at www.sgi-usa.org

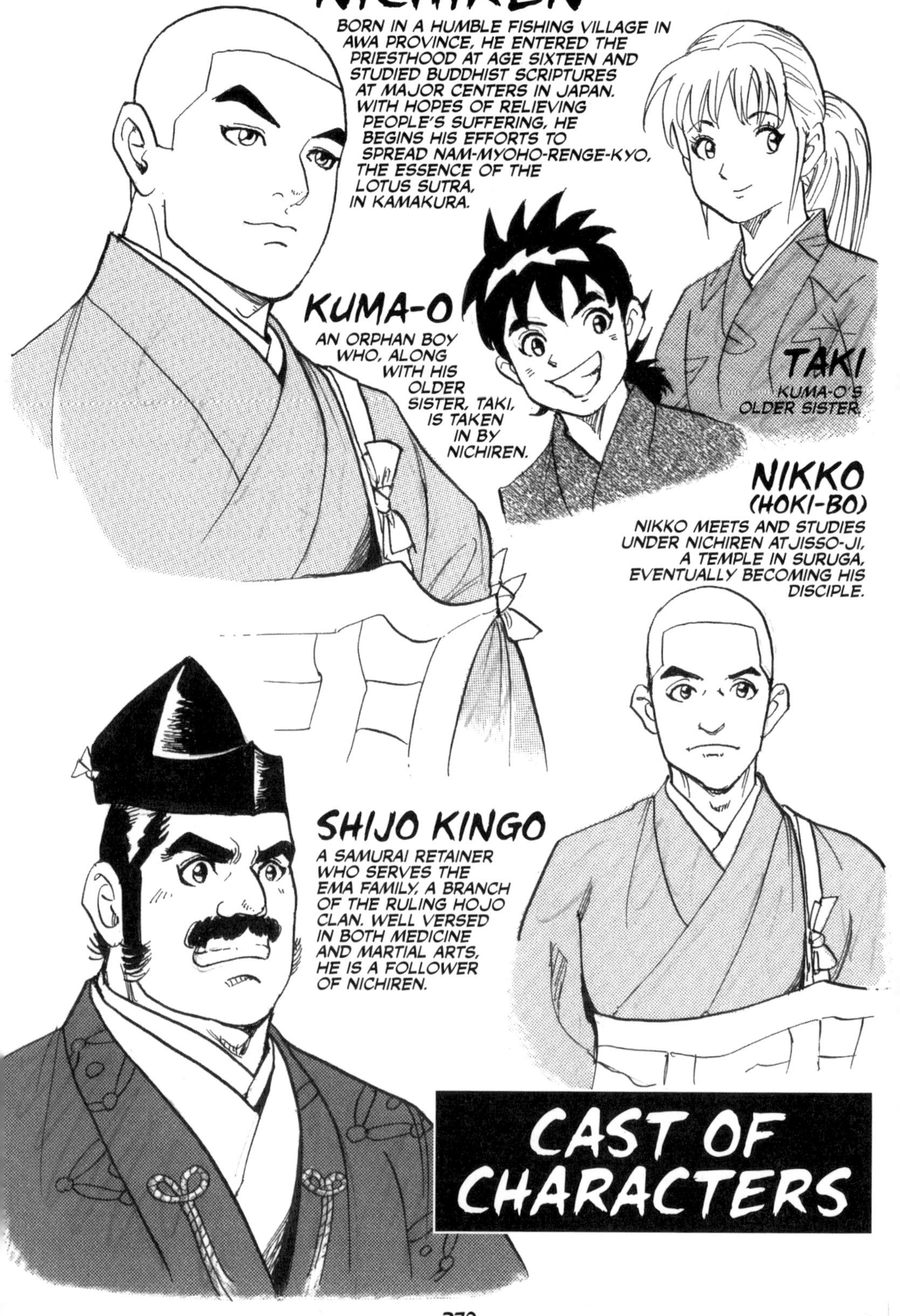
NICHIREN
BORN IN A HUMBLE FISHING VILLAGE IN AWA PROVINCE, HE ENTERED THE PRIESTHOOD AT AGE SIXTEEN AND STUDIED BUDDHIST SCRIPTURES AT MAJOR CENTERS IN JAPAN. WITH HOPES OF RELIEVING PEOPLE'S SUFFERING, HE BEGINS HIS EFFORTS TO SPREAD NAM-MYOHO-RENGE-KYO, THE ESSENCE OF THE LOTUS SUTRA, IN KAMAKURA.
KUMA-O
AN ORPHAN BOY WHO, ALONG WITH HIS OLDER SISTER, TAKI, IS TAKEN IN BY NICHIREN.
TAKI
KUMA-O'S OLDER SISTER.
NIKKO
(HOKI-BO)
NIKKO MEETS AND STUDIES UNDER NICHIREN ATJISSO-JI, A TEMPLE IN SURUGA, EVENTUALLY BECOMING HIS DISCIPLE.
SHIJO KINGO
A SAMURAI RETAINER WHO SERVES THE EMA FAMILY, A BRANCH OF THE RULING HOJO CLAN. WELL VERSED IN BOTH MEDICINE AND MARTIAL ARTS, HE IS A FOLLOWER OF NICHIREN.
CAST OF CHARACTERS

HEI NO SAEMON

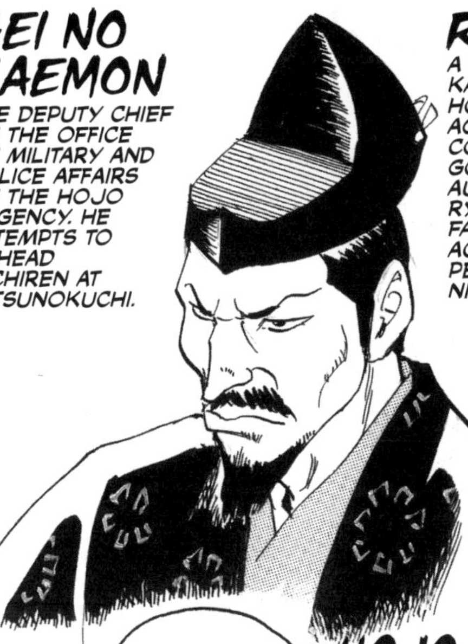

THE DEPUTY CHIEF OF THE OFFICE OF MILITARY AND POLICE AFFAIRS OF THE HOJO REGENCY. HE ATTEMPTS TO BEHEAD NICHIREN AT TATSUNOKUCHI.

RYOKAN

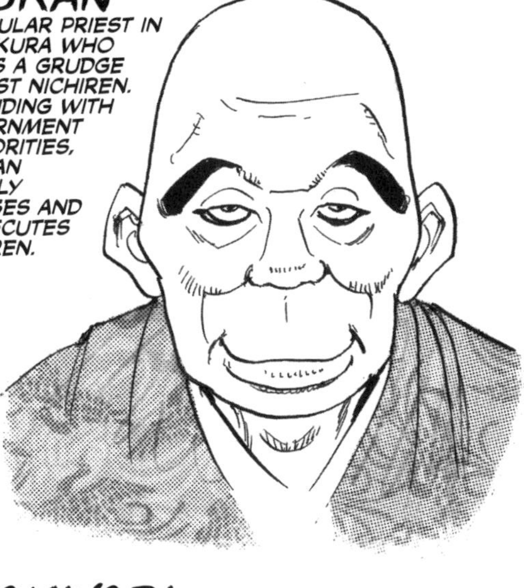

A POPULAR PRIEST IN KAMAKURA WHO HOLDS A GRUDGE AGAINST NICHIREN. COLLUDING WITH GOVERNMENT AUTHORITIES, RYOKAN FALSELY ACCUSES AND PERSECUTES NICHIREN.

HOJO TOKIYORI

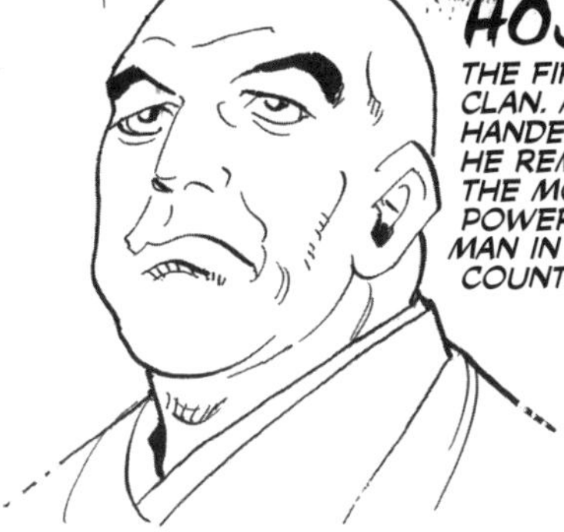

THE FIFTH REGENT OF JAPAN'S RULING HOJO CLAN. ALTHOUGH HE HAS RETIRED AND HAS HANDED HIS TITLE TO HOJO NAGATOKI, HE REMAINS THE MOST POWERFUL MAN IN THE COUNTRY.

HOJO SHIGETOKI

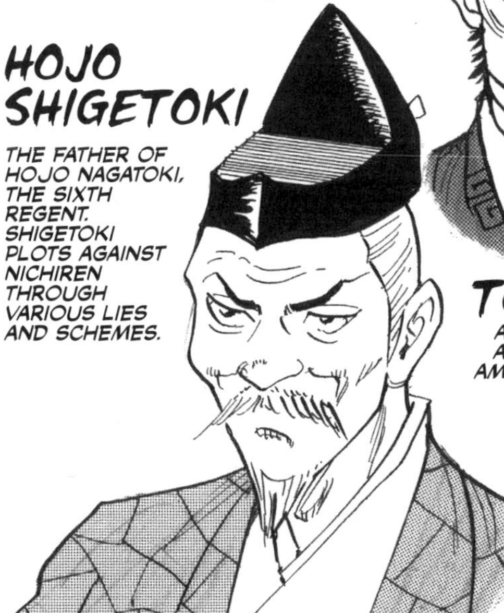

THE FATHER OF HOJO NAGATOKI, THE SIXTH REGENT. SHIGETOKI PLOTS AGAINST NICHIREN THROUGH VARIOUS LIES AND SCHEMES.

TOJO KAGENOBU

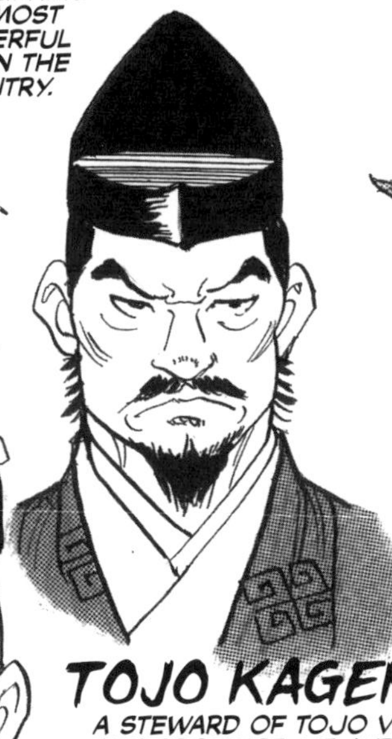

A STEWARD OF TOJO VILLAGE IN AWA PROVINCE. HE AND HIS MEN AMBUSH NICHIREN UPON NICHIREN'S RETURN TO HIS HOMETOWN.

YUKI

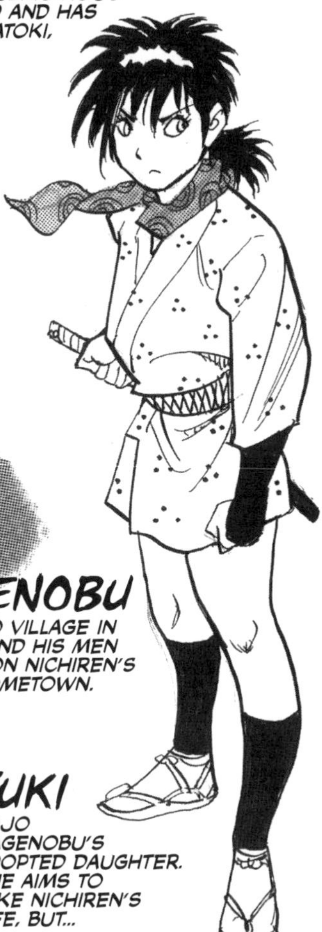

TOJO KAGENOBU'S ADOPTED DAUGHTER. SHE AIMS TO TAKE NICHIREN'S LIFE, BUT...

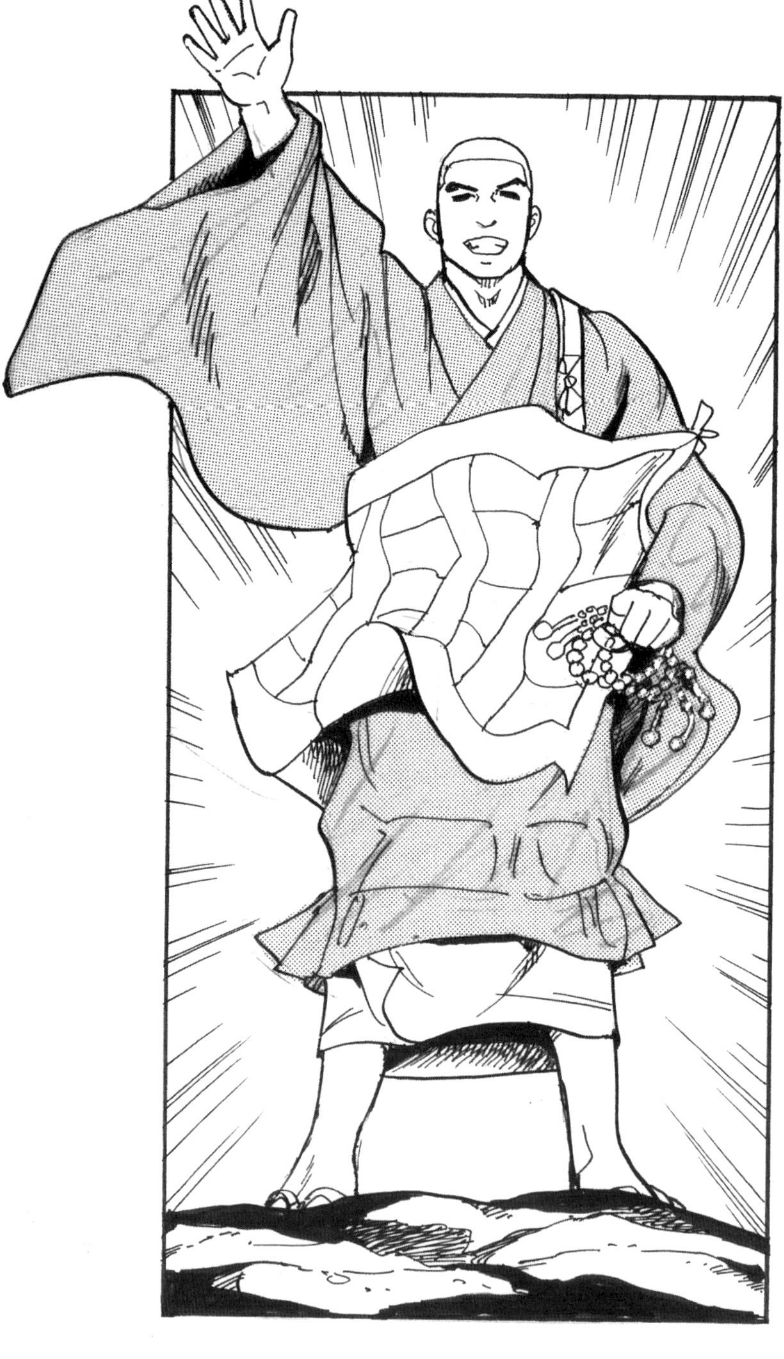